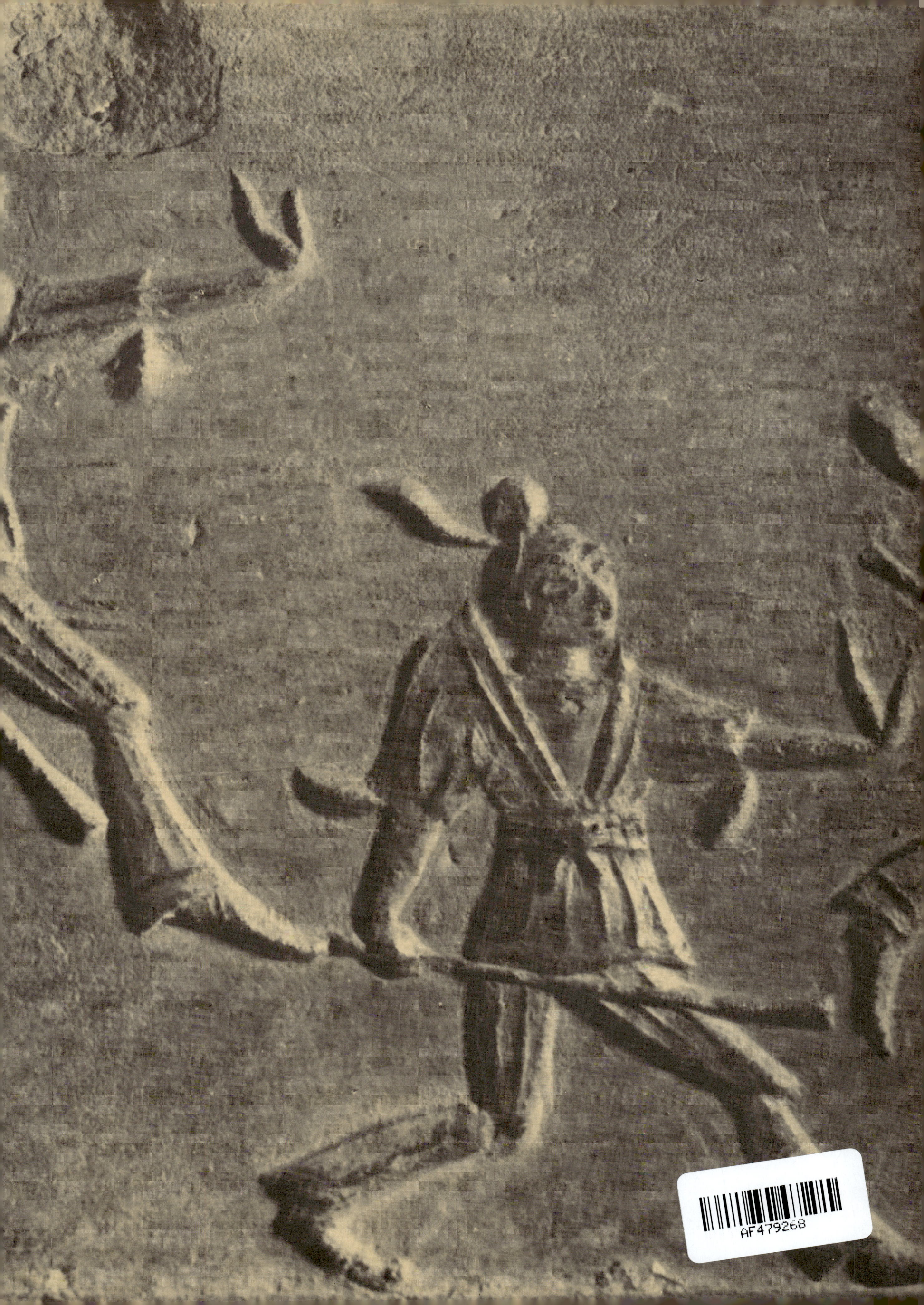

ARTS OF CHINA

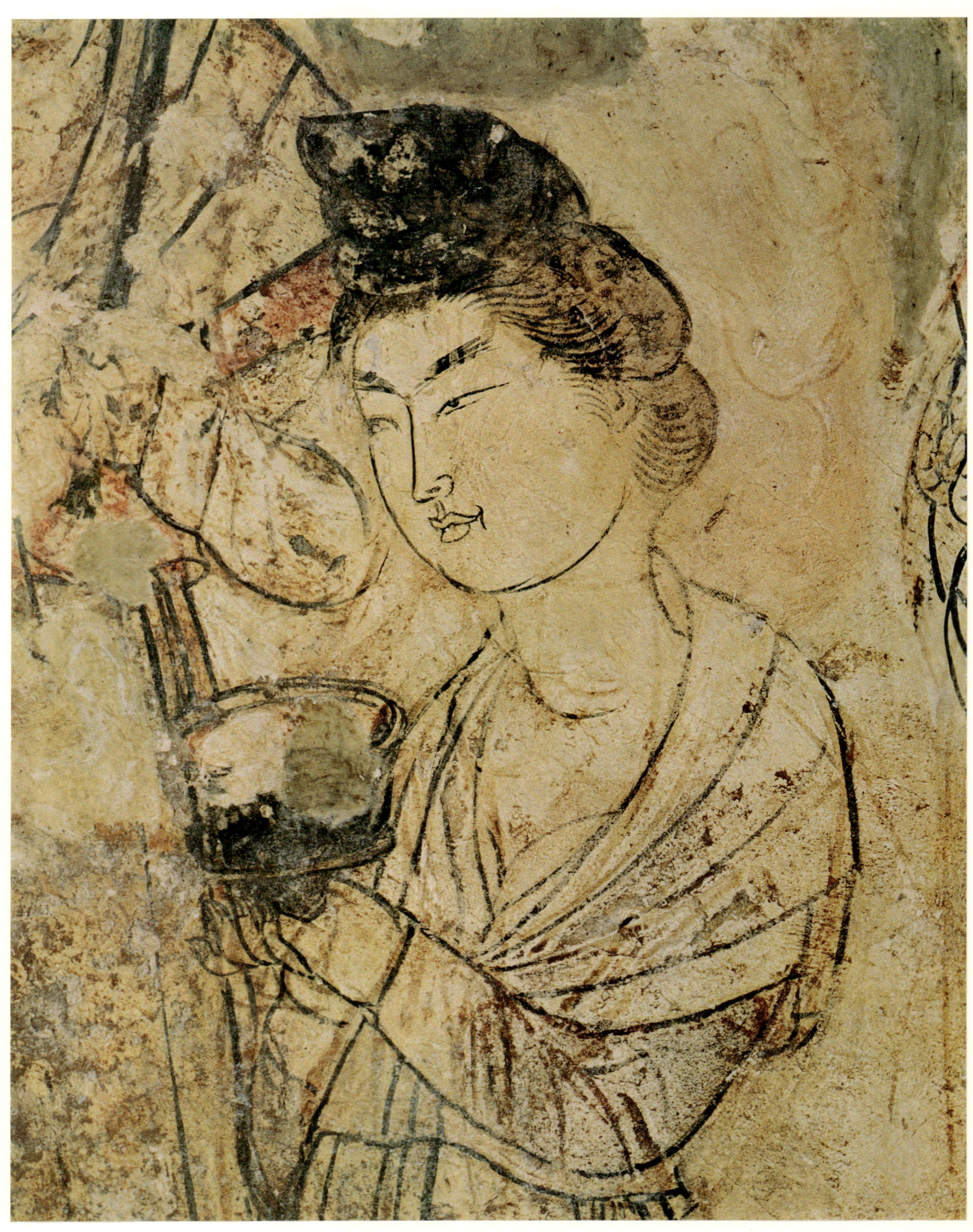

ARTS OF CHINA

Neolithic Cultures to the T'ang Dynasty

RECENT DISCOVERIES

TERUKAZU AKIYAMA

KŌSEI ANDŌ

SABURO MATSUBARA

TAKASHI OKAZAKI

TAKESHI SEKINO

Coordinated by MARY TREGEAR

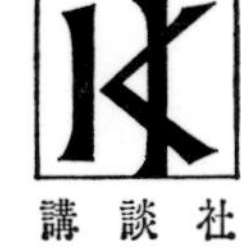

KODANSHA INTERNATIONAL LTD.

Tokyo, Japan & Palo Alto, Calif., U.S.A.

DISTRIBUTORS:

British Commonwealth (excluding Canada and the Far East)
WARD LOCK & COMPANY LTD.
London and Melbourne

Continental Europe
BOXERBOOKS, INC.
Zurich

The Far East
JAPAN PUBLICATIONS TRADING COMPANY
C.P.O. Box 722, Tokyo

Published by KODANSHA INTERNATIONAL LTD., 2-12-21 Otowa, Bunkyo-ku, Tokyo, Japan and KODANSHA INTERNATIONAL/USA, LTD., 577 College Avenue, Palo Alto, California 94306. Printed in Japan.
Library of Congress Catalog Card No. 68–17454

First edition, 1968

Contents

Foreword

Some years ago Kodansha embarked on the project of producing a comprehensive survey of the arts of China as part of the company's ambitious World Art Series. After extensive consultation with the leading Oriental art historians of Japan, it was decided to publish an entirely new series of three volumes: recent archaeological discoveries of material from Neolithic times into the T'ang dynasty; Buddhist cave-temple art; and paintings in Chinese museums.

The first volume in the series fills the long-recognized need for a comprehensive examination of the most recent archaeological discoveries in China. Although all of the material has appeared piecemeal in various learned journals and monographs—publications whose subscription is limited mostly to scholars who read Chinese—there had been no expository, general survey of the major findings with quality photographic reproductions and accurate identifications meaningful to the scholar, and in a format with text satisfying the need of the general art enthusiast.

The project for this volume was entrusted to a distinguished panel of Japanese scholars on Chinese art, headed by Professor Yoshiho Yonezawa, Japan's and one of the world's leading authorities on Chinese painting and general editor also of Volume III, and including Professors Terukazu Akiyama, Kōsei Andō, Saburō Matsubara, Takashi Okazaki and Takeshi Sekino. Fortunately all these scholars had traveled to China to inspect the new material and their firsthand intimacy with the objects provides the basis of the descriptive text.

The second volume, Chinese Buddhist cave art, again fills the long-recognized need for an extensive coverage of these sometimes transcendent wall paintings and sculptures in high-quality color reproduction. Professors Matsubara and Akiyama wrote the text and explanatory notes and supervised the selection of plates for this volume. To complete the series, the third volume presents paintings in Chinese museum collections from the T'ang dynasty to the present, with text by Professors Yonezawa, Michiaki Kawakita and Kei Suzuki.

The general acclaim following publication of the three volumes in Japan and the immediate use made in the Americas and Europe of these books, even though they are in Japanese, strongly emphasized the need for the present English-language edition.

The present edition retains the same basic content as the original Japanese volumes, but with a considerable amount of new material added by the authors especially for the English translation—notably, in this volume, an extended contribution by Professor Matsubara and tomb diagrams by Professor Akiyama. Volume II will be greatly expanded by the inclusion of detailed explanations to the captions to the plates. Professor Yonezawa will also expand his valuable contribution to Volume III, to which he will add an overall summary encompassing the three volumes.

For the English translation and supervision Kodansha International has been very fortunate in securing the services of Miss Mary Tregear, Dr. Alexander C. Soper and Dr. George Hatch. It is expected that Dr. Soper's Volume II will be available later this year, while Dr. Hatch's Volume III will be ready in early 1969. None of these books would have been available without the generous cooperation of the Chinese People's Association for Cultural Relations and Friendship with Foreign Countries and the Japan-China Cultural Exchange Association, and Kodansha International wishes to record its appreciation to these organizations' officers in China and Japan.

THE EDITORS

Preface

For the Western reader the special interest of this volume is twofold: it lies both in the very fine illustrations made available by the Chinese authorities and in the approach of the Japanese authors. The opportunity to study fine photographs, with full references, of many of the most interesting finds from controlled excavations undertaken in China since 1949 must be welcomed by all interested in Chinese art. The present volume, on finds of the early periods, includes much important material to add to our understanding of the regional development of style and techniques. The quality of the pictures makes them important study material of objects which most Western students have been unable to see for themselves.

In accordance with the publication policy, the translation preserves the form of the original and the viewpoints of the Japanese scholars writing for the general reader in their country. In itself this is of interest and also provides an opportunity of reading scholars, eminent in their own country as authorities on Chinese art, who rarely publish in English. The translation has been prepared with the active cooperation of the authors and remains close to the original text. This often results in interesting emphasis and comment, though the Western reader may find occasionally that discussion assumes a knowledge of history and literature more readily available to the Oriental reader. However, a glossary has been included to assist in the identification of the many special terms and place names which naturally appear in characters in the Japanese text.

MARY TREGEAR

Oxford, 1968

NEOLITHIC CULTURES TO THE T'ANG DYNASTY

RECENT DISCOVERIES

I. Neolithic, Yin and Chou—Arts of the Peasant and Aristocrat

PREHISTORIC ARTS The deep loess of Honan, Shensi and Shansi in North China was laid down in the later part of the last ice age. At the end of this period the rainfall was low over this area, but a subsequent increase in rainfall gave rise to many rivers, notably the Yellow River, which carved its way through this fertile plain. This combination of fertile soil and ample water supply created conditions ideal for the agriculture that has flourished in this area from Neolithic times until the present day. Numerous prehistoric earthenwares, the first art objects to appear in China, were among the loveliest flowers to bloom in the loess plains.

The Neolithic culture of North China can be broadly divided into two types: the Yang-shao and Lung-shan cultures. These are named after the sites where typical remains were first discovered, namely: Yang-shao village in the Min-ch'ih District of Honan Province, and Ch'eng-tzu-yai near the town of Lung-shan, in the Li-ch'eng District of Shantung Province. An earthenware painted with beautiful decorations (Painted Pottery), is peculiar to the Yang-shao culture (Pls. 1–6, 24–30), while the Lung-shan culture is typified by burnished Black Pottery (Pls. 32–35). There has been much controversy about the possible relationship between these two cultures. But the findings from the excavations of 1956 and 1957 near Miao-ti-kou in the Shan District of Honan established that the Lung-shan culture succeeded that of Yang-shao, and indeed is the continuation of it.

Remains of the Yang-shao culture settlements have been found over a wide area of the middle reaches of the Yellow River, covering northern Honan, southern Shansi, and central Shensi. Remains of variants of the Yang-shao culture have been found also in association with the mixed farming and grazing culture that flourished in Kansu and Ch'ing-hai along the upper part of the Yellow River. On the other hand, the Lung-shan culture is thought to have developed first in the Shansi or Honan area and to have extended west as far as Kansu, east to Shantung, north as far as Liaotung and south into Chekiang. In Chekiang this culture persisted into the Western Chou dynasty and in Liaotung into the Eastern Chou. Although there were other Neolithic cultures with individual characteristics in central China, they were all to some extent influenced by either the Yang-shao or Lung-shan cultures. This may serve as a brief preliminary to the discussion of the prehistoric arts of China that follows.

With the establishment of settled agriculture by the Neolithic peoples, everyday utensils in earthenware made their appearance. The shaping and decorating of these jars and bowls is the earliest artistic activity in China. This artistic activity was limited to pottery of a certain quality, for not only is there no sign of artistic embellishment of stone implements of the period, but there is also a class of coarse, rough pottery that is almost entirely undecorated. In both these cases the explanation must lie in the practical intention of the tools and pots. However there is a strong decorative style both in the Painted and Black Pottery that is of some artistic interest.

The Painted Pottery was made of a fine clay and built up by hand or by the coil method to make a thin-bodied ware. The surface was burnished and the piece fired in an oxidizing fire of at least 1000 degrees centigrade. The result is a reddish-bodied earthenware. As a rule, the painting, applied before firing, was in black only, but, in some cases, black and/or red was used over a white slip. The majority of pieces found in the middle Yellow River region are large and small bowls; jars are very rare (Pl. 4). The decoration is of leaf motifs, curved lines, whorls, spots and crisscross motifs painted with an easy grace. By comparison, among the wares of the upper Yellow River, those of the Ma-chia-yao type, which include both Pan-shan and Ma-ch'ang types, are very much more beautiful, and of a higher quality both in form and decoration. The Pan-shan wares are mostly short-necked, round-bodied jars, with whorl, crisscross, checker, zigzag and wavy motifs painted in red and black. Ma-chia-yao wares are typically small bowls or tall-necked jars. Painted in black only, the decoration features very beautiful whorl motifs and frog-like figures (Pl. 24). Ma-ch'ang ware, mostly jars and tall-stemmed bowls (*tou*), are painted in black and red in diaper, crisscross and zigzag motifs (Pl. 26). Of these three Kansu types, the Pan-shan wares are certainly the most handsome (*see* Pl. 26 Note). Other sites showing Painted Pottery culture settlements in this upper Yellow River area are Hsin-tien (Pl. 29), T'ang-wang (Pl. 28), Ssu-ma and Sha-ching (Pl. 30). In all these places, bronze implements were also found, and the pottery shows clear regression in both style and quality. The sites can thus be taken to be of a later date.

There are two theories on the origin of the Painted Pottery in China. Some European and American scholars are of the opinion that the culture is related to the painted pottery of western Asia, which they take to be the prototype for the Chinese wares. Chinese scholars, on the other hand, believe the Painted Pottery to be indigenous, and to have originated in the Yellow River basin. There seems to be some evidence to suggest a connection, however indirect, with the west, but the nature of the relationship is not yet clear.

The Black Pottery characteristic of the Lung-shan culture is a development of the Painted Pottery. It retained the fine quality, thin body and burnished surface of the earlier ware. However, reduction firing was employed, and the resulting dark, carbon-impregnated surface took on a black, lacquer-like luster when smoked and burnished a second time. In contrast to the colored brightness of the Painted Pottery, the Black wares appear austere and very plain. But these thin, wheel-made wares with an almost metallic sheen have a beautiful simplicity entirely typical of the culture. This Black ware was made in a great variety of shapes, including cauldrons, cups, bowls, jars and dishes and even stemmed shapes reminiscent of modern forms (Pls. 32–35). A sharpness of angle recalling bent sheet metal and flat-bottomed shapes with three short legs can be said to be forms peculiar to the Black Pottery.

Although it seems evident that there is some stylistic connection between the Lung-shan Black Pottery and the bronze vessels of the Yin and Chou dynasties, this does not necessarily indicate a simple imitation of the ceramics by the bronze-makers. Indeed, the influence may have been the reverse, since the Black Pottery culture persisted in some areas through the Yin and Chou periods.

Apart from the two main cultures of Yang-shao and Lung-shan, the culture found at Ning-yang District, Shantung must be mentioned. The ceramics found at this site are thought to be in the general line of the Lung-shan culture, but the decoration of wares in black and white is evidently a link with the Yang-shao tradition.

It has been assumed that the pottery and stone implements of these Neolithic cultures were made as they were needed by ordinary people. But in view of the complicated structure of the kilns found at Yang-shao and Lung-shan culture sites, it is very difficult to believe that the Painted and Black wares were not made by skilled artisans. Perhaps the coarser earthenware was made by the ordinary people for their everyday use, while the Painted and burnished Black wares, because they were quasi-ritual or decorative pieces, were made by skilled specialist craftsmen. This possibility is further supported by the use of the potter's wheel for the more refined wares, at least by the Lung-shan potters, and the use of a sophisticated kiln. The great beauty and skill that this pottery shows is probably due to the refinement of a technique that had become a very specialized craft. If this was the case, these early specialist ceramists were creating works of art in styles to the taste of the period. It is possible to recognize and classify various styles even of these Neolithic potters. Where a style is approved by public taste, it will be imitated and become an established type. But another style that does not fit with the taste of the period will be dropped. Thus the types basic to these Neolithic cultures reveal the aesthetic taste of the primitive farmers of North China.

It is usually held that the art of primitive farmers is symbolic and conceptual, while that of the primitive hunter tends to be intuitive and realistic. This seems natural when one considers that hunters depict in their artistic work the animals that they know well and can master. But farmers, with their natural respect and awe for the forces of nature that so ruthlessly control their livelihood, seek to express more religious or introspective feelings in their art. So it is that the Neolithic farmers used abstract and geometric forms, thought to be symbolic, that typify the decoration of the Painted Pottery. Yet there are rare exceptions where pottery of the period has been found painted with man and animal motifs. Notable among these are the human faces and fish on the wares excavated at Pan-po, Sian, Shensi (Pls. 1, 2), fish and birds on wares excavated at Pei-shou-ling, Pao-chi District, Shensi, and frog-like designs painted on wares found at Miao-ti-kou (Pl. 24) and also on the Painted Pottery of the Ma-chia-yao type in the Kansu region. In addition to these examples of a relatively realistic animal decoration on pottery, there are a few examples of this period of work in relief and in the round: the clay disc owl mask found at Hua District, Shensi (Pl. 39); the potsherd found at Fu-feng District, Shensi that shows a human mask (Pl. 40), and finally the three potsherds from Miao-ti-kou that show the relief representation of a gecko-like creature (Pl. 38). All these examples are unusual for their period, and indeed, seen singly, it would be very difficult to ascribe them to their correct culture. Thus, they may be taken as examples of the work of artists of the period, working outside the established style of their time, whose work was never accepted by the public taste of the period. As such, we must admire them as the work of realistic artists working against a strong symbolic tradition. The skillful analysis of this blending process between originality and imitation is perhaps one of the most important ways of clarifying the fundamental nature of prehistoric art.

THE ARTS OF YIN AND WESTERN CHOU The Neolithic cultures were based on a family clan structure that controlled a communal life in which there was little or no accumulation of wealth; the riches of this society were perishable and the harvests were distributed among the clan. With the use of bronze, the social structure changed radically. The family clan collapsed, social strata appeared, and the first state was formed. Those able to produce bronze weapons conquered their rivals and then established a dynasty and set up a state.

The first archaeologically known state in China is that of the Yin dynasty. Although it is not clear how or when this dynasty was established, it is known that the capital of the state in the later stage of the dynasty was near the present city of An-yang in Honan Province. There is discussion as to the exact dates of the Yin dynasty, but there is general agreement that it covers a three hundred year period between the fourteenth and eleventh centuries B.C. Extensive excavations of the area of the "Wastes of Yin" near An-yang, the site of the later Yin capital, have been carried out during the last forty years. The site of a grand palace, many large and small graves and the numerous valuable articles discovered within them have provided important material for the study of the culture and arts of the Yin dynasty. Before the 1950's, these An-yang sites were the sole area of known sites of this period. But within the last seventeen years, many other sites, revealing both the early and middle stages of this dynasty, have been found, and news of these finds is awaited with keen interest by academic circles throughout the world. Notable among these sites, all in central and northern China, are those at Ch'eng-chou, Hui District, and Lo-yang, all in Honan Province.

While the Yin dynasty flourished in the area of present-day Honan, a new state was emerging to the west in present-day Shensi; this became the Chou state. Gradually this state gained ascendency over the Yin state and eventually conquered it, replacing the dynasty. At first the capital was at Hao-ching (southwest of Sian), Shensi, but in 770 B.C. the capital was moved to Lo-yi, Honan (southwest of Lo-yang). This movement of the capital marks the division of the dynasty into the so-called Western and Eastern Chou dynasties. The dynasty fell to the Ch'in in 249 B.C.

Although the Chou state surpassed the Yin in military power, culturally it had little to offer, and for the most part it sought to continue the culture of the earlier dynasty. Both the Yin and the Western Chou were, of course, Bronze Age cultures, but it is important to remember, in considering the arts of the period, that the use of bronze was limited to weapons and ritual vessels for the use of the ruling class. The ordinary people still used wood and stone implements and lived in pit dwellings much as they had in the Neolithic period. Thus the bronze art that we are considering was produced by specialist craftsmen for an elite.

The most typical products of this art are the bronze ritual vessels called either *tsun-yi* or *yi-ch'i*. Such vessels were used in temples at festivals, in rituals possibly for royal ancestors, for use as eating and drinking vessels at banquets and as musical instruments. The shapes and decoration, no less than the exceptional quality of casting technique, are unique in the world. A great many such vessels have been found, but the finest have all come from the large tomb near Hou-chia-chuang, An-yang, Honan. Among these finds is the largest bronze vessel so far found, the Ssu Mu Wu *ting* (Pls. 9, 10), a large, four-legged *ting* (cauldron) that weighs 875 kilograms. The Hou-chia-chuang pieces all date from the late Yin dynasty and show an excellence of technique and intricacy of design that could not be surpassed even today.

The beginnings of this magnificent casting technique is still a mystery. Many strange bronze vessels thought to be of a middle Yin dynasty date have been found in recent years at Hui District and Ch'eng-chou and other sites in northern and central China. They are atypical, thin-walled, less well cast, bear no inscriptions, and are characterized by decoration cast in raised lines, circular and zigzag patterns (Pl. 41). They are believed to be older than the bronze vessels of the An-yang area and to belong to the middle of the Yin period, thus constituting simpler precursors of the later Yin pieces. But this problem cannot be so simply resolved: both Dr. Sueji Umehara and the author believe that they cannot possibly be of such antiquity. At present it can only be said that the origins of the Yin bronze vessels are unclear. A good guess, if one must be hazarded, is perhaps that of Dr. Umehara, who holds that the vessels were bronze copies of well-developed, wooden sacrificial vessels, and thus were from the start extremely complex and divorced from practical use.

There are some fifty kinds of bronze vessels of the Yin and Western Chou periods, referred to by a complex nomenclature in the Chinese Classics, which can be divided into four categories with respect to use: wine vessels, food vessels, water vessels, and musical instruments. Space does not allow a discussion of all these categories, but a representative selection is shown in the plates and these are discussed in the plate notes. Though it has been supposed here that the prototypes of these bronzes were wooden vessels, there are many cases in which even earlier models may have been found in clay or horn vessels. It is both the shapes and the very complex decoration that characterize these Chinese bronzes. Although some rare pieces show a realistic style of decoration, this is exceptional and outside the main tradition (Pl. 45). The main tradition is typified by the symbolic, highly stylized decoration.

Perhaps the most remarkable of the highly symbolic representations of imaginary animals is the *t'ao-t'ieh* (Pl. 47). This is a weird animal mask, the most striking feature of which is the eyes. The origin and meaning of this mask is not clear, but it seems at least certain that the mysterious light of the eyes was intended to ward off evil demons. Other designs are those of the *k'uei-feng* (a mythical bird), the *k'uei-lung* (a *k'uei-feng* with an elongated dragon-like trunk), and the *hui-lung* (a serpent-like dragon with no feet). The spaces between the principle designs are almost without exception filled in with *lei-wen* (a squared whorl) as a background motif (Pl. 10). The *lei-wen* is very popular with the Chinese, and has been used symbolically in their arts from ancient times to the present day. The elegance of these bronzes is now enhanced by the surface patina acquired through long years of burial; but the original effect, probably a metallic shine much like polished brass, would certainly impress us today as more grotesque than beautiful.

The overriding quality of symbolism and formalization of Chinese art in this period allowed very little individuality of expression to the artist. The atmosphere of gloom unrelieved by lightness or gaiety is expressed in fantastic and complex designs. The grotesque *t'ao-t'ieh* glowers, and a ferocious tiger bites the head of the ghost of a man (Pl. 9, 43, 44). This is a world of terror, and there is a quality of threatening stillness in these dignified bronze vessels. They are the symbols of the authority and wealth of a ruling class, disguised as the ritual objects of the magic-religion of the state. As such, they aim to inspire fear and cannot admit of any freedom and naturalness of expression. At the same time, the remarkable technical perfection of these works could only have been achieved through the efforts of generations of specialist craftsmen pursuing their own unique vision of beauty. Notable among the art objects of this period are bronze-edged tools, the famous Yin White Pottery, glazed ware, pottery with impressed designs, ivory and bone items, stone sculpture, and jade objects. Through all these media, a consistent period style and the beginnings of a genuine tradition of "Chinese art" are detectable. The Western Chou dynasty continued the tradition of Yin bronzes, albeit with some changes; but the White Pottery and stone sculpture had already disappeared, and it is generally a rather depressing period in Chinese art.

The arts of the common people in the Yin and Western Chou dynasties contrasted strongly with those of the ruling class. Among the earthenwares of the classless Neolithic period, the lovely designs of the Painted Pottery and the simple, engraved patterns of the Black Pottery are outstanding. But in the Yin dynasty, the arts of the common people were completely stagnant, and there is very little worthy of mention. The gray pottery that met their daily needs carries no other decorative elements than a rather forlorn impressed rope design. The plainness of these vessels stands in sharp contrast to the splendid intricacy of the arts of the ruling class. The common people, to some degree, must also have aspired to aesthetic expression. In coming to the cities they must have gazed upon grand architectural structures, seen the splendidly attired members of the privileged classes, and come into contact with richly adorned artifacts of many kinds. There must have been a reason why there is so little evidence of aesthetic feeling in their own works.

Since ancient times in China, in all strata of society from the emperor to the common people, there have existed severe restrictions on many aspects of artistic expression. With regard to clothing, for example, a complex class system governed the shape of caps and the design of ceremonial dress. Yellow was designated the imperial color, red that of the privileged classes, and blue that of the commoners. In line with this, such symbolic designs as the *t'ao-t'ieh,* which appear on Yin and Chou bronzes, must have been the prerogative of kings and those immediately below them. It is further possible that not only these symbolic motifs, but all manner of decorative embellishment was limited to the ruling classes. If this was indeed the case, then commoners would have had no opportunity to express their creative and aesthetic sensibilities.

The shining, bizarre bronze vessels and the symbolic designs worked upon them express the concept of beauty of a primitive farming people. Irrespective of class distinctions, these objects can be taken as the final selective result of their aesthetic value judgments. The common people, too, when they had the opportunity, must have been driven by a desire to imitate these bronzes and their designs even more than by any wish for an expression of their own originality. Thus the yellow pottery that belongs to the Lung-shan tradition was perhaps made in imitation of the color of the bronze vessels. Thus also, black pottery jars that reflect clearly the shapes of the bronze vessels have been discovered. Further, in the southeast coastal region, the *lei-wen* motif, which is thought to have been the monopoly of the ruling classes, seems to be common on the impressed pottery excavated there. Fragments of pottery impressed with the *t'ao-t'ieh* design have also been found in a residential area in the vicinity of Nanking, but these are very unusual. Oppressed by a central authority whose control over their creativity was not always complete, the use of such designs as the *lei-wen* by the common people of the time seems almost stealthy and somewhat pathetic.

THE ARTS OF CH'UN CH'IU AND WARRING STATES PERIODS As stated above, the removal of the capital to the east in 770 B.C. marked the division of the dynasty into the Western and Eastern Chou periods. The first half of the Eastern Chou period, from the transfer of the capital to the partition of Chin into the three states of Han, Wei, and Chao in 403 B.C., is also called the Ch'un Ch'iu, or "Spring and Autumn" period. This is because it corresponds to the period covered by the *Ch'un Ch'iu Annals,* a history of the state of Lu attributed to Confucius. The starting date of this period is sometimes given as 722 B.C., to correspond with the first entry in the *Ch'un Ch'iu* in the first year of the reign of Duke Yin of Lu. The period from the tripartite division of Chin to the unification of the country by the state of Ch'in in 221 B.C. is called the Warring States period, again on the basis of a history of the period called the *Chan Kuo Ts'e,* or *The Annals of the Warring States.*

The Eastern Chou period witnessed the complete eclipse of Chou dynastic power, and the appearance of great feudal lords such as the Five Hegemons of the Ch'un Ch'iu period and the Seven Heroes of the Warring States, who partitioned the country among themselves. The peaceful dream of the Western Chou was broken, and China was torn by continuous dissension and warfare. However, the appearance of iron agricultural implements at the beginning of the Ch'un Ch'iu period signaled an important revolution in agriculture. Ox-drawn plows were introduced, and large-scale irrigation works constructed. The result of these innovations was a conspicuous rise in agricultural efficiency, an expansion of the area under cultivation, and a rapid enlargement of the harvest. The consequent accumulation of wealth stimulated the development of a money economy. The use of bronze coins and a flourishing commerce brought prosperity to cities and strength to the states. Thus the temporarily stagnated culture of ancient China was given a great push forward. This background makes possible an explanation of the greatly expanded walled cities and tombs of the Ch'un Ch'iu and Warring States periods, and of the many grand relics found in them. The result of this concentration of wealth in urban centers was to greatly enrich the lives of city-dwellers. The new atmosphere thus engendered gave rise to the diverse speculations of the "hundred philosophers" in the field of thought, and to new, tradition-breaking trends in the arts.

Although remains of this period were of course known earlier, it was not until the scientific excavations carried out in China since the revolution of 1949 that the great body of material of this period was brought to light. Since 1954, careful exploration has been made of the Eastern Chou site in the southwest suburbs of Lo-yang, which site appears to be a Chou capital during the Ch'un Ch'iu period. Out of the 260 tombs found at Chung-chou-lu in Lo-yang itself, seventy-four are of the Ch'un Ch'iu period. The finds from this site show some very fine material (Pl. 15). The excavations of 1956–57 in the Kuo state cemetery at Shang-ts'un-ling, Shan District, Honan, revealed some 234 tombs of the late Western Chou and early Ch'un Ch'iu periods. From this place come two bronze swords and three bronze mirrors that are the earliest examples of their kind yet found. Also in 1955 the Ts'ai Hou (Marquis of Ts'ai) tomb was excavated at Shou District, Anhui (Pls. 13, 57). The bronze vessels from this site have added much to the establishment of dating standards for such vessels of this period.

Some three thousand Warring States tombs have been discovered, five times more than those of the Western Chou and Ch'un Ch'iu periods. In the last several years, in a wide area stretching from Liaotung in the north to Szuchwan, Hupei, and Hunan in the south, excavations of Warring States tombs have been carried out. In the territory of the three Chin states around Lo-yang and Hui District in Honan, over one thousand tombs have been found in some twenty sites. Another fifteen hundred have been found at sites in Ch'ang-sha, Hunan, and Hsin-yang, Honan, within the territory of the old state of Ch'u. Particularly at Ch'ang-sha, scholars have been surprised at the appearance of such treasures as carved planks set at the bases of coffins, bronze swords encased in black-lacquered scabbards, leather shields on which cloud-dragon designs are painted in vermilion and yellow on a black background, male and female wooden figures that show the customs of the times, a painting of a dragon, a tiger, and a woman drawn on silk, inscribed bamboo slips and the brushes used to write them, a large wooden lute (*se*), and a steelyard scales with its weights.

Large cities have been excavated at many places. At Hou-ma Municipality, Shansi, the site of the ancient capital of the Chin and Wei states was investigated in 1956. In 1958, the site of the Yen capital of Hsia-tu was excavated at Yi District in Hopei, and the old capital of the Ch'i state was studied at Lin-tzu District in Shantung. Semicircular eave end-tiles and square bricks impressed with beautiful designs, and potsherds with impressed inscriptions were unearthed from the old Ch'i capital. In 1959, four bronze founding furnaces and thirty thousand clay molds (Pls. 74–76) were found south of the Wei-Chin capital site at Hou-ma, and pottery kilns were discovered at Wu-an, Hopei, and Lo-yang in Honan, adding much information to our knowledge of the casting and molding techniques of the time. The nineteen wooden carts found at Liu-li-ko in Hui District, Honan, in 1950, and the various lacquer ware taken from Ch'ang-t'ai-kuan, Hsin-yang District, Honan, in 1957 and 1958 reveal superior woodworking and lacquer techniques. These are but a few items turned up by the new excavations recently carried out.

The craftsmen of the Ch'un Ch'iu and Warring States periods were divided into two groups, state and private. In the Ch'un Ch'iu period, the older clan-based units of craftsmen were gradually dissolved and drawn into state enterprises, while an independent handicraft industry also began to arise among the people—a trend that gathered strength in the Warring States period. In the "Treatise on Crafts" ("K'ao-kung-chi") section of the *Rites of Chou* (*Chou Li*), the specializations of state craftsmen are divided into thirty items within six larger fields such as woodworking, metalworking, etc.; and the chapter on the "Accumulation of Goods" ("Huo-chih Lieh-chuan") in the *Historical Records* (*Shih Chi*) by Ssu-ma Ch'ien records the accumulation of great wealth by the operators of iron foundries and salt works. State craftsmen polished their techniques under government sponsorship, while private craftsmen must have directed their work to meet the demands of wealthy patrons for whom money was no object. The result was an amazing development of technical perfection in many aspects of applied arts.

First, in the field of metalworking, the use of openwork in bronze made many new designs possible. A cloud-whorl pattern in gold or silver was in popular use on the surfaces of bronze implements and mirrors, carriage fittings and buckles (Pls. 16, 17). Both inlay and plating techniques are to be seen. In the former, silver and gold were laid into the cast depression of the design; in the latter, thin gold or silver plating was attached to the surface, or the design painted on with a thin brush after mixing the powdered metals with some sort of adhesive substance. In addition, decorative stone inlay (Pl. 17) and the inlay of animal figures in copper was also used on bronze. The fine working of gold and silver itself was also much improved, and decorative objects with designs impressed on gold plate, variously designed gold buckles, silver lidded vessels and carved images appear. Rare treasures testifying to the beauty and skill of metalworking were excavated at a Warring States tomb at Ku-wei-ts'un in Hui District, including a carriage shaft with a horse's-head decoration affixed to the tip (Pl. 16), and buckles on which jade and glass are inlaid on a gold-plated silver base (Pl. 17).

The artistic techniques of ceramic materials also show remarkable progress in this period. In addition to the gray pottery of everyday use, there are glazed wares, impressed wares, pottery on which designs have been burnished with a spatula, and painted pottery in multi-colored designs. Clay tiles and bricks for use as building materials, often with beautiful impressed designs (Pls. 92–97) seem to have become common in the Ch'un Ch'iu and Warring States periods. There are also lovely figures and models etc., employing Black Pottery techniques, which appear to have been made specifically for burial purposes.

Perhaps it is in the field of lacquerwork that the craftsmen of this period excelled. Furniture, weapons, musical instruments and funerary objects were all decorated with lacquer painting in red, black, yellow and green (Pls. 19–21, 90, 98–108, 110). From the evidence of the pieces found, it would seem that the craft had already reached a high technical perfection by the Warring States period (Pl. 90). This is illustrated in a charming story related in the *Book of Han Fei-tzu,* a legalist-philosopher of the third century B.C.:

> "A man was commissioned to do paintings on a whip for the Chou emperor. Upon presenting it for inspection after three years' labor, it appeared no different from an ordinary lacquered whip. The emperor flew into a rage, but the craftsman said, 'Build a wall eighty feet high with an eight-foot window, then examine your whip again by the light of that window at sunrise.' The emperor did this, and found that his whip was complete with all manner of dragons and serpents, birds and beasts, carriages and horses."

Though this may be no more than apocryphal, it does perhaps indicate the extent to which fine lacquer painting had developed at this time.

Many other objects have been found in excavations of this period to show the craftsmen's mastery in other media, including jade, colored glass, and textiles, both silk and hemp weaving (Pl. 112). Some very strange wood carvings in the Ch'u state tombs at Hsin-yang show the high development of this craft (Pl. 98). But it is surprising that stone carving is very rare indeed, the exception being the pieces found at Ch'ang-sha.

It is perhaps no exaggeration to say that these crafts, mastered in the Warring States period, are the basis of all the applied arts of China through the ages. In general character, too, the arts of this period show a remarkable contrast to the solemnity and formalism of the preceding age. This can be seen very clearly in a comparison of bronze vessels. In place of the heavy, intricately decorated pieces of the Yin and Western Chou, the later pieces are thin and smooth with simple and light decoration. The animal motifs have dissolved and appear in fragments as elements in a design. Often the inlay designs depict scenes of hunting and banquets (Pls. 23, 77). We are no longer conscious of the ritual purpose of the vessels, nor are they symbolic of authority. In lacquer decoration, the scenes are even lighthearted and humorous: hunters carry home their kill tied to a pole, a man takes a walk with a dog. The lively animal designs seen on the semicircular eave end-tiles of the Ch'i state, and the lifelike tiger torso depicted on the water pipe from the Yen state are noteworthy (Pl. 91). A round, fat bronze horse (Pl. 65), a wooden phoenix with flapping wings and uplifted coxcomb (Pl. 105), a clay figure carrying a child on its back are but a few of the many realistic pieces that could be mentioned.

Why did this great change come about? Where did such cheerfulness and lightness come from? One clue to the answers may lie in the contact of many Chinese states with their neighbors to the north. In the Ch'un Ch'iu and Warring States periods, contacts between Chinese states and peoples of the north increased greatly. This trend was particularly evident with the states of Yen, Chao, and Ch'in. The territorial expansion of the Yen state into the northeast, and the use of barbarian dress and mounted archers by King Wu-ling of Chao are well known. It is conceivable that fresh perspectives were brought to the solemnity and formalism of Chinese art by the dynamic realism of Scythian art objects from the north.

The social changes of the time must also have played a part. In the Warring States period, the authority of the Yin and Chou tradition began to crumble, the control of thought and discussion was loosened, and the common people became much more active and vigorous. The usurping of power by rebellious officials, the elevation of commoners to the position of prime minister, the great accumulation of wealth by merchants, the arrogance of political opportunists who traversed the country, the flourishing of the hundred schools of philosophy, are all new phenomena without precedent.

Under these circumstances, the oppression of the ordinary people and, more particularly of the artist, was lifted, and a freedom of new expression arose. The arts that had served the authority of the state religion were released, and now served the ordinary people and the wealthy. However, the grave and abstract tradition was not entirely lost; it persisted beside the new realism through the Ch'in and Han periods, and thereafter colored the long tradition of Chinese art.

TAKESHI SEKINO

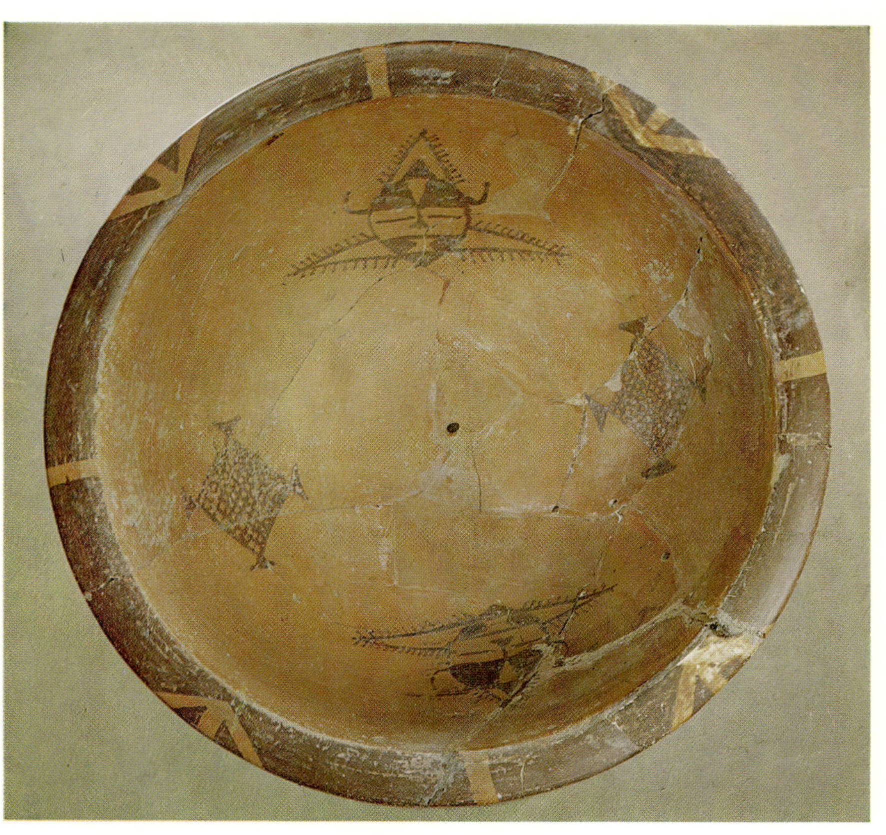

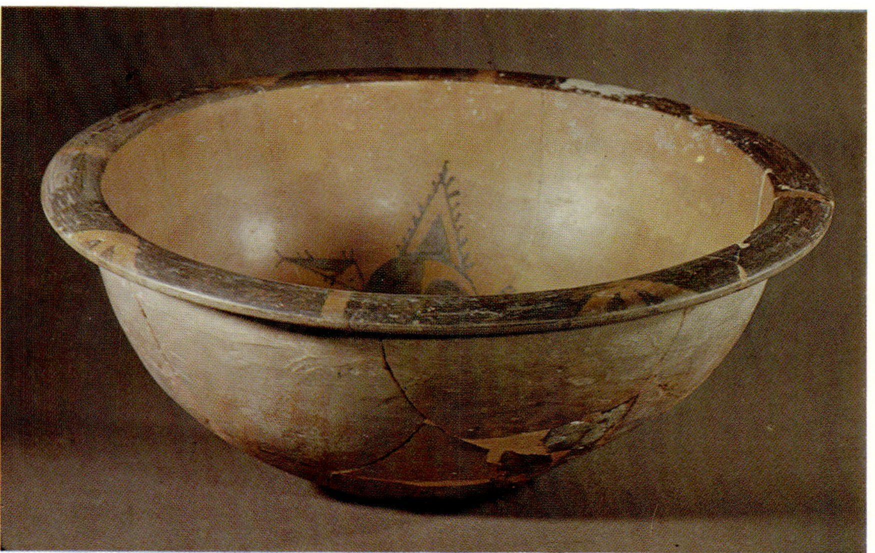

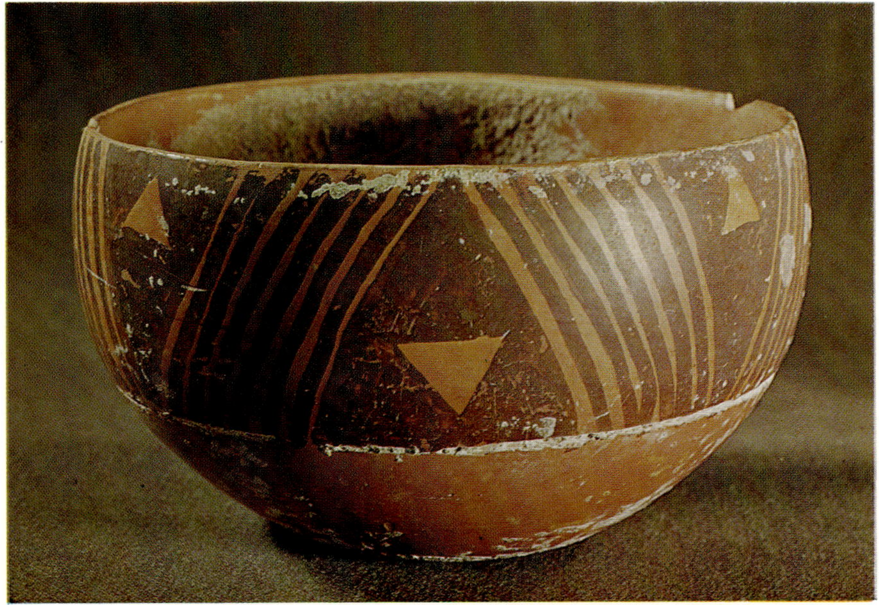

1–3. Painted Pottery, red earthenware with black slip decoration. Yang-shao type. Neolithic period. Excavated at Pan-p'o-ts'un, Sian, Shensi.

1. *Bowl. height: 16.4 cm. (6.5 in.); diameter: 44.5 cm. (17.5 in.)*
2. *Bowl used as the cover of a jar burial. height: 18.0 cm. (7.1 in.); diameter: 38 cm. (14.95 in.)*
3. *Cup. height: 13.0 cm. (5.1 in.); diameter: 12.0 cm. (4.7 in.)*

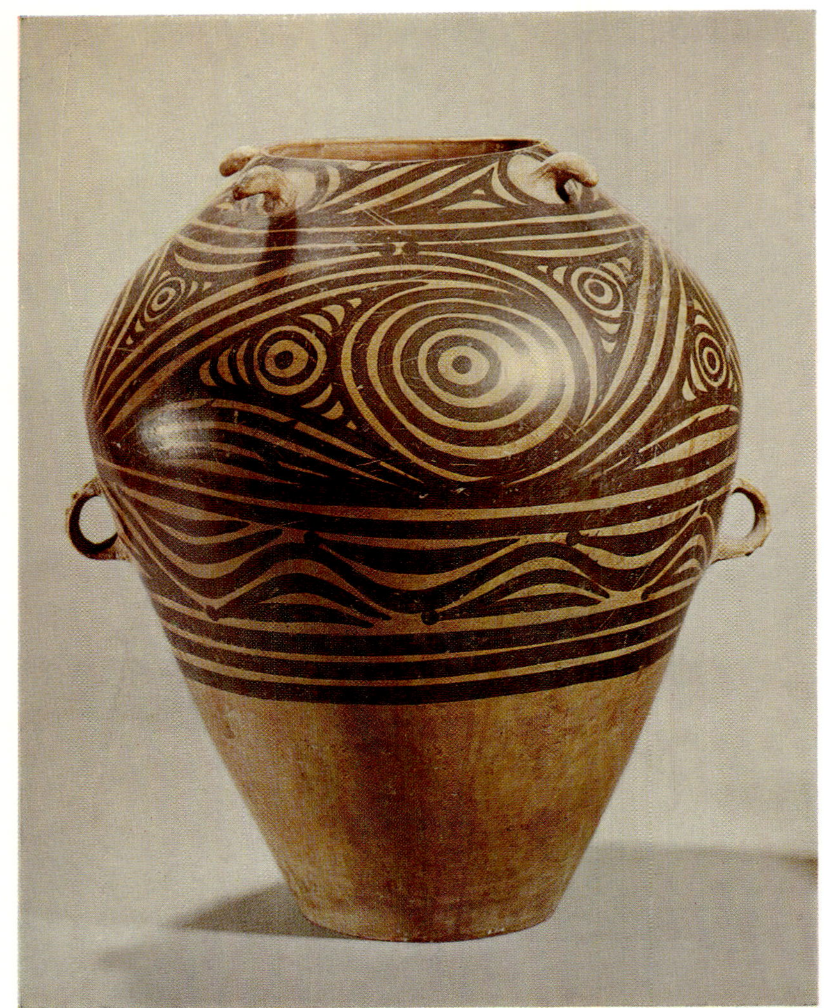

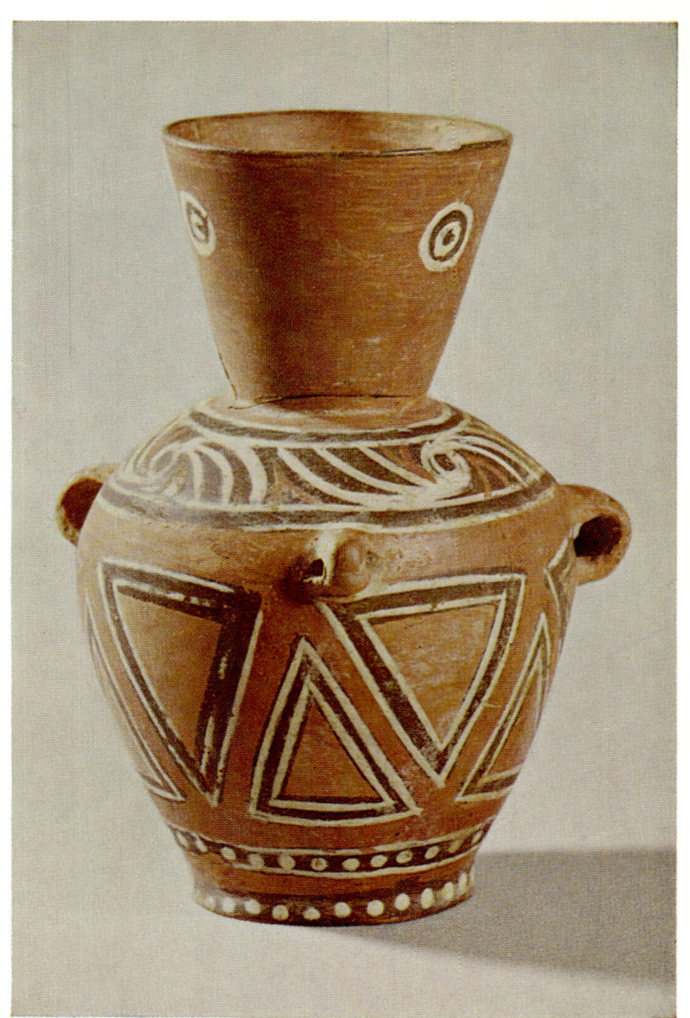

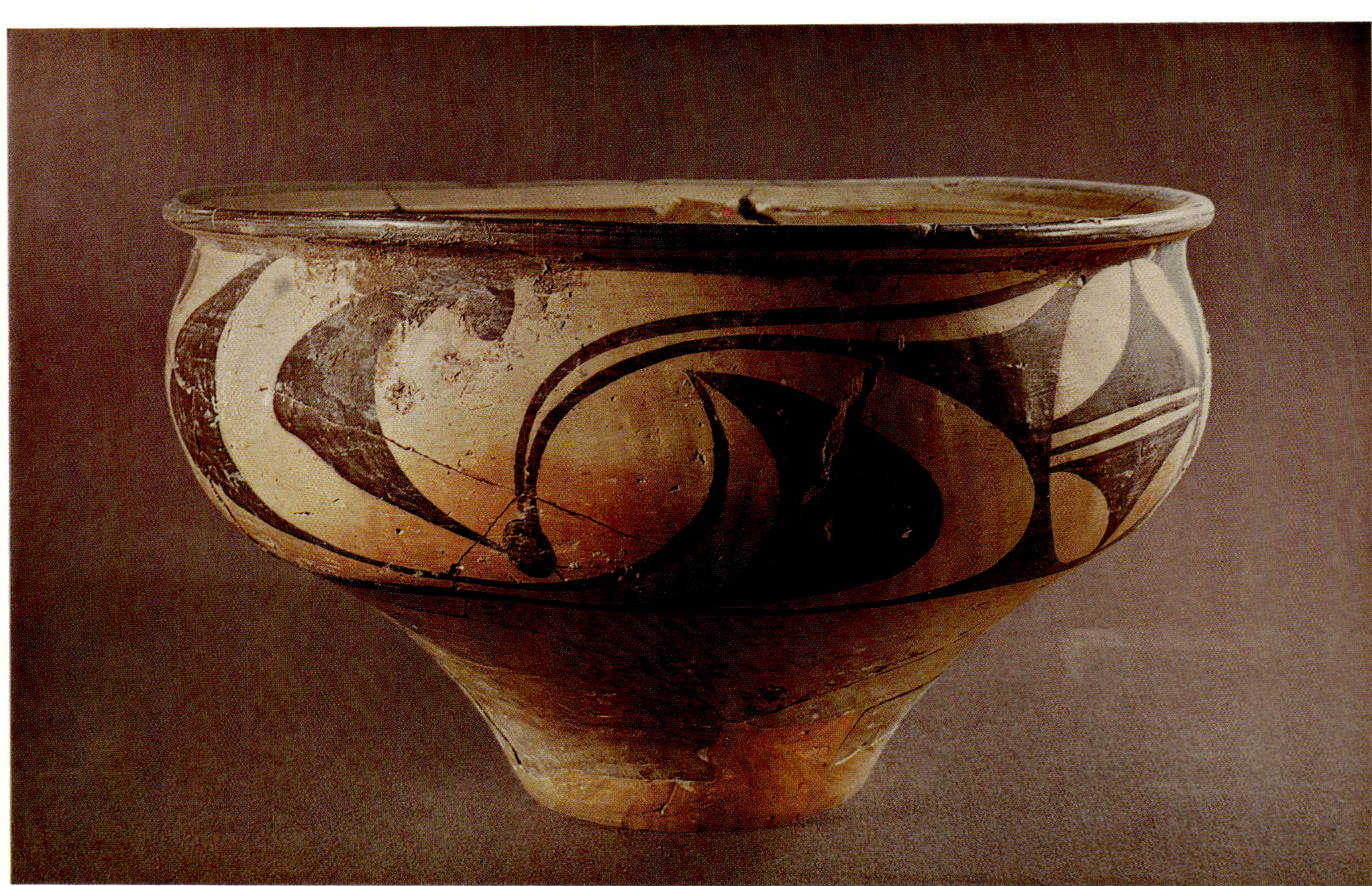

6. Painted Pottery bowl, red earthenware with black slip decoration. Yang-shao type. Neolithic period. Excavated at Miao-ti-kou, Shan District, Honan.
height: 22.5 cm. (8.9 in.); diameter at mouth: 36.5 cm. (14.4 in.)

◀4. *(left)* Painted Pottery jar, red earthenware with black slip decoration. Ma-chia-yao type. Neolithic period. Excavated at San-p'ing, Lin-hsia District, Kansu.
height: 48.0 cm. (18.9 in.)

◀5. *(right)* High-collared Painted Pottery jar, red earthenware with black and white slip decoration. Thought to be Yang-shao type. Late Neolithic period or early Yin dynasty. Excavated at Pao-t'ou, Ning-yang District, Shantung.
height: 17.2 cm. (6.9 in.)

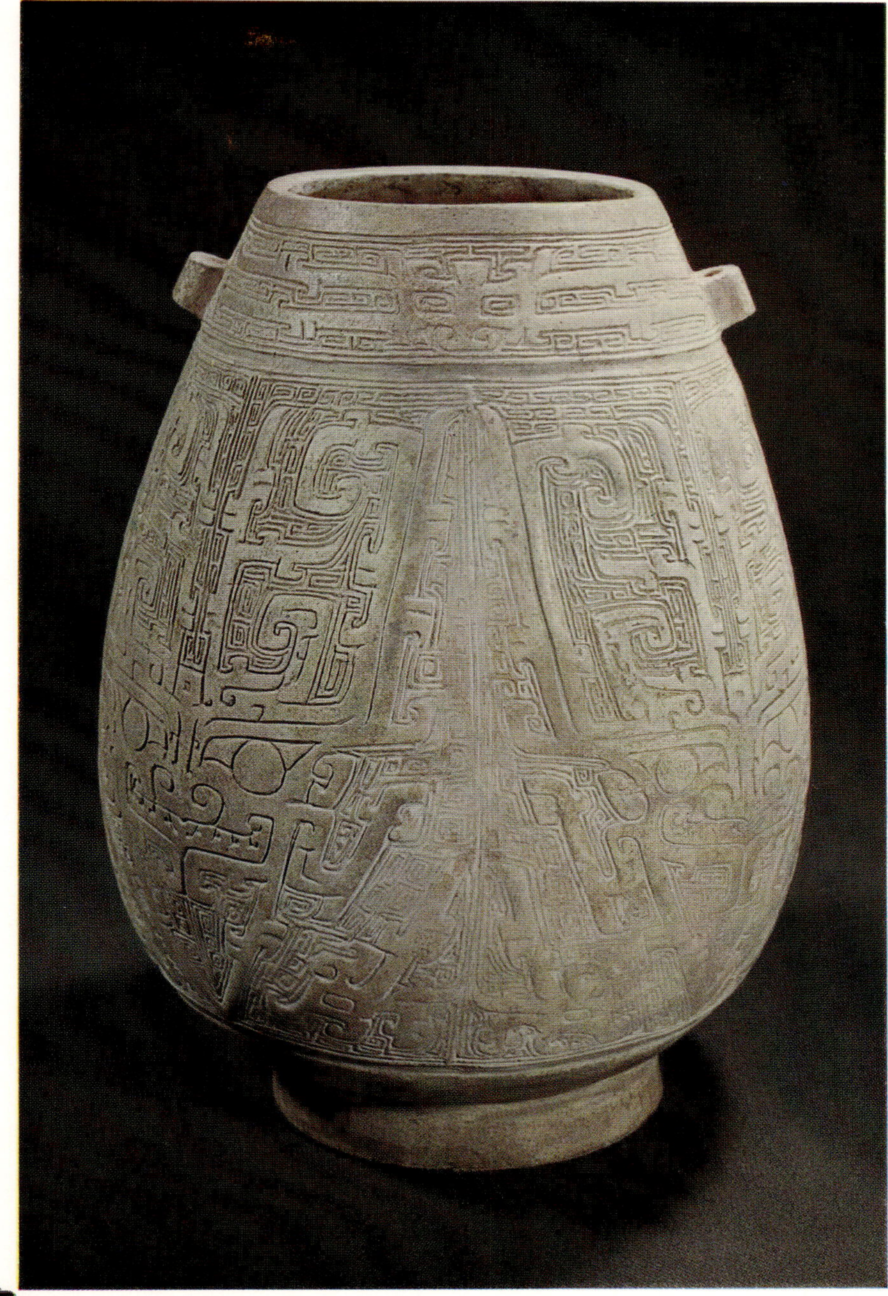

7. Jar, white earthenware. Yin dynasty. Excavated at An-yang District, Honan.
height: 18.5 cm. (7.3 in.); diameter: 17.6 cm. (6.9 in.)

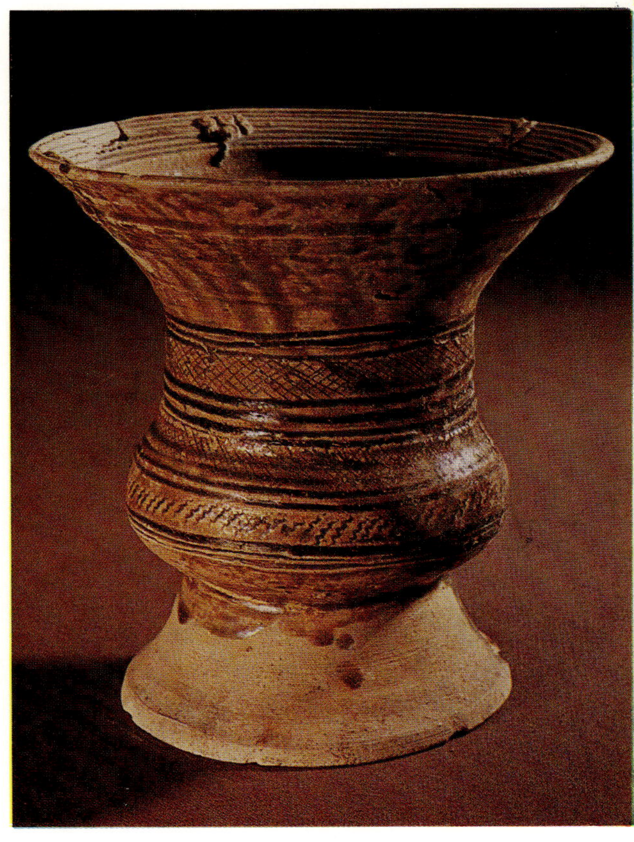

8. *Tsun*, earthenware with yellow-brown glaze over incised decoration. Western Chou dynasty. Excavated at T'un-hsi Municipality, Anhui.
height: 18.5 cm. (7.3 in.); diameter: 17.6 cm. (6.9 in.)

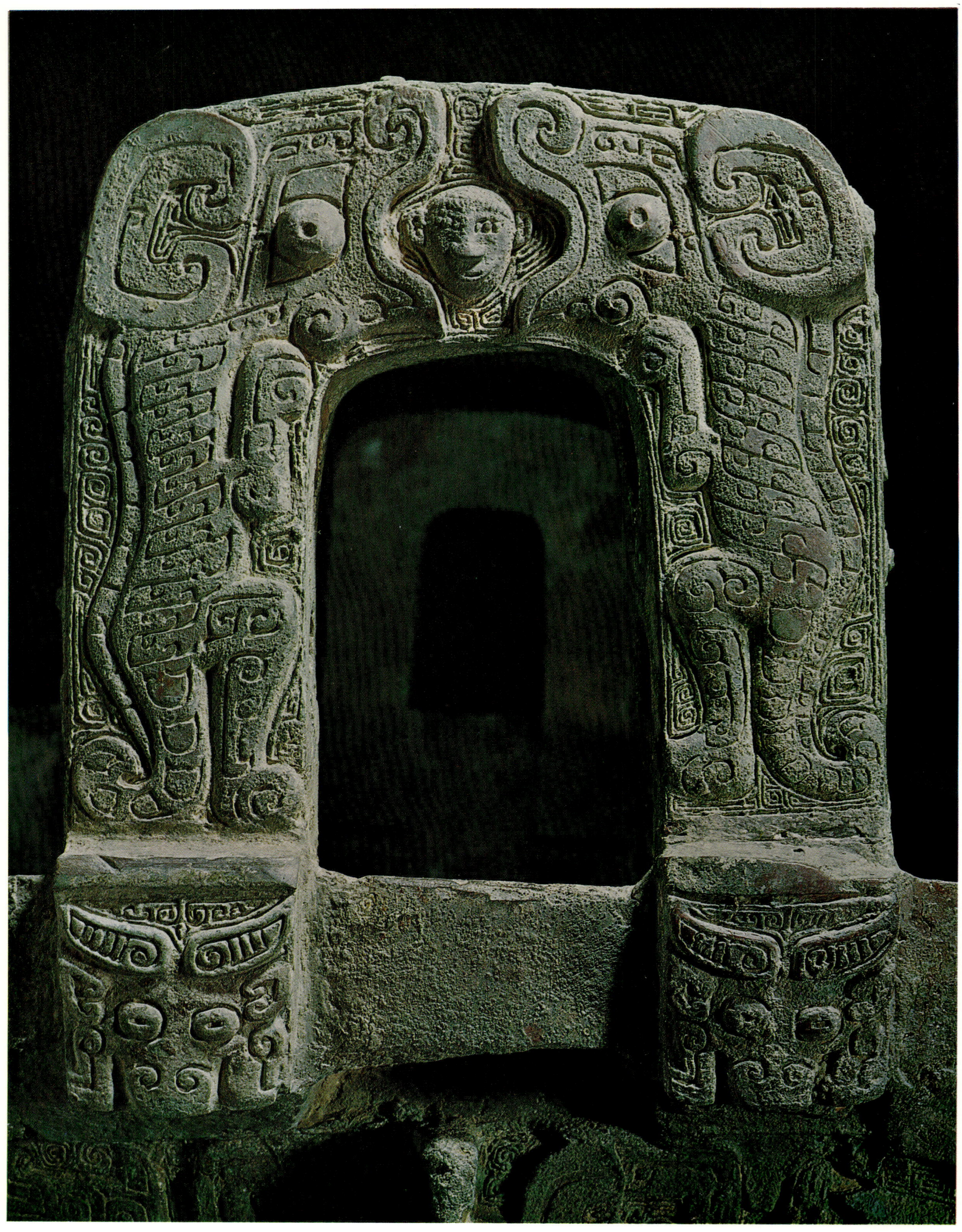

9. Lug-handle of Ssu Mu Wu *ting* (*see* Pl. 10).

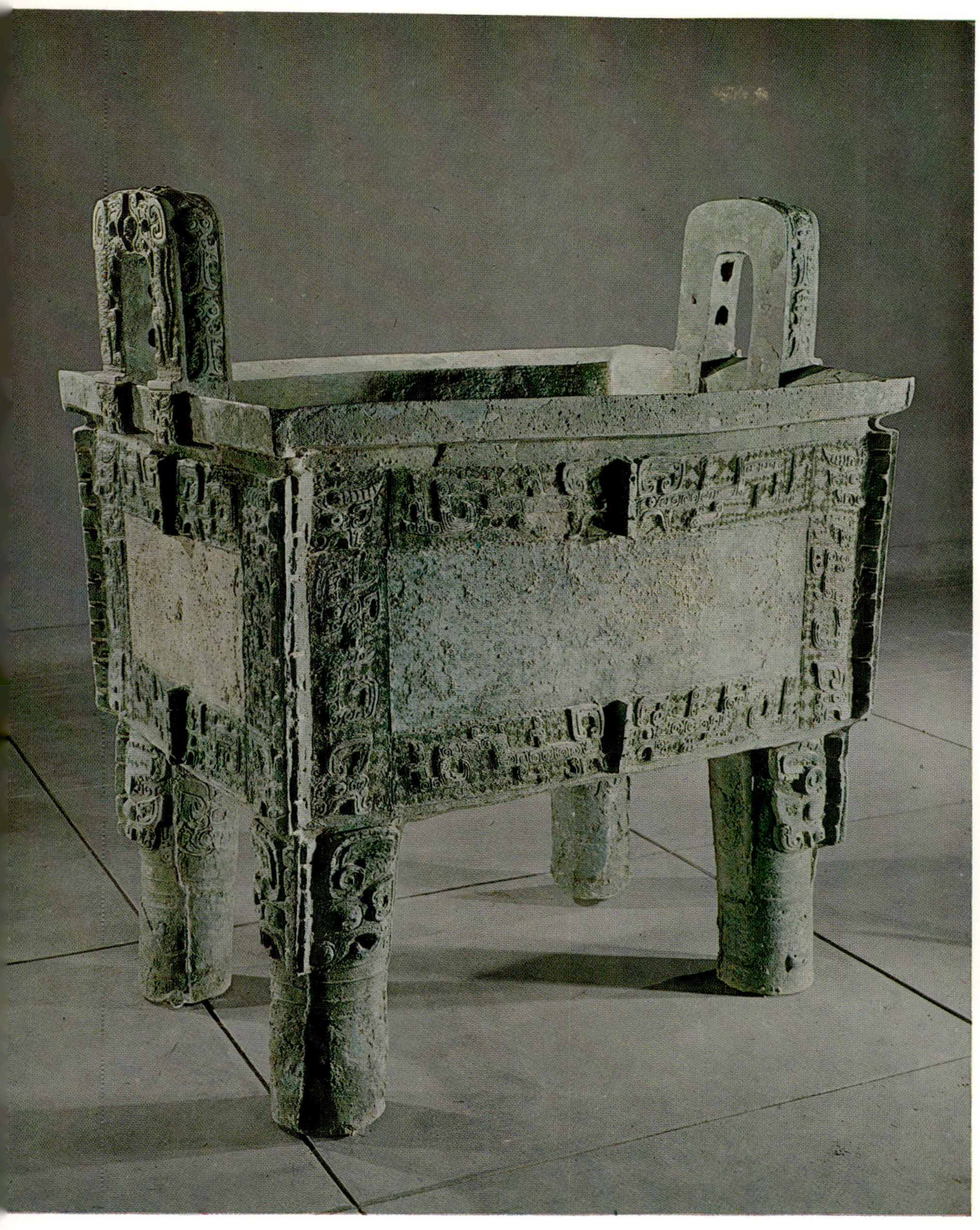

10. Ssu Mu Wu *ting*, bronze. Yin dynasty. Excavated at Wu-kuan-ts'un, An-yang District, Honan.
height: 133 cm. (52.4 in.); length: 110 cm. (33.3 in.); weight: 875 kg. (1929 lbs.)

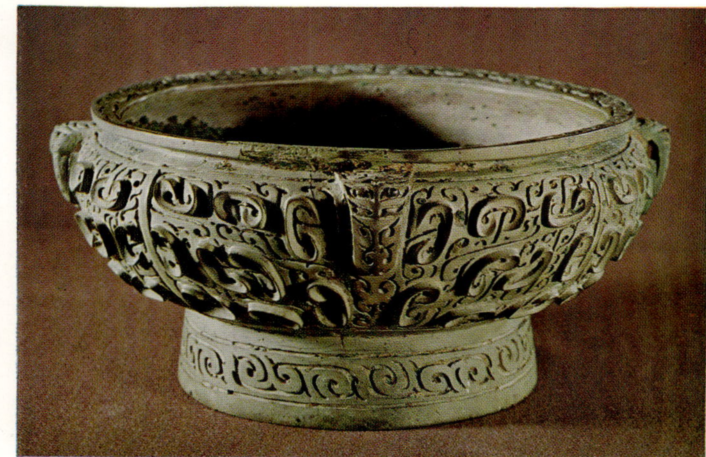

11. *Kuei*, bronze. Western Chou dynasty. Excavated at Shang-ts'ao-lou-ts'un, Ch'ang-hsing District, Chekiang.
height: 10.0 cm. (3.9 in.); diameter: 18.1 cm. (7.1 in.)

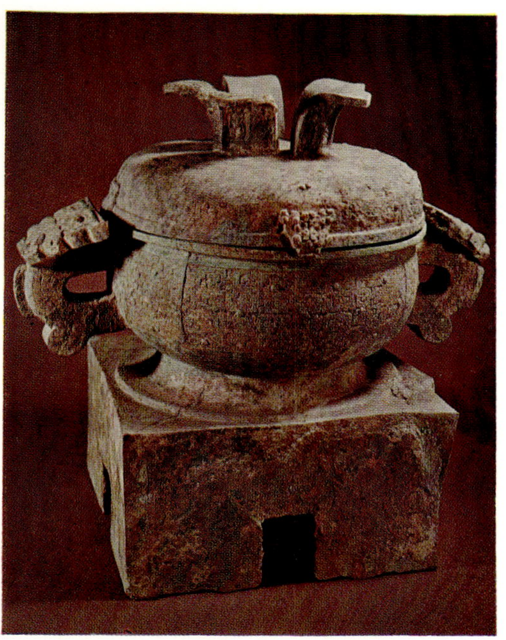

13. Marquis of Ts'ai *kuei*, bronze. Ch'un Ch'iu period. Excavated from the Marquis of Ts'ai tomb, Shou District, Anhui.
height: 36.0 cm. (14.2 in.); diameter: 23.8 cm. (9.5 in.)

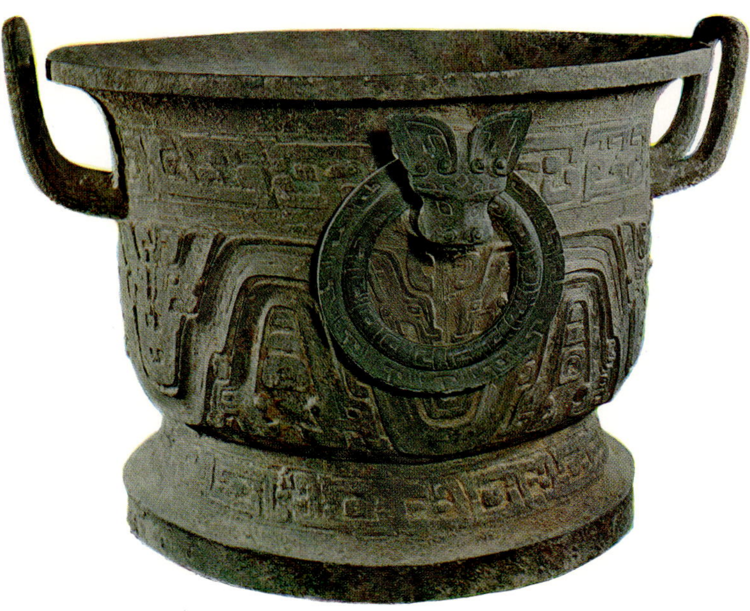

12. *Yü*, bronze. Late Western Chou dynasty. Excavated at Ch'i-chia-ts'un, Fu-feng District, Shensi.
height: 36.0 cm. (14.2 in.); diameter: 47.0 cm. (18.5 in.)

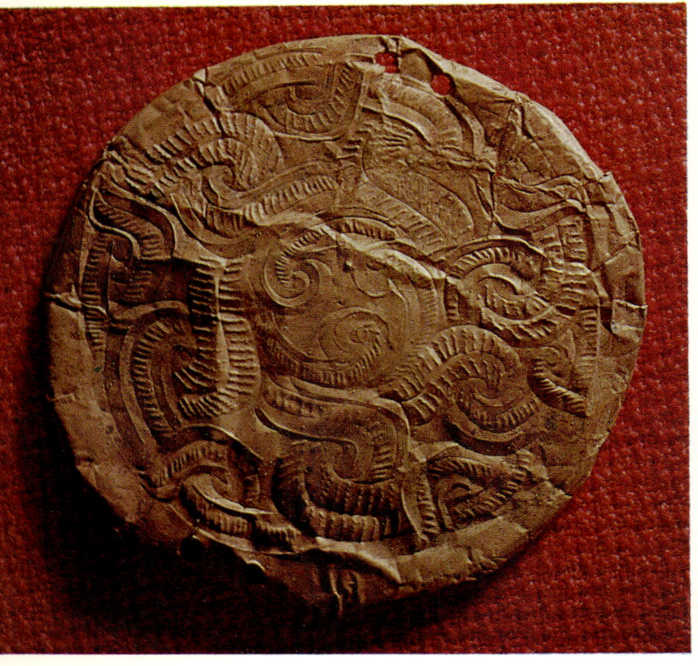

14. Gold plaque, perhaps used as a costume decoration. Ch'un Ch'iu period. Excavated from the Marquis of Ts'ai tomb, Shou District, Anhui.
diameter: 5.2 cm. (2.0 in.)

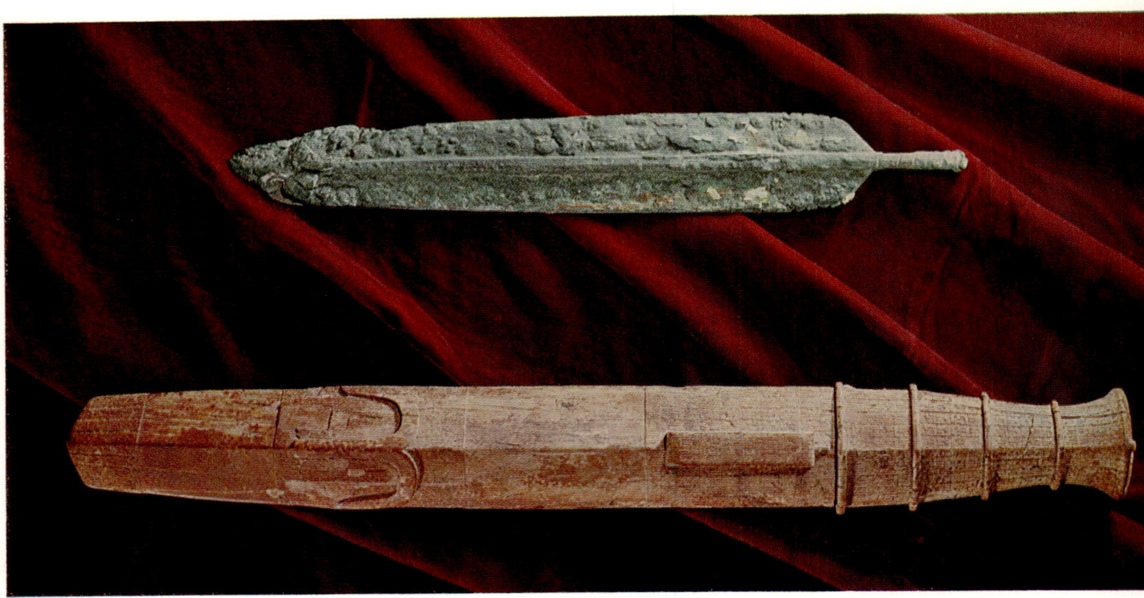

15. Bronze sword with carved ivory hilt and sheath. Ch'un Ch'iu period. Excavated at Chung-chou-lu, Lo-yang, Honan.
blade length: 28.5 cm. (11.2 in.)

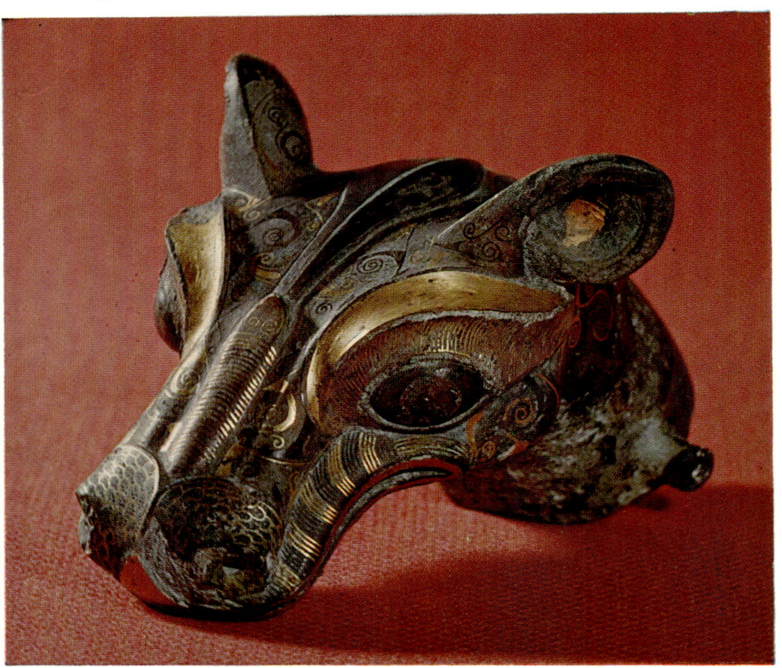

16. Finial in the shape of a horse's head, bronze inlaid with gold and silver. Warring States period. Excavated at Ku-wei-ts'un, Hui District, Honan. *length: 13.3 cm. (5.2 in.)*

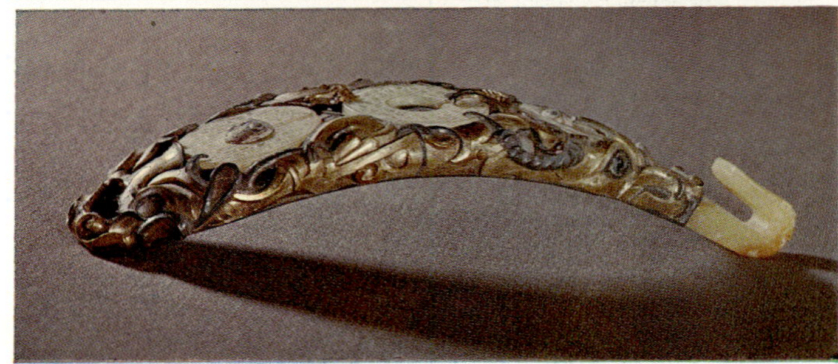

17 (a, b). Belt hook, silver and gilt with jade and glass insets. Warring States period. Excavated at Ku-wei-ts'un, Hui District, Honan.
length: 18.4 cm. (7.3 in.); width at center: 4.9 cm. (1.9 in.)

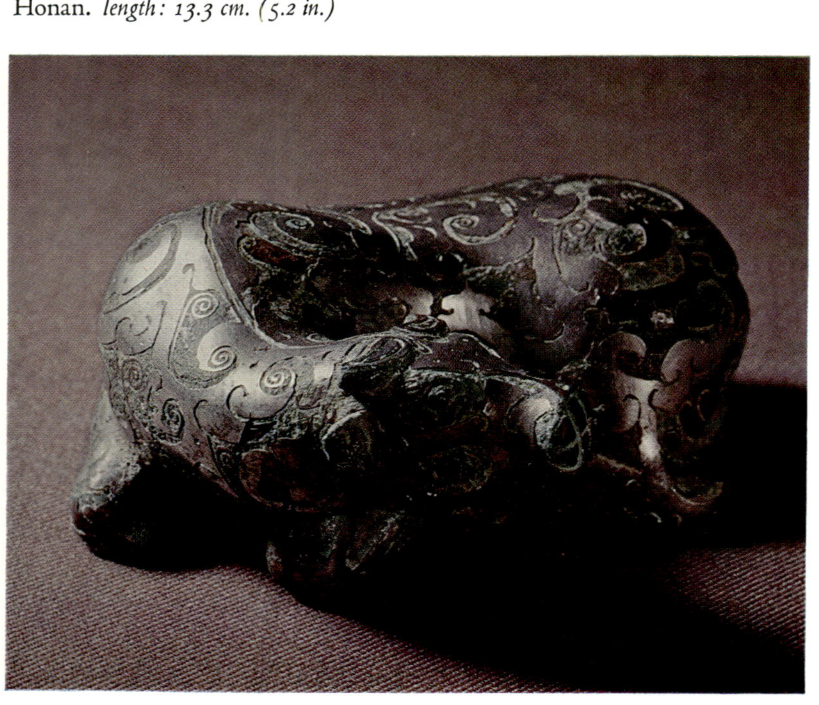

18. Buffalo, bronze inlaid with white metal. Warring States period. Excavated at Ch'iu-chia Hua-yüan, Shou District, Anhui.
length: 10.0 cm. (3.9 in.)

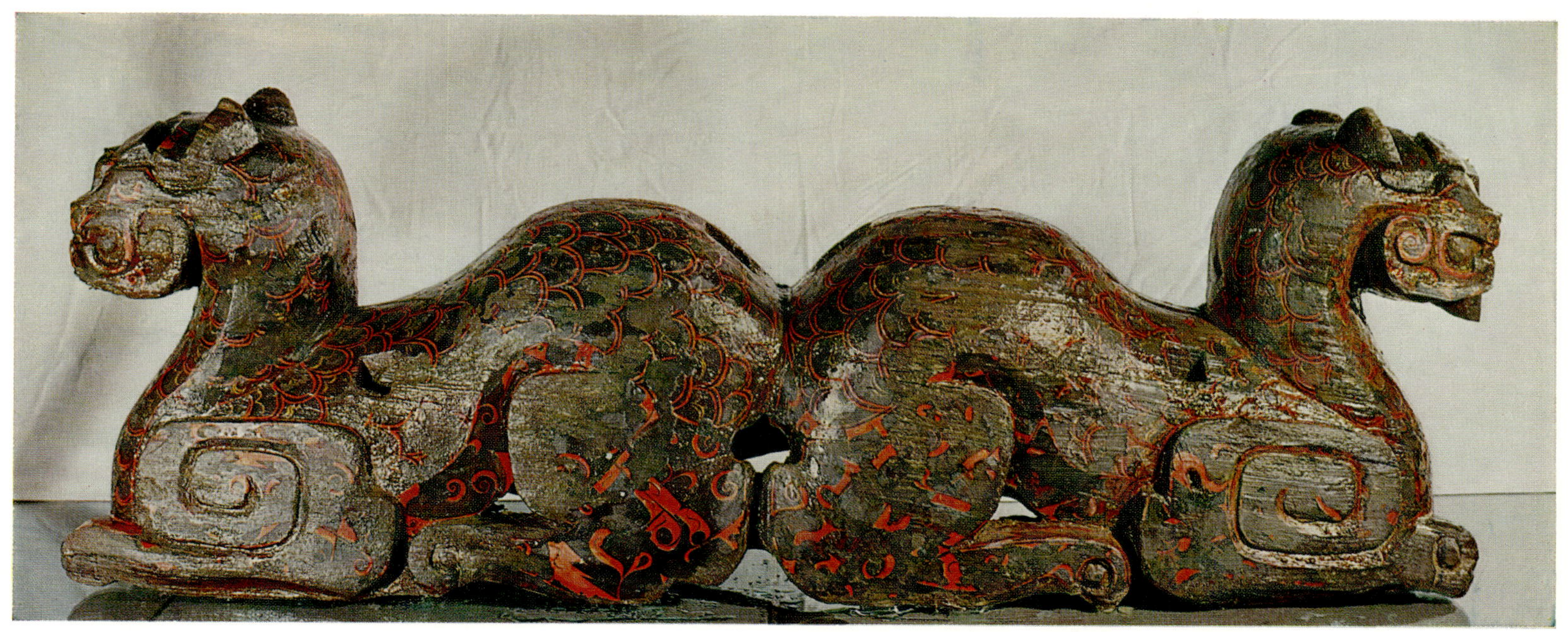

19. Pair of tigers, carved wood with black, red and yellow lacquer decoration; possibly the stand for a drum. Warring States period. Excavated from tomb No. 2, Chang-t'ai-kuan, Hsing-yang District, Honan.
height: 39.0 cm. (15.3 in.); length: 108 cm. (42.6 in.)

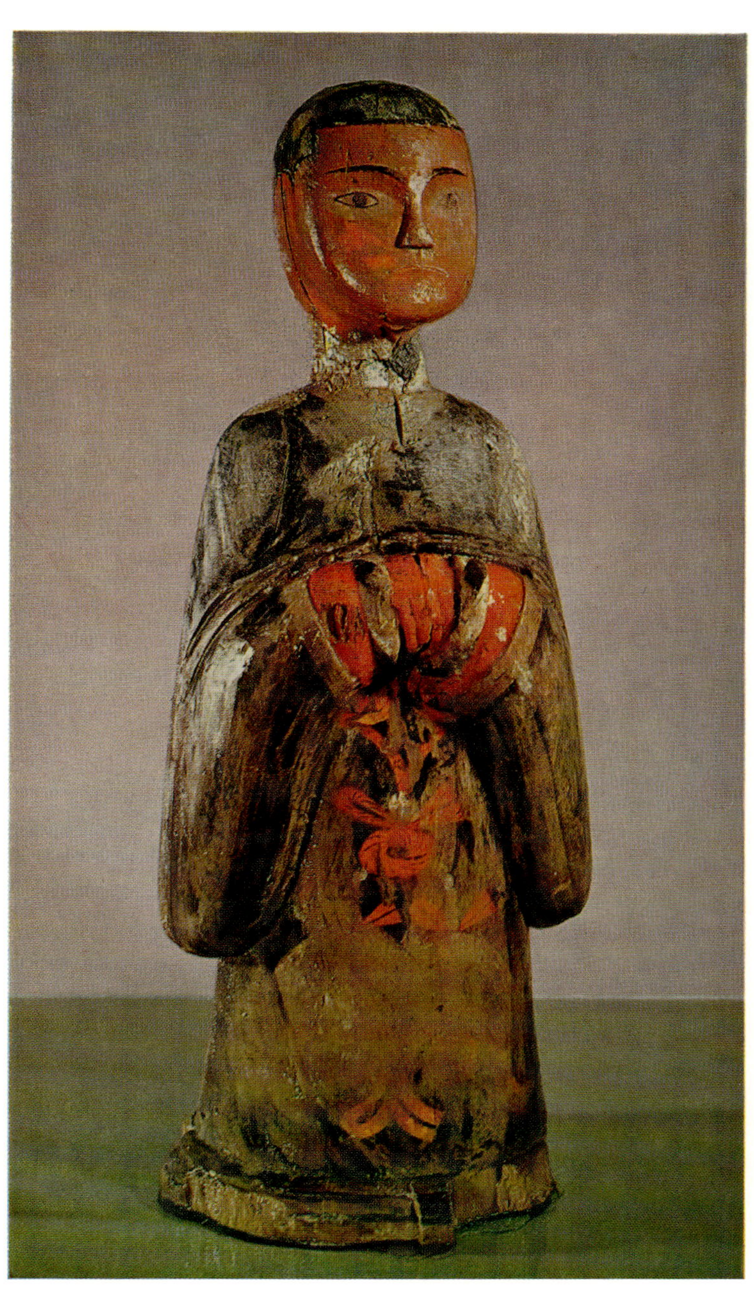

20. Male figure, carved and lacquered wood. Warring States period. Excavated from tomb No. 2, Chang-t'ai-kuan, Hsing-yang District, Honan.
height: 64.0 cm. (25.2 in.)

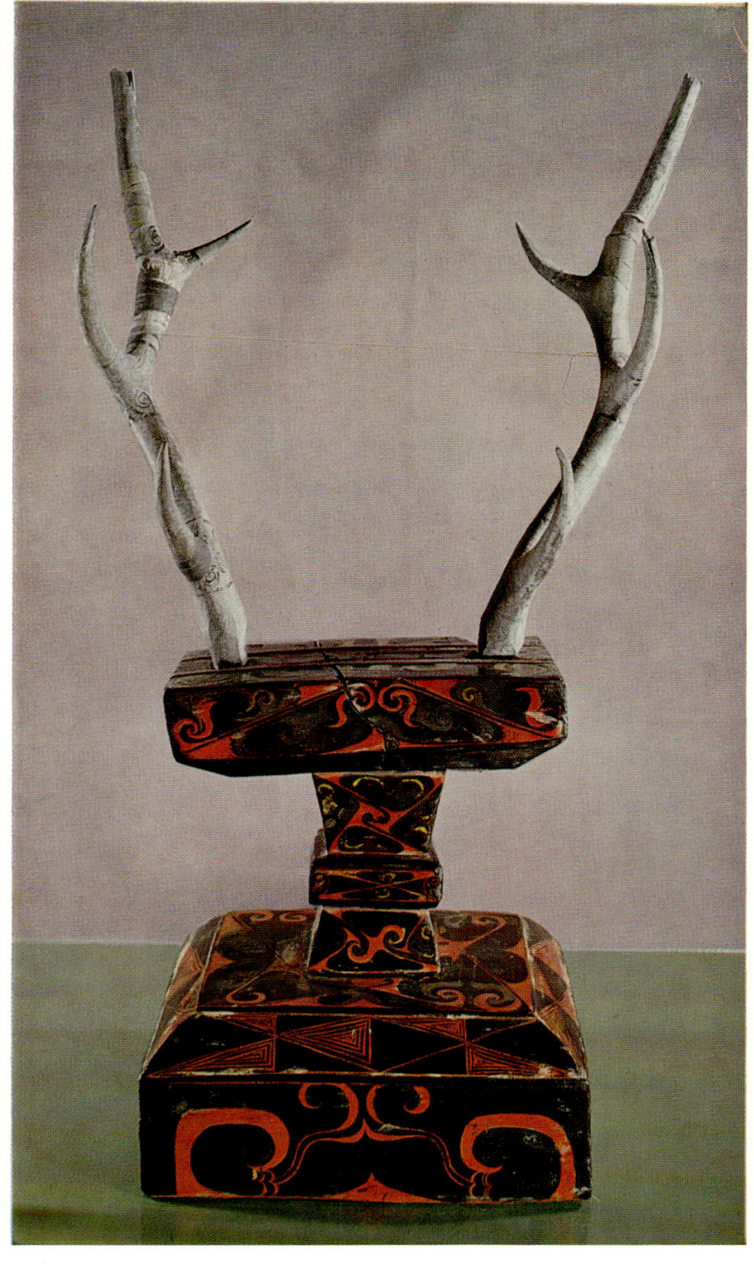

21. Stand surmounted by deer antlers, lacquered wood. Warring States period. Excavated from tomb No. 2, Chang-t'ai-kuan, Hsing-yang District, Honan.
height: 88.6 cm. (34.0 in.)

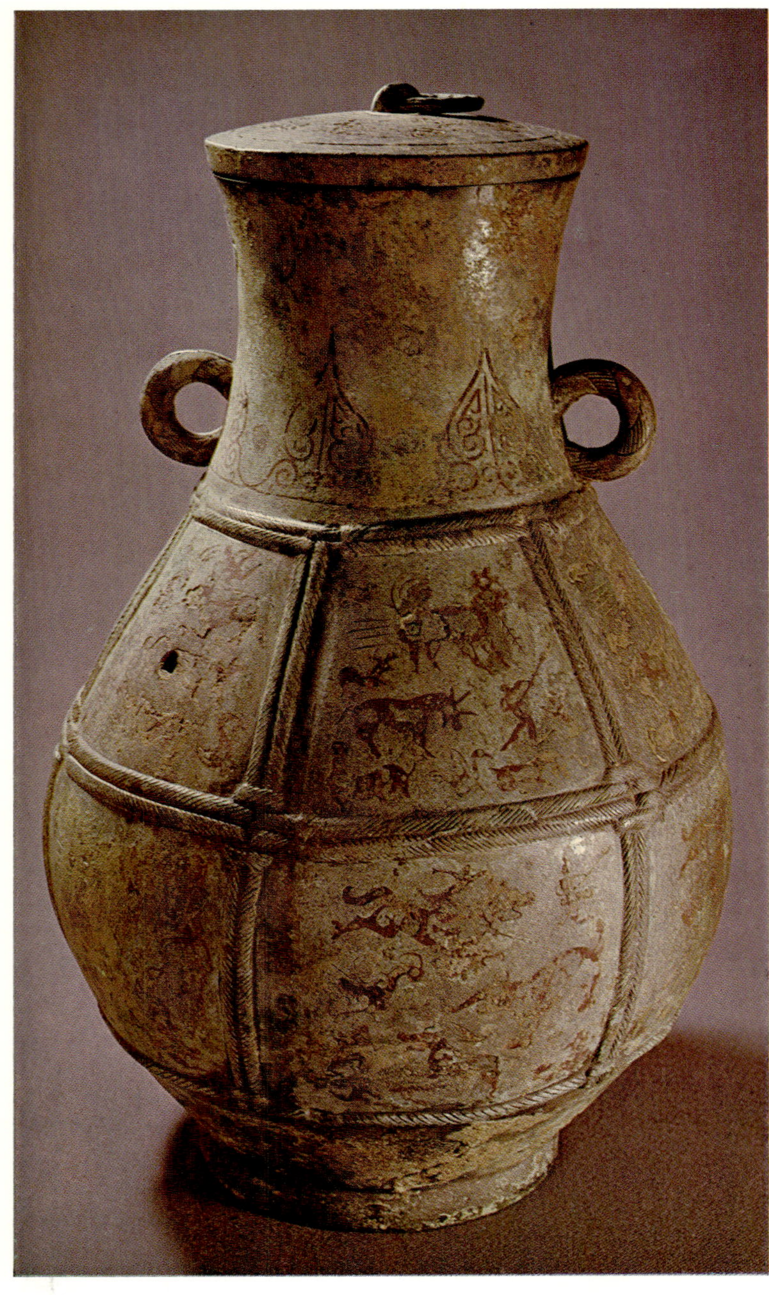

22. Covered *hu*, bronze with inlaid copper decoration. Warring States period. Excavated from tomb No. 5, Chia-ko-chuang, T'ang-shan Municipality, Hopei.
height: 34.9 cm. (13.8 in.)

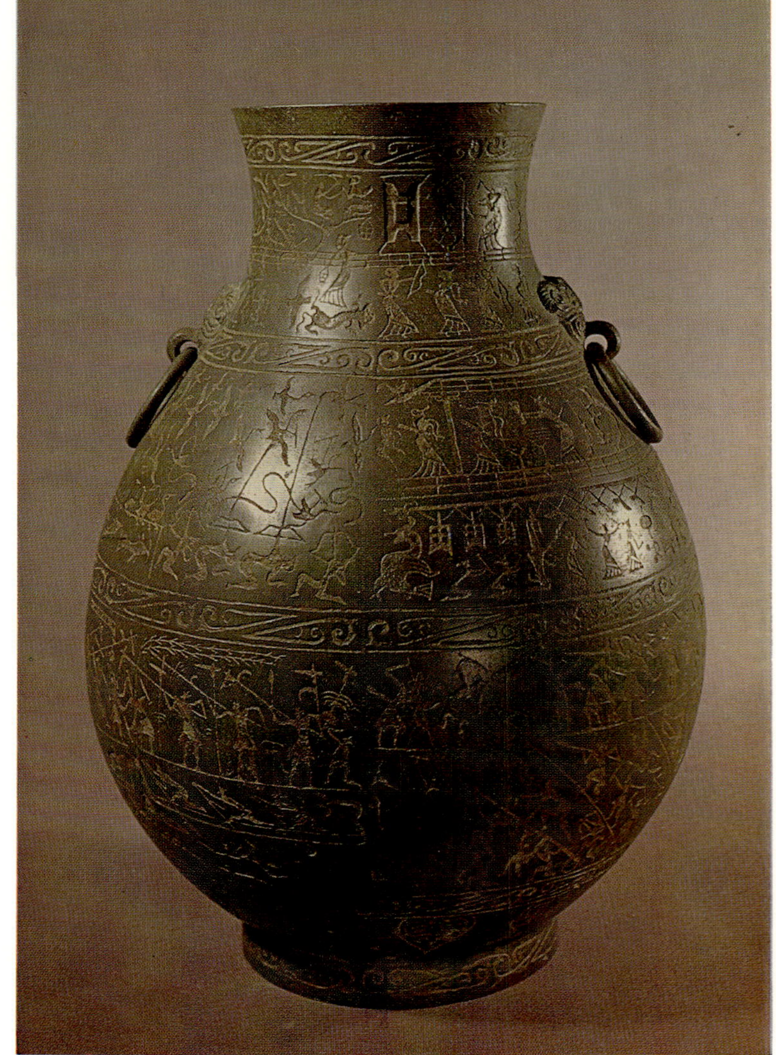

23. *Hu*, bronze with cast decoration, probably originally inlaid. Warring States period. Provenance unknown.
height: 31.7 cm. (12.5 in.); diameter at mouth: 11.0 cm. (4.3 in.)

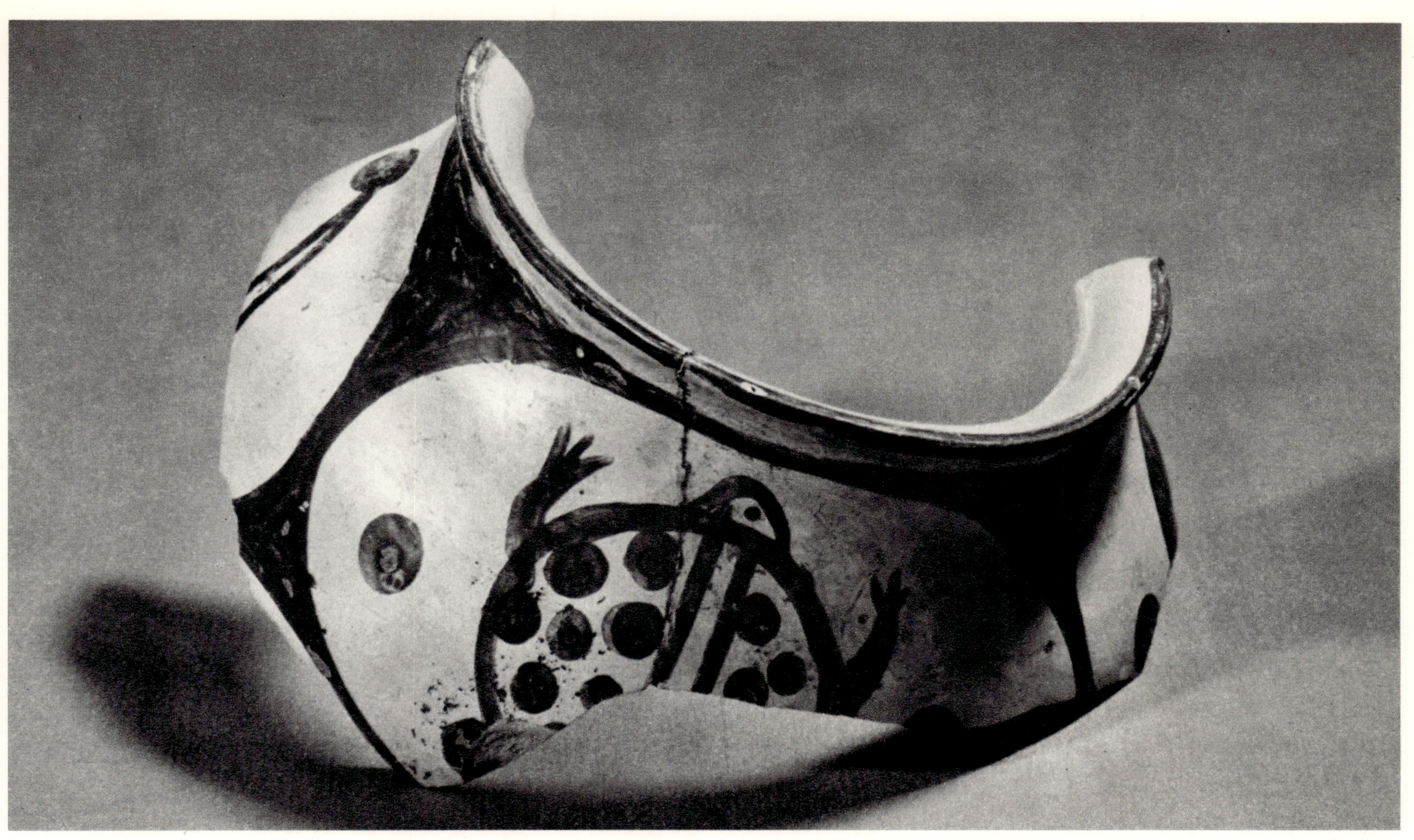

24. Painted Pottery jar shard, earthenware with slip decoration. Yang-shao type. Neolithic period. Excavated at Miao-ti-kou, Shan District, Honan.
length: 17.1 cm. (6.7 in.); width: 8.7 cm. (3.4 in.)

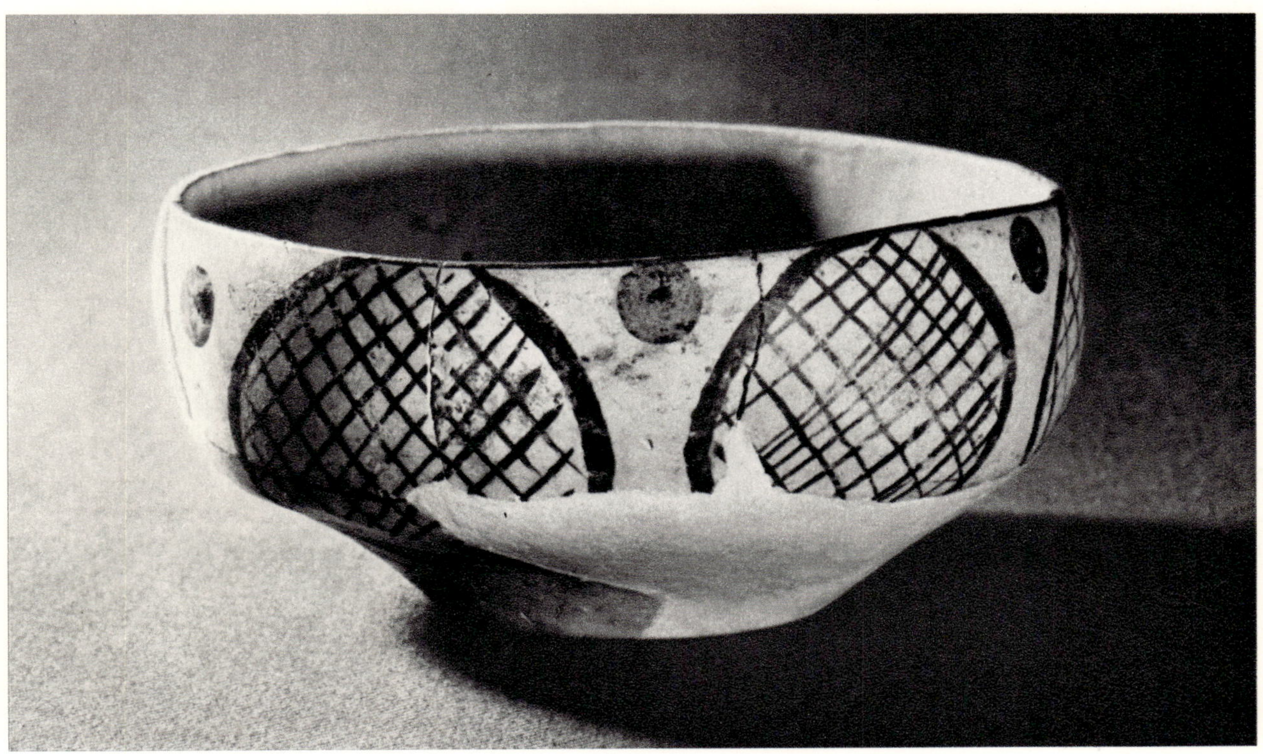

25. Painted Pottery cup, earthenware with black slip decoration. Yang-shao type. Neolithic period. Excavated at Miao-ti-kou, Shan District, Honan.
height: 6.3 cm. (2.46 in.); diameter at mouth: 12.9 cm. (5.1 in.)

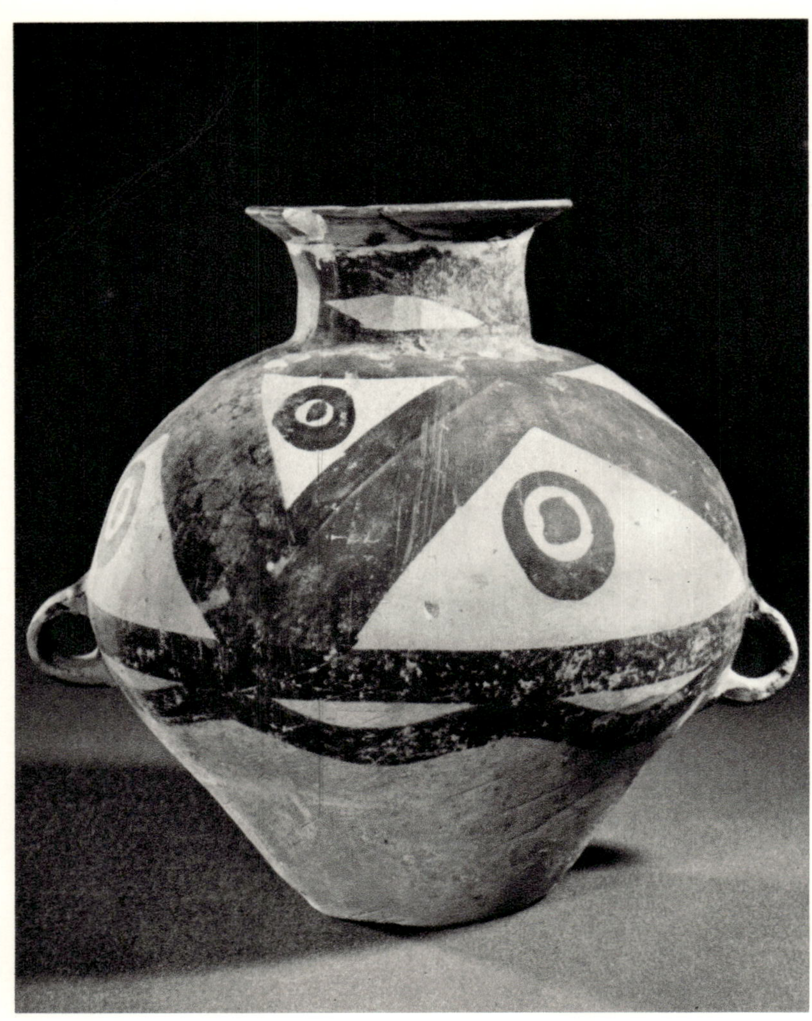

26. Painted Pottery jar, earthenware with slip decoration. Ma-ch'ang type. Neolithic period. Excavated at Pai-tao-kou-p'ing, Lan-chou, Kansu.
height: 22.2 cm. (8.8 in.)

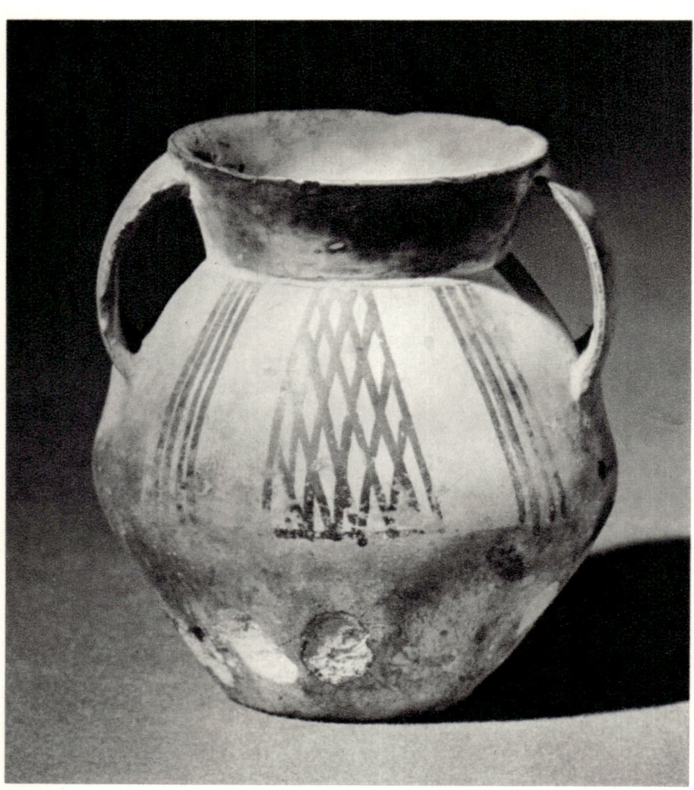

27. Painted Pottery two-handled jar, earthenware with slip decoration. Ch'i-chia type. Stone-and-Bronze period. Excavated at Tu-chia-ts'un, Lin-t'ao District, Kansu.
height: 13.0 cm. (5.1 in.)

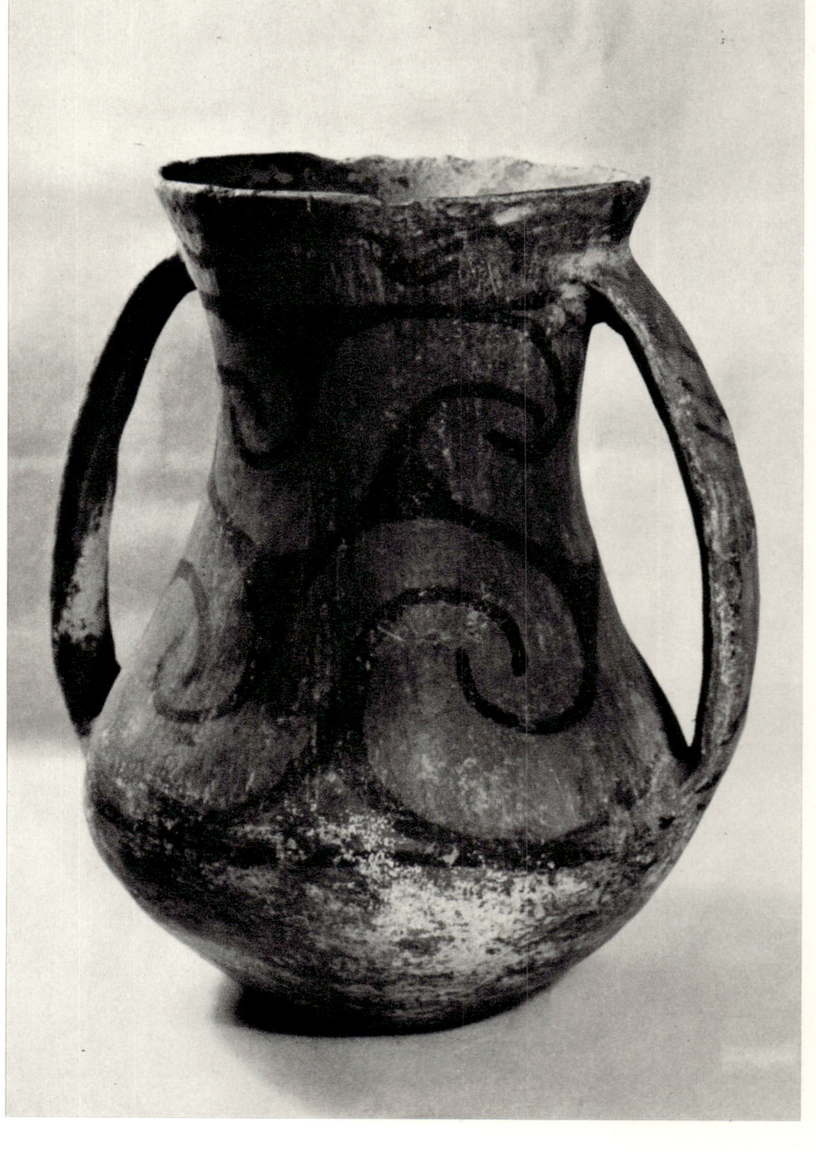

28. Painted Pottery two-handled jar, red-slip-coated earthenware with black slip decoration. T'ang-wang type. Stone-and-Bronze period. Excavated at T'ang-wang-ch'uan, Tung-hsiang Autonomous Region, Kansu.
height: 23.5 cm. (9.3 in.); diameter at mouth: 13.0 cm. (5.1 in.)

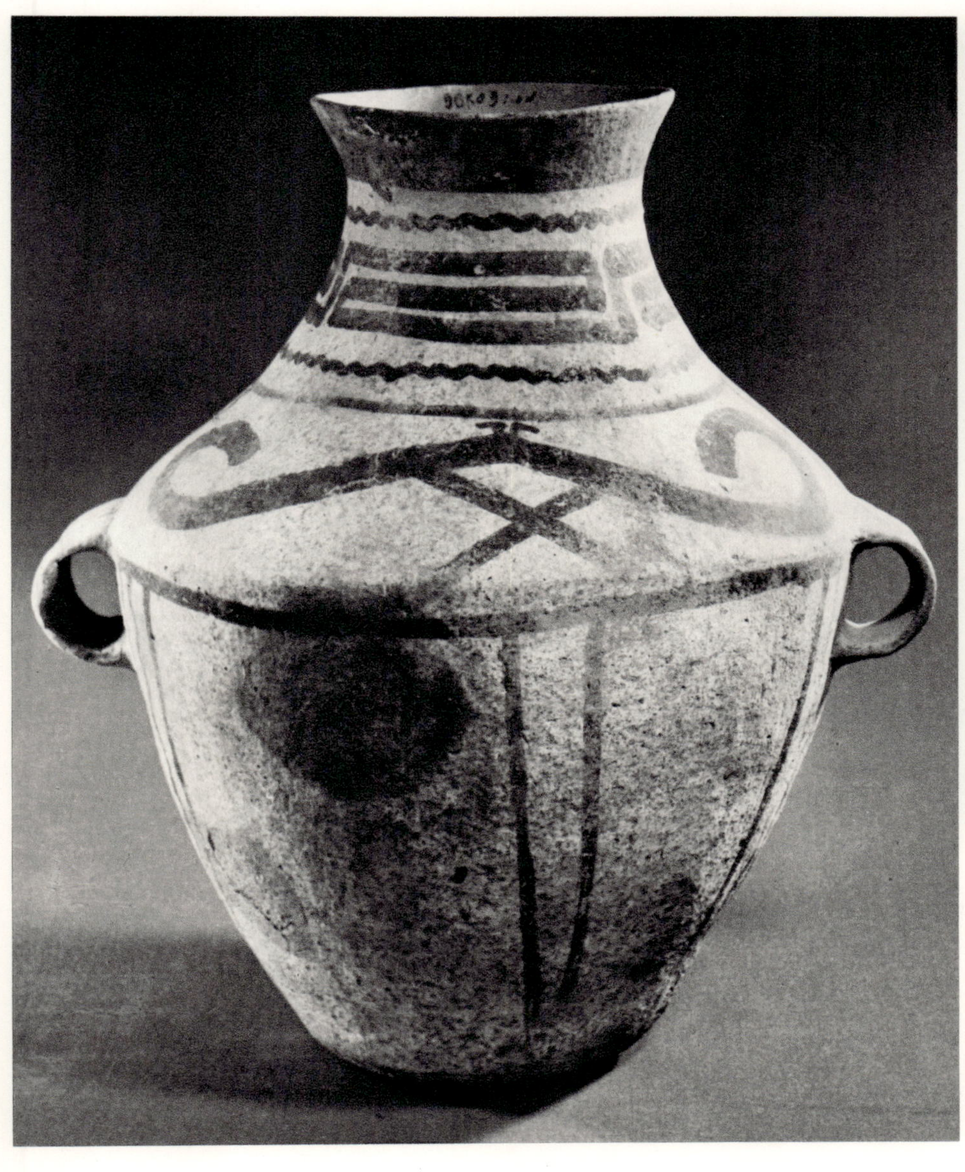

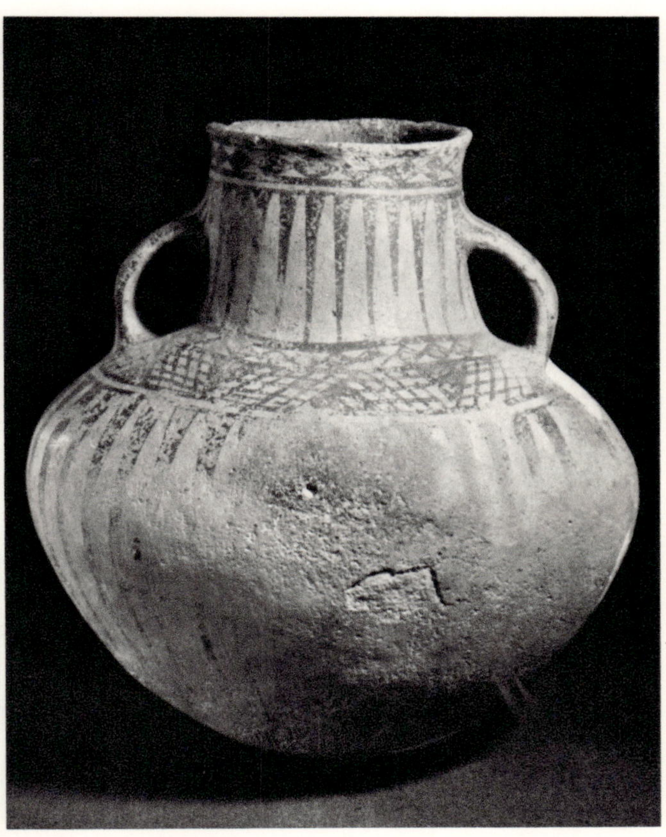

30. Painted Pottery two-handled jar, earthenware with red slip decoration. Sha-ching type. Bronze Age. Excavated at Tung-chia-t'ai, T'ien-chu District, Kansu.
height: 20.2 cm. (8.0 in.)

29. Painted Pottery jar, white-slip-coated earthenware with slip decoration. Hsin-tien type. Stone-and-Bronze period. Excavated at Kuo-chia-p'ing, Lin-t'ao District, Kansu.
height: 42.0 cm. (16.5 in.)

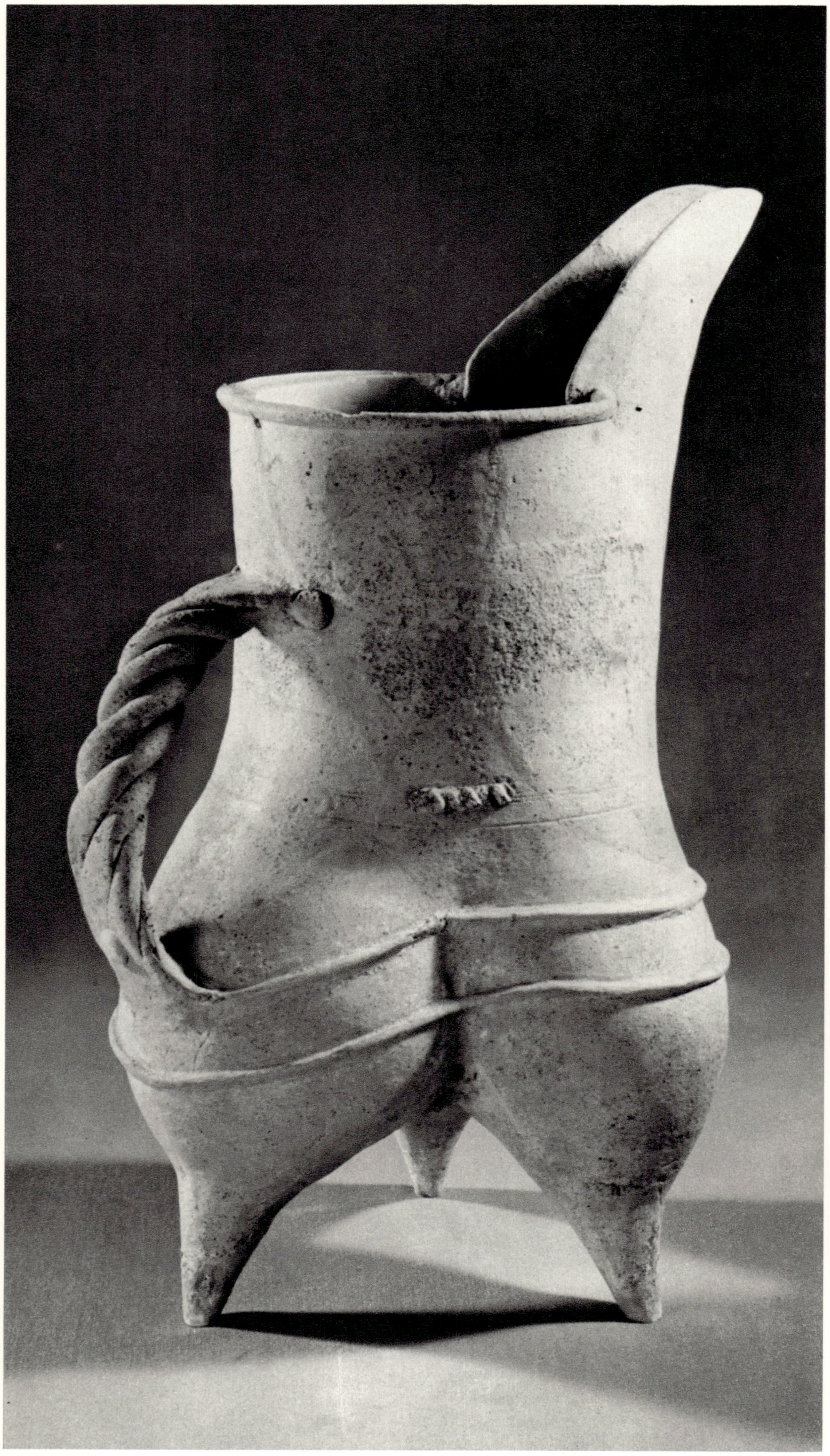

31. Spouted *kuei*, earthenware. Late Lung-shan type. Late Neolithic period. Excavated at Liang-ch'eng-chen, Jih-chao District, Shantung.
height: 33.5 cm. (13.2 in.)

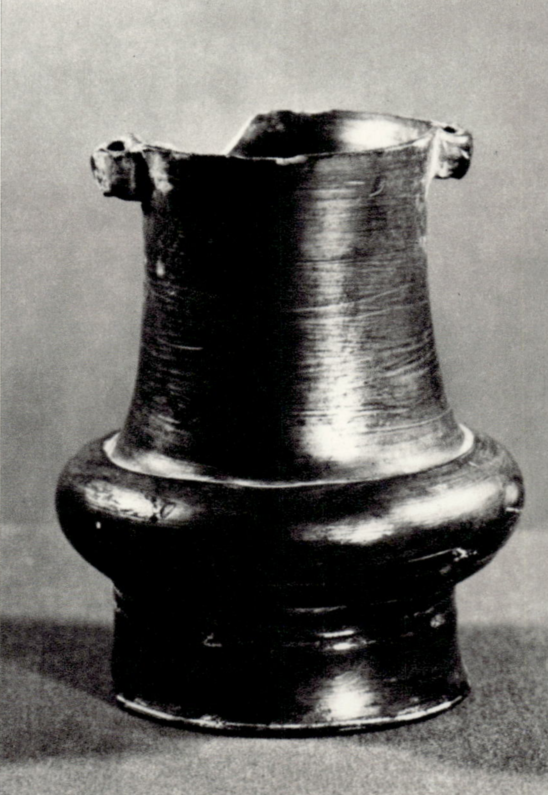

32. Black Pottery *hu*, burnished black earthenware. Neolithic period. Excavated at Liang-chu-chen, Hangchow, Chekiang.
height: 12 cm. (4.7 in.); diameter at mouth: 6.5 cm. (2.56 in.)

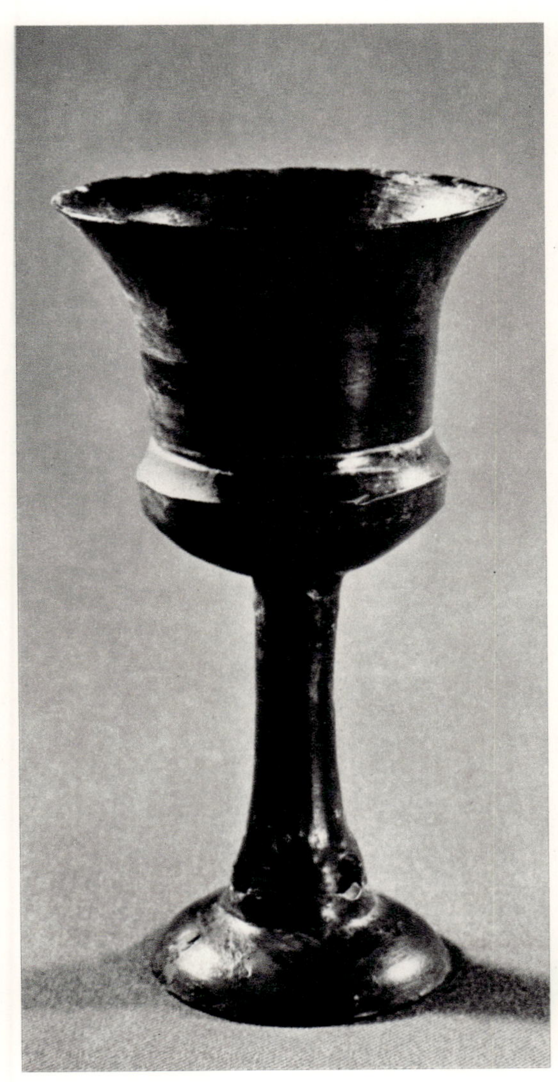

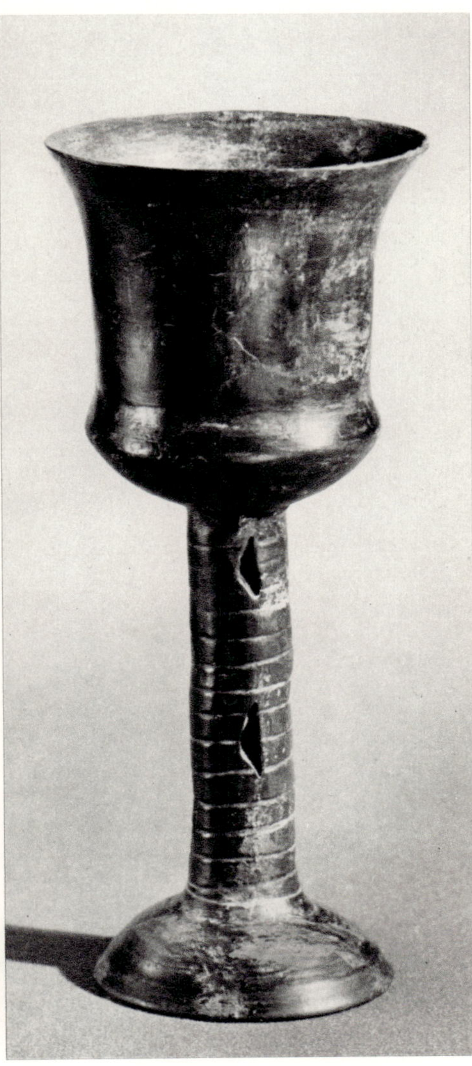

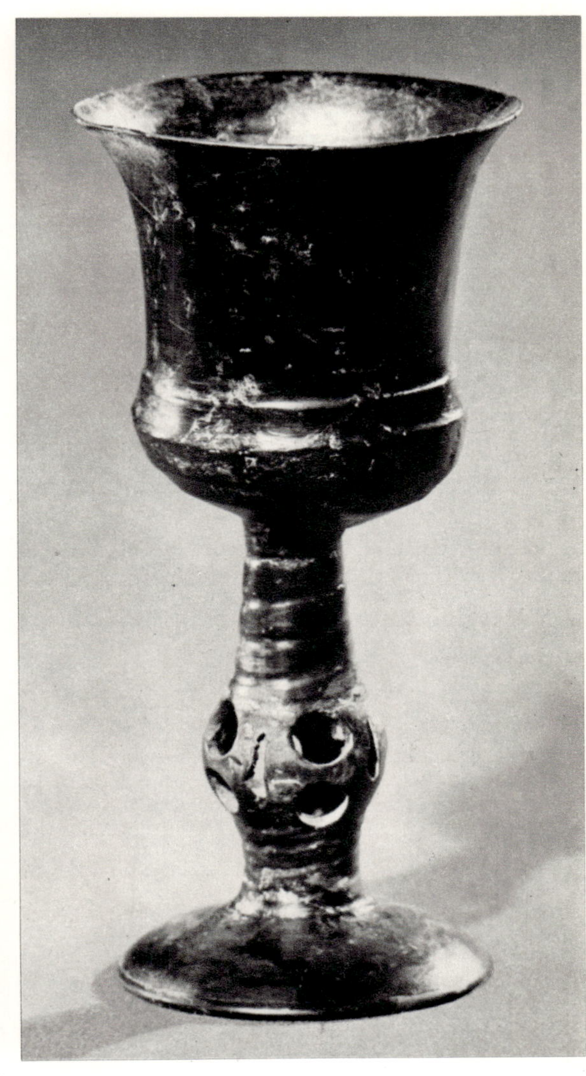

33–35. Black Pottery stemmed cups, burnished black earthenware. Neolithic period. Excavated from tombs in Ching-chih-chen, An-ch'iu District, Shantung.
heights: [*33*] *18.3 cm. (7.2 in.)*; [*34*] *18.9 cm. (7.5 in.)*; [*35*] *19.2 cm. (7.6 in.)*

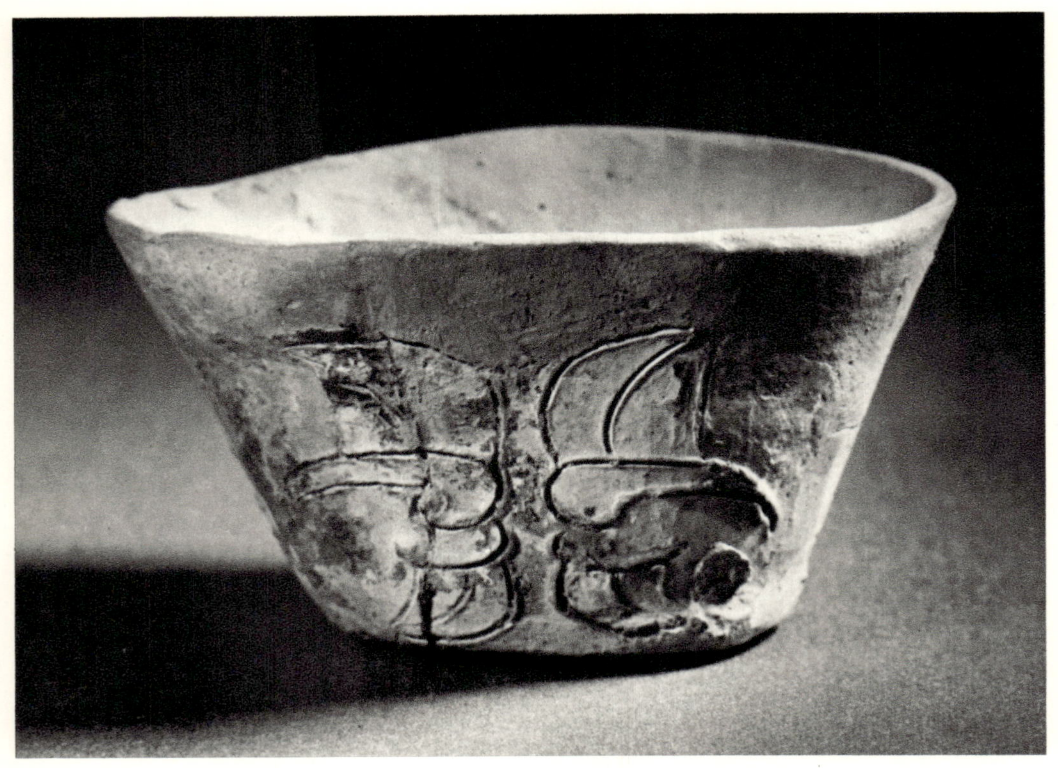

36. Cup, earthenware with incised decoration. Neolithic period. Excavated at Shih-chia-ho, T'ien-men District, Hopei.
height: 5.5 cm. (2.17 in.); diameter at lip: 9.8 cm. (3.8 in.); diameter at base: 5.3 cm. (2.0 in.)

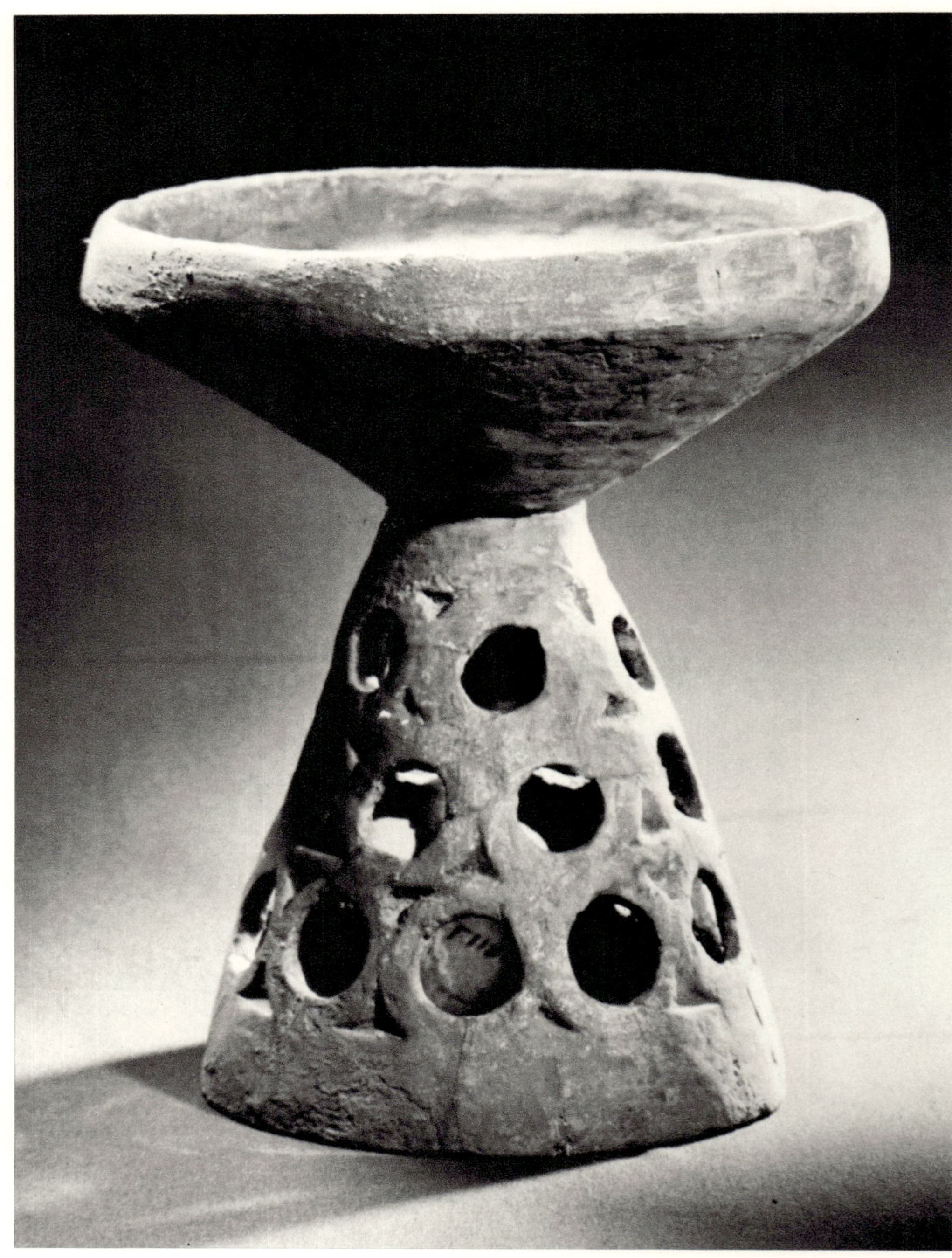

37. *Tou*, red earthenware. Ch'ing-lien-kang type. Neolithic period. Excavated at Hua-t'ing-ts'un, Hsin-yi District, Kiangsu.
height: 26.8 cm. (10.5 in.); diameter at lip: 22.6 cm. (8.9 in.); diameter at base: 17.1 cm. (6.7 in.)

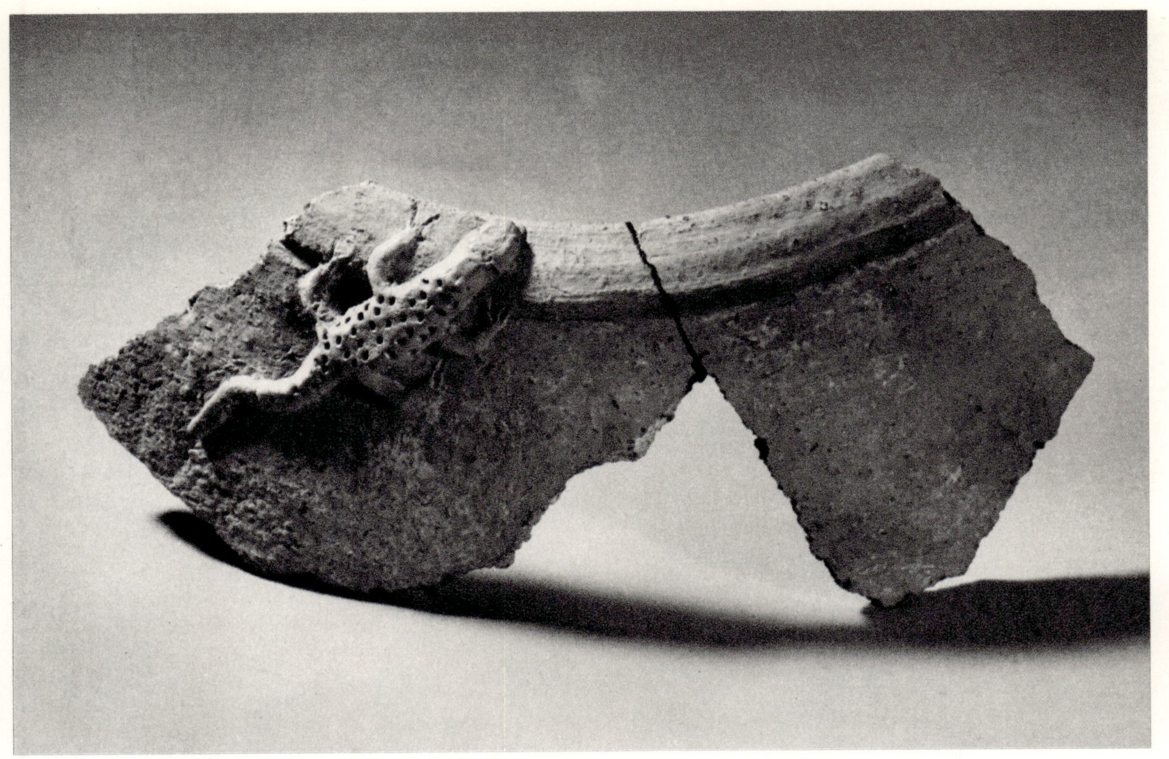

38. Gecko in high relief on a rough, red earthenware shard. Neolithic period. Excavated from a Yang-shao culture stratum at Miao-ti-kou, Shan District, Honan.
height: 8.5 cm. (3.35 in.); width: 19.0 cm. (7.5 in.)

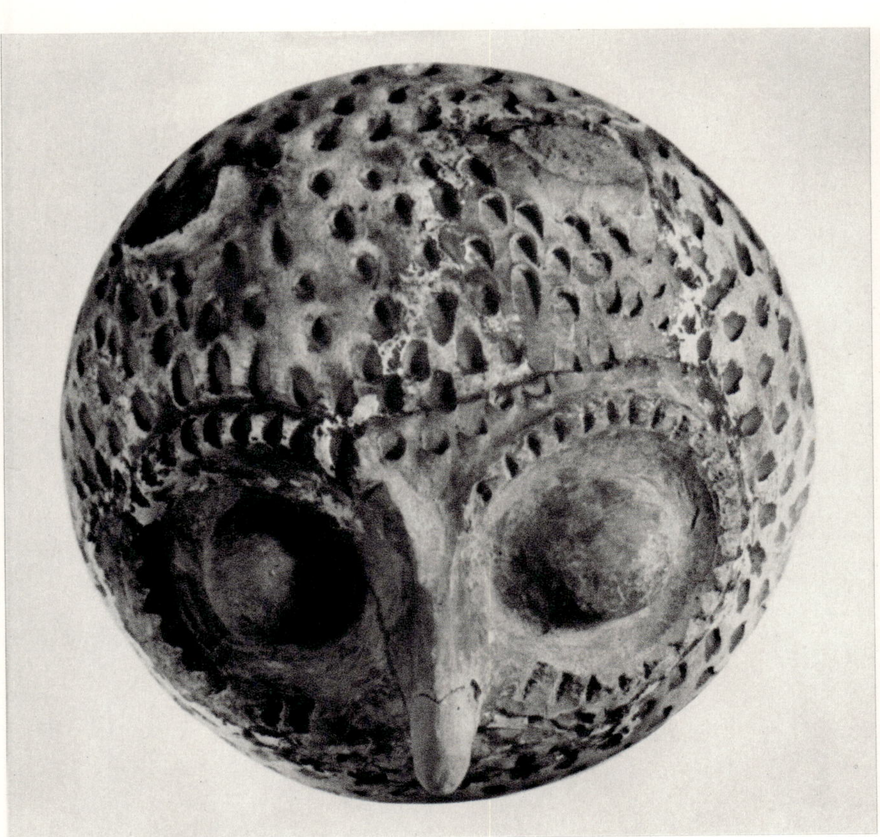

39. Horned owl mask, earthenware. Yang-shao type. Neolithic period. Excavated at Hua District, Shensi.
diameter: 14.0 cm. (5.5 in.)

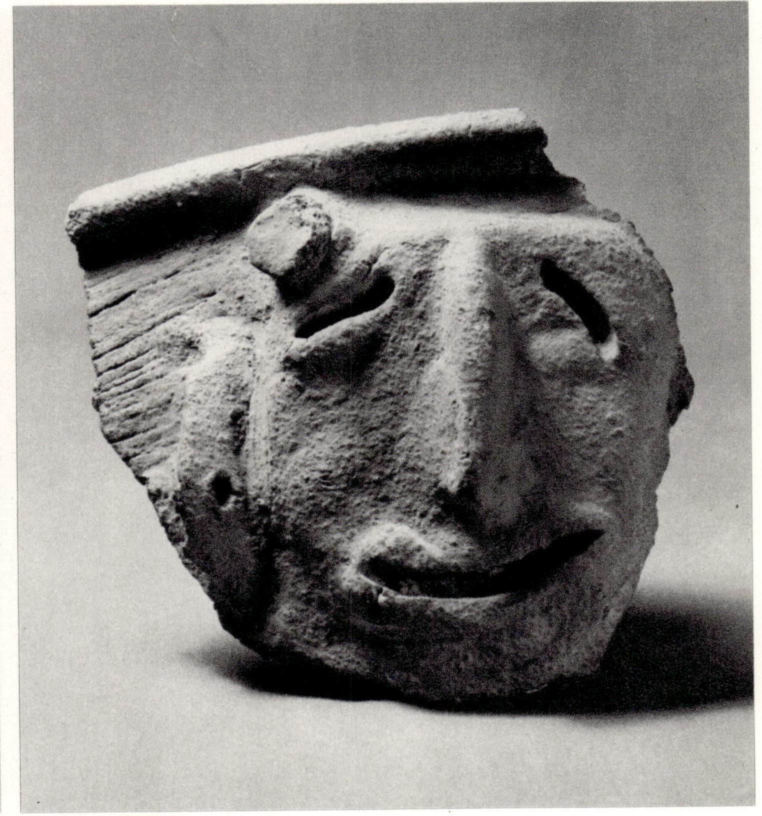

40. Human mask, coarse earthenware shard. Yang-shao type. Neolithic period. Found at Fu-feng District, Shensi.
height: 11.0 cm. (4.3 in.); width: 11.7 cm. (4.6 in.)

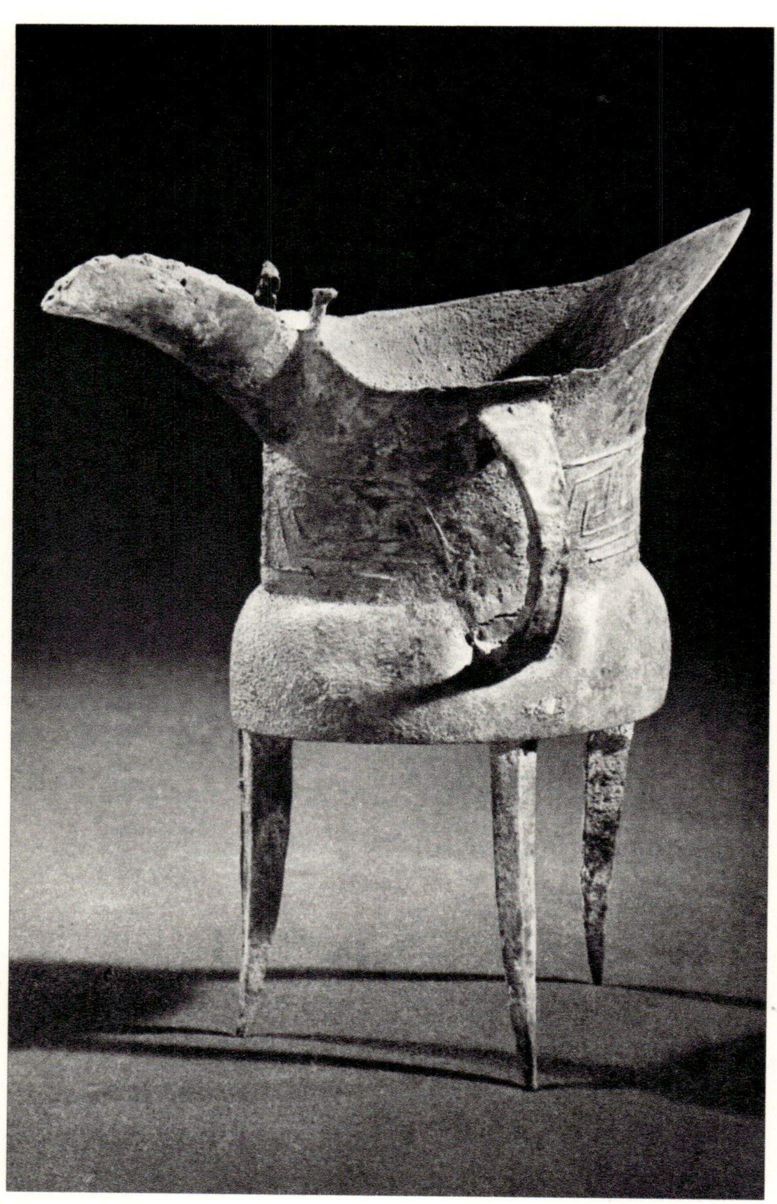

41. *Chüeh*, bronze. Yin dynasty. Excavated at Liu-li-ko, Hui District, Honan.
height: 14.2 cm. (5.6 in.)

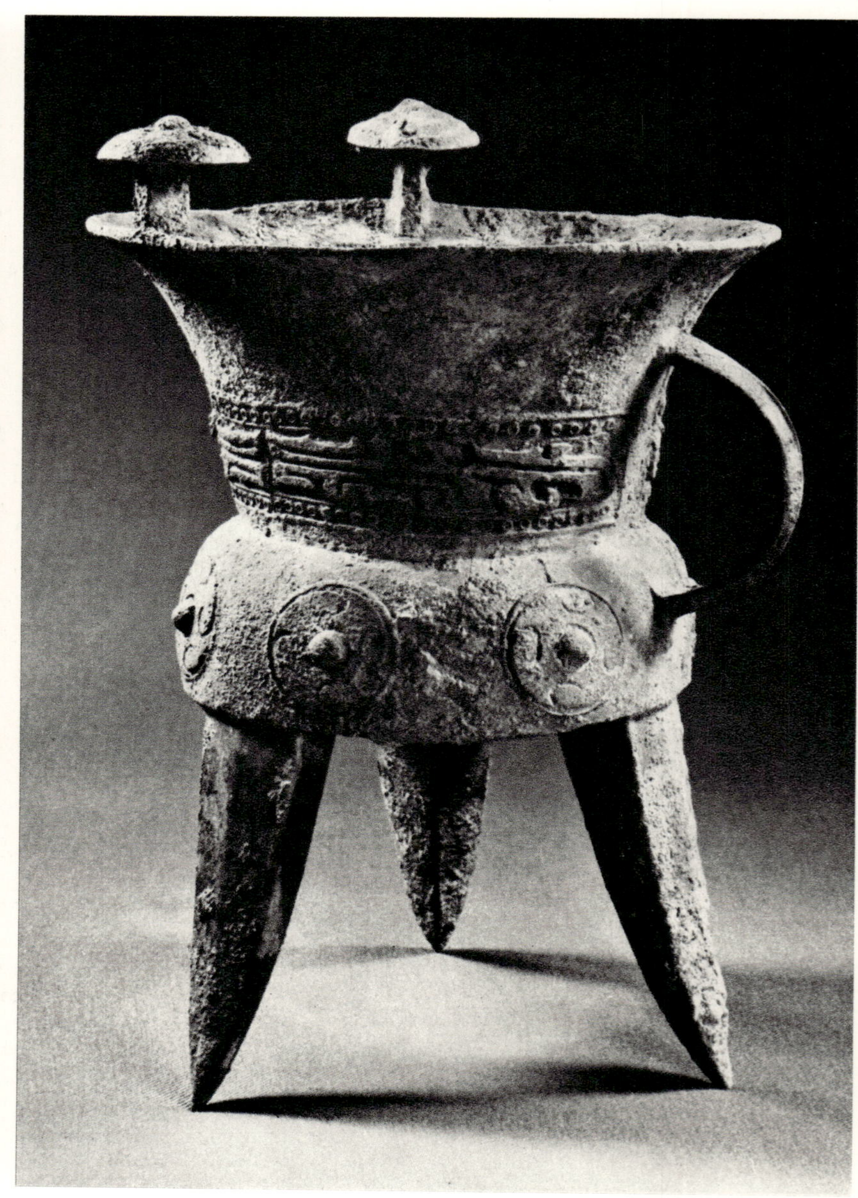

42. *Chia*, bronze. Yin dynasty. Excavated at Pai-chia-chuang, Ch'eng-chou Municipality, Honan.
height: 26.0 cm. (10.2 in.)

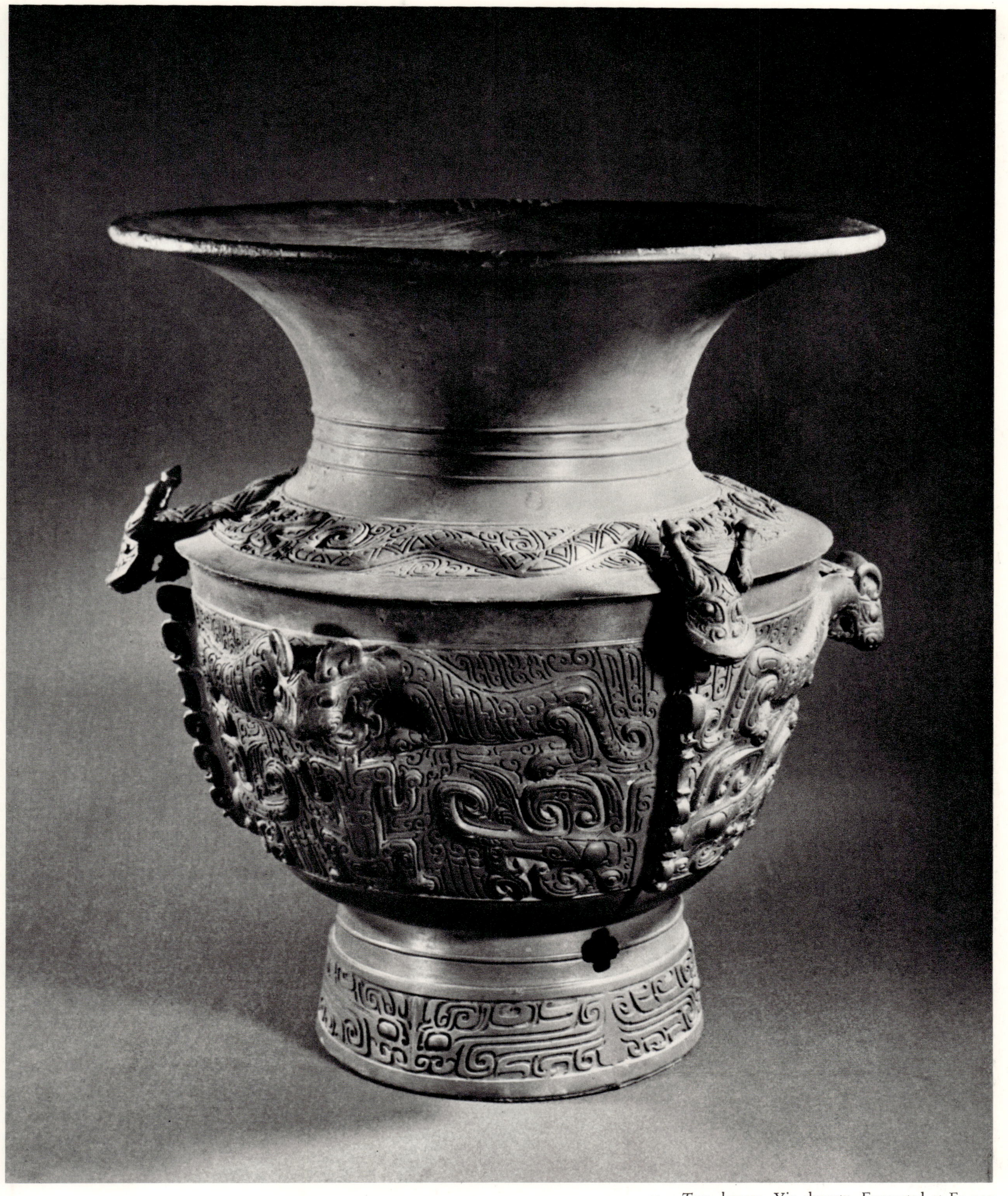

43. *Tsun*, bronze. Yin dynasty. Excavated at Fu-nan District, Anhui.
height: 50.5 cm. (19.9 in.)

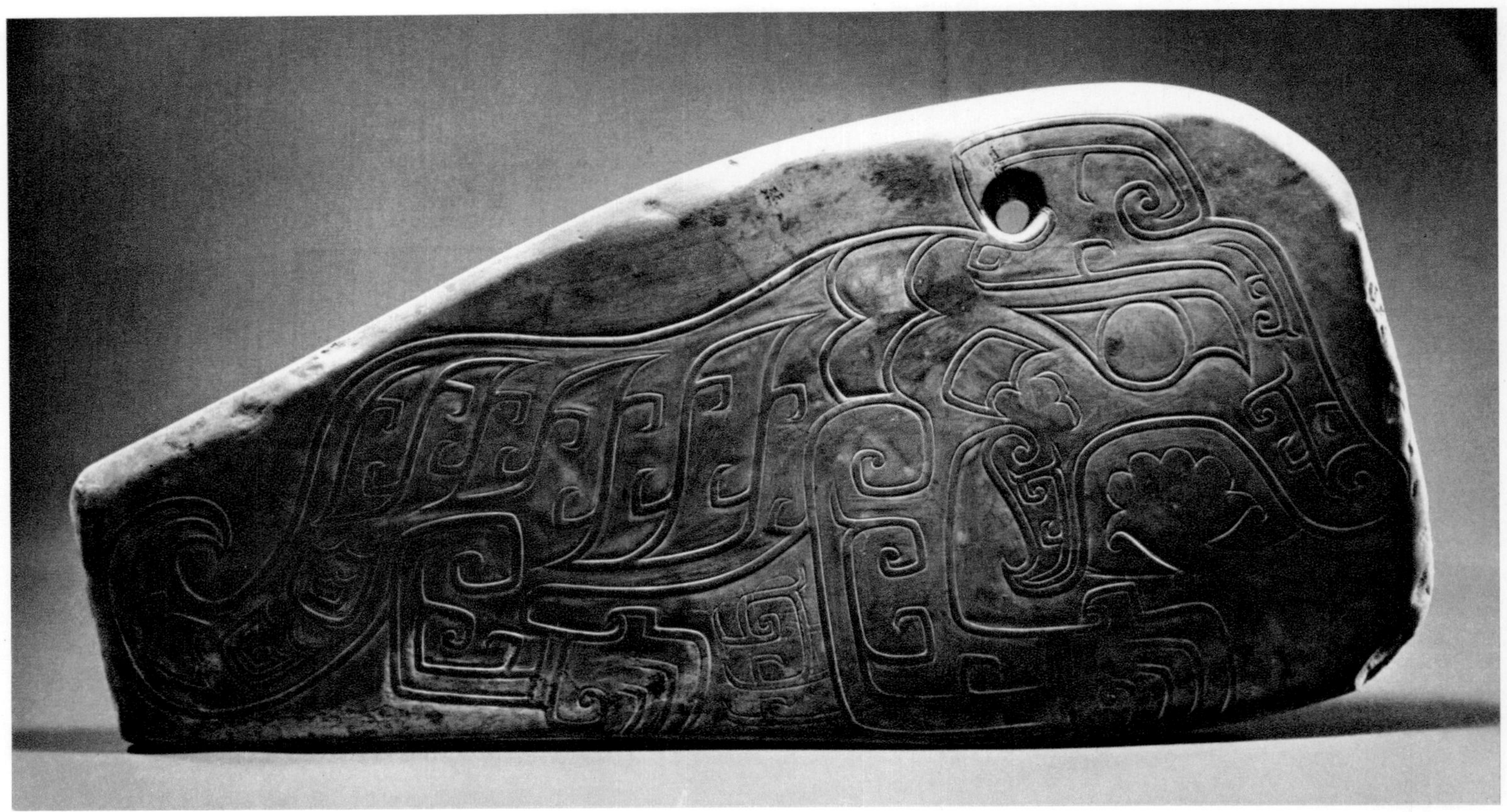

44. Chime, stone. Yin dynasty. Excavated from the Great Tomb at Wu-kuan-ts'un, An-yang District, Honan.
length: 84.0 cm. (33.0 in.)

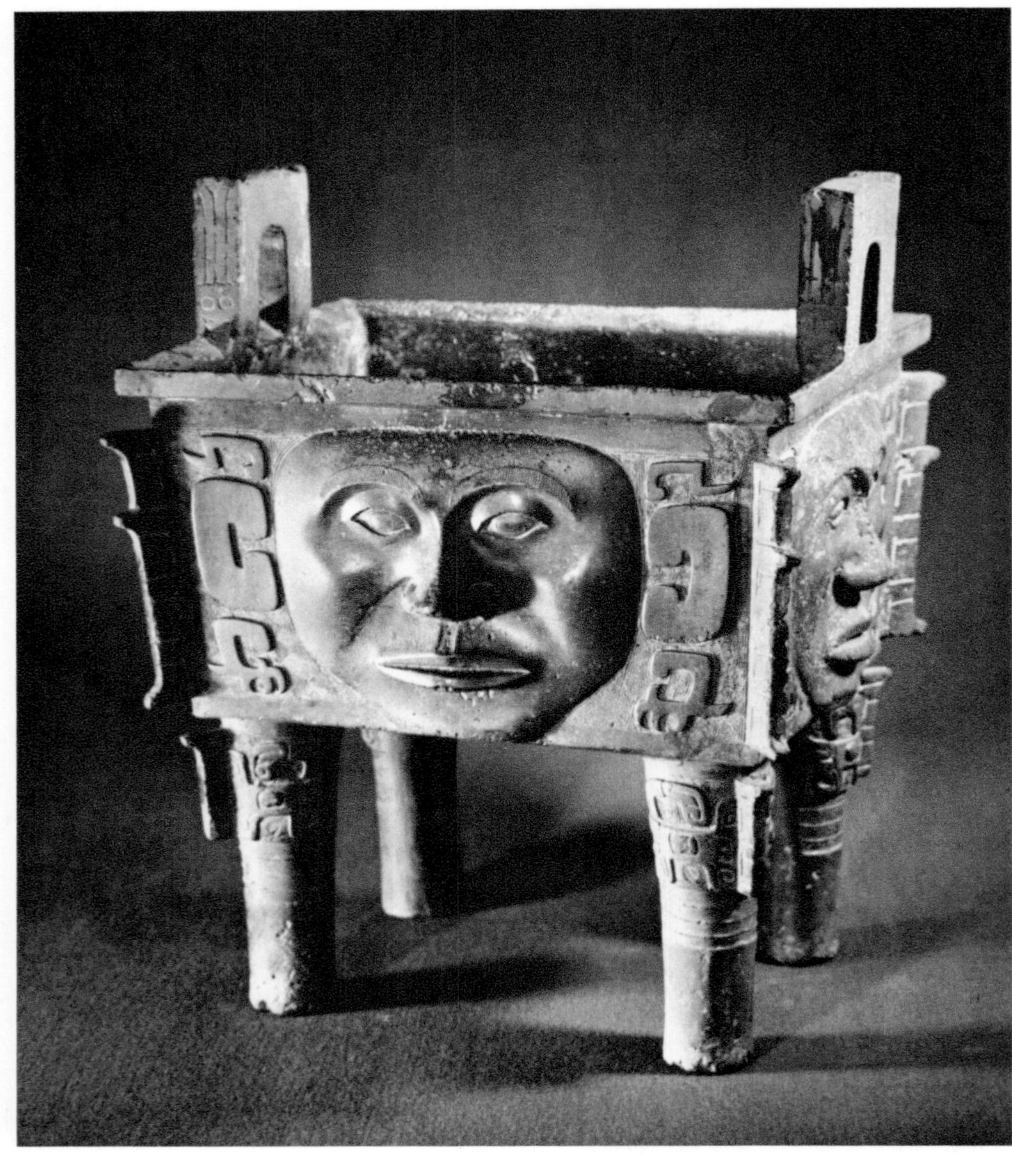

45. Rectangular *ting* with human mask decoration, bronze. Late Yin dynasty. Excavated at Ning-hsiang District, Hunan.
height: 38.5 cm. (15.5 in.); leg height: 14.4 cm. (5.7 in.)

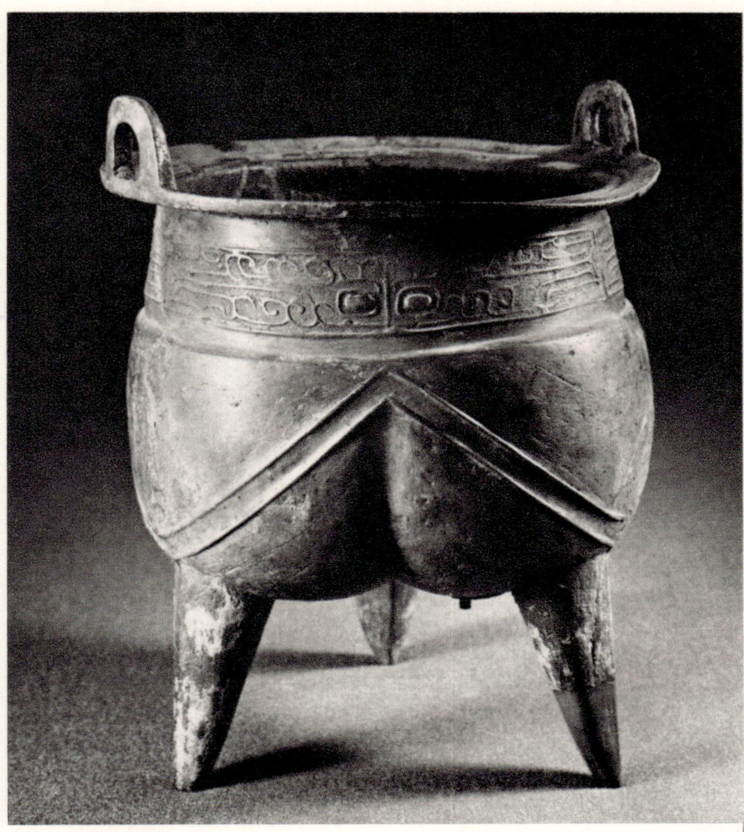

46. *Li*, bronze. Yin dynasty. Excavated at Liu-li-ko, Hui District, Honan.
height: 18.0 cm. (7.1 in.)

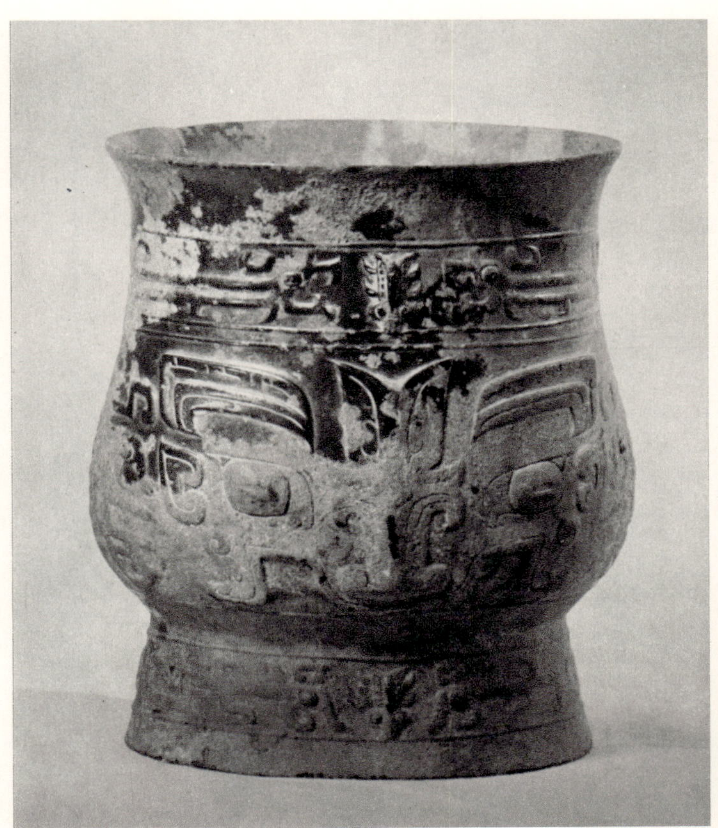

47. *Chih*, bronze. Yin dynasty. Excavated at Ch'ing-hua-chen, Ch'i-shan District, Shensi.
height: 17.0 cm. (6.7 in.); diameter at lip: 13.5 cm. (5.3 in.)

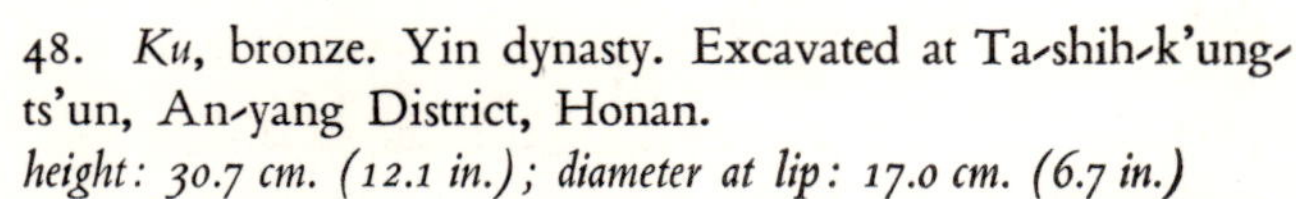

48. *Ku*, bronze. Yin dynasty. Excavated at Ta-shih-k'ung-ts'un, An-yang District, Honan.
height: 30.7 cm. (12.1 in.); diameter at lip: 17.0 cm. (6.7 in.)

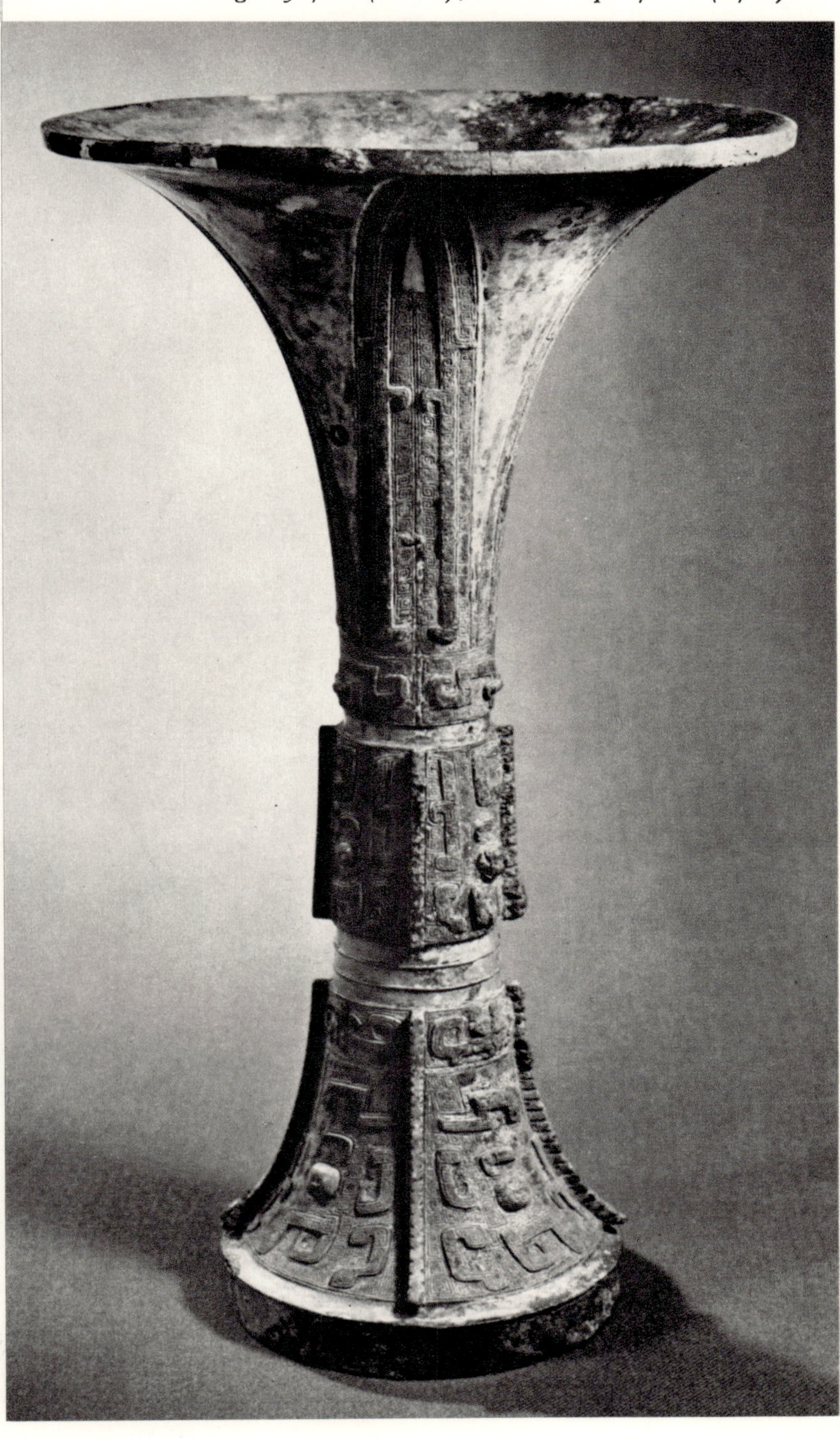

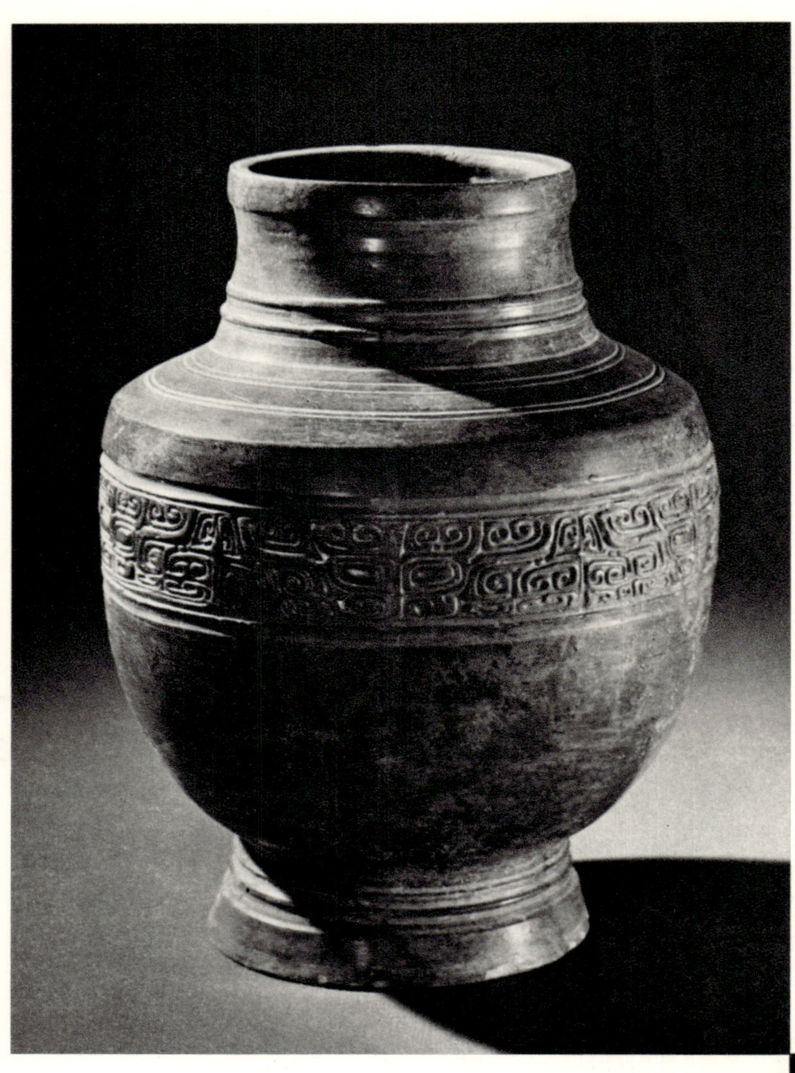

49. *Hu*, burnished earthenware with impressed design. Yin dynasty. Excavated at Ch'eng-chou Municipality, Honan.
height: 35.0 cm. (13.8 in.)

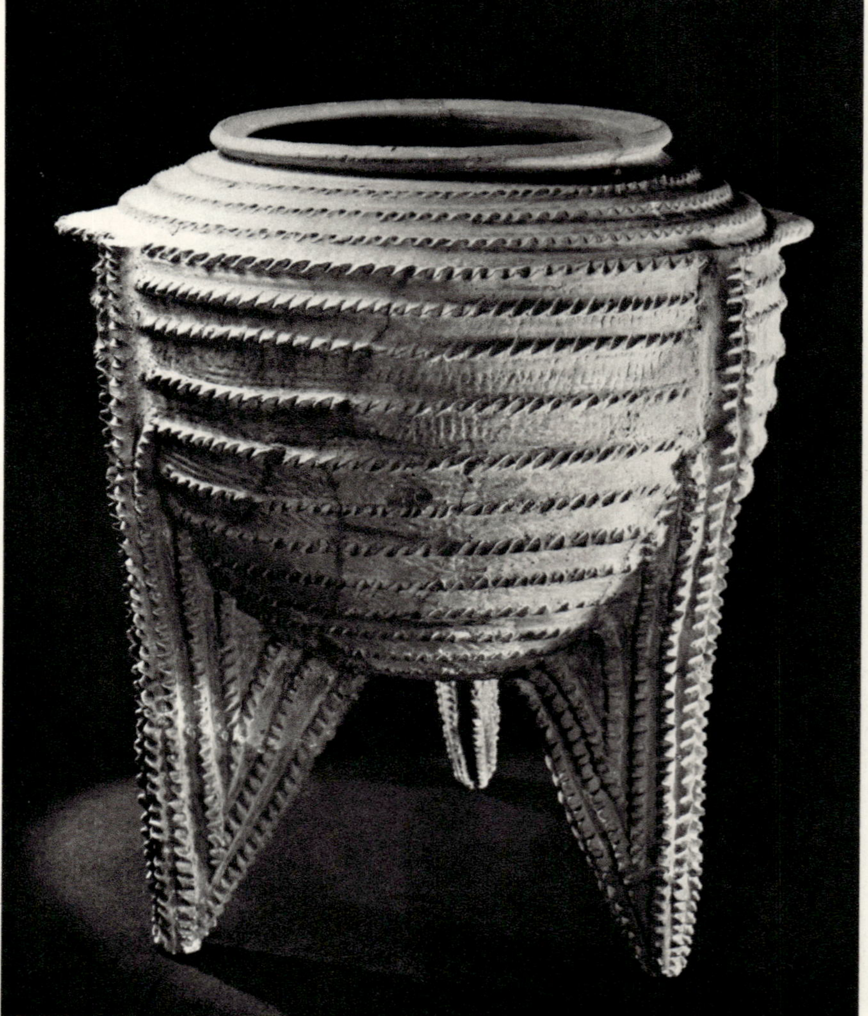

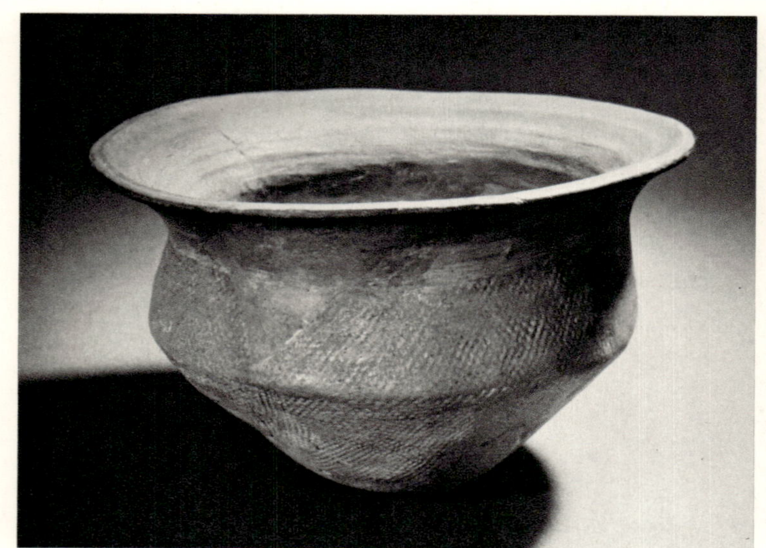

50. *Tsun*, earthenware with yellowish-green glaze. Yin dynasty. Excavated at Erh-li-kang, Ch'eng-chou Municipality, Honan.
height: 14.8 cm. (5.8 in.); diameter at mouth: 19.0 cm. (7.5 in.)

51. Three-legged *ting*, gray earthenware. Yin dynasty. Excavated at Ch'i-li-p'u, Shan District, Honan.
height: 38.0 cm. (14.95 in.)

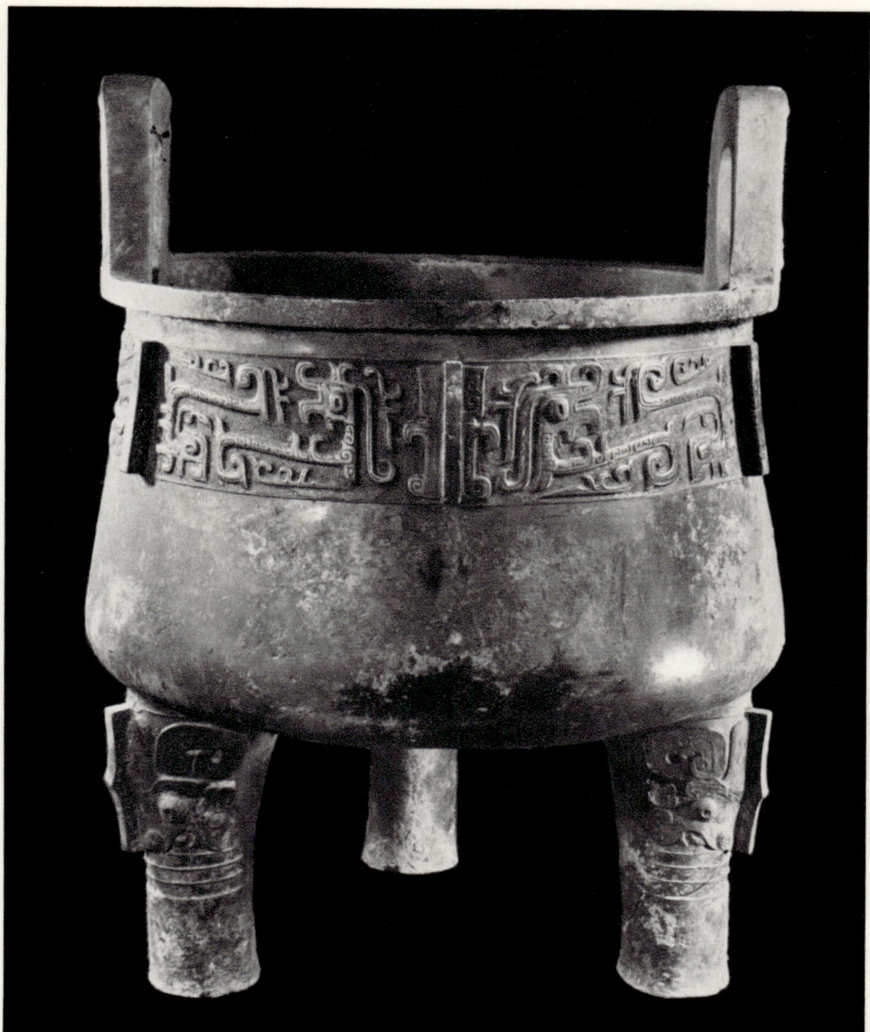

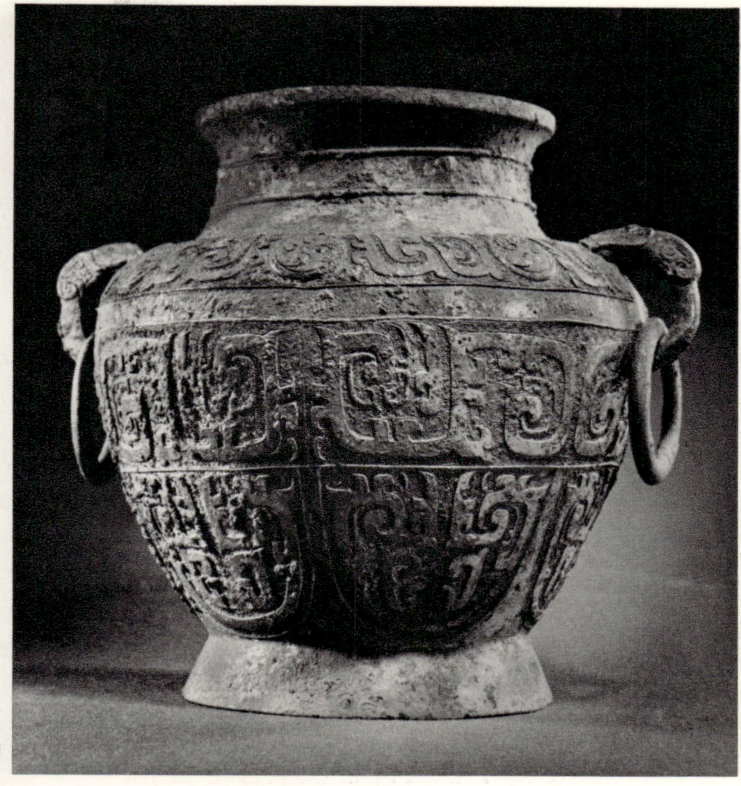

53. *Lei*, bronze. Middle Western Chou dynasty. Excavated at P'u-tu-ts'un, Ch'ang-an District, Shensi.
height: 24.8 cm. (9.7 in.); diameter at lip: 15.5 cm. (6.1 in.)

52. Three-legged *ting*, bronze. Early Western Chou dynasty. Excavated at Ch'i-shan District, Shensi.
height: 89.5 cm. (35.2 in.); leg height: 30.0 cm. (11.8 in.); diameter at lip: 61.3 cm. (24.1 in.)

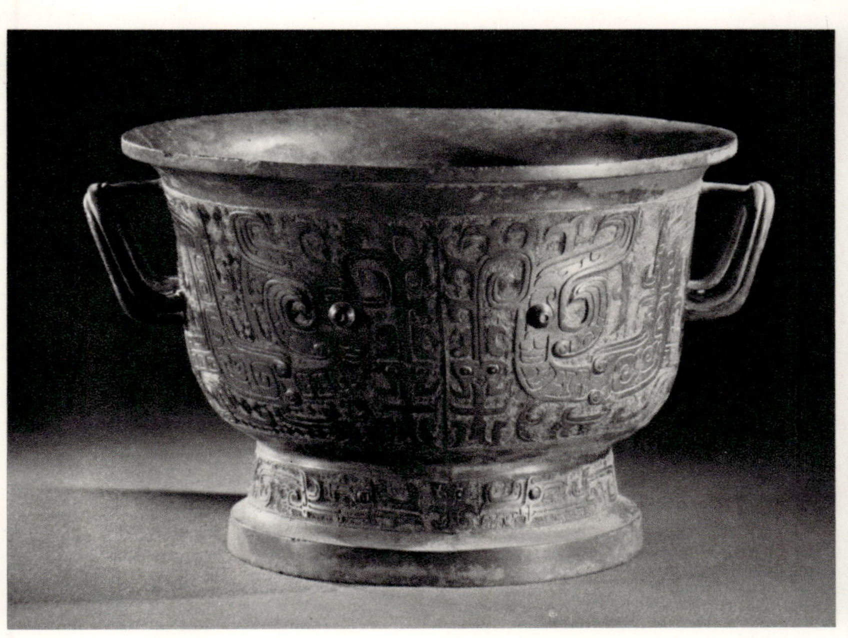

54. Marquis of Yen *yü*, bronze. Western Chou dynasty. Excavated at Ma-ch'ang-kou, Ling-yüan District, Liaoning.
height: 24.0 cm. (9.4 in.)

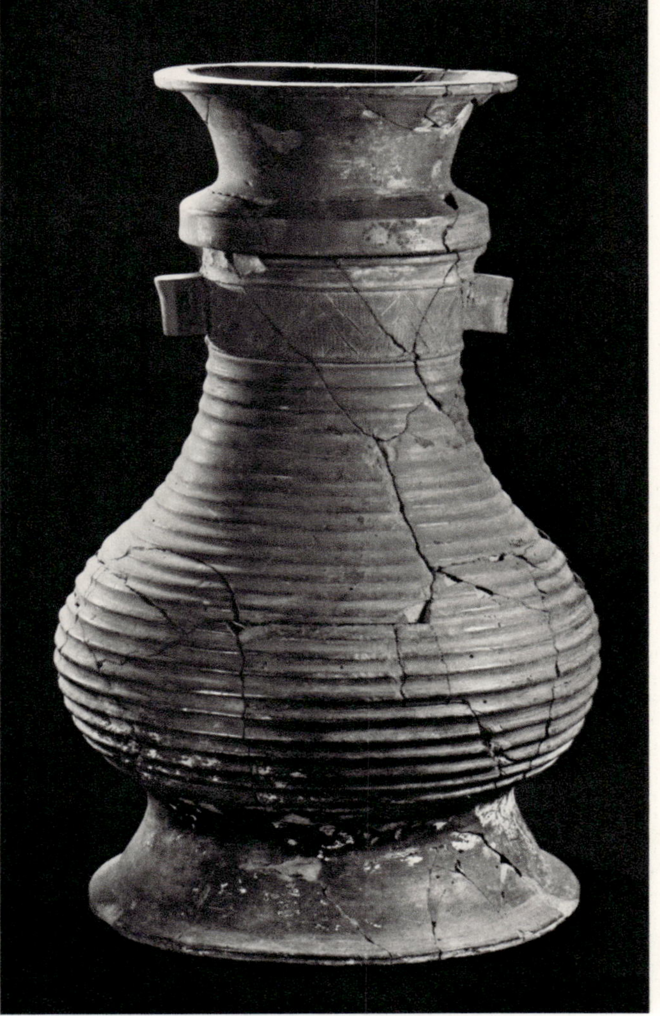

55. Covered *hu*, unglazed earthenware. Western Chou dynasty. Excavated at Chang-chia-p'o, Ch'ang-an District, Shensi.
height: 39.1 cm. (15.3 in.)

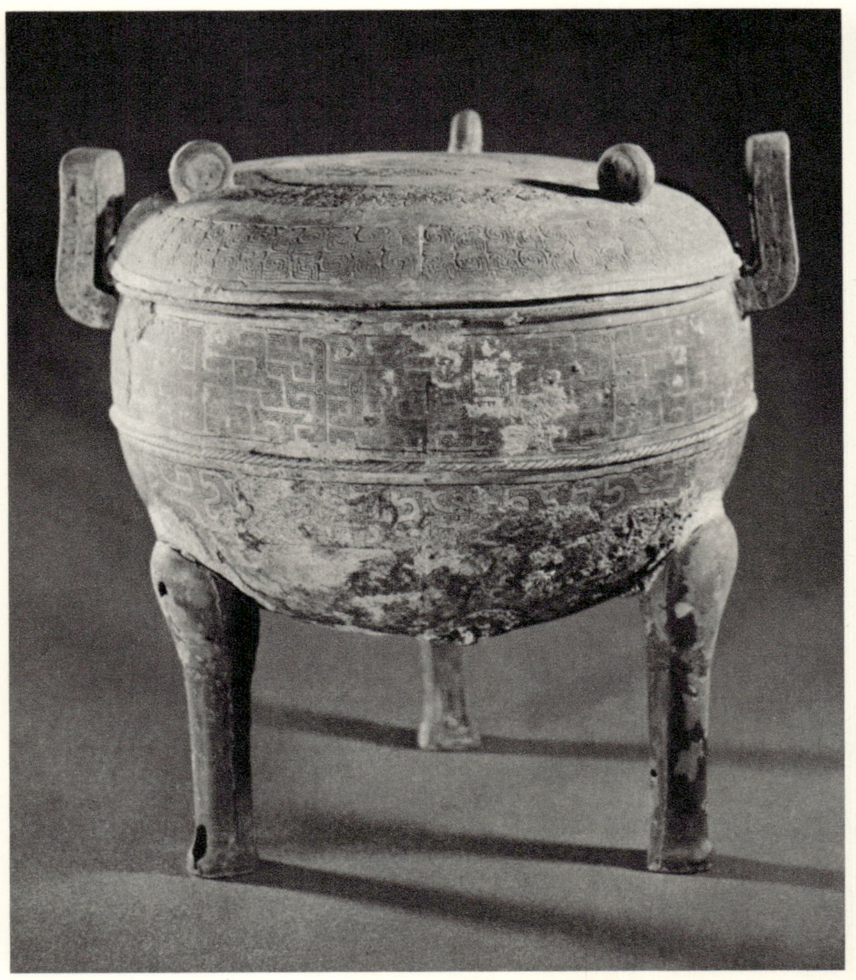

56. Covered *ting*, bronze. Ch'un Ch'iu period. Excavated at Chung-chou-lu, Lo-yang Municipality, Honan.
height: 33.0 cm. (13.0 in.); diameter of body: 30.0 cm. (11.8 in.)

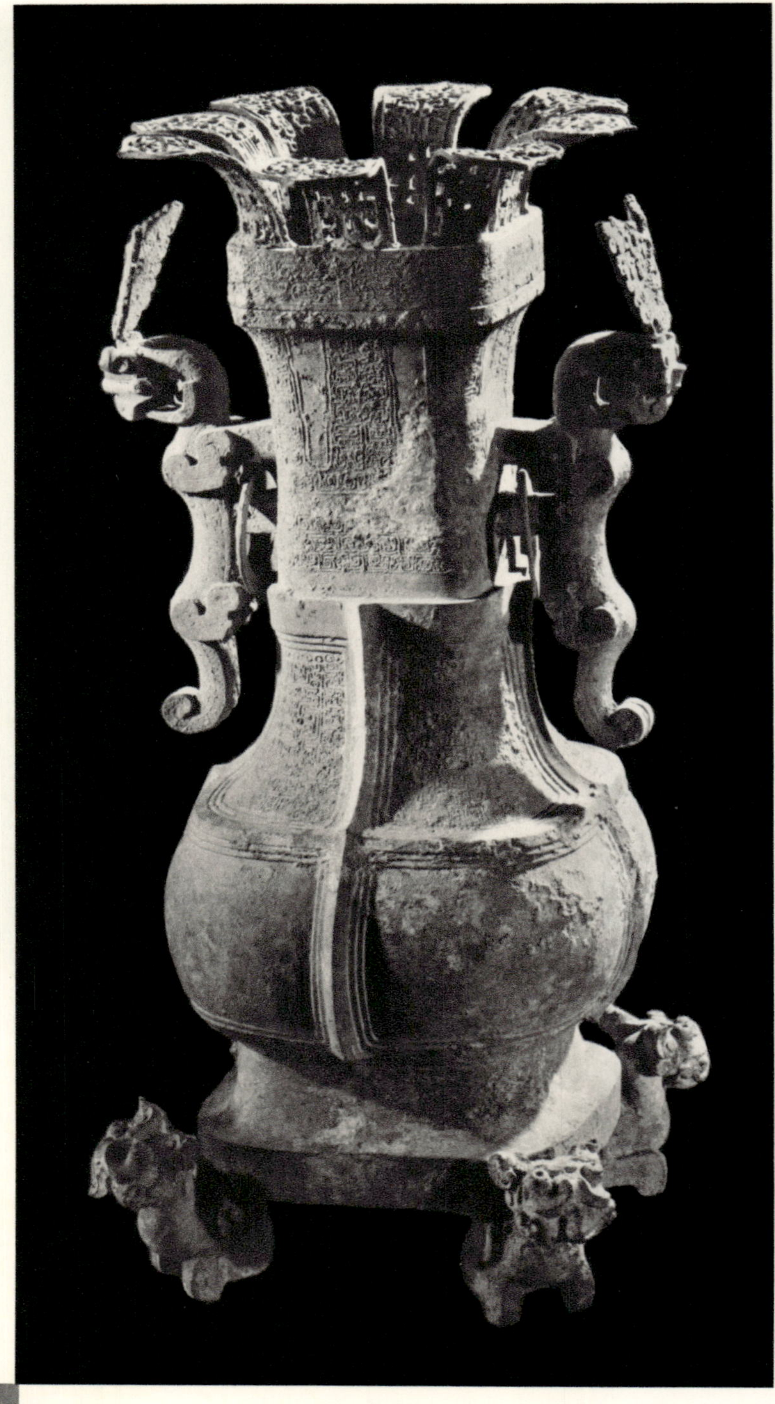

57. Marquis of Ts'ai *hu*, bronze. Late Ch'un Ch'iu period. Excavated from the Marquis of Ts'ai tomb, Shou District, Anhui.
height: 80.0 cm. (31.5 in.); diameter at lip: 18.5 cm. (7.3 in.)

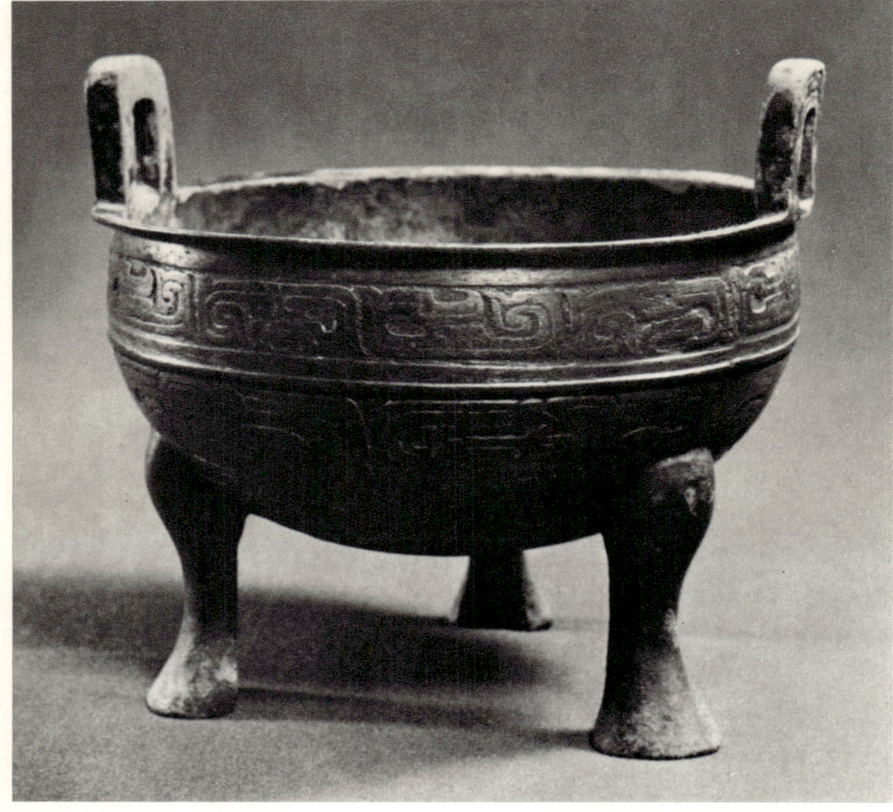

58. *Ting*, bronze. Ch'un Ch'iu period. Excavated at the Kuo state cemetery, Shang-ts'un-ling, Shan District, Honan.
height: 15.7 cm. (6.2 in.); diameter at lip: 16.0 cm. (6.3 in.)

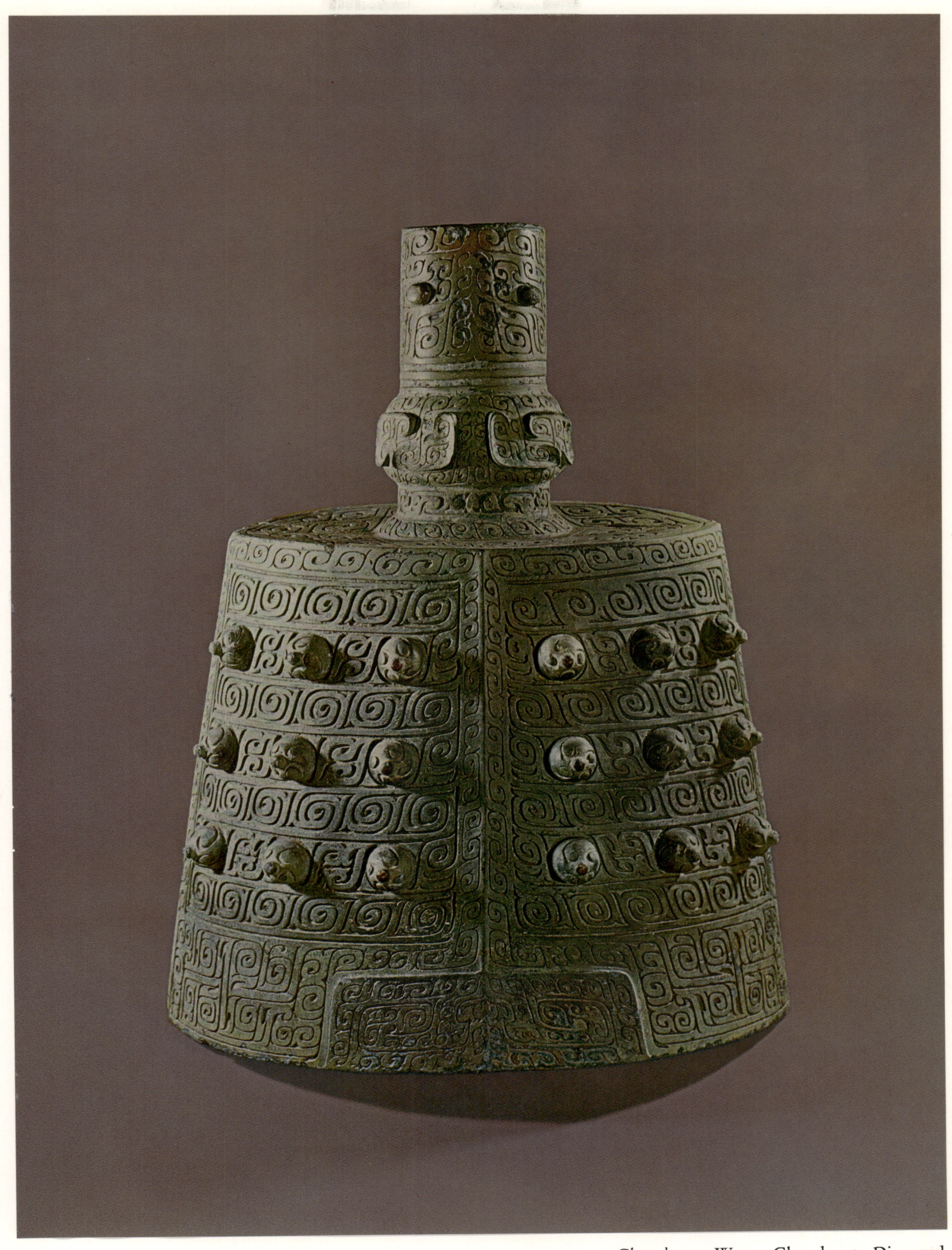

59. *Chung*, bronze. Western Chou dynasty. Discovered at Ch'ang-hsing, Chekiang.
height: 52.0 cm. (20. 5 in.)

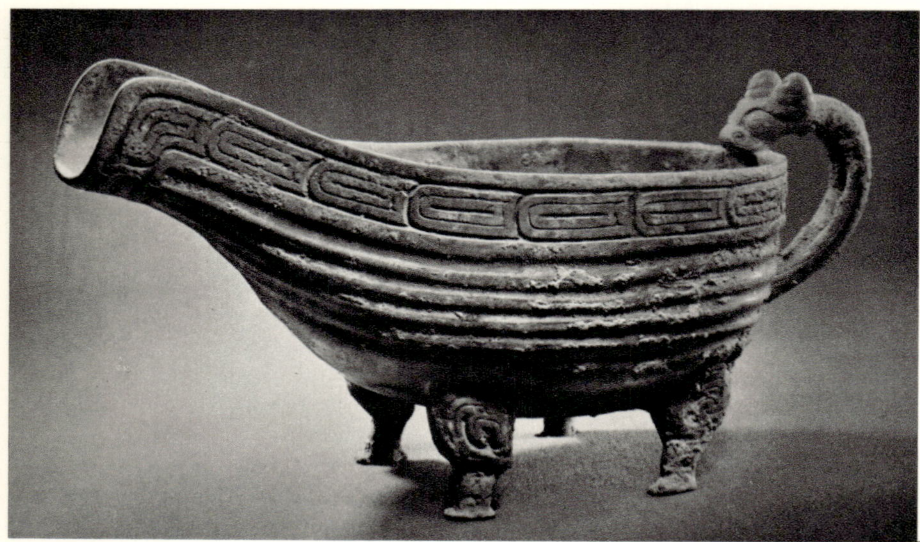

60. *Yi*, bronze. Ch'un Ch'iu period. Excavated at the Kuo state cemetery, Shang-ts'un-ling. Shan District, Honan.
height: 17.8 cm. (7.0 in.); length: 35.0 cm. (13.5 in.)

61. Covered *ling*, bronze. Ch'un Ch'iu period. Excavated at Yi-shui District, Shantung.
height: 53.5 cm. (21.1 in.)

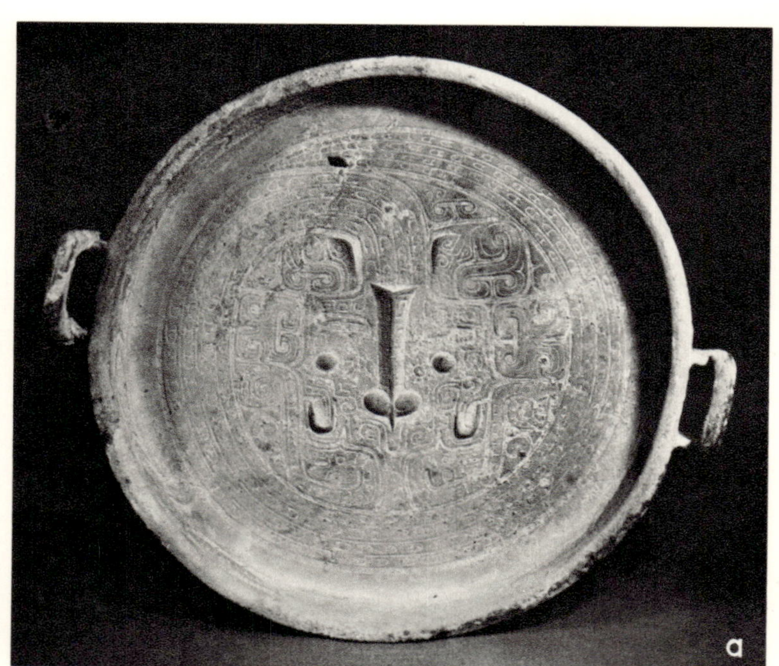

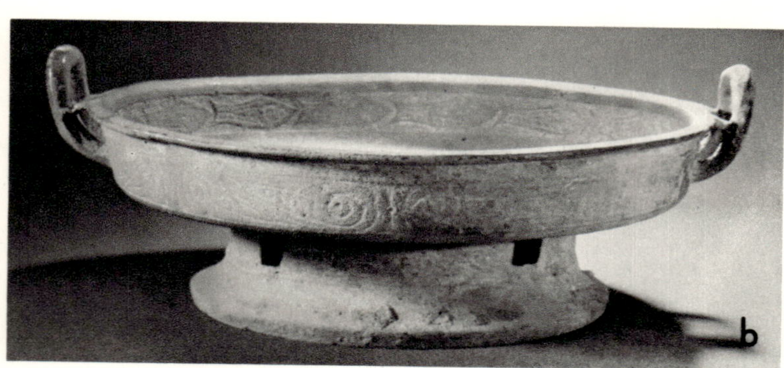

62 (a, b). *P'an*, bronze. Ch'un Ch'iu period. Excavated at the Kuo state cemetery, Shang-ts'un-ling, Shan District, Honan.
height: 14.2 cm. (5.6 in.); diameter at lip: 34.5 cm. (13.6 in.)

63. Covered jar, gray earthenware. Ch'un Ch'iu period. Excavated at the Kuo state cemetery, Shang-ts'un-ling, Shan District, Honan.
height: 30.0 cm. (11.8 in.)

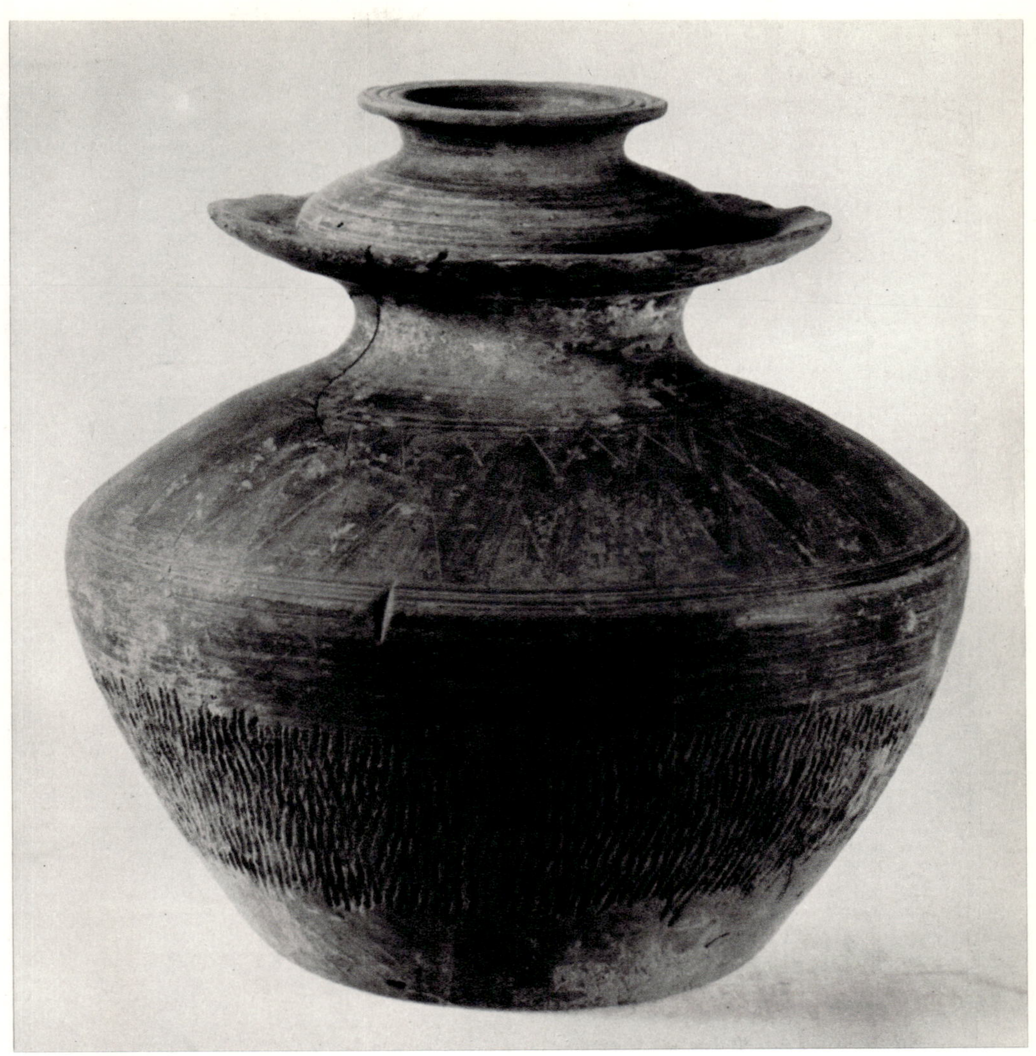

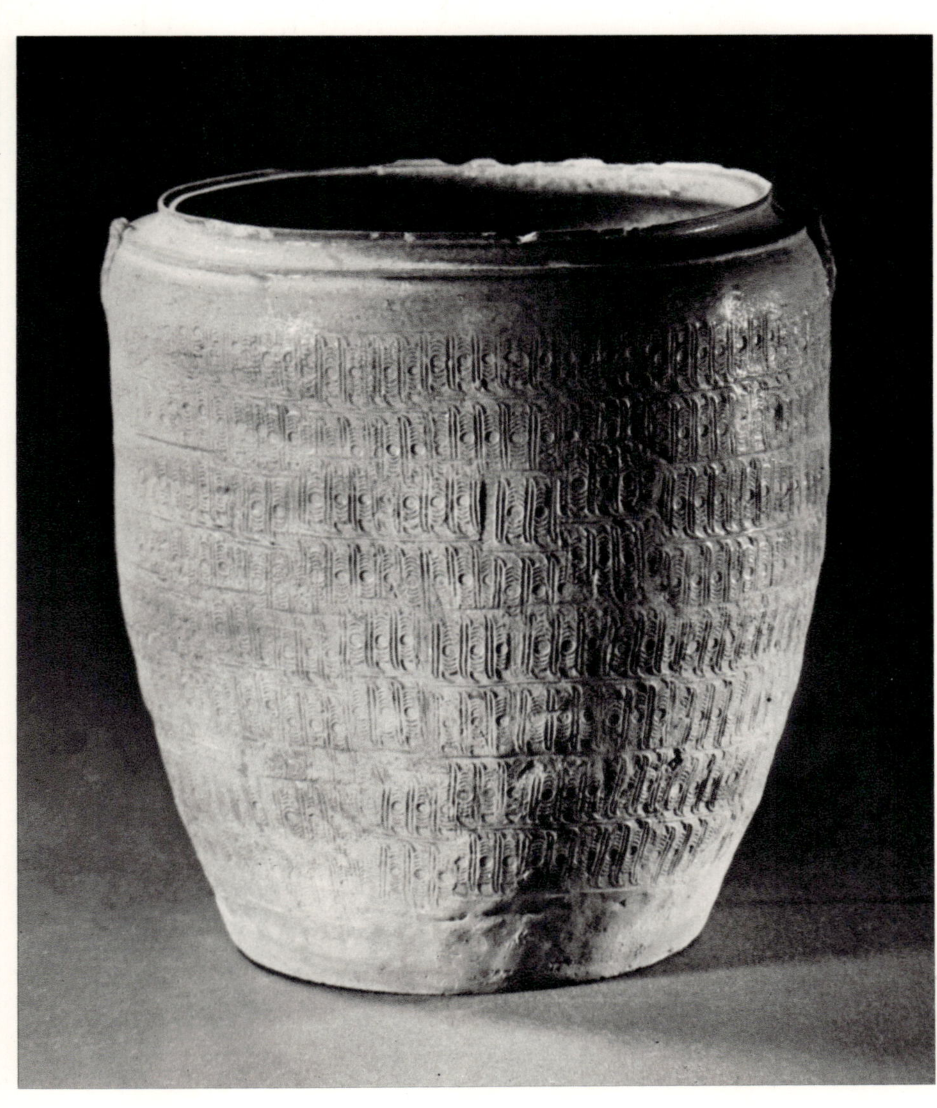

64. *T'an*, glazed earthenware with impressed design. Ch'un Ch'iu period. Excavated at Chen-tse District, Kiangsu.
height: 29.7 cm. (11.7 in.)

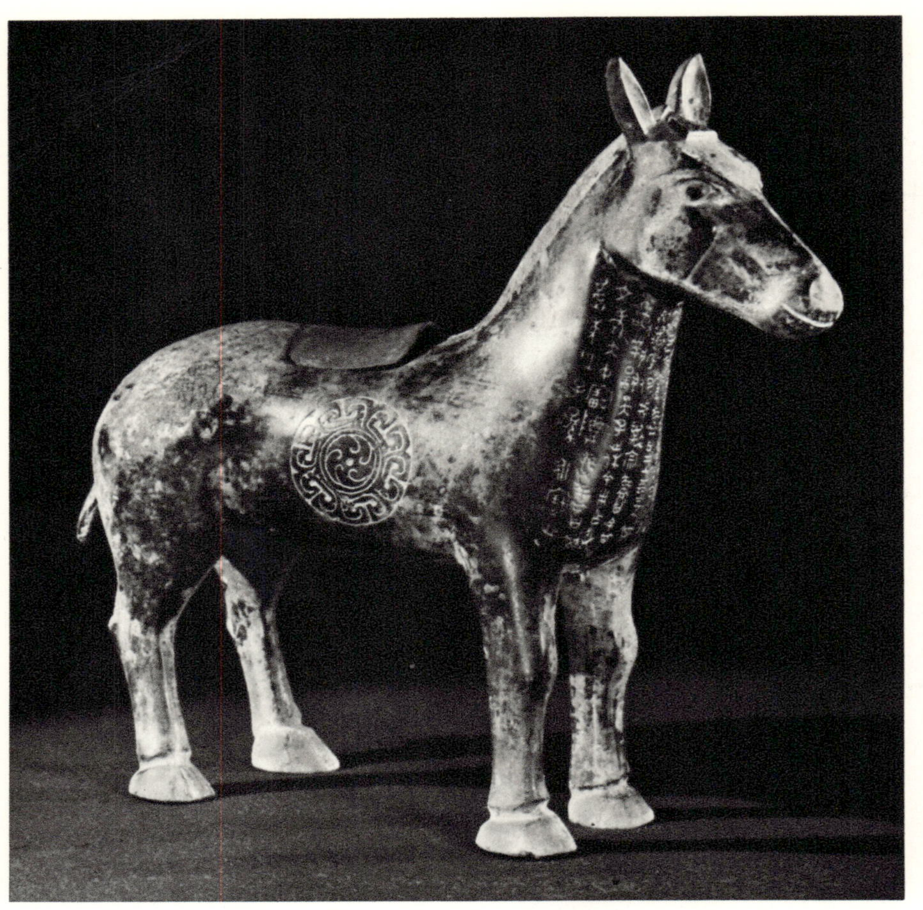

65. Horse-shaped *tsun*, bronze. Western Chou dynasty. Excavated at Li-ts'un, Mei District, Shensi.
height: 32.4 cm. (12.8 in.)

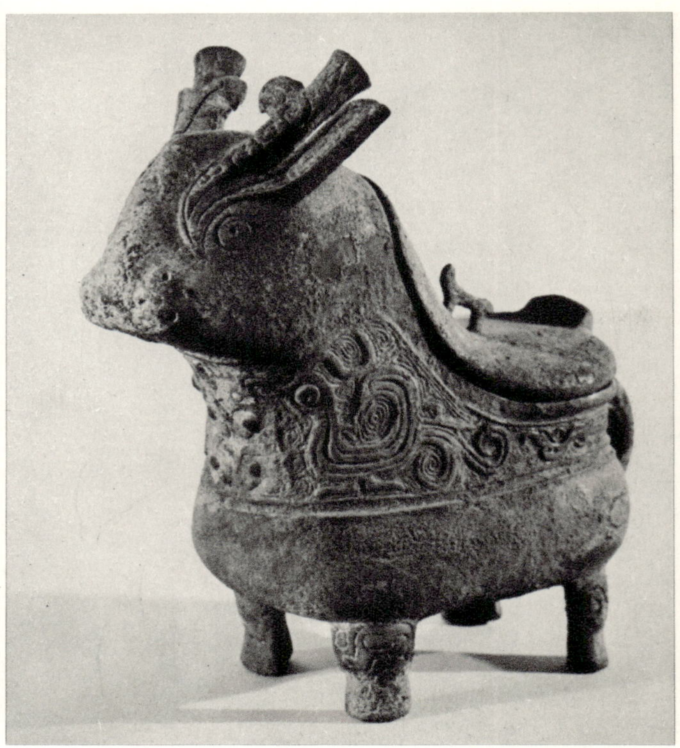

66. Covered *ssu kuang*, bronze. Early Western Chou dynasty. Excavated at Yen-tun-shan, Chen-chiang Municipality, Kiangsu.
height: 21.2 cm. (8.4 in.)

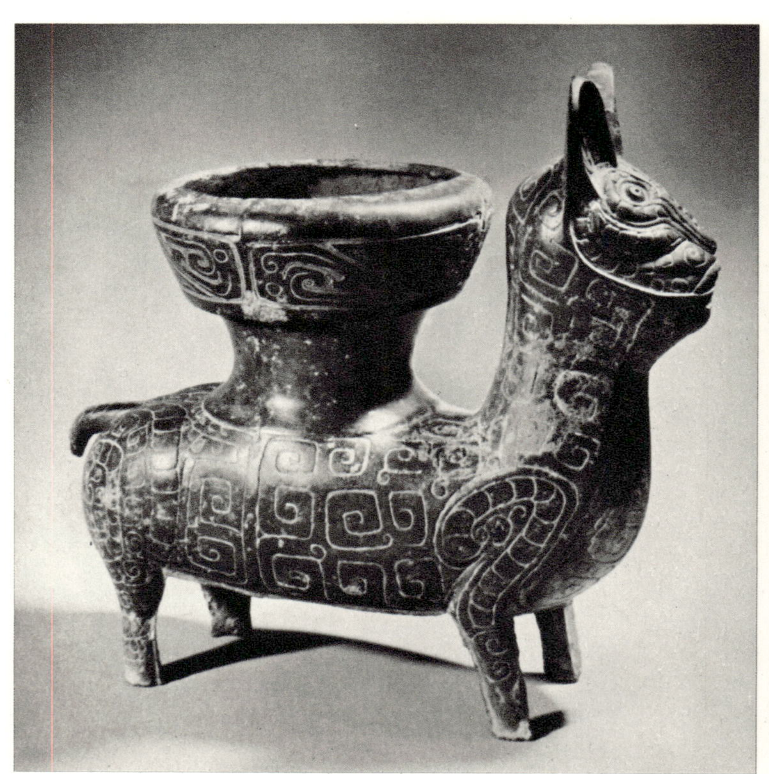

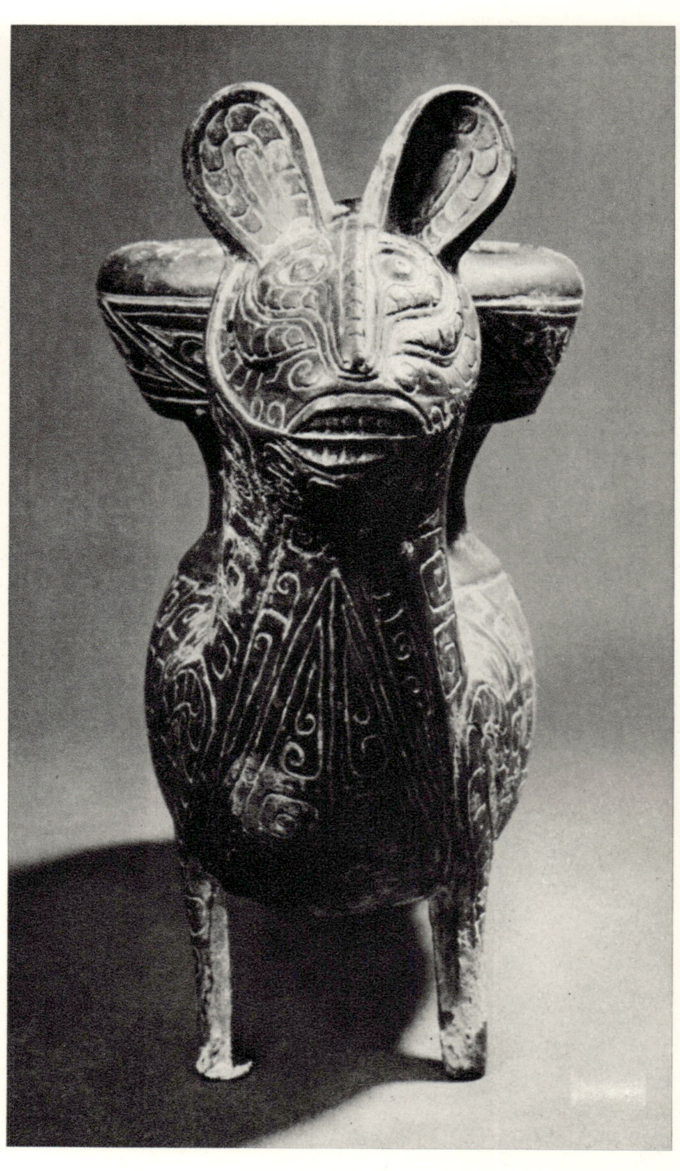

67–68. Animal-shaped *tou*, bronze. Ch'un Ch'iu period. Excavated at the Kuo state cemetery, Shang-ts'un-ling, Shan District, Honan.
height: 29.0 cm. (11.4 in.); length: 31.5 cm. (12.4 in.)

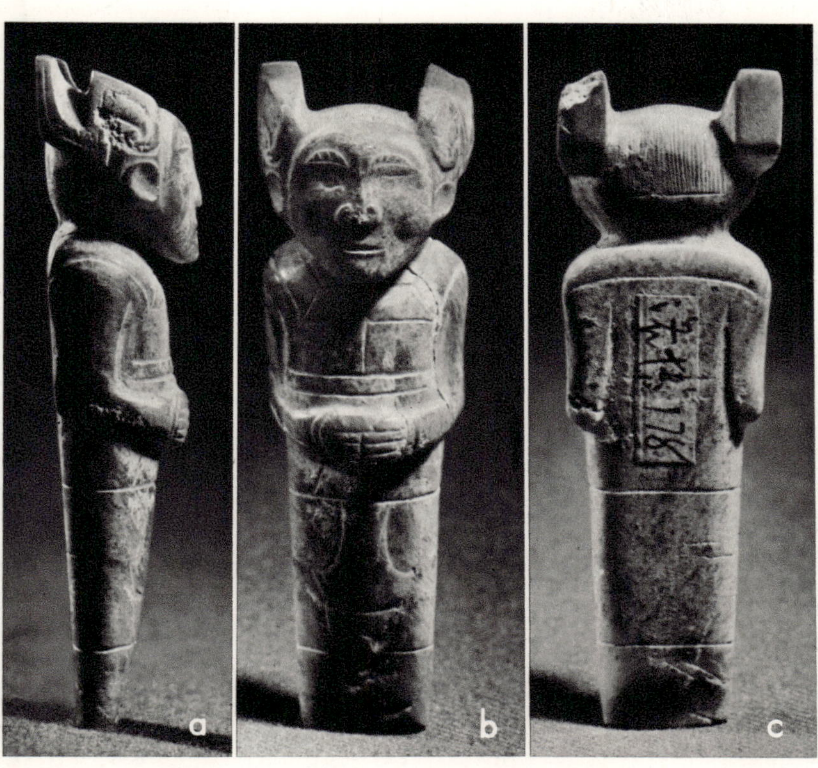

69 (a–c). Male figure, jade. Western Chou dynasty. Excavated at Tung-chiao, eastern outskirts of Lo-yang Municipality, Honan.
height: 7.4 cm. (2.9 in.)

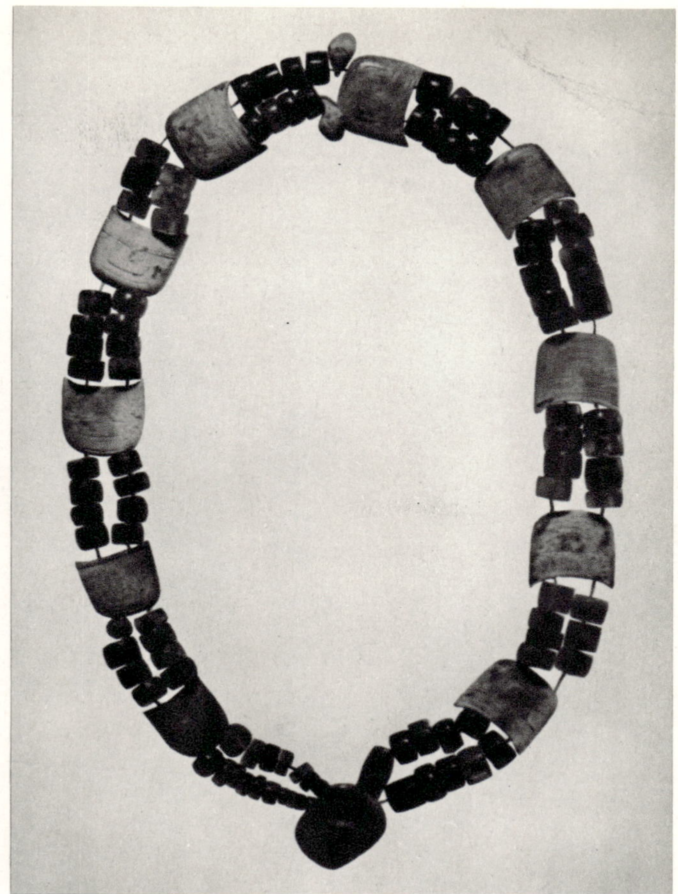

70. Necklace, stone and jade. Ch'un Ch'iu period. Excavated at the Kuo state cemetery, Shang-ts'un-ling, Shan District, Honan.

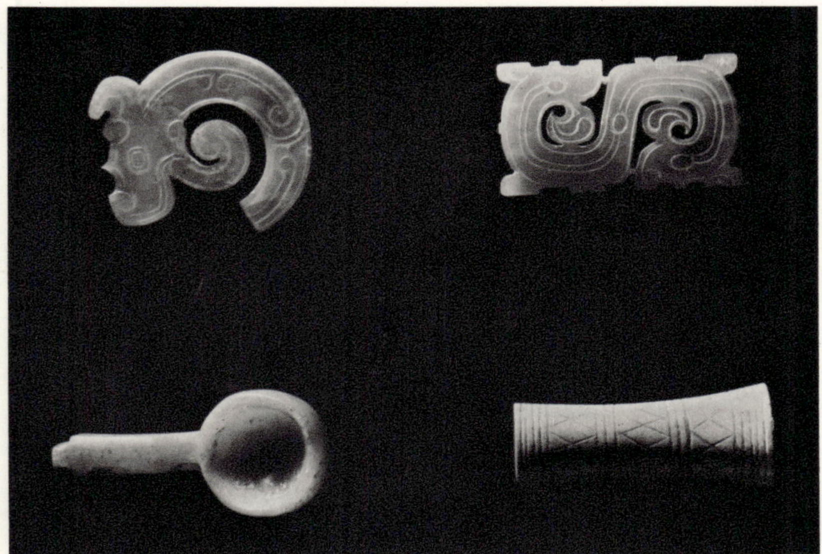

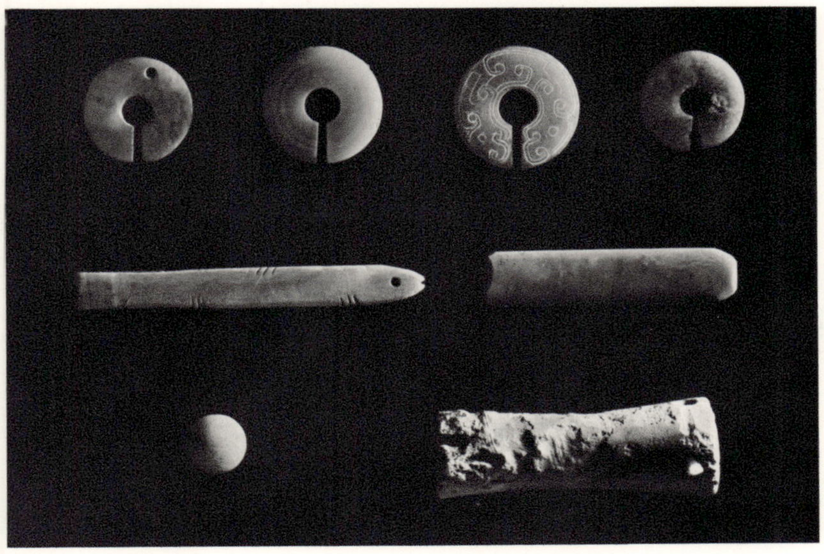

71–72. Ornaments, stone and jade. Ch'un Ch'iu period. Excavated at the Kuo state cemetery, Shang-ts'un-ling, Shan District, Honan.

71. Flat animal plaques; spoon-shaped and cylindrical ornaments.

72. upper row: jade *chüeh*; middle row: fish-shaped and rectangular jade strip; lower row: spherical and cylindrical ornaments.

73. Mirror, bronze. Ch'un Ch'iu period. Excavated at the Kuo state cemetery, Shang-ts'un-ling, Shan District, Honan.
diameter: 6.7 cm. (2.6 in.)

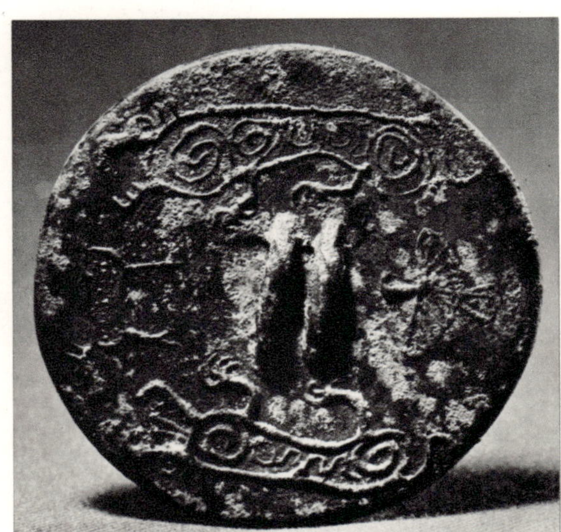

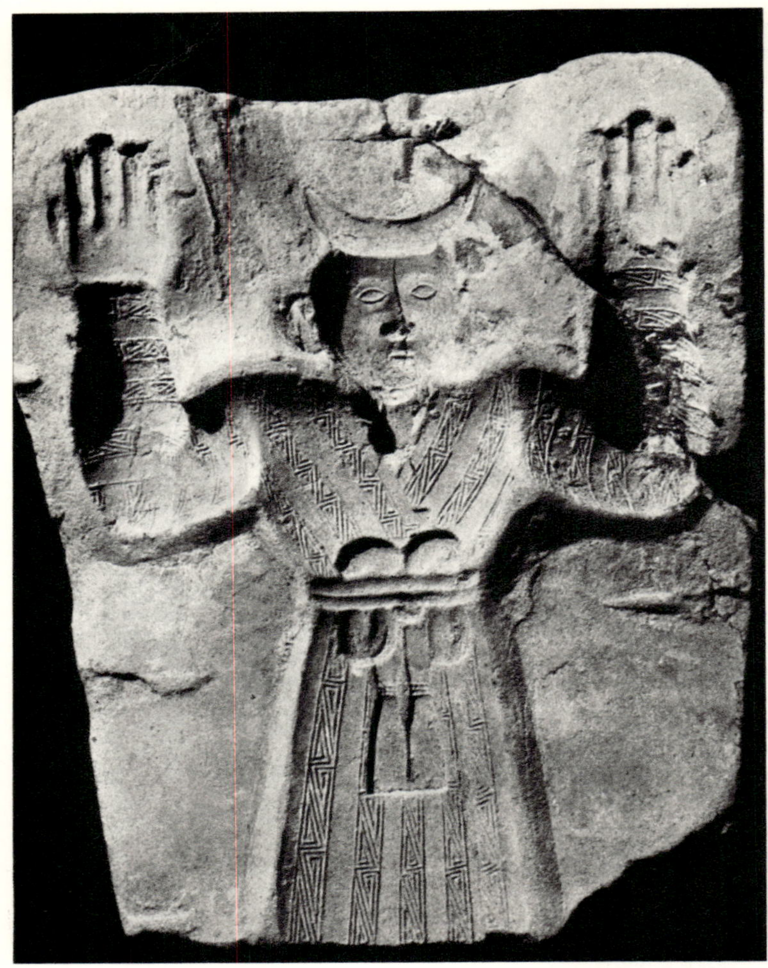

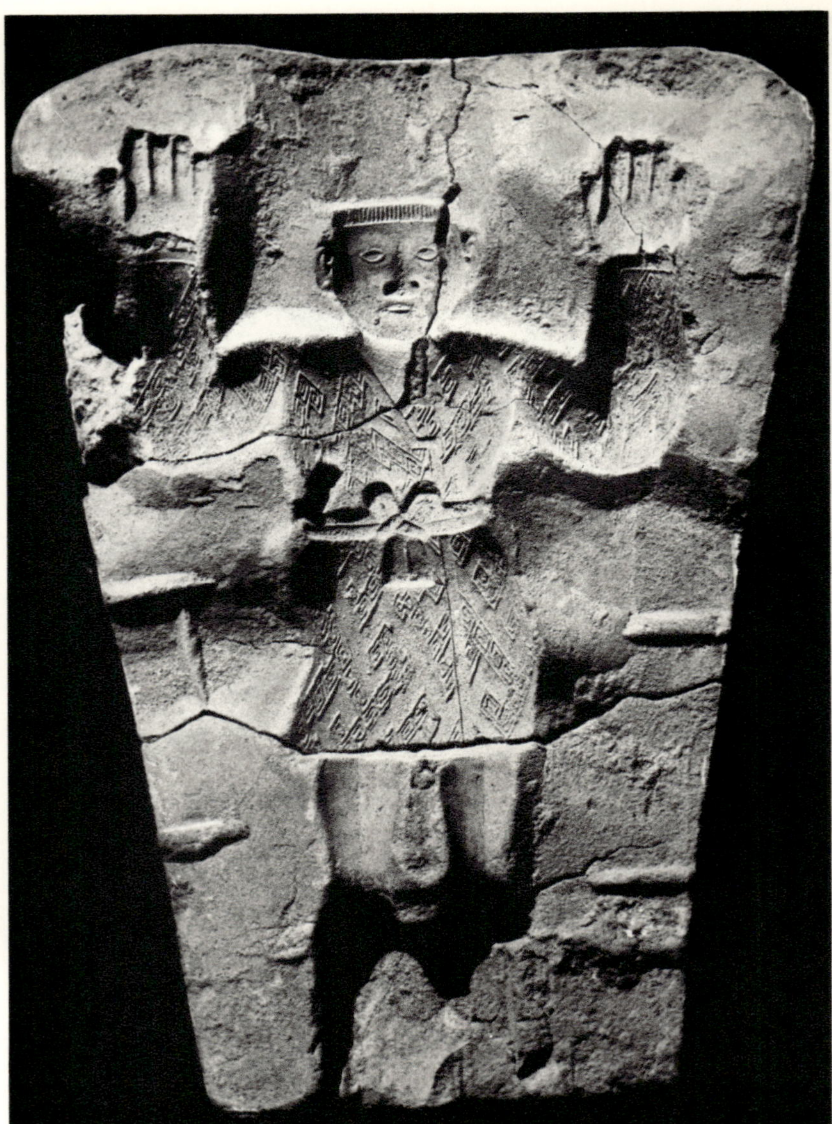

74–76. Relief, "replica" molds for bronze casting, earthenware. Late Ch'un Ch'iu or early Warring States period. Excavated from an Eastern Chou site at Hou-ma Municipality, Shansi.

74. *Female figure. height: 8.5 cm. (3.35 in.)*

75. *Male figure. height: 10.5 cm. (4.1 in.)*

76. *Semicircular plaque in two sections. diameter: 23.0 cm. (9.1 in.)*

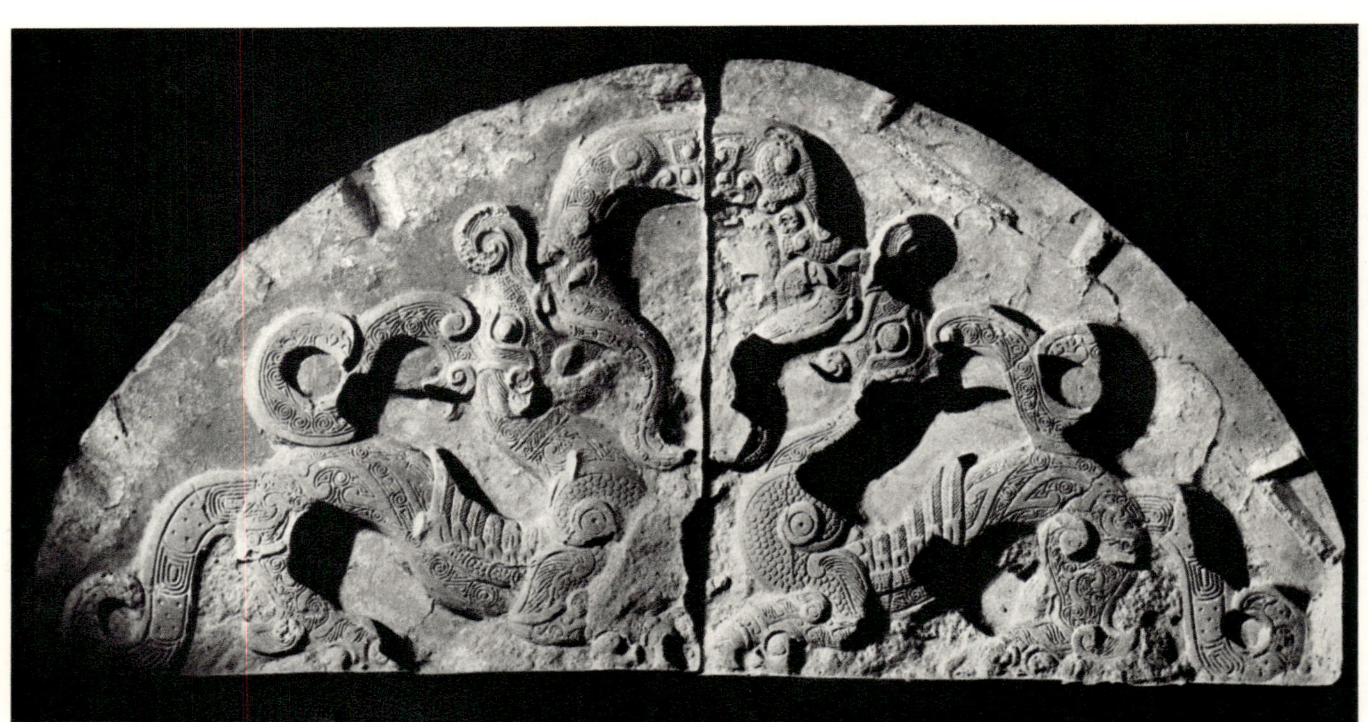

77 (a–d). Details of a *hu* (same as Pl. 23), bronze with cast decoration. Warring States period. Provenance unknown.

b. *Banqueting scene.*

c. *Hunting scenes and mulberry leaf picking.*

d. *Water battle scene.*

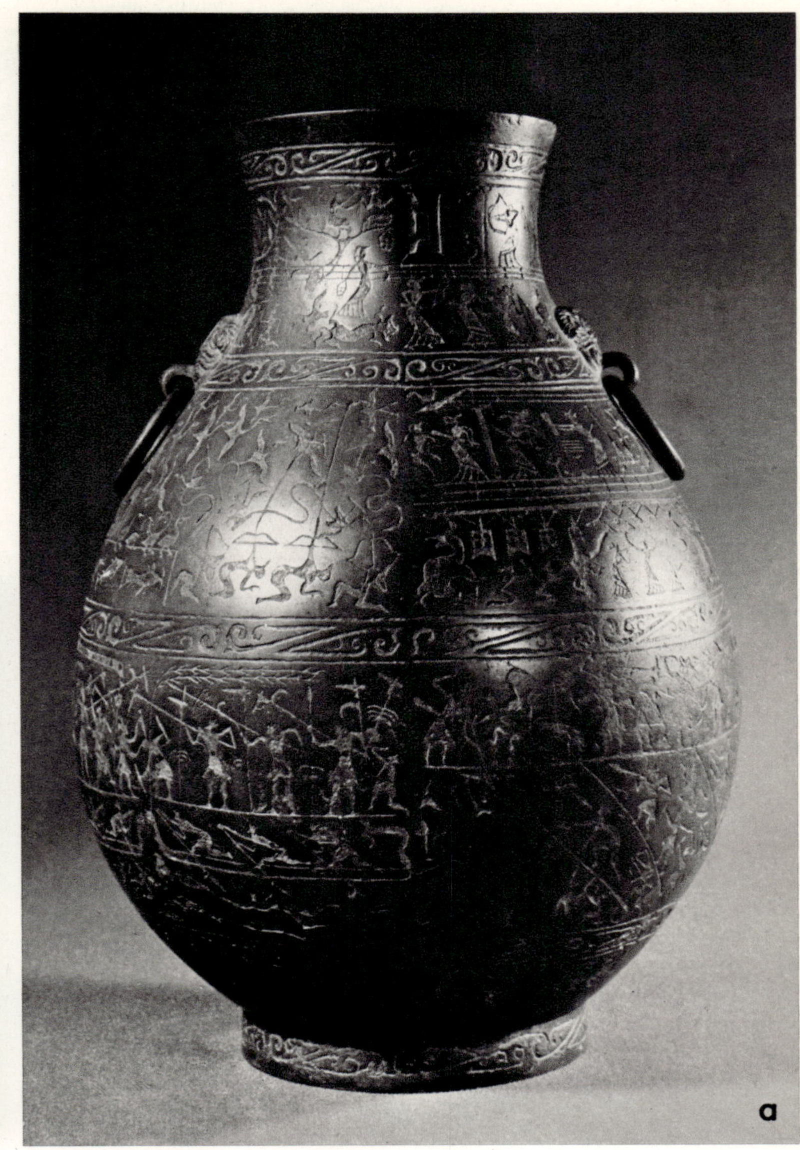

a

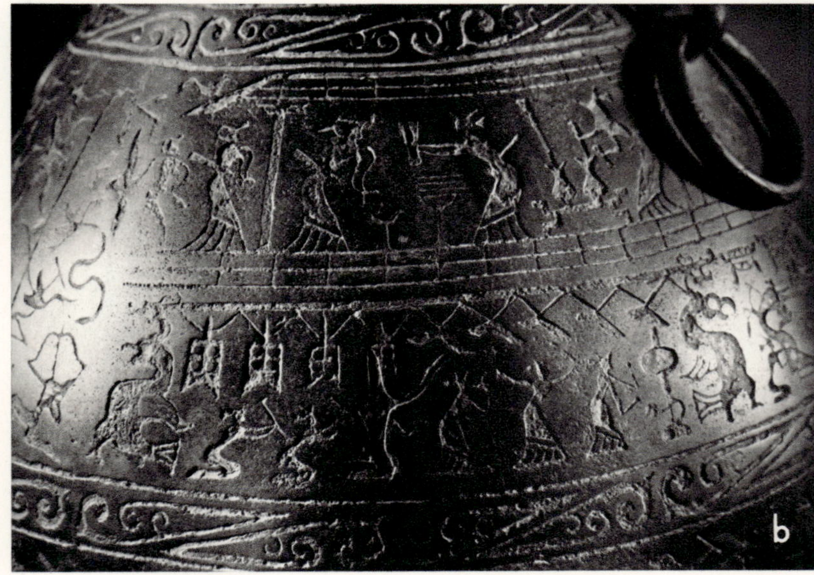

b

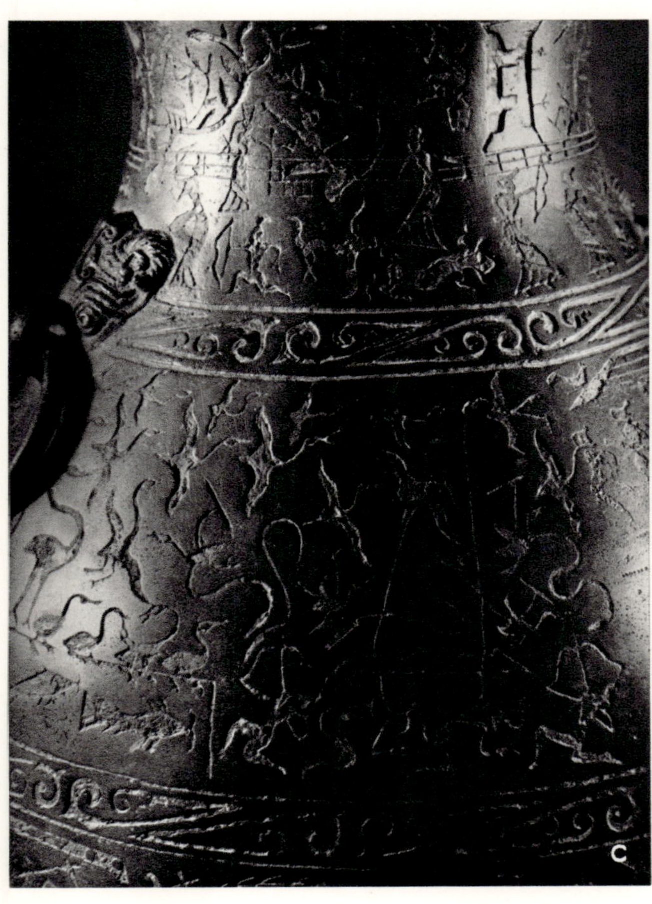

c

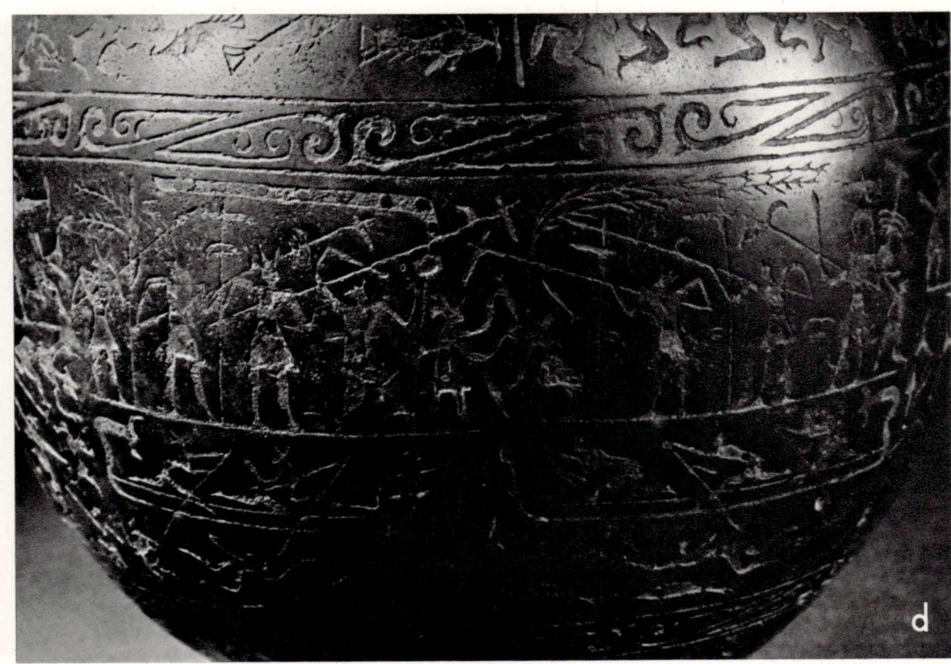

d

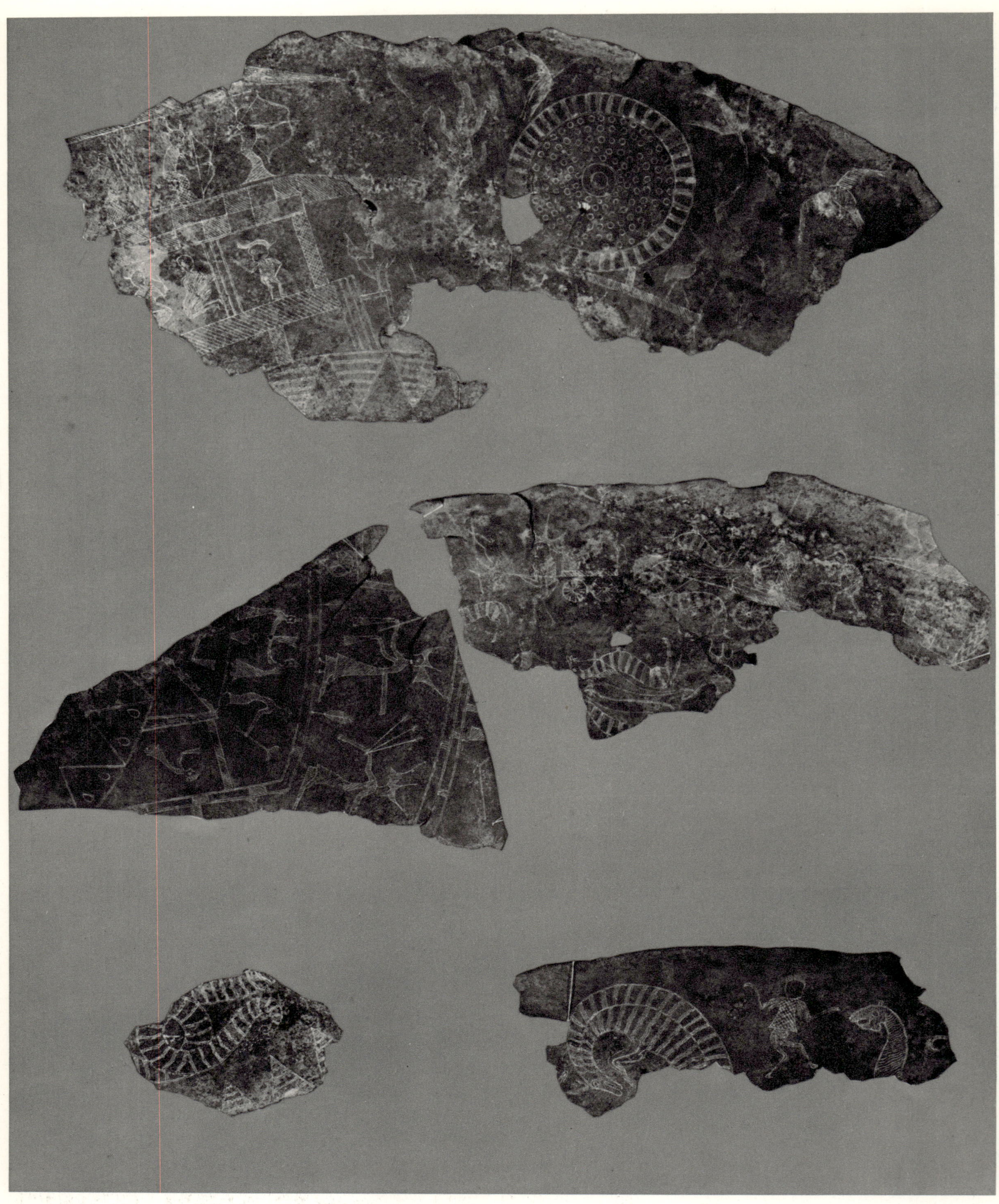

78. Fragments of a bronze vessel thought to be a *chien*. Warring States period. Provenance unknown.

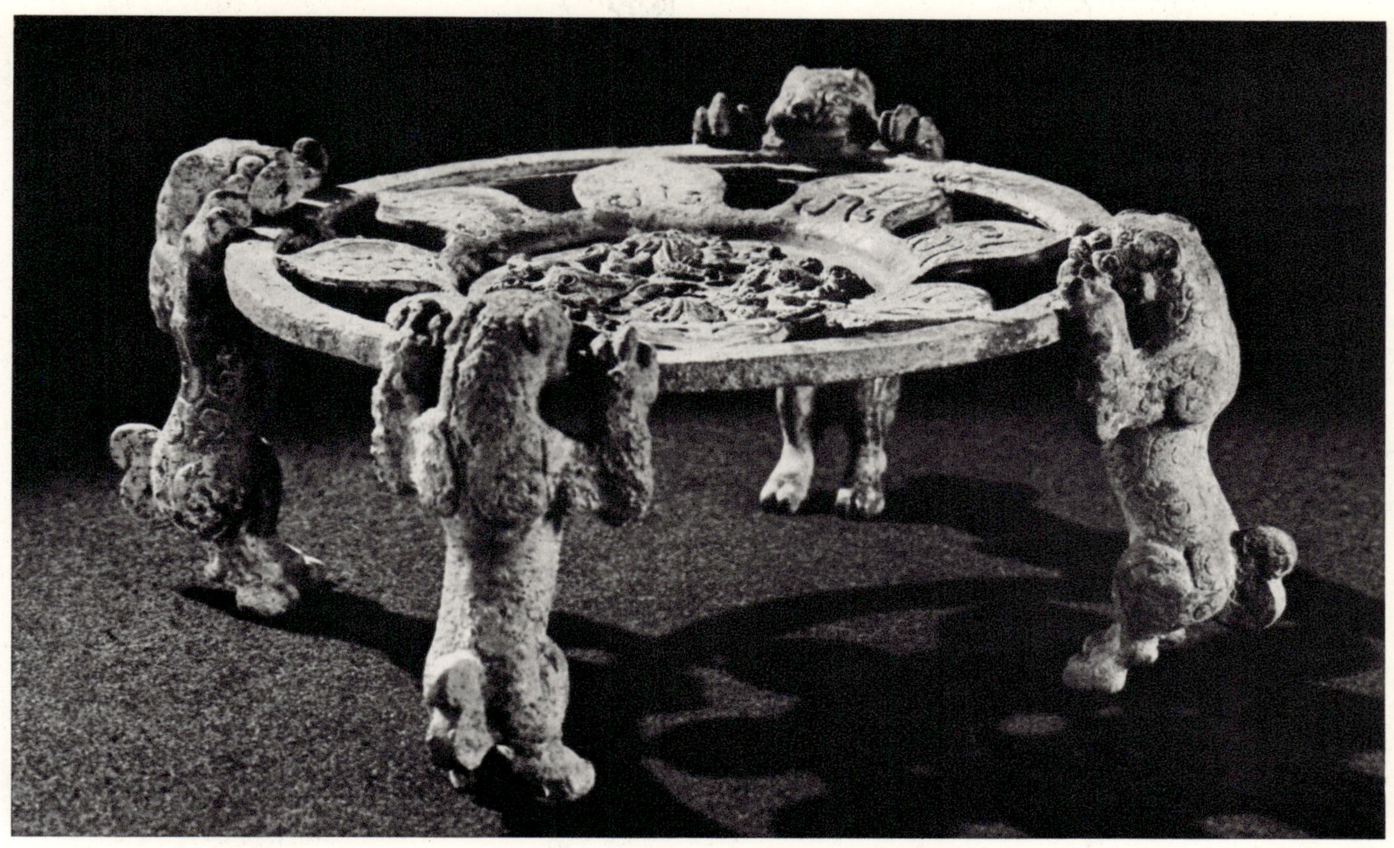

79. Circular stand with tiger-shaped legs, bronze. Warring States period. Excavated at Hou-ch'uan, Shan District, Honan.
height: 8.0 cm. (3.15 in.)

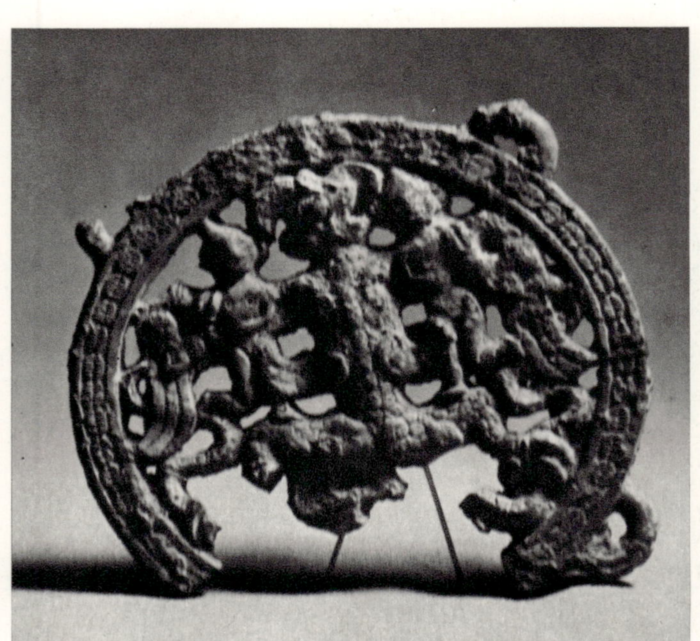

80. Openwork ornament, bronze. Early Warring States period. Excavated at Chung-chou-lu, Lo-yang Municipality, Honan.
diameter: 8.1 cm. (3.2 in.); thickness: 0.5 cm. (0.2 in.)

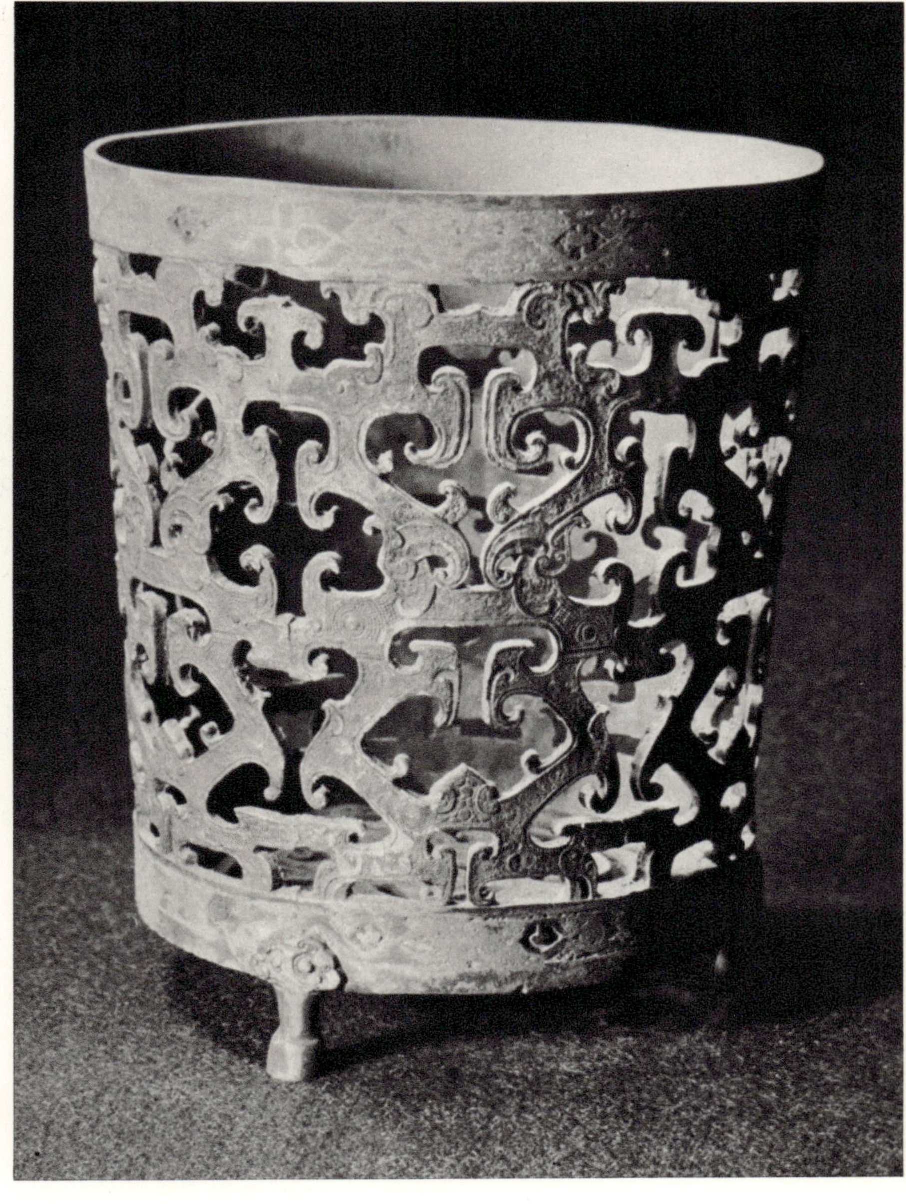

81. *Lien*, bronze. Warring States period. Excavated at Ch'ang-t'ai-kuan, Hsin-yang District, Honan.
height: 14.0 cm. (5.5 in.)

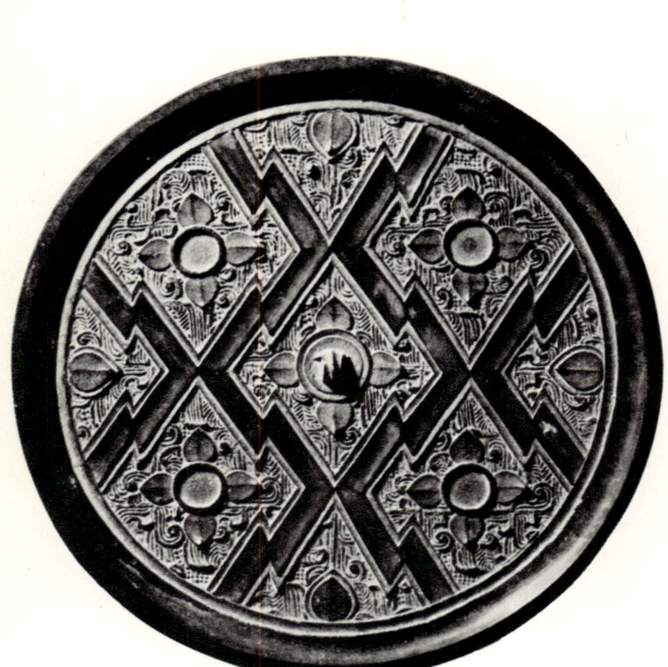

82. Mirror with quatrefoil decoration, bronze. Warring States period. Excavated at Liao-chia-wan, Ch'ang-sha Municipality, Hunan.
diameter: 11.9 cm. (4.7 in.)

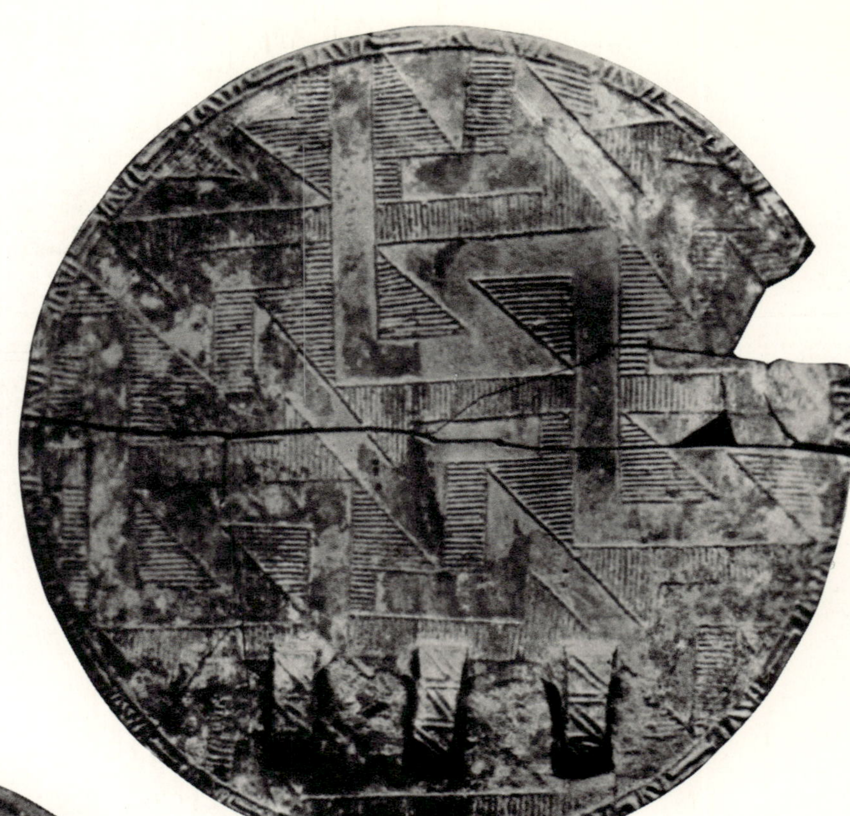

83. Mirror with multiple loop-handles, bronze. Warring States period. Excavated at Shih-erh-t'ai-ying-tzu, Chao-yang District, Liaoning.
diameter: 22.5 cm. (8.9 in.); height of loop: 0.5 cm. (0.2 in.)

84. Mirror with *shan* pattern, bronze. Warring States period. Excavated at Yüeh-liang-shan, Ch'ang-sha Municipality, Hunan.
no measurement given

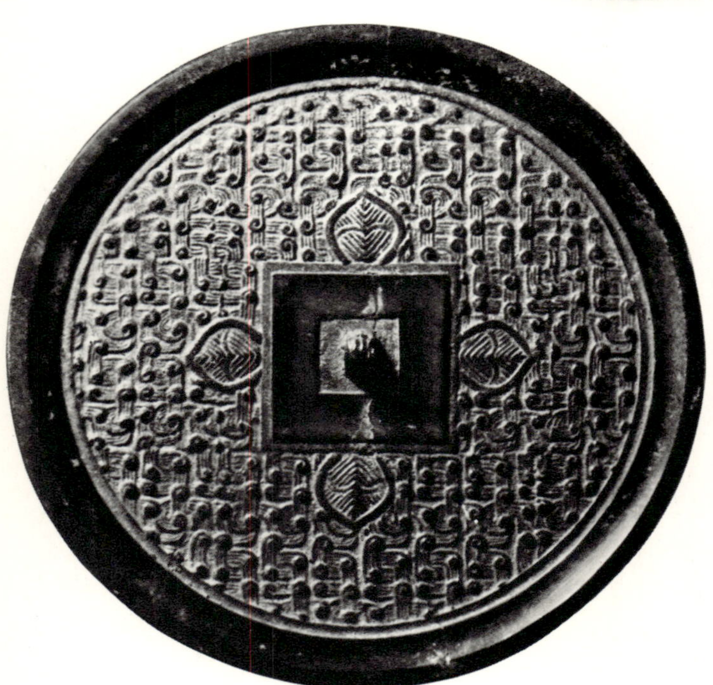

85. Mirror, bronze. Warring States period. Excavated at Yüeh-liang-shan, Ch'ang-sha Municipality, Hunan.
diameter: 12.3 cm. (4.8 in.)

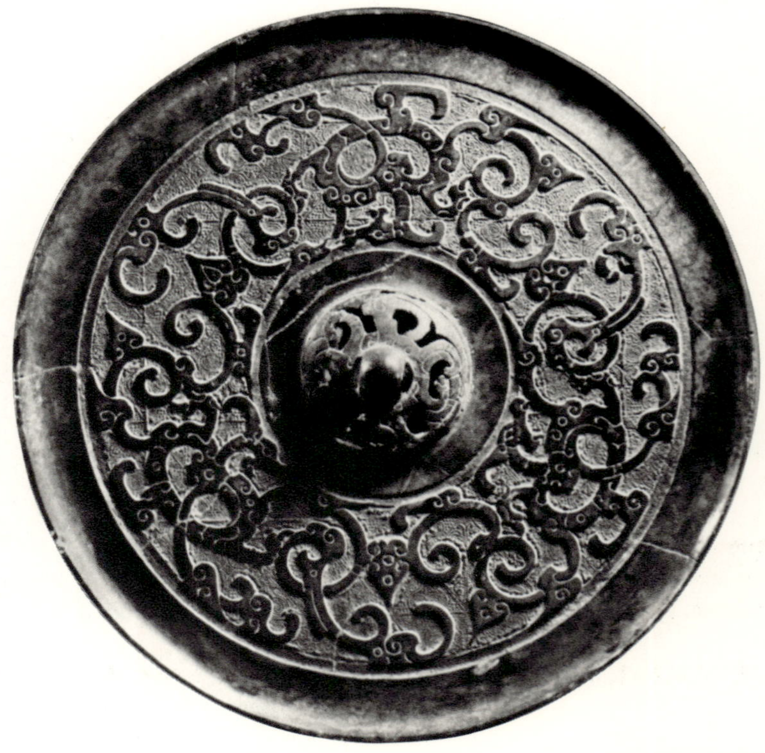

86. Mirror with hemispherical, openwork knob and intertwined-dragon pattern, bronze. Late Warring States period. Excavated at Tzu-tan-k'u, Ch'ang-sha Municipality, Hunan.
diameter: 16.5 cm. (6.5 in.)

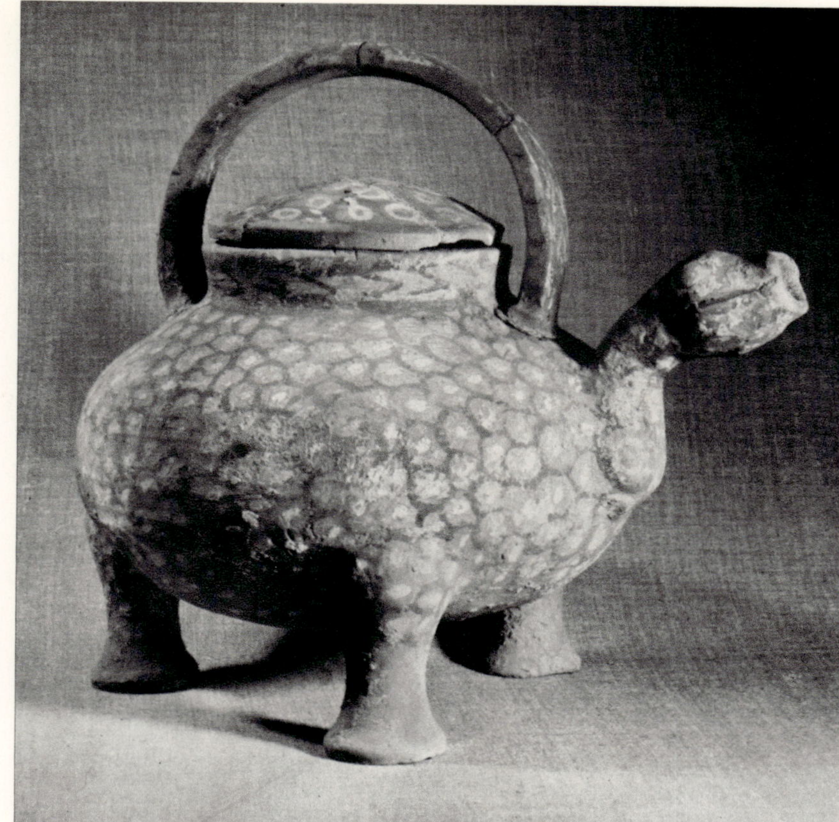

87. *Ho*, earthenware with slip decoration. Warring States period. Excavated at Tung-tung-ts'un, Hsing-t'ai Municipality, Hopei.
height: 27.0 cm. (10.6 in.); diameter at belly: 23.0 cm. (9.1 in.)

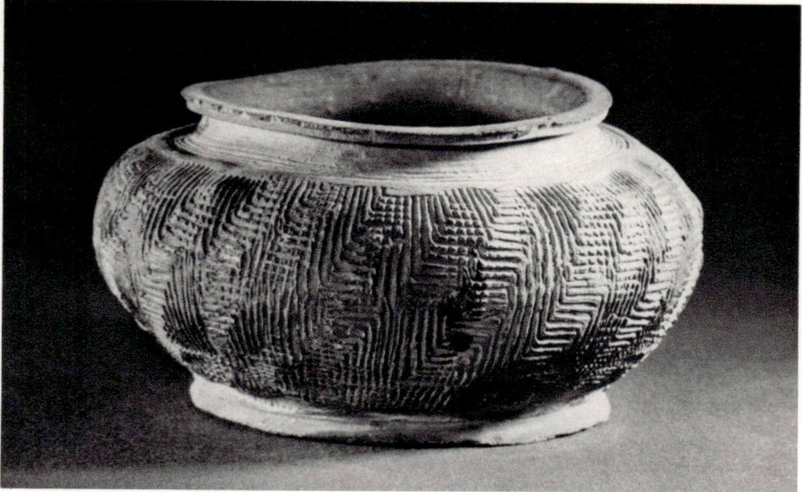

88. Jar, unglazed earthenware with impressed design. Warring States period. Excavated at She-chu, Li-yang District, Kiangsu.
height: 10.0 cm. (3.9 in.); diameter at belly: 18.0 cm. (7.1 in.)

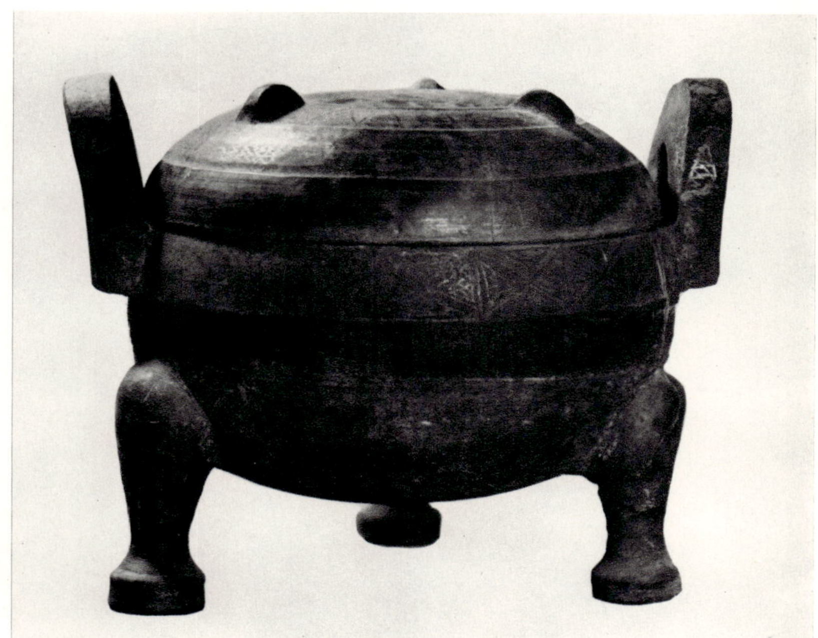

89. Covered *ting*, dark-gray earthenware with "graphite" decoration. Warring States period. Excavated at Erh-li-kang, Ch'eng-chou Municipality, Honan.
height: 23.4 cm. (9.3 in.)

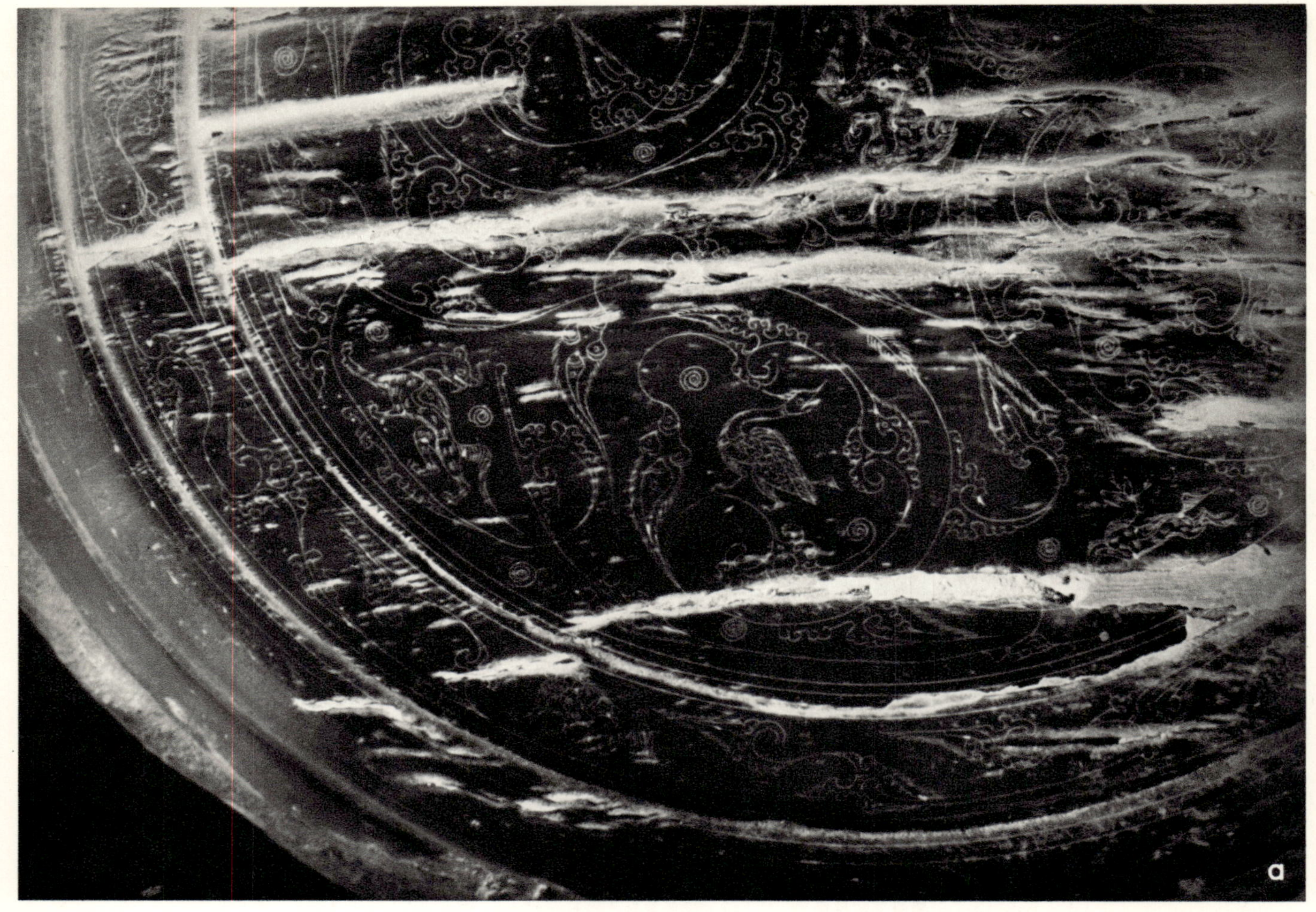

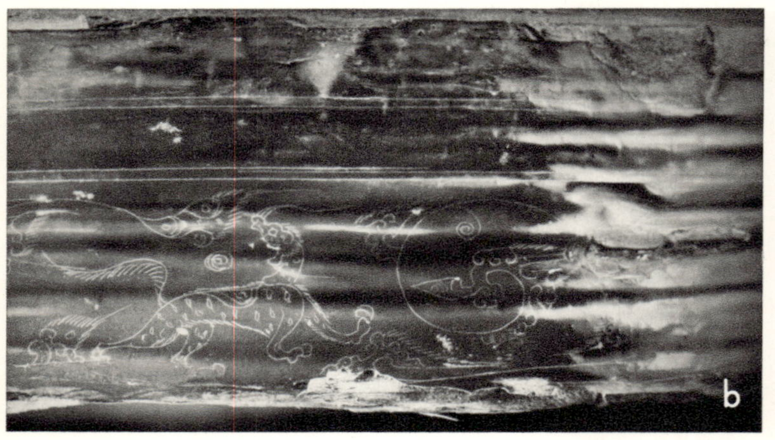

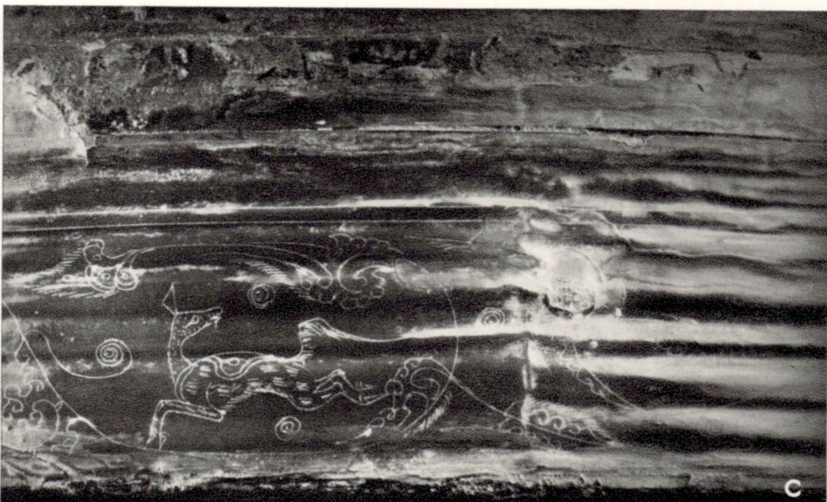

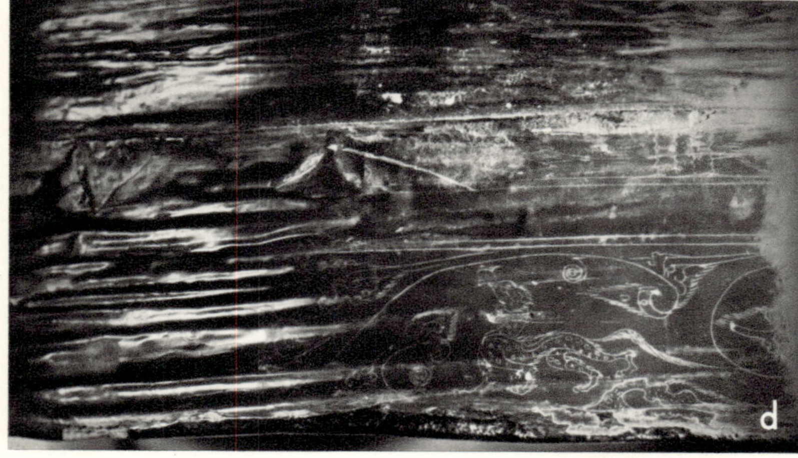

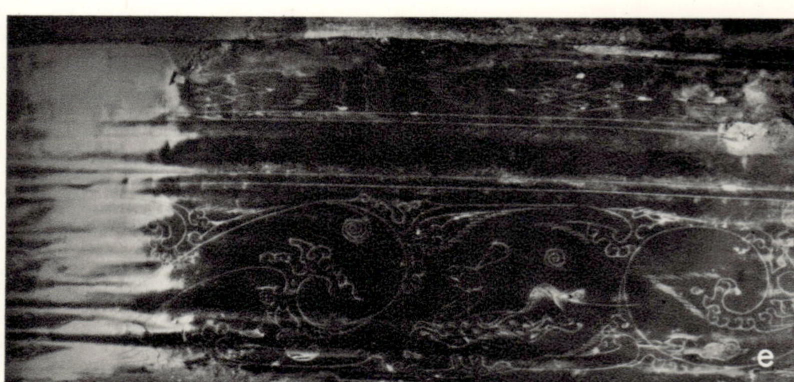

90 (a–e). Details of the engraved decoration on a lacquered *lien*. Warring States period. Excavated at Ch'ang-sha Municipality, Hunan.

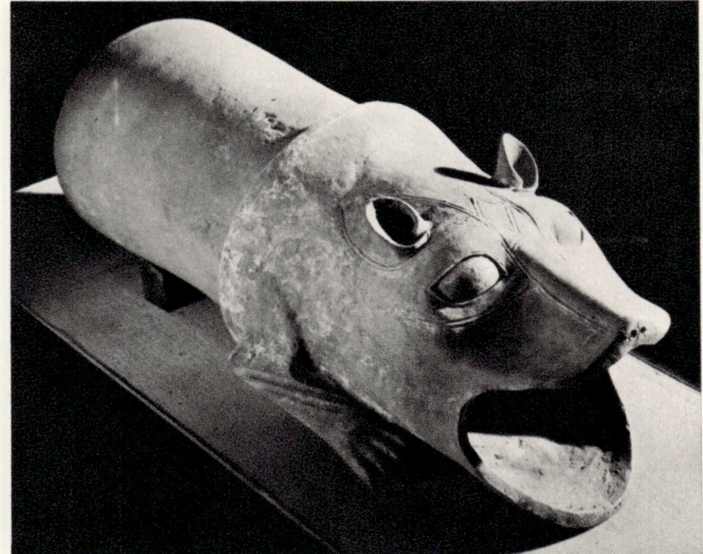

91. Tiger-headed waterspout, earthenware. Warring States period. Excavated at the site of Yen-hsia-tu, Yi District, Hopei.
length: 120 cm. (47.2 in.); mouth height: 36.5 cm. (14.4 in.); mouth width: 34.0 cm. (13.4 in.)

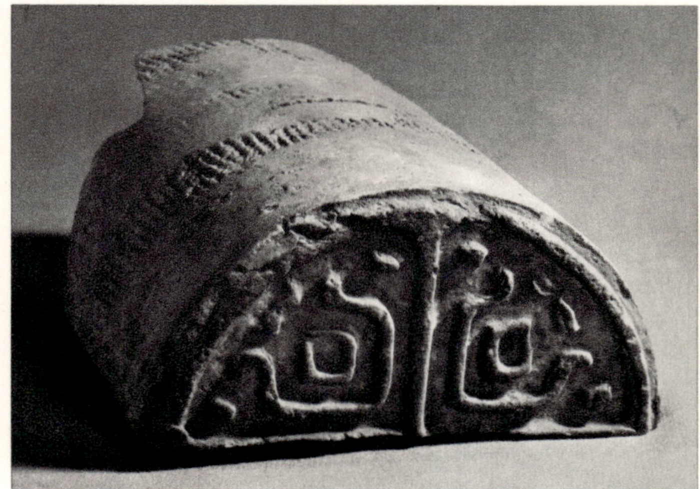

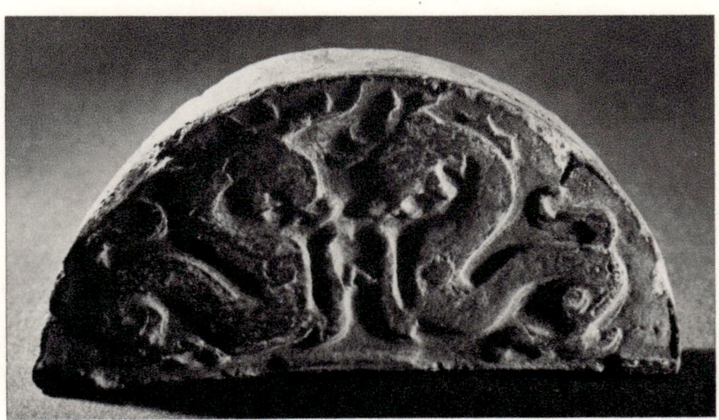

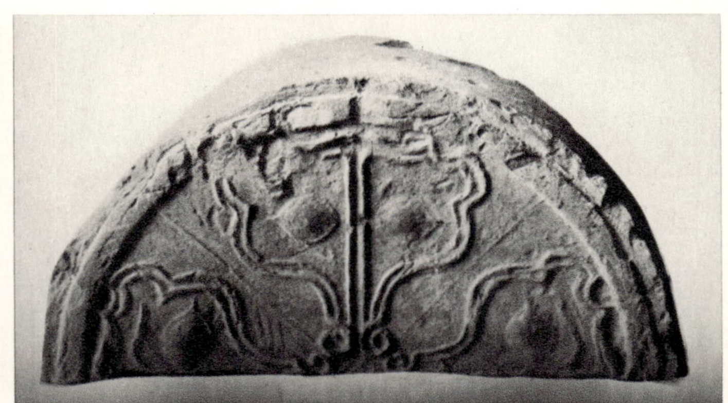

92–94. Semicircular eave end-tiles, earthenware. Warring States period. Excavated at Chung-chou-lu, Lo-yang Municipality, Honan.
92. no measurement given
93. diameter: 18.2 cm. (7.2 in.)
94. height: 6.0 cm. (2.36 in.); diameter: 12.5 cm. (4.9 in.)

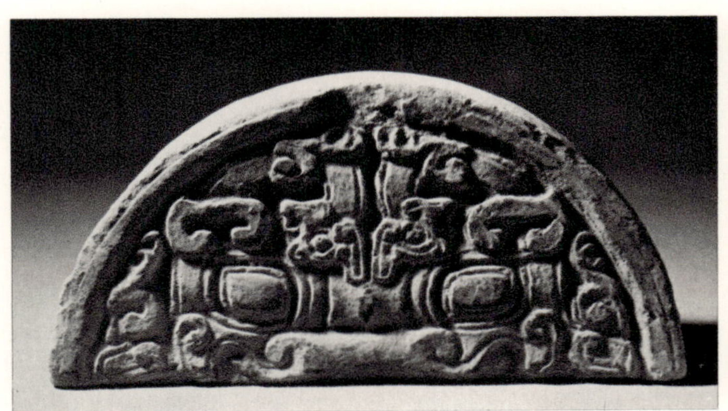

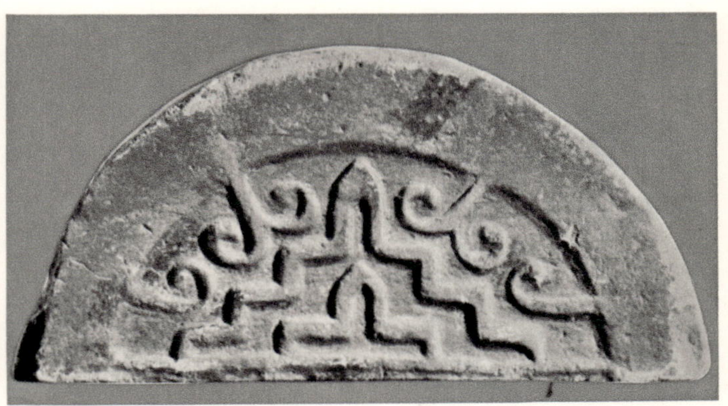

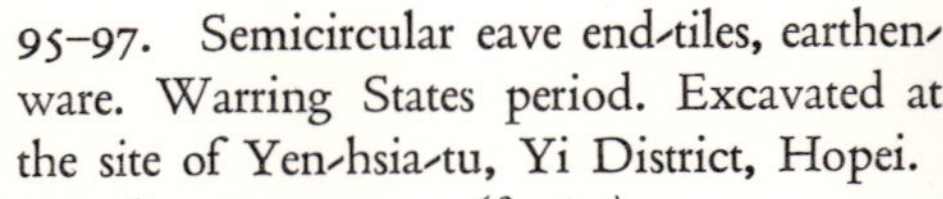

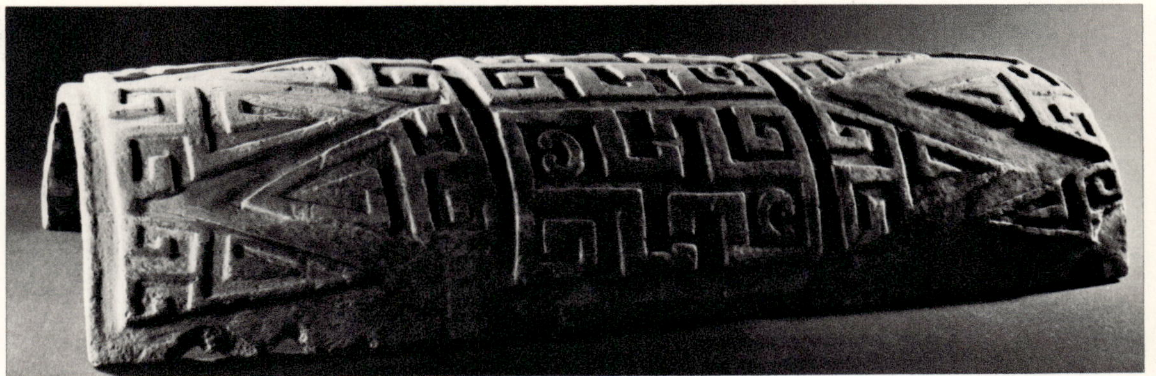

95–97. Semicircular eave end-tiles, earthenware. Warring States period. Excavated at the site of Yen-hsia-tu, Yi District, Hopei.
95. diameter: 21.5 cm. (8.5 in.)
96. diameter: 17.3 cm. (6.8 in.)
97. Curved tile. length: 92.5 cm. (36.4 in.); diameter: 38.0 cm. (14.95 in.)

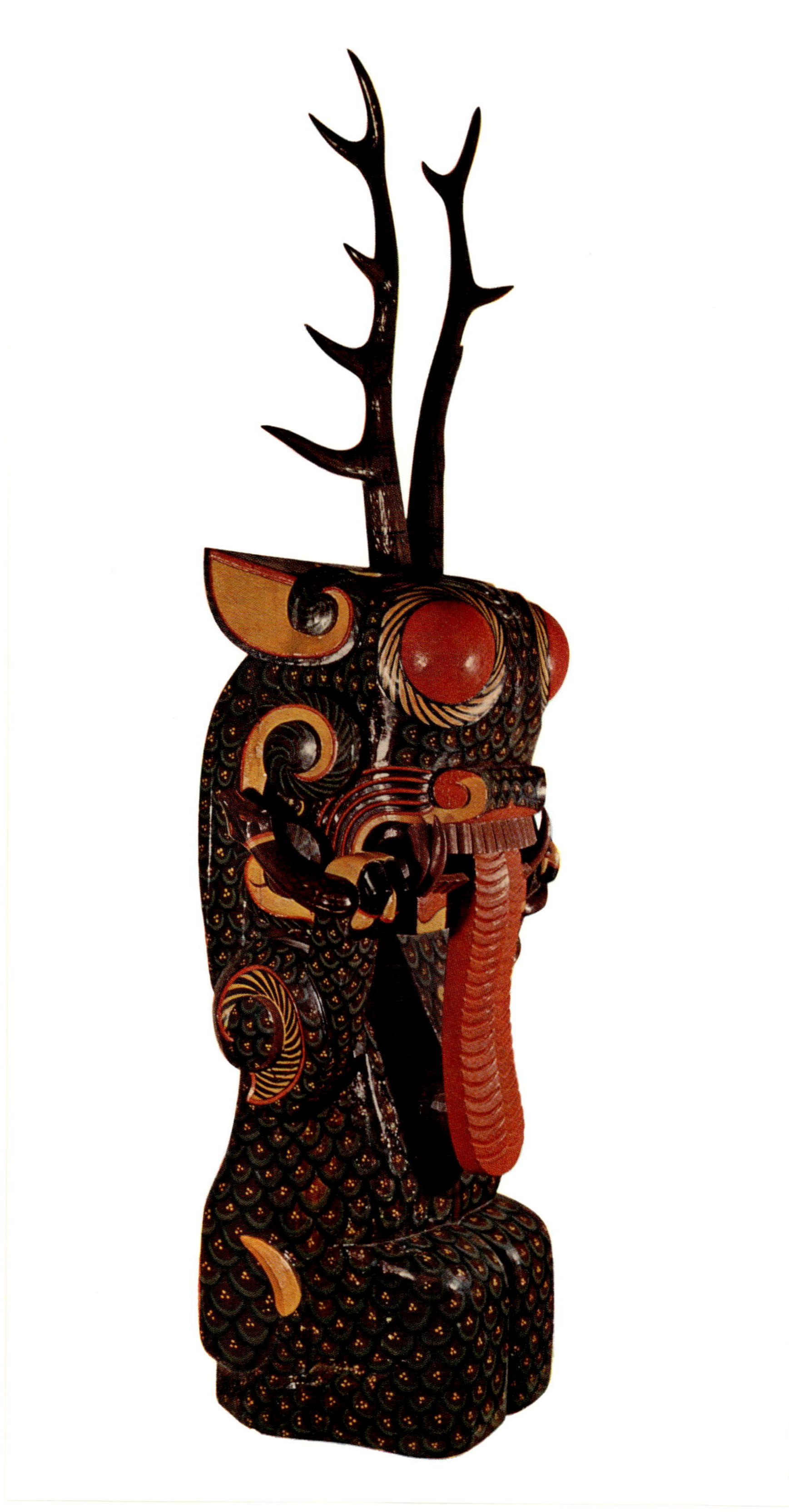

98. Horned animal eating a snake, carved and lacquered wood. Warring States period. Excavated at Ch'ang-t'ai-kuan, Hsin-yang District, Honan.
height: 195 cm. (76.7 in.)

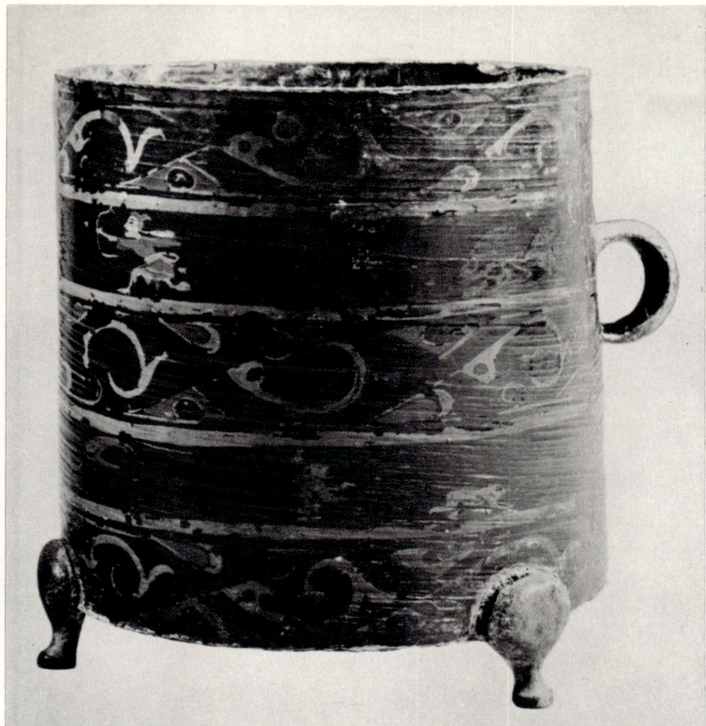

99. *Lien*, black and red lacquer. Warring States period. Excavated at Yen-chia-tsui, Ch'ang-sha Municipality, Hunan.
height: 12.3 cm. (4.8 in.); diameter at lip: 11.4 cm. (4.5 in.)

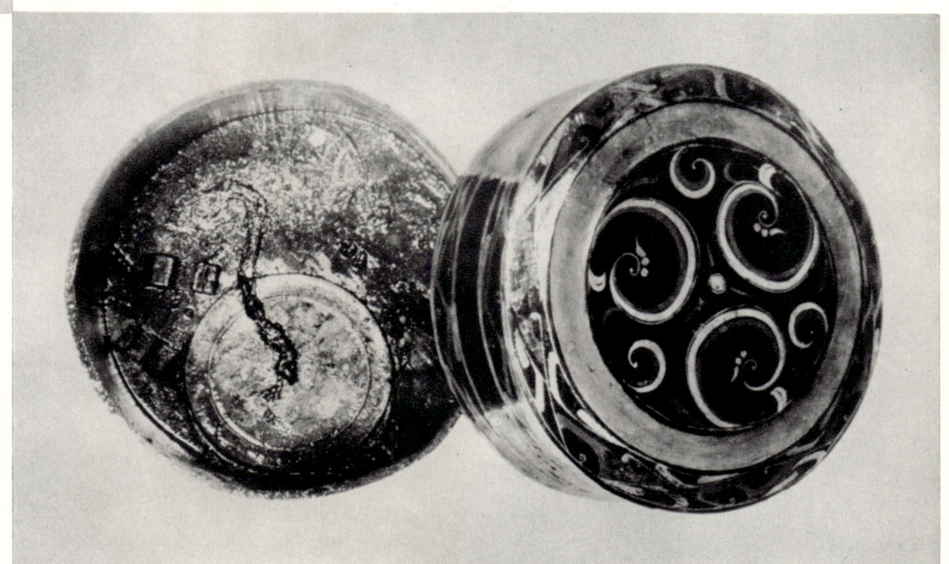

100. Wooden box, black and red lacquer. Warring States period. Excavated at Tso-chia-kung-shan, Ch'ang-sha Municipality, Hunan.
height: 9.5 cm. (3.74 in.); diameter: 21.0 cm. (8.3 in.)

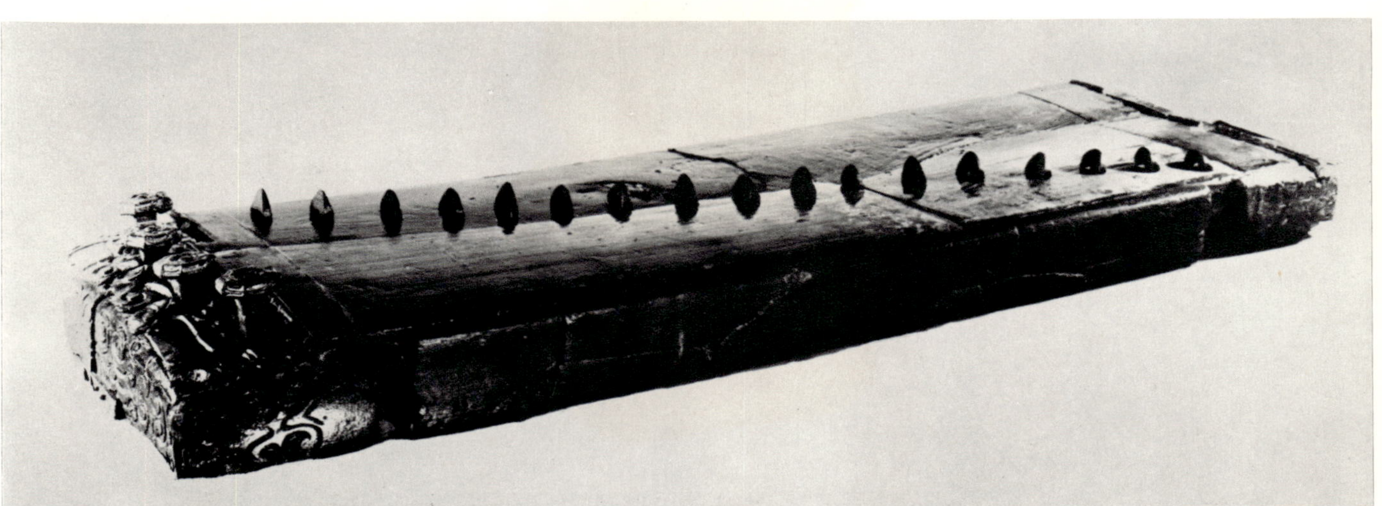

101. Twenty-five-stringed *se*, wood with lacquered end-sections. Warring States period. Excavated from tomb No. 2, Ch'ang-t'ai-kuan, Hsin-yang District, Honan.
height: 8.0 cm. (3.15 in.); length: 147 cm. (57.8 in.); width: 45.0 cm. (17.7 in.)

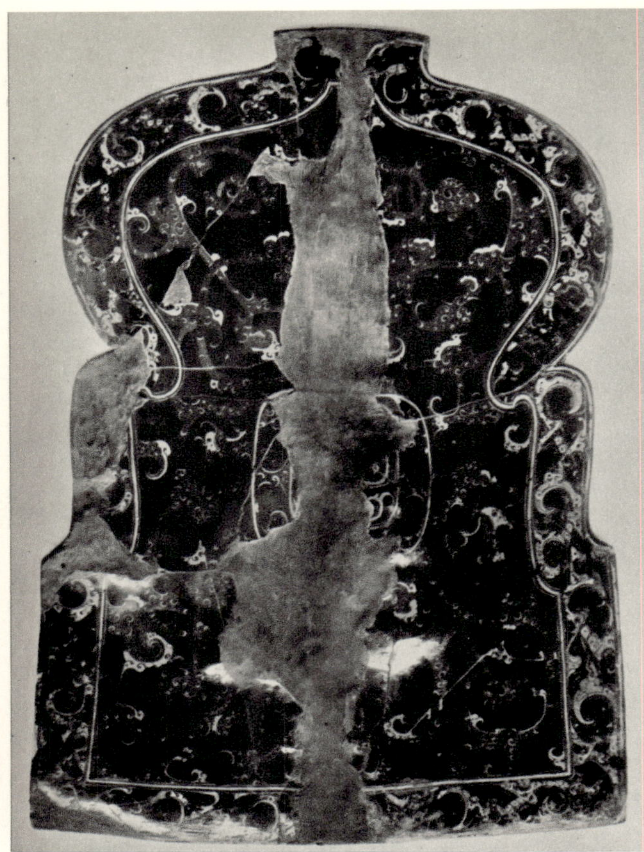

102. Inner surface of leather shield, red, yellow and black lacquer. Warring States period. Excavated at Wu-li-p'ai, Ch'ang-sha Municipality, Hunan.
height: 63.0 cm. (24.8 in.)

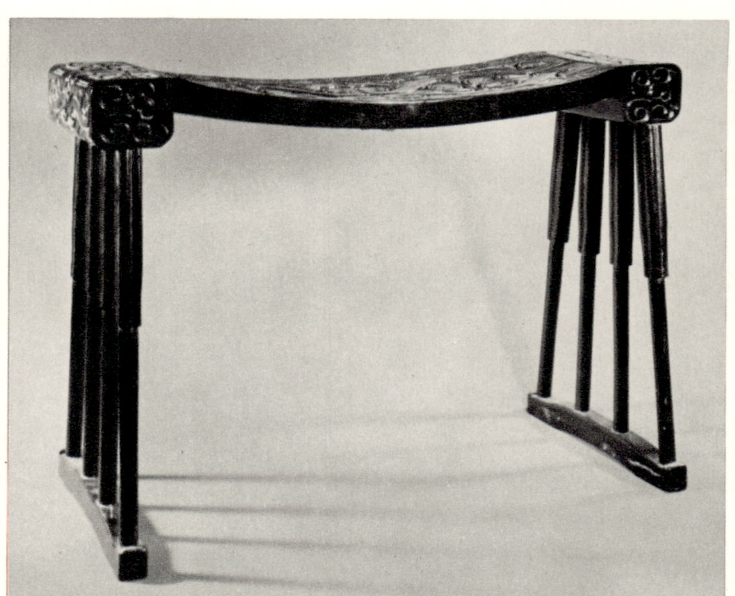

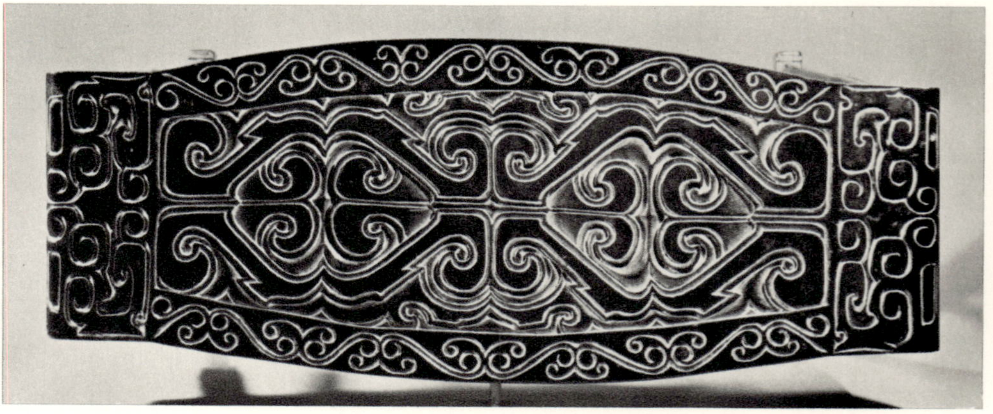

103–104. Armrest, carved lacquer. Warring States period. Excavated from tomb No. 1, Ch'ang-t'ai-kuan, Hsin-yang District, Honan.
height: 48.0 cm. (18.9 in.); width: 23.8 cm. (9.35 in.)

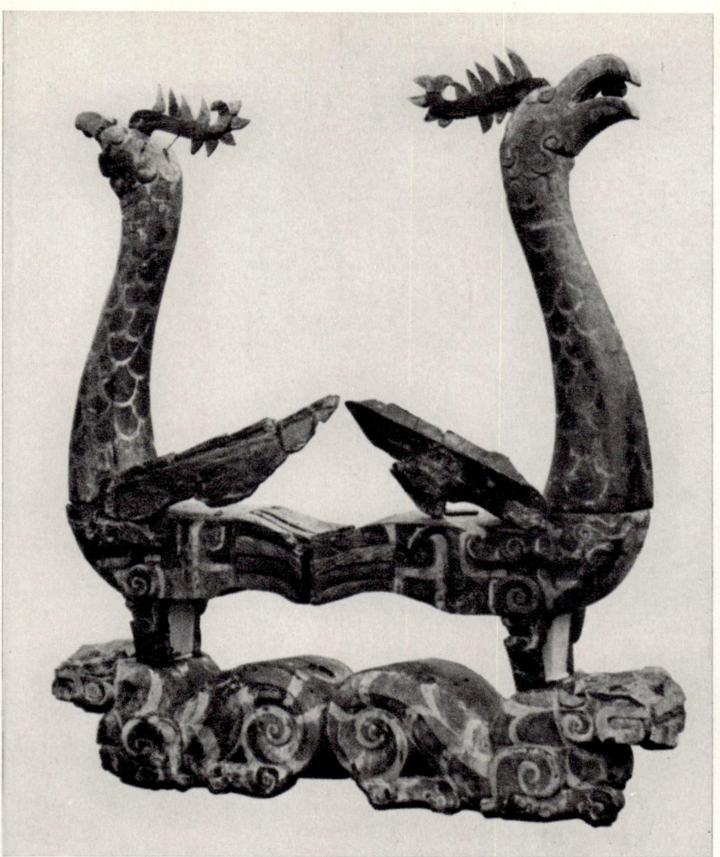

105. Phoenixes, lacquered wood. Warring States period. Excavated at Ch'ang-t'ai-kuan, Hsin-yang District, Honan.
height: 163 cm. (64.1 in.)

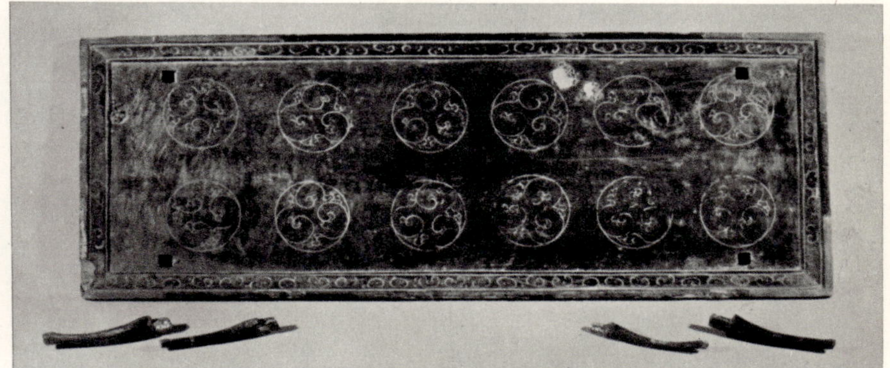

106. Table, lacquered wood. Warring States period. Excavated at Ch'ang-sha Municipality, Hunan.
length: 39.0 cm. (15.3 in.)

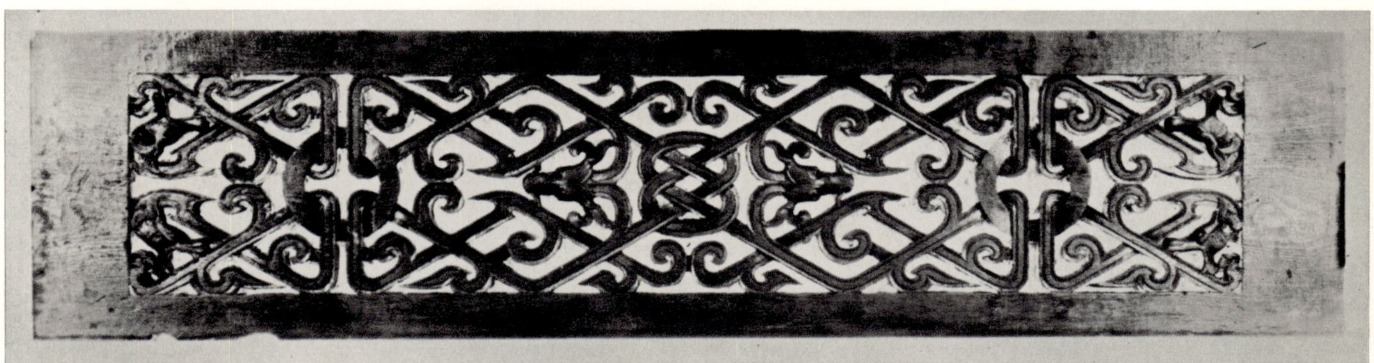

107. Openwork panel, wood. Warring States period. Excavated at Yang-t'ien-hu, Ch'ang-sha, Hunan.
length: 183 cm. (72 in.); width: 45.0 cm. (17.7 in.); thickness: 4.0 cm. (1.58 in.)

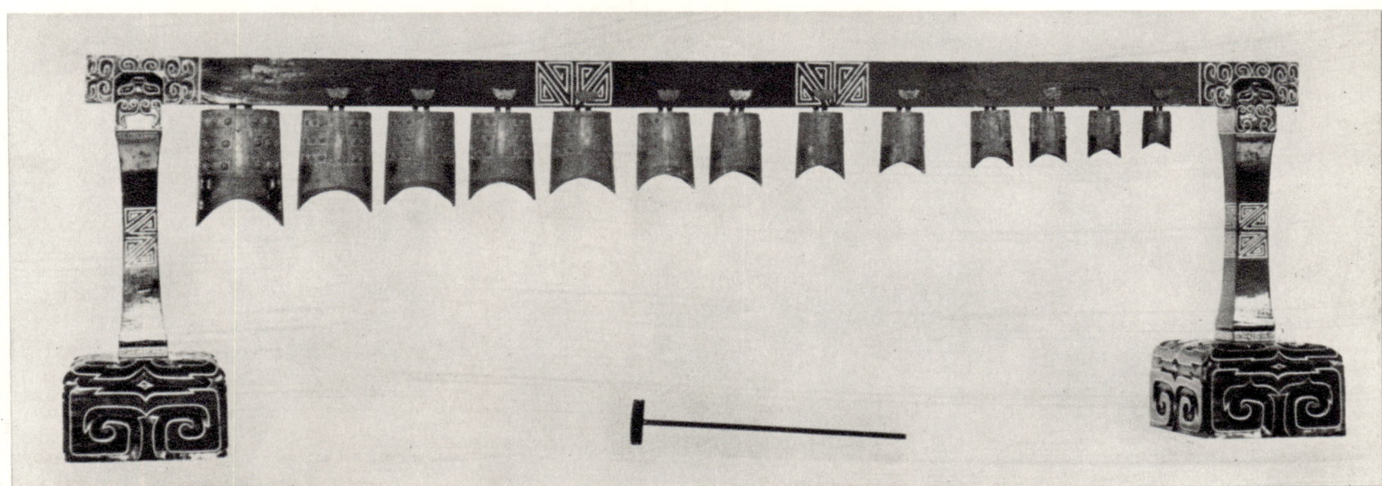

108. Set of thirteen bells, bronze. (Reconstructed rack, lacquered wood.) Warring States period. Excavated from tomb No. 1, Ch'ang-t'ai-kuan, Hsin-yang District, Honan.
length: 242 cm. (95.3 in.)

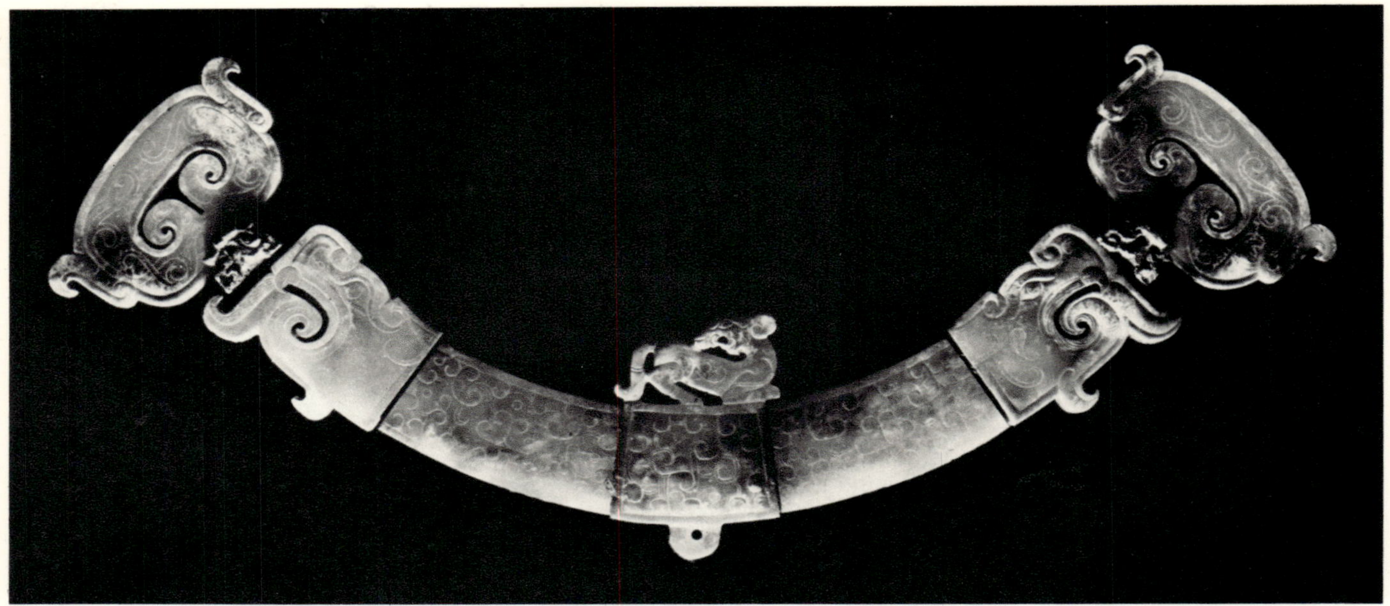

109. *Huang*, white jade. Warring States period. Excavated at Ku-wei-ts'un, Hui District, Honan.
length: 20.4 cm. (8.1 in.)

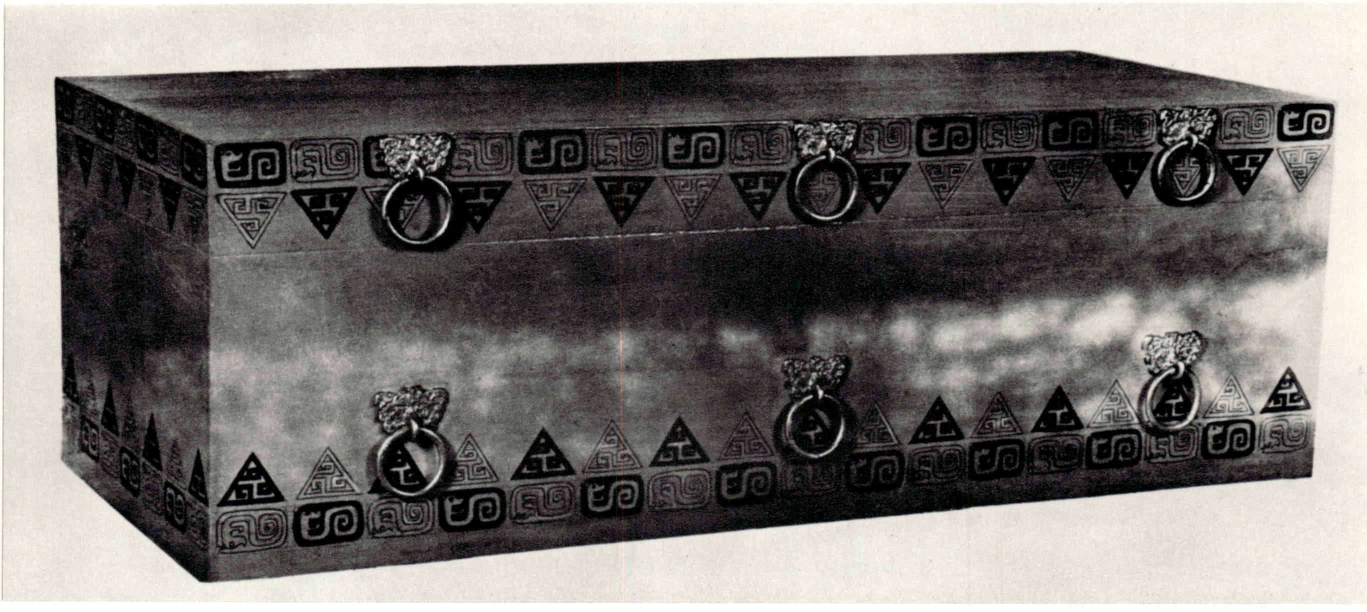

110. Reconstructed coffin, lacquered wood. Warring States period. Excavated at Ku-wei-ts'un, Hui District, Honan.
length: 234 cm. (93.2 in.)

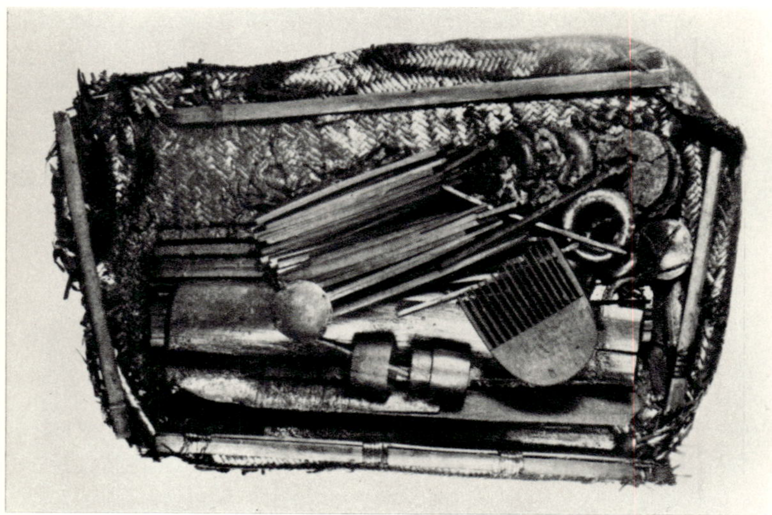

111. Bamboo basket containing writing tools and other objects. Warring States period. Excavated at Tso-chia-kung-shan, Ch'ang-sha Municipality, Hunan.
length: 35.0 cm. (13.8 in.)

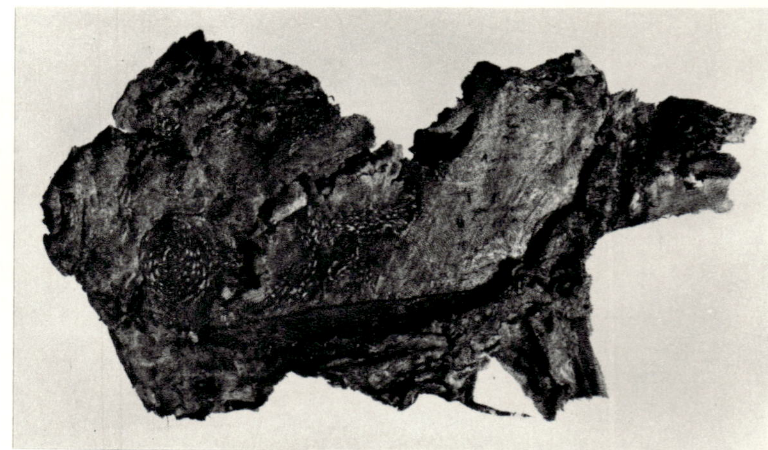

112. Fragment of yellowed silk. Warring States period. Excavated at Ch'ang-sha Municipality, Hunan.
length: 15.0 cm. (5.9 in.)

II. *Han to T'ang—Transition and Innovation in Art*

HAN TO SIX DYNASTIES In 221 B.C., Shih Huang-ti of Ch'in established the first great Chinese empire, with its capital at Hsien-yang. On his death in 209 B.C., however, the empire collapsed and confusion reigned again until the Emperor Kao-tsu of the Former Han (206-194 B.C.) eventually gained control and established a new capital, with palaces and city walls, at Ch'ang-an. Under the Ch'in the territories of the seven states were reorganized into provinces and prefectures controlled by a central government. The Han dynasty reinstated this system, and the empire was maintained under a strong central authority throughout the Former and Later Han—a period of some four centuries of peace.

During the Warring States period, industries and crafts had been developed in individual states, and in some cases techniques of metalwork, lacquerwork, jade carving and other crafts had already been brought to near perfection. The Han empire, an empire comparable in its scale to the Roman, absorbed these and in many cases standardized their products, thus facilitating a shift to mass production. The greatly expanded class of officials in the provinces and prefectures, and the powerful provincial families, created a great demand that made it necessary for a supply of these standardized objects of industrial art to be constantly at hand.

The empire expanded territorially by leaps and bounds during the reign of the Han Emperor Wu-ti (140–86 B.C.) and communication was established with areas as far apart as the "Western Regions" (i.e. Central Asia), and Nan-hai, the far southeast of the continent. A colony was set up in Lo-lang in Korea (near present-day Pyongyang) and defenses were secured against the marauding nomads on the northern borders. At home, cultural and administrative institutions were established and the system of "Rites," based on Confucianism, was drawn up. Materials were brought from afar for the crafts of China, and the standardized works produced were widely distributed throughout the territories of the empire. This is witnessed by, for instance, articles discovered in tombs at Lo-lang, the most distant prefecture of the empire, which included not only bronze vessels and mirrors and silk fabrics from central China, but jade from Central Asia, lacquer ware from Szuchwan and carved tortoiseshell from Nan-hai—and these, moreover, not as individual pieces, but in complete sets.

The majority of the artisans and craftsmen of the Han dynasty were state employed, the industry and the crafts being controlled by officials of the central government. In the capital there were three official agencies handling such matters: the K'ao-kung-shih, the Tung-yüan-chiang and the Shang-fang. The K'ao-kung-shih made furniture, etc. for the imperial family; the Tung-yüan-chiang made *ming-ch'i*, the objects buried with the dead in their tombs; and the Shang-fang articles of specially high quality for the imperial family's use (this is the Shang-fang often found in inscriptions on mirrors; in the middle Later Han the Shang-fang was divided into three sections: "left," "center," and "right."). Apart from these three main organizations, there were temple craftsmen and the "East and West Weaving Workshops," two separate groups of textile craftsmen working for the imperial family.

There were similar agencies in the provinces, too; weapons-makers were distributed in six centers,[1] the two textile centers were in present-day Shantung and Honan,[2] while two centers in present-day Szuchwan[3] produced mainly gold and silver work, though the lacquer industry also flourished there. The expenditure on these works was enormous. It is recorded in the biography of Kung Yü in the *Han Shu* (*The Book of Han*) that in the reign of the Emperor Yüan-ti (48–32 B.C.) five million *ch'ien* each was spent annually by the commanderies of Kuang-han and Shu alone, while fifty million was spent by the three main organizations. To cover this expenditure a government monopoly of the salt and iron industries was established. This was administered from some seventy-six centers throughout the country.

BRONZE VESSELS By the Warring States period, the bronze vessels used for ritual purposes had discarded grotesque motifs such as the *t'ao-t'ieh* and adopted lighter patterns based on the intertwined-dragon motif (Pl. 86). Techniques such as gold plating, gold inlay and the inlay of precious stones were perfected (Pls. 15, 18), and forms for vessels such as the *chung* and *ting* were firmly established. The bronze vessels of the Former Han took over what had been perfected in the preceding period, but turned to mass production and standardization, with the gradual loss of surface decoration. Besides traditional shapes such as the *chung* and *ting*, vessels such as the incense burner, the *lien* and—in Later Han times—the *hsi* also appeared; these were more for practical use than for ceremonies or ornaments. Types of bronze vessels include the *chung*, *fang*, *ting* (cauldron), *yen* (a kind of steamer in two parts), *ho* (a vessel for mixing the five flavors), *mou* (an iron pan), *Po-shan-lu*, *hsiang-lu* (incense burners), *yi* (a type of washbasin), *teng*, *lien*, *shui-ti* (container for holding water used in mixing Chinese ink), and *hsi*.

The *chung* shape is a goblet with no surface decoration except a simple belt around the belly and animal masks with ring-handles on the shoulder. Some have a swinging chain loop-handle and others a tall foot-ring (Pl. 135). The *fang* is a square jar. The *ting* has no surface decoration, but both the *chung* and *ting* may have simple inscriptions giving the name of the emperor's tomb or the government official for whom it was made.[4] However, most Han marks are not cast, but incised, giving the name of the craftsman, date of production, name of the owner, grade of the vessel, or words of good luck.

The custom of burning incense spread during the Han dynasty, and the incense burner was added to the list of bronze vessels. The "hill" shape burner was especially popular and continued after the general production of other shapes had ceased[5] (Pl. 137). The *teng* is a lamp and has many variants, some with a human figure supporting the burners (Pl. 132), or with long-legged supports. The *lien*, a cylindrical container for women's toilet articles, was also made in bronze. The *hsi* is a type of basin produced in the Later Han period, largely at Chu-ti and T'ang-lang in southwestern Szuchwan. These basins are usually decorated with twin fish or ducks at the bottom inside and have a maker's mark of date and place of manufacture and a good luck phrase.

From the Later Han period on, the production and use of the traditional bronze vessels diminished, and for burial with the dead, ceramic *ming-ch'i* superseded bronze. Indeed after the Three Kingdoms period, such traditional shapes as the *chung* and *ting* completely disappeared, and it seems that only a few vessels for everyday use, such as incense burners and measures, persisted.

BRONZE MIRRORS The technique of making metal mirrors, particularly of white bronze, was perfected in the Warring States period. These objects (Pls. 82-86) are polished on one side for reflection and have a protuberance with a hole passing through it in the center of the other. The mirror can be held either by a cord threaded through the hole or it can be placed on a stand, as illustrated in one of the scenes in the handscroll by Ku K'ai-chih, the "Admonitions of a Preceptress to a Lady About to Enter the Court" now in the British Museum. Techniques of decoration were more or less perfected by this period, the area around the knob on the back of the mirror being covered with a design that sometimes used gold or precious-stone inlay.

At first, the craftsmen of the Former Han probably carried on the styles of their predecessors, but in time they produced distinctive types of mirrors of their own, and the so-called Former Han type of mirror came into being, with characteristic designs, such as "stars-and-clouds," "grasses-and-leaves," "arc design," "circle-and-volute." These are plain, having no overall decoration, but have a heavy, rounded knob on the back and inscriptions, which may be quite elaborate.[6] Long inscriptions are particularly common on the arc design and circle-and-volute type mirrors. Another type of mirror perfected around the period 9–23 A.D. is the so-called *Fang-*

ko juei-chü ssu-shen mirror[7] (Pl. 144). Normally this design included a wide cloud-scroll border, with a main field of decoration symmetrically arranged and consisting of angles and circles with the four animal guardians of the four directions in thread relief. A series of rectangles arranged within the border contains the twelve characters representing the astrological "stems" (symbols used separately or in combination to denote the passage of time, i.e. hours, days, weeks and the cycle of years used in dating). The design is highly symbolic and contains many allusions to metaphysical ideas then current. The long inscriptions usually incorporated in the design often give the name of the maker.[8]

In the Later Han period the "wild animal" motif appeared alongside the arc design and Four Guardians mirrors. In Szuchwan, again, animal-mask mirrors and in Chiang-nan "mythical beast" mirrors were made, and centers for the production of high-quality mirrors seem to have grown up outside the capital. Particularly interesting are the mythical beast mirrors, believed to have been produced in Chiang-nan, which were made during the period from the Wu state of the Three Kingdoms on into the Southern Dynasties. The fact that higher levels of techniques were preserved under the Southern Dynasties as compared with the neglect of such techniques under the Northern Dynasties is also borne out by the existence of a fine specimen of a mythical beast mirror of the Ch'i state dated 498 A.D. The same type of mirror was to become the ancestor of the mirrors of Sui times.

LACQUER WARE Lacquerwork techniques had also been perfected in the Warring States period and were continued by the Han craftsmen, under the auspices of the government agencies, with a high degree of specialization in the production process. From inscriptions on their work, it is clear that official craftsmen working in lacquer were stationed at Shou, Kuang-han, Tzu-t'ung and Wu-tu, all commanderies (*chün*) of what is now Szuchwan, According to the geographical treatise of the *Book of Former Han*, official lacquer-workers were also at Huai District, Honan, and at Ch'eng-tu, Szuchwan. The records show a well-organized industry in which the officials were rated in grades and the processes involved were divided into eight separate stages.[9] The types of lacquerwork were differentiated by the body material used. The usual base is, of course, wood. *Chia-chu*, used especially in the manufacture of bowls and cups, is built up of alternate layers of lacquer and hemp cloth, while what is termed *lan-t'ai* uses bamboo basketwork as its base. The most famous example of this latter work is the lacquer-painted basket found at Lo-lang and now in the National Museum, Seoul. There are two traditional styles of decoration. In one, a design or picture is painted in black, red or yellow on a black or red ground (Pl. 115); there are some fine examples of such work done with delicate brushwork on a smooth ground. The other involves patterns, pictures of animals, etc., done in needle engraving. It is from lacquer painting that we catch some glimpse of the quality of fine painting in the early periods in China.

JADE AND GLASS The jade used in the Han dynasty is nephrite. This came, notably, from Lan-t'ien District, Shensi and from Khotan in Sinkiang Province, and was carved for ritual or ornamental objects such as those in Plates 145–149. Jade was used for *p'ei-yü*, *tsang-yü*, sword decorations, seals, and various vessels as well as for carved figures of human beings and horses. Of these, the *p'ei-yü* and *tsang-yü* are the most noteworthy. *P'ei-yü* embraces various types of rings (Pls. 149, 158), of which there are three categories—*pi*, *huan*, and *yüan*—defined according to the relative proportion of the diameter of the central hole of the body of the ring. Some *pi* have a "rice-grain" pattern of raised dots (Pl. 158), others a pattern of engraved dragon-whorls (Pl. 149); they vary greatly in size, the smallest being under ten centimeters in diameter and some of the largest reaching twenty-two centimeters. From painted portraits and other evidence, it seems that at least the *pi* and *huan* rings were worn as costume ornaments, though they undoubtedly could also have a ritual significance derived from a much earlier use.

The *tsang-yü* is a class of burial object, ritual pieces carved in many shapes to be placed in the orifices of the body on burial, and have various names depending on whether they were intended to be placed in the eyes, nose, ears, mouth, anus or clasped in the hands. The small cicada shape was traditionally placed in the mouth, possibly with some allusion to the apparent resurrection of the insect as a handsome winged creature at one stage of its life cycle.

Weapons in the Han dynasty, by now made exclusively of iron, were sometimes embellished with carved jade (Pls. 145–148). The hilt of a sword might be decorated at the pommel and have a rhomboid jade guard (Pl. 147). The surface of the sheath might also be decorated with jade fittings designed to take a cord for suspending at the waist, or finished at the tip with a shaped piece of jade. This sword decoration is often very beautifully carved with dragon designs, and records show that "jade-embellished swords" were very costly items.

Glass was produced in China in a variety of shapes, including cups, bowls, *pi*, *huan* and earplugs. With the *pi* and *huan*, the material was merely used as a substitute for jade; the *pi* are usually about ten centimeters in diameter and decorated with the rice-grain motif. Dr. Yoshito Harada has put forward the view that the earplug rings, for which the ears were pierced, were a custom adopted from the barbarians living in the south. Many terms were used for glass in the Han dynasty: *liu-li*, *po-li* and *huo-ch'i-chu*. *Liu-li* is an abbreviation for *pi-liu-li*, thought to be a transliteration of the Sanscrit term *vaidūrya* (lapis lazuli or beryl). This seems to support the view that there is a close connection between the glass of the West and that made in China. However, analysis of the *pi*-type glass shows it to be a lead glass, distinct from the soda-lime glass of the West, and the similarity in composition of the lead glass and the green lead glaze of Han tomb wares seems adequate proof of the production of lead glass in China. This fact in itself does not exclude the possibility that soda-lime glass was brought to China overland by the Central Asian Silk Road or by sea from the south. Indeed, in the "Ode to a Glass Bowl," the Chin dynasty poet P'an Ni describes it as coming:

"... through the desert over the steep K'unlun mountains ..."

It is said that the value of domestic glass decreased, and it lost its appeal, when merchants of the Ta Yüeh-chih state began to produce multi-colored glass even more lustrous than that of the West at P'ing-ch'eng (present-day Ta-t'ung) during the reign of T'ai Wu-ti of Northern Wei (424-465 A.D.). It is possible that the glass from the Feng family tombs at Ching District, Hopei may be of this type (Pls. 162, 163). It is said that in the last twenty years of the sixth century, one Ho Ch'ou made glass in the Sui state. It is interesting that a period of active production of glass in China should again correspond to a period of lively exchanges with the West.

TEXTILES During the Han period there were official textile centers at Lin-tzu in the Ch'i Commandery and Hsiang-yi in the Honan Commandery, and it is recorded that several thousand people were working at the Ch'i centers alone. Silk brocade was the specialty of Hsiang-yi, while high quality *ping-wan* (white silk of close, smooth texture), and *ch'i* (open-weave, variegated, thin silk) and embroidery were made at Lin-tzu. Apart from these two centers, there were, in the Former Han dynasty, two imperial workshops in the capital known as the East and West Weaving Workshops, but by the end of the Former Han period, the East Weaving Workshop had ceased production. From the Three Kingdoms period on, Szuchwan was known for the production of brocade, Shu *chin* (the brocade of Shu, one of the Three Kingdoms) being particularly famous. Brocade was of the warp-design type, and from the end of the Former Han on, a greater variety of designs were developed, cloud-scrolls and pictorial patterns being introduced. Han silk fabrics have been found in such outlying sites as Lo-lang in Korea, Nia in Sinkiang Province and Noin Ula in Outer Mongolia (Pl. 120). A few of these textiles have inscriptions woven into the fabric.

Embroidery, chiefly done in chain stitch, was more highly prized than brocade, not only because it required more labor, but because richer colors and designs were possible (Pls. 117–119).

The dress of various grades of court officials during the Han dynasty was strictly controlled by regulations as set out, for example, in the "Treatise on Ceremonial Dress" ("Yü-fu-chih") of the *Book of Later Han.* These laws required a considerable wardrobe of silk gowns to be kept by each official for ceremonial occasions, and this alone would explain the size of the Chinese silk industry. The quality of Chinese silk was already well known in the West, where the country was known as the "silk country." Silk was transported to the West by the great route linking the Chinese and Roman empires via Central Asia—the celebrated "Silk Road."

INDUSTRIAL ARTS OF THE SUI AND T'ANG DYNASTIES Wen-ti of Sui, joining the forces of Ch'i with his own, conquered Ch'en and set up a capital at Ta-hsing, the city known as Ch'ang-an under the T'ang dynasty. His successor, Yang-ti, established a city at Lo-yang and built the great canal between North and South China. Thus were the foundations laid for the power of the Sui and T'ang dynasties. The Sui dynasty did not survive for long, but the T'ang Emperor T'ai-tsung, who assumed the throne in 627 A.D., carried on the work started. The T'ang dynasty marked a time of great prosperity for China. In addition to the two great cities in the north, Ch'ang-an and Lo-yang, the cities of Yang-chou on the canal and Ch'eng-tu in Szuchwan were thriving centers, and industries sprang up all over the country. It is particularly significant here that the Southern Dynasties territories—the so-called Chiang-nan area—which had been developed at a rapid rate since the split of dynasties, saw an enormous population increase, and such crafts as metalwork, lacquer ware, weaving, and ceramics showed a particular increase in importance.

The capital, Ch'ang-an, is said to have had a population of one million at one time. This included a number of Western craftsmen, and the culture of T'ang in its heyday had a pronounced cosmopolitan character, which was reflected in its industrial arts. In both the Sui and T'ang dynasties, craftwork was administered from the capital with a well-ordered bureaucratic organization distinguishing crafts and types of produce.[10] At this time, too, there was a great concentration of craftsmen in the capital. Records show that the Shao-fu-chien and Chiang-tso-chien, inspectorates charged with official manufacturing and engineering, employed respectively 19,850 and 15,000 men.

BRONZE Bronze ritual vessels as known in the Yin, Chou and Han dynasties were now no longer produced, but there was a continued demand for bronze wares for everyday use, such a lamps, incense burners and water ewers. The level of techniques was high, and in the mid-eighth century, an official bronze foundry was built at Chü-yung District, Kiangsu where it is said that such masterpieces as the phoenix-headed ewers were produced. Yang-chou was a famous center of bronze manufacture during the T'ang period, the mirrors produced there being especially famous.

Mirrors mark the highest point reached by Sui-T'ang metalwork. Besides the commoner square and round mirrors (Pls. 166, 171, 172, 175), six- and eight-lobed shapes (Pls. 173, 174, 176, 177) appeared in the T'ang dynasty, and various types of decoration with precious materials also became popular (Pl. 128).

Sui dynasty mirrors are usually decorated with Four Guardians, mythical beast and "floral roundel" motifs. The Four Guardians mirrors obviously hark back to mirrors of Han times. Thus the arrangement of the patterns and the inscriptions is derived from the mythical beast mirrors. The inscriptions on Sui mirrors are in four-character lines composed in a very literary style, in striking contrast to the Han and Six Dynasties inscriptions, which simply record dates and phrases wishing good luck.[11]

Decoration such as the floral roundels had a strong Western element, the most striking being the so-called sea-horse-and-grapes motif. This new and brilliant design was a combination of Western-style grapevine arabesques with mythical animals. Many examples of this type of mirror have been preserved, pointing to a large production; they must have well suited the early T'ang taste for flamboyant richness of decoration.

Besides the mirrors with patterns of "floral scrolls" and the like, others have a pair of phoenixes and a pair of lions, or a dragon encircling the central knob; some illustrate various stories and legends such as that of the Hare in the Moon (Pl. 176), or episodes from Confucian lore, while others show popular customs such as hunting (Pl. 175) and ball games. In 729, the fifth day of the eighth month, the emperor's birthday, was proclaimed a public festival to be known as *Ch'ien Ch'iu Chieh*, the "One Thousand Autumns Festival." On this occasion the various officials declared their wish to present the emperor with mirrors and "presentation purses," and on the same day the following year one hundred officials presented the gifts, and the emperor gave a gold mirror and a purse of pearls to each official above the fourth grade. An eight-lobed dragon mirror (Pl. 173) discovered at Kuo-chia-t'an in Sian bears the two characters *ch'ien-ch'iu* ("thousand autumns"), and is therefore regarded as one of the special mirrors made for this ceremony. There is further evidence in the poem by Po Lo-t'ien:

> "The mirror is ready for presentation at the Palace of Paradise. The chief official at Yang-chou packed it himself, for humble men should not reflect themselves in this mirror. This mirror, with the design of the flying dragon on the back is called 'the mirror of the emperor'. . . ."

From this we can infer that the flying dragon design was associated with the special mirrors for the emperor, and that such a mirror was actually made at Yang-chou for presentation to the Emperor.

Among the many mirrors decorated with other materials are those with a silver plate on the back, usually decorated with a high-relief design on a ground of fish-roe tooling (Pl. 177); those in which designs are cut out of thin gold or silver sheets fixed to the back of the mirror with lacquer and burnished till the design appears through the lacquer; and those with designs in mother-of-pearl, malachite, tortoiseshell or amber applied in the same way. These sumptious pieces were particularly popular in the second quarter of the T'ang dynasty, and well typify the taste of the time. There are a number of fine examples preserved in the Shōsōin in Japan, and others have been excavated recently from sites in and near Sian and Lo-yang (Pl. 128).

SILVER According to the records of the time, silverwork was often used for gifts by the emperor both to his own officials and to foreign envoys. Around the end of the Northern and Southern Dynasties period, silver coins were introduced from the West and in T'ang times rapidly came into general use in China among the aristocracy and for trade with distant regions. The Sassanian peoples used silver as the basis for their currency and the influence of Sassanian culture is very apparent in T'ang silverwork. The silver vessels of T'ang are of a great variety of shapes, including cups, bowls, boxes, etc. (Pls. 178–183). The surface is often decorated with fine, engraved line designs of birds, flowers, and animals, etc., with a fish-roe tooled background (Pls. 181–183). They are very brilliant, and even include well-organized scenes of hunting and human figures. The silver and gilt dish with lion design (Pl. 180) found recently at Pa-fu-chuang, northern Sian, together with spoons dated 743 and 751 A.D., is made by the same technique as a silver and gilt dish with flower decoration in the Shōsōin collection, and is believed to have been buried at the time of the An Lu-shan rebellion. Another silver and gilt dish was also found recently at the site of the Hsing-ch'ing Palace built between 713 and 756 A.D. This very large piece—eighty-four centimeters in diameter—gives us some idea of the splendor of the silverware used at the banquets of this period.

TEXTILES Early T'ang was an important period of change for Chinese brocade and damask weaving techniques. With the T'ang dynasty, brocades with the design in the woof as well as the warp put in an appearance. Damask weaving techniques also became more diversified, and various fabrics with many different surface patterns emerged. Woof-design brocade could utilize as many as eight colors, in place of the three colors used previously—as seen, for example, in the brocade known as *hua-wen-chin*, which became popular in the second quarter of the T'ang dynasty and displayed many rich gradations of color. Where designs are concerned, Chang Yen-yüan, in the *Li-tai Ming-hua Chi*, mentions figured silks that a man called Tou Shih-lun of Yi-chou(Ch'eng-tu) wove in early T'ang times. The imperial storehouses, he records, had specimens of both damask and brocade, with designs of paired partridges, fighting rams, unicorns, phoenixes and other fabulous animals; they were known as *jui-chin* ("jade-token brocade") and *kung-ling* ("court damask"). Again, the "Yi-wen-p'ao" chapter of the *T'ang Hui Yao* (*State Regulations of T'ang*) records that in 694 the emperor granted an embroidered robe to each official above the third grade. Each rank was allocated its own animal or bird motif for this robe.[12]

Eizo Ōta considers that the famous figured brocades with lion-hunting and rhinoceros designs in the Hōryūji and Shōsōin collections are probably of the *jui-chin* type. One can probably detect in the *jui-chin* designs—especially the "confronted motif"—and in the woof-weave techniques involved, a strong influence from Sassanian Persia. Besides these fabrics, the same period produced *to-chin*, a brocade patchwork of sewn patches, and dyeing techniques such as tie-and-dye and batik.

THE SHŌSŌIN The Shōsōin treasure-house was built by the Dowager Empress Kōmyō in the sixth month of 756 A.D. in order to house the treasures and personal belongings of the Emperor Shōmu, and the storehouse and its contents were dedicated to the Vairocana image (the "Great Buddha") at the Tōdaiji Temple in Nara. T'ang culture was in its heyday at the time, and many works of industrial art were brought back from China by Japanese missions sent to that country. They are included in the collection, along with other works that Japanese craftsmen produced under their influence. The Shōsōin collection contains examples of both Chinese and Japanese craftsmanship in great variety. The collection includes an enormous range of objects: furniture, writing equipment, books, clothing, games, eating and drinking vessels, drugs, mirrors, masks, weapons, jewelry, musical instruments, Buddhist ritual objects, etc. The materials and techniques cover most of those known in China; metalwork (plating, wrought work, carving, inlay, etc.), lacquer ware (nacre inlay, *heidatsu* [Japn.], *maki-e* [Japn.], etc.), ceramics (*san-ts'ai*), glass, wood and bamboo work, horn work, dyeing and weaving. Some of the objects—for example, the fine "sea-horse-and-grapes" mirror in the southern wing and the eight-lobed mirror with a design of hermit, crane and twin dragons in the northern wing—are undoubtedly of Chinese manufacture, but it is probable that some of the mirrors and *san-ts'ai* earthenware are of Japanese make. Many objects show a marked influence from the West, and much of the material used, such as ivory and rhinoceros horn, as well as various types of incense, etc., probably came from outside the limits of Chinese territory, and give a vivid idea of the cosmopolitan nature of T'ang culture at its height. One looks for renewed study of the Shōsōin collection in view of the new material made available by excavation at Ch'ang-an, Loyang, and elsewhere.

CERAMICS FROM THE HAN TO THE T'ANG DYNASTY A hard stoneware was produced by the Later Han dynasty, but true porcelain, nonporous and translucent, was not perfected until Sung times. Whereas glass was not seriously developed in China, the ceramic tradition is long and continuous, the aim always being to produce something to rival jade itself. The Han to T'ang period brought the first signs of greatness in the history of Chinese ceramics.

The most common ware of Han is called Grayware; everyday articles such as pots, jars, cups, etc. are of a heavy earthenware, bluish gray in color, and are turned on the wheel. Some have a smooth, burnished surface, but jars and the like were finished with a mat- or rope-impressed decoration. The type of ware with slip decoration (Pls. 113, 114) is thought to have been typical of burial wares and not for daily use.

The glazed wares of Han are in two distinct classes: the green and the "gray" glazes. The green glaze color is derived from copper oxide in a low-fire (700–800°C.) lead glaze, giving a rich blue-green color. With exposure over the centuries, this tends to deteriorate due to the layering of the glaze, which allows water to get in, resulting in very beautiful irridescent effects. The green glaze was used chiefly on replicas of bronze vessels for use as *ming-ch'i* and on clay figures of men, horses, etc.; it was seldom used on articles of everyday use. It seems that the green glaze was perhaps thought to resemble the green patina of the bronze, and used as a substitute. The "gray" glazed earthenware has been shown to have existed as early as the Yin and Chou dynasties. Specimens from the Later Han dynasty have been found in tombs of central and southern China. It is a high-fire glaze and ware and is usually regarded as the forerunner of the Yüeh-type Greenware of the later periods.

This Yüeh-type Greenware has been found in great quantity recently in tombs around Nanking—the capital of the Three Kingdoms state of Wu and also of the Southern Dynasties state—and at Kiangsu and Chekiang, which lay in its territories. From dated tombs of this southern area,[13] many vessels of practical use, including cups, *hu*, ewers, lamps and urinals, have been found, together with *ming-ch'i* representing objects such as stoves, wells, mills, animal pens, etc. (Pls. 152–157). Some of these pieces bear dated inscriptions, which give them a special importance. The most famous of these are the decorated urn excavated from Shao-hsing, Chekiang, which is inscribed with the date 260 A.D., the lamp (Pl. 153) dated 265 A.D., from Nanking, and the *hu-tzu* or urinal giving the date 251 A.D. (Pl. 152). This piece, excavated at Chao-shih-kang, a district of Nanking, gives a place of production assigning it to the Shao-hsing area of Chekiang, a district of the old state of Yüeh, from which the kilns and ware got their name. The discovery of the sites of the Yüeh kilns in the period up to 1937 owed much to scholars such as Yasuo Yonaiyama, Yūzō Matsumura, A.D. Brankston, J.M. Plumer and Ch'en Wan-li. To their work Fujio Koyama and other Japanese scholars have added invaluable studies, and since the war scholars in China have been conducting further research. Many Six Dynasties kilns have been identified[14] in Chekiang and Fukien, though it is not as yet possible to differentiate with certainty the products of each, since they are so similar. Another kiln at Yi-hsing District, Kiangsu, also produced Greenware, and it has been identified in the Chou Ch'u tomb at Yi-hsing and in tombs in Nanking. However, the largest quantity of the finest Greenware, of which the *hu-tzu* (Pl. 152) is an example, undoubtedly came from the central kilns in the Shao-hsing area, and especially the Chiu-yen group. This Greenware of the Yüeh area, in general, gained great popularity throughout China and was produced in many kilns, principally in Chekiang. With the growth of the tea drinking custom, this elegant Greenware came further into prominence. A passage in the *Ch'uan Fu* by Tu Yü of Chin says: "Ceramic cups should be used for tea drinking and the best ware is Tung-ou." The Tung-ou referred to is in the Yüeh area.

From the finds in the Feng family tombs at Ching District, Hopei, it is clear that Greenware was also produced in the Northern Dynasties region. Pieces found include large *hu* vases with lotus flower decorations, which show a strong Western influence in their design (Pl. 122). Greenware kilns of the Sui dynasty have been found at Ku-pi-ts'un in Tz'u District, Hopei, and bowls, tall goblets and jars from the kiln were found in the Pu Jen tomb at An-yang, Honan. These can be labeled collectively "Northern Greenware."

A great change in economic life and communications between north and south took place in the Sui and T'ang dynasty. Luxury ceramics had a good market in Ch'ang-an and Lo-yang and other big cities. Not only the Yüeh type of ceramic was popular, but the aristocrats of the capital cities had a taste for white wares and for *san-ts'ai*. White ware was produced at many kilns, both north and south,[15] but the wares of Hsing-chou in Hopei are the most representative. The pieces traditionally known as Hsing-chou ware normally use white clay with a thin, transparent glaze and a fine crackle, but the kiln site, unfortunately, has not been discovered. Kilns for both white wares and *san-ts'ai* have been found at Kung District in Honan. These wares are believed to be those referred to in the *Yüan-ho Chün-hsien Chih*, where it says: "White stoneware was presented to the emperor from Honan in the K'ai-yüan era" (713–742 A.D.).

Ch'ang-nan is the old name for the place in Fou-liang District, Kiangsi, that from the Sung dynasty on was called Ching-te-chen. It is said that, at the beginning of the T'ang dynasty, two skilled potters at this place produced plain white wares comparable to fine jade. The large white stoneware circular inkstone now in the Haji shrine in the Dōmyōji Temple, Osaka is thought to be a Ch'ang-nan piece of T'ang times. The Chi-chou kilns at Chi-an, Kiangsi, are of course most famous for their Sung *temmoku*-type wares, but it has been confirmed that phoenix-headed ewers and other superior white stoneware was made here in the T'ang dynasty. Besides the white ware, *san-ts'ai* wares further enriched the lives of the aristocrats of the second quarter of the T'ang dynasty. A low-fire, lead-glaze ware, it used various colors—green obtained from copper and red, yellow, brown and black from ferrous oxide—that produced remarkably beautiful effects in various combinations on a white body. Where the body is not of white clay, it is coated with a white slip engobe. Typical *san-ts'ai* combines white, yellow and green, but the whole class is known as *san-ts'ai*, or "three color" ware, even where other colors are used. A blue glaze was also used at this time, and not infrequently was added to the other colors common in *san-ts'ai*. *San-ts'ai* ware was used for vases, spouted ewers, phoenix-headed ewers, three-legged jars, cups, basins, and also in all the rich variety of tomb models (*ming-ch'i*), which are more fully discussed in

Chapter V. The phoenix-headed and spouted ewers are obviously influenced from the West, and along with the *san-ts'ai* camels, foreigners and the like bear witness to Ch'ang-an's taste for the exotic.

In the T'ang dynasty, attempts were made to assess the relative qualities of the ceramics produced. Lu Yü, writing in his *Ch'a Ching* (*Classic of Tea*), has a famous passage in which he evaluates the teacups produced throughout the country:

> "So far as porcelain is concerned, the best cups are those made in Yüeh-chou, the second at Ting-chou, the third at Wu-chou, fourth at Yo-chou and fifth at Shou-chou and Hung-chou. Some people place Hsing-chou wares above those of Yüeh, but I cannot agree with this. While Hsing-chou wares can be compared with silver, I would compare those of Yüeh-chou with jade."

Many Yüeh kilns of the T'ang and Sung dynasties have been identified by Chinese scholars. Some examples of fine quality pieces exported to both Japan and to the Middle East have been identified as from the Shang-lin Lake area. Notable among these are the Yüeh-yao types found by J. Plumer at Samarra, in Iraq. Greenware has also been found at all the kiln sites mentioned in the *Ch'a Ching*. In addition to these, a fine quality of Greenware has been found at Yao-chou in Shensi and at Wen-chou, Chekiang.[16] The achievement of such a widespread high quality of Greenware must surely indicate a long history of fine potters working toward the jade-like ware perfected by the tenth century.

Takashi Okazaki

NOTES

1.	Huai District, Honei Commandery 懐県，河内郡	in present-day	Hopei
	Yung-yang District, Honan Commandery 滎陽県，河南郡		Honan
	Yang-ts'ui District, Ying-ch'uan Commandery 陽翟県，潁川郡		Anhui
	Wan District, Nan-yang Commandery 宛県，南陽郡		Honan
	Tung-p'ing-yang District, Chi-nan Commandery 東平陽県，済南郡		Shantung
	Feng-kao District, T'ai-shan Commandery 奉高県，泰山郡		Shantung
2.	Lin-tzu District, Chi Commandery 臨淄県，済郡		Shantung
	Hsiang-yi District, Ch'en-liu Commandery 襄邑県，陳留郡		Honan
3.	Shu Commandery 蜀郡	near Ch'eng-tu	Szuchwan
	Kuang-han Commandery 広漢郡		Szuchwan

4. Typical inscriptions of this type are: 孝文廟鼎 ("*ting* of the Hsiao-wen Temple") and 中私官鐘 ("*chung* of the Chung Sung office").

5. The "hill" shape, which is called Po-shan-lu (博山炉) in Chinese, apparently takes its name from the Po Shan (Po Hill) in Ch'ing-chou, Shantung. It is recorded that in the reign of the Emperor Wu-ti (32-6 B.C.) there was a famous maker of Po-shan incense burners called Ting Huan (丁緩) working in Ch'ang-an.

6. There are many examples of simple phrases of good luck:

    日有喜 ("may the sun bring happiness")
    常得意 ("may your wishes be constantly fulfilled")

    Longer phrases may well be quotations from such works as the *Ch'u Tz'u* (楚辞).

    内清質以昭明，光輝象夫日月
    心忽揚而願忠，然雍塞而不泄 （内区）

7. This design is often misleadingly classified in Europe as "TLV type." This description refers only to the angles in the design and of course can have no relevance to the significance of the whole design. Up to the present no analysis of the meaning of this distinctive mirror decoration has been universally accepted.

    The mirror design classification appearing in the Japanese text is the result of the original research of Dr. Sueji Umehara. Dr. Umehara's terms have been translated into the appropriate English equivalents, though this Japanese system does not always recognize the conventional classification used by Western art historians.

Mirror design type	*Japanese term*
stars-and-clouds	星雲文鏡
grasses-and-leaves	草葉文鏡
arc design	銘帯内行花文鏡
circle-and-volute	銘帯重圏文鏡
wild animal	獣帯鏡
Four Guardians	四神鏡
mythical beast	画文帯神獣鏡
floral roundels	団華文鏡
sea-horse-and-grapes	海獣葡萄鏡
floral scrolls	宝相華文鏡

8. Many inscriptions incorporate the family name of the maker, as for example, 杜氏作 ("made by the Tu clan").

    王氏作竟四夷服　　多賀新家人民息
    胡虜殄滅天下復　　風雨時節五穀熟
    長保二親子孫力　　官位尊顕蒙禄食
    伝告後世楽毋亟　　大利今

9. The workmen in the stages of production of lacquer ware were classified as follows:

素工	Su-kung, those who made the wooden body
髹工	Hsiu-kung, those who put on the undercoating of lacquer
上工	Shang-kung, those who put on the top coating of lacquer
銅釦黄塗工	T'ung-k'ou huang-t'ou-kung, those who produced metal fittings
画工	Hua-kung, those who painted the decoration
涓(彫)工	T'iao-kung, those who wrote the inscription
清工	Ch'ing-kung, those in charge of the finishing
造工	Tsao-kung, the craftsman in overall charge of the work.

    The names of these craftsmen may appear in the inscription, as is seen in the following from a piece of Han lacquer found near Pyongyang in Korea: 元始三年蜀郡西工。造乘輿髹彫画木黄耳棓。客一升十六籥。素工豊。

10. There were three main inspectorates (監; *chien*) controlling the craftwork: 少府 Shao-fu, 将作 Chiang-tso, and 軍器 Chün-ch'i. The Shao-fu inspec-

torate was further divided into five bureaus (署; *shu*): 中尚, 左尚, 右尚, 染織, 掌治. The Chiang-tso inspectorate had many subdivisions: 左校, 右校, 中校, 甄官, 百工, 就谷 The Chün-ch'i inspectorate was simply divided into the 弩坊署 and 甲坊署.

11. The following are quotations from mirrors of the Sui dynasty:

From Kuo-chia-t'an, Sian:

仙人竝照　智水斉名　花朝艶采　月夜流明　龍盤五瑞　鸞舞双情
伝聞仁寿　始験銷兵

From San-ch'iao, Sian:

盤龍麗匣　舞鳳新台　鸞驚景見　日曜花開　団疑璧転
月似輪廻　端形鑑遠　胆照光来

12. The animal and bird motifs designated for various ranks are as follows:

王	Prince	Coiled dragon or deer
宰相	Minister	Phoenix
尚書	Secretary	Pair of geese
(左右) 衛将軍	Wei-chiang-chün	Pair of *ch'i-lin*
(左右) 武衛	Wu-wei	Pair of oxen
(左右) 韜衛	T'ao-wei	Pair of leopards
(左右) 玉鈴衛	Yü-ling-wei	Pair of pheasants
(左右) 監門衛	Chien-men-wei	Pair of lions
(左右) 金吾衛	Chin-wu-wei	Pair of *ch'ih*

13. Tomb sites in the southern region in which Greenware has been found:

Dynasty	*Date of tomb*		*Location*
Wu	272 A.D.	溧陽県	Li-yang District, Kiangsu
Wu	273 A.D.	趙史岡	Chao-shih-kang, Nanking
Wu	276 A.D.	黄岩県	Huang-yen District, Chekiang
Western Chin	285 A.D.	丁甲山	Ting-chia-shan, Nanking
Western Chin	297 A.D.	宜興県	Yi-hsing District, Kiangsu
Eastern Chin	361 A.D.	西善橋	Hsi-shan-ch'iao, Nanking
Liu-Sung	428 A.D.	黄岩県	Huang-yen District, Chekiang
Liu-Sung	447 A.D.	黄岩県	Huang-yen District, Chekiang

14. Some of the Six Dynasties kilns making Greenware:

Kiln	*Location*
Te-ch'ing 徳清	Te-ch'ing District, Chekiang 徳清県
Chiu-yen 九厳	Shao-hsing District, Chekiang 紹興県
Fuchou T'ai-chou 福州台州	Fuchou Municipality, Fukien 福州市
Shang-hsün 上薫	Hsiao-shan District, Chekiang 蕭山県
Wang-chia-lou 王家漊	Shao-hsing District, Chekiang 紹興県

15. These kilns include:

Kiln	*Location*
Hsing-chou 邢州	Nei-ch'iu District, Hopei 内邱県
Ch'ang-nan 昌南	Fou-liang District, Kiangsi 浮梁県
Chi-chou 吉州	Chi-an Municipality, Kiangsi 吉安市
Ta-i 大邑	Ta-i District, Szuchwan 大邑県

16. Greenware kilns of the T'ang dynasty include:

Kiln	*Location*
Ting-chou 鼎州	Ching-yang District, Shensi 涇陽県
Wu-chou 婺州	Chin-hua District, Chekiang 金華県
Yüeh-chou 岳州	Hsiang-yin District, Hunan 湘蔭県
Hung-chou 洪州	Nan-yang Municipality, Kiangsi 南陽市
Shou-chou 寿州	Hui-nan Municipality, Anhui 淮南市
Yao-chou 耀州	Tung-shan District, Shensi 銅山県
Hsi-shan 西山	Wen-chou Municipality, Chekiang 温州市

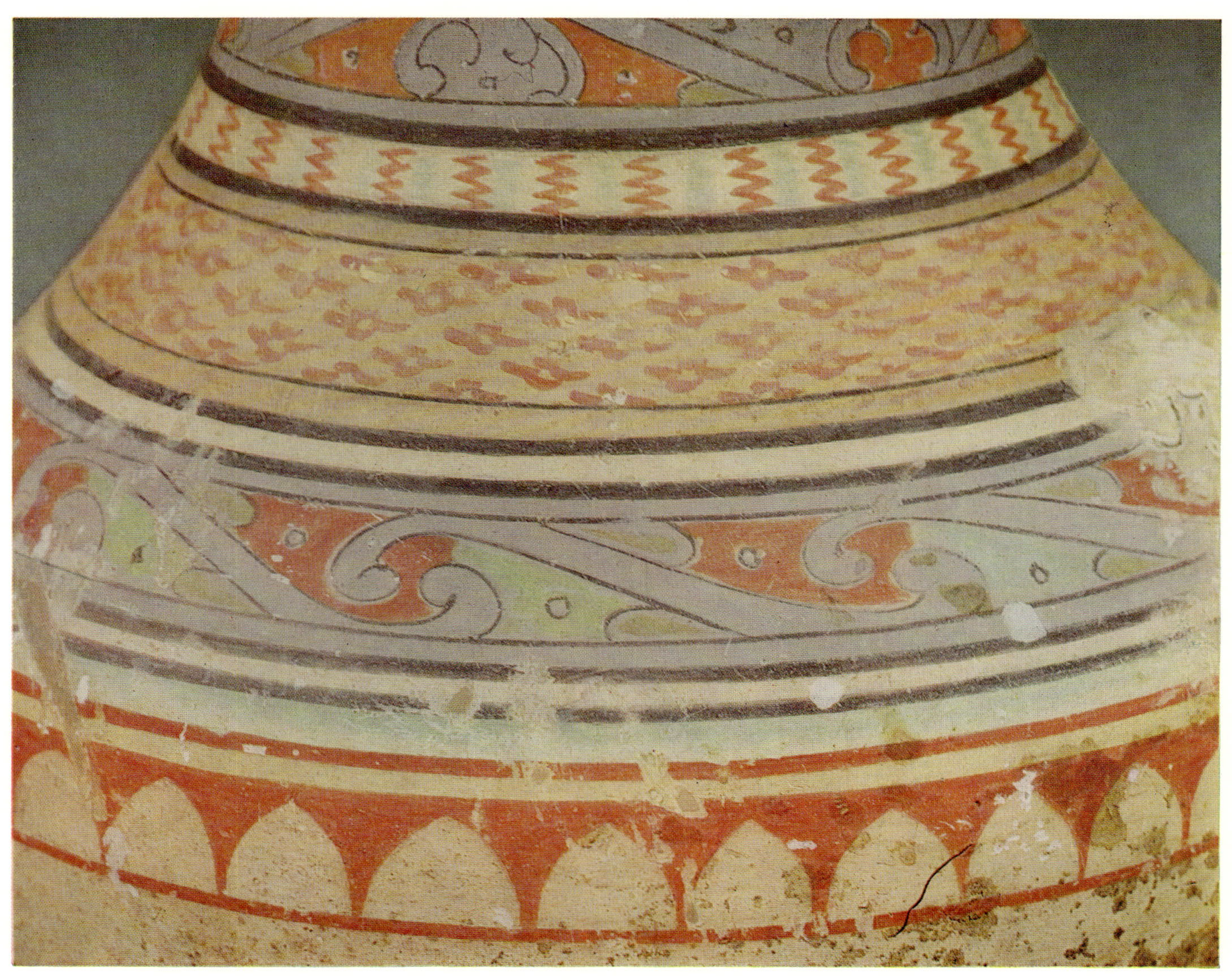

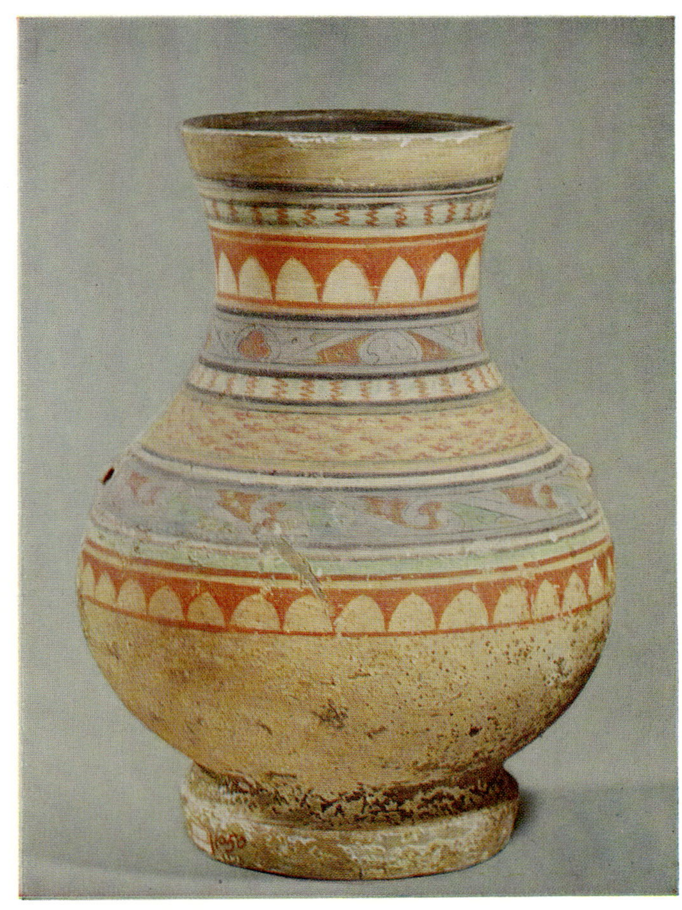

113–114. Jar, earthenware with slip decoration. Former Han dynasty. Exacavated from a Han tomb at Shao-kou, Lo-yang Municipality, Honan.
no measurement given

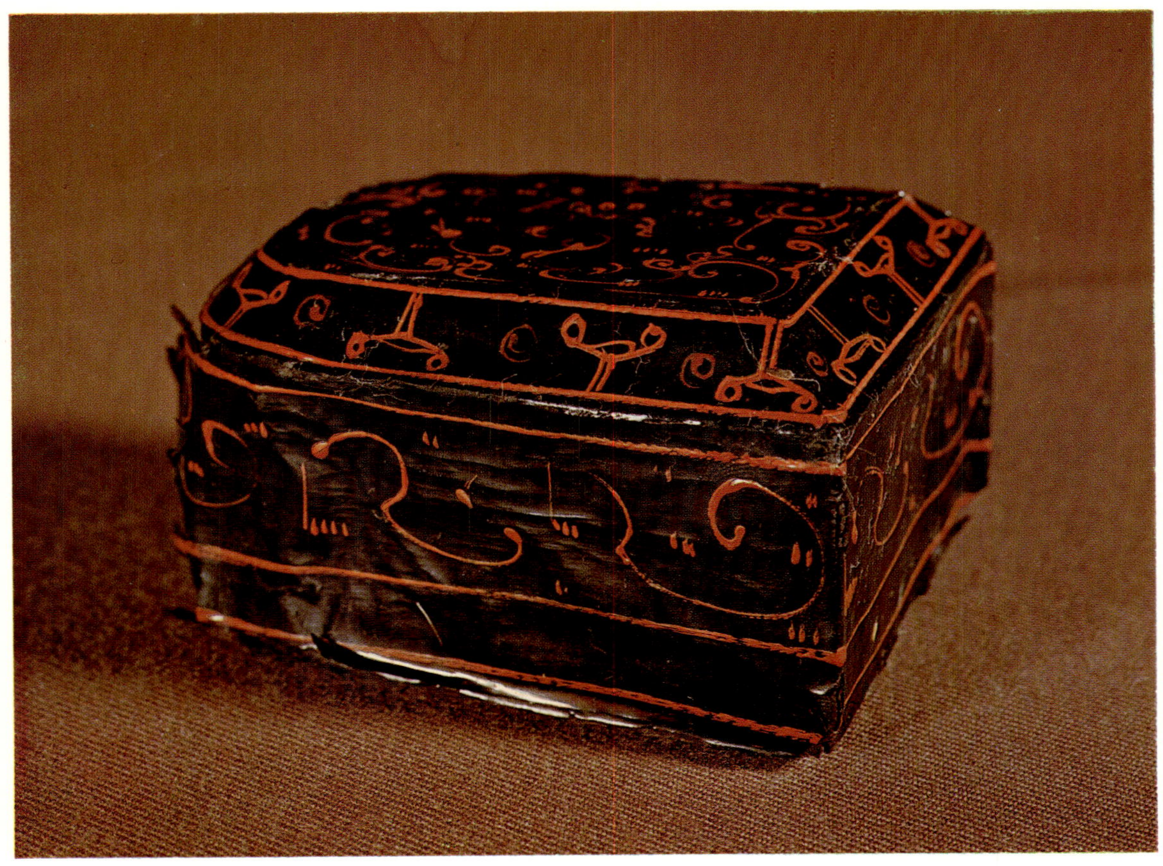

115. Horsehoof-shaped box, lacquer on cloth. Former Han dynasty. Excavated from a Han tomb at Feng-huang-ho, Yang-chou Municipality, Kiangsu.
height: 5.4 cm. (2.1 in.); height: 8.2 cm. (3.2 in.); width: 6.0 cm. (2.36 in.)

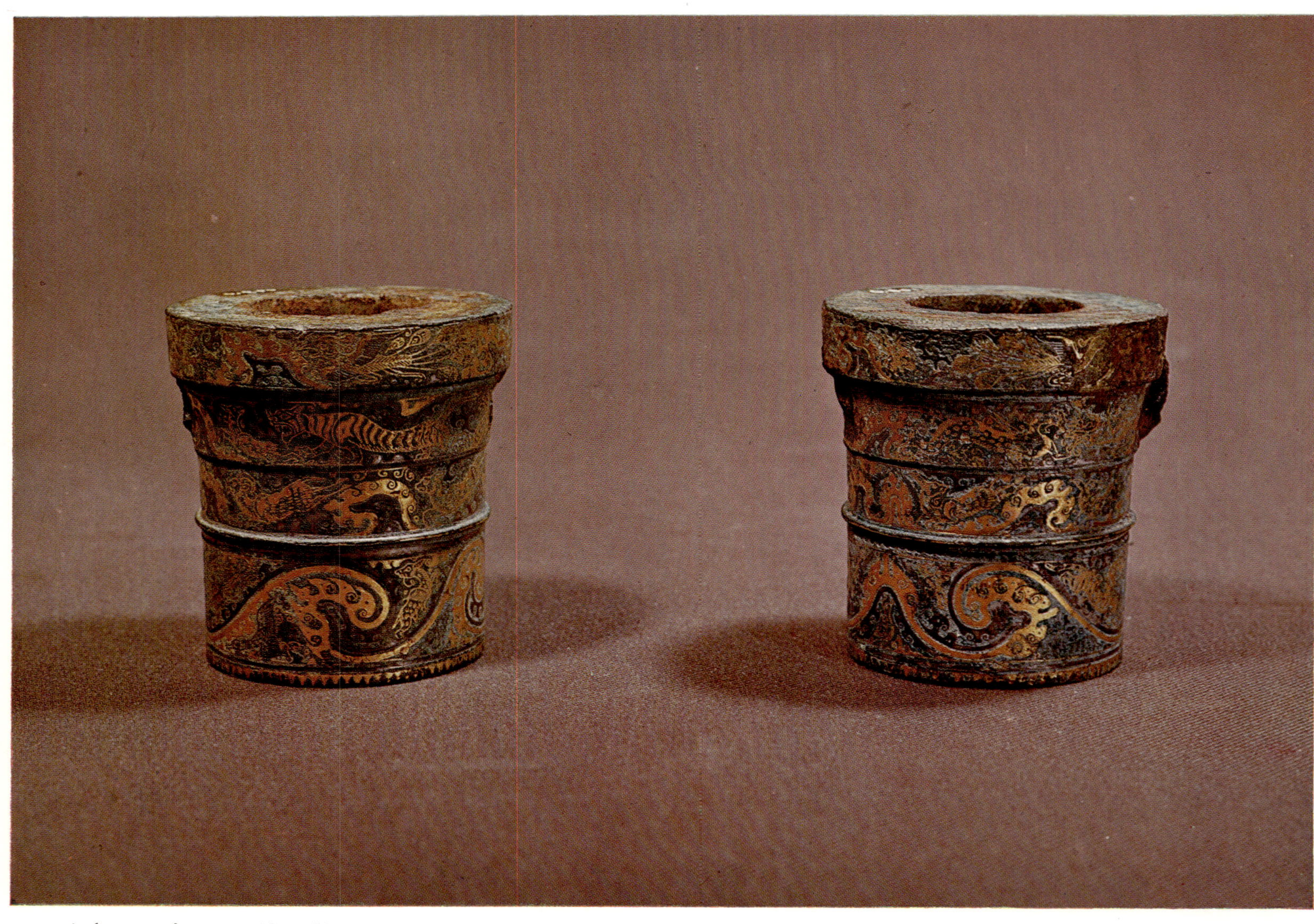

116. Axle caps, bronze with gold and silver inlay. Han dynasty. Excavated at Ning District, Shantung.
height: 6.8 cm. (2.7 in.)

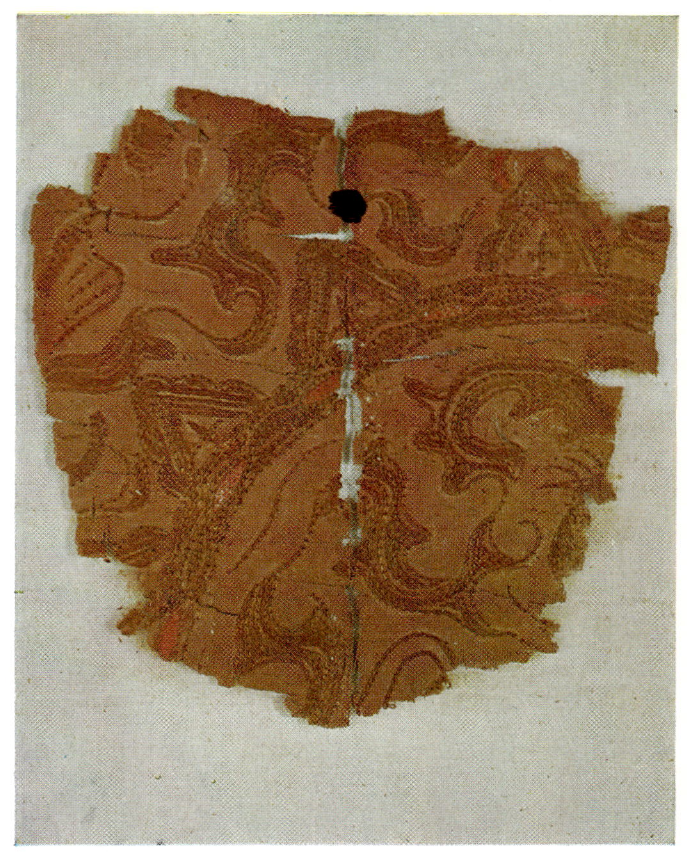

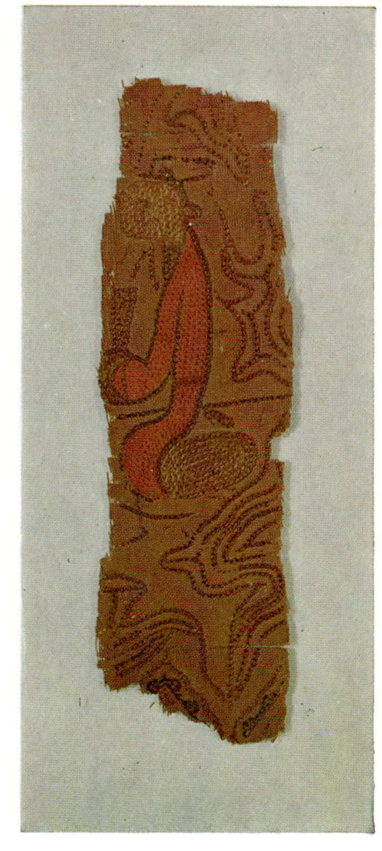

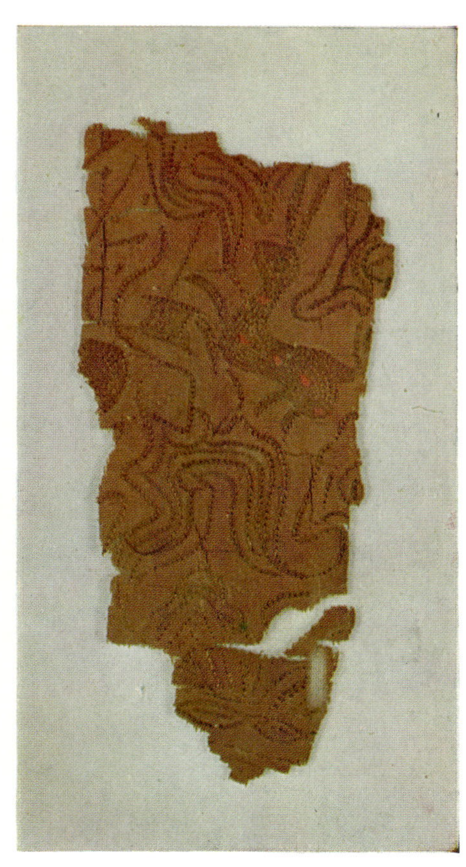

117–119. Fragments of embroidered silk. Han dynasty. Excavated from a Han dynasty tomb at Huai-an District, Shansi.
117. 6.5 × 6.5 cm. (2.56 × 2.56 in.)
118. 8.0 × 2.3 cm. (3.15 × 0.91 in.)
119. 7.0 × 3.5 cm. (2.76 × 1.38 in.)

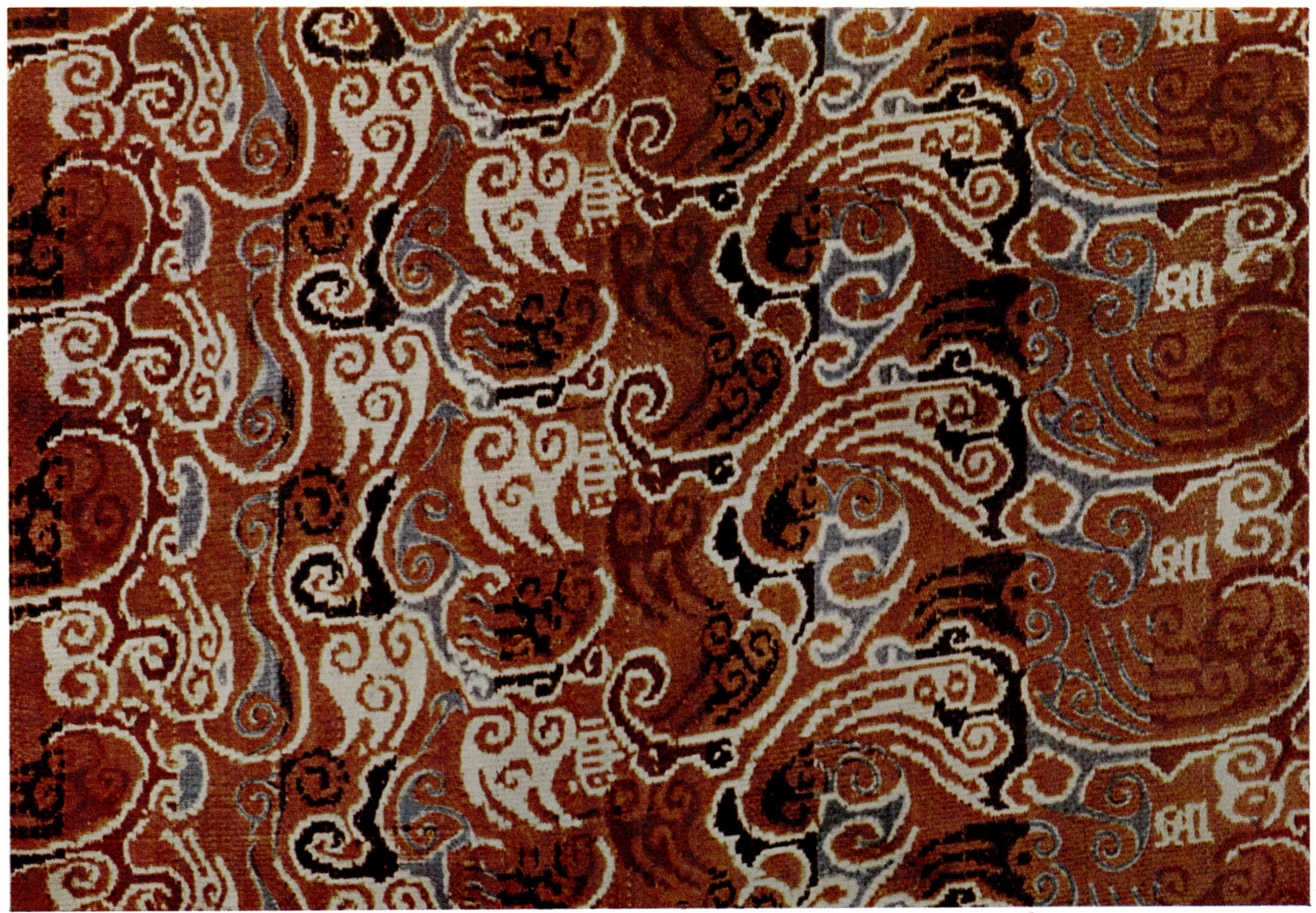

120. Detail of brocade from a man's jacket. Later Han dynasty. Excavated at Min-feng District, Uighur Autonomous Region, Sinkiang.

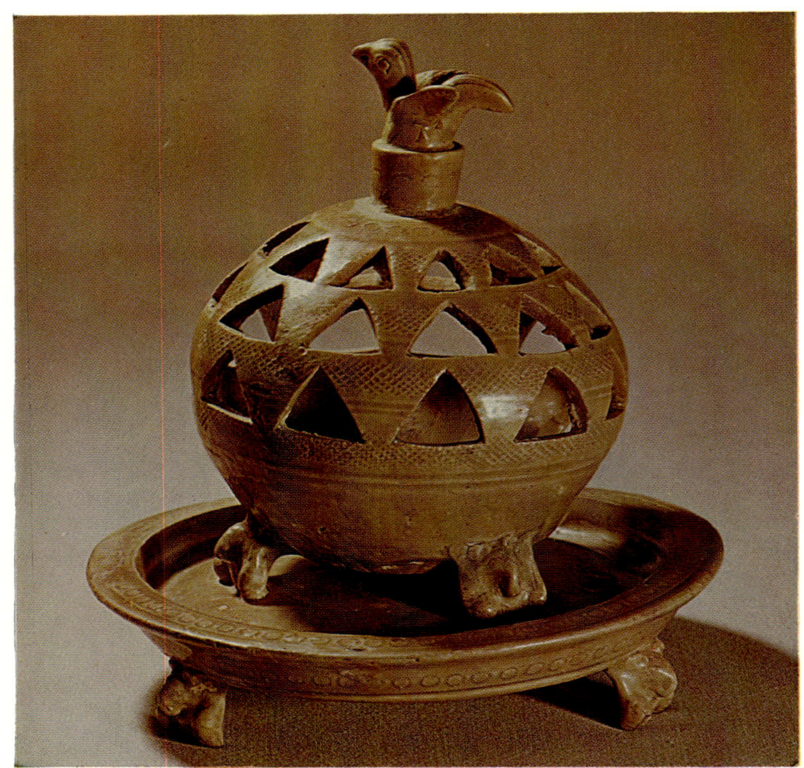

121. Incense burner, Greenware. Chin dynasty. Excavated at a Western Chin tomb, Yi-hsing District, Kiangsu.
height: 19.5 cm. (7.7 in.)

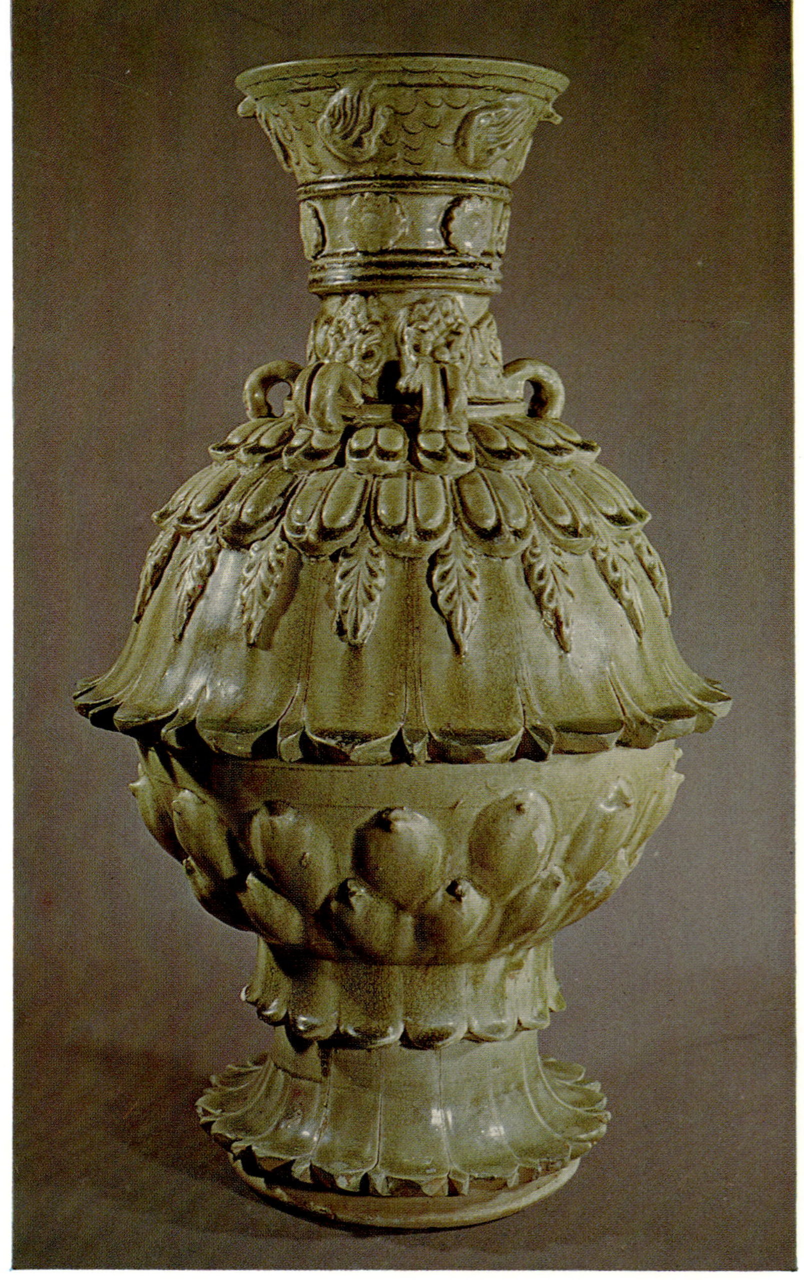

122. Large jar, Greenware. Northern Dynasties. Excavated from the Feng family tombs, Ching District, Hopei.
height: 66.5 cm. (26.2 in.); diameter: 19.2 cm. (7.6 in.)

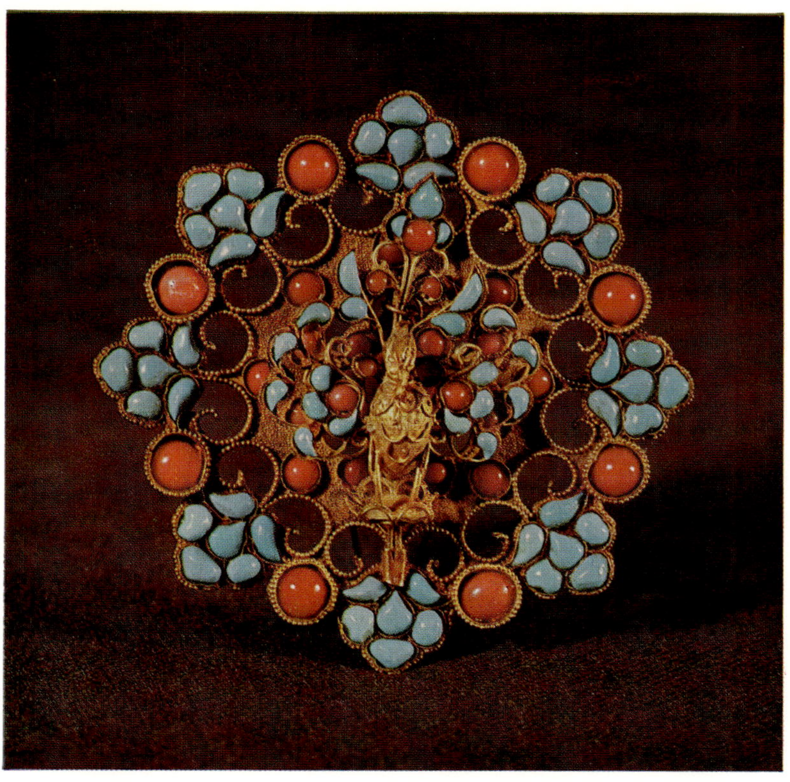

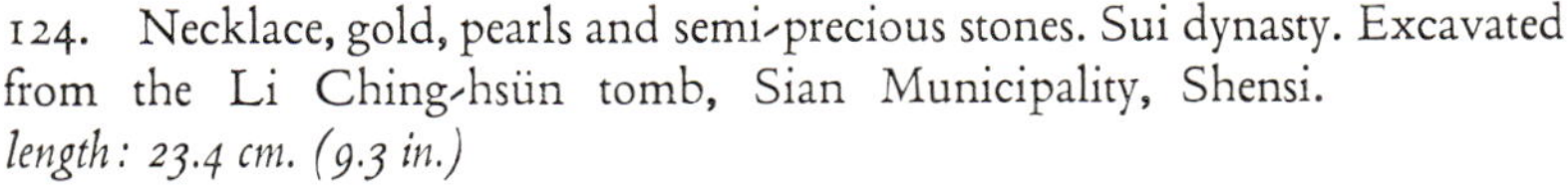

123. Jewelry, gold, coral and turquoise. T'ang dynasty. Excavated from a tomb at Han-sen-chai, eastern outskirts of Sian Municipality, Shensi. *diameter: 7.0 cm. (2.76 in.)*

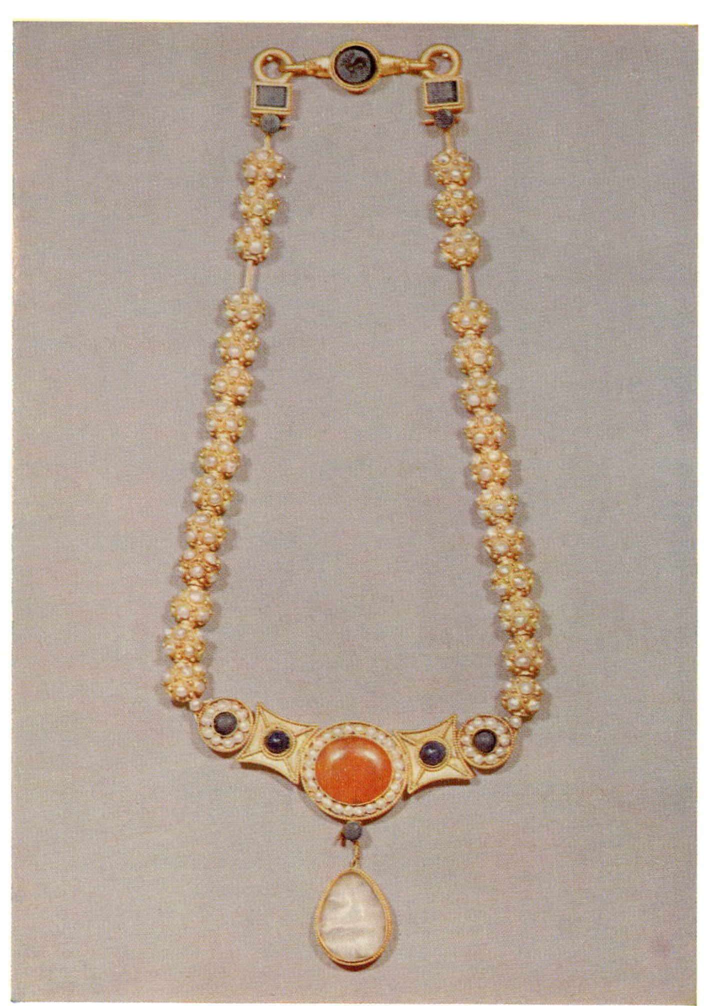

124. Necklace, gold, pearls and semi-precious stones. Sui dynasty. Excavated from the Li Ching-hsün tomb, Sian Municipality, Shensi. *length: 23.4 cm. (9.3 in.)*

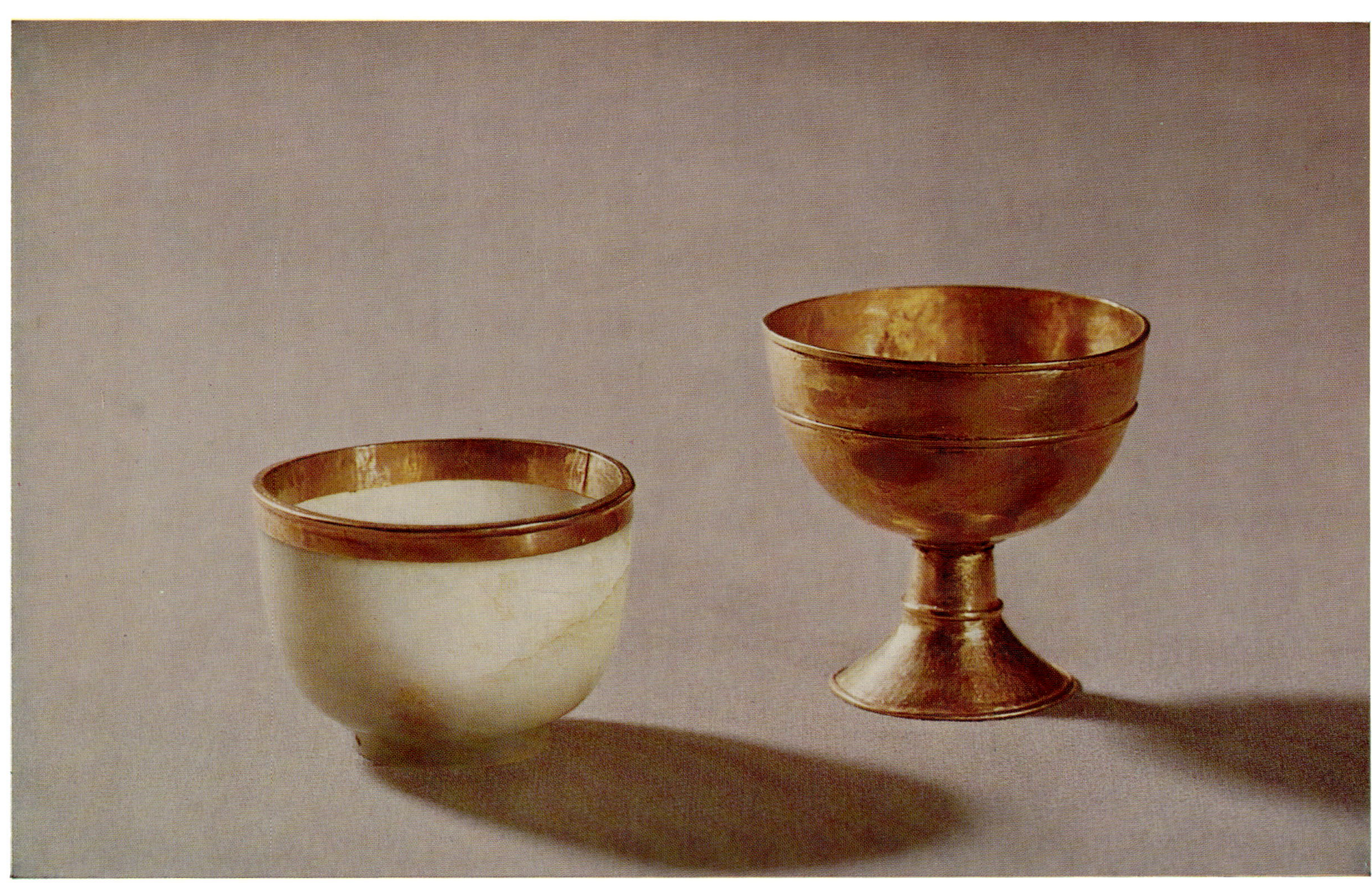

125. White jade cup and gold, stemmed cup. Sui dynasty. Excavated from the Li Ching-hsün tomb, Sian Municipality, Shensi.
Jade cup. height. 4.1 cm. (1.6 in.); diameter: 5.6 cm. (2.2 in.)
Stemmed cup. height: 6.0 cm. (2.36 in.); diameter: 5.8 cm. (2.25 in.)

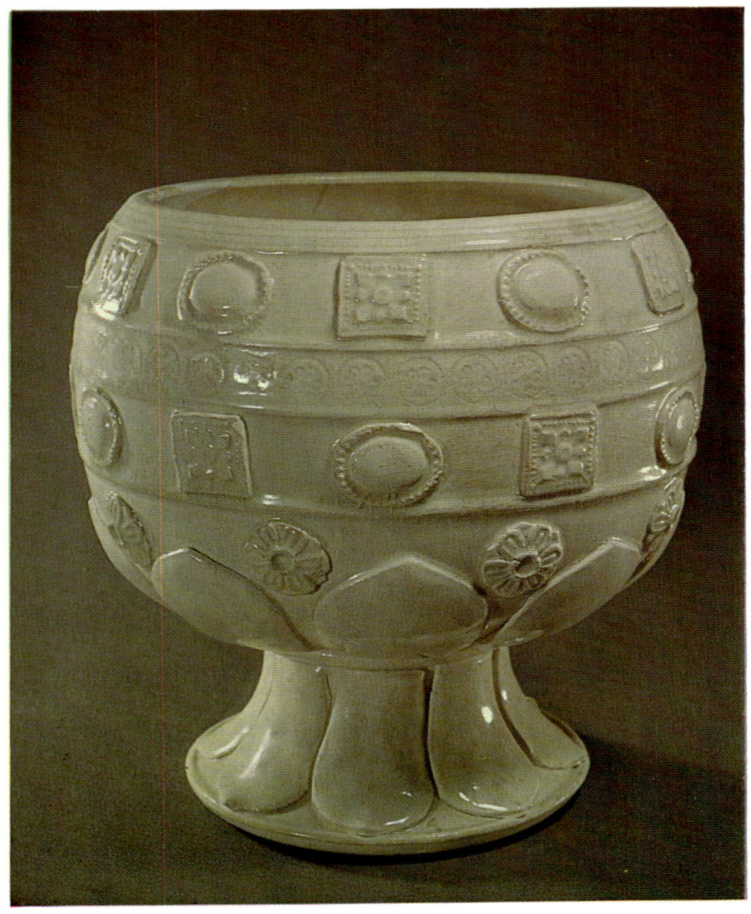

126. Stemmed bowl, green-white ware. T'ang dynasty. Excavated from a T'ang dynasty tomb at Han-sen-chai, eastern outskirts of Sian Municipality, Shensi.
height: 23.0 cm. (9.1 in.)

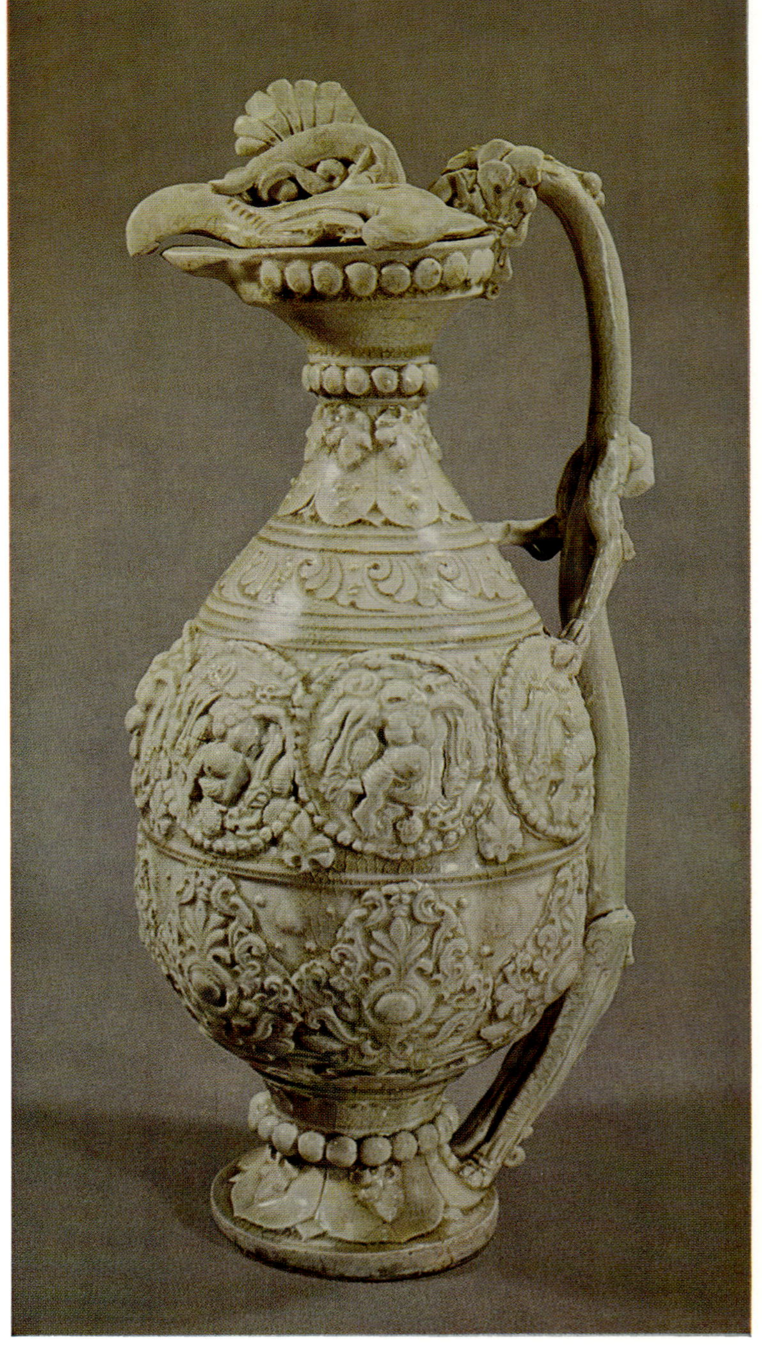

127. Bird-headed ewer, Greenware. T'ang dynasty. Excavated at Chi District, Honan.
height: 41.2 cm. (16.2 in.); diameter at mouth: 9.4 cm. (3.7 in.); diameter at base: 10.0 cm. (3.9 in.)

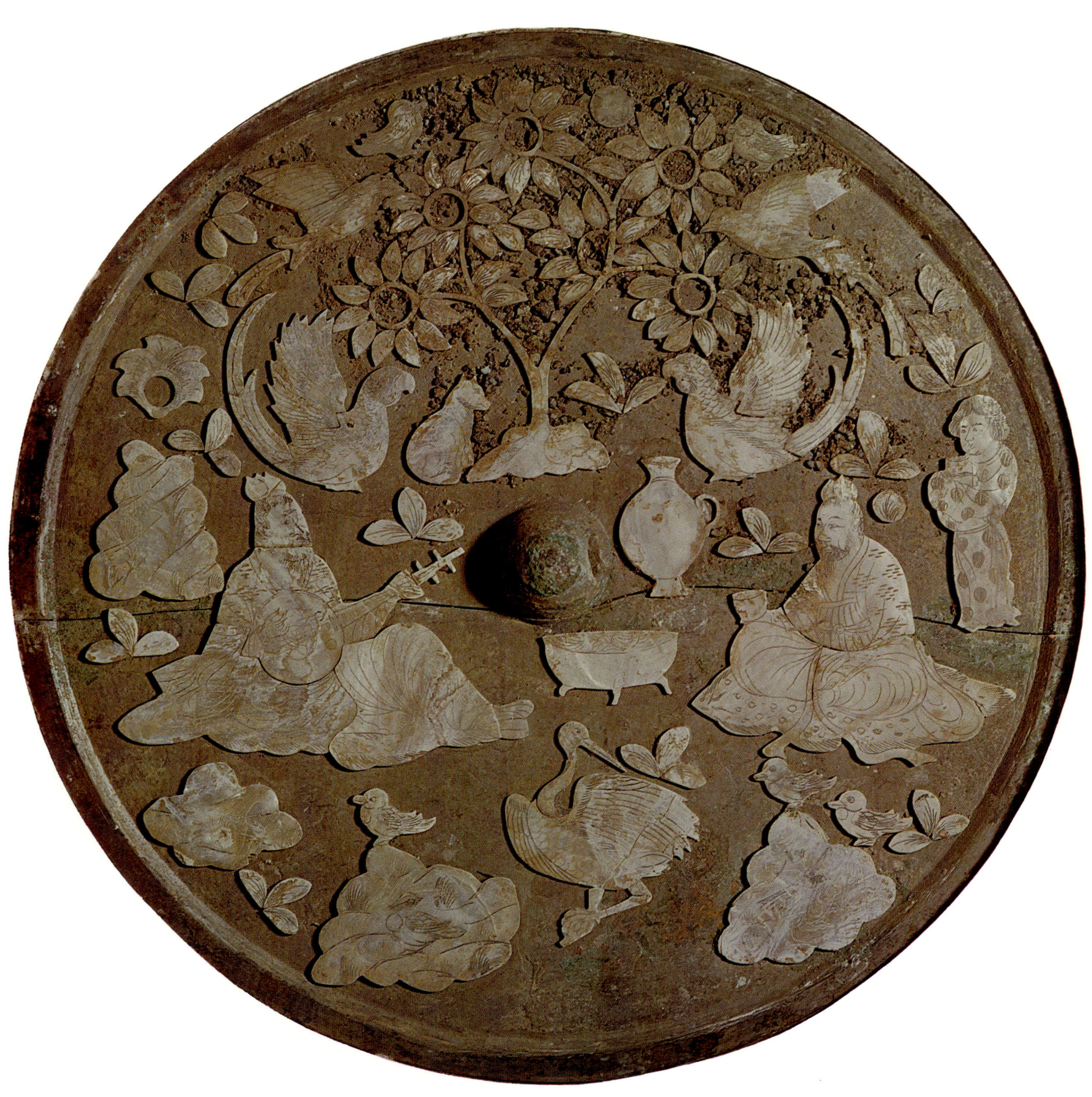

128. Mirror, nickel with mother-of-pearl and traces of lacquer. T'ang dynasty. Excavated from a T'ang dynasty tomb, west of the Chien River, Lo-yang Municipality, Honan.
diameter: 25.0 cm. (9.8 in.)

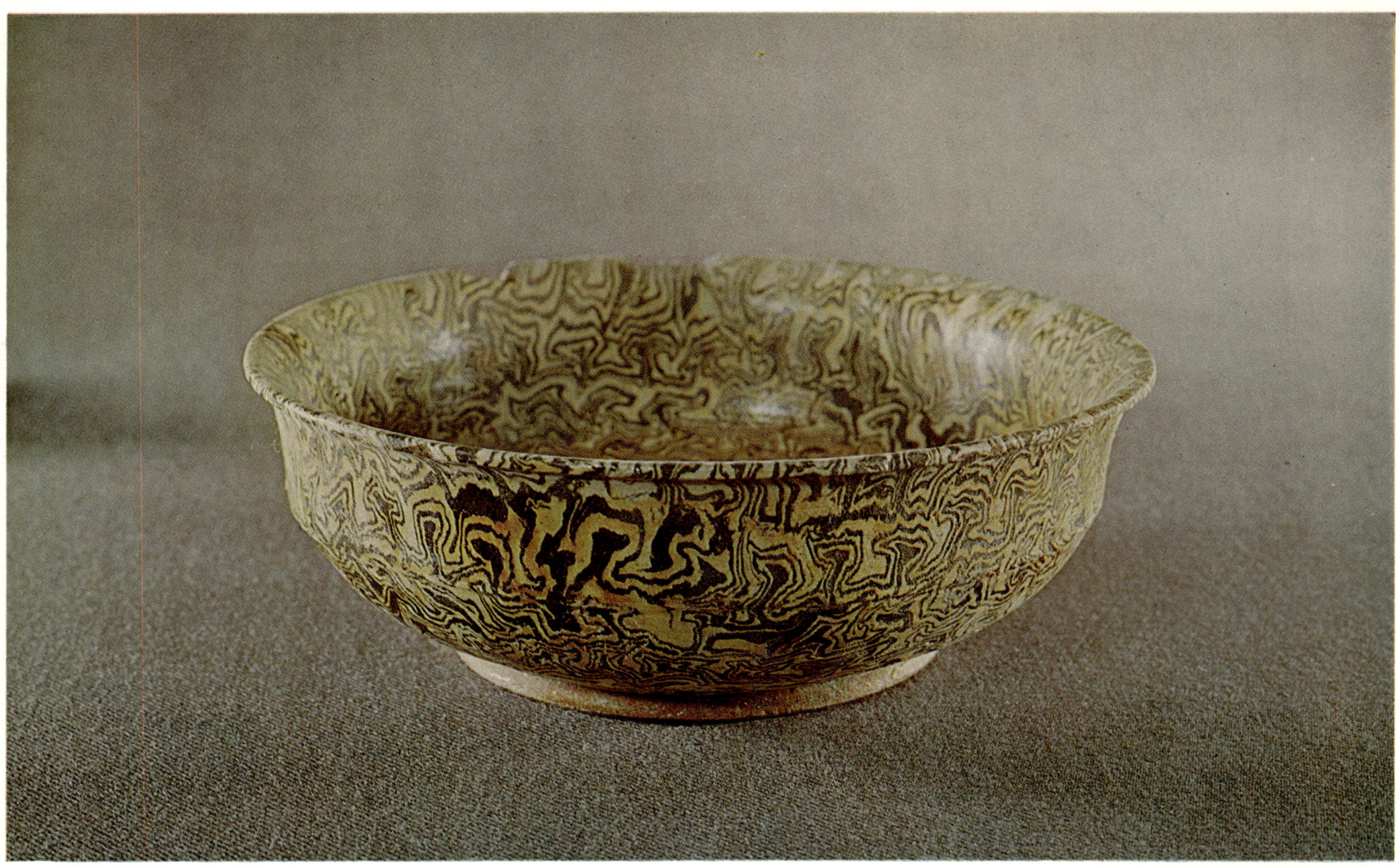

129. Small bowl, marbled ware. T'ang dynasty. Excavated from a T'ang dynasty tomb at Wang-chia-kung, Sian Municipality, Shensi.
height: 6.0 cm. (2.36 in.); diameter: 16.1 cm. (6.3 in.)

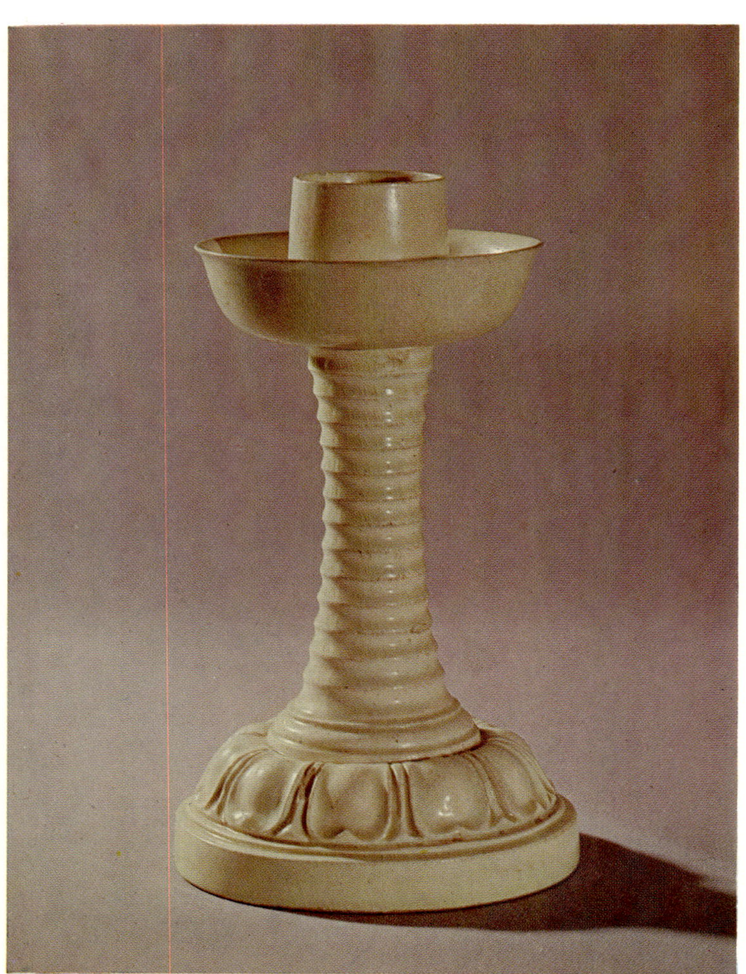

130. Stemmed lamp, white-glazed stoneware. T'ang dynasty. Excavated from a T'ang dynasty tomb at San-men-chia, Shan District, Honan.
height: 30.3 cm. (11.9 in.)

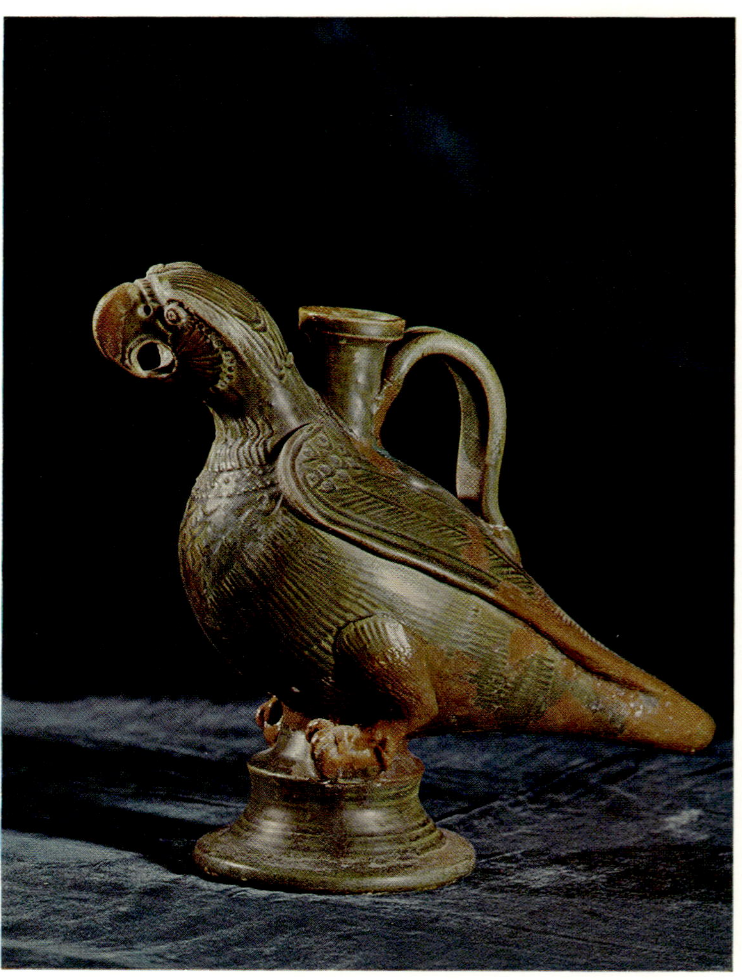

131. Parrot-shaped ewer, green- and yellow-glazed earthenware. T'ang dynasty. Excavated from tomb No. 3, T'u-ch'eng-tzu, Horin Gohl, Inner Mongolia.
height: 19.5 cm. (7.7 in.)

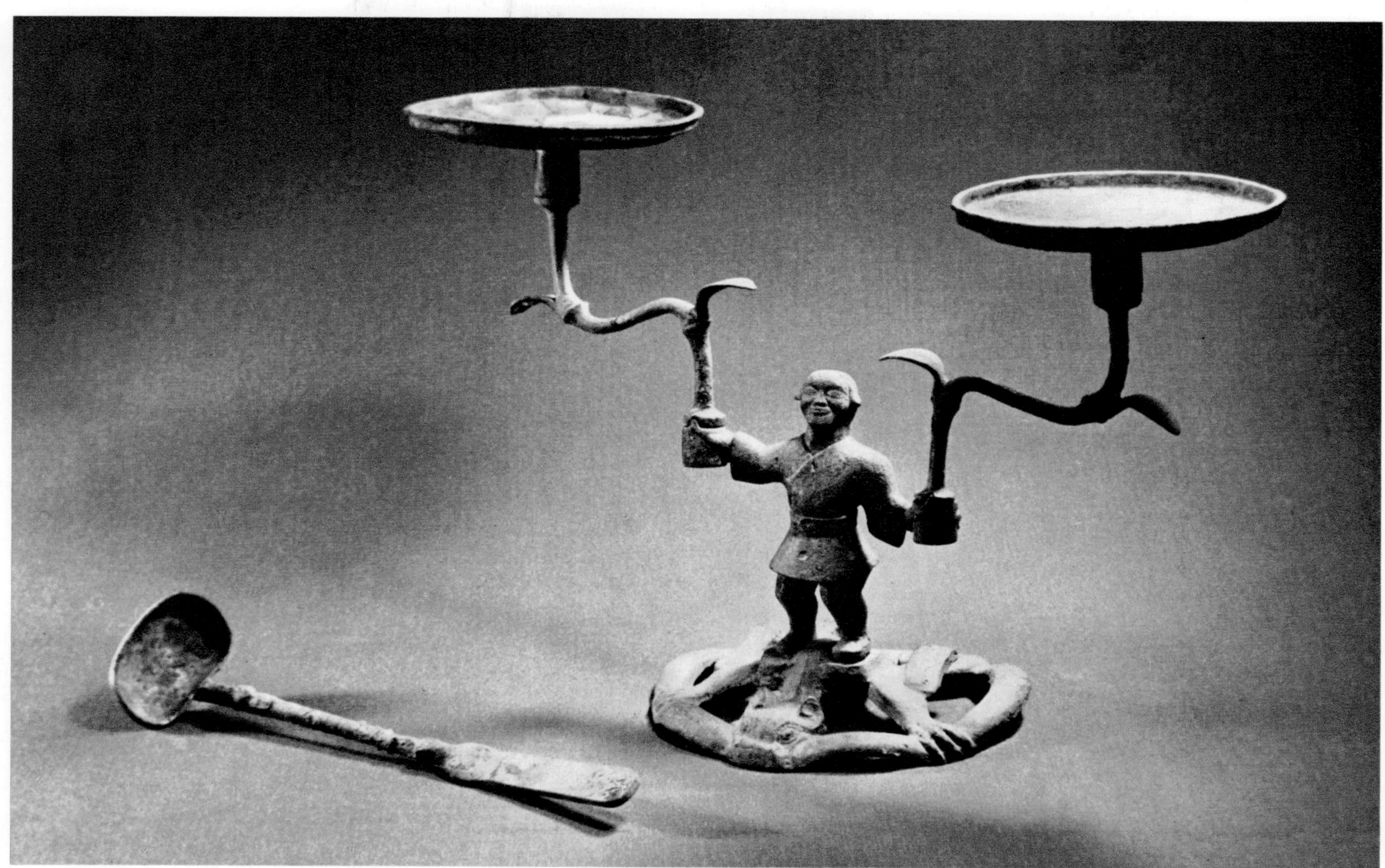

132. Lamp and spoon, bronze. Han dynasty. Excavated from a Han dynasty tomb at Pu-k'ou-ts'un, Chu-ch'eng District, Shantung.
lamp height: 21.3 cm. (8.4 in.); spoon length: 22.2 cm. (8.8 in.)

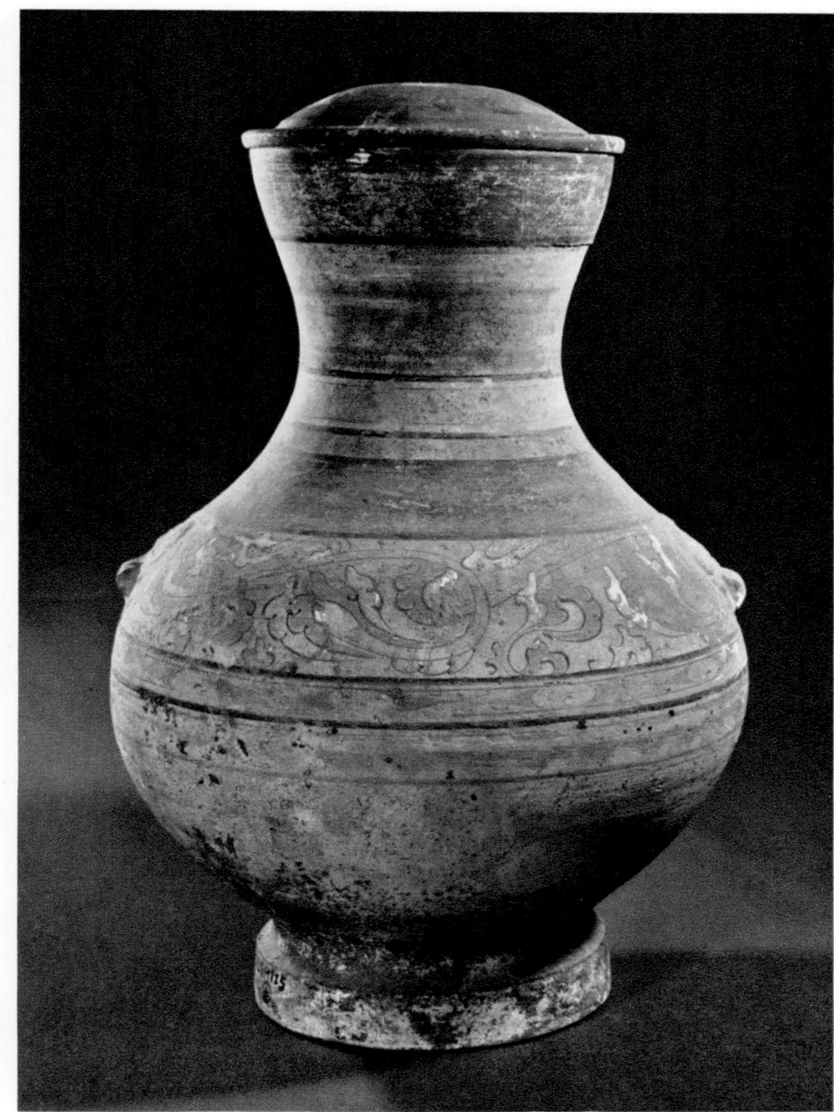

133. Covered jar, earthenware with slip decoration. Former Han dynasty. Excavated from a Han dynasty tomb at Shao-kou, Lo-yang Municipality, Honan.
height: 48.0 cm. (18.9 in.)

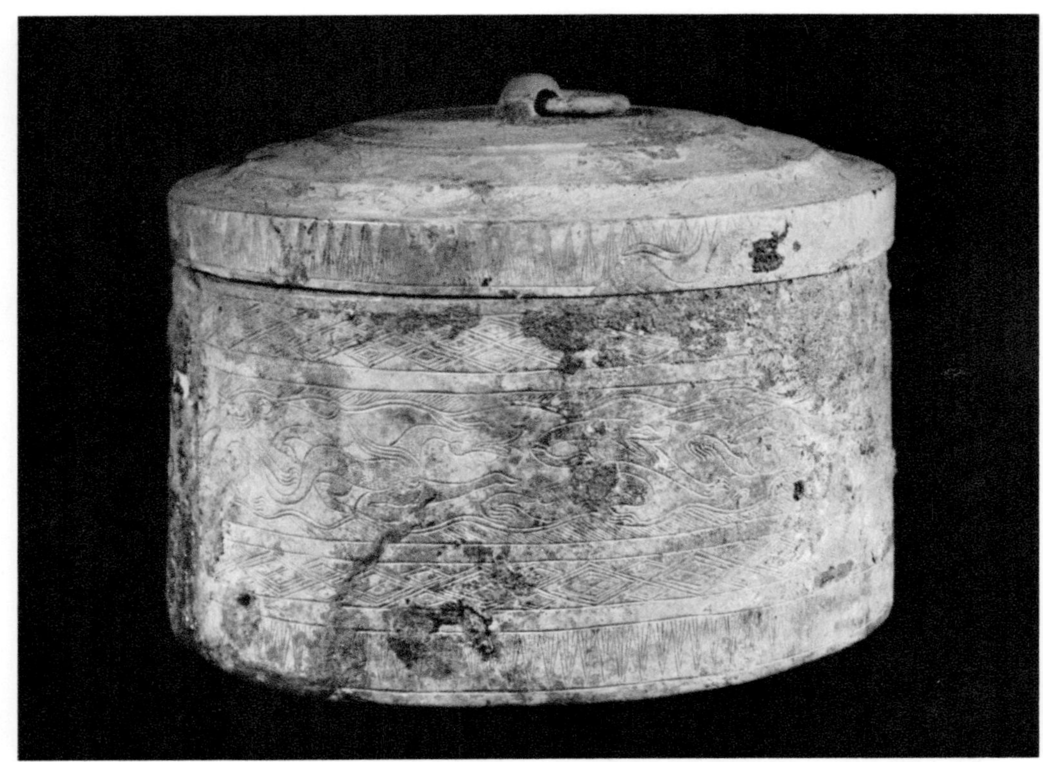

134. *Lien*, bronze. Han dynasty. Excavated from a Han dynasty tomb at Chiang-chia-shan, Heng-yang Municipality, Hunan.
height: 12.2 cm. (4.8 in.); diameter at lip: 15.7 cm. (6.2 in.)

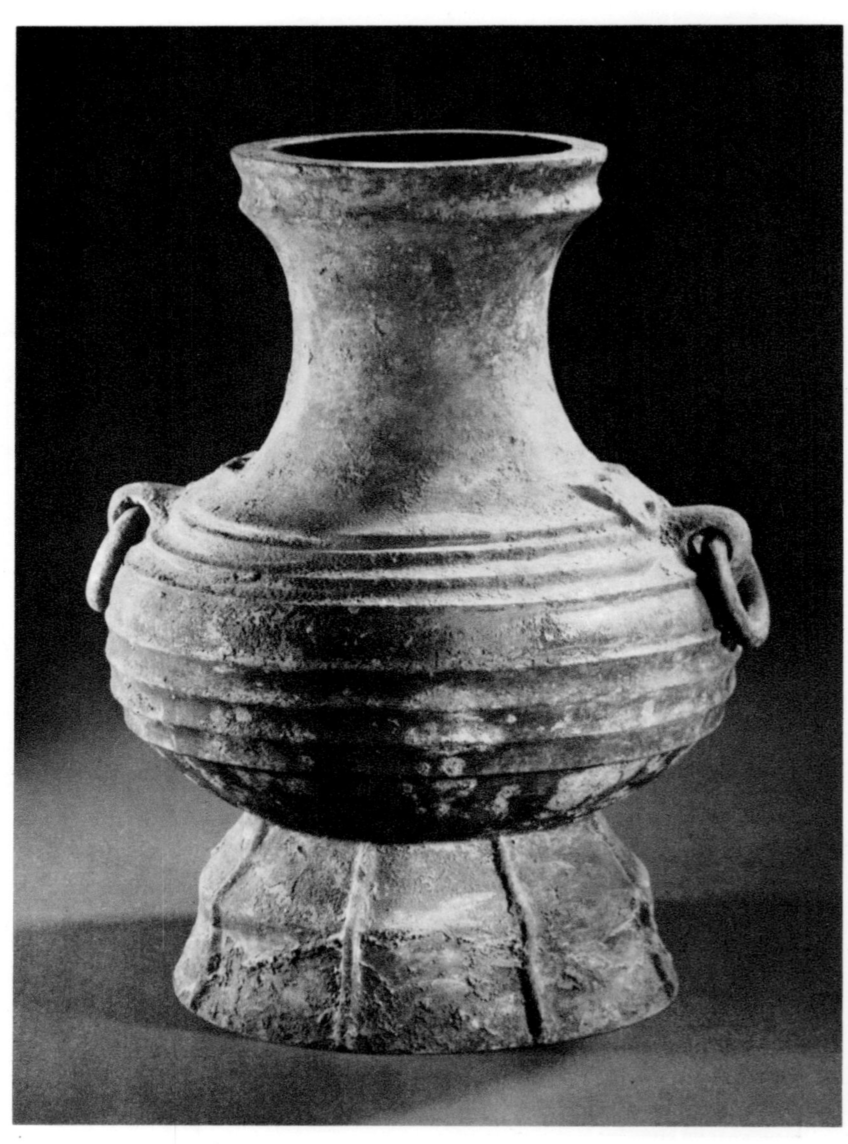

135. *Chung*, bronze. Han dynasty. Excavated from a Han dynasty tomb at Shuang-shan-ch'u, Yi District, Shantung.
height: 36.0 cm. (14.2 in.); diameter at lip: 17.0 cm. (6.7 in.)

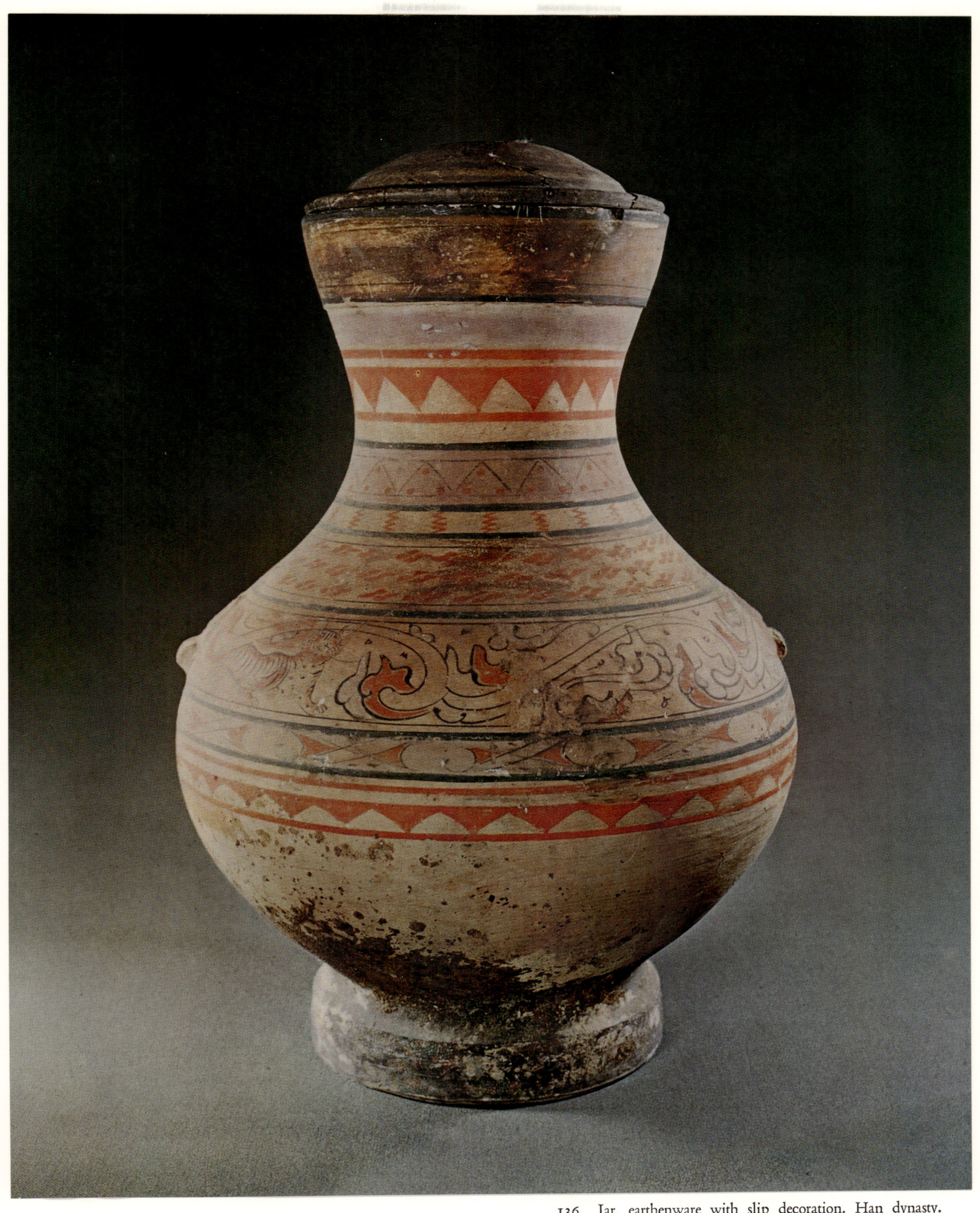

136. Jar, earthenware with slip decoration. Han dynasty. Excavated from a Han dynasty tomb at Shao-kou, Lo-yang Municipality, Honan.
height: 48.0 cm. (18.9 in.)

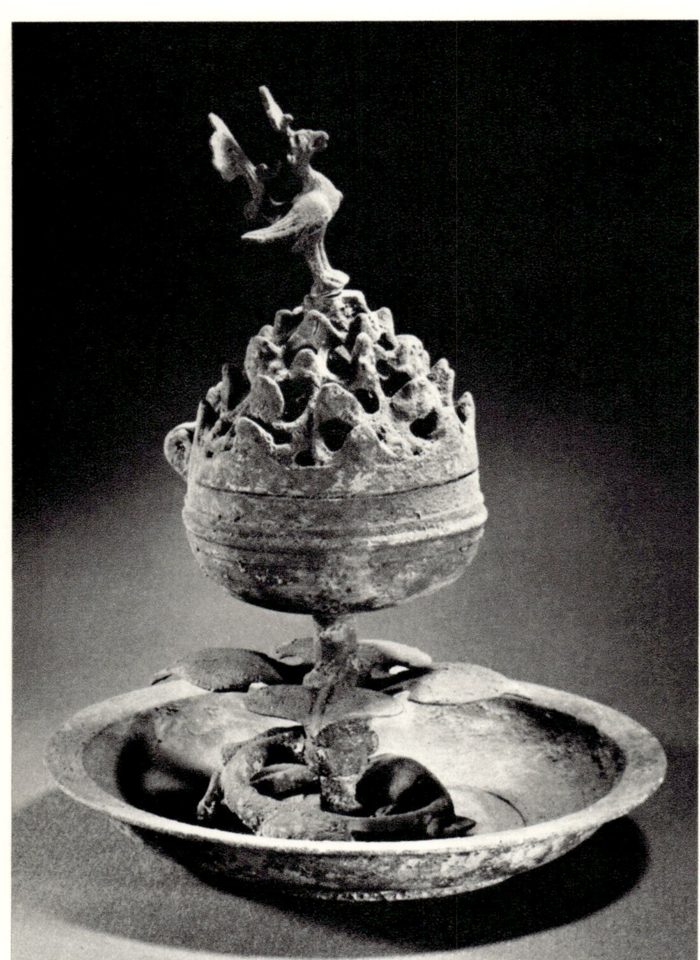

137. Hill-shaped incense burner, bronze. Han dynasty. Excavated from a Han dynasty tomb at Shuang-shan-ch'u, Yi District, Shantung.
height: 29.0 cm. (11.4 in.)

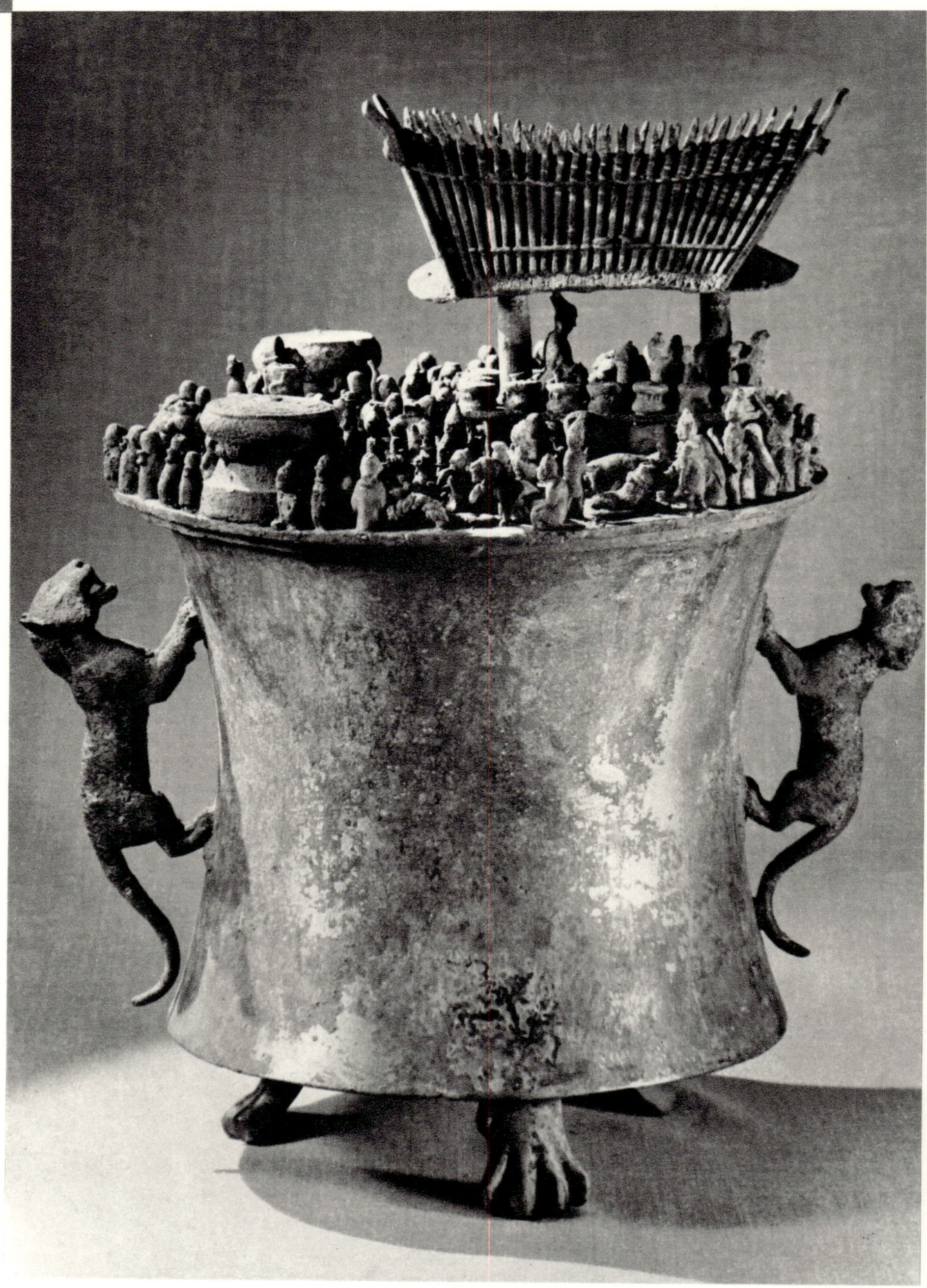

138. Cowrie container, bronze. Former Han dynasty. Excavated at Shih-chai-shan, Chin-ning District, Yünnan.
height: 53.0 cm. (20.8 in.)

139. Men dancing with saucers, bronze. Former Han dynasty. Excavated at Shih-chai-shan, Chin-ning District, Yünnan.
height: 11.5 cm. (4.5 in.)

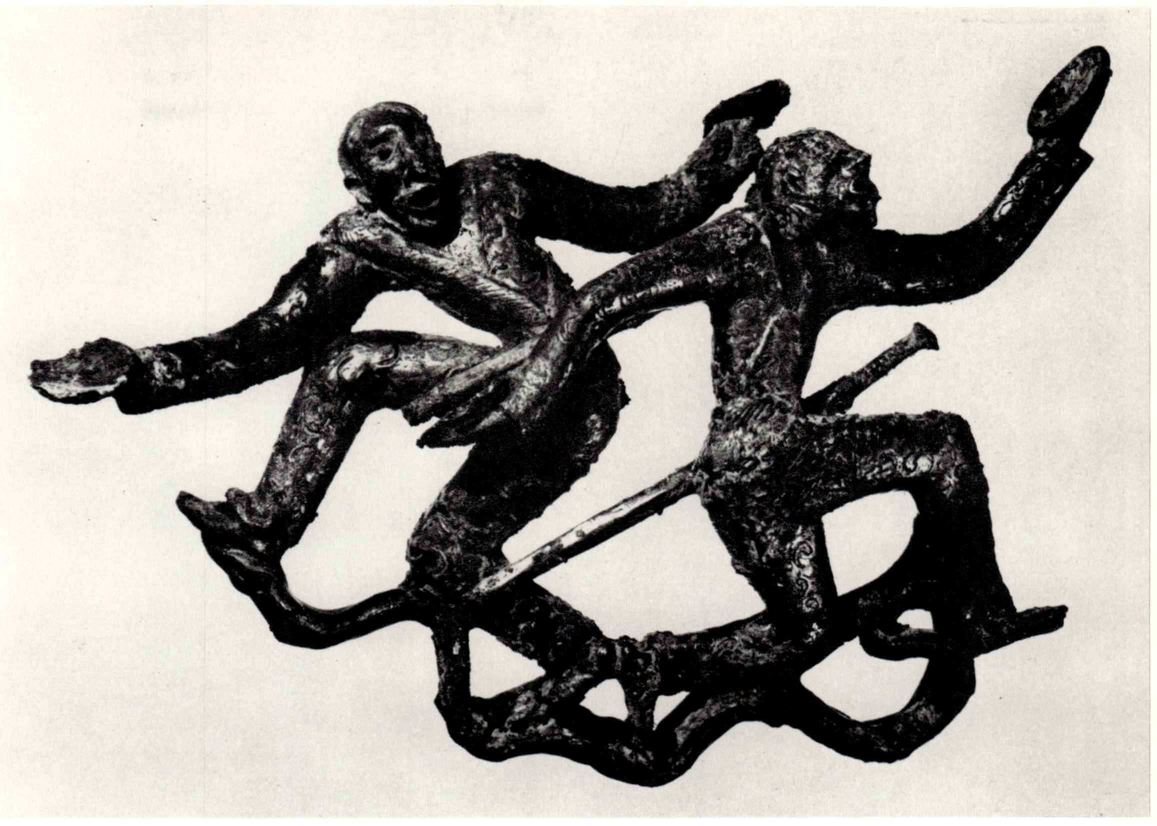

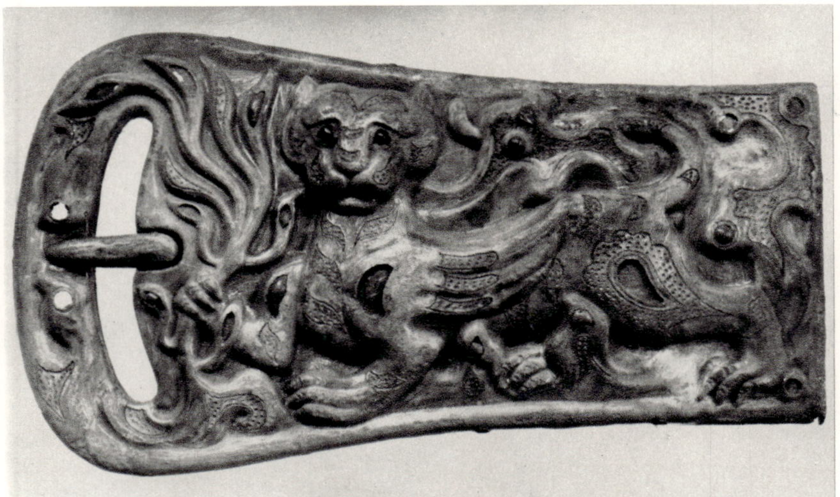

140. Belt buckle, gold relief with agate, turquoise, and silver-foil inlay. Former Han dynasty. Excavated at Shih-chai-shan, Chin-ning District, Yünnan.
length: 10.1 cm. (3.9 in.)

141 (a, b). Iron sword with bronze handle and gold-decorated sheath. Former Han dynasty. Excavated at Shih-chai-shan, Chin-ning District, Yünnan.
length of sword: 49.0 cm. (19.3 in.)

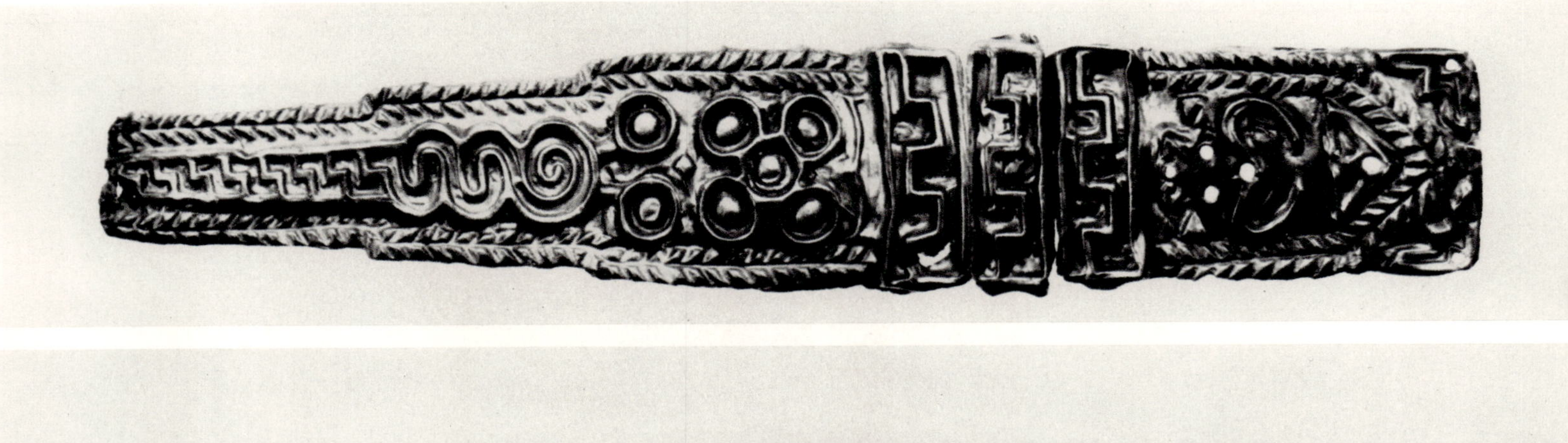

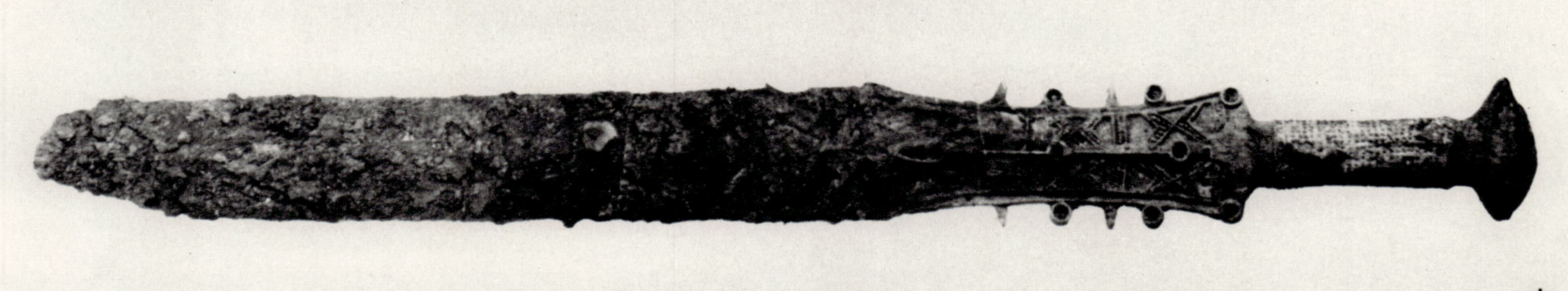

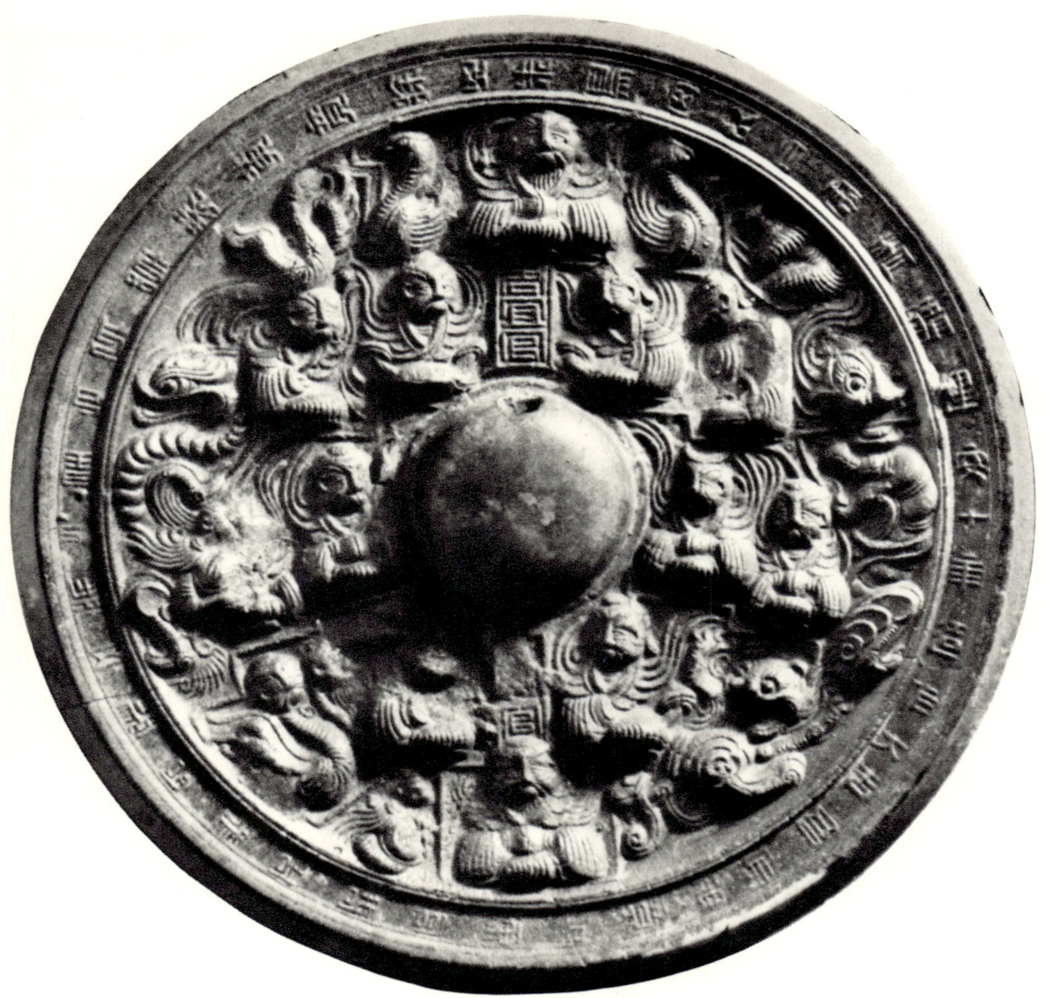

142. High-relief mirror, bronze. Later Han dynasty (dated 205 A.D.). Excavated from a Han dynasty tomb at Che Shan, Wu-hu Municipality, Anhui.
diameter: 13.5 cm. (5.3 in.); thickness: 0.4 cm. (0.15 in.)

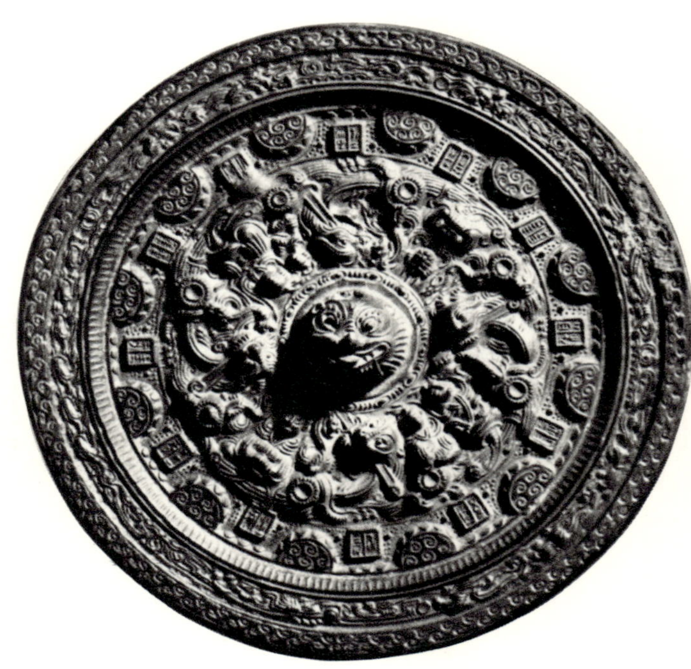

143. High-relief mirror, bronze. Later Han dynasty. Excavated from a Han dynasty tomb at Li-chu, Shao-hsing Municipality, Chekiang.
diameter: 13.0 cm. (5.1 in.)

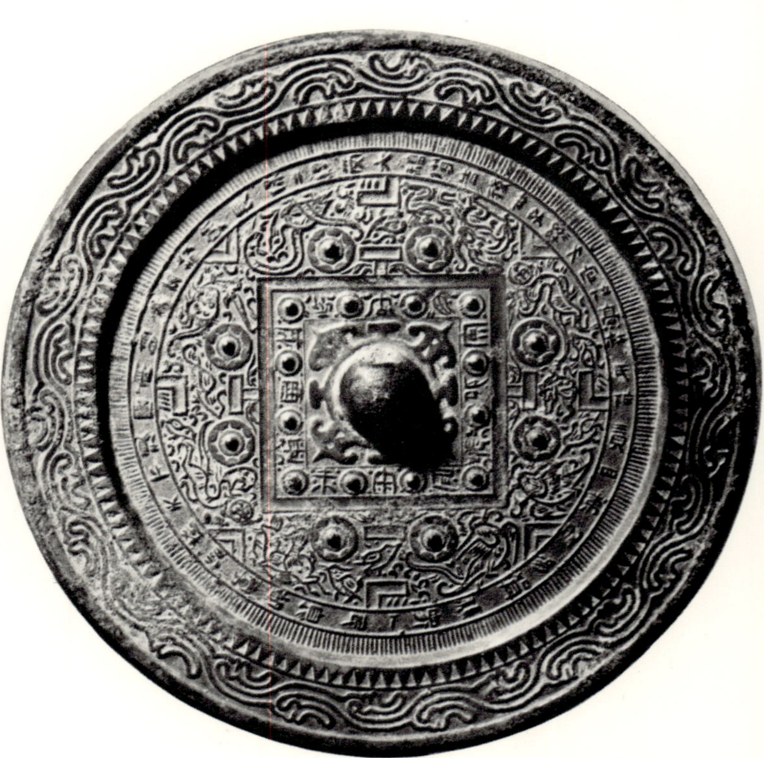

144. Mirror, bronze. Wang Mang interregnum, Han dynasty. Excavated from a Han dynasty tomb at Ho-chia-ts'un, western outskirts of Sian Municipality, Shensi.
diameter: 20.3 cm. (8.0 in.)

145–147. Sword fittings, carved jade. Han dynasty. Excavated from a Han dynasty tomb at Jung-yüan, Ch'ang-sha Municipality, Hunan.
lengths: [*145*] *5.9 cm. (2.3 in.);* [*146*] *5.8 cm. (2.25 in.);* [*147*] *5.6 cm. (2.2 in.)*

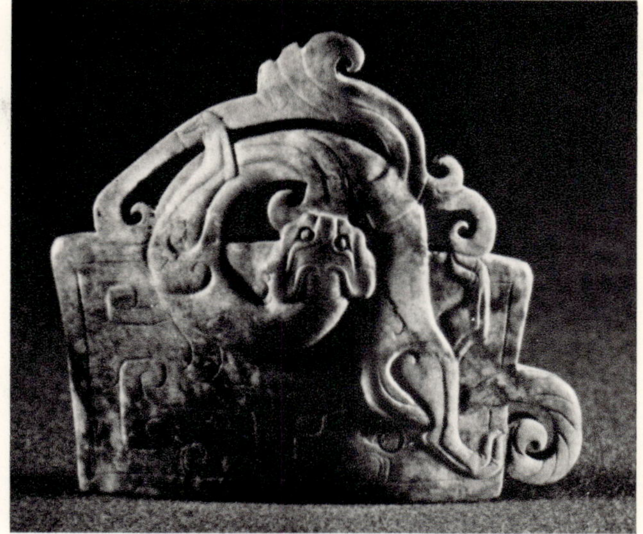

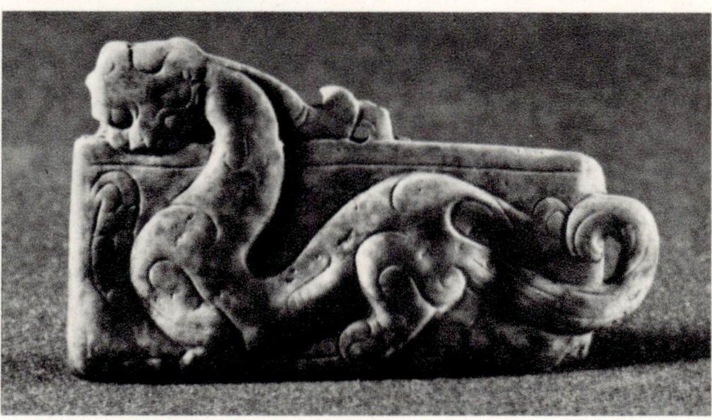

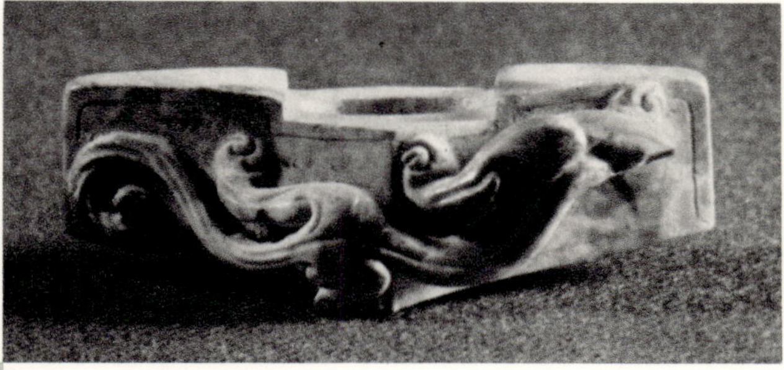

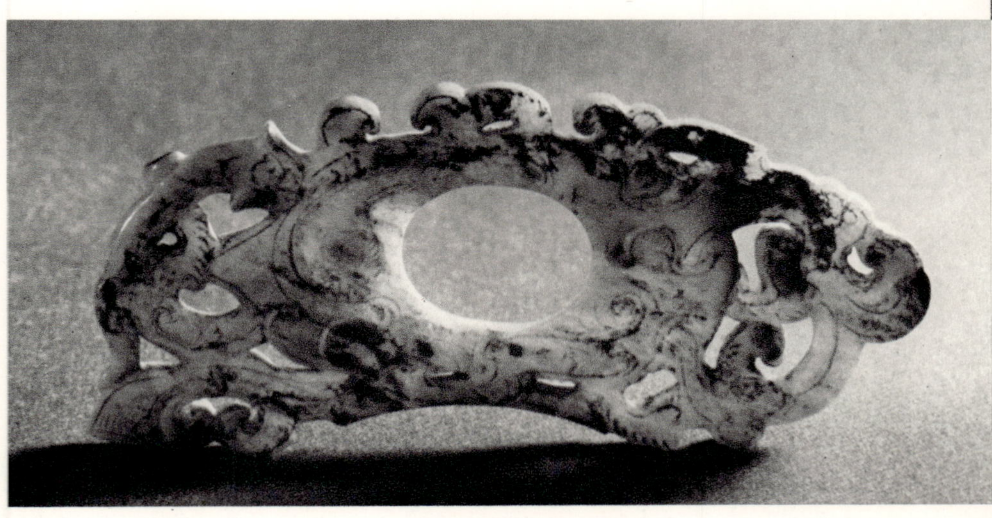

148. *P'ei,* carved jade. Wang Mang interregnum, Han dynasty. Excavated from a Han dynasty tomb at Wu-li-p'ai, Ch'ang-sha Municipality, Hunan.
length: 9.2 cm. (3.6 in.); width: 3.7 cm. (1.46 in.); thickness: 0.5 cm. (0.198 in.)

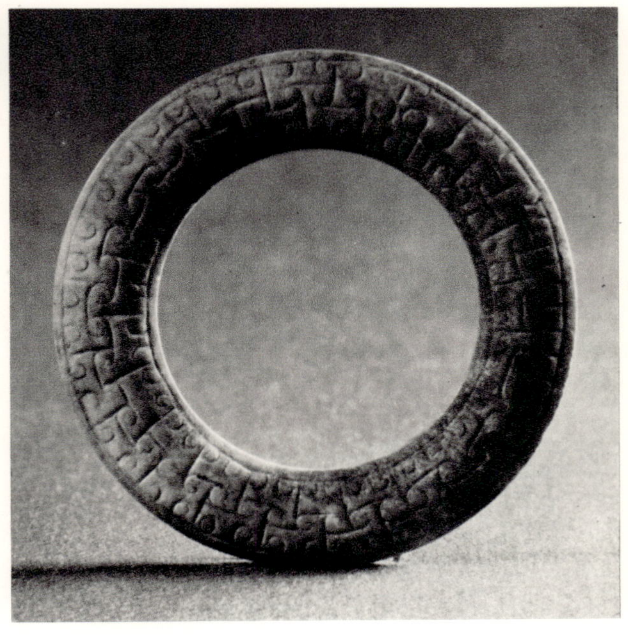

149. *Yüan,* jade. Han dynasty. Excavated at Jung-yüan, Ch'ang-sha Municipality, Hunan.
outer diameter: 5.5 cm. (2.17 in.); inner diameter: 3.4 cm. (1.46 in.)

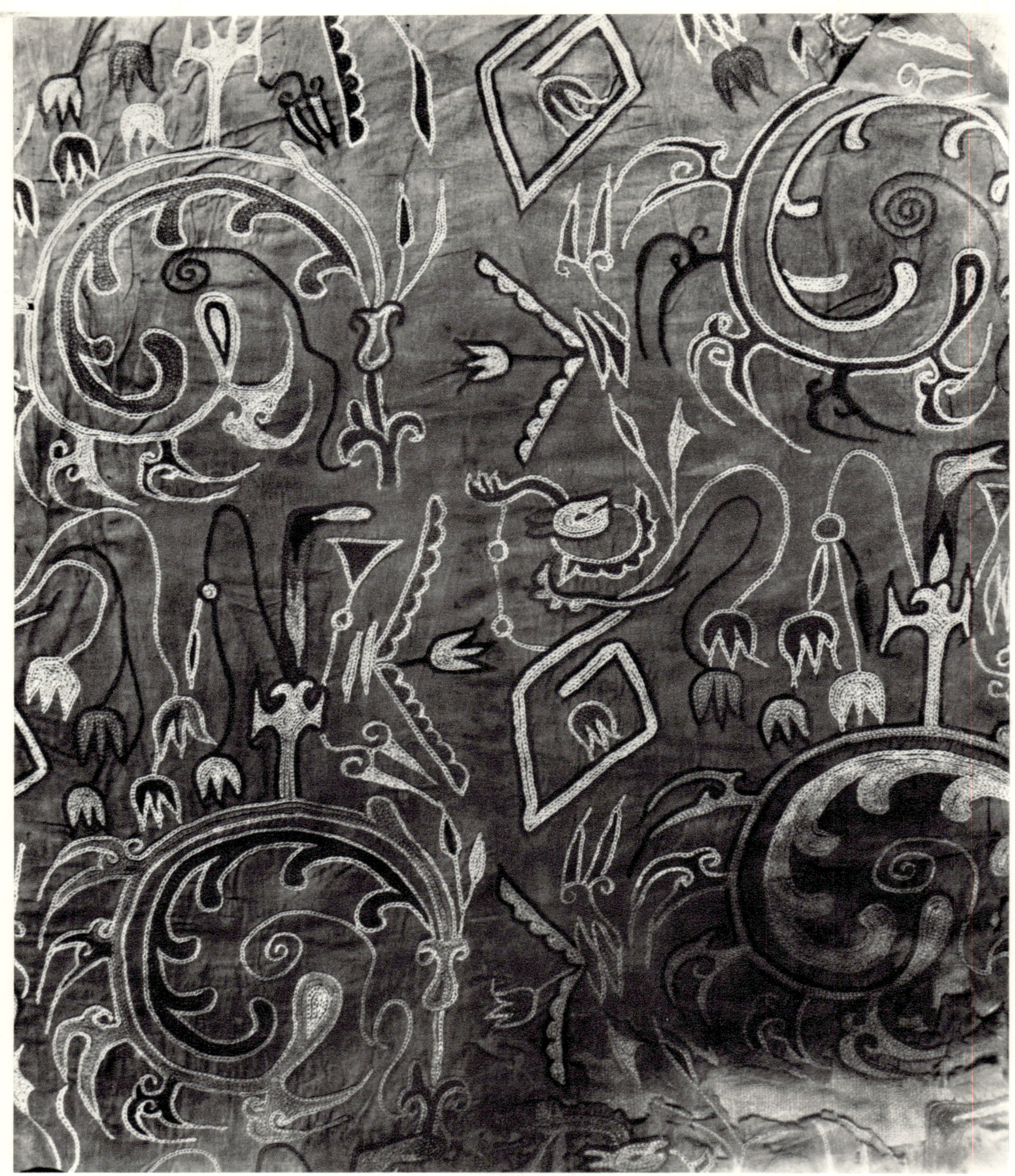

150. Green silk embroidered with animal and flower motifs in polychrome chain stitch. Han dynasty. Excavated at Min-feng District, Uighur Autonomous Region, Sinkiang.

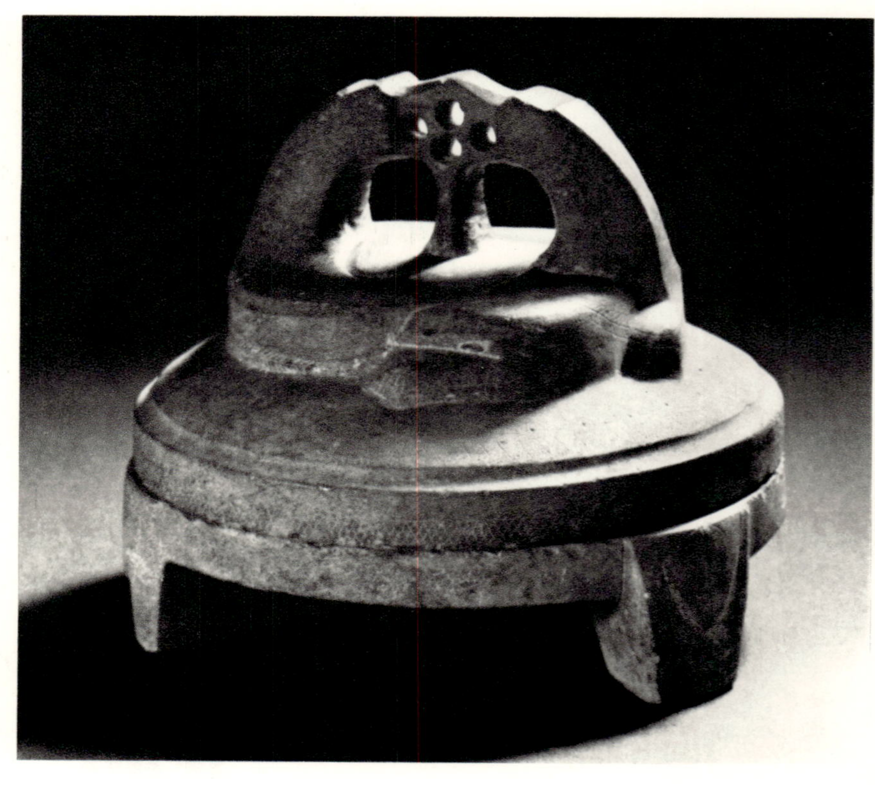

151. Inkstone, gray-blue stone. Han dynasty. Excavated from a Han dynasty tomb at Li-ko-tuo, T'ai-ho District, Anhui.
height: 14.3 cm. (5.6 in.); diameter: 15.8 cm. (6.2 in.)

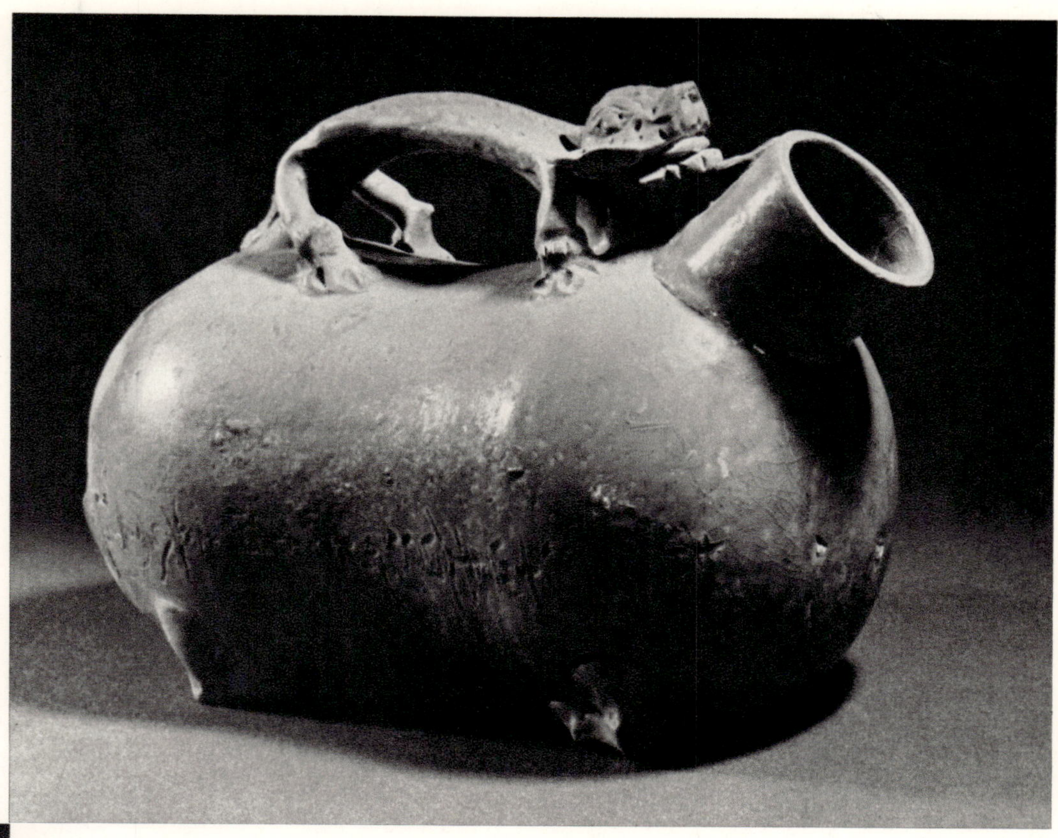

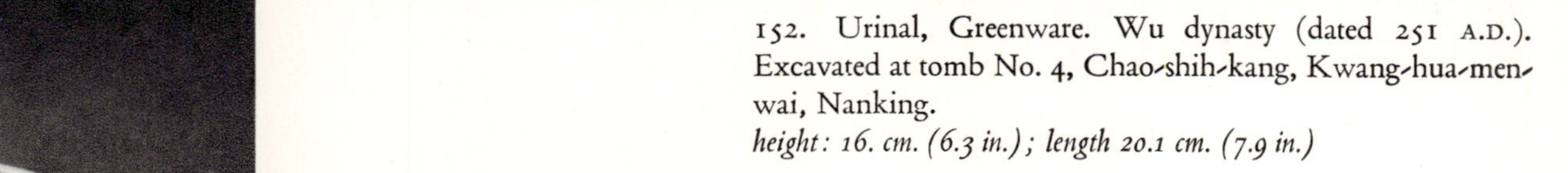

152. Urinal, Greenware. Wu dynasty (dated 251 A.D.). Excavated at tomb No. 4, Chao-shih-kang, Kwang-hua-men-wai, Nanking.
height: 16. cm. (6.3 in.); length 20.1 cm. (7.9 in.)

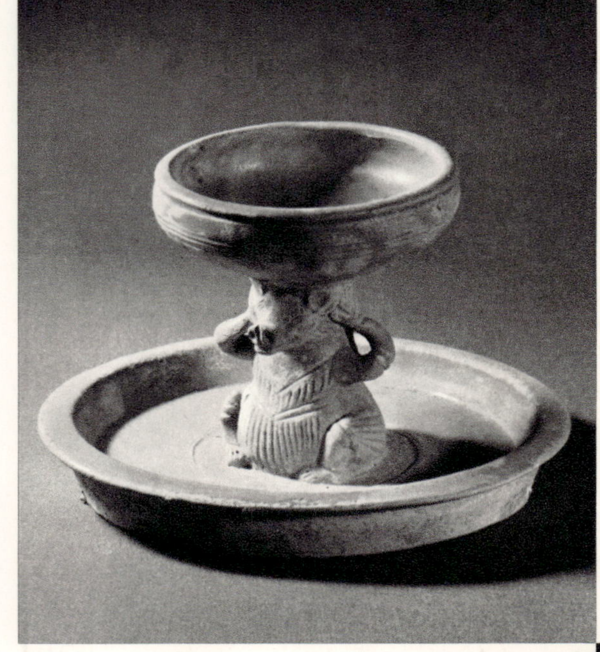

153. Lamp, Greenware. Wu dynasty (dated 256 A.D.). Excavated at Ch'ing-liang-shan, Nanking.
height: 12.3 cm. (4.8 in.); top diameter: 9.5 cm. (3.74 in.); base diameter: 15.2 cm. (6.0 in.)

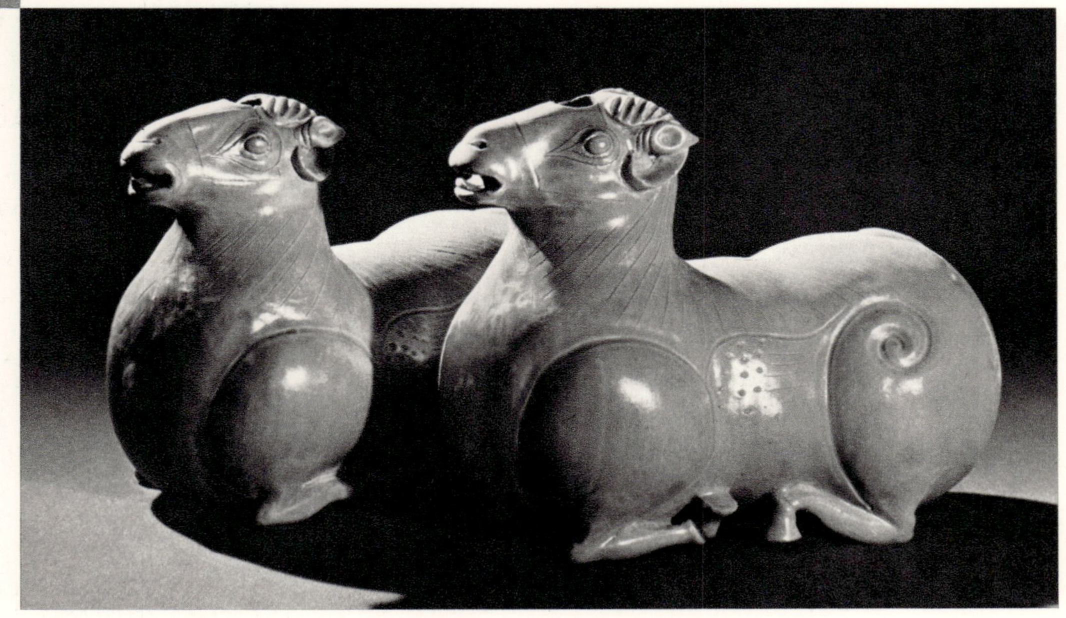

154. Ram-shaped water pots, Greenware. Wu dynasty. Excavated from a tomb constructed in 265 A.D., Nanking.
[*right*] *height: 24.9 cm. (9.8 in.); length: 31.7 cm. (12.5 in.)*
[*left*] *height: 23.4 cm. (9.3 in.); length: 32.0 cm. (12.6 in.)*

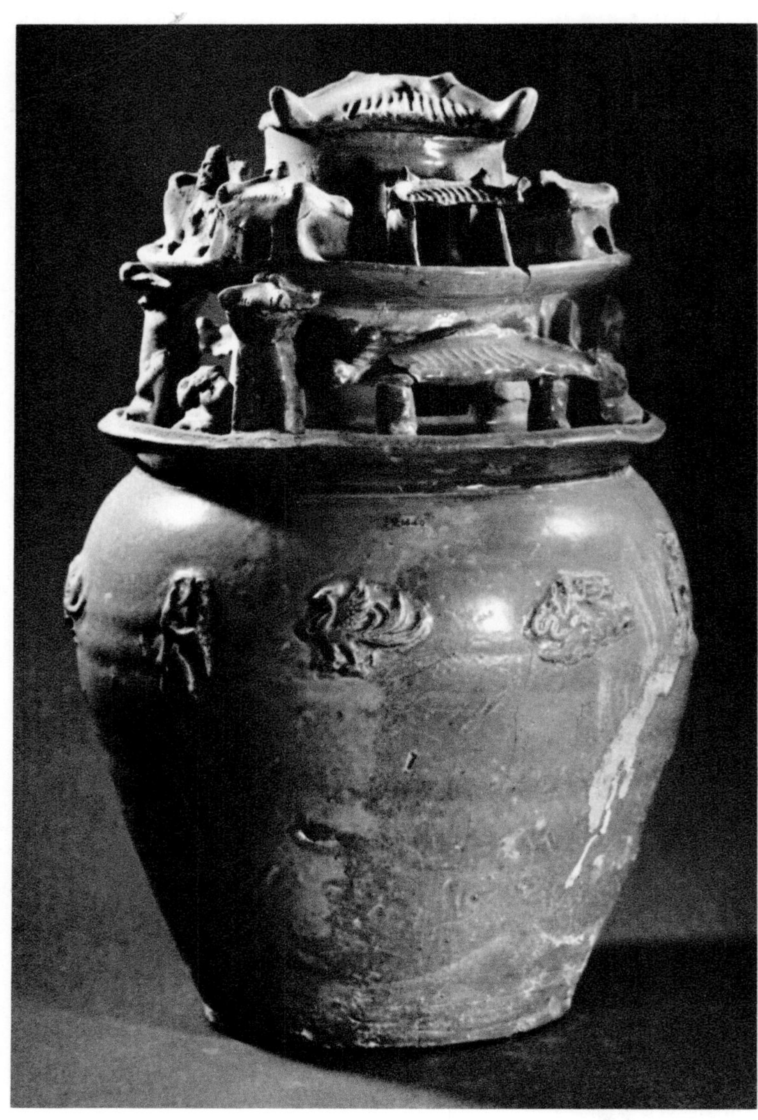

155. Urn, Greenware. Chin dynasty (dated 300 A.D.). Excavated from a Chin dynasty tomb at Chu-chi District, Chekiang.
height: 39.0 cm. (15.3 in.)

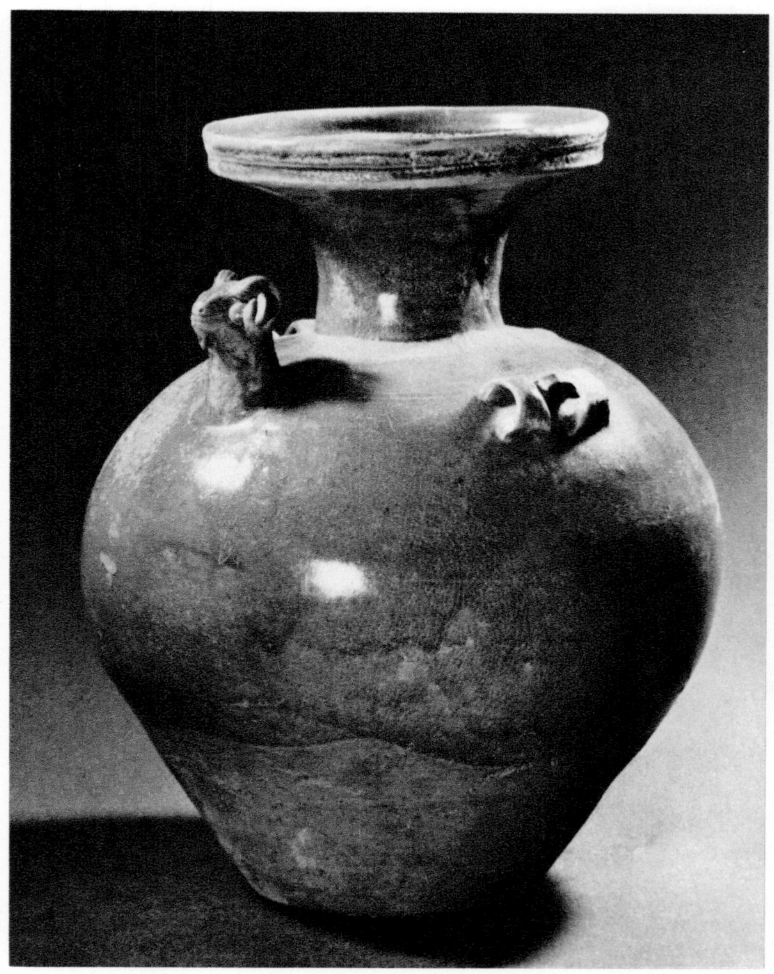

156. Ram-spouted jar, Greenware. Six Dynasties. Excavated at Mu-fu-shan, Nanking.
height: 35.7 cm. (14.1 in.); diameter at lip: 18.3 cm. (7.2 in.)

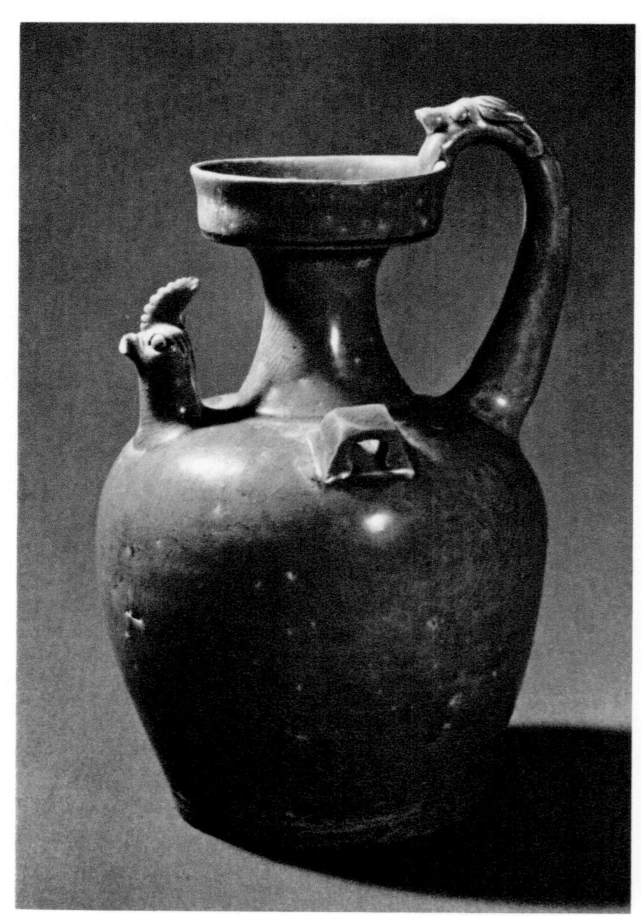

157. Chicken-spouted ewer, Greenware. Liu-Sung dynasty. Excavated from a Liu-Sung dynasty tomb at Hsiu-shui-ling, Huang-yen District, Chekiang.
height: 13.5 cm. (5.3 in.); diameter: 12.0 cm. (4.7 in.)

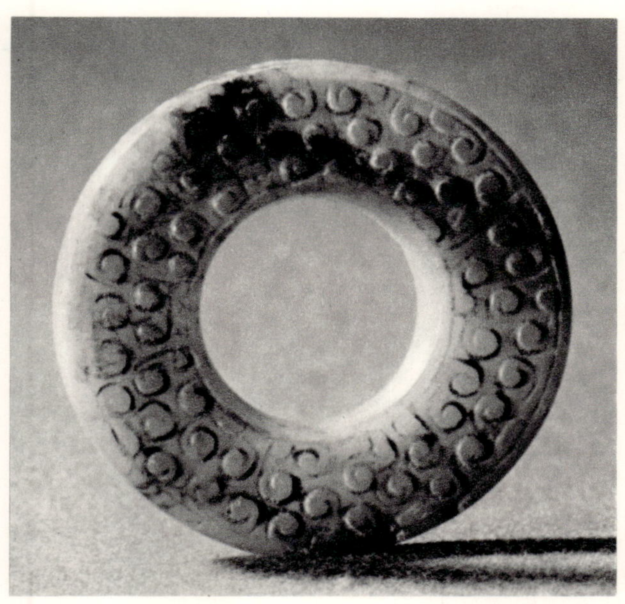

158. Ring with "rice-grain" pattern, jade. Northern and Southern Dynasties. Excavated at Hsi-shan-ch'iao, Nanking.
outer diameter: 5.4 cm. (2.1 in.); inner diameter: 2.5 cm. (0.98 in.); thickness: 0.6 cm. (0.24 in.)

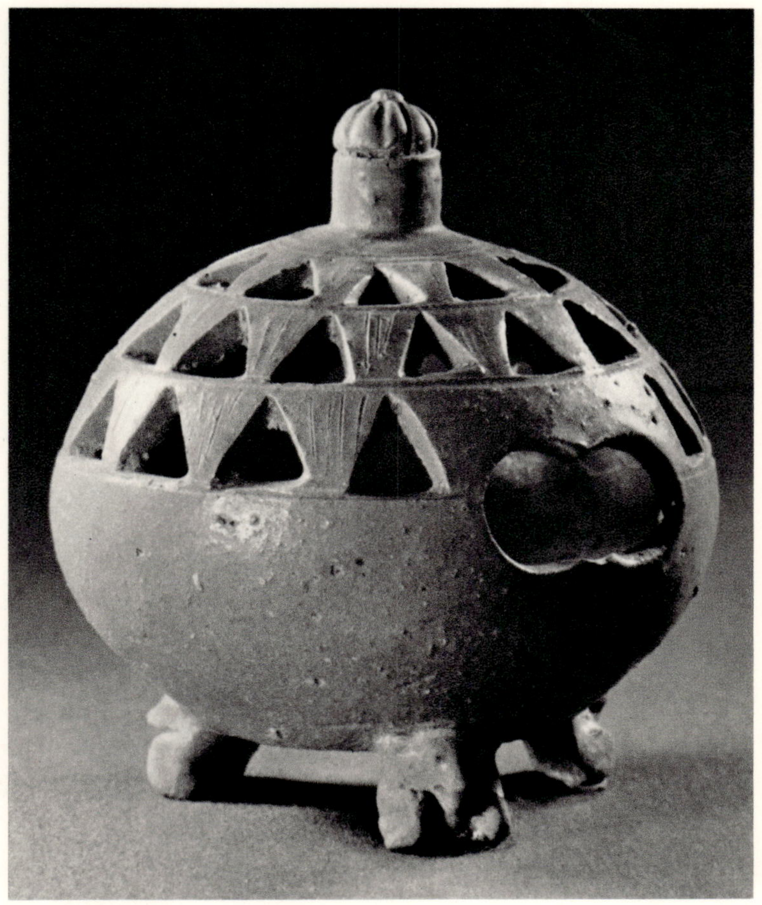

159. Incense burner, Greenware. Chin dynasty. Excavated from a Chin dynasty tomb at Yi-hsing District, Kiangsu.
height: 13.5 cm. (5.3 in.); diameter: 12.0 cm. (4.7 in.)

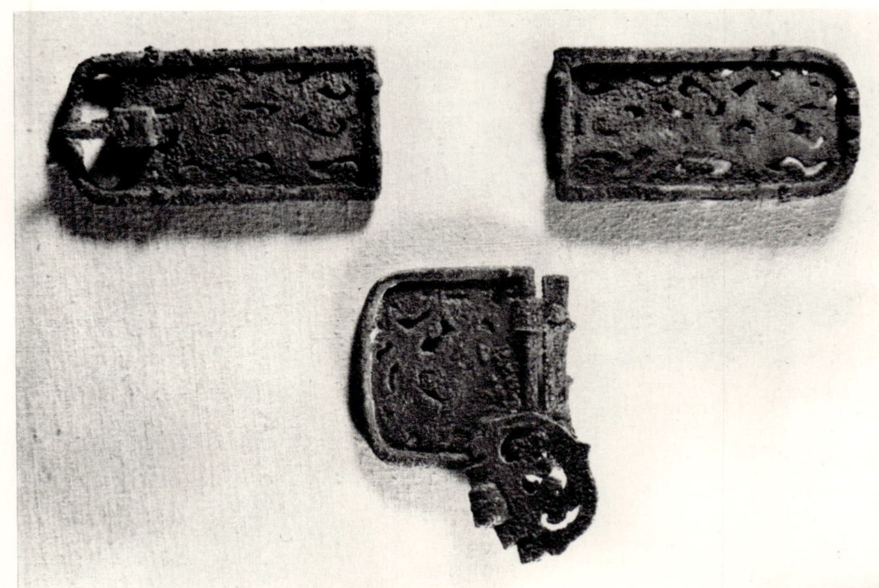

160. Belt fittings, metal. Western Chin dynasty. Excavated from a Chou family tomb at Yi-hsing District, Kiangsu.
length: approx. 6.5 cm. (2.56 in.); width: approx. 3.5 cm. (1.38 in.)

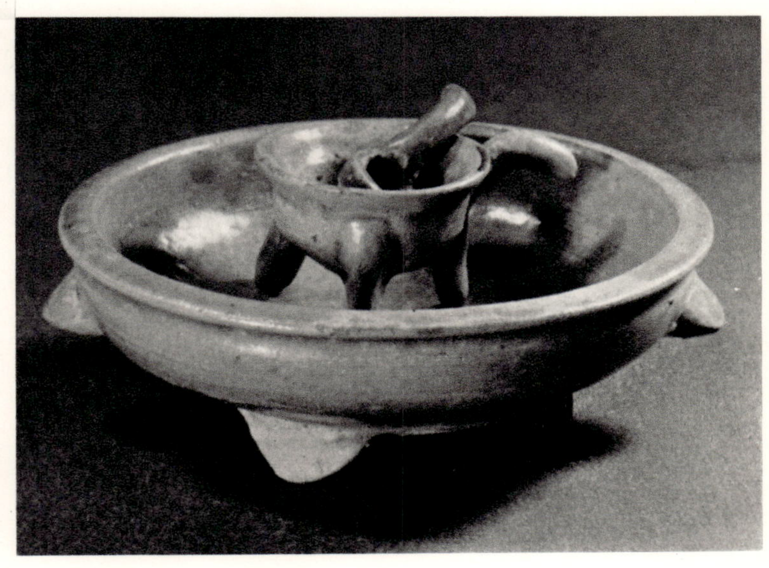

161. Cooking vessel model, Greenware. Western Chin dynasty. Excavated from a Chou family tomb, Yi-hsing District, Kiangsu.
height: 8.3 cm. (3.25 in.); diameter 11.7 cm. (4.6 in.)

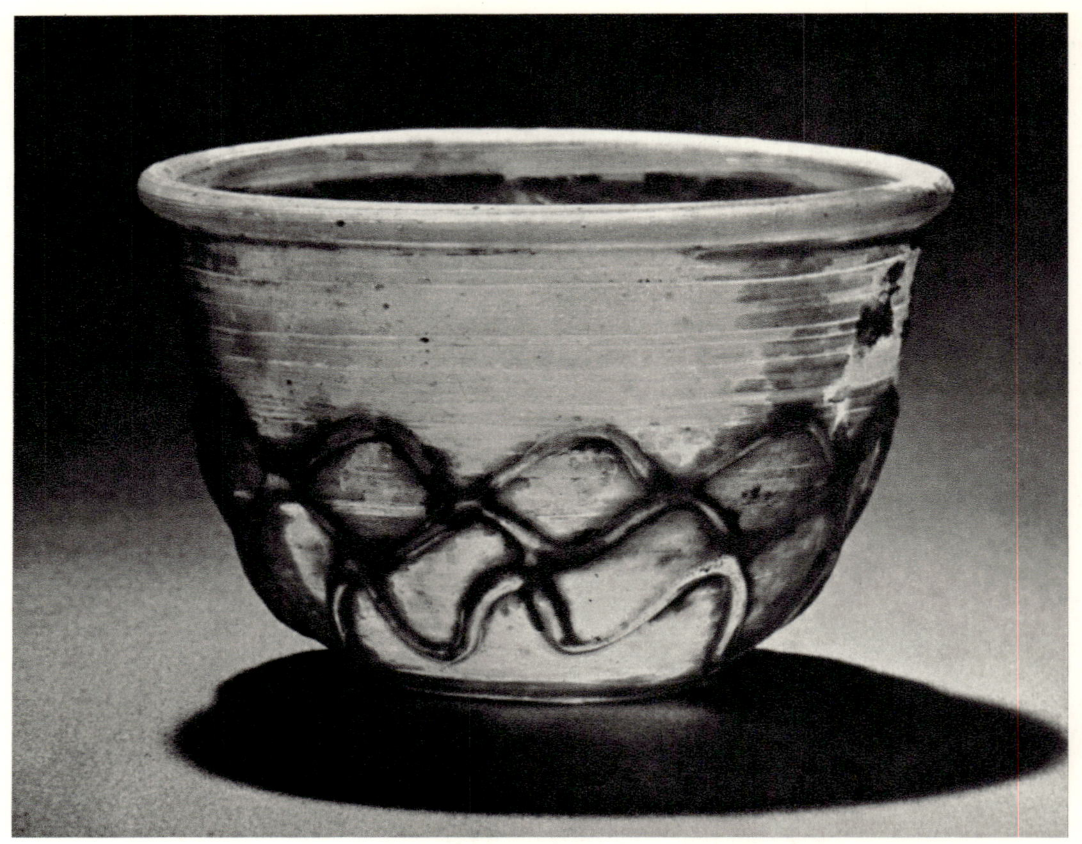

162. Glass bowl. Northern Dynasties. Excavated from the Feng family tombs, Ching District, Hopei.
height: 6.7 cm. (2.6 in.); diameter; 10.3 cm. (4.0 in.)

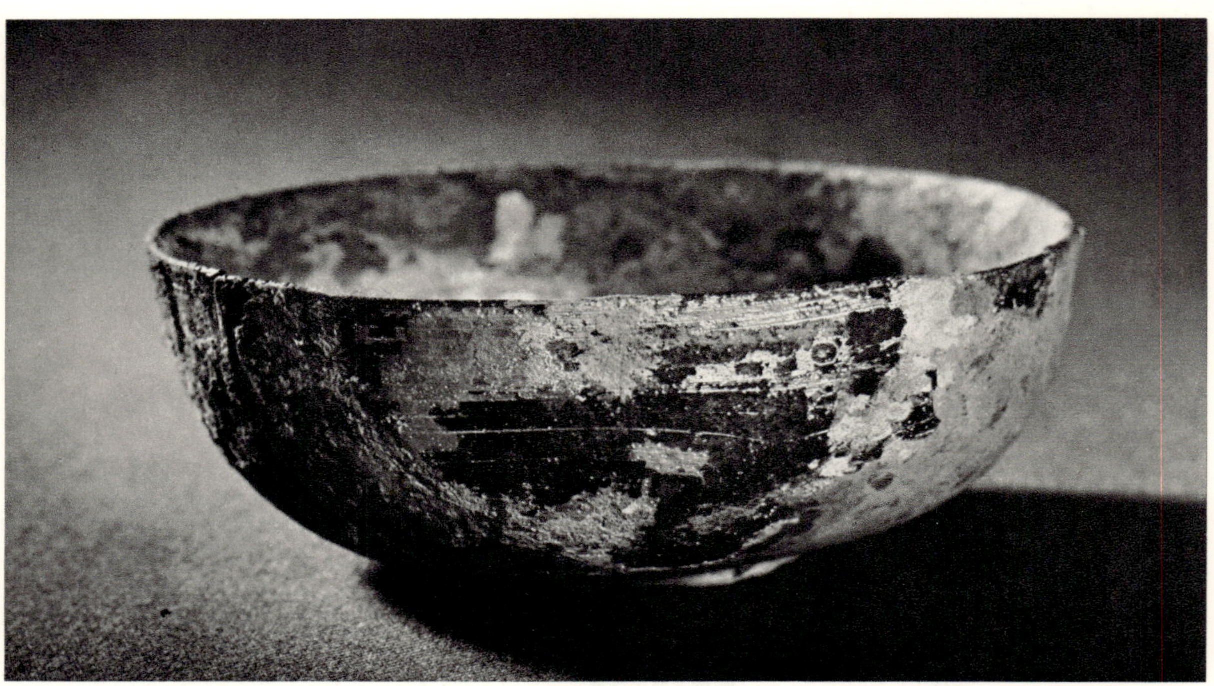

163. Glass bowl. Northern Dynasties. Excavated from the Feng family tombs, Ching District, Hopei.
height: 4.4 cm. (1.7 in.); diameter: 11.4 cm. (4.5 in.)

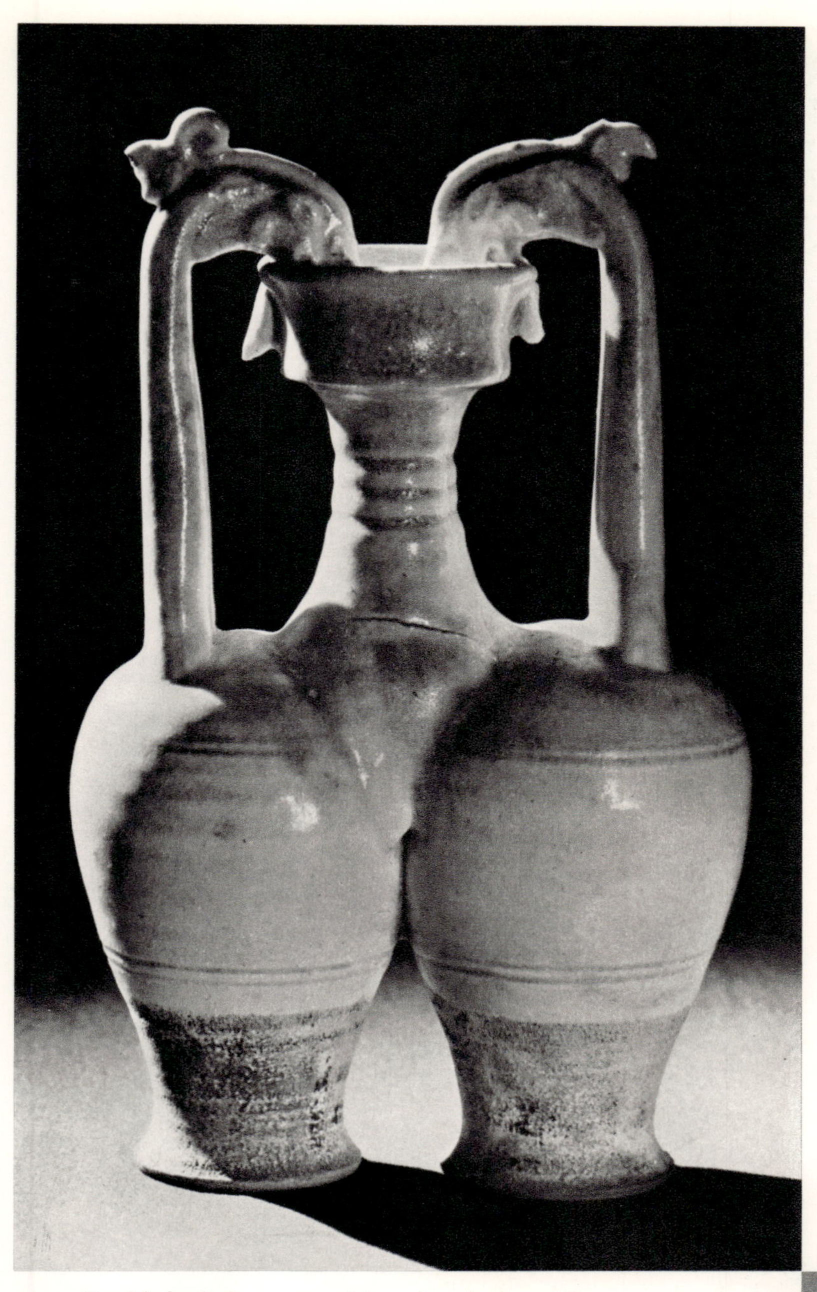

164. Double-bodied ewer, white clay body with transparent glaze. Sui dynasty. Excavated at the Li Ching-hsün tomb, Sian Municipality, Shensi.
height: 18.6 cm. (7.3 in.)

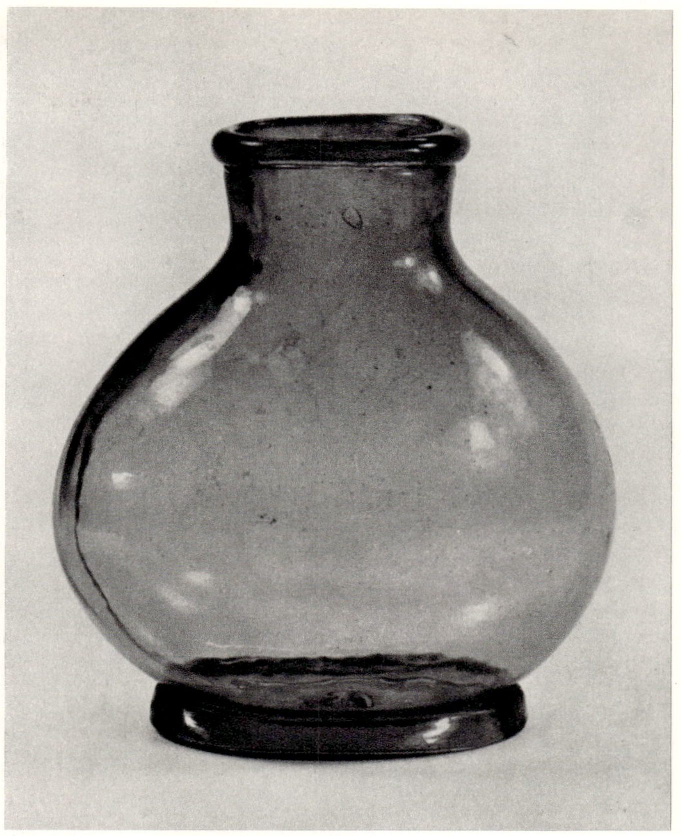

165. Bottle, green transparent glass. Sui dynasty. Excavated from the Li Ching-hsün tomb, Sian Municipality, Shensi.
height: 12.5 cm. (4.9 in.)

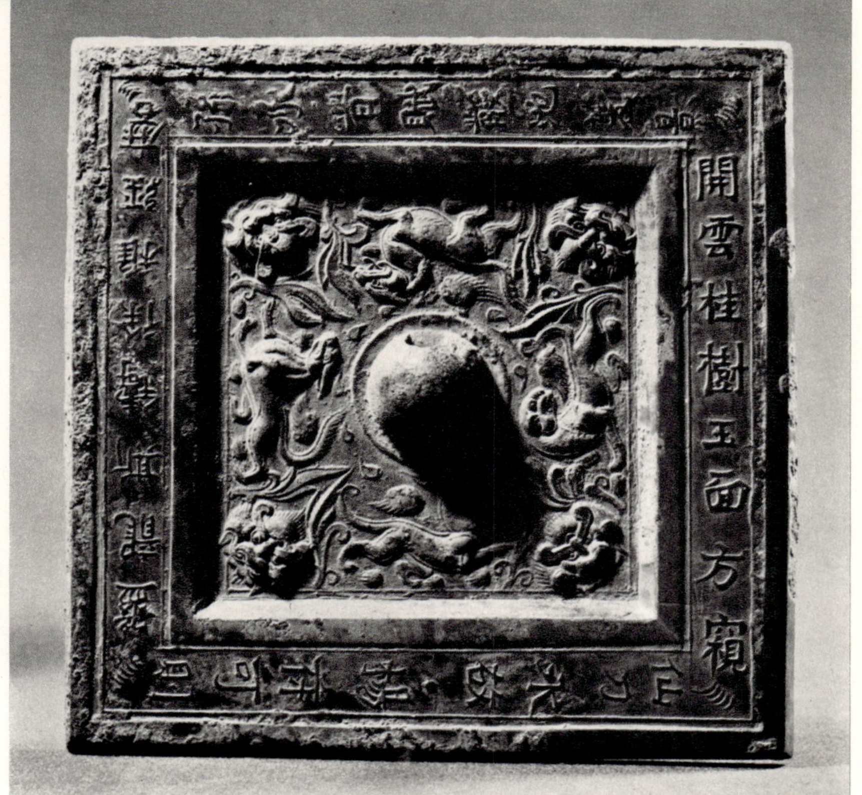

166. Rectangular mirror, bronze. Sui dynasty. Excavated from a Sui dynasty tomb at Kuo-chia-t'an, eastern outskirts of Sian Municipality, Shensi.
diameter: 14.7 cm. (5.8 in.)

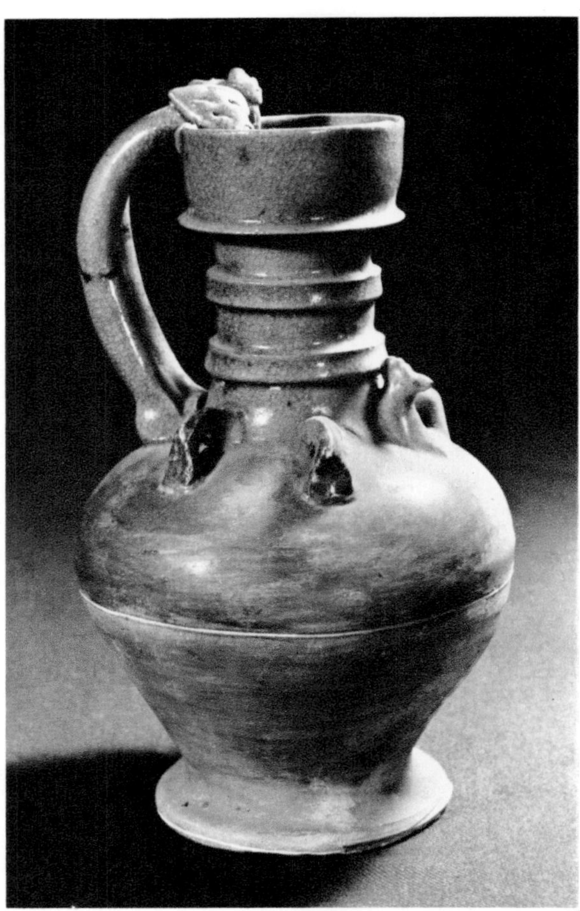

167. Chicken-spouted ewer with dragon handle, Greenware. T'ang dynasty. Excavated from the Li Shuang tomb, Yang-t'ou-chen, Sian Municipality, Shensi.
height: 19.7 cm. (7.8 in.)

169. Four-handled jar, Greenware. T'ang dynasty. Excavated from a T'ang dynasty tomb at Yang-t'ou-shen, Sian Municipality, Shensi.
height: 30.0 cm. (11.8 in.)

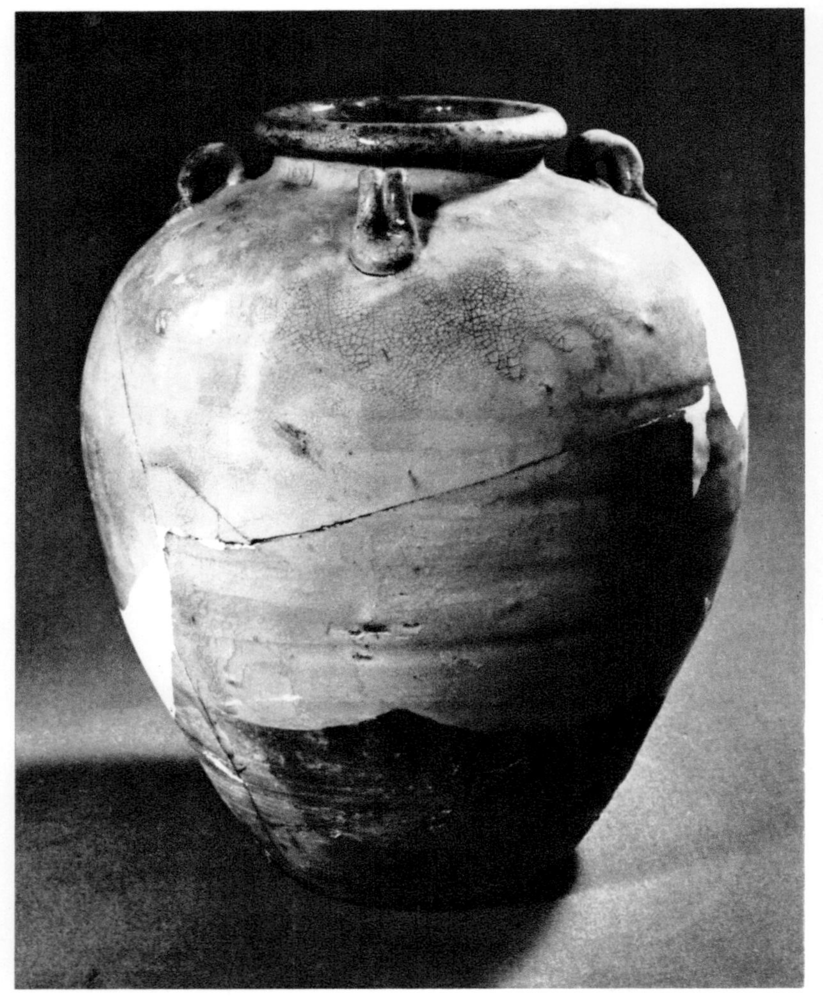

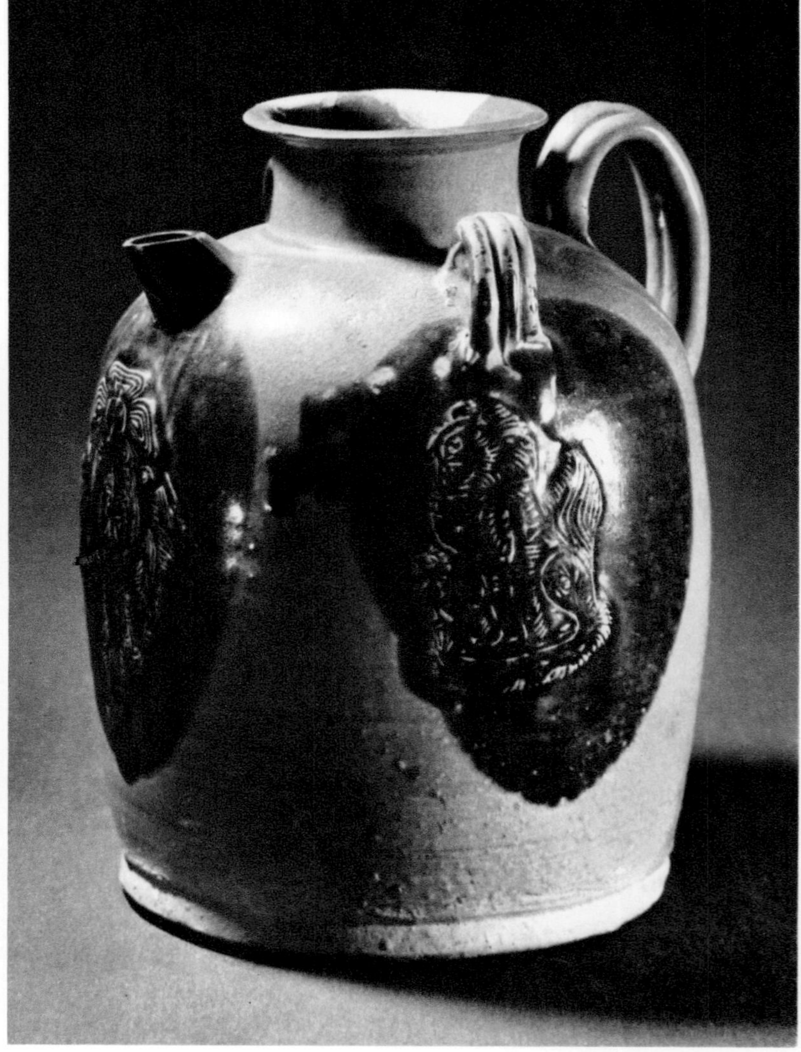

168. Spouted jar, pale-gray clay body with greenish-yellow glaze and dark-brown splashes. T'ang dynasty. Excavated from the site of the Wa-cha-p'ing kiln, Ch'ang-sha Municipality, Hunan.
height: 22.5 cm. (8.9 in.); diameter at lip: 8.0 cm. (3.15 in.)

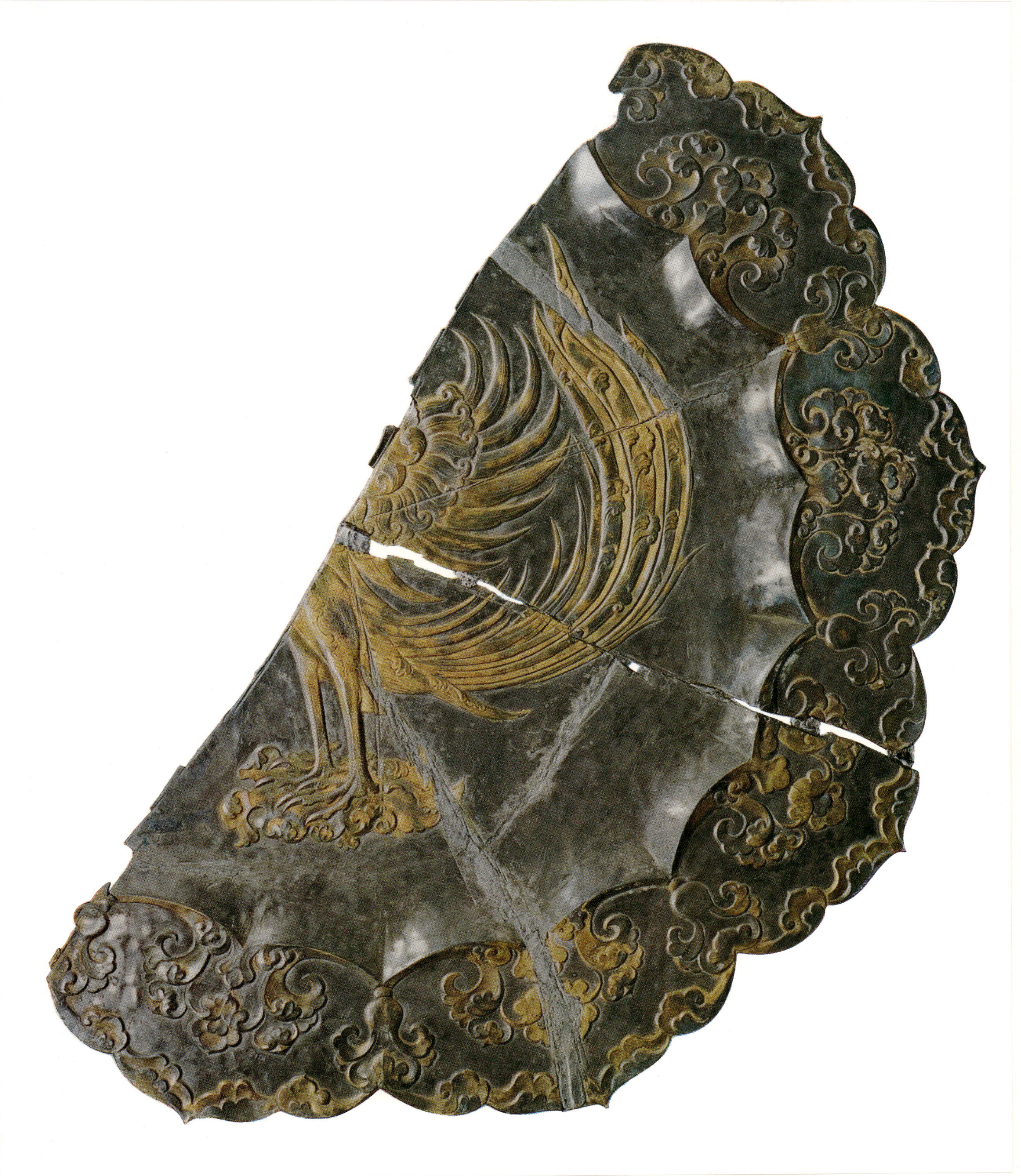

170. Plate fragment, silver and gilt. T'ang dynasty. Excavated west of Han-sen-chai, Sian Municipality, Shensi.
diameter: 84.0 cm. (33.0 in.)

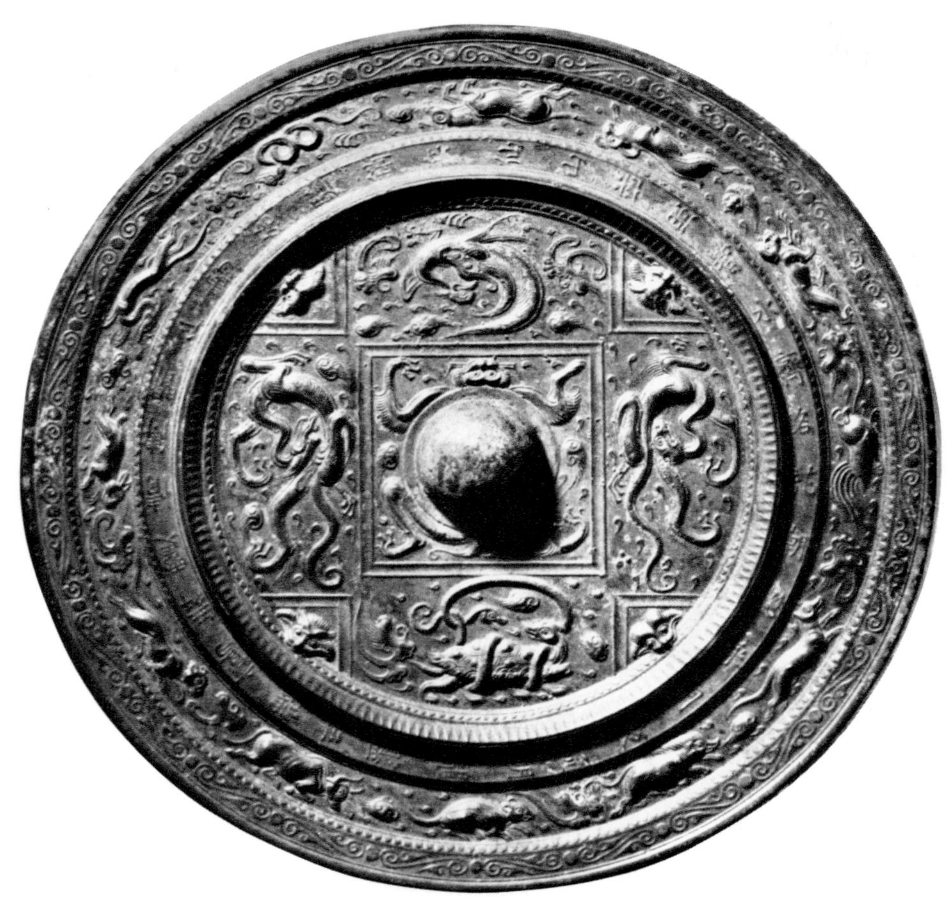

171. Mirror with animal decoration, bronze. T'ang dynasty. Excavated from a T'ang dynasty tomb at Ssu-mao-ch'ung, Ch'ang-sha Municipality, Hunan.
diameter: 22.0 cm. (8.7 in.)

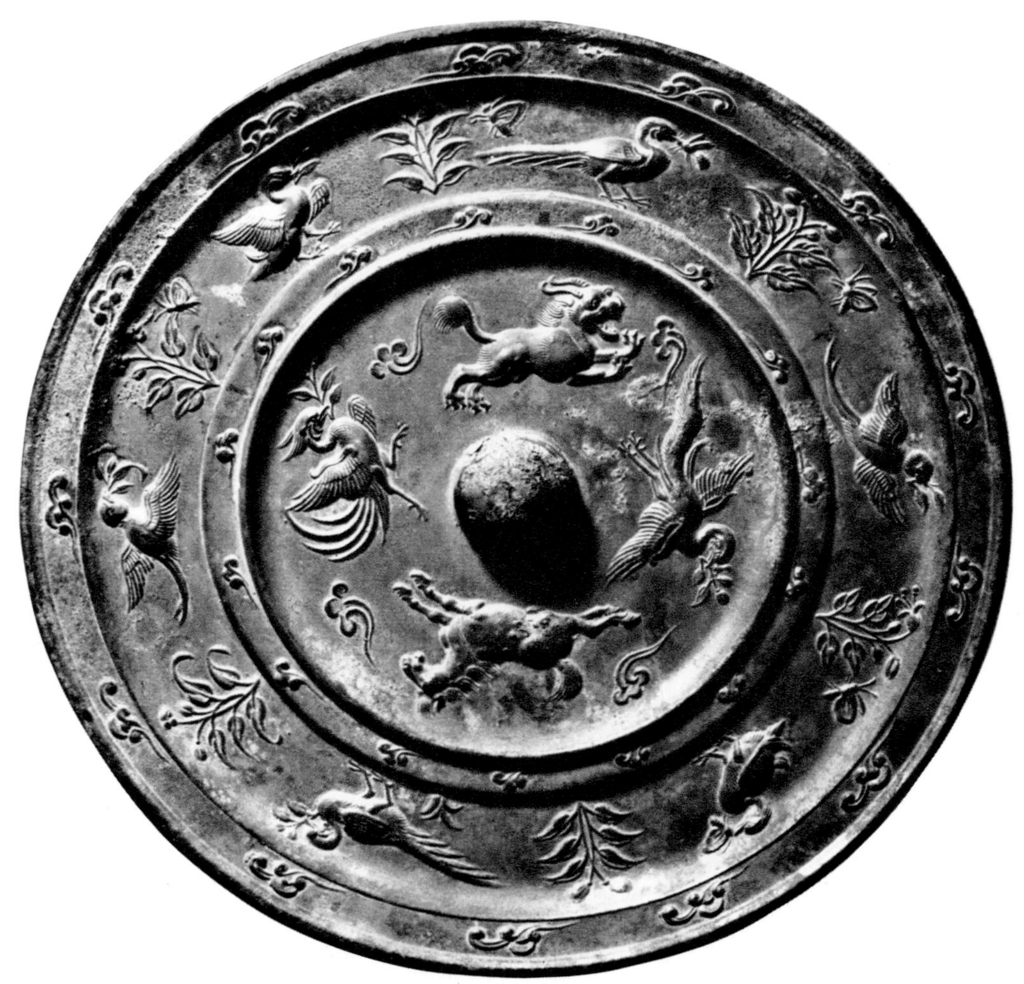

172. Mirror with animal, bird and flower decoration, bronze. T'ang dynasty. Excavated from a T'ang dynasty tomb at Han-sen-chai, eastern outskirts of Sian Municipality, Shensi.
diameter: 24.0 cm. (9.4 in.)

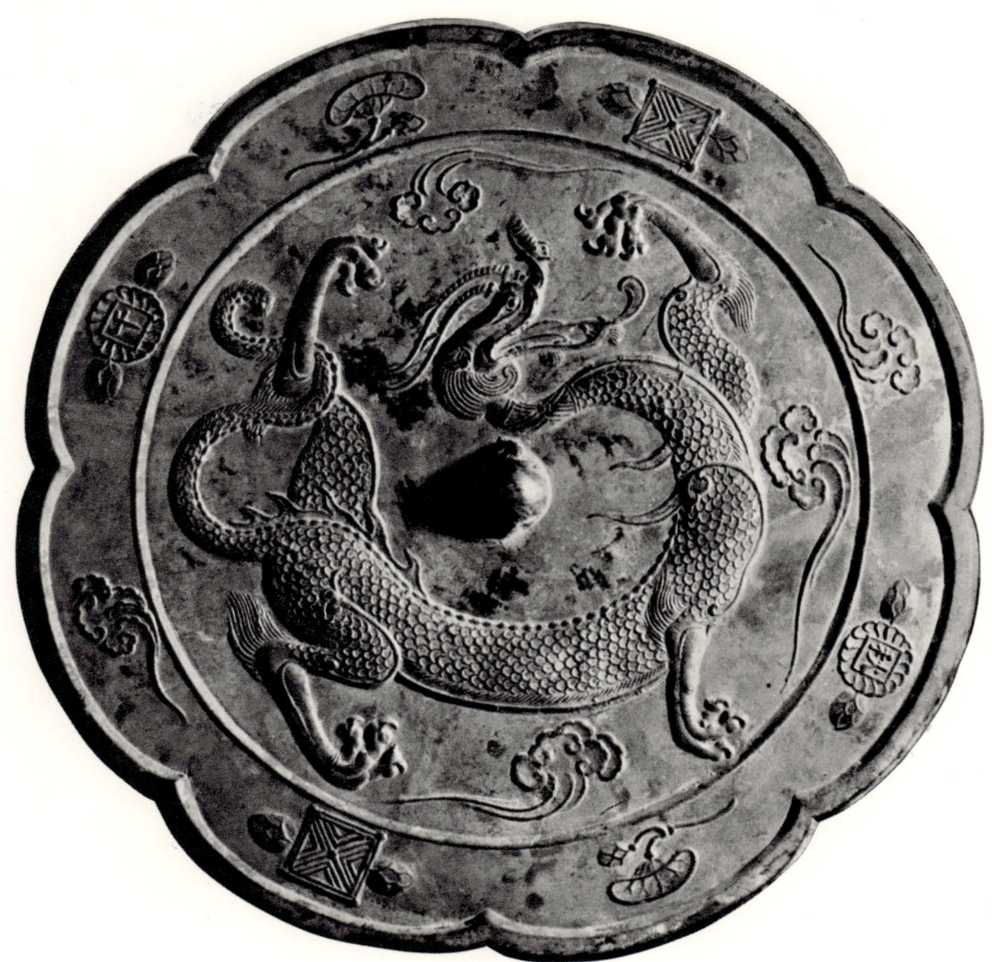

173. *Ch'ien-ch'iu* mirror, bronze. T'ang dynasty. Excavated from a T'ang dynasty tomb at Kuo-chia-t'an, eastern outskirts of Sian Municipality, Shensi.
diameter: 26.1 cm. (9.4 in.)

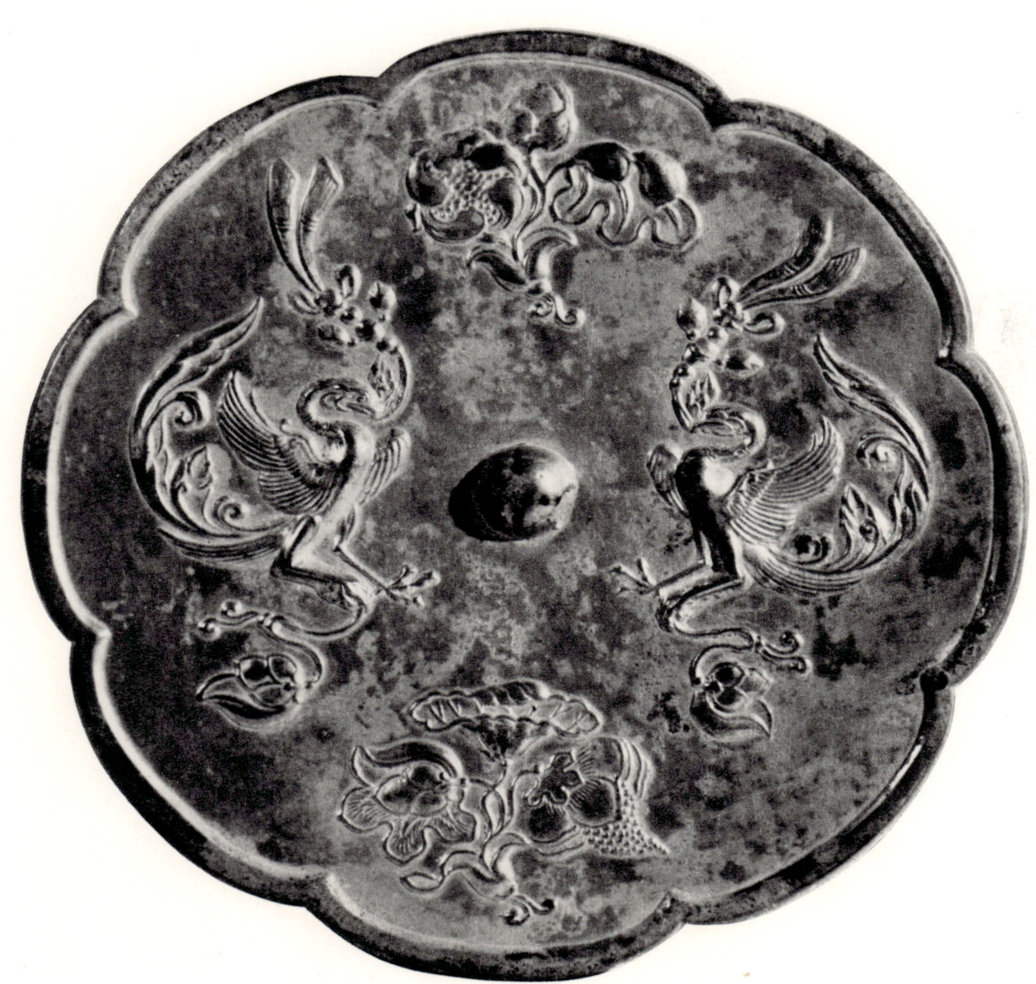

174. Mirror with bird and flower decoration, bronze. T'ang dynasty. Excavated from a T'ang dynasty tomb at Kao-lou-ts'un, eastern outskirts of Sian Municipality, Shensi.
diameter: 24.0 cm. (9.4 in.)

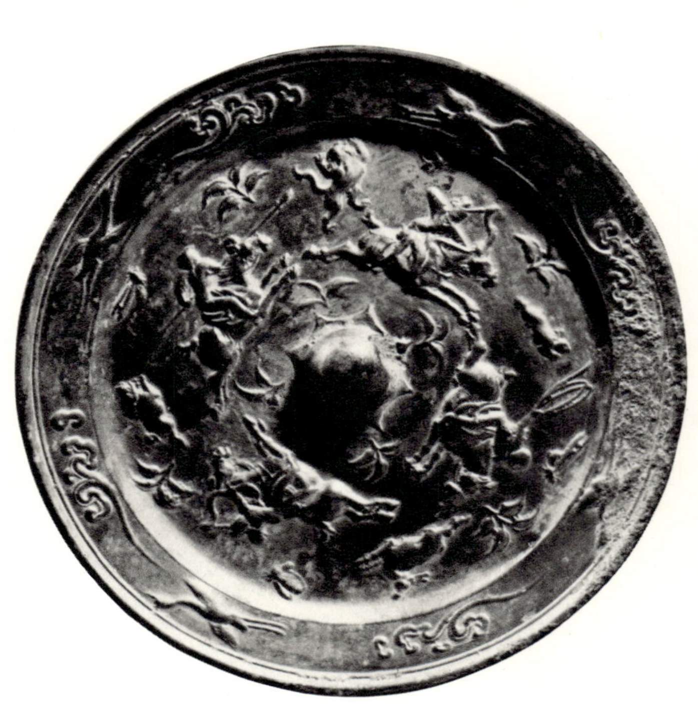

175. Mirror with hunting scene, bronze. T'ang dynasty. Excavated from a T'ang dynasty tomb at Wang-chia-fen, eastern outskirts of Sian Municipality, Shensi.
diameter: 15.0 cm. (5.9 in.)

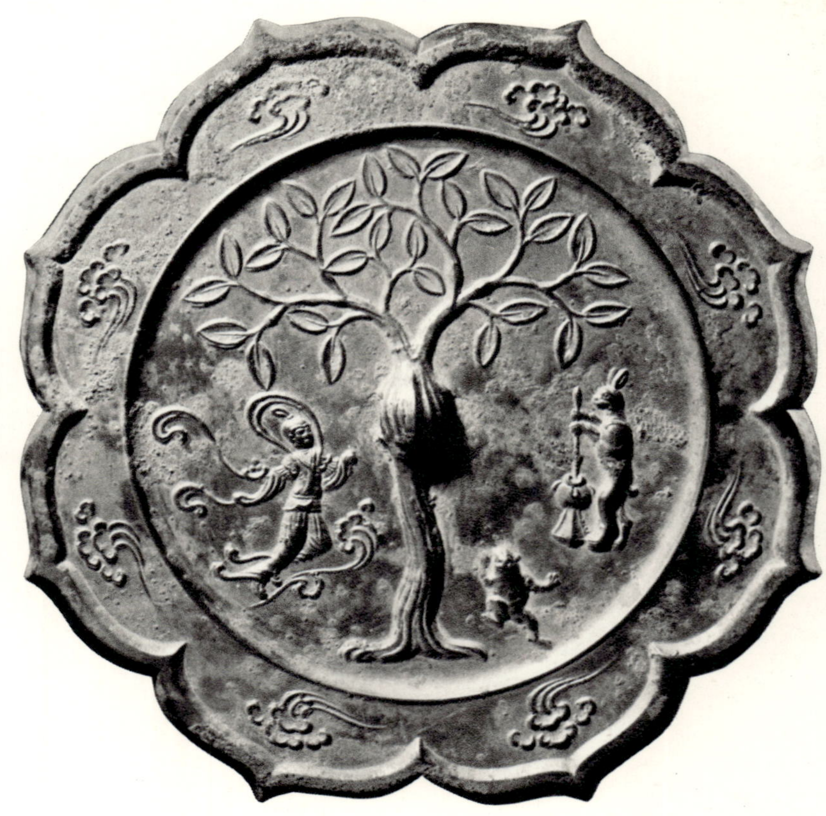

176. Eight-lobed mirror, bronze. T'ang dynasty. Excavated from a T'ang dynasty tomb at Sian Municipality, Shensi.
diameter: 21.0 cm. (8.3 in.)

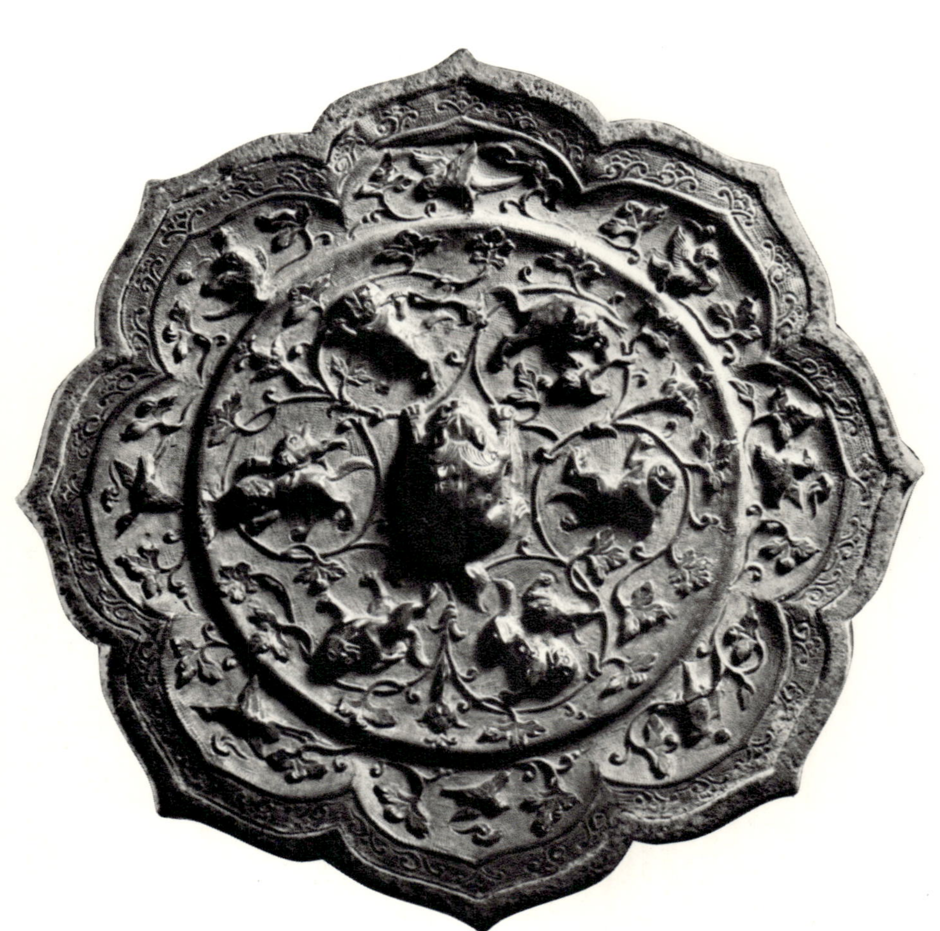

177. Eight-lobed mirror, silver plate on white bronze body. T'ang dynasty. Excavated from a T'ang dynasty tomb at Han-sen-chai, eastern outskirts of Sian Municipality, Shensi.
diameter: 21.0 cm. (8.3 in.)

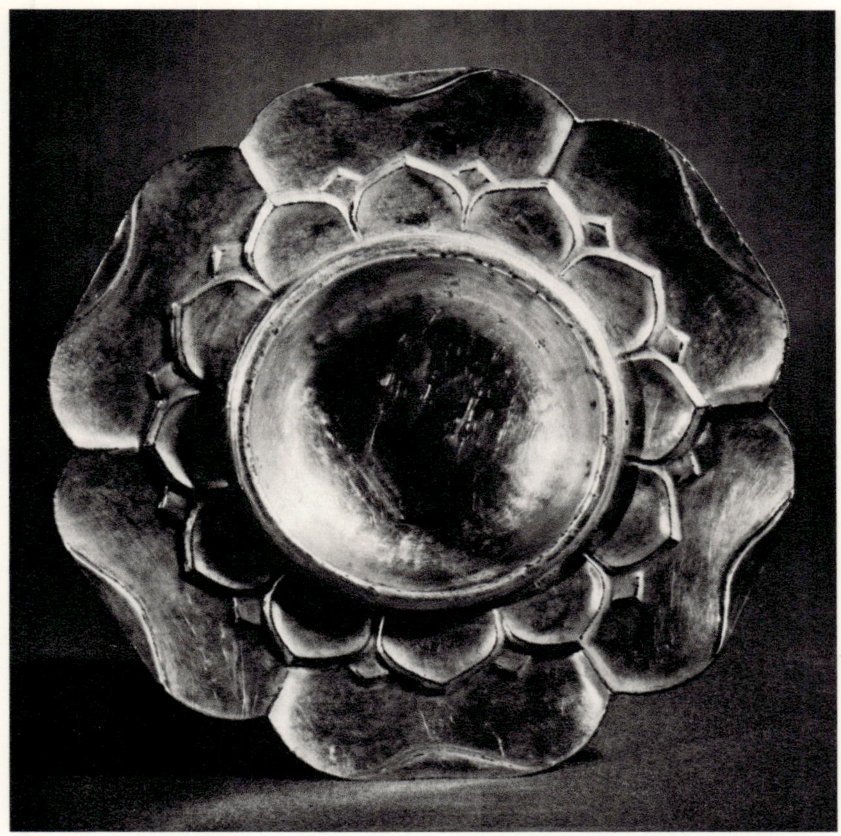

178–179. Six-lobed cup stand, silver and gilt. T'ang dynasty. Excavated at Ho-p'ing-men-wai, Sian Municipality, Shensi. *height: 4.5 cm. (1.77 in.)*

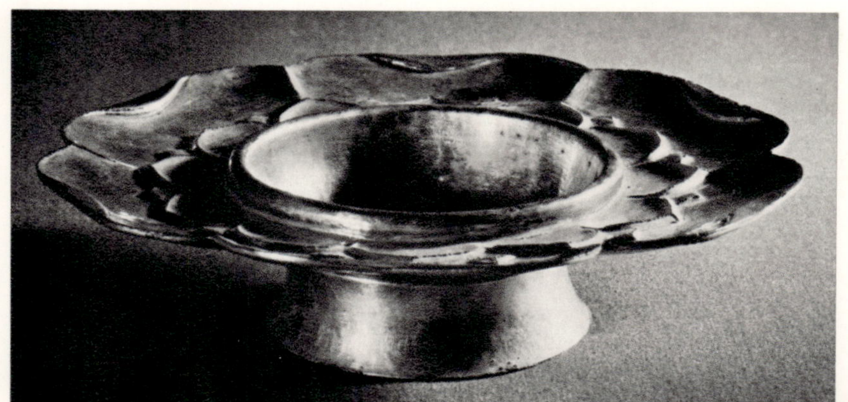

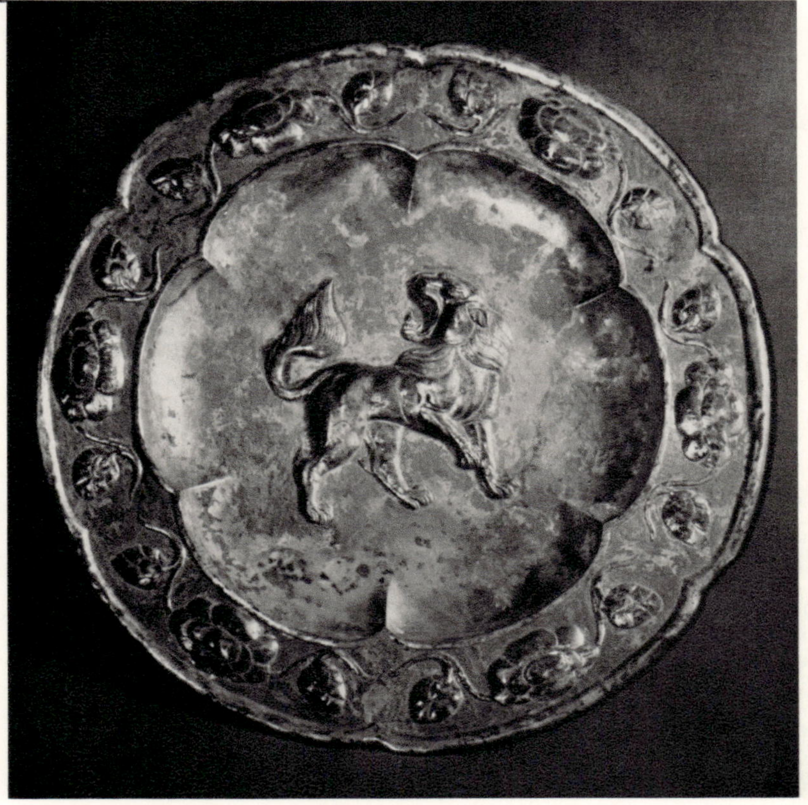

180. Six-lobed dish on three legs, silver and gilt. T'ang dynasty. Excavated at Pa-fu-chuang, northeastern outskirts of Sian Municipality, Shensi. *height: 9.0 cm. (3.54 in.); diameter: 34.8 cm. (13.7 in.)*

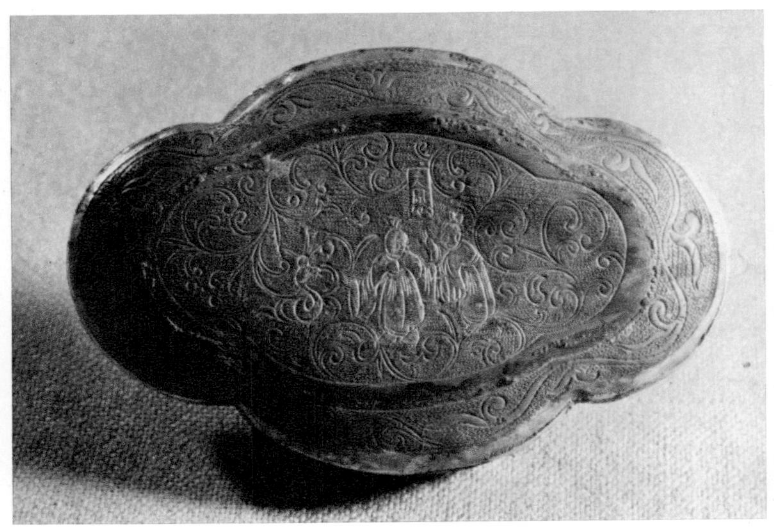

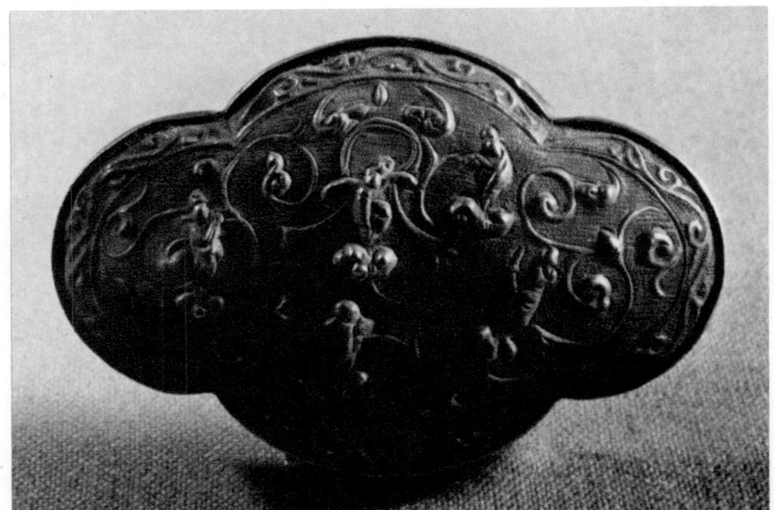

181–183. Covered box, silver and gilt. T'ang dynasty. Excavated at Hung-ch'ing-ts'un, southeast of Sian Municipality, Shensi.
height: 2.0 cm. (0.79 in.); length: 5.0 cm. (1.97 in.)

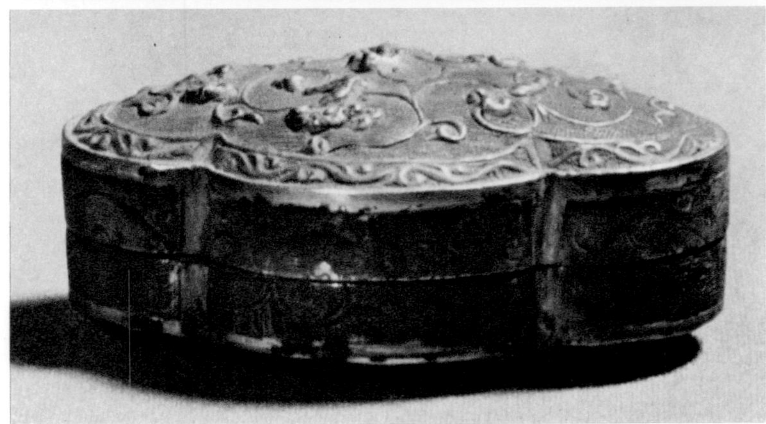

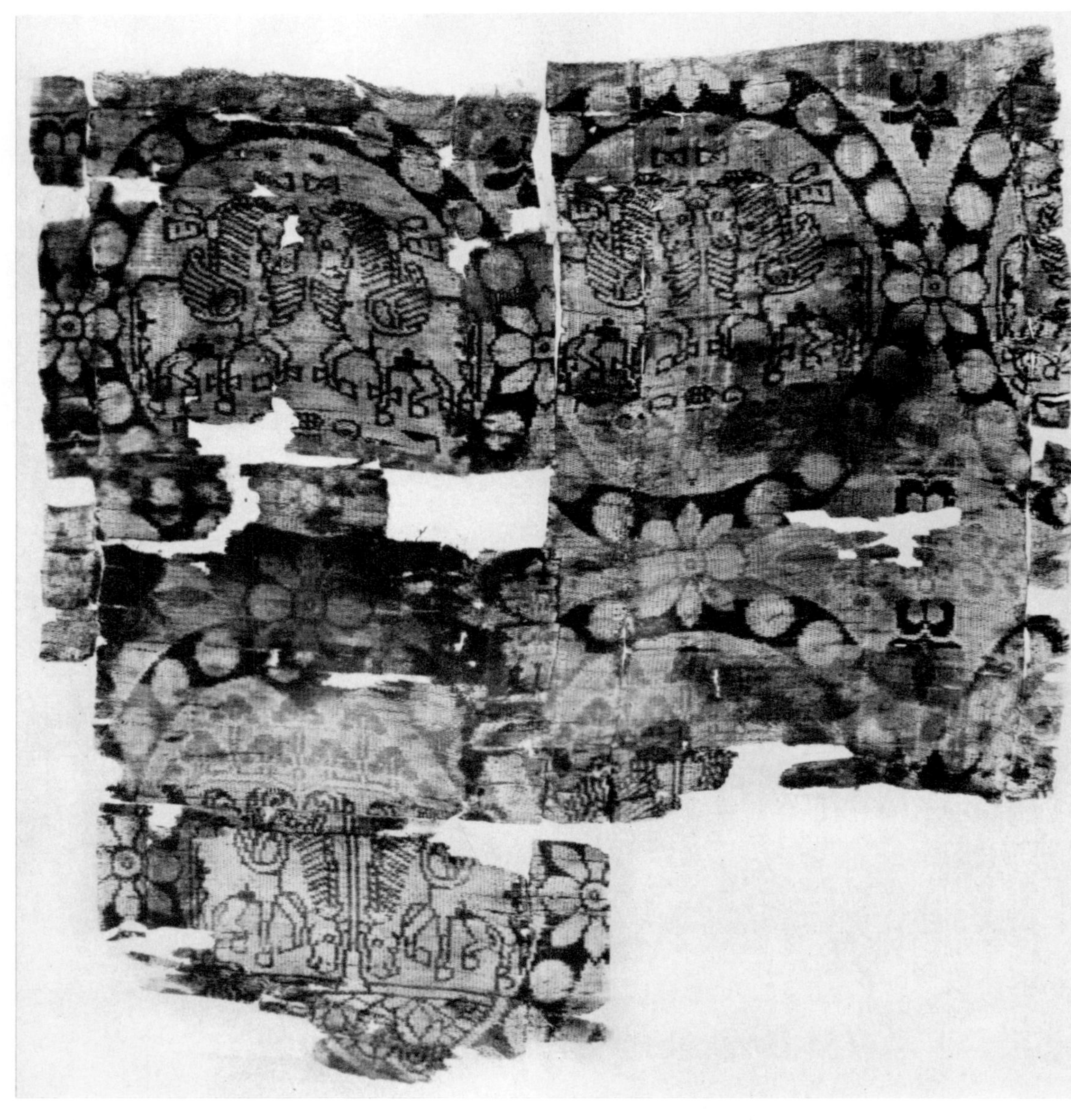

184. Brocade fragment, woven in blue, green and red on a yellowish-orange base. T'ang dynasty. Excavated from an Astana grave at Turfan, Uighur Autonomous Region, Sinkiang.

III. *Painting—The Embellishment of Tombs*

TOMB DECORATION By the beginning of the Ch'in dynasty, Chinese tombs were already elaborately constructed and beautifully decorated and furnished. The legendary Li-shan mausoleum, said to have been built by Shih Huang-ti before his death (209 B.C.), is well known. From the Han dynasty on, under the influence of Confucius' teaching of honor to ancestors, the custom of such lavish burial had become more widespread, so that elaborate tombs were constructed not only for emperors but also for aristocrats, lords and bureaucratic officials. Remains of such Han burials have been found in many parts of Asia.

These tombs are indeed underground treasuries, because it is in these burials that the arts of these ancient times have been most effectively preserved. This is especially true of painting, for a great wealth of pictorial decoration of all sorts is to be found here. The lacquer and earthenware are decorated with an infinite variety of painted designs, and many of the interior stone or brick chambers are decorated with beautiful wall paintings. The stone walls of some are engraved with figures in low relief, while the brick walls have been decorated with impressed scenes, both of which lend a richness to studies of pictorial expression of the Han dynasty.

PAINTED OBJECTS The discovery of many lacquer-painted objects at the provincial Han dynasty site of Lo-lang in Korea opened the eyes of the world to the beauty of Han dynasty lacquer painting. The famous woven-bamboo, lacquered box found at this site shows some of the finest painting known of this period. However, comparison with the many examples found recently at Ch'ang-sha (Pls. 90, 187) shows that the works of the Ch'u state (one of the Warring States in southern China), though lacking some of the exactness of the later, northern Han pieces, have a greater movement and a basic concern with spatial relationship.

Painting on earthenware (Pls. 113, 114) is carried out in slip colors over a white slip engobe, the whole design often being strengthened by a black line. Designs commonly appear on burial jars used as vessels for grain, where, besides the various traditional decorative motifs, the symbolic animals of the four directions (dragon, tiger, phoenix, tortoise) appear. The painting of even such humble wares shows the vivacity and mastery of line of this period. A further instance of painting on ceramics is the figure scenes on the miniature tower found at Hsing-yang District, Honan, in 1958 (Pls. 188, 246). Here a servant kneels before his master and, in the lower register, a man and a woman are seen dancing. These figures are expressed very simply and directly, but with great individuality in action and expression.

BRICK TOMBS A finer quality of the same technique is shown on the painted bricks. These cannot be called wall painting in the accepted sense—in which the whole wall surface is treated as a decorative unit—for here only parts of the tomb structure are embellished with painting on the bricks. The shape and pictorial composition of the decorated bricks was determined by their location in the tomb: rectangular bricks are found on lintels and beams, while gables have a triangular shape. These painted bricks seem to have developed in the Former Han period. The best-known examples in the West are the figure-painted bricks found at Pa-li-t'ai, Lo-yang, which are now in the collection of the Boston Museum of Fine Arts. But at the time of the construction work on the new city of Lo-yang, many Han dynasty tombs with beautiful painted bricks were excavated, and two large tombs have been removed in Wang-ch'eng Park in Lo-yang and reconstructed there. The paintings in one of these tombs comprise a series of figures, perhaps relating the main events of the deceased's life, on the lintel of a doorway between the inner and outer chambers and also on the upper part of the inner chamber.[1] When seen in 1960, they still retained their vivid and clear colors. The bright color tone and the light and soft touch of the brush are the most impressive features of the paintings. These bright colors (especially the pale purple, green and rose) are also found commonly on the slip-painted earthenware of the period and clearly typify one aspect of Han painting that has not been fully recognized to date.

HAN TOMB PAINTING Mural painting in the usual sense, in which scenes are painted over a wall surface, are found in many tombs over a wide area far from the capital of the period. Notable among the Han tombs are those at Ying-ch'eng-tzu and Liao-yang District (Pls. 205–207), Liaoning; Wang-tu District, Hopei (Pl. 211); Liang-shan District, Shantung (Pl. 203) and Tun-k'o-tun, Inner Mongolia. Of these, the wall painting at tomb No. 2, Ying-ch'eng-tzu, shows primitive but strong, freely drawn figures. Those at Wang-tu perhaps are more precisely drawn, but are full of expression. The colors at Wang-tu, which are shaded, are used boldly and somewhat heavily, filling in the line drawing.

In general, the painting of the Han period, on whatever medium, is still archaic. Figures appear almost exclusively in side view, and spatial relationships in depth are still expressed diagrammatically, the nearer objects being lower. There is as yet little compositional unity of the picture space, the elements of which are placed haphazardly on the wall surface. However, the sophistication of brush technique and considerable subtlety in the interpretation of movement and expression is already striking. The portraits and legendary scenes were important expressions of the Confucian ideals espoused at the time. Genre scenes (processional scenes and pictures of acrobats and entertainers) were also in fashion and most vividly show the artistic temperament of the time.

Apart from painting, much stone relief carving has been found on tomb chambers and on small stone temples and gateways of this period. The most famous are those at Hsiao-t'ang-shan (first century A.D.) and the Wu family shrine (second century A.D.), both in Shantung. The Hsiao-t'ang-shan carvings are engraved in line relief, while the Wu shrine scenes of legendary and historical stories are carried out in a very flat relief. Although powerfully composed, the individual forms are hard, and here again the spatial relationships are expressed diagrammatically. An interesting example was found in the third-century stone tomb at Yi-nan, also in Shantung, in which fine detail lines are incised both on the wall surface and on the flat, excised figures, adding vivid movement to the composition. The molded bricks found in Szuchwan show a fluid line and a developed spatial expression characterizing the advanced artistic sense in the area of the Shu state of the Minor Han period (221–263 A.D.).

SIX DYNASTIES TOMB PAINTING The fact that the art of painting developed quickly, both technically and aesthetically, during the Wei, Chin and Northern and Southern Dynasties periods is clear not only from the objects of the time, but also from a study of the literature. The names of artists are first recorded in this period, and books were written discussing theories of aesthetics and problems of technique. The best-known artists of this period are Ku K'ai-chih, the literati painter of Eastern Chin, and the two professional painters, Chang Seng-yao of Liang, and Lu T'an-wei of the Liu-Sung state. The literature discussing the art of the time (fourth through sixth centuries) reflects the gradual systemization of Chinese aesthetics.

The study materials confirming the development of painting in this period are divided into two types: silk scroll paintings such as the famous "Admonitions" handscroll of Ku K'ai-chih (known today only from the T'ang dynasty copy), and excavated tomb paintings and materials. These tomb paintings were first brought into prominence by the Korean Koguryŏ state wall paintings. The earliest Koguryŏ paintings are found in fourth- and fifth-century tombs at Chi-an District, on the northern bank of the Ya-lu River (for example, the Wrestlers Tomb and the Dancers Tomb), showing a vivid use of strong color and expressive movement. In tombs of later periods (500–650 A.D.) near Pyongyang, the paintings show a striking refinement, sophistication and development. In the Northern and Southern Dynasties tombs discovered in the central area of China since 1949, no large tomb wall paintings such as occur in the Koguryŏ tombs have yet been found. Two tombs are specially noteworthy. First, the fifth-century tomb excavated at Teng District, Honan (Pls. 189, 190, 204, 214–216), which has paintings of warriors and flying figures at either side of the gate and painted relief bricks in the inner chambers. These examples of varied legendary and historical subjects represent the advanced techniques of the metropolitan area. The two large brick walls found near Nanking (Pl. 217) show a relief of eight men among trees, including the "Seven Worthies of the Bamboo Grove." The figures of these men typify the technique and style of figure drawing of the Southern Dynasties; the line is sinuous and the forms slender, where the northern artists used a crisp and formalized idiom. The large number of wall paintings of the same period found in such Buddhist cave temples as Mai-chi-shan and Tun-huang are well known and will be discussed in Volume II of this series.

T'ANG TOMB PAINTING The changes in painting that took place during the Sui and early T'ang periods were of the utmost importance in the traditions of Chinese painting as a whole. It is in T'ang painting that the classical style of Far Eastern painting is first realized. Before 1949, we had been able to assess the development of T'ang painting only from the wall paintings of cave temples in outlying districts, from paintings on textiles (usually silk) and paper unearthed at Central Asian sites, and from the treasures in the Shōsōin in Japan. But, since 1949, many T'ang dynasty tombs have been discovered within the boundaries of the two ancient dynasty capital cities of Sian (Ch'ang-an) and T'ai-yüan. The wall paintings of the Sian area, which are listed in the Table (p. 108), were executed from the mid-seventh to the ninth century, and show the course of T'ang dynasty painting. Especially, the Sian paintings of the later half of the seventh and beginning of the eighth century are of the highest quality and clearly display the rapid developments in painting.

The first entry in the Table on page 108 is the 658 A.D. tomb of Chih-shih Feng-chieh. Here the fluent painting of a dancing girl shows a strong influence of Northern and Southern Dynasties style with its movement expressed in soft flowing lines. The Li Shuang tomb, built some ten years later, has many figure paintings (Pls. 192, 193, 226) with a spontaneous style, a rich ink stroke and a simple, light treatment. Most of the figures are filled in with a red pigment, though the beginnings of polychrome treatment can be seen in the green sleeves of the figure in Plate 192.

About half a century later are the three important tombs of the Princess Yung-t'ai (700 A.D.) (frontispiece, Pls. 191, 230), Wei Chiung (708 A.D.) (Pls. 219–225), and the Lady Hsüeh (701 A.D.) (Pls. 197, 228). The differences of quality of the paintings in these tombs reflect the social statuses of the persons buried and the consequent quality of the artists employed rather than the relative dates of working. It is evident from the thoughtful and often sensitive overpainting on a preliminary drawing and the much wider range and splendor of color that much care was taken by the artists working on the Princess' tomb. With these paintings we can imagine the brightness of the court life of the time. The paintings of this tomb seem to have been done by a master artist of the period. In contrast, the almost perfunctory painting in ink on a roughly prepared wall of the Lady Hsüeh tomb is perhaps more typical of tomb painting in its simplicity of color and treatment. However, a growing sureness of drawing shows even through this relative crudity. The figures of the Wei Chiung tomb, also in this free style, have perhaps greater refinement and are more elaborately expressed.

In the Su Ssu-hsü tomb (745 A.D.) (Pls. 194–196), a certain decadance has begun to be apparent: the painting of the male dancer and musicians on the east wall of the tomb chamber is poorly drawn, but has some complexity of composition. Considering the quality of the painting recorded in T'ang documents, such as wall paintings in the temples of Ch'ang-an by such master artists as Wu Tao-hsüan at this period, it seems clear that wall painting in tombs belongs to a different stratum of art: the materials and care taken were different, as were the kind of artists. There is a readily appreciable difference between decoration made for a subterranean chamber, which would not be seen more than once, and that for a sumptuous city temple visited frequently by fashionable worshipers. The tomb paintings are probably representative of the common level of painting of the time. The Princess Yung-t'ai tomb is perhaps the one exception that shows some of the great painting of T'ang times, and it is for this reason that it is of great importance.

TERUKAZU AKIYAMA

1. 洛陽西漢墓壁画, 文物精華, 1964, No. III. This important Han tomb has been reported only in this article, complete with color plates and diagrams.

Table of Tombs with Wall Paintings in the Sian Area

TOMB	LOCATION	BURIAL DATE	EXCAVATION DATE
Chih-shih Feng-chieh	No. 1, Kuo-tu-chen, Sian	658 A.D.	1957
Li Shuang	No. 1, Yang-t'ou-chen, Sian	668 A.D.	1956
Princess Yung-t'ai	Liang-shan-lu, Ch'ien District, Sian	706 A.D.	1960
Wei Chiung	No. 1, Nan-li-wang-ts'un, Sian	708 A.D.	1959
Lady Hsüeh	No. 4, Ti-chang-wan, Hsien-yang	710 A.D.	1953
Feng Fan-chou	No. 2, Erh-chi-fu, Hsi-kao	729 A.D.	1954
Su Ssu-hsü	No. 59 M-1, Ching-wu-lu, eastern outskirts of Sian	745 A.D.	1952
Chang Ch'ü-she	No. 33, Ti-chang-wan, Hsien-yang	747 A.D.	1953
Kao Yüan-kuei	No. 5, Yi-chi-fu, Hsi-kao	756 A.D.	1955
Kao K'o-ts'ung	No. 1, site 803, Hsi-kao	847 A.D.	1954

IV. Monumental Animal Sculpture

❀ To decorate and make the exterior of tombs as imposing as possible has been a custom common to both East and West in all ages. However, in China it took a special form during the Han and succeeding periods. From this time it became the custom to set up stone pillars, tables and gates to the tomb and to place imposing stone carvings of human beings and animals on either side of the path leading to it. In many cases these were of a splendor to match the brilliance of the interiors of the tombs: massive pieces of rock carved in the hope of achieving physical permanence.

This monumental sculpture, which flourished from Han into T'ang times, has a threefold significance in the history of Chinese art. In the first place, the tomb sculpture of the Han period is the first genuine sculpture found in China. Secondly, the stone animals of the Southern Dynasties show the style of the Chiang-nan region at its most typical. Thirdly, tomb sculpture provides an unbroken picture of the Chinese sculptural tradition from Han to T'ang. In this section, discussion is confined to the animal carvings found among the tomb sculpture of each succeeding period.

❀ STONE ANIMALS OF THE HAN PERIOD The stone animals set before the tomb of Huo Ch'ü-ping, erected in the Former Han period, are early examples of the tomb sculpture of the Han dynasty. These are carved in granite and include horses, cows and pigs. Details, including the facial features, are not particularly skillfully expressed, but the whole effect makes good use of the massiveness inherent in the material. Outstanding among the carvings is the stone horse standing quietly over a fallen warrior, one of the northern barbarians defeated by Huo Ch'ü-ping (Pl. 237). This piece has been famous since early T'ang times and now stands in the Shensi Museum. A rectangular block with no sense of movement and carved in a manner resembling bas-relief, the work relies for effect solely on the material itself. Yet the very size (188 cm. tall) makes it a fittingly impressive and imposing adornment for the tomb of a general who played a part in Wu-ti's subjugation of the Hsiung-nu.

In contrast to the much more human qualities of the *ming-ch'i* found within the tombs, with their associations of affection for the departed, the stone figures placed before the tombs are relatively intellectual and severe. The need to make them as imposing as possible demanded two of the essential attributes of sculpture: size and volume. As a result the tomb carvings of the Han period represent the first true sculpture in China. It is distinct from the carvings of the Yin, Chou and Warring States periods, when there was no clear distinction between sculpture and applied art.

In general style and in the satisfying solidity one can detect certain elements in common with the Warring States bronze horse found at Chin-ts'un, Honan. This is an indication that this first "true" sculpture was by no means a completely unheralded manifestation of the Han period. Nevertheless, the appearance of large-scale, carved stone figures is an epoch-making event in the history of Chinese art, and one cannot dismiss lightly the theories of those who see in the introduction of such animal sculpture an influence from the culture of the West.

Apart from this work at the tomb of Huo Ch'ü-ping, not a single specimen of Former Han tomb sculpture is known. However, it is recorded that stone horses were also set up in front of the tomb of Kuang

Wu-ti, the first emperor of Later Han. Although these do not survive, one can thus assume that the tradition of making horse sculptures was carried through to the Later Han period. Other animal sculptures from the Later Han known today include a pair of stone lions at the ancestral shrine of the Wu family at Chia-hsiang District, Shantung; a *t'ien-lu* and *pi-hsieh* at the tomb of Sung Tzu in Nan-yang District, Honan; and a pair of stone lions at the tomb of Kao Yi at Ya-an District, Szuchwan.

The stone animals were made in pairs so that they could be arranged in an orderly right-left symmetry on either side of the path leading to the tomb. In this respect they are quite different from the stone animals of the Huo Ch'ü-ping tomb, which were erected simply to mark the existence of the tomb and were arranged with no relationship to each other. This kind of change probably marks the establishment of a recognized form for tomb sculpture. The sculpture itself, as is evident from the stone lions at the Wu family shrine (147 A.D.), has become considerably more realistic compared with the somewhat symbolic treatment of the Huo Ch'ü-ping carvings.

The stone lions at the Wu shrine are particularly valuable in that the name of the sculptor is known—Sun Tsung. The massive bodies show the S-curve that characterizes the stone animals of Later Han. There is, however, a greater sense of power, and the wings, which rather surprisingly spring from the shoulders of the lions, are a sign of influences from the art of western Asia during this period. During the period from Han to T'ang, tomb sculpture is characterized by the frequent occurrence of imaginary beasts. Thus the figures at the Sung Tzu tomb (*ca.* 167 A.D.) at Nan-yang referred to above are of the kinds known as *t'ien-lu* and *pi-hsieh*. It was probably believed that such menacing figures enhanced the dignity of the tomb and served to glorify the memory of the deceased.

The closing years of the Han dynasty have left us, among other works, the stone lions at the tomb of Kao Yi, Prefect of Yi-chou, Szuchwan (see above). These date from about 209 A.D. and despite the undoubted excellences of detail, when considered as a whole they show a tendency toward formalization and a two-dimensional quality compared to the Wu shrine lions. The treatment of the wing feathers, for example, shows a mere perfunctory orderliness. However, in the resilient S-curve of the bodies, the vigorous forward thrust of the chests, and the relaxed, widespread stance, these lions have a genuine dignity and nobility.

The changes undergone by Han animal sculpture between about 117 B.C., when the Huo Ch'ü-ping horse was made, and around 209 A.D., the date of the Kao Yi tomb, mark an obvious progress. One should of course also take into account the possibility that the assurance and nobility of the Kao Yi tomb figures may be local attributes of the art of the Szuchwan area. The constant characteristics of the Han period animal sculpture could be summed up as being those of simplicity and majesty. These characteristics cover both the Huo Ch'ü-ping horse, with its completely static treatment, and the stone animals of Later Han with their proud stance, head high and chest thrust out. Both possess in full measure the imposing quality necessary to monuments of this kind, and in both the carving of the stone qualifies them as genuine works of sculpture. The carving is indeed far more advanced than that of the stone human figures that are another feature of tomb sculpture of the same period.

The surviving stone human figures of the Han period include a pair at the Chung-yueh-miao shrine on Mt. Ch'ung-shan, Teng-feng District, Honan, and two figures at the tomb of Lu Wang at Chüeh-hsiang-pu, Ch'u-fu District, Shantung. These are rudimentary in the extreme, being little better than carved pillars, with even the facial features only vaguely indicated. This is typical of the greater skill in the representation of birds and animals rather than of human beings shown in much art of the Han dynasty, which characteristic is but a continuation of the progress made in animal sculpture in the period of the Warring States.

The custom of placing stone carvings before tombs was continued through Three Kingdoms and Chin times, good examples being the lions at T'ung-ch'iao-t'ai, Ts'ao-wei. Also significant is a stone horse, dating from the Hsia state (407–431 A.D.) of the Five Barbarians and Sixteen Kingdoms period (304–439 A.D.). This work, found at Ch'a-chia-chai, Ch'ang-an, was installed at Shensi Museum in 1954. It is 200 centimeters high and 225 centimeters long and is important for its inscription (大夏真興六年) (424 A.D.), which serves as a basis for dating other stone animal sculpture. Moreover, the strong resemblance, despite the great gap in time, between this fifth-century work and the Huo Ch'ü-ping tomb stone horse, though undoubtedly due partly to a local cultural survival, serves to prove the persistence of Han culture even into the Five Barbarians period.

STONE ANIMALS OF THE SOUTHERN DYNASTIES When the Three Kingdoms and Chin gave way to the Northern and Southern Dynasties, it was the stonemasons of the Southern Dynasties, moving to the Chiang-nan region, who carried on and further developed the Han tradition. Possibly because tomb sculpture of this type was a cultural feature peculiar to the Han people, it seems to have more or less died out in the territories controlled by the non-Han Northern Dynasties, despite the strong trend toward assimilation of Han culture in other fields.

In the Southern Dynasties (in the Liu-Sung, Ch'i, Liang and Ch'en states; 420–589 A.D.), stone animals, pillars and gates were erected before the tombs of emperors and of the aristocracy. Examples include the Ch'ü-ning *ling* of Sung Wu-ti, the Yung-an *ling* of Ch'i Hsüan-ti, the Ching-an *ling* of Ch'i Wu-ti, the Hsiu-an *ling* of Ch'i Ching-ti, the Hsing-an *ling* of Ch'i Ming-ti, the Hsiu *ling* of Liang Wu-ti, the tomb of Liang Hsiao-hsiu and that of Liang Hsiao-chi, and the Wan-an *ling* of Ch'en Wu-ti. In the course of this period, stone animal sculpture underwent a number of stylistic changes that gradually created a definite style peculiar to the Southern Dynasties.

Stone animals were so popular for the tombs of the Southern Dynasties that it is to be expected that more will be excavated in the future. Unfortunately, many sculptures have remained underground because the exact sites of the tombs are not known; however, investigations by the Chinese government in 1956 alone resulted in the discovery of nineteen sites in the Nanking area and ten in that of Tan-yang. For example, the site of the Yung-ning tomb of Wen-ti of Ch'en was discovered to be at a place called Shin-tzu-ch'ung, northeast of Tzu-chin-shan outside the Ch'i-lin gate, Nanking, and here a *pi-hsieh* was unearthed. A *t'ien-lu* was found at the Ch'ü-ning tomb of Wu-ti of the Liu-Sung state in the Ch'i-lin-pu of Nanking. The most worthwhile find of all however, was of the stone animals unearthed in 1956 from the Hsiao-hung tomb of the Liang dynasty between the Ch'i-lin gate and the Hsieh-ho gate, Nanking. (Pl. 239). These are extremely well preserved, and in their majesty and power and the rhythm of their poses are at least the equal of other Southern Dynasties stone beasts already known.

Apart from these, stone figures of the Liao period that have long been particularly famous are the lions at the tomb of Hsiao-hsiu near the Yao-hua gate, Nanking (*ca.* 518 A.D.). They are characterized by their overall massiveness and their outthrust chests, while details such as the sharply curved lines of the manes show a great delicacy and refinement of workmanship. Both the Hsiao-hung and Hsiao-hsiu tombs constitute genuine sculpture in the sense that they are carved in the round; in this they afford a clear contrast with, for example, the stone animals of the Southern Ch'i, and are a sign that the stone animal carvings of the Southern Dynasties had come to maturity.

Features common to all the Southern Dynasties stone animals are their massiveness and a clear-cut quality, shown in the incisive treatment of the wing feathers. This achieves a combination of majesty and grace. These creatures with their proudly raised heads, open mouths and swelling chests clearly carry on the tradition of the stone animals of the Han period, yet some of them, such as those of the Liang period, combine a far greater massiveness than the Han work with a lightness and freshness that is just the reverse of their somewhat stolid Han counterparts. Where Han sculptors preferred unity of style and tended to be bound by considerations of form, these later works give an impression of spontaneity and cheerfulness; the same is true when they are compared with Northern Dynasties animal sculpture as typified by the lions in the cave-temples at Lung-men. Only a truly remarkable technique could have enabled the stonemasons of the Southern Dynasties to breathe such noble artistic life into such massive boulders of rock.

One can gain almost no idea of the sculptural style of the Southern Dynasties from its Buddhist sculpture, since all we possess of the latter are a few stone Buddhas with Southern Dynasties inscriptions unearthed in the Szuchwan region. Thus it is to the figures of the Chiang-nan area centering on Nanking that we must turn for our knowledge of the Southern Dynasties style. Today this animal sculpture is playing a very significant role, in the absence of specimens of Buddhist sculpture, in proving just how greatly the Southern Dynasties style differed from that of the Northern Dynasties. In this sense it is a very important field of study in relation to the history of Chinese sculpture as a whole.

STONE ANIMALS OF THE T'ANG DYNASTY With the T'ang period, tomb sculpture became still more popular. The earliest specimens extant are a pair of stone tigers before the tomb of the Emperor Kao-tsu built at the beginning of the Chen Kuan reign of the Emperor T'ai-tsung (627–650 A.D.) (Pl. 240). These animals are full of power; they stand with all four feet planted on the ground, and there is a fine balance between the head and the trunk. Unlike the imaginary beasts of the Han and the Southern Dynasties periods, they are close to real tigers and the style is extremely realistic. In this, they mark a clear new point of departure for tomb sculpture, contrasting strongly as they do with the earlier fondness, especially in the Han dynasty, for imaginary beasts carved in a relatively symbolic style.

The next work that should be mentioned here, though different from other sculpture, is a work of the mid-seventh century—the reliefs known as the "Six Swift Horses" that were originally at the tomb of T'ai-tsung at Li-ch'üan District, Shensi (Pl. 241). These representations of favorite horses of the Emperor T'ai-tsung were carved on six stone blocks and set up within the gateway of the tomb; they are closer to carving in the round than relief work. The treatment of the resilient curves of the horses' backs and bellies is particularly skillful, and the arrangement of the horses in space is very effective. Here realism is carried still further than in the Kao-tsu tigers.

As scarcely needs pointing out, the superb new realism found in these stone carvings of T'ang is part of the new realism that affected all art in early T'ang times. They are, in a sense, the best indicators of the course taken by this new realism in sculpture, since Buddhist sculpture in early T'ang was less affected by the new trend, doubtless because it was not a dominant current of sculpture at this time.

At the height of the T'ang period, in the reign of the Empress Wu Tse-t'ien (684–705 A.D.), the realistic trend saw its finest flowering in all fields of sculpture. Most important among surviving works of this period are the sculptures in front of the tomb of Kao-tsung at Ch'ien District, Shensi. They include winged horses, ostriches, lions and horses. The winged horses (Pl. 242) are heavily built with thick legs and the "flying" cloud-scroll patterns of the wings are a reflection of the grace and brilliance so typical of the age. The idea of the winged horse itself was an influence from the cultures of western Asia; however it is also characteristic of this age that, despite the fanciful nature of the subject, the sense of actuality should be greater than in the figures of the Han and Six Dynasties periods. This richness and brilliance marks the peak of T'ang tomb sculpture; after this there is a decline, a tendency towards formalism. The stone human and animal figures that stand in front of the Shun *ling* at Hsien-yang District, Shensi (Pl. 243), dating to the latter half of the reign of the Empress Wu, are a case in point. Thus the stiff, lifeless treatment of the figures resembling giraffes cannot be attributed solely to the imaginary nature of the subject, but must be put down in part to the stylistic characteristics of the period.

Of course, even among these figures at the Shun *ling*, one can find considerable elements of realism: the powerful forelegs and fierce gaze of the pairs of lions that stand on all four sides of the tomb. Somewhat later, however, with the sculpture at the Jui-tsung and the Su-tsung tombs, there is a marked loss of life and power compared with the Buddhist sculpture of the same period, and little of the characteristic virtues of stone carving are in evidence.

As is stated above, the advance in realism seen in early T'ang times, as in the tigers of the Kao-tsu tomb, was skillfully applied in later years to animals that were in themselves fanciful. This produced a blend of the symbolic and the realistic that is one of the characteristic features of Chinese sculpture as a whole.

The tradition of tomb sculpture from Han to T'ang is a long one. It faithfully reflects the sense of form of each succeeding period and in this respect it must be accorded a place in the history of Chinese sculpture not inferior to that held by Buddhist sculpture.

SABURO MATSUBARA

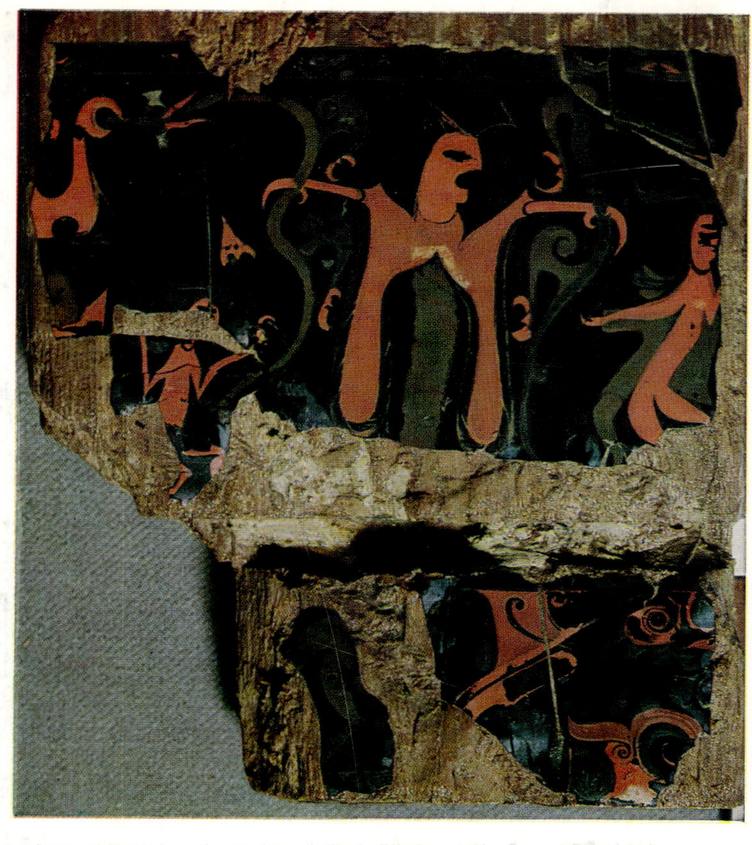

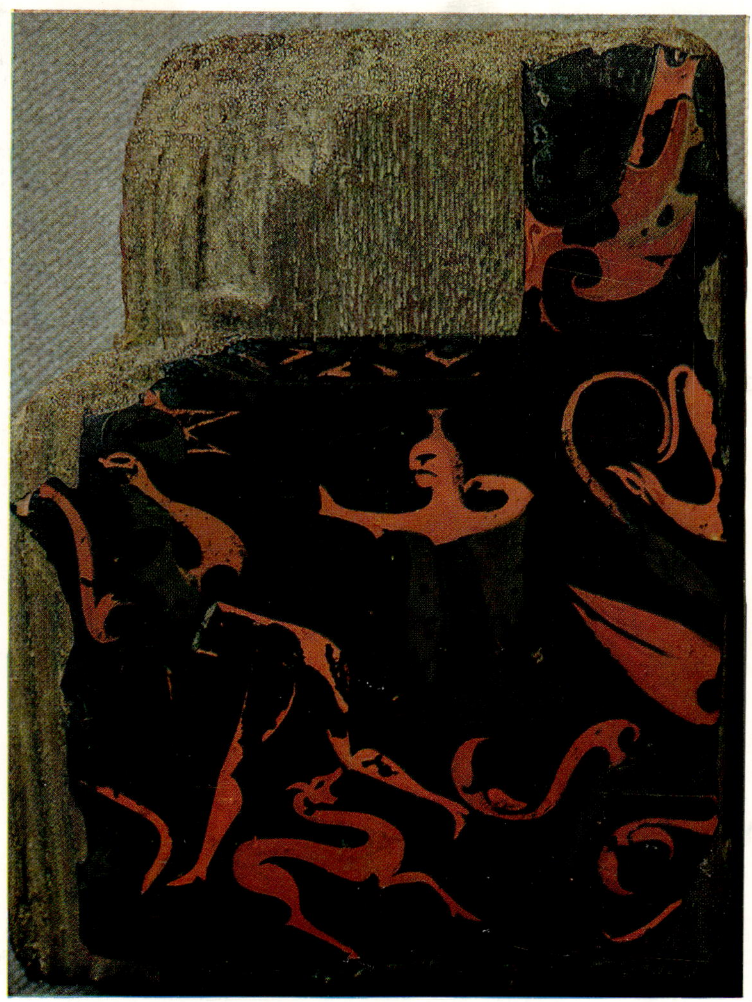

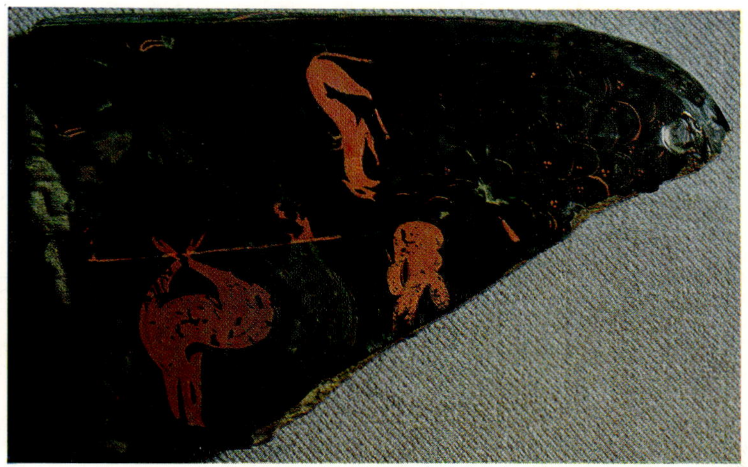

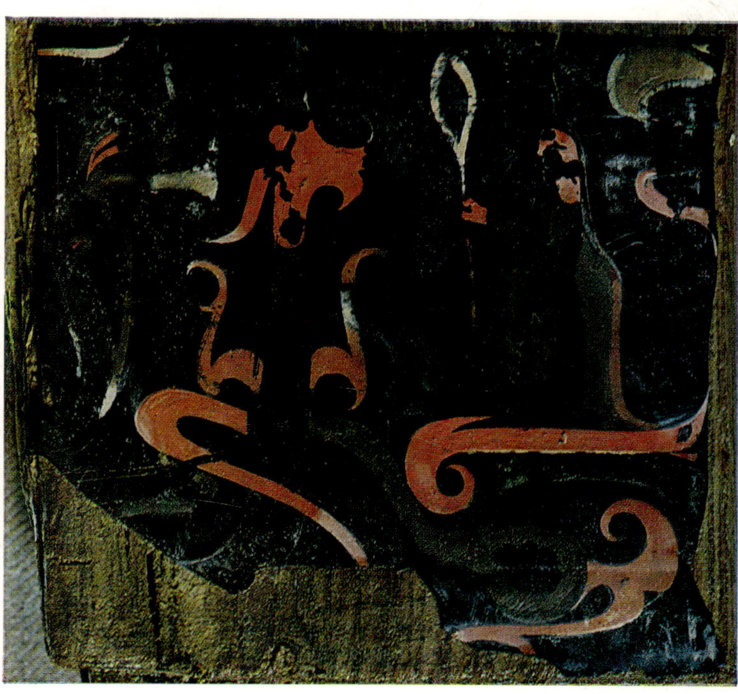

185. Fragments of a lacquered *se*. Warring States period. Excavated from tomb No. 1, Chang-t'ai-kuan, Hsing-yang District, Honan.

a. *8.3 × 7.0 cm. (3.25 × 2.76 in.)*
b. *10.0 × 8.0 cm. (3.9 × 3.15 in.)*
c. *6.5 × 10.8 cm. (2.56 × 4.2 in.)*
d. *10.2 × 7.0 cm. (4.0 × 2.76 in.)*

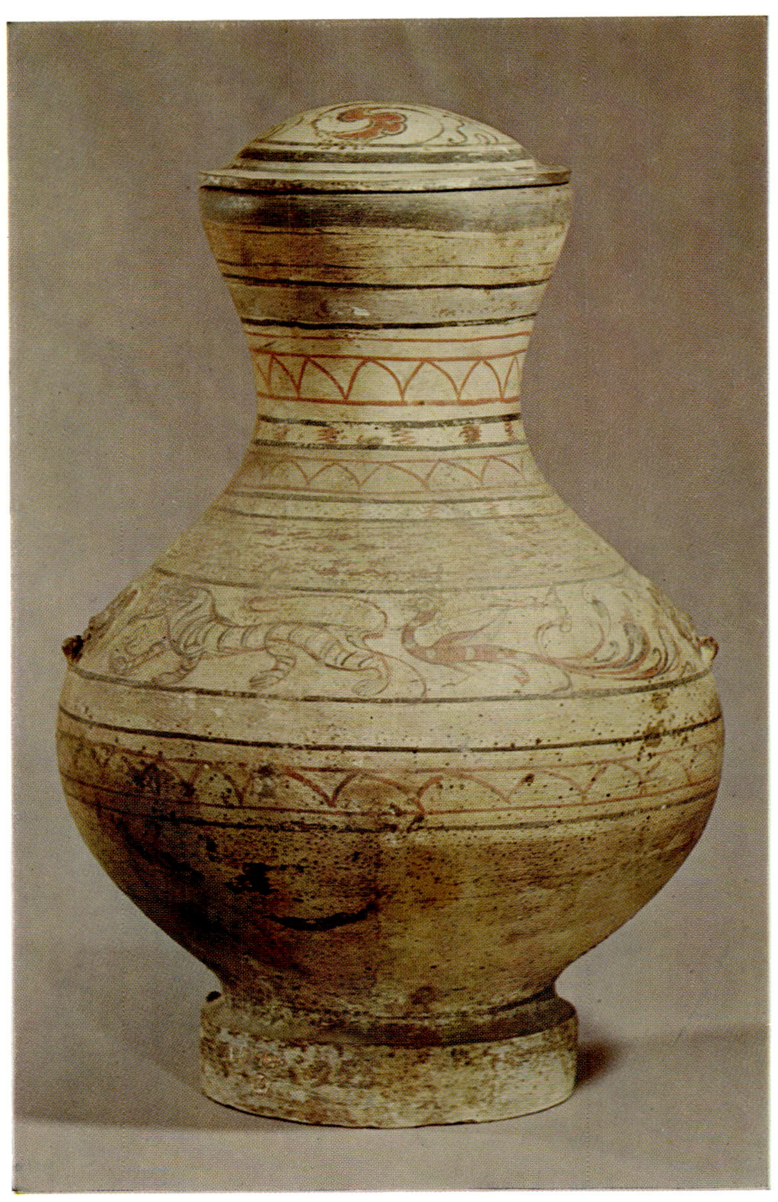

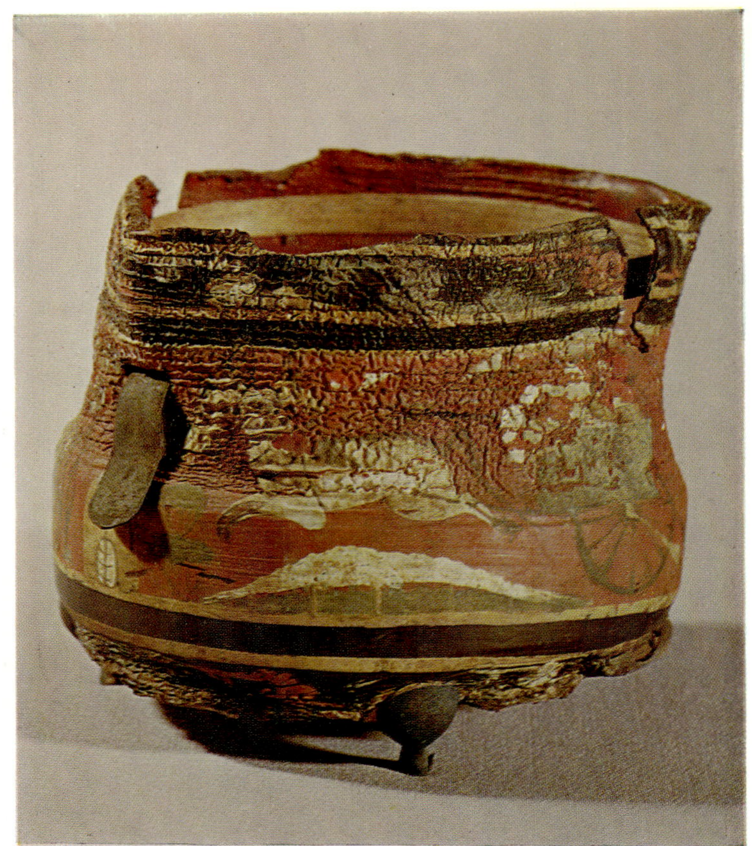

187. *Lien*, lacquer on wood. Han dynasty. Excavated from a tomb at Ch'ang-sha Municipality, Hunan.
height: 11.1 cm. (4.3 in.)

186. Jar, earthenware with slip decoration. Former Han dynasty. Excavated from tomb No. 50, Shao-kou, Lo-yang Municipality, Honan.
height: 50.1 cm. (19.7 in.)

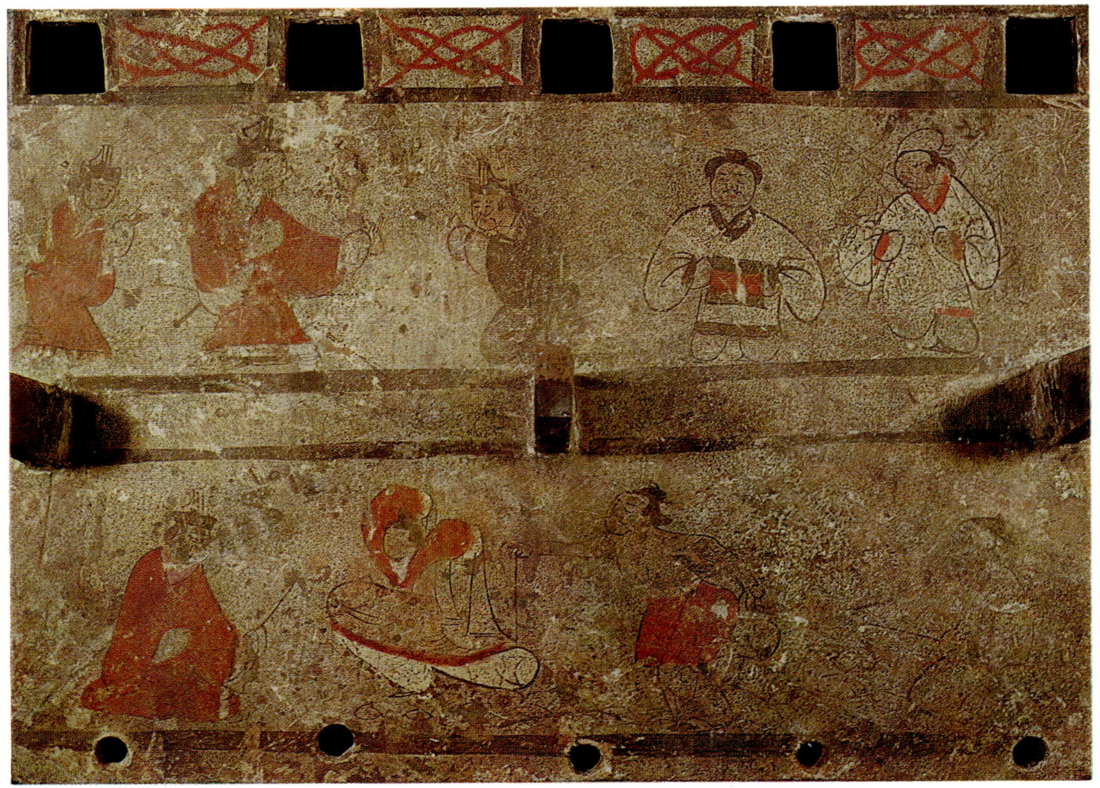

188. Ceramic building, detail (entire building pictured in Pl. 246). Han dynasty. Excavated at Ho-wang-ts'un, Hsing-yang District, Honan.
height of building: 77.0 cm. (30.3 in.)

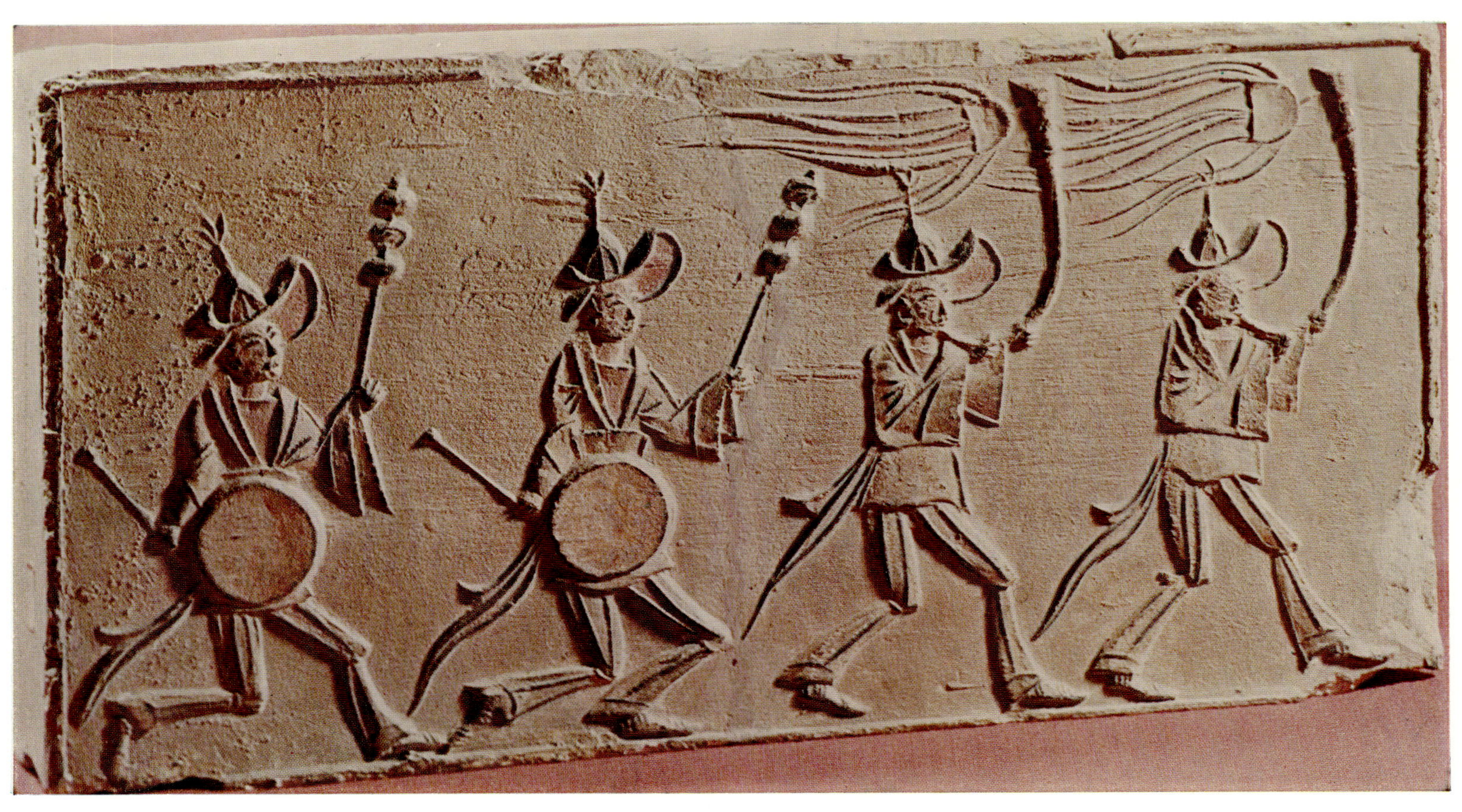

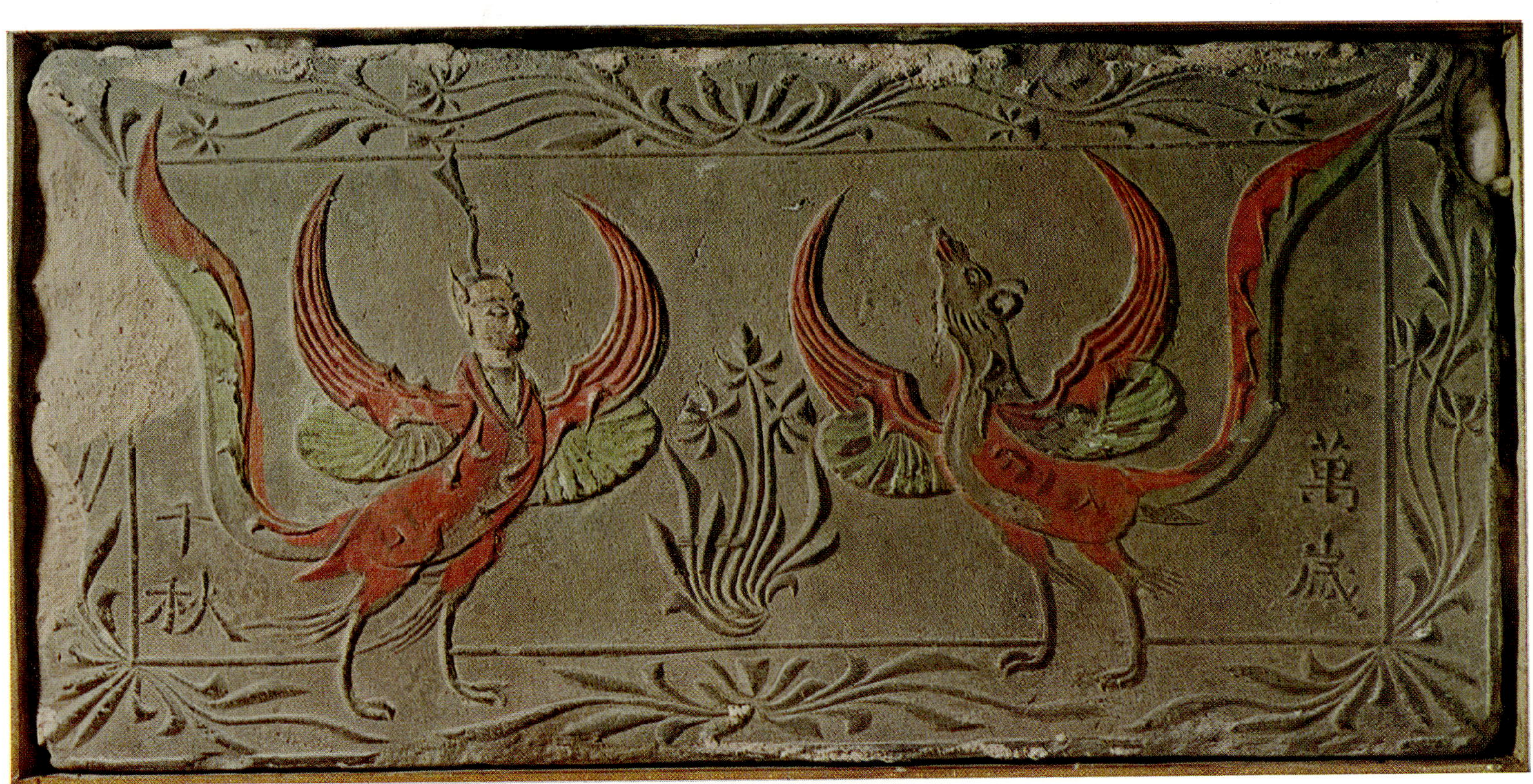

189–190. Mold-impressed bricks from the coffin chamber and passageway of a tomb. Southern Dynasties (fifth century). Excavated at Hsüeh-chuang-ts'un, Teng District, Honan (*see* Pls. 214–216).
brick height: 19.0 cm. (7.5 in.); width: 38.0 cm. (14.95 in.); thickness: 6.0 cm. (2.36 in.)

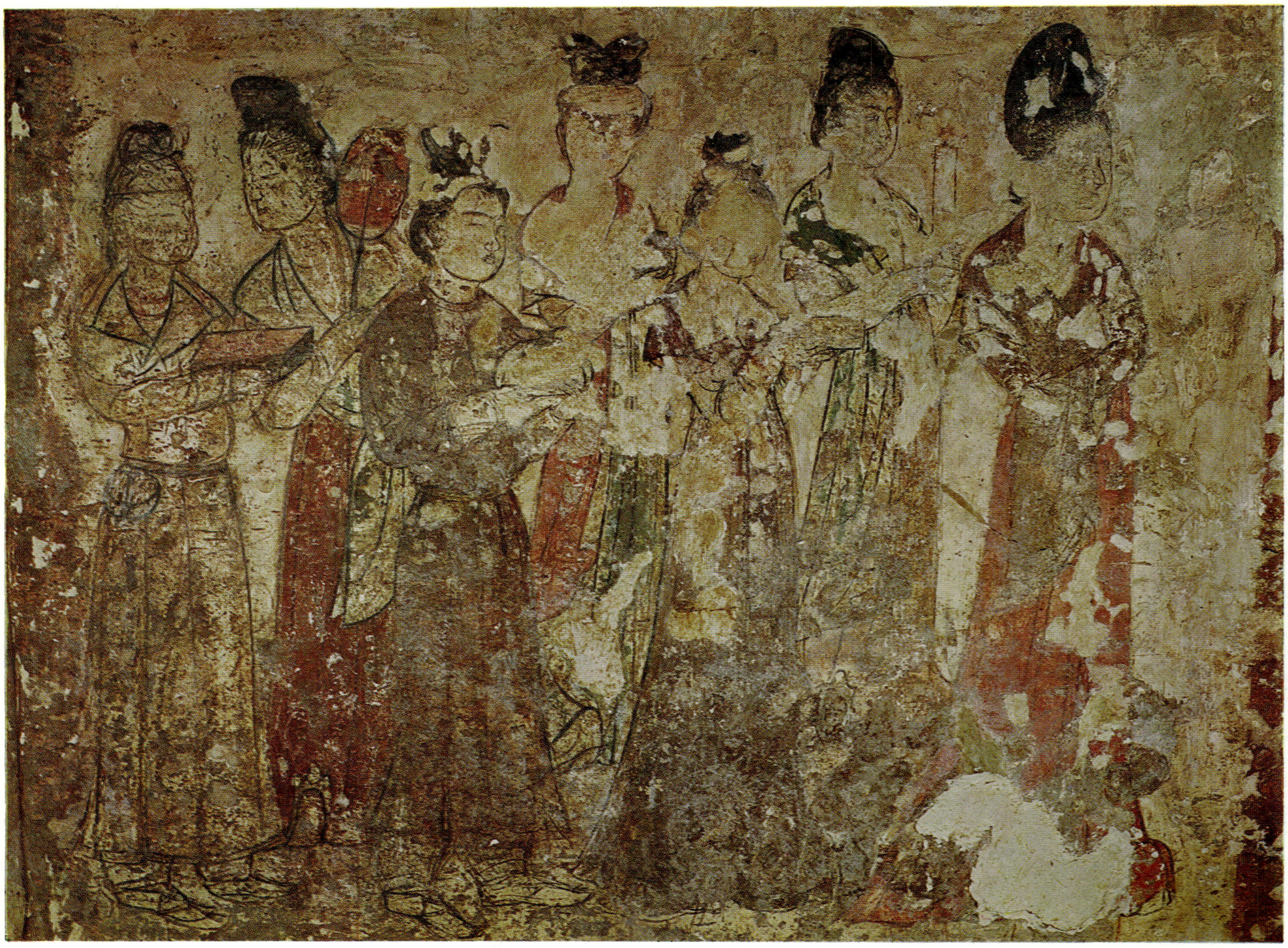

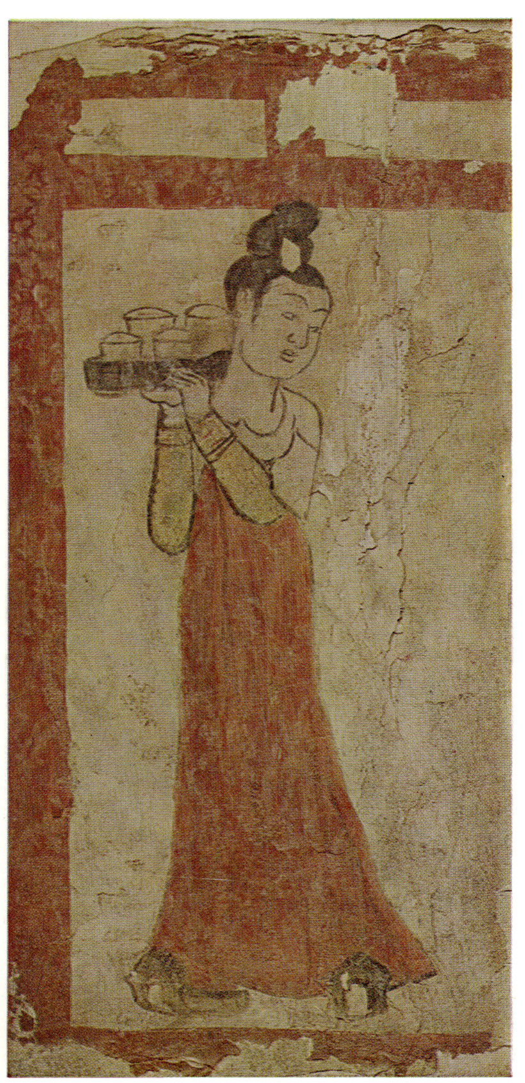

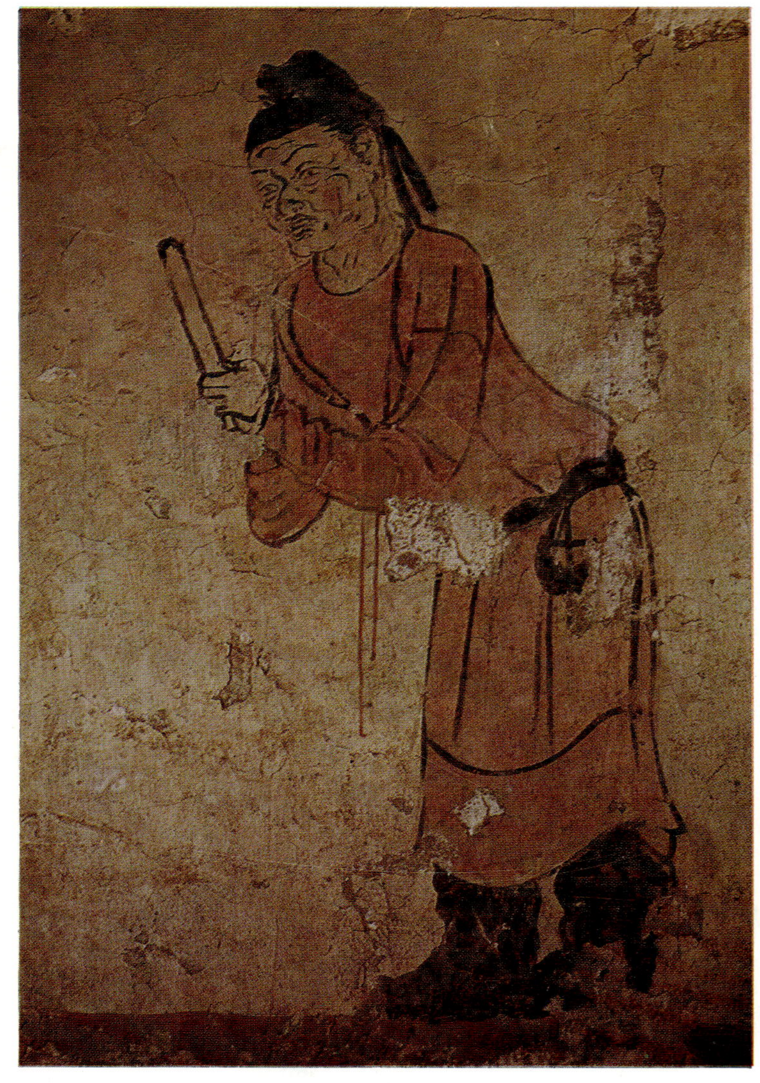

192–193. Tomb wall paintings. T'ang dynasty (668 A.D.). From the tomb of Li Shuang, Yang-t'ou-chen, southern outskirts of Sian Municipality, Shensi.

192. 177.5 × 90.0 cm. (69.8 × 35.4 in.)

193. 123 × 90.0 cm. (48.4 × 35.4 in.)

◀ 191. Tomb wall painting. T'ang dynasty (706 A.D.). From the east wall of the front chamber, Princess Yung-t'ai tomb, Liang-shan, Ch'ien District, Shensi. *wall height: 198 cm. (77.9 in.); wall length: 420 cm. (165.5 in.)*

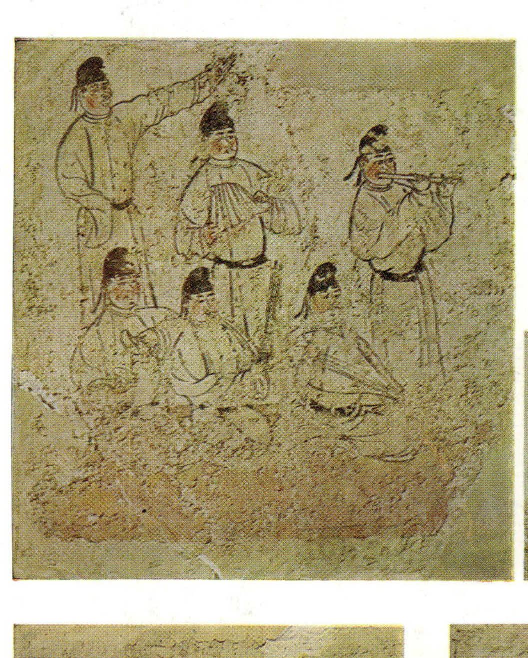

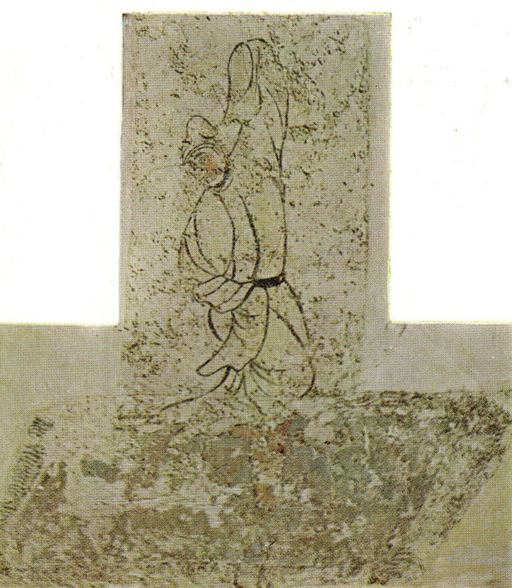

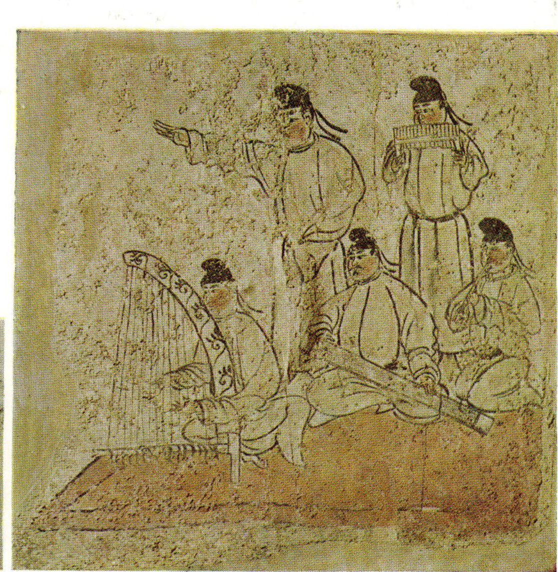

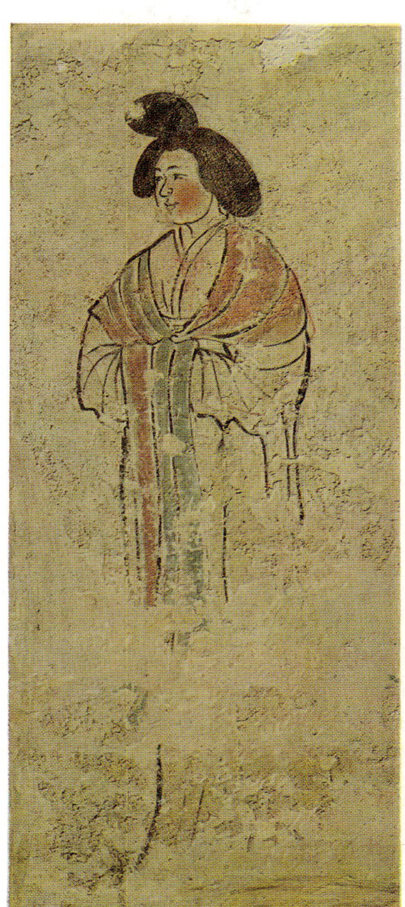

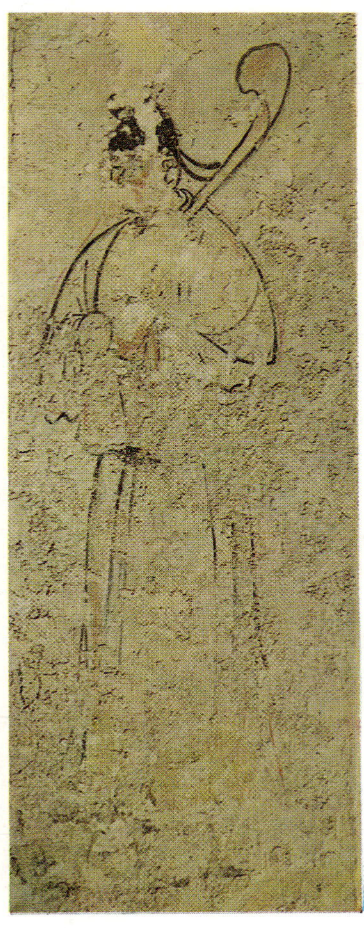

194–196. Tomb wall paintings. T'ang dynasty (745 A.D.). From the tomb coffin chamber of Su Ssu-hsü, Ching-wu-lu, eastern outskirts of Sian Municipality, Shensi.
194 (a–c). From the east wall. height: 153 cm. (60.2 in.)
195. From the north wall. height: 130 cm. (51.1 in.)
196. From the north wall. height: 120 cm. (47.2 in.)

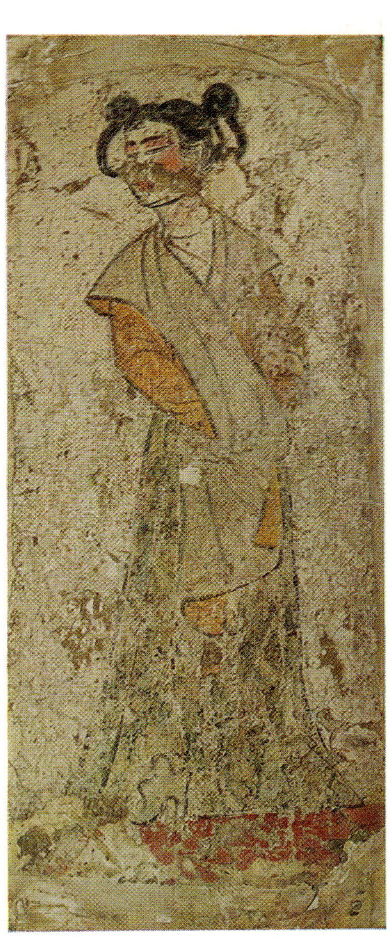

197. Tomb wall painting. T'ang dynasty (710 A.D.). From the tomb of Lady Hsüeh, Ti-chang-wan, Hsien-yang, Shensi. *height: 113 cm. (44.4 in.); width: 48.0 cm. (18.9 in.)*

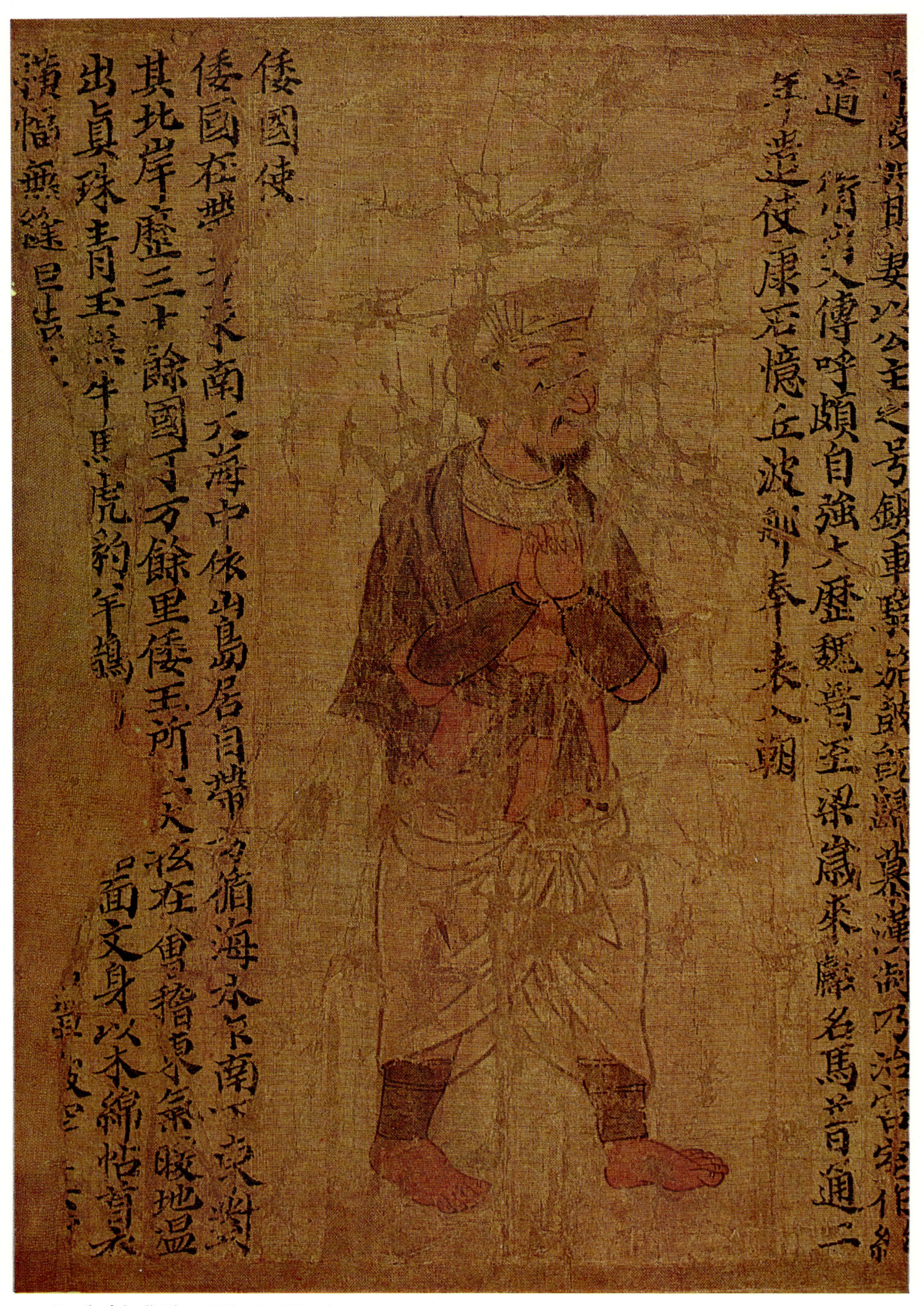

198. Detail of the "Tribute Office Scroll," color on silk. Copy (1077 A.D.) of the original by Hsiao Yi (539 A.D.)
no measurement given

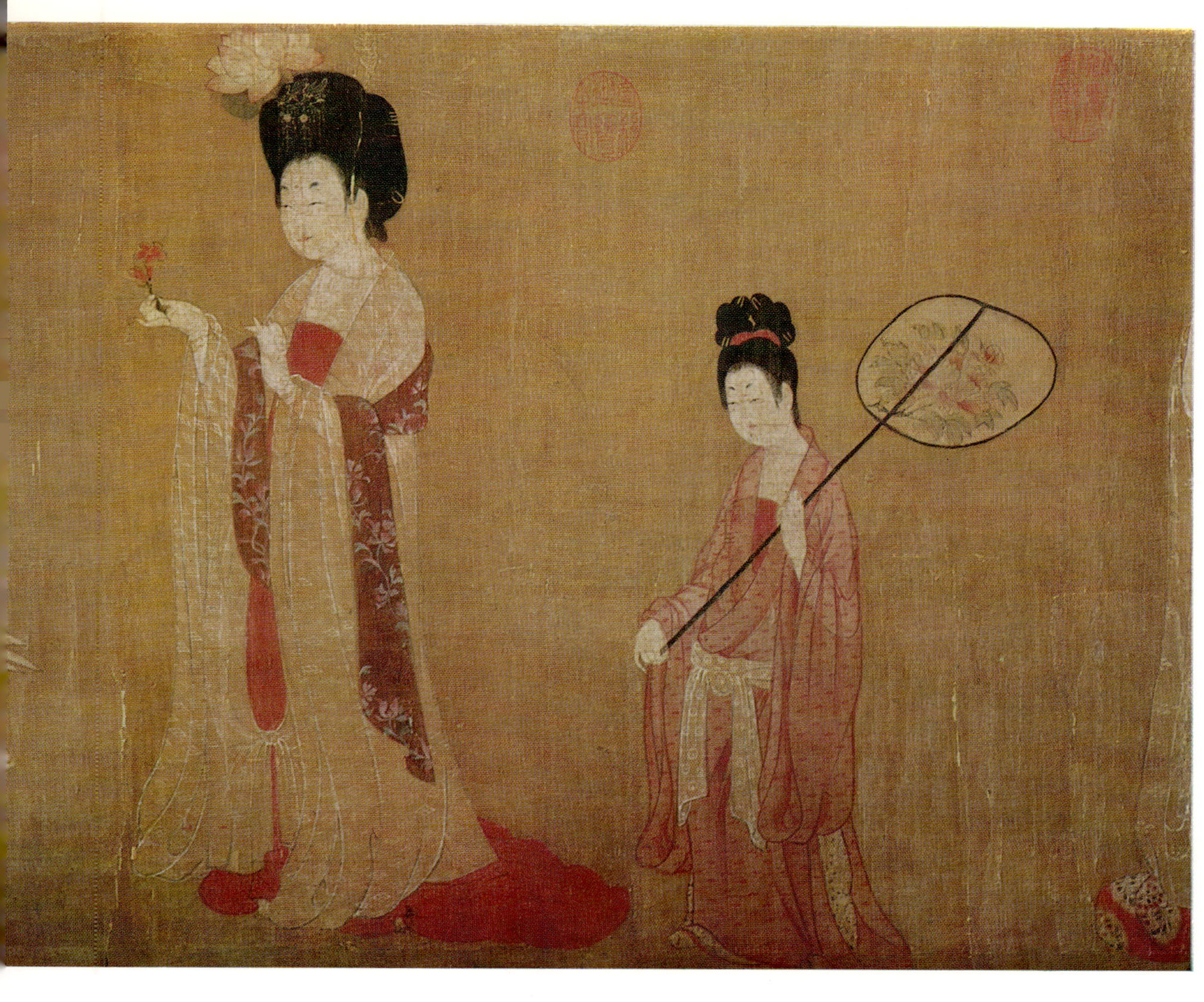

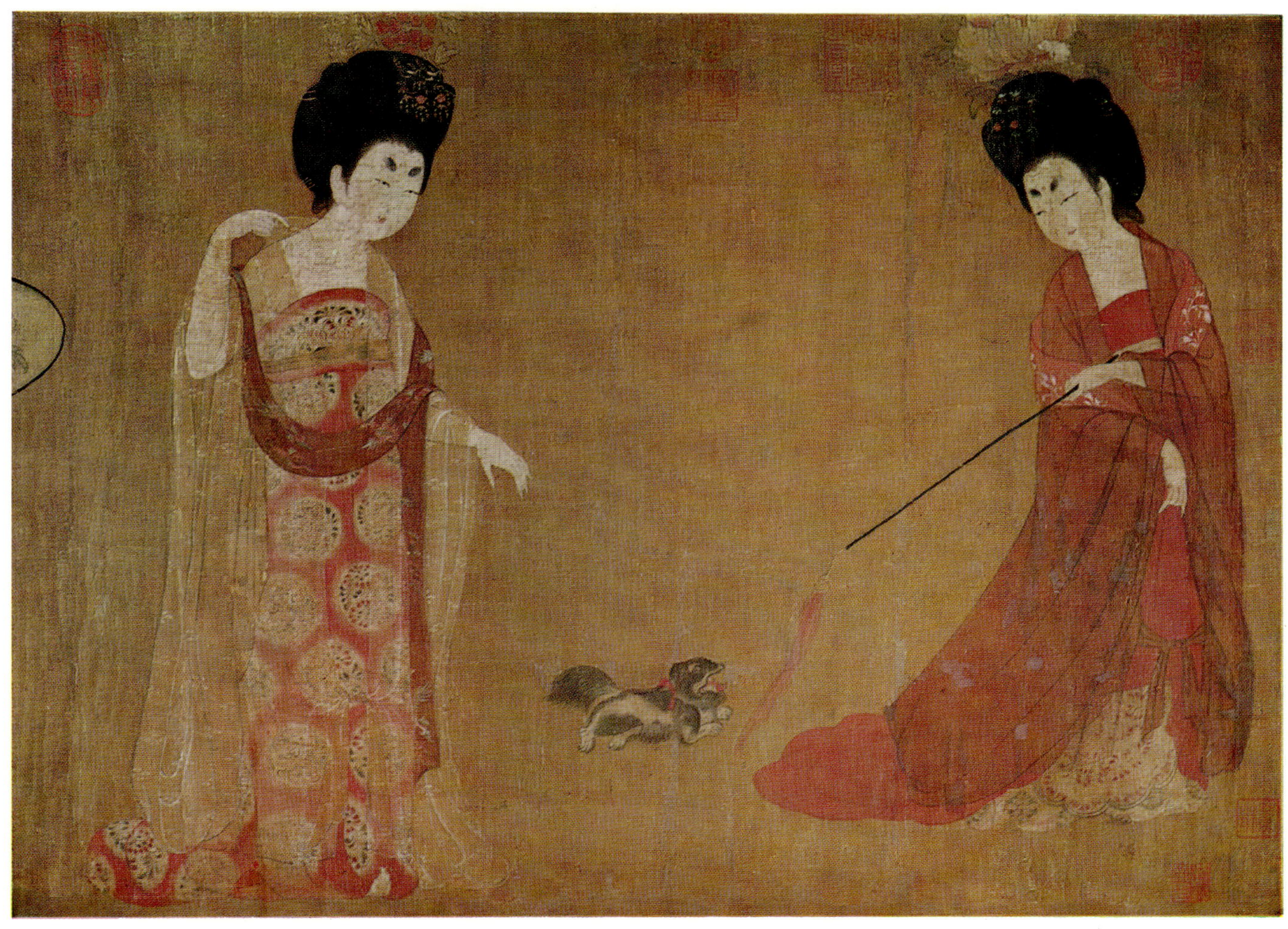

199. Detail of "Ladies-in-Waiting" scroll by Chou Fang, ink and color on silk. T'ang dynasty.
length: 45.8 cm. (18.0 in.)

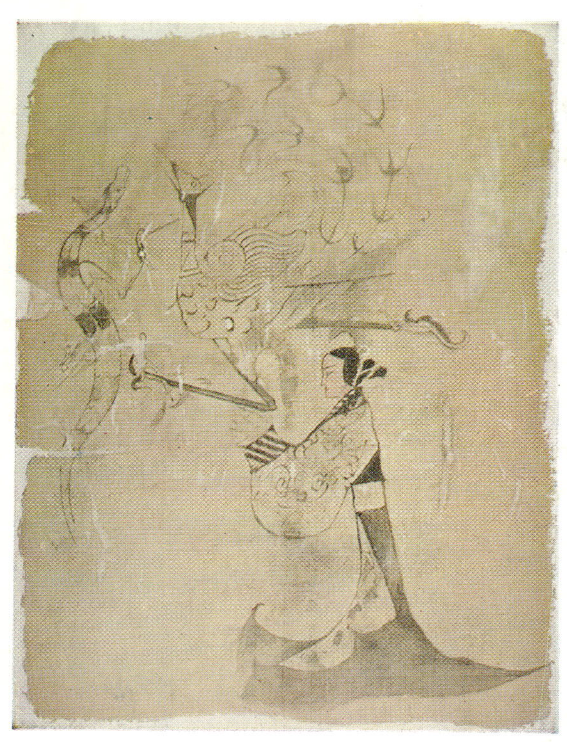

200. Copy of a painting on silk. Warring States period. Original excavated at Ch'en-chia-ta-shan, Ch'ang-sha Municipality, Hunan.
length: 29.2 cm. (11.5 in.); width: 20.8 cm. (8.2 in.)

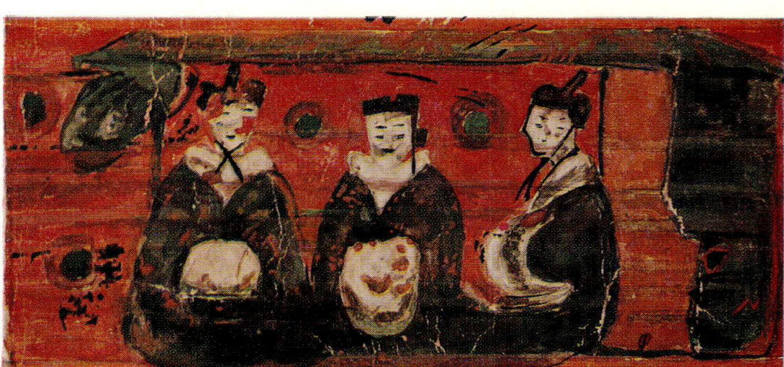

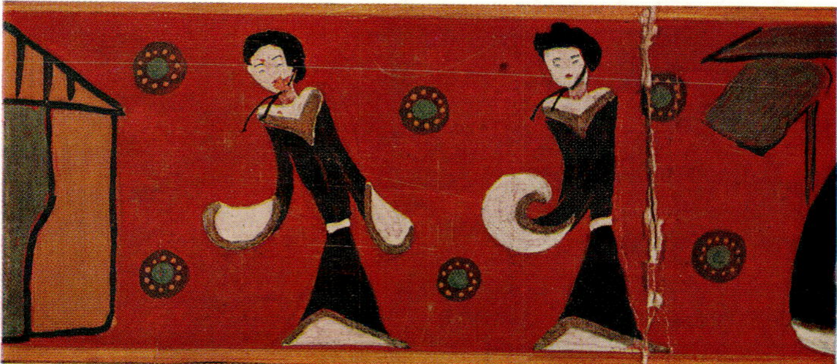

201–202. Reconstructed details of lacquer painting on a *lien*. Han dynasty. Excavated at Ch'ang-sha Municipality, Hunan.
lien *height: 18.0 cm. (7.1 in.);* lien *diameter: 12.0 cm. (4.7 in.)*

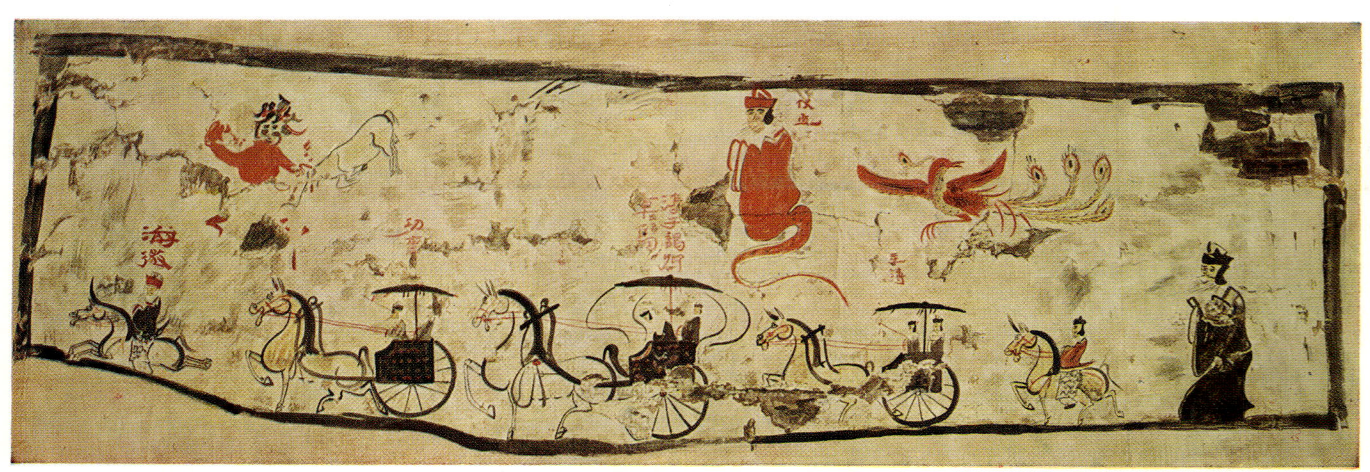

203. Carriage procession, copy of a tomb wall painting. Later Han dynasty. From a stone coffin tomb at Hou-yin-shan, Liang-shan District, Shantung.
height: 62.0 cm. (24.4 in.); width: 202 cm. (79.6 in.)

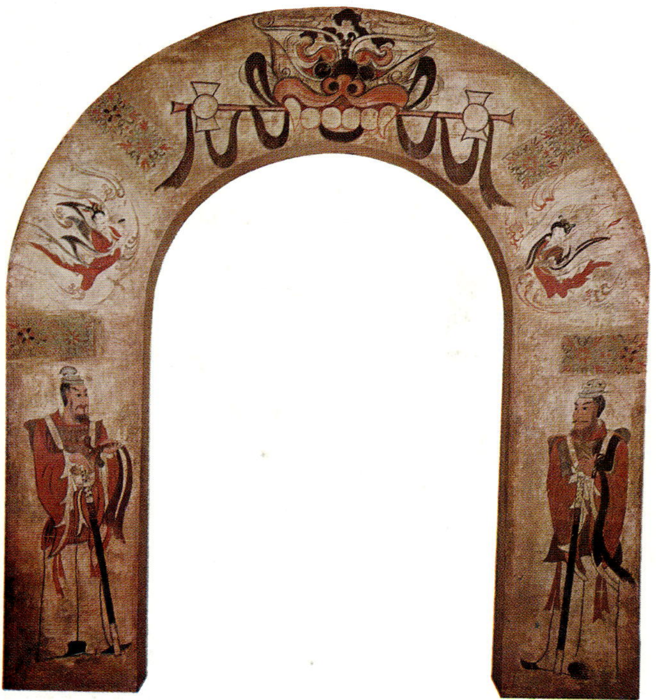

204. Reconstruction of the painting on a tomb gateway. Southern Dynasties (fifth century). From a tomb at Hsüeh-chuang-ts'un, Teng District, Honan.
gate height: 300 cm. (118.2 in.); gate width: 270 cm. (106.8 in.); width of each pier: 60 cm. (23.6 in.)

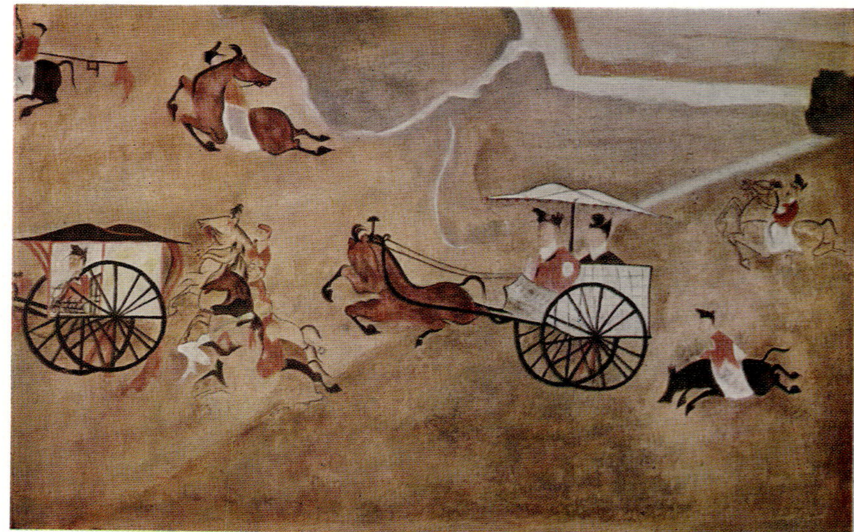

205. Detail of a tomb wall painting. Han dynasty. From a stone coffin tomb at Pei-yüan, Liao-yang District, Liaoning.

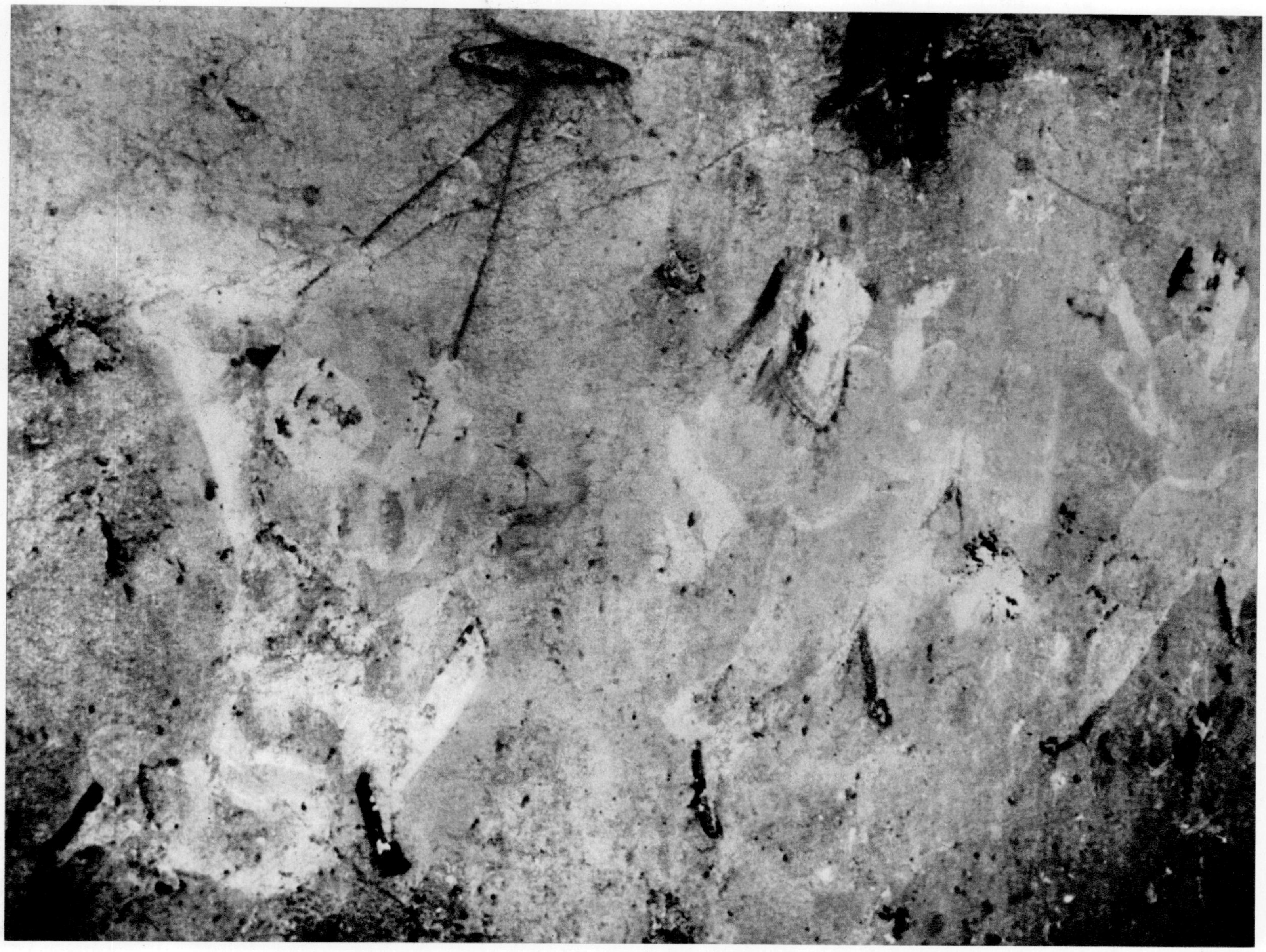

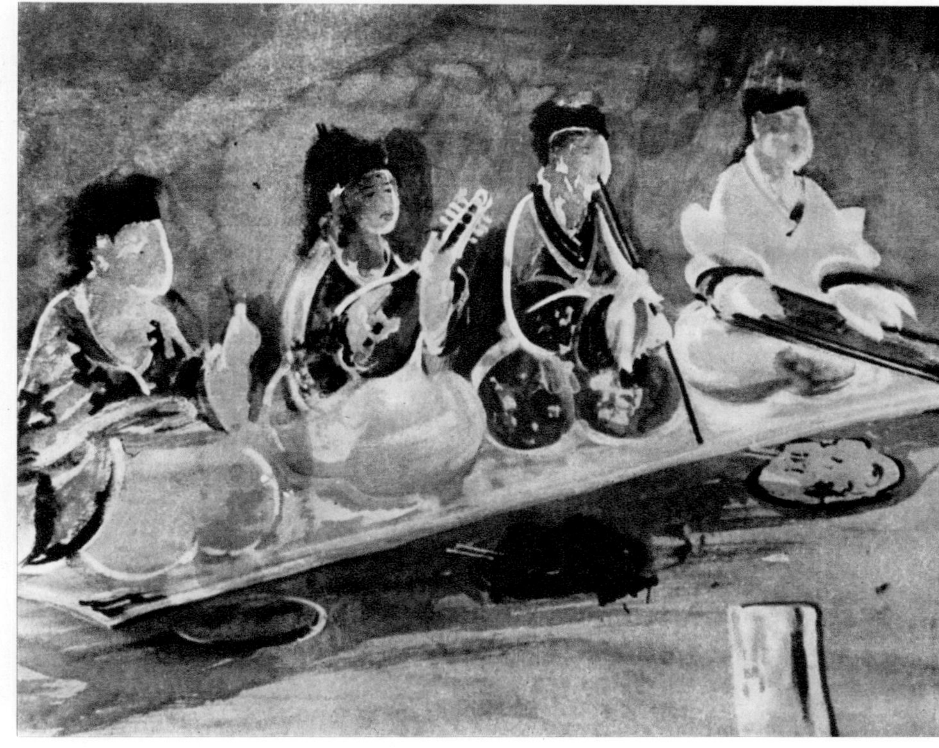

206–207. Details of a tomb chamber wall painting. Han dynasty. From a tomb at Pang-t'ai-tzu, Liao-yang District, Liaoning.
wall height: 130 cm. (51.1 in.); wall width: 200 cm. (78.8 in.)

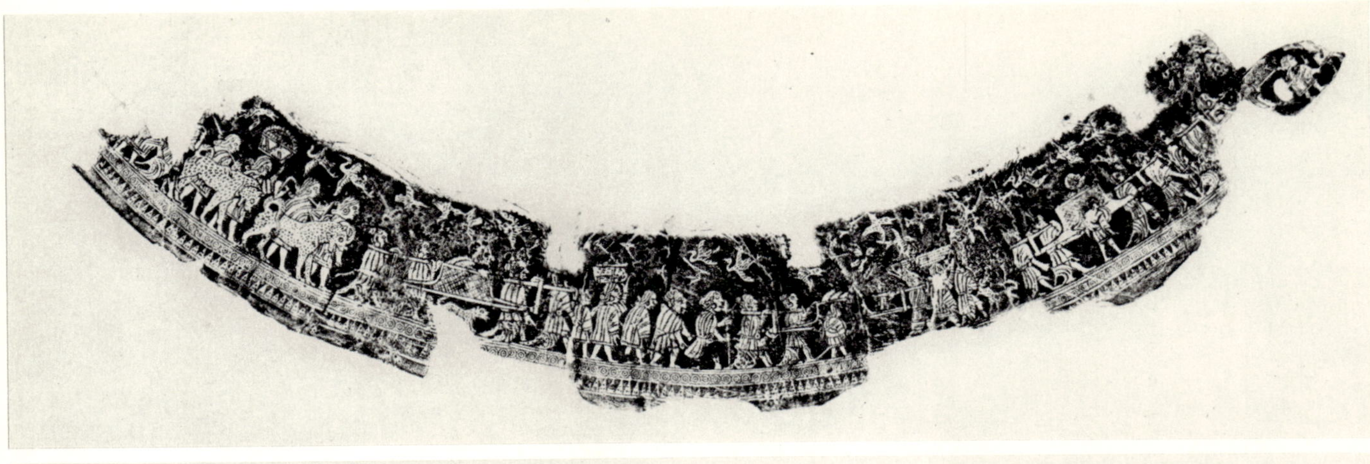

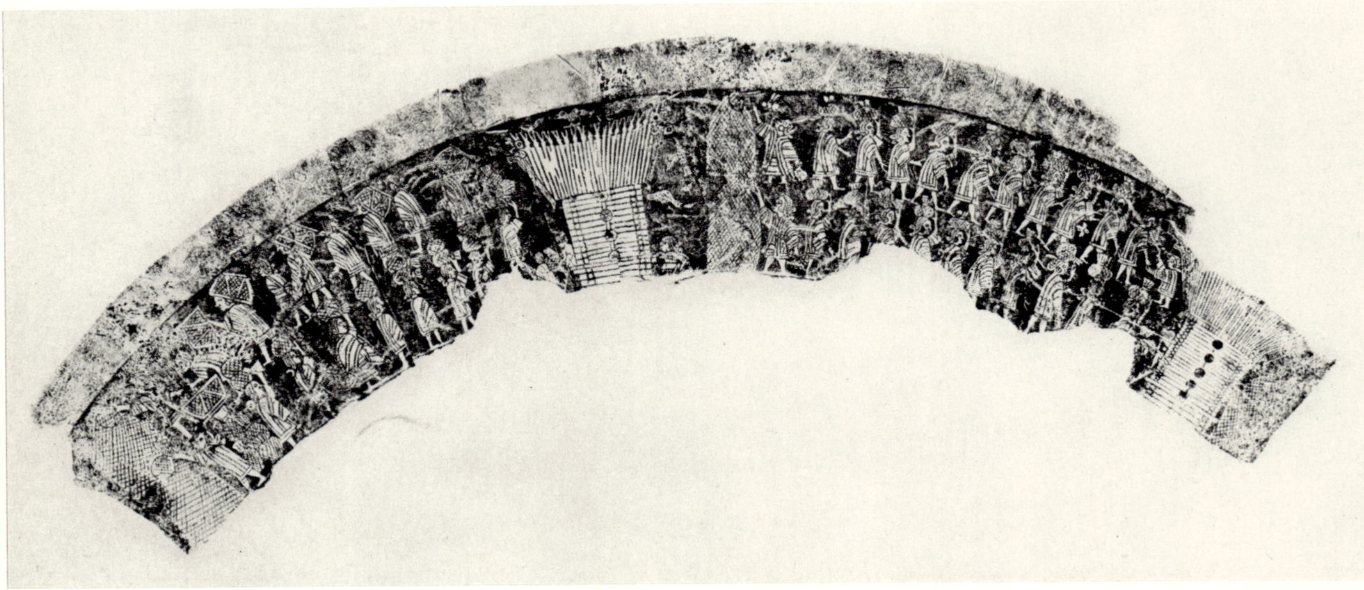

208. Rubbings of the engraved decoration on a cowrie container, bronze. Former Han dynasty. Excavated at Shih-chai-shan, Chin-ning District, Yünnan.

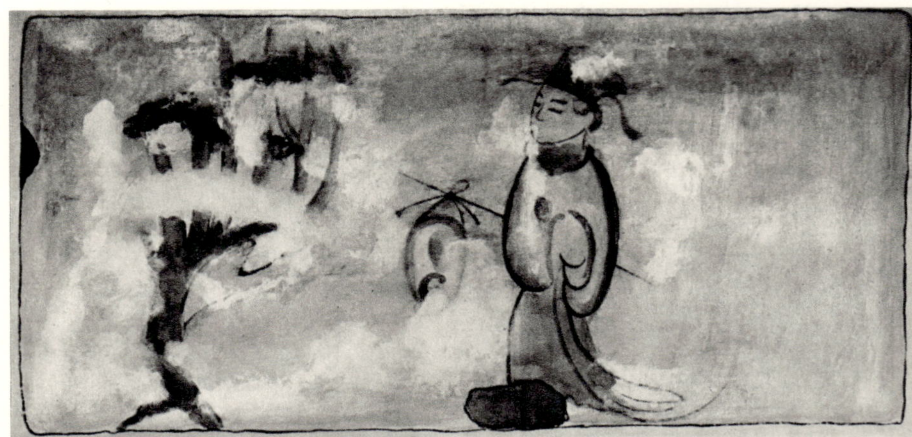

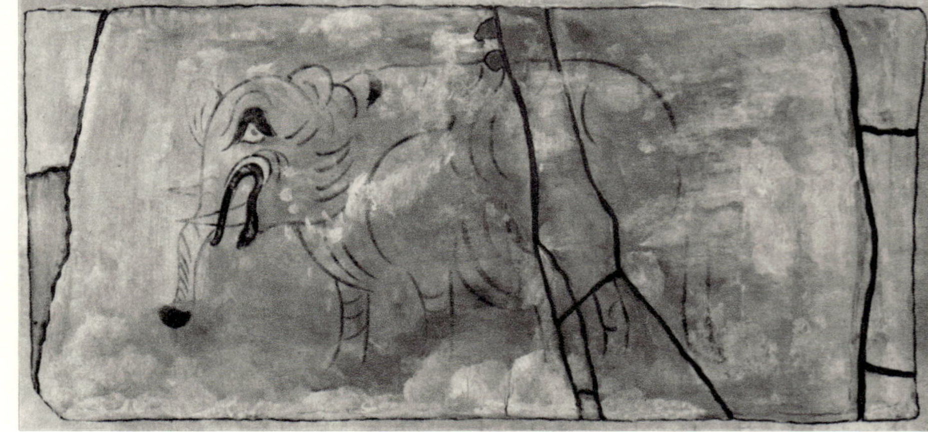

209–210. Painted bricks. Han dynasty. From the antechamber, south wall, tomb No. 1, Chiu-ch'üan, Kansu.
height: 17.0 cm. (6.7 in.); width: 36.0 cm. (14.2 in.); thickness: 5.0 cm. (1.97 in.)

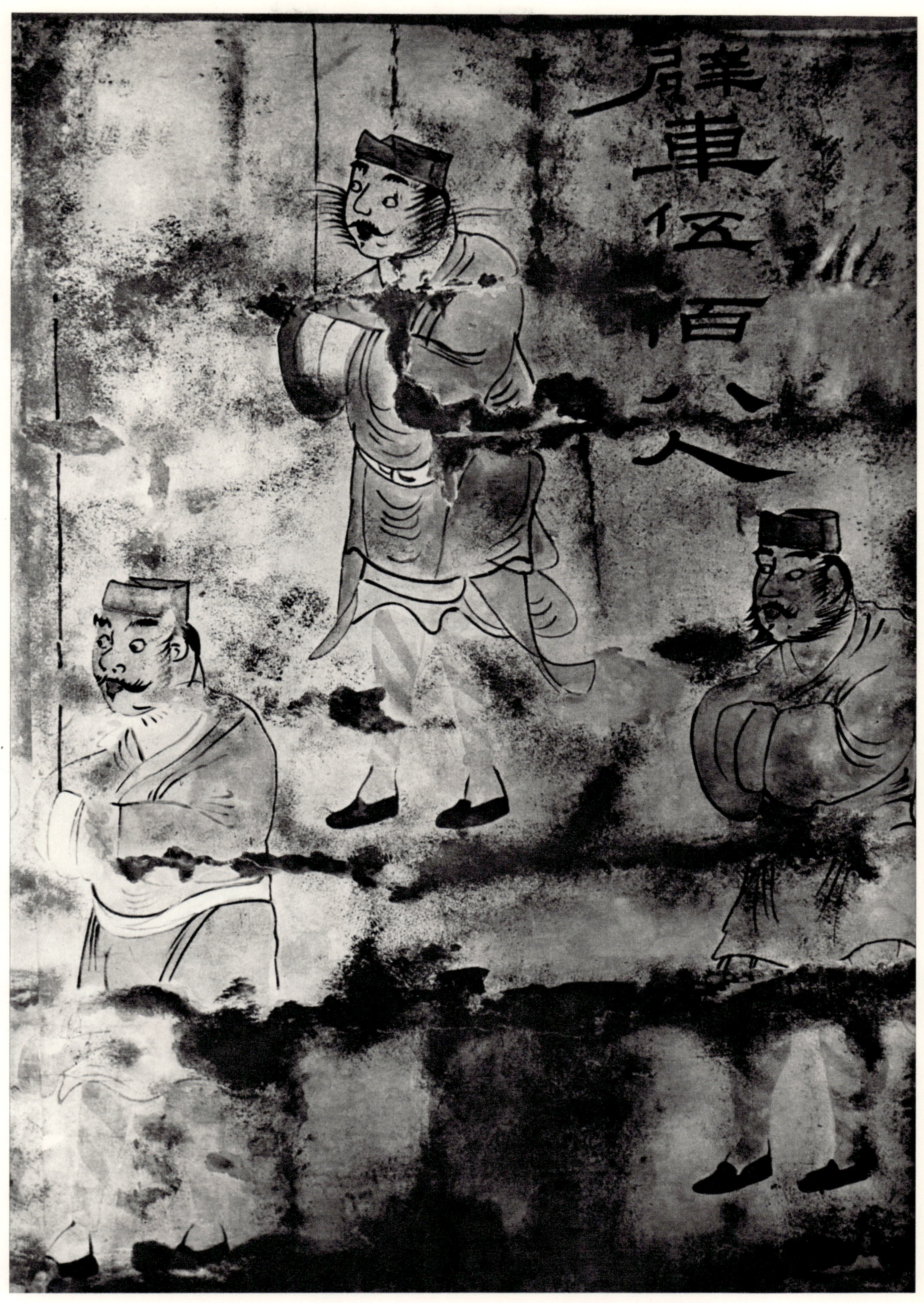

211. Detail of a tomb wall painting. Later Han dynasty. From the antechamber of tomb No. 1, So-yao-ts'un, Wang-tu District, Hopei.
height: 140 cm. (55.2 in.)

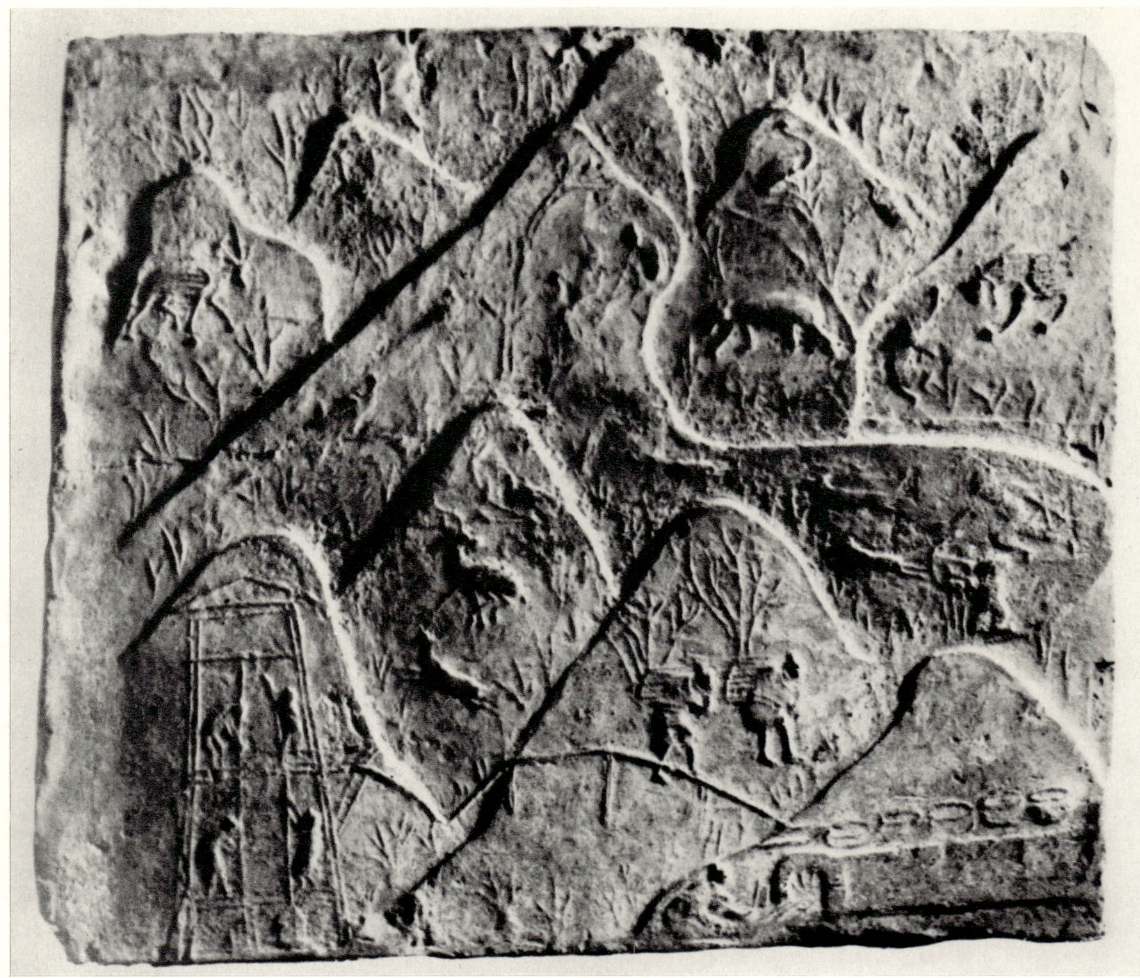

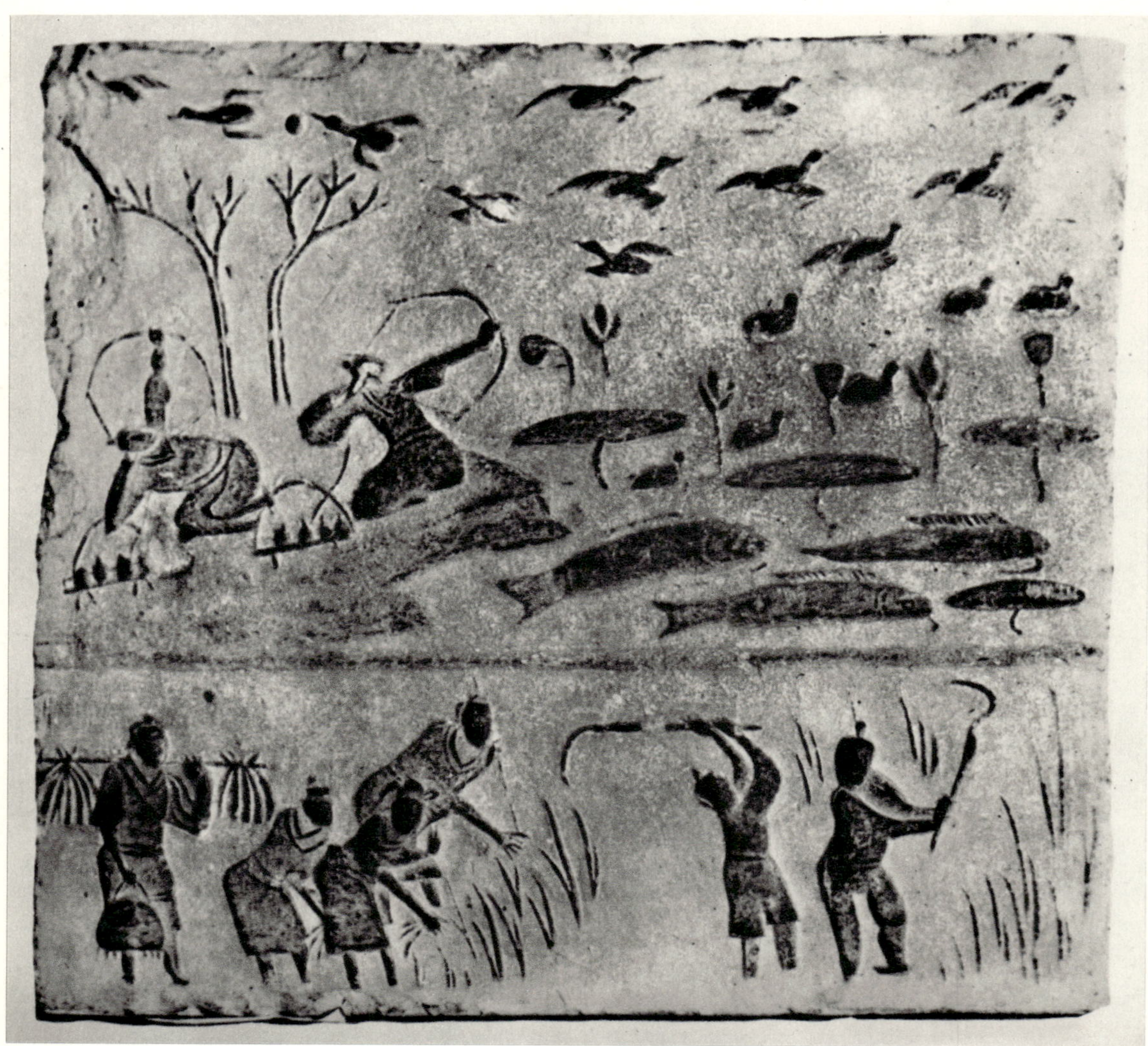

212–213. Relief bricks. Later Han dynasty. From tombs No. 1 and 2, Yang-tzu-shan, Ch'eng-tu, Szuchwan.
212. Salt-making scene, tomb No. 1. width: 46.7 cm. (18.4 in.)
213. Genre scene, tomb No. 2. width: 45.8 cm. (17.6 in.)

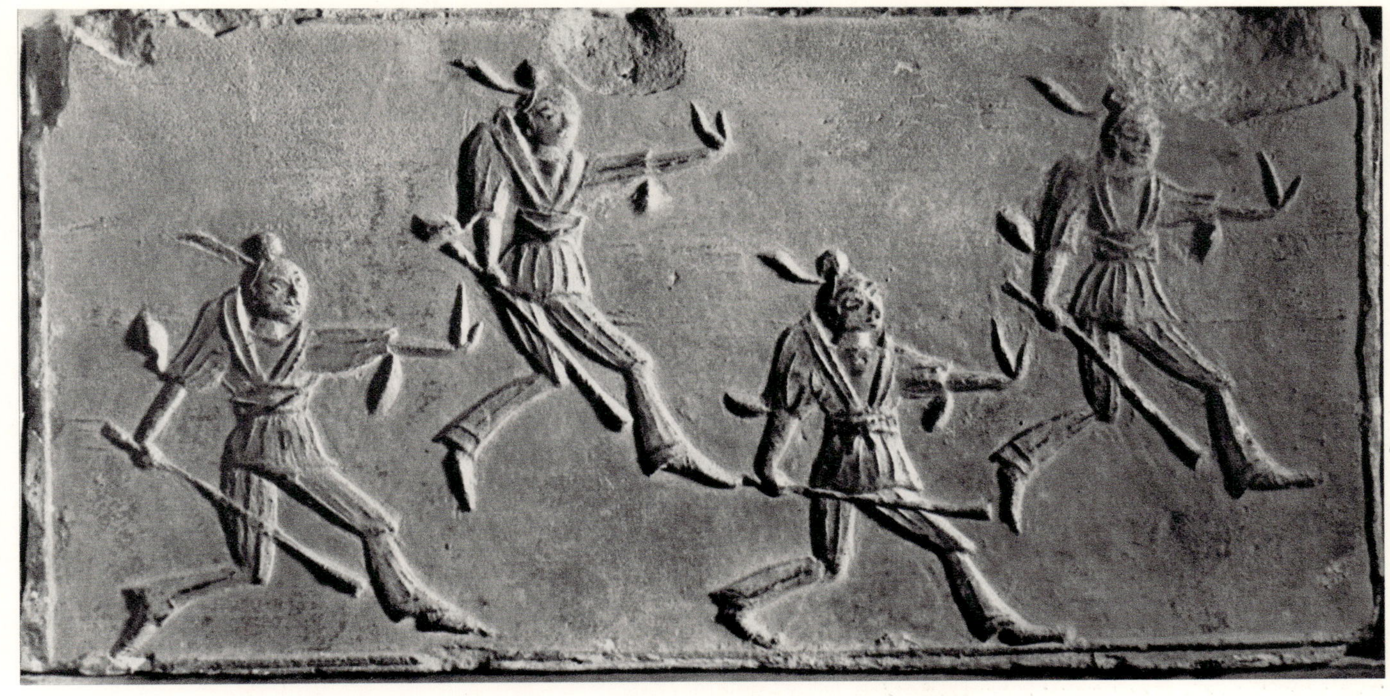

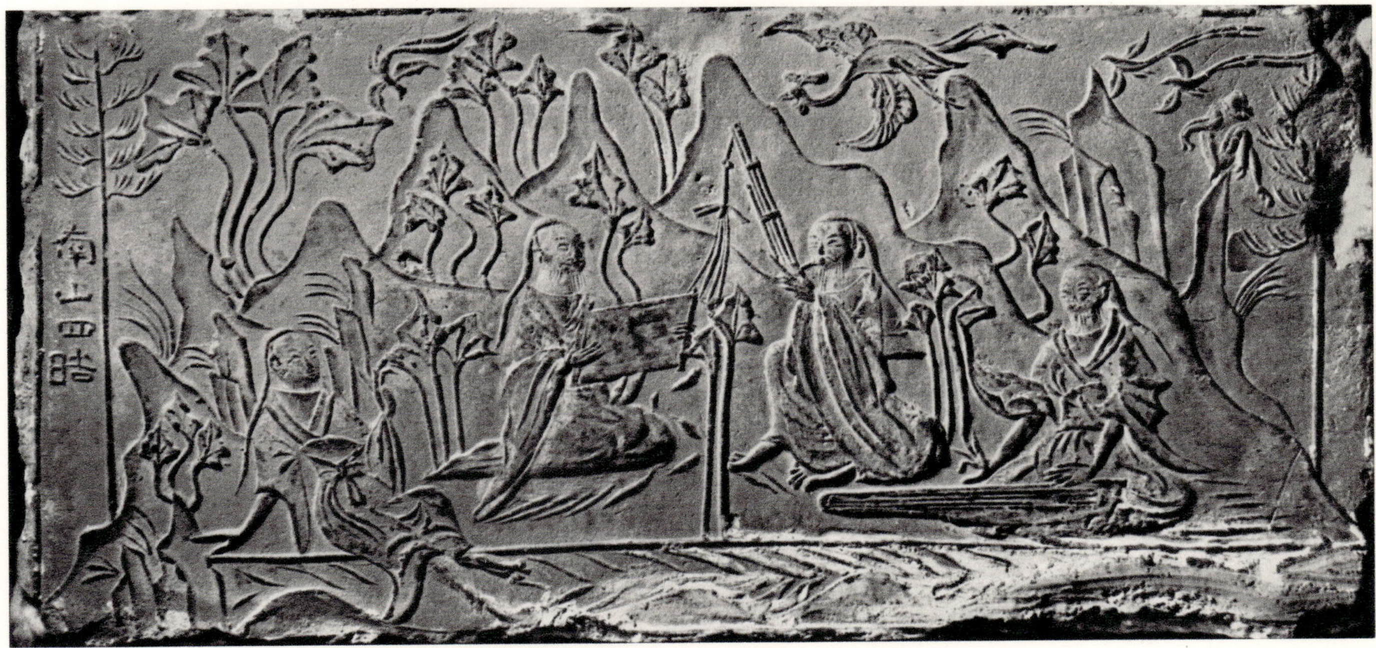

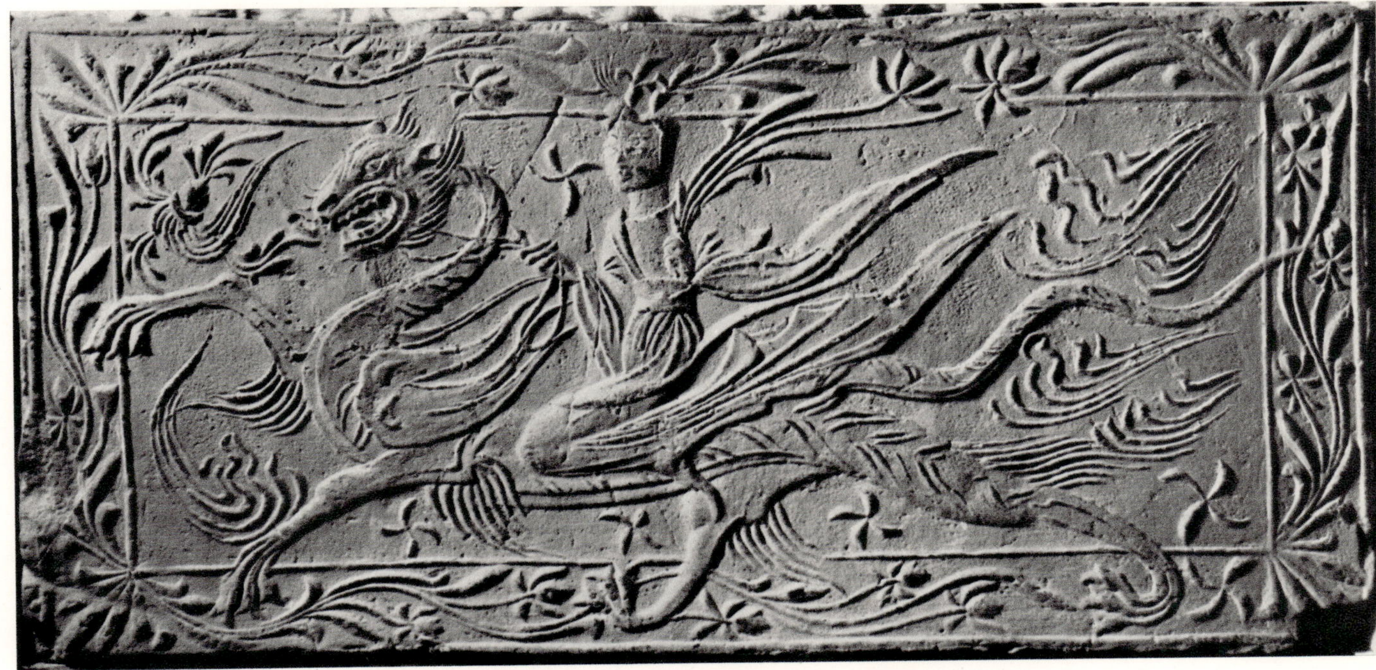

214–216. Mold-impressed bricks from the coffin chamber and passageway of a tomb. Southern Dynasties (fifth century). Excavated at Hsüeh-chuang-ts'un, Teng District, Honan (*see* Pls. 189–190).
brick height: 19.0 cm. (7.5 in.); width: 38.0 cm. (14.95 in.); thickness: 6.0 cm. (2.36 in.)

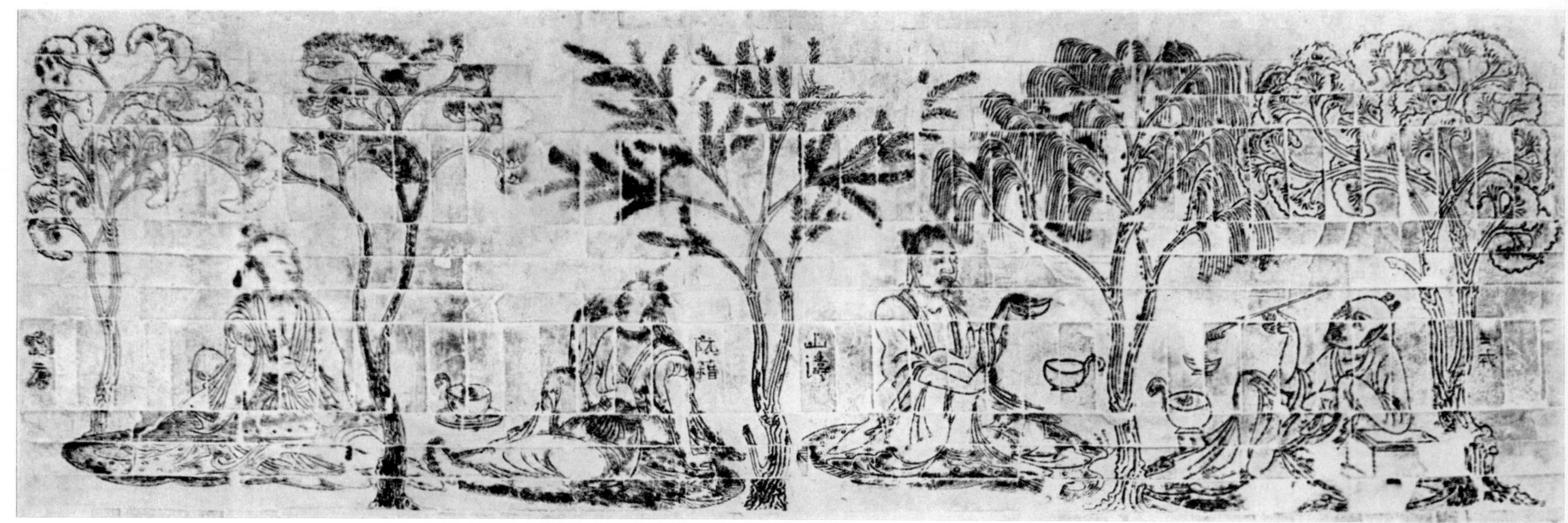

217. Rubbing of impressed-brick wall decoration. Late Eastern Chin or Liu-Sung dynasty (early fifth century). From a tomb at Hsi-shan-ch'iao, Nanking.
height: 80.0 cm. (31.5 in.); width: 240 cm. (94.6 in.)

218. Details of the "Tribute Office Scroll," color on silk. Copy (1077 A.D.) of the original by Hsiao Yi (539 A.D.).
no measurement given

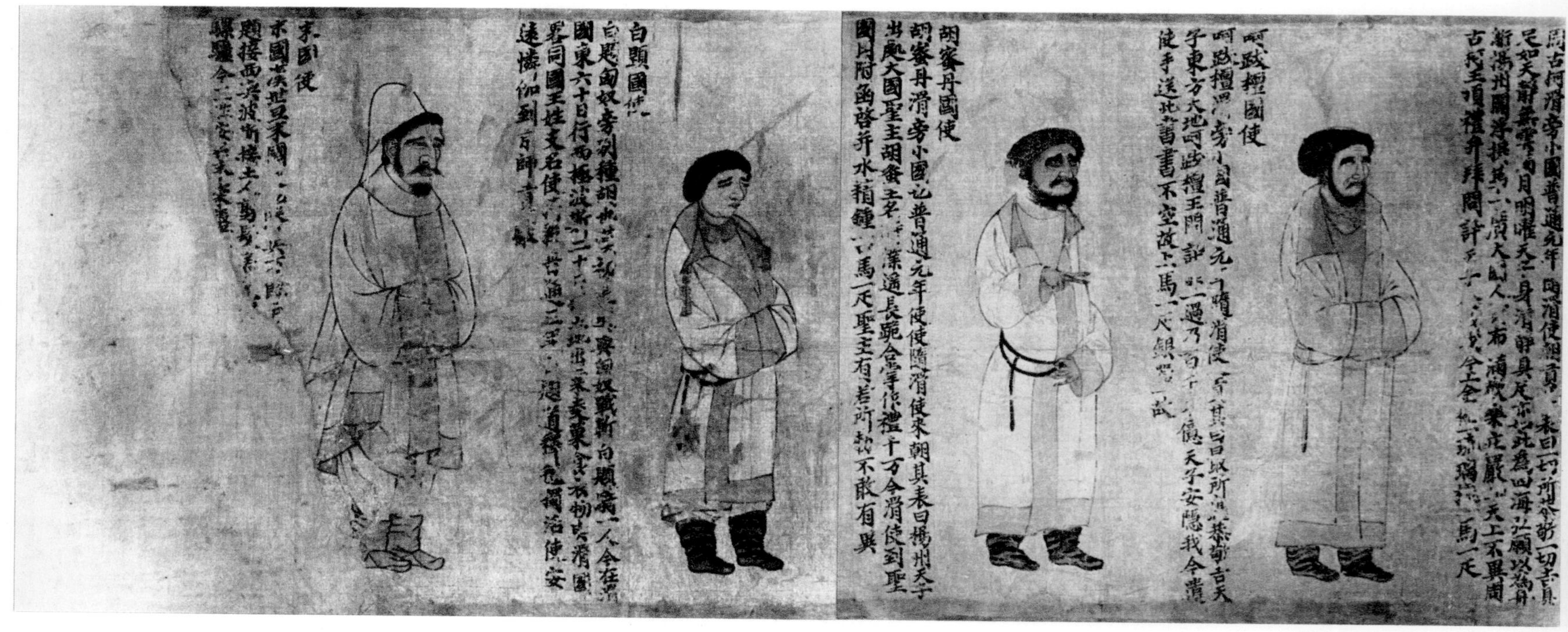

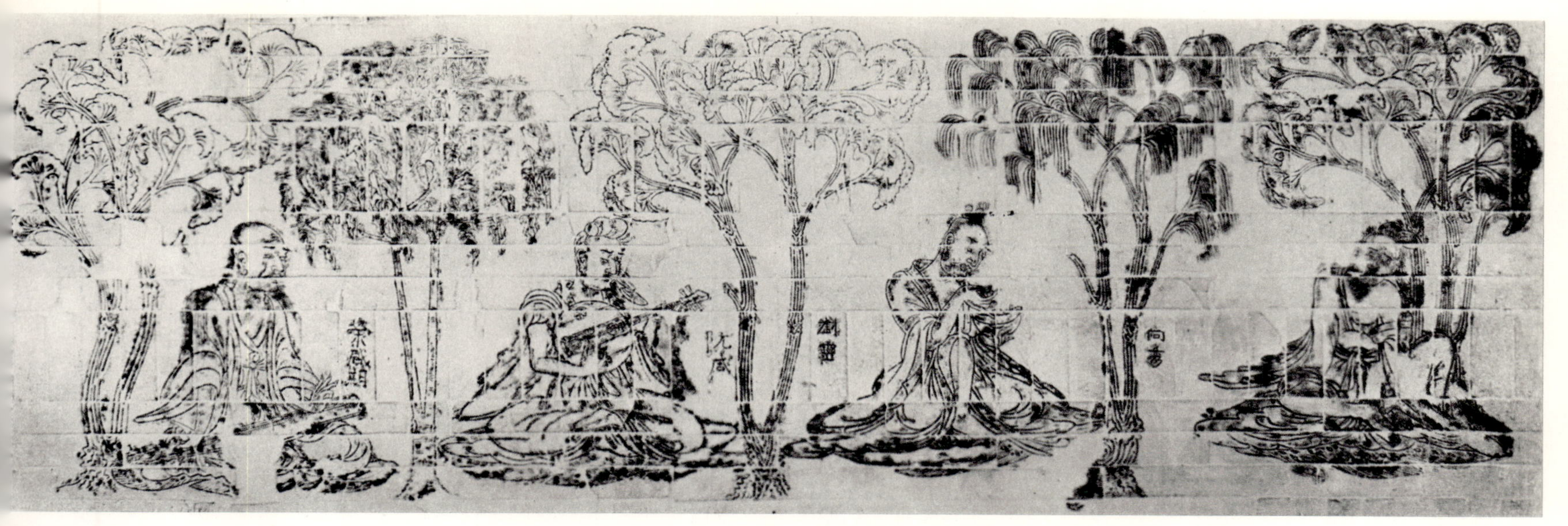

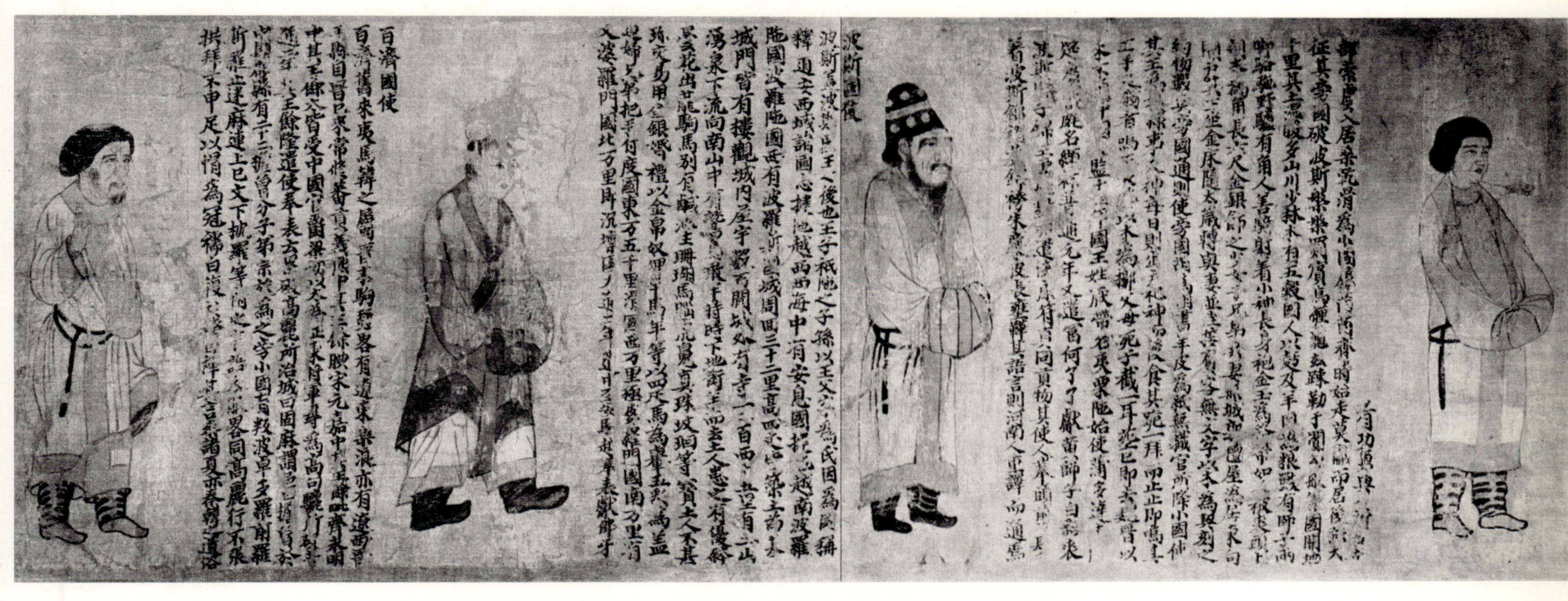
百濟國使
波斯國使

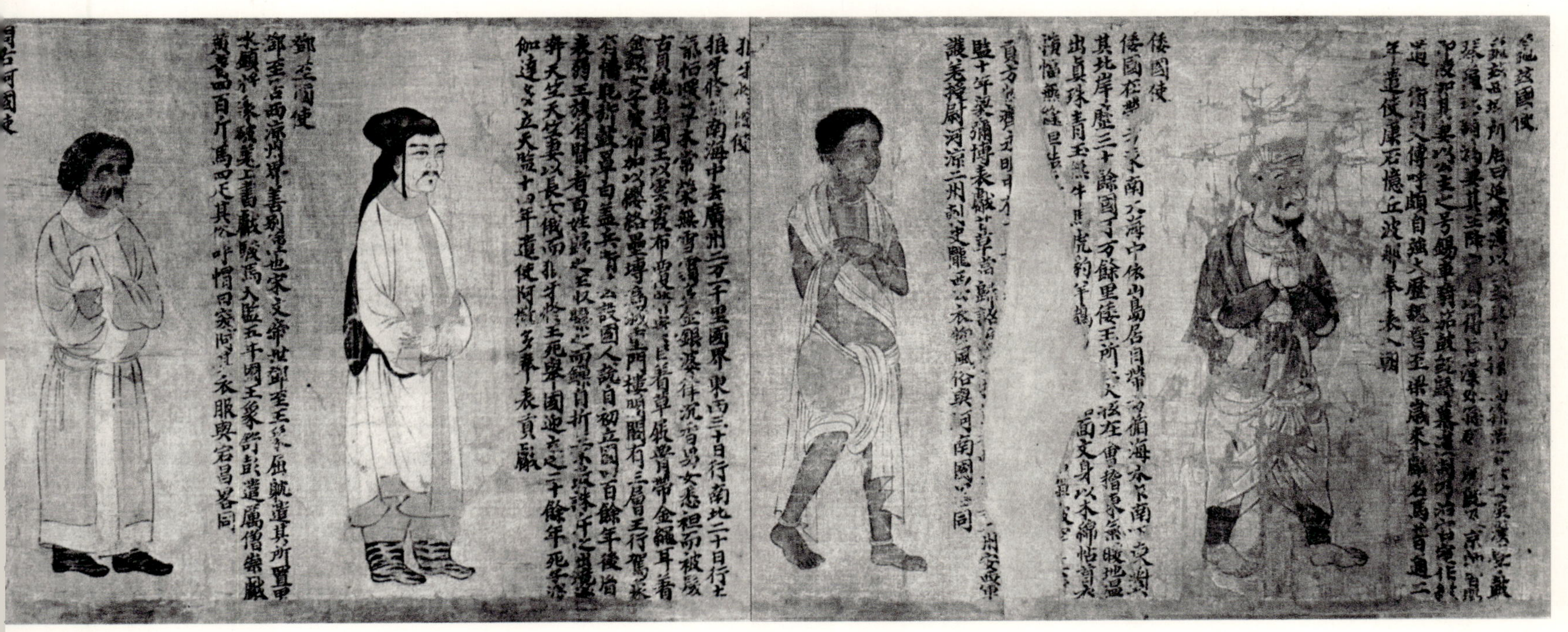
倭國使
鄧至國使

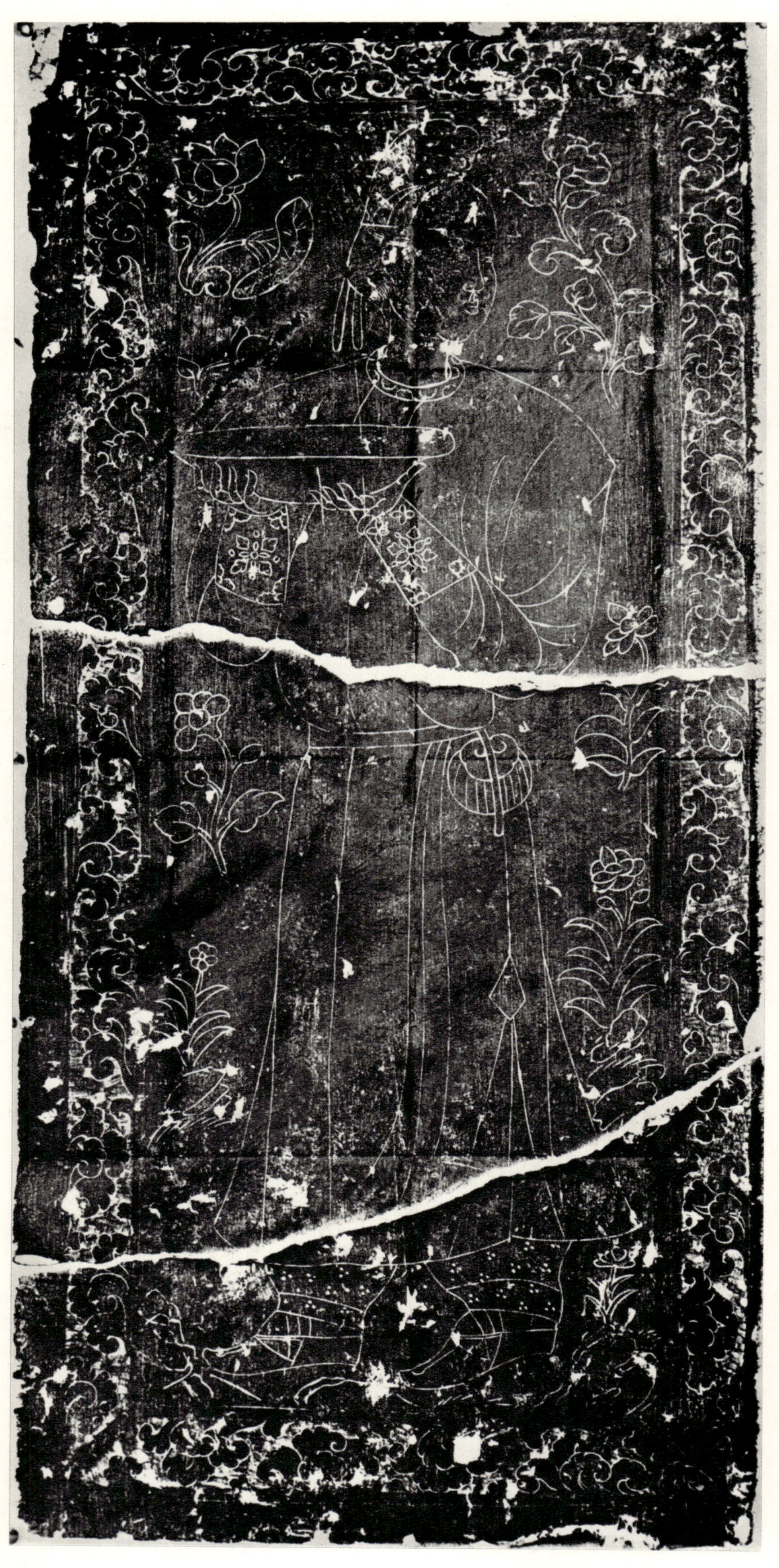

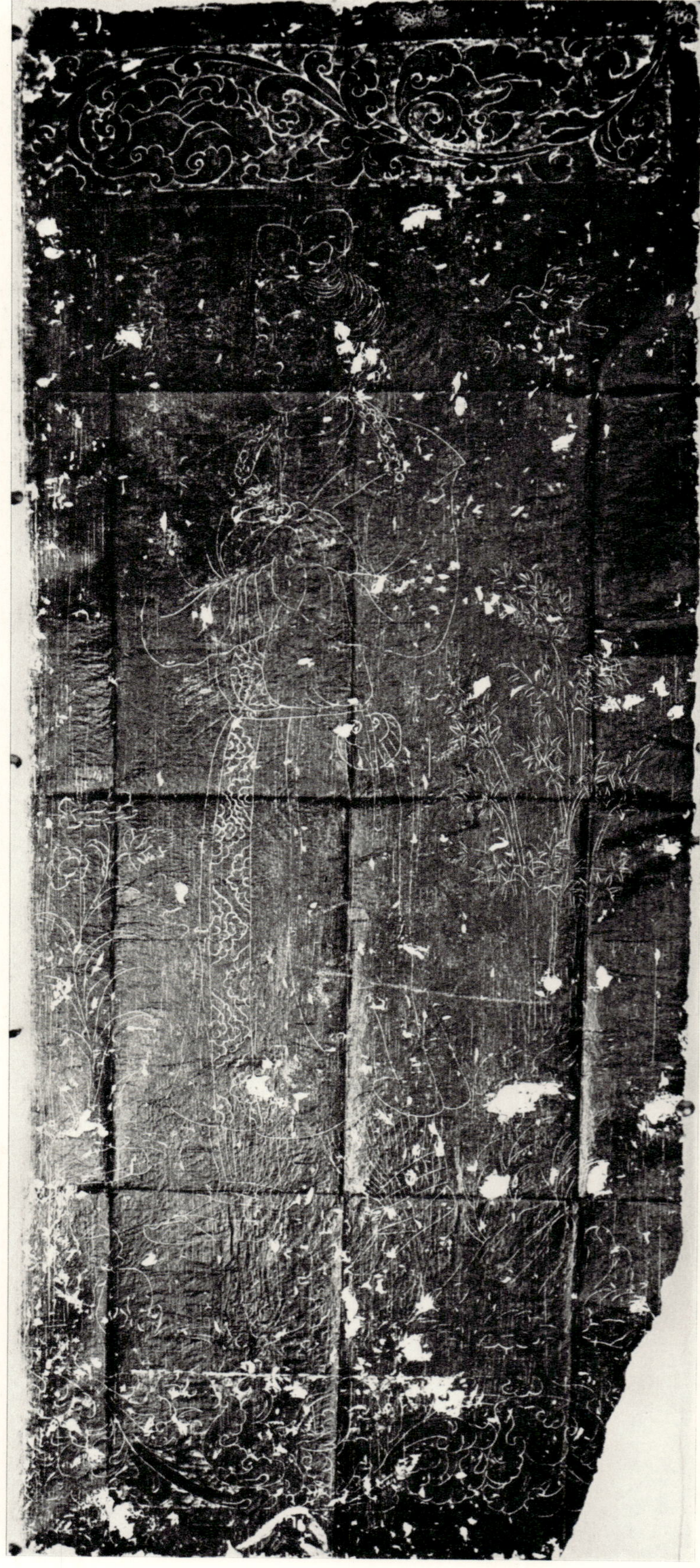

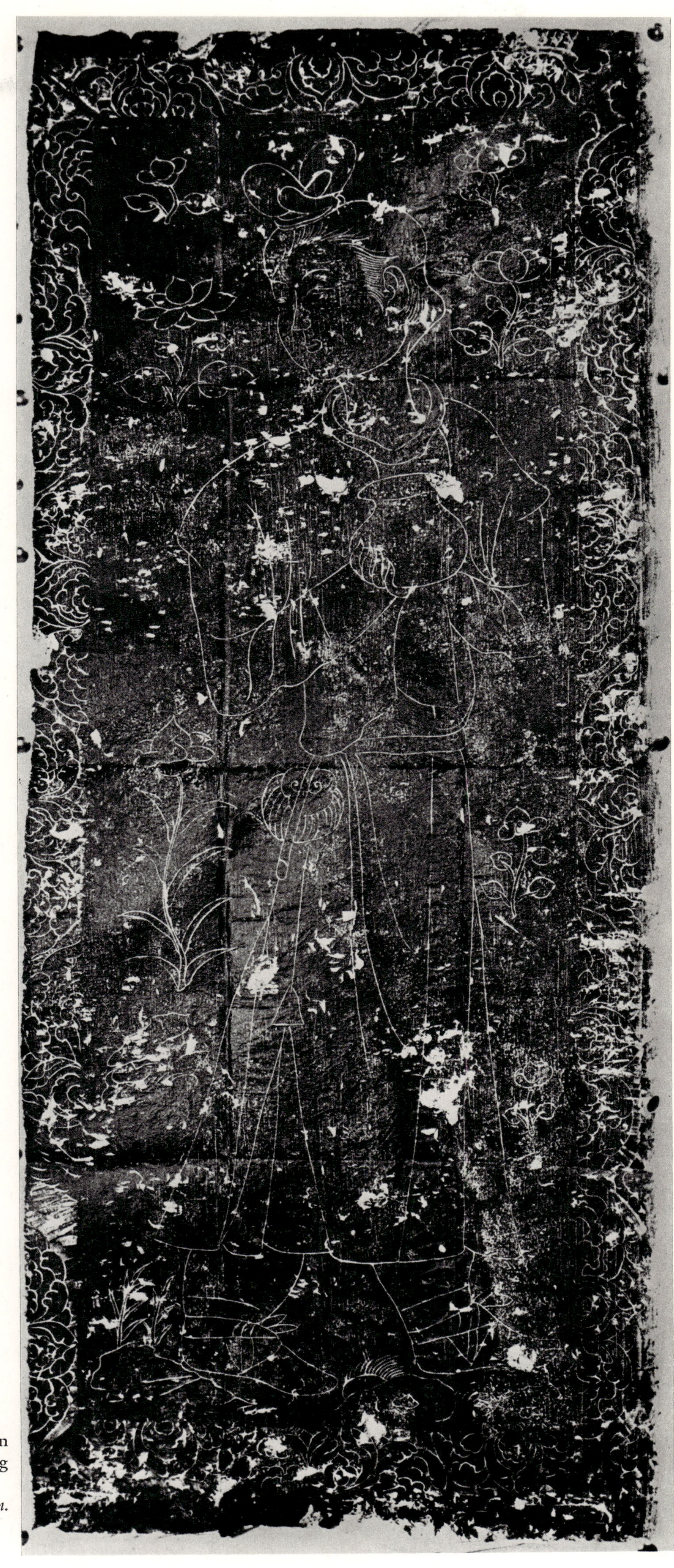

219–221. Engraved slabs from the case of a stone coffin (details). T'ang dynasty (708 A.D.). From the Wei Chiung tomb at Nan-wang-ts'un, Ch'ang-an District, Shensi.

219, 220 (facing page). height: 100 cm. (39.4 in.); width: 42.0 cm. (16.5 in.).

221. height: 103 cm. (40.5 in.); width: 40.0 cm. (15.75 in.)

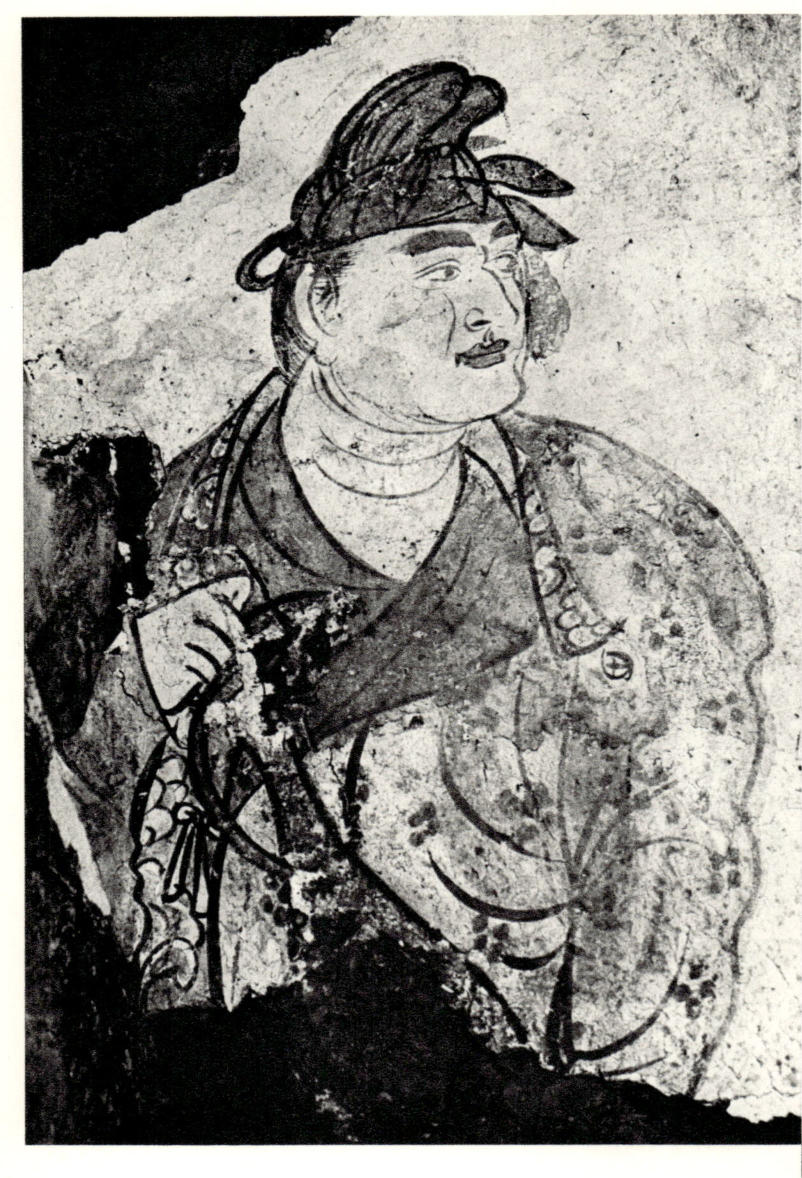

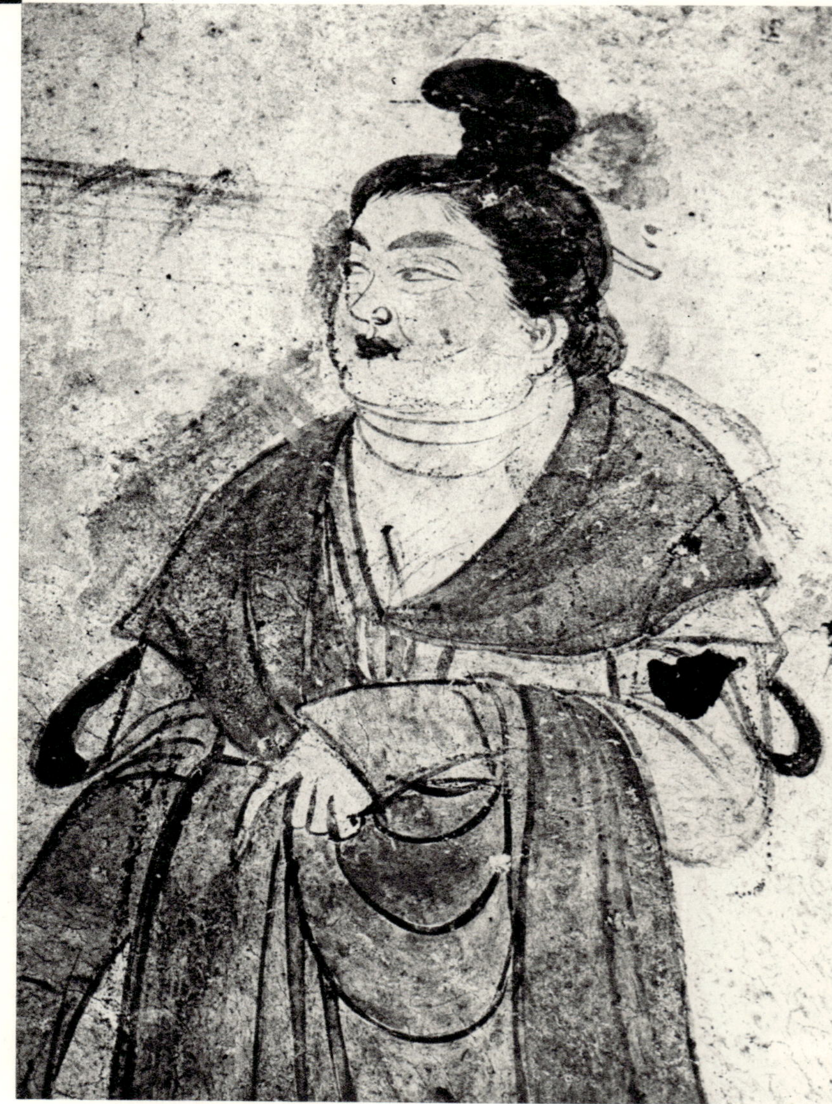

222–225. Details of wall paintings from a tomb coffin chamber. T'ang dynasty (708 A.D.). From the Wei Chiung tomb at Nan-wang-ts'un, Ch'ang-an District, Shensi.

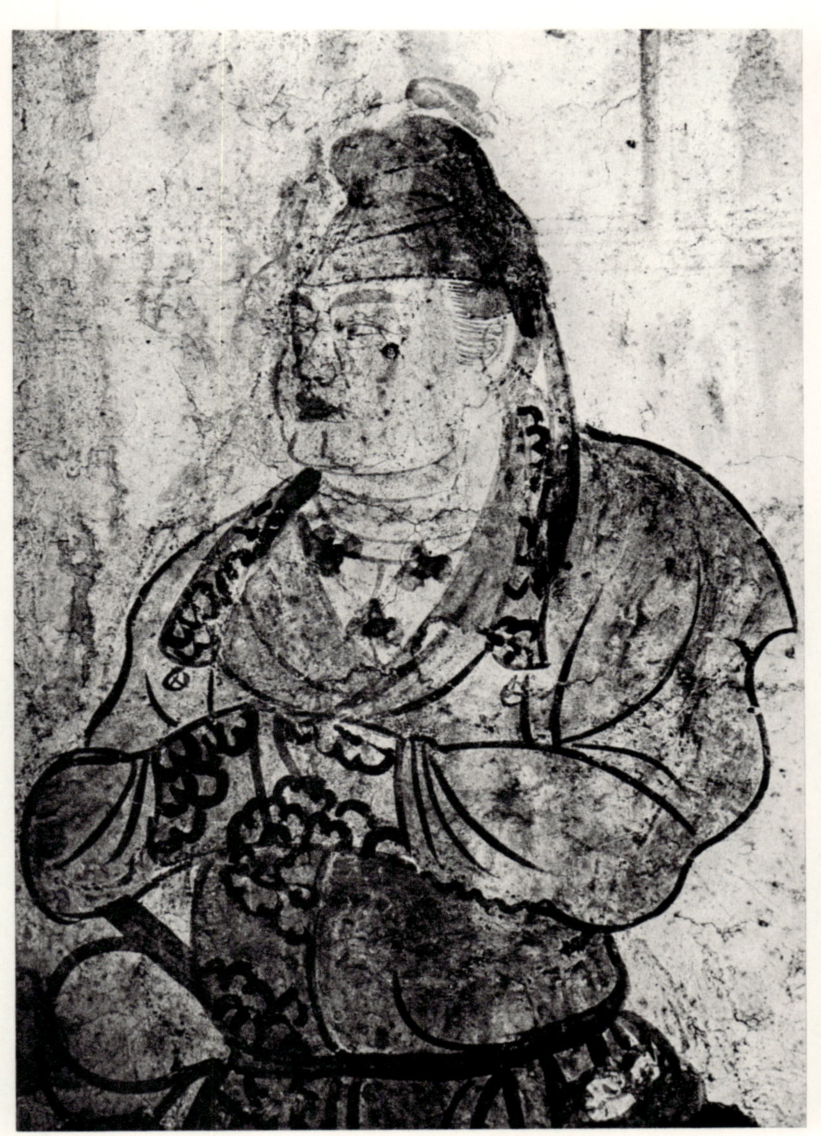

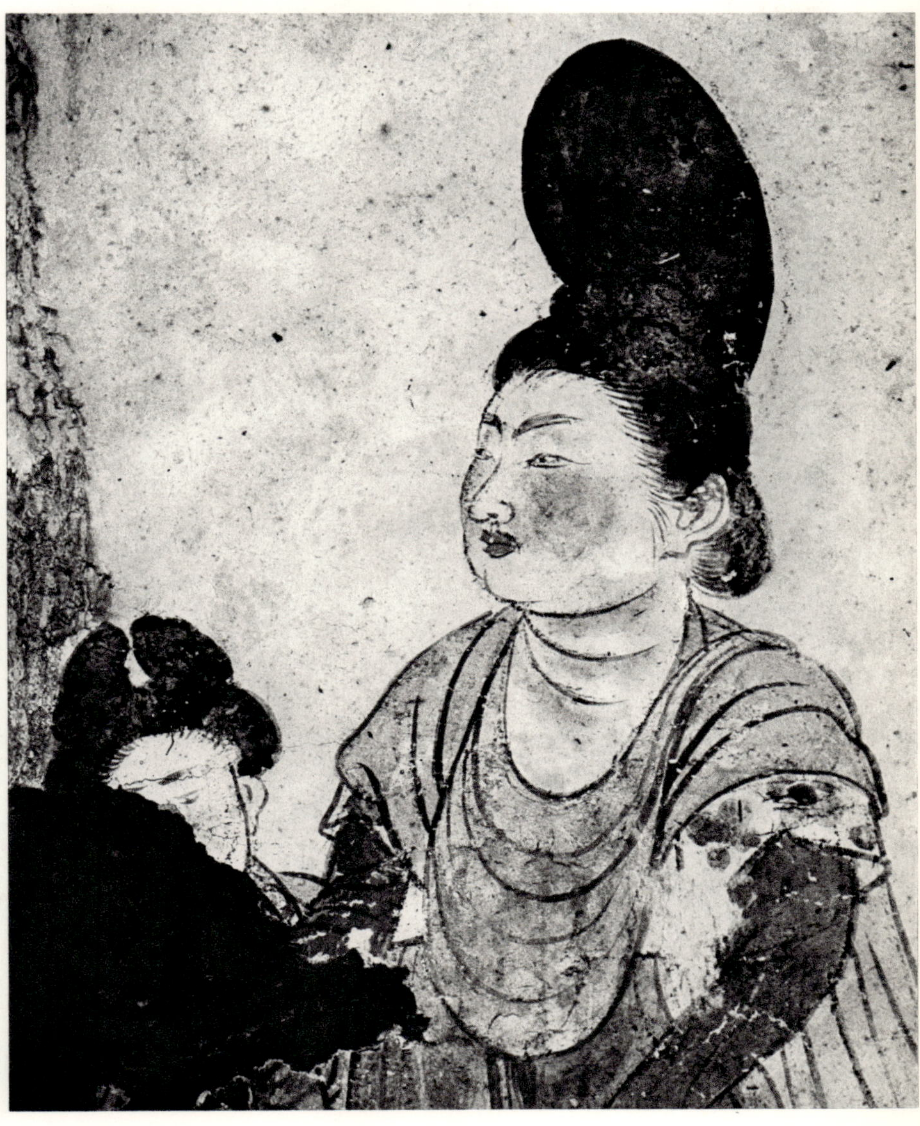

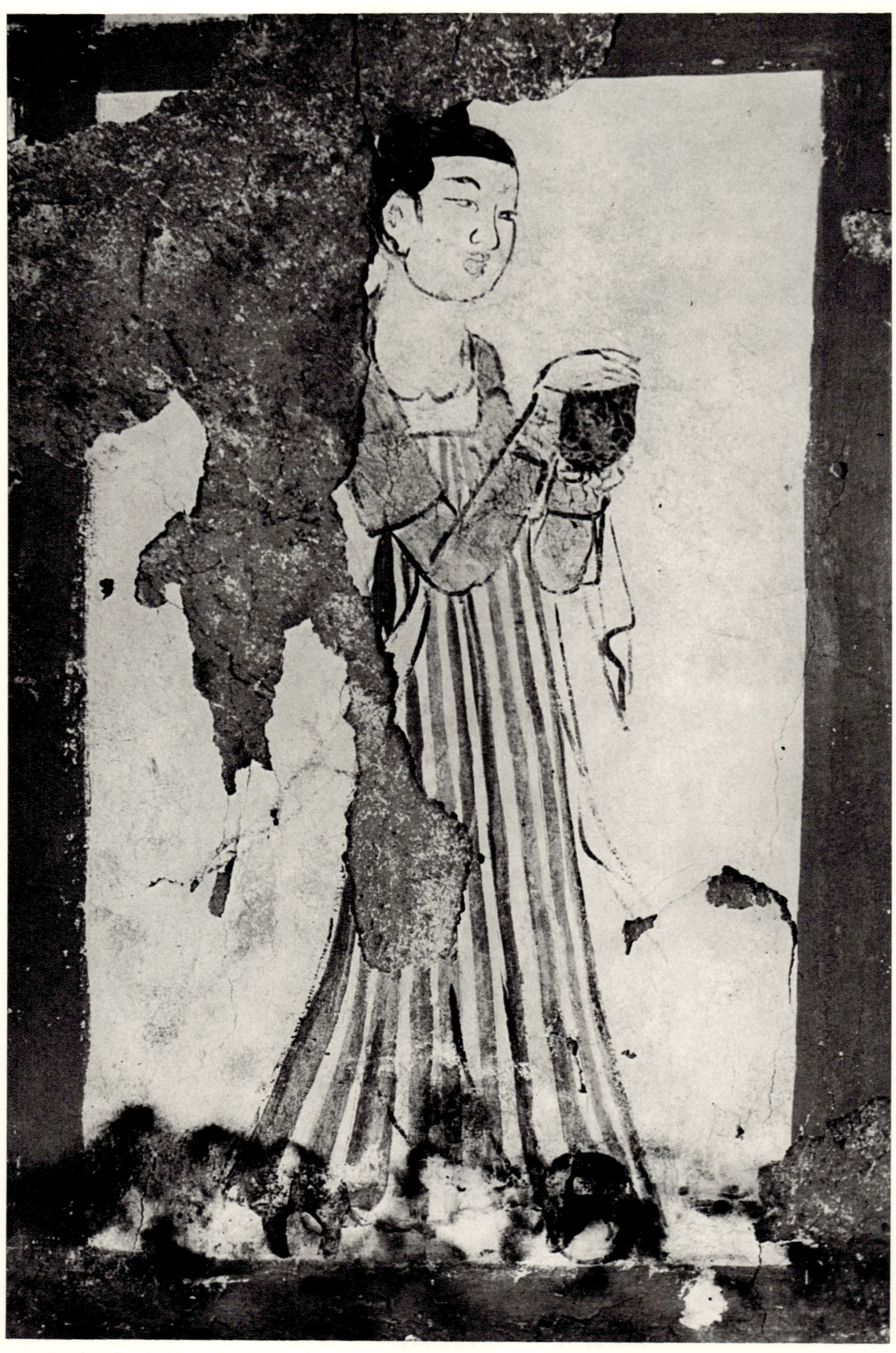

226. Tomb wall painting. T'ang dynasty (668 A.D.). From the tomb of Li Shuang, Yang-t'ou-chen, southern outskirts of Sian, Shensi (*see* Pls. 192, 193).
no measurement given

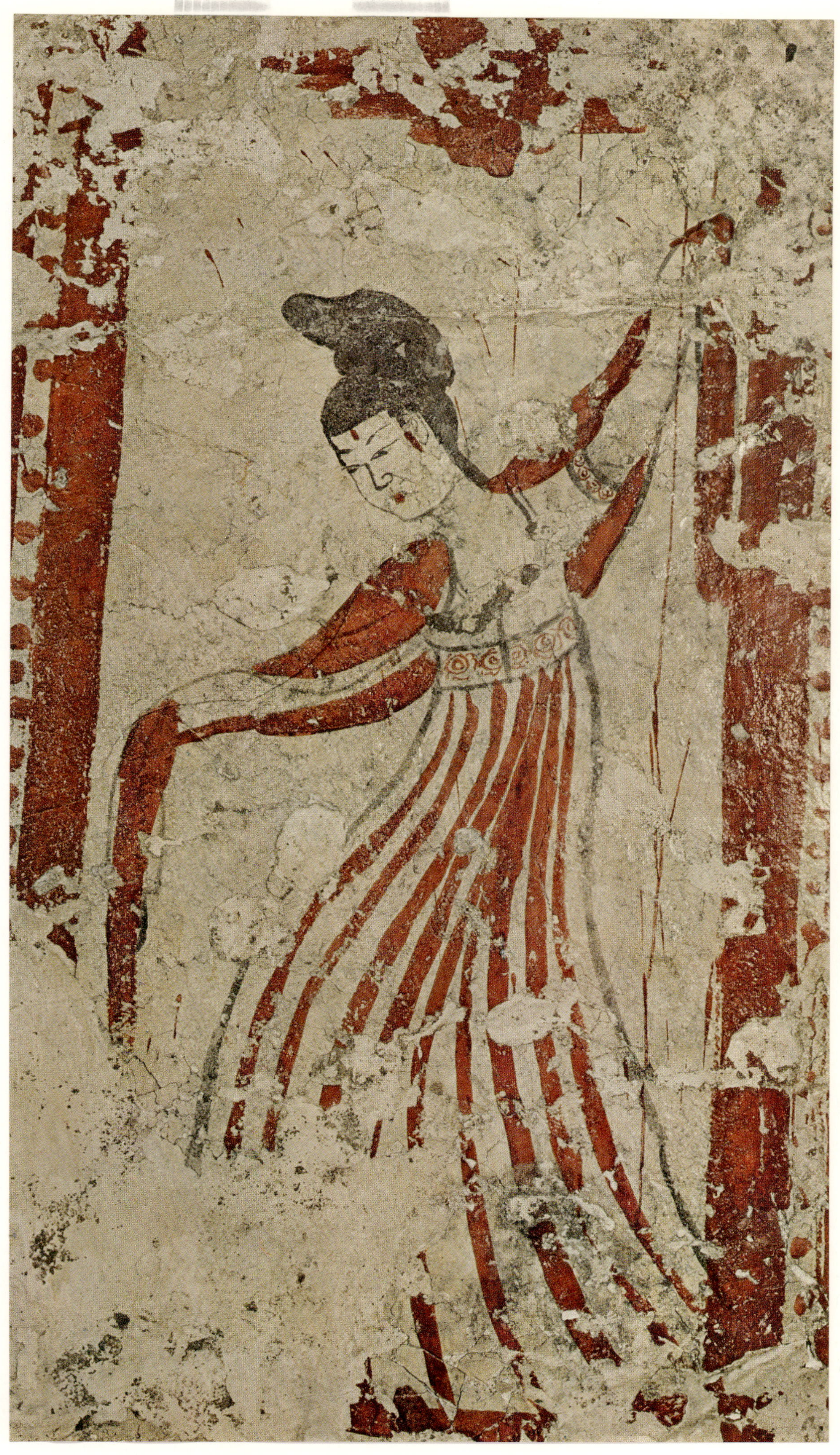

227. Tomb wall painting. T'ang dynasty (658 A.D.). From the tomb of Chih Shih Feng Chieh, Kuo-tu-chen, Sian Municipality, Shensi.
height: 116 cm. (35.7 in.); width: 72.0 cm. (28.4 in.)

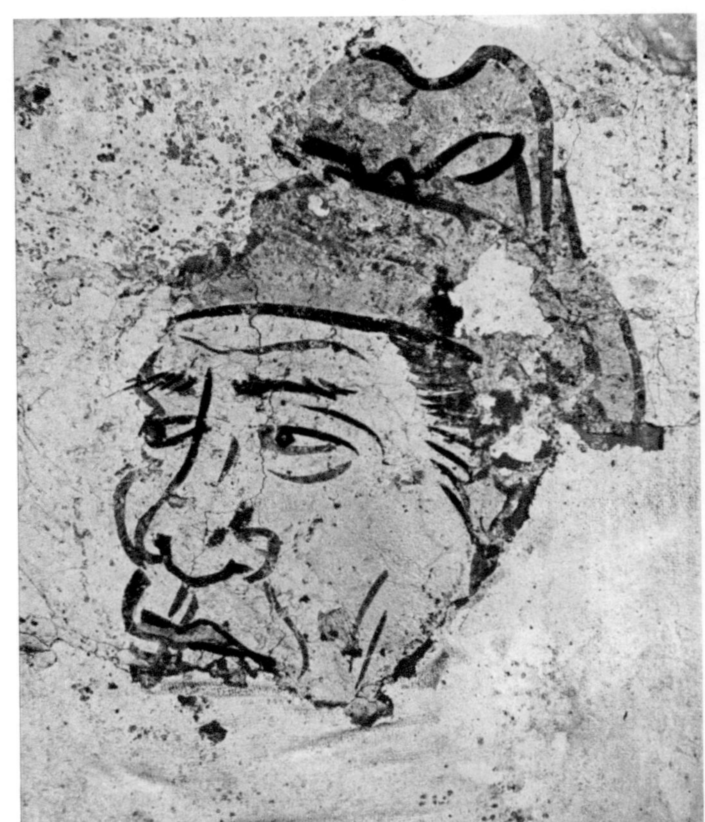

228. Tomb wall painting. T'ang dynasty (710 A.D.). From the tomb of Lady Hsüeh, Ti-chang-wan, Hsien-yang, Shensi (*see* Pl. 197).
no measurement given

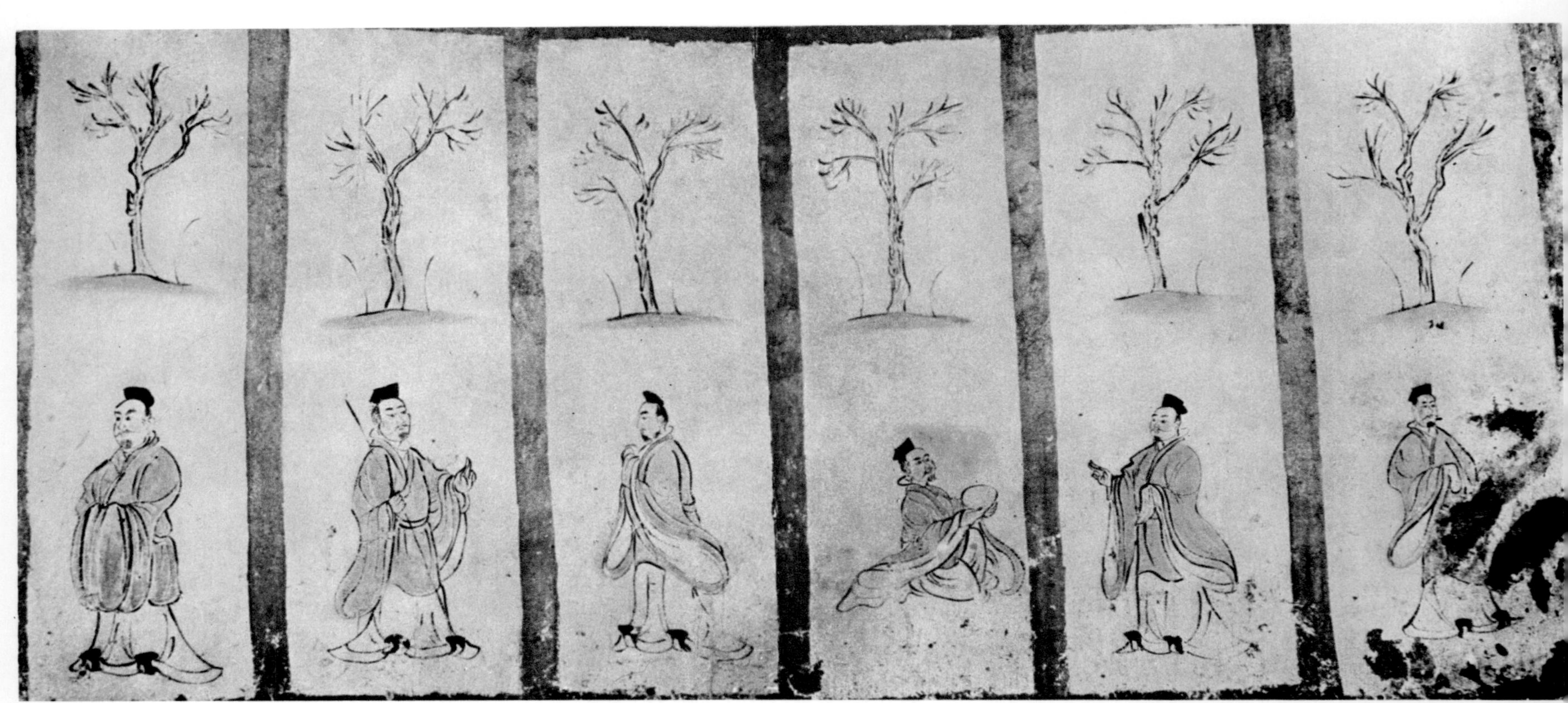

229. Tomb wall painting. T'ang dynasty (745 A.D.). From the west wall of the Su Ssu-hsü tomb, Ching-wu-lu, eastern outskirts of Sian Municipality, Shensi (*see* Pls. 194–196).
height: 70.0 cm. (27.6 in.)

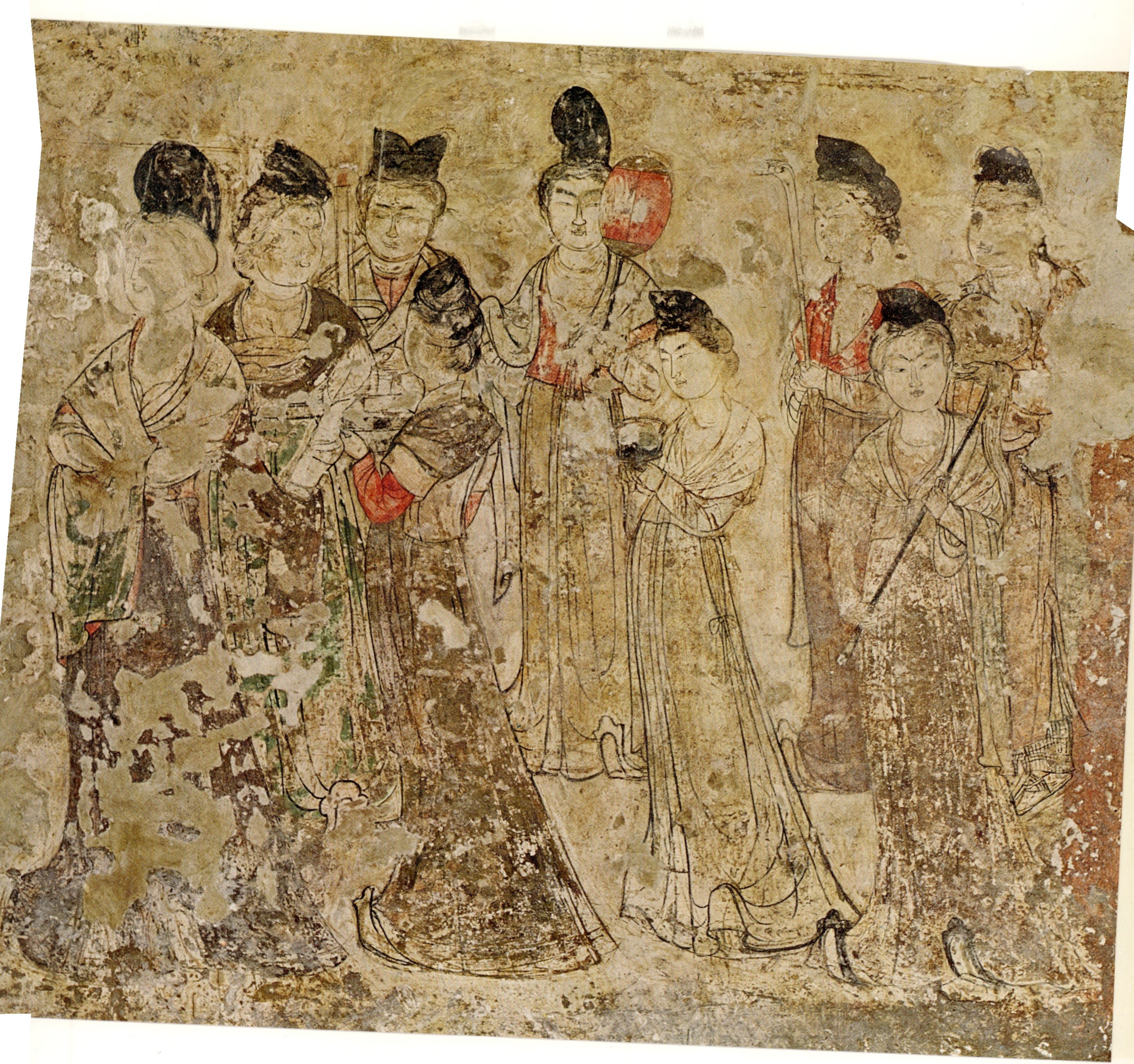

230. Tomb wall painting. T'ang dynasty (706 A.D.). From the east wall of the front chamber, Princess Yung-t'ai tomb, Liang-shan, Ch'ien District, Shensi.
wall height: 198 cm. (77.9 in.); wall length: 420 cm. (165.5 in.)

231–232. Details of tomb wall painting. Early T'ang dynasty. From tomb No. 4, Chin-sheng-ts'un, southern outskirts of T'ai-yüan Municipality, Shansi.
231. height: 71.3 cm. (28.1 in.)
232 (facing page). height: 74.3 cm. (29.3 in.)

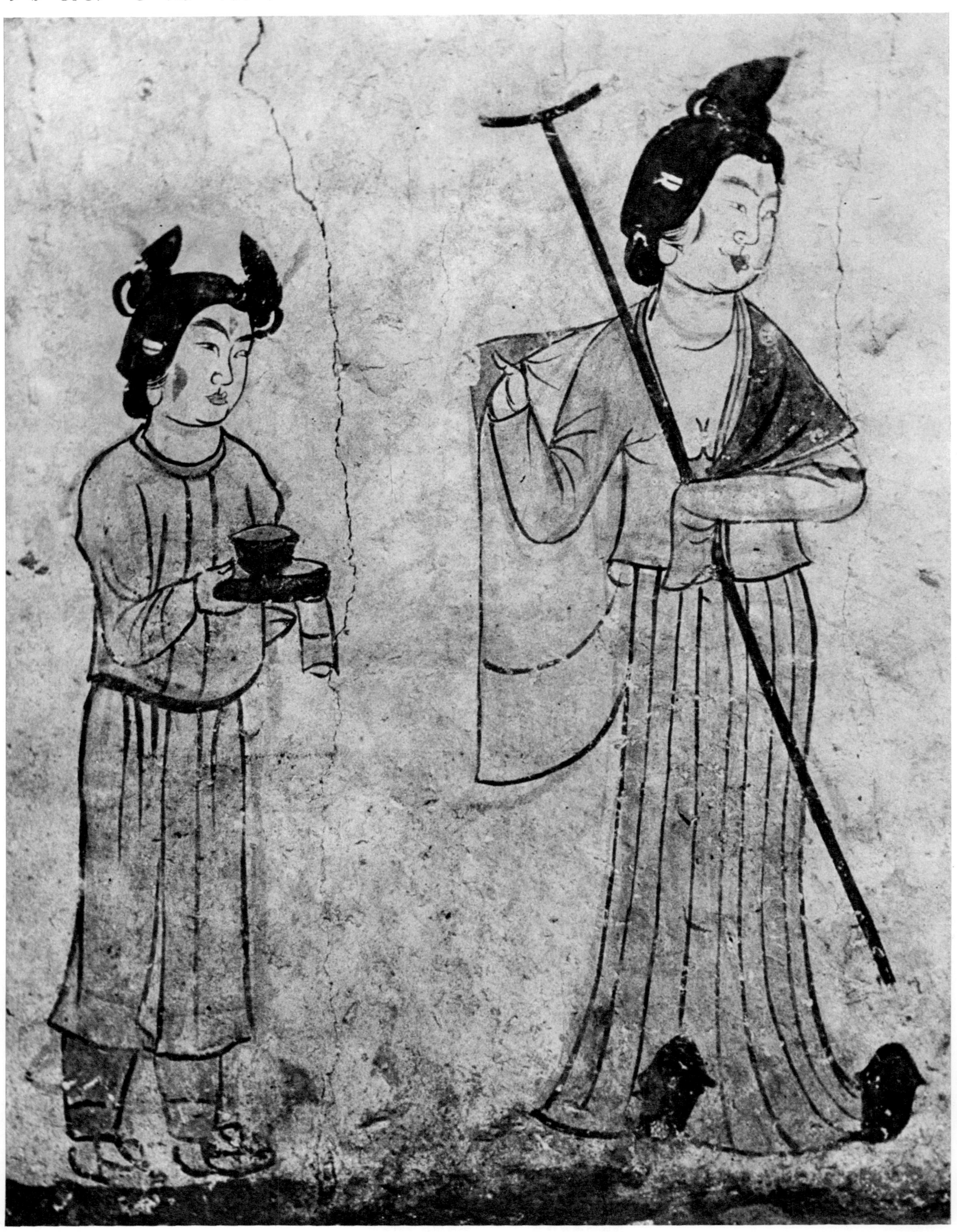

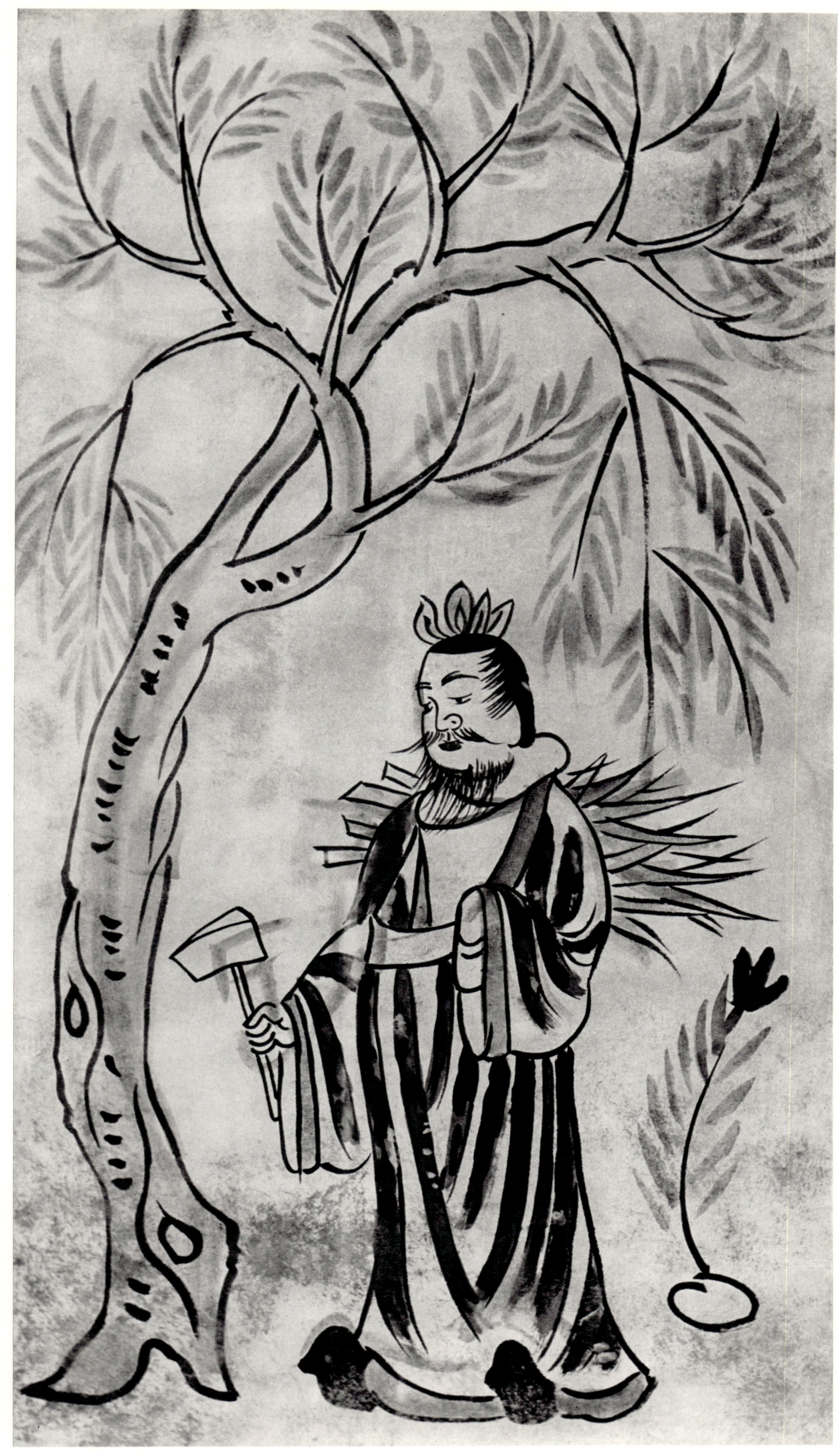

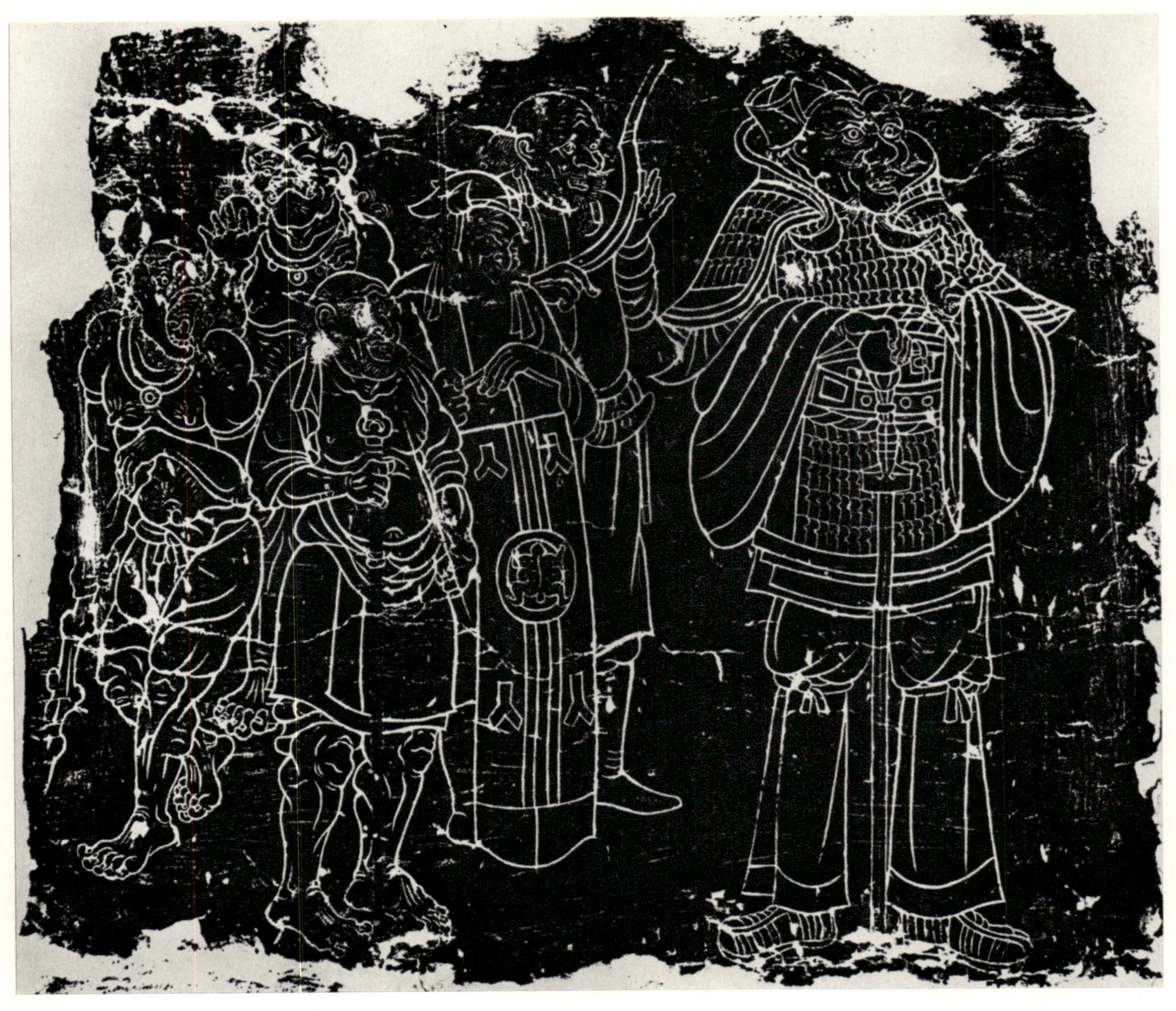

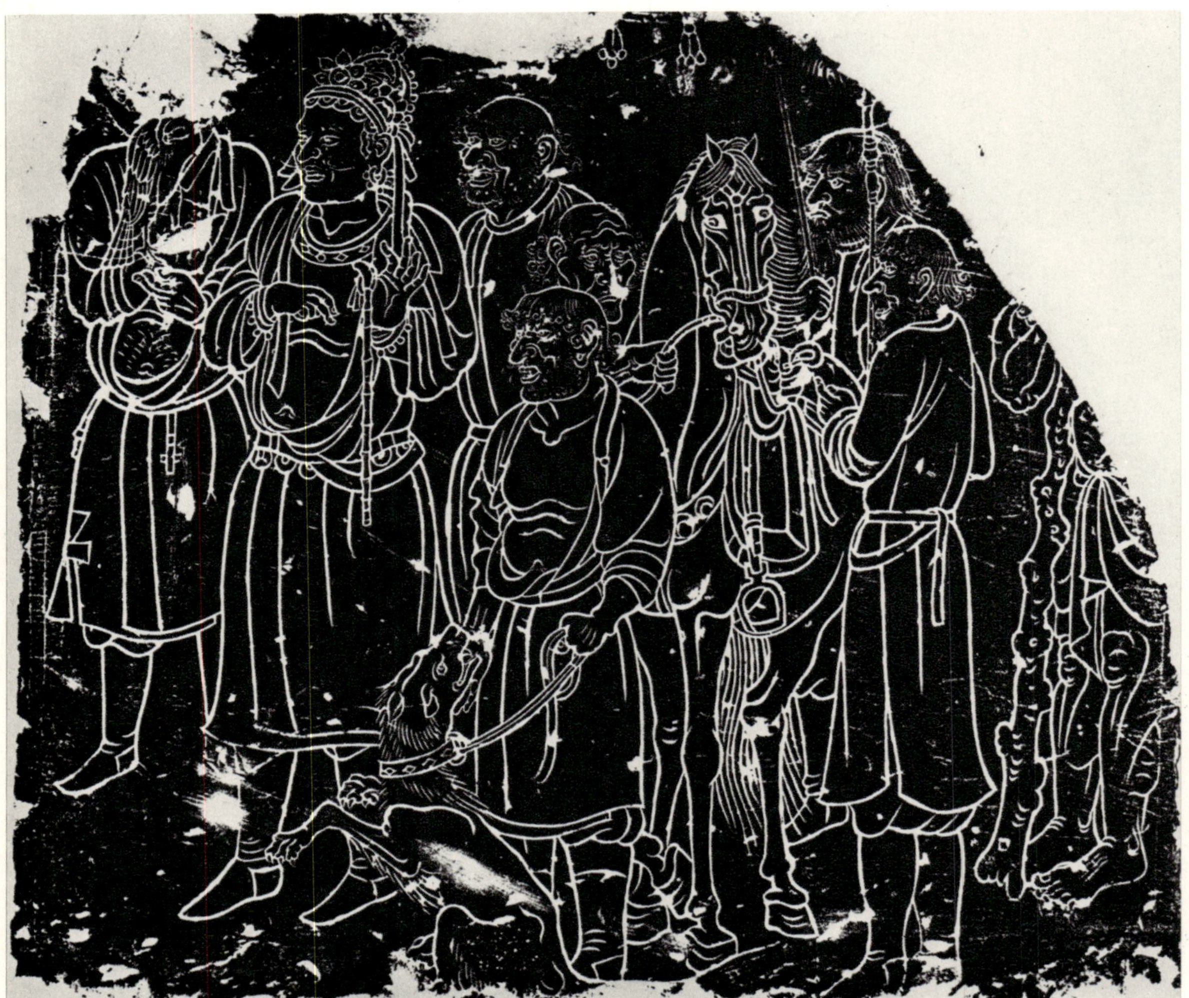

233–234. Rubbings of stone line engravings of Buddhist figures, warriors and guardians. T'ang dynasty (663 A.D.). From the base of the Priest Tao-yin tablet at Pei-lin, Sian Municipality, Shensi.
height: 37.0 cm. (14.6 in.); width: 43.0 cm. (16.9 in.)

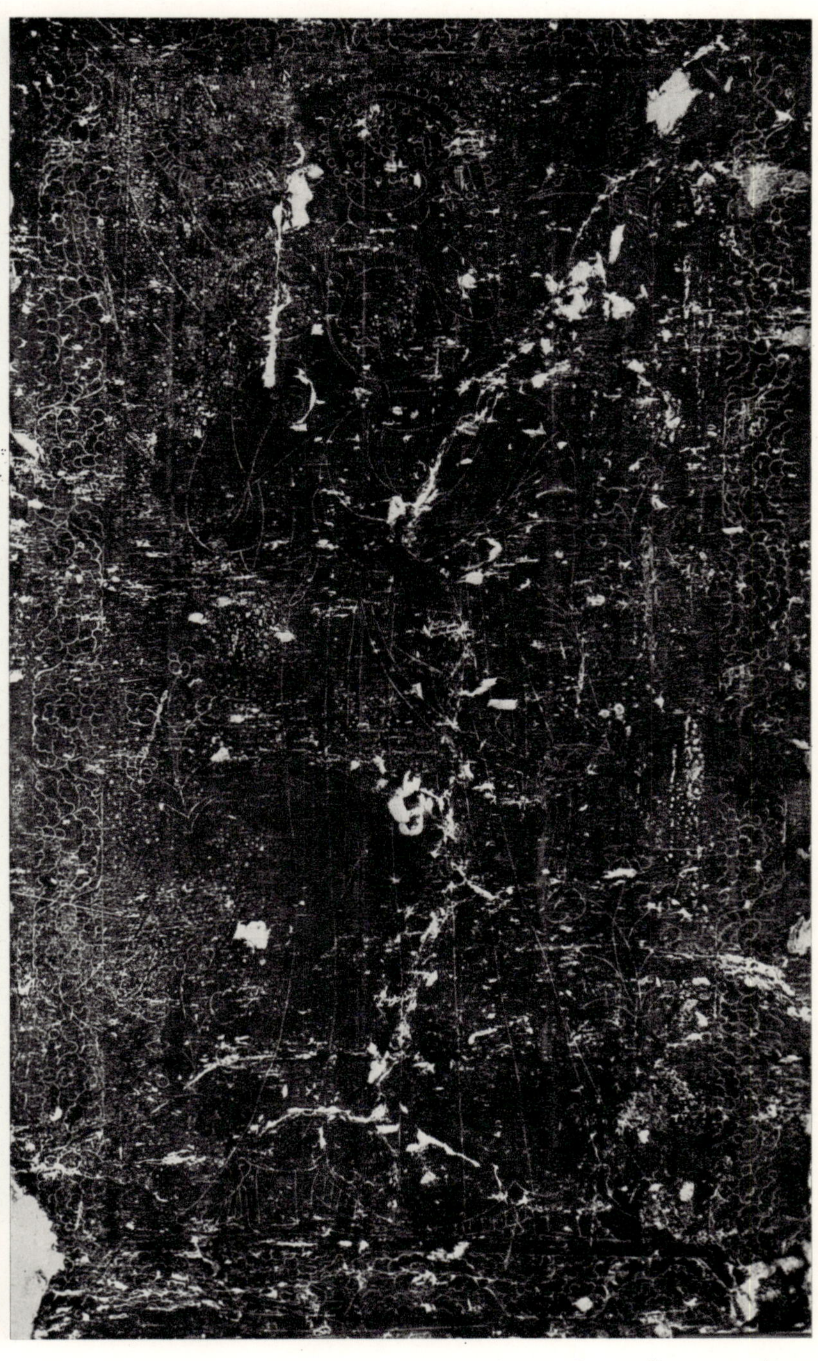

235–236. Rubbings of stone line engravings. T'ang dynasty. From the Wei Hsü tomb, southern Ch'ang-an District, Shensi.
length: 121 cm. (47.6 in.); width: 75.0 cm. (29.6 in.)

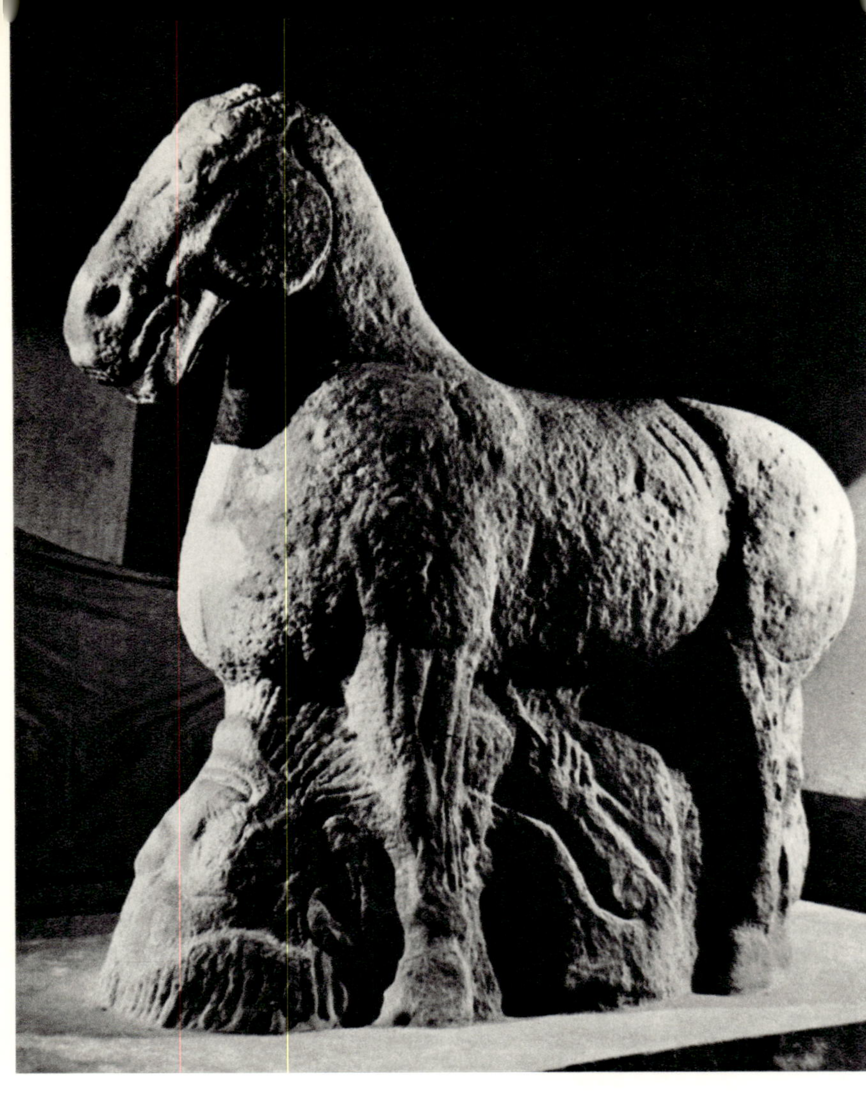

237. Horse standing over a captive, stone. Former Han dynasty (*ca.* 117 B.C.). From the tomb of General Huo Ch'ü-ping, Hsing-p'ing District, Shensi.
height: 188 cm. (74.1 in.); length: 190 cm. (74.9 in.)

238. Mythical animal, stone. Southern Ch'i dynasty (*ca.* 498 A.D.). From the Hsing-an tumulus, Tan-yang, Kiangsu.
height: 260 cm. (102.4 in.); length: 310 cm. (122.1 in.)

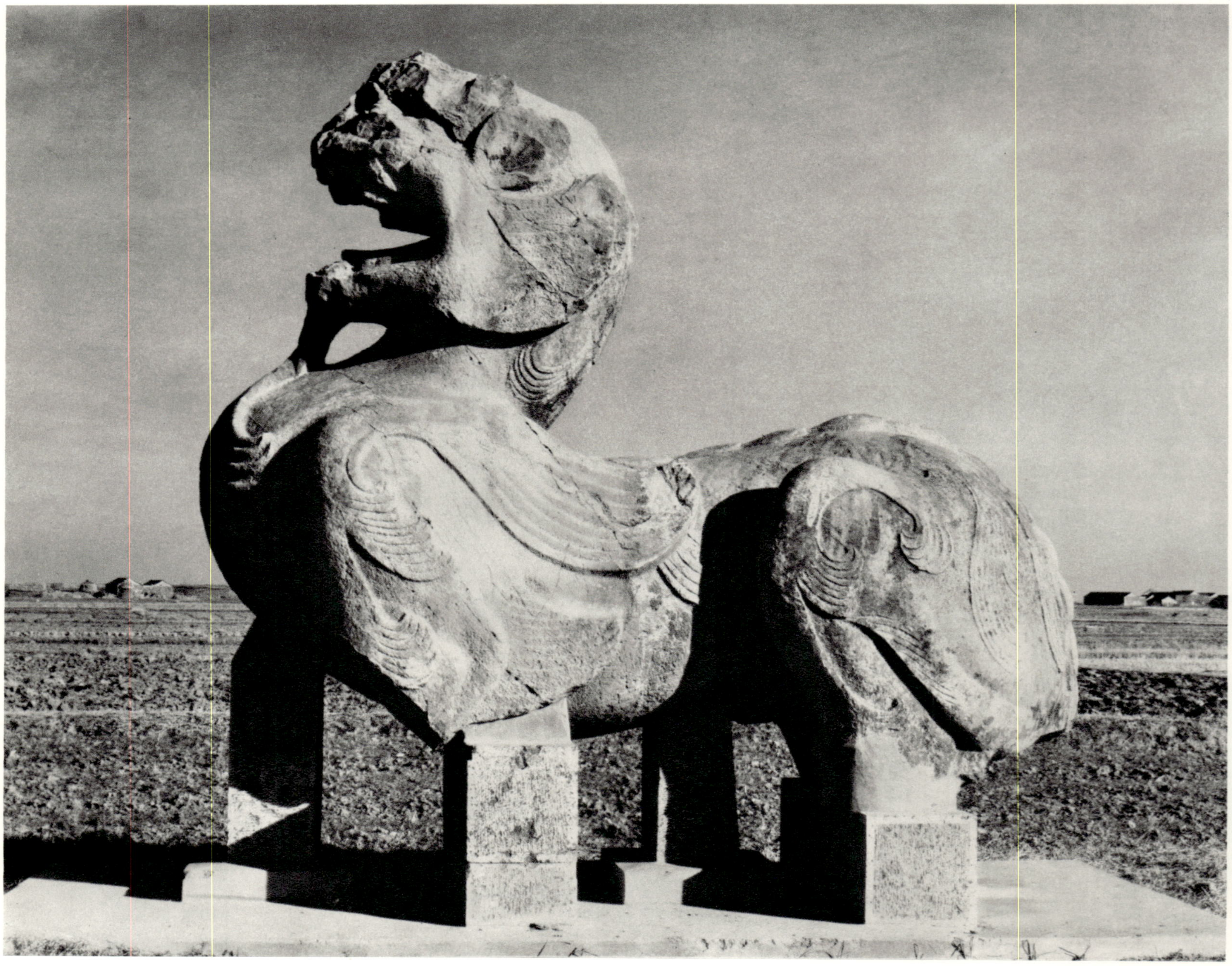

239. Mythical animal, stone. Liang dynasty (*ca.* 526 A.D.). From the Hsiao-hung tomb, Ch'i-lin-men, Nanking.
height: 280 cm. (110.3 in.); length: 300 cm. (118.2 in.)

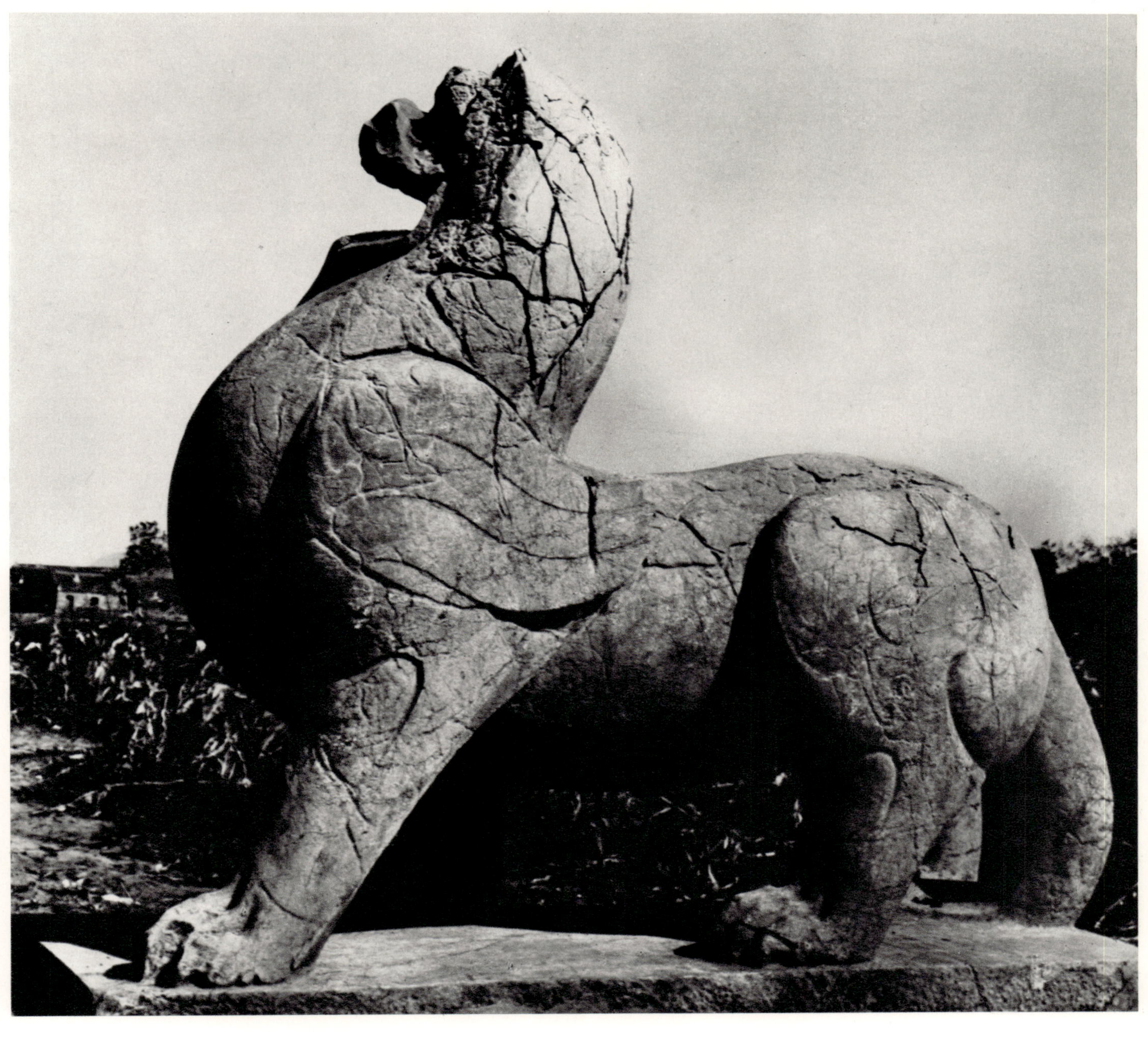

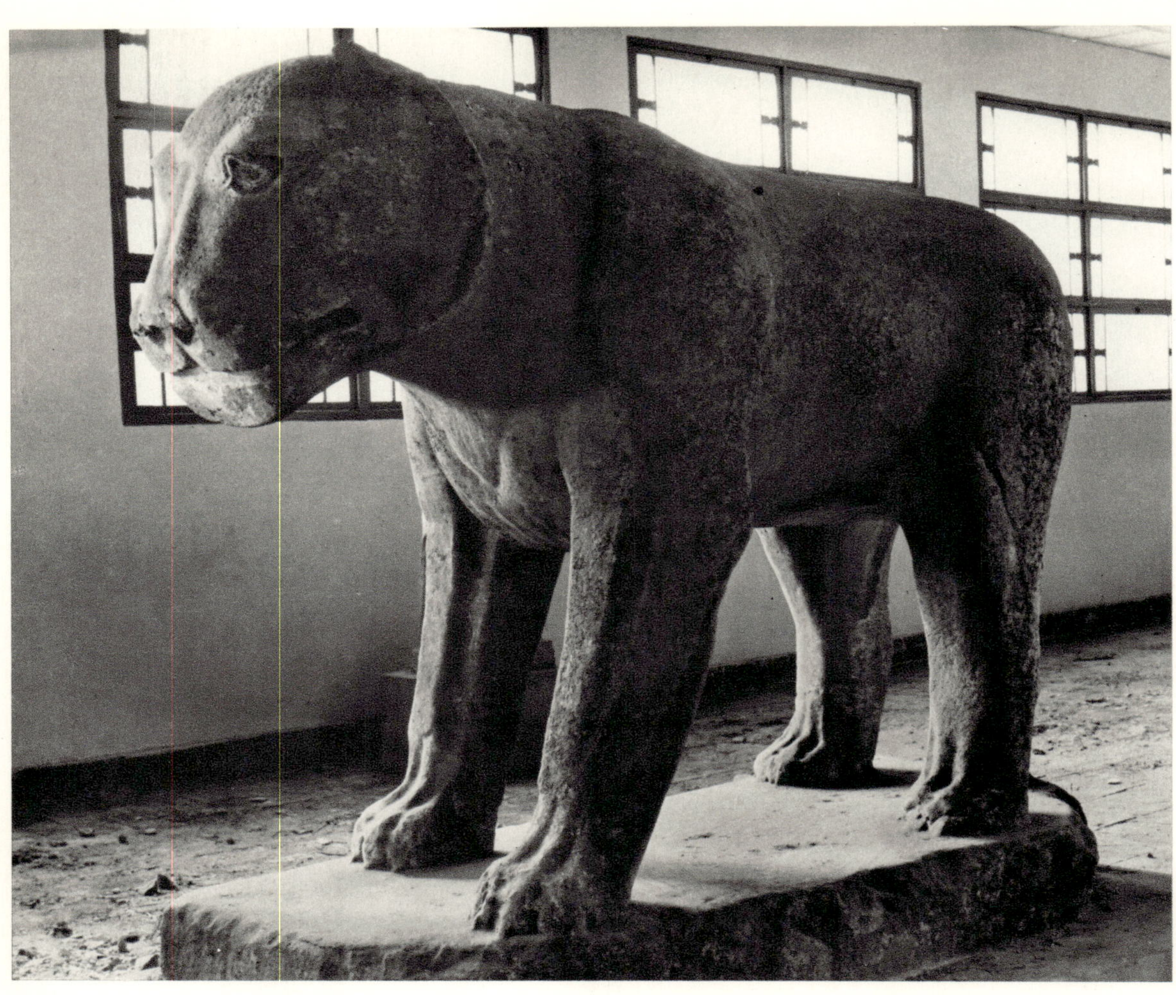

240. Tiger, stone. T'ang dynasty (*ca.* 635 A.D.). From the tomb of the Emperor Kao-tsu, the Hsien *ling*, San-yüan District, Shensi.
length: approx. 300 cm. (118.2 in.)

241. The "White-Hoofed Horse" of T'ai-tsung, stone relief carving. T'ang dynasty (seventh century). Originally from the Chao *ling*, Li-ch'üan District, Shensi.
height: 170 cm. (67.0 in.); width: 205 cm. (80.8 in.)

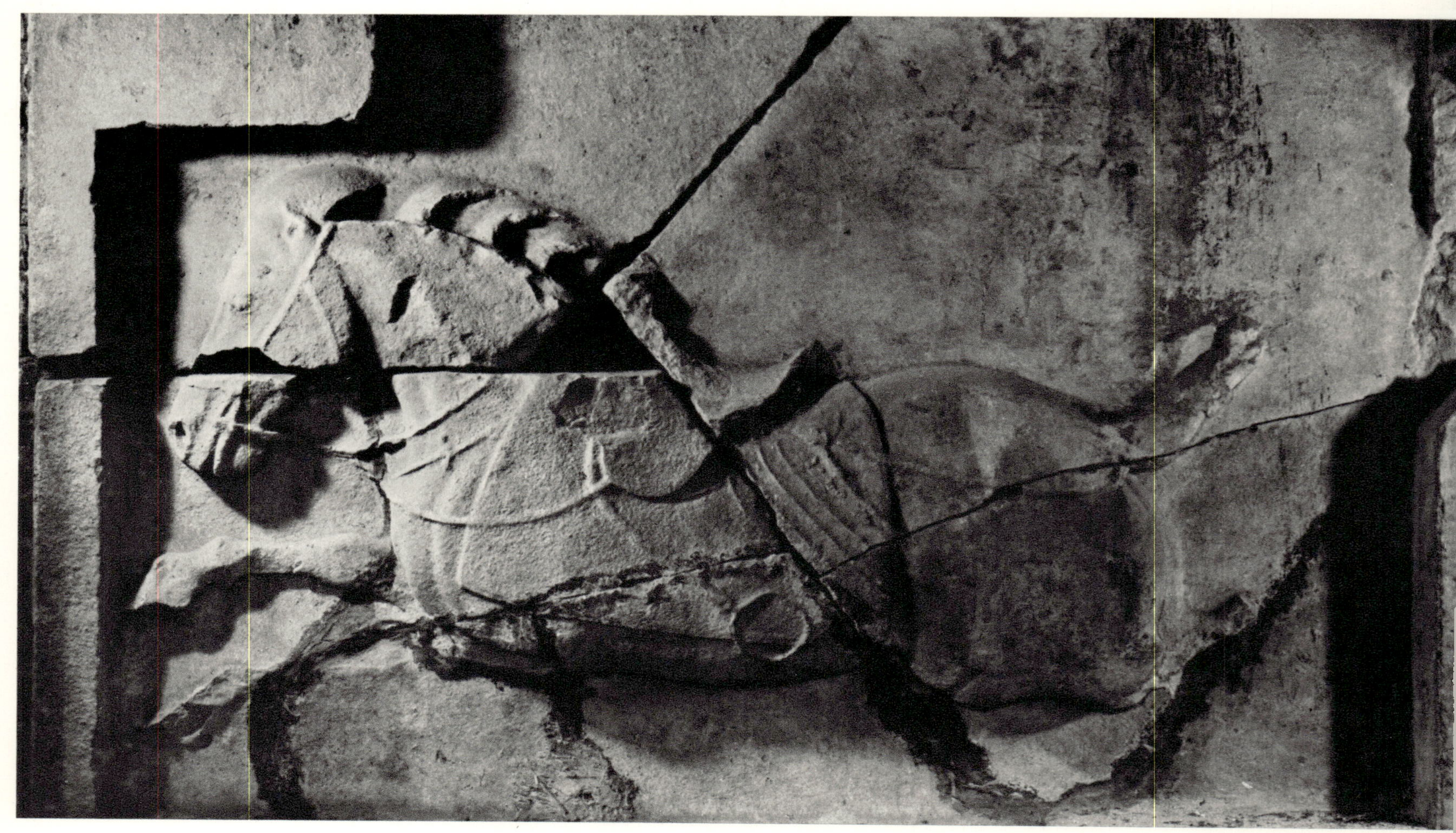

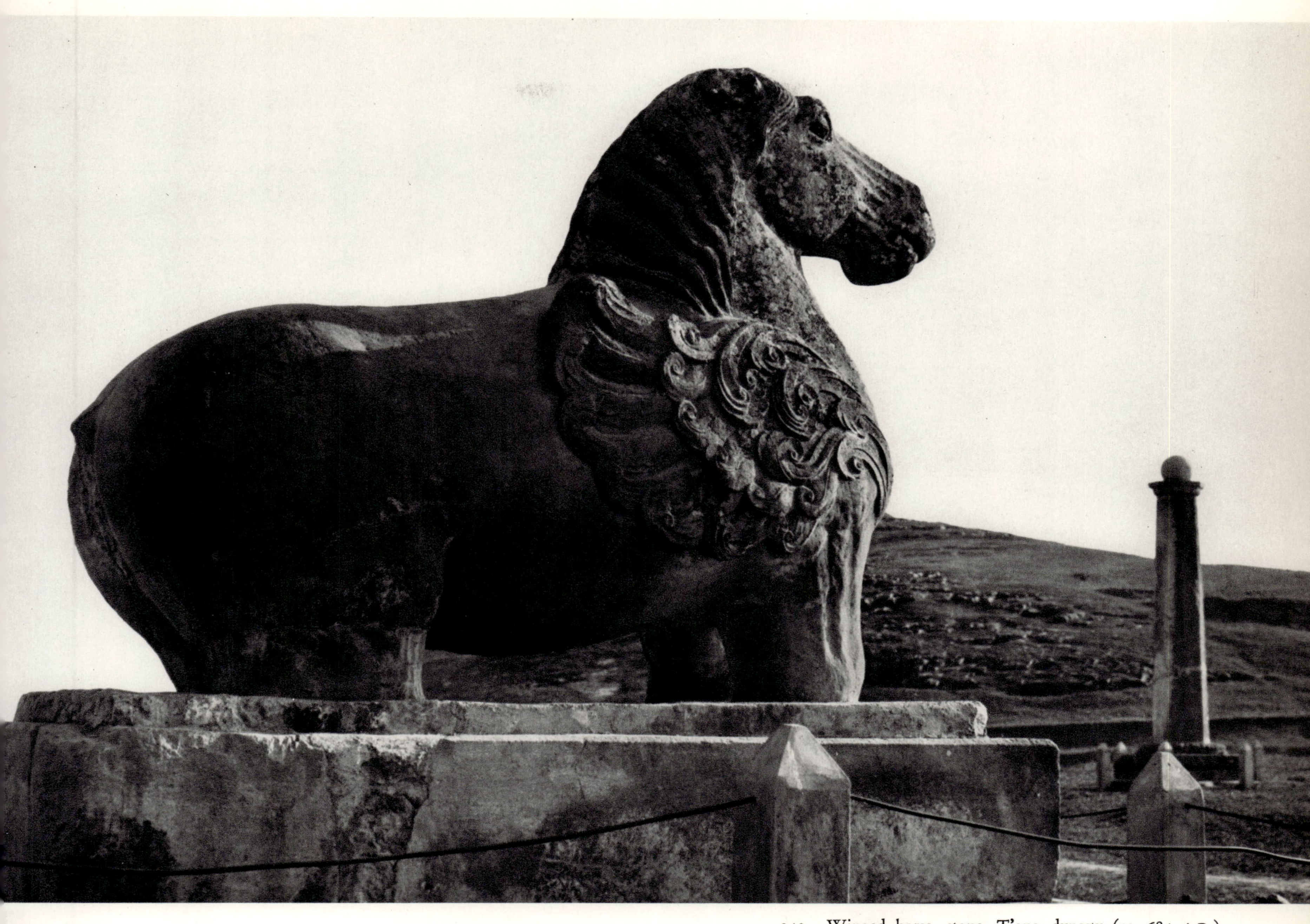

242. Winged horse, stone. T'ang dynasty (*ca.* 684 A.D.). From the Ch'ien *ling*, Ch'ien District, Shensi.
height: approx. 400 cm. (157.6 in.)

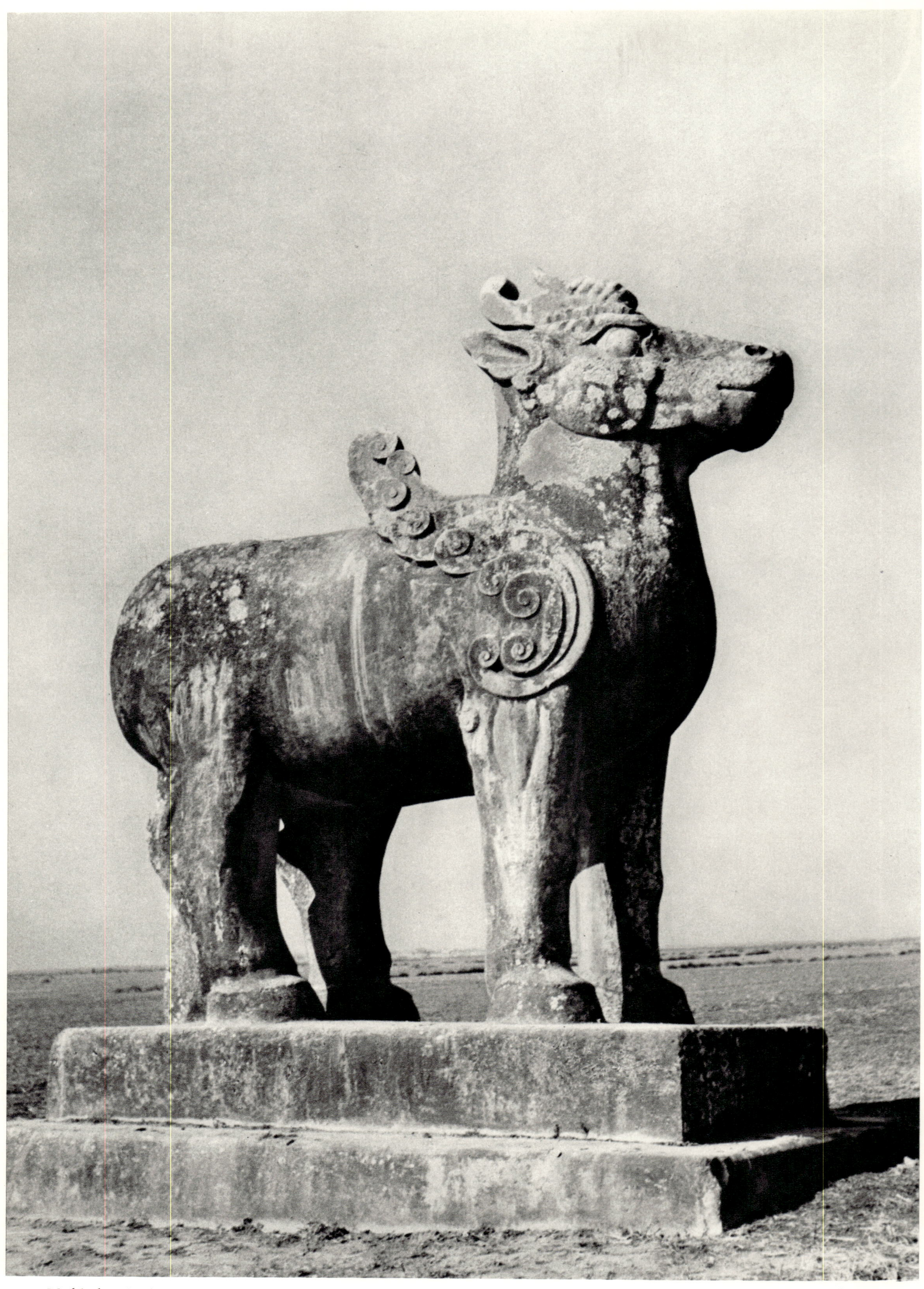

243. Mythical animal, stone. T'ang dynasty. From the Shun *ling*, Hsien-yang District, Shensi.
height: approx. 480 cm. (189.1 in.)

V. Burial Objects—Models of Worldly Comfort

MING-CH'I As with the *haniwa* of Japan, it was the custom in ancient China, instead of making living sacrifices, to bury models of people, animals, articles of everyday use, and buildings with the dead. These are commonly known as *ming-ch'i* (spirit objects), though the terms *yung* (jointed human figurines) and *ni-hsiang* (clay figures, because of the material often used) are also employed. The origin of this custom of making burial models in China is not clear. Some small clay models of human figures were discovered in a late Yin tomb at Hsiao-t'un, An-yang, in Honan, but these are too crude to merit attention as works of art. No Chou dynasty *ming-ch'i* have been found; however, the *Yi Li (Book of Etiquette and Ceremonial)* directs that "the *ming-ch'i* are to be placed to the west of the vehicle," which suggests that objects were being buried with the dead, whatever the materials used. A further entry in the same work says: "The *ming-ch'i* are for the use of spirits, and the sacrificial vessels are for the use of men," which shows that objects made specifically for burial with the dead, rather than for practical use, were already being made. Moreover, a passage in the *Chou Li* (*The Rites of Chou*) describes the procedure for a funeral as follows: "At a funeral, prepare vehicles and a procession, at the graveyard mount a ceremonial guard and then place the *hsiung-ch'i* in the pit." The term *hsiung-ch'i* has long been accepted as meaning *ming-ch'i,* and this quotation indicates that the custom of burying *ming-ch'i* with the dead was quite widespread by the time of Confucius (sixth century B.C.). Indeed, Confucius himself says: "The earthen chariots and straw figures, which have existed since ancient times, are really *ming-ch'i,* and I feel no objection to burying them. However, I am opposed to the use of *yung,* which seems too much like the sacrifice of living people." One can infer from this reference that the technique of representing human beings in *ming-ch'i* had achieved a certain realism.

It is only recently that attention has come to be directed to *ming-ch'i* as works of art or as subjects of serious study. Innumerable tomb models of all sorts must have been made over the millennia, and considerable numbers of them subsequently unearthed, but the only recorded reference is that of a ceramic *ting* noted in the twelfth-century catalog *Po Ku T'u.*

It was Lo Chen-yü, one of the most eminent Chinese scholars of the twentieth century, who first pointed out the value of tomb models as art and as reference material in the study of Chinese history. Mr. Lo first came across two ancient earthenware tomb figures in a Peking shop in 1907. The shopkeeper treated them as of no value, explaining their presence in his stock by saying they had been dug from an ancient tomb in Honan but were generally regarded as of no value, and he had acquired them free along with some art objects he had bought. Lo Chen-yü promptly offered to buy any similar pieces, not necessarily human figures, and left a list of types of *ming-ch'i* as listed in the *T'ang Hui Yao* (*State Regulations of T'ang*). The result was that the next spring the dealer brought a large and varied collection of *ming-ch'i* from Honan. These included, besides human figures, farm buildings, animals, birds, wells, kitchen utensils, musicians, etc. Lo bought the whole lot, and soon merchants began to bring them from further afield, notably from Sian. From his collection Lo Chen-yü selected a number of outstanding pieces and reproduced them in his four-volume *Ku Ming-Ch'i T'u-Lu* of 1916.

In Japan, Dr. Kōsaku Hamada of Kyoto University was one of the first to collect and study *ming-ch'i.* His book, *Illustrated Notes on Ancient Ming-ch'i Figures (Komeiki Deizō Zusetsu)*, was published in 1924. Dr. Yaichi Aizu of Waseda University also began collecting around 1916, and for many years lectured at the university on the subject. His large collection of *ming-ch'i* is now displayed in the Aizu Memorial Hall at that university.

Before Mr. Lo drew attention to the *ming-ch'i*, there had been very little material for the study of sculpture in ancient China, and almost nothing was known of the plastic arts previous to the Han period. Even for the Han dynasty, the material was limited to the famous reliefs at the Wu family shrine and stone figures at places such as Ch'ü-fu and Sung-shan. The following period, too, was represented only by stone reliefs from a few places such as the caves at Ta-t'ung and Lung-men. Thus it was a revelation to find in these tomb models—probably dismissed in their day as the work of mere craftsmen—works of considerable artistic merit that added much to any study of the plastic arts.

Today, discussion of the plastic energy and the techniques of Chinese sculpture is unthinkable without reference to the *ming-ch'i*. It is the discovery of *ming-ch'i* that has made clear the true worth of this sculpture and filled in a historical gap. Nor is the question simply one of the plastic arts, since the *ming-ch'i*, including as they do almost every kind of article in everyday use at the time—and in more detail than, say, the Japanese *haniwa*—give a very vivid picture of life at the time, known to us hitherto only by written records, and have been invaluable to students of history and ethnology.

In the past, unfortunately, as Mr. Lo points out, the *ming-ch'i* reached the hands of the scholar only after being dug up by riflers of ancient tombs who passed them on to the curio dealers with whom they were in league, and from whom, in turn, they had to be bought. Thus there was no clue to when the objects were produced, and little chance of estimating their age by means of other objects excavated with them. Thus they could be classified only very vaguely as Han, Six Dynasties, T'ang, and so on. Since 1949, however, Chinese scholars have been engaged in steady research and excavation, and their findings have been made public. This already has extended our knowledge greatly, and further great strides can be expected in the future.

THE WARRING STATES PERIOD Nearly forty years ago, a number of wooden figures, believed to date from the Warring States period, appeared on the curio market, excavated from tombs at Ch'ang-sha in Hunan. Carved from a single piece of wood, they have flat bodies and stand straight and square, with right-left symmetry. The head is flattish, with a pointed chin and nose. Both hands are raised forward. The skirt is flared from the sash outward, and covers the ankles. The whole effect is extremely static.

Since 1949, similar finds from many excavations of Warring States tombs in the Ch'ang-sha area have confirmed the dating of these figures. Especially interesting was a group of more than fifty from the Warring States tombs with wooden burial chambers excavated at Yang-chia-wan on the outskirts of Ch'ang-sha in 1953 and 1954. A variation of the type was discovered at Yang-t'ien-hu (Pl. 260). Here the eyes and brows and garments are painted and the arms carved separately, being pegged to the bodies. It is significant here, too, that the treatment of these wooden figures, with their static quality and right-left symmetry, resembles that of the human figures found on the painted-chariot *lien* (Pl. 187) of the Former Han period, also excavated at Ch'ang-sha. A set of seated musicians carved in wood was also found at tomb No. 6, Yang-chia-wan, Ch'ang-sha—a charming group, very vividly portrayed in the act of playing their various instruments.

As for clay *ming-ch'i*, several specimens of pottery figures about five centimeters high have been found at Fen-shui-ling, Ch'ang-chih Municipality, Shansi Province (Pl. 259). These also have their hands held forward and wear skirts that cover their ankles. They include a woman carrying an infant on her back. Sculpturally speaking, they represent no advance whatsoever on the wooden figures of Yin times, but are believed to date from the Warring States period.

Visiting a friend in Shanghai in the summer of 1941, I was shown several small earthenware figures, which I was told had been discovered recently at Hui District in Honan, about eighty kilometers south of Chang-te. These figures of about seven to eight centimeters in height are very simply modeled, with a short, thick neck, a flat face with a small projection for the nose, and no carved eyes. All wear long-sleeved garments that hide the hands, and the women wear long, spreading skirts covering the ankles. The material is a black, smoothly polished earthenware, with red painting on the faces and garments, forming a vivid contrast. Almost all of the figures are represented in dance poses, the movement lively and the simplified modeling of the limbs fresh and very striking. They can be called the earliest known example of anything approaching true sculpture in China, and are incomparably better than any other sculpture of the same period.

Recently many more of these figures have been found; they are usually referred to as Black Pottery, and have attracted much attention among scholars. Apart from the human figures, they include animals, mirrors of the same style as Warring States period mirrors, and many replicas of bronze and lacquer wares, notably belt hooks, cups, and vessels that are apparently incense burners. On these, the red-painted decoration is in exactly the same style as that of the Warring States bronze and lacquer pieces from Chin-ts'un on the outskirts of Lo-yang. I myself bought, at a Peking curio shop, a mirror of polished black earthenware with a beautiful animal-coil decoration in red on the back.

The question remains of whether the differences between the static Ch'ang-hsia type *ming-ch'i* and the active Black Pottery figures of Honan should be seen as a difference of period or of district. To decide this definitely will require discoveries from a more extended range of sites, but judging from the state of culture in various regions during the Warring States period the difference would seem to be a regional one. Besides those already mentioned, the small standing and squatting figures in silver and bronze found in tombs of the late Warring States period at Chin-ts'un in Lo-yang, as well as the bronze warrior figures excavated at Fen-shui-ling in Ch'ang-chih Municipality, can probably be considered to date from the same period, but in general the costly metal *ming-ch'i* tended gradually to give way to ceramics.

HAN DYNASTY After the long, unsettled period of the Warring States and the short-lived Ch'in dynasty, China was unified under one great imperial dynasty. The new stability of society brought increasing affluence, and the corresponding development of the industrial arts extended even to the *ming-ch'i* required by burial customs of the time, which became more elaborate and varied, while regional differences tended to decrease.

Representative of the *ming-ch'i* of the period are those made for the imperial family. A factory, the Tung-yüan-chiang, was established to supply its needs, and the "Treatise on Rites and Ceremonies" in the *Han Shu* (*Book of Han*) gives a comprehensive list of requirements for an imperial burial. This includes thirty-six human figures, musical instruments, eating and drinking vessels, furniture, kettles and wine casks—in all, some forty different kinds of articles totaling two hundred objects, in addition to nine chariots. *Ming-ch'i* were similarly buried with aristocrats and local lords, the number varying in proportion to their rank. It is not surprising, therefore, that very many examples from this period have survived to the present day.

Ceramic *ming-ch'i* of the Han period may be glazed or unglazed. The glazes used are brown or green, more often used separately, but occasionally found together. Unglazed pieces are low-fired, are usually a dark, almost black, gray and are often painted in colors over a white slip coating (Pls. 186, 246). They were formed either by hand, on the potter's wheel, or by mold. The use of molds shows that *ming-ch'i* were mass produced. There are naked human figures made of clay that, it would seem, were dressed in clothes at the time of burial. In some cases the heads only were made of clay, being fixed to a wooden body, while in the case of horses, sometimes the head or both head and body were made of clay, the rest being made of wood.

The human figures can be divided into two large groups: one of very lively figures, performing dances or a kind of sword dance, and one of static, symmetrical, standing figures. The first of these seems to be in the tradition of the polished Black Pottery figures of the Warring States. They are full of life and movement. Modeled by hand and further shaped with a spatula, they tend to be intellectualized, where the Warring States figures rely on feeling. The Han people, who built up a great empire, appreciated clarity and exactitude, reason and logic, and in their art they sought to organize and make more precise the realism that came in from the west during the Warring States period. Dancers, acrobats, musicians and dwarfs figure largely in their visual arts, and the subjects favored were scenes from historical legends. Naturally, this general preference is reflected in the *ming-ch'i*. Especially fine examples are the set of dancer and musicians and the dancing warrior in the

Aizu Collection at Waseda University. The static figures derive from the wooden figures from Ch'ang-sha (Pl. 260), which themselves seem to derive from the straw figures mentioned in the Chou dynasty writings.

Among the *ming-ch'i* of the early Han, there are many earthenware figures similar to the wooden figures from Ch'ang-sha. The head is still flat and the neck short and thick; the whole impression is one of heavy gloom and sadness. Wooden figures were still produced in some places in the Han dynasty (Pls. 266–274). Those found at Feng-huang-shan near Ch'eng-tu, Szuchwan (Pls. 268–270) have some similarities with the Ch'ang-sha figures, although they wear jackets and trousers in place of the long garment of the more easterly style.

The coexistence of both the "northern" (typified by the Black Pottery) and "southern" (typified by the Ch'ang-sha figures) style *ming-ch'i* in the same place is probably a result of the unification of the country achieved under the Han dynasty. By the later part of the dynasty they both became more elaborate and expressive. The static, standing figures, moreover, became more realistic in the treatment of flesh (Pls. 289-291). The gray-clay servingwoman in the Aizu Collection is splendidly modeled in the round (*see* Pl. 289). Wearing many layers of garments, worn in much the same way as the Japanese kimono is worn today, the figure is much more three-dimensional in its treatment, though still standing quite straight. The copious hair is bound back; the facial expression is one of profound sorrow. The dynamic style, on the other hand, is very effectively used in the dancers, musicians and storyteller figures found in the late Han tombs near Ch'eng-tu (Pls. 281–285, 287). These cheerful, individual figures have something in common with the Buddhist sculpture of the Six Dynasties. The Szuchwan figures can be said to lack in grace of movement, but they are all lively. However, other provincial styles seem to have remained somewhat old-fashioned, stiff and coarse (Pls. 262–265).

In general, the animal *ming-ch'i* of Han, of which there are a great many, are more vital than those of human beings. This is perhaps especially true of the horses, shown with long nose, proudly erect mane and standing with feet firmly planted on the ground. Some are saddled, some unsaddled. In the strength and spirit of their stance, they well deserve the epithets "dragon horse" or "dragon-footed" bestowed on them. Some of the horse models are without legs or even without body or legs. It is presumed that these were originally of wood that decayed in burial. Such a horse with clay head and body and wooden legs still attached used to be exhibited at the former Lü-shün museum. Some of the horses of the later Han from Szuchwan are well fleshed and realistic in a way reminiscent of Roman marble horse sculptures. Dogs are unmistakably Chinese, with upstanding ears and squat, barrel bodies. Those dug up at T'ien-hui-shan have a realistic air that supports the evidence for a unique artistic tradition in this area at this time (Pls. 244, 304, 305).

Besides these, there are other domestic animals and birds—ducks, sheep, pigs, chickens, etc.—some of them of great charm, and also some wild animals such as tigers. The use of wood for animal *ming-ch'i* through the Han dynasty is instanced by the discovery of wooden animals and chickens in tombs in Kansu and fine wooden oxen (Pl. 267) and bears from Szuchwan.

The Han *ming-ch'i* of articles of everyday use include stoves, kettles, jars, *ting* and all manner of domestic utensils, etc. known at this time. They are usually plain gray ware and unglazed, with the occasionally glazed pieces more elaborately made. There are even model kitchens complete with all kinds of utensils and even food that give a vivid idea of life at the time. The buildings include carefully made, interesting examples of the many-storied pavilions of which the Han people were so fond (Pls. 317-320). Where ordinary houses are concerned, there are many auxiliary buildings of the kind found within a residential compound (Pls. 321, 322), but very few models of dwelling houses as such. This is probably because the burial chamber itself was to be regarded as the dwelling house of the deceased. Roofs are tiled and either gabled or hipped. Different types of tile are distinguished, and some bear the same patterns as the real thing. The models are often green glazed, though some were unglazed and painted with rich colors (Pl. 246). All manner of outbuildings are included within a rectangular or round enclosure—sheep pens, privies, and chicken houses. Besides these, there are granaries, millhouses, storage sheds, pigsties, etc. Among the most interesting are the mills and well heads. The mills contain miniature grinding stones operated by foot or by hand, and sometimes have men working them. Well heads (Pls. 311, 313) are square, rectangular or cylindrical, often with a roof into which is fixed the pulley for the rope. Some have a shallow trough for washing clothes. These also sometimes bear carvings of the deities of the four directions and other figures. These miniatures may not be precise representations of their real counterparts, but they certainly give us a concrete image of the everyday life and objects of the Han dynasty.

SIX DYNASTIES It is believed that the *ming-ch'i* showed little development and that there was a deterioration in the Han style during the period from the third century on into the fifth century. This seems to have been particularly true of the Southern Dynasties, and the *ming-ch'i* from the recently excavated tombs of this period near Nanking are of little artistic interest. The general judgment has yet to be substantiated, however, and we must await more material for study. One point of interest, nevertheless, is seen in the Chin dynasty figures excavated at Nanking. Although artistically mediocre, standing stiff and static with little movement (Pls. 333, 336, 338), the oval face characteristic of Han figures disappears in favor of a square chin. This was to persist for a long time in the sculpture of later periods. Another point of note is that the *ming-ch'i*, in general, are more cheerful in mood than those of the contemporaneous Northern Dynasties.

There was a large output of models in the Northern Wei state, most of the types imitating those of the Han dynasty. Without exception, they were made by mold. Many of these are slip decorated, but no glazed models have been found in the central plains (*chung-yüan*) area. The clay has a bluish-black color. Both human and animal figures have stands under their feet for added stability—probably an influence from the Buddhist art then flourishing. The flatness of the human figures is probably due partly to the persistence of the Han style and partly to the technical problems involved in using molds. Some, in fact, are modeled only in the front, and these may be a reflection of Buddhist sculpture, with its emphasis on the frontal view for use in temples. It is not easy to be sure to what extent this marked characteristic is due to a definite stylistic preference and how much to technical expediency, and this point must perhaps remain a matter of opinion. However, in the study of this period in history, any discussion of Chinese sculpture should take into account the probable interaction of Buddhist and non-Buddhist styles, in which discussion the consideration of *ming-ch'i* must play an important part.

The facial expressions are rather more individual, and express a variety of emotions such as rage, surprise, amusement, etc. The skirts are not as exaggerated as in the Han figures, but some are still flared from a narrow waist. The graceful female figure with hair dressed high and wearing a long-sleeved, high-waisted gown is quite beautiful (Pl. 329). The shape of the mouth and the slight smile; the posture, with sunken chest and abdomen well forward; and the upright, symmetrical stance have much in common with the Buddhist figure sculpture of the time. However, by comparison, the modeling of the eyes seems far more naturalistic. Some of the figures of warriors are more active, though this was true also of the Han figures. There are many equestrian figures, both men and women. As might be expected under the rule of a nomadic, equestrian people, the horses are particularly fine among the animal figures; they show a variety of poses, and are often brilliantly caparisoned (Pl. 339, 340). There are also figures of camels. The dogs include some floppy-eared foreign breeds, and there are even figures of women fondling pet dogs. The models of buildings are very disappointing, losing all the splendor of the Han pieces.

T'ANG DYNASTY The T'ang dynasty, which built up an extensive empire across the face of Asia, also constructed a fabulous empire below the ground. Even the royal tombs of Egypt cannot equal the splendor of the T'ang tombs, rich in every sort of embellishment, including sculpture.

By the seventh and eighth centuries, the T'ang empire was a cosmopolitan society to which many travelers came. Foreigners settled in the country, and large cities such as Ch'ang-an and Lo-yang were exotic with many races and customs. People from Persia, Arabia, India, and the southern countries; Turks from Central Asia, Japanese and Koreans—people of all races and colors mixed freely in the great cities, and Caucasian girls were employed in the pleasure gardens. The same cosmopolitan prosperity is evident in the tombs, and the *ming-ch'i* reached their highest peak of development. Records show that in the middle T'ang period there was a great vogue for *ming-ch'i* among the aristocracy and bureaucracy; the human figures became more lifelike than ever, and at funerals people would parade brilliant and elaborate examples in the streets. It was a more resplendent version of the custom followed until recently in China of parading paper models of human figures, objects of everyday use, houses and even cars at a funeral procession.

A special government office, the Chen-kuan-shu, supervised the production of *ming-ch'i* at Court, but the *ming-ch'i* custom eventually became so popular and the objects so lavish that the authorities were moved to issue ordinances regulating the number to be used according to the rank of the deceased, forbidding the burial of precious metals such as gold, silver and bronze, and permitting only earthenware models. In the reign of Hsüan-tsung, the regulations stated that those above the third rank were allowed ninety *ming-ch'i*, those above the fifth rank, sixty, and those above the ninth rank, up to forty. In 741 A.D., these numbers were further reduced, but the vogue was so strong that it is doubtful whether the ordinances were observed.

Unfortunately, very little is known of the *ming-ch'i* of the early seventh century, i.e. from Sui to early T'ang times, and since little is known even of other sculpture at this time, further information on the subject could be very enlightening. At present two main groups have been identified, one apparently the successor to the Northern Wei-Northern Ch'i type and the other believed to be the prototype of the later T'ang *ming-ch'i*. These last are glazed white, yellow, or purple, but are still symmetrical in their postures and show little of the movement of the later masterpieces (Pls. 342–352). Finds of *ming-ch'i* that can be dated at least approximately include those from tombs in the Sian area, dated between 642 and 678 A.D. (*see* Table, p. 108). Types are much the same as those already discussed, but two new figures typical of this period appear—the earth spirit and guardian demons, while models of buildings and vessels show a relative decline.

Most of the male figures are shown in official costume (Pls. 370, 371), but warrior figures wear armor similar to that seen on the Four Kings and Twelve Generals of Buddhist sculpture. It seems likely that this armor was in fact the type normally worn at the time. Among the warrior figures are many bearded foreigners, evidence of the use of foreign mercenaries at this time. Foreign troops figured in the An Lu-shan rebellion in the Hsüan-tsung reign, and foreign mercenaries were also used to put it down and save the T'ang regime. Round blue eyes, big noses, curly red hair and costume resembling a modern overcoat often appear in the non-warrior figures, also (Pls. 253, 255), as well as near-naked slaves with ebony skins and reddish hair, and illustrate the extent of the influx of foreigners into Chinese society at this time. There are figures of falconers wearing long, loose garments with broad, turned-back collars and even some men wearing a coat slung over their shoulders, unbuttoned. This fashion appears to have been common in the Caucasus from early times, and recurred, though the garment is shorter, in mid-nineteenth-century military costume in Europe. A considerable number of the male figures of the middle T'ang are very large, and some of the *san-ts'ai* ("three-color") glazed figures stand nearly six feet tall.

As pointed out by Dr. Seiryō Hamada, the female figures are of two main types: slender graceful girls, and plump, Junoesque matrons. The first type seems to be in the tradition of the Six Dynasties figures, being tall and thin with a delicate face, hair dressed high and long skirts (Pls. 369, 378). Some of these figures represent noble ladies with formal coiffure, dressed in the style of the sculptured figures of Srimaha and Sarasvati, but a *san-ts'ai* seated figure found in tomb No. 90 (Pl. 378) at Wang-chia-fen-ts'un, Sian, has a whitish, sleeveless upper garment with brown borders, a dark-green skirt with floral pattern, a very high hairstyle, round face smiling slightly and raised hands. This is one of the most beautiful female figures found since 1949. Although it is assumed to be of middle T'ang date, there is no way of dating it exactly. However, the figures of maidservants found in the Princess Yung-t'ai tomb (706 A.D.) are some guide to the dating of this slender type (Pls. 247, 249). The ordinary woman has a simple upper garment and skirt, the latter often having a stripe, which was probably the fashion around the beginning of the eighth century. It is interesting that few women are shown working in the T'ang dynasty *ming-ch'i*, whereas this had been a popular subject in the Six Dynasties.

The plump women have round cheeks, usually a flattish nose, and hair swept in drooping wings topped by a long coil, and wear loose, sweeping gowns with narrow sleeves or full skirts hitched high at the waist (Pls. 369, 372). This type was first recognized in the painting known as "The Beauty Standing Under a Tree" on the famous screen in the Shōsōin repository, Japan, and the type has taken its name from the title of this painting. However, similar figures appear in other paintings of the T'ang period, in the sculpture of the *apsaras* (a type of angel) of the Nara period in Japan, as well as in Central Asian art of the same period. It seems clear from this evidence that this must have been a type of beauty much in favor throughout many lands. Until the excavations of recent years, little was known of the date of the first appearance of this type of figure in *ming-ch'i*, but today we can be more explicit with the support of dated finds. Of these, the very fine piece found at the Hsien-yü T'ing-hui tomb (723 A.D.) at Nan-ho-ts'un, west of Sian, seems to represent an early stage in their production (Pl. 250). The woman holding a baby in her arms, found in the Shih Ssu-li tomb (744 A.D.) to the east of Sian, is one of the most developed examples of this type of figure, which is also represented in models found in the Wu Shou-chung tomb (748 A.D.) at Kao-lou-ts'un, Sian. Judging from the number of pieces found, it would seem that this style of female figure was most popular from 704 A.D. until the fifties of the same century. It was in 745 A.D. that Hsüan-tsung, the emperor during this time, took a daughter of the Yang family as one of his concubines—this was the famous Yang Kuei-fei, who is recorded as having been a plump beauty. Indeed, her rival, Mei-fei, spitefully nicknamed her Fei-pei, "Fat Maidservant." She was doubtless chosen because hers was a type of beauty currently in fashion. In any event, the previously held theory that the plump beauty figures were made in admiration of the royal favorite have been disproved by the discovery of so many models of this type dating from well before her rise to favor.

The large number of models of camels once again reflects the commerce with Western countries at this time. Some are shown standing, others squatting at rest or neighing. Some have their drivers with them, usually foreigners dressed in a costume reminiscent of modern Western dress. The magnificent animal carrying a band of musicians on its back—48.5 centimeters in height, with the human figures adding another eleven centimeters or so—found in the Hsien-yü T'ing-hui tomb (Pl. 251), is an exceptionally fine example. Such camels did in fact parade the main streets of Ch'ang-an at times of temple festivals and the like. The opulence of these figures reflects the great wealth of the gentry then gathered in the cities, while the striking vitality and inventiveness is witness to the immense energy of the craftsmen of the day.

As in other ages, the horses represent the very best in the animal *ming-ch'i*. They are of all colors and gorgeously caparisoned. By comparison with the Han or Six Dynasties horses, these are full of movement, and one can almost hear them champing and snorting as they paw the ground (Pls. 254, 256, 381, 383, 384). There are some fine equestrian figures, too, including women (Pls. 379, 380, 382). There are bullocks and bullock carts, and the strange figures, with human bodies dressed in official robes but with animal heads, one for each sign of the Chinese zodiac. They are usually unglazed and made of a red oxidized earthenware. Typical examples of these came from the Shih Ssu-li tomb (744 A.D.) already mentioned and the Chu T'ing-ch'i tomb (808 A.D.) at Hsiao-t'u-men, Sian.

The enormous variety of receptacles and models of articles of everyday use among the *ming-ch'i* is too extensive to be listed. However, the *san-ts'ai* chest unearthed along with the seated female figure (Pls. 376, 377) from a tomb at Wang-chia-fen-ts'un, the *san-ts'ai* chest in the St. Louis Art Museum and the chest in the Buffalo Natural Science Museum are exceptionally beautiful and elaborate examples. It would seem that *san-ts'ai* ceramic pieces found in tombs include some made for everyday use and not specifically as *ming-ch'i*. The models of buildings also include some beautiful *san-ts'ai* pieces. The roof is usually gabled and the front divided by pillars into three "bays," the central bay usually being open, while the outer two have walls pierced by barred windows. Some years ago I saw what was undoubtedly a model of a Buddhist structure in the Honan museum—made of uncolored tile, but with a hipped and gabled roof, double doors at the front flanked by barred windows, decorations covering the nailheads, and characteristic ornaments on the main and subsidiary roof ridges. Such models are very unusual, for Buddhist elements are rare in *ming-ch'i*. The models of granaries are about 11.7 centimeters high and have gabled and tiled roofs. The side walls have small windows, while the front and back suggest brick walls. The wooden parts are indicated roughly by incised lines made with a spatula. Well heads are square and lavatories, now separate from pigsties, have a stool in the center.

Both refined white clay and a slightly pinkish clay were used in T'ang *ming-ch'i.* It used to be a Peking curio dealer's rule of thumb that the white clay figures came from Lo-yang and the pink from Ch'ang-an, but recent finds of both at both sites have refuted this theory. It seems from the damaged part of a late Six Dynasties figure in the author's possession that the pink clay was already in use before the T'ang. Also, the white clay of a green-glazed model jar from the Hsiao family tomb at Ching District, Hopei (late Six Dynasties) makes it clear that the white clay was also used earlier than the T'ang dynasty. Pieces fired with this white clay take a brilliant white finish more striking than anything known before, and when used under the *san-ts'ai* glazes, it gives a smooth, glossy surface; it is one of the great contributions to the ceramic tradition of China. Besides the primary colors, all kinds of intermediate colors were used, producing color effects of a high degree of complexity. The gray pottery was no longer used.

The *san-ts'ai* of the T'ang period marks the highest artistic achievement of the *ming-ch'i.* The term *san-ts'ai* denotes chiefly the use of soft green, yellow and reddish-brown glazes on a white body fired at 700–800° centigrade. The green color derives from copper and the red and yellow from iron, and mixtures of these colors occurred. In addition, a cobalt blue was sometimes added to the glaze. Occasionally these colors are used singly or two at a time, in which case they should perhaps strictly be regarded as a monochrome or two-color class. However, it is the usual practice to term any low-fire, glazed, white bodied *ming-ch'i* of T'ang times as T'ang *san-ts'ai* regardless of the number of colors used. The colored glazes all applied at once tend to run together, or melt together in the kiln, resulting in fortuitous effects of color that give this whole class a special charm that the makers must surely have deliberately taken into account.

Low-fire, single-color glazed *ming-ch'i* were already being made in the Sui dynasty, when the glaze was brown, yellow, or white, and achieved quite a good texture and color. This glaze continued into the T'ang dynasty, as shown in finds dated at 682 and 703 A.D. The real, distinctive *san-ts'ai* seems to have been achieved in the reign of the Emperor Hsüan-tsung, then, after the An Lu-shan rebellion of 750 A.D. the decline appears to have been rapid. A few later *san-ts'ai* pieces have been found as far afield as Japan and the Liao state, but in all cases they are much inferior to the pieces of T'ang at its zenith. It seems that almost all the best *san-ts'ai* dates from the first half of the eighth century. Nor was the geographical distribution so widespread as with other *ming-ch'i,* being almost entirely limited to around Lo-yang and Ch'ang-an. This, and the gorgeousness of the pieces themselves, indicates that *san-ts'ai ming-ch'i* were the prerogatives of the aristocracy and the wealthy of the big cities. In the cosmopolitan mixture of motifs used at this time, particularly, there is a strong flavor of Sassanian art.

Though the highest quality *ming-ch'i* were limited to Shensi and Honan, and particularly to Lo-yang and Ch'ang-an, many provincial types were made. The most significant of these are the clay models found in middle T'ang tombs in Astana, Turfan, Sinkiang Province. These models are made on a core of grass or wood fibers, which was subsequently coated with clay modeled into a figure, which was then painted very richly on a white ground. A great variety of figures have been found, including officials, ladies, foreigners, equestrian figures, horses, and camels. It cannot be said that their treatment is either free or elaborate, and they have a rustic unsophisticated air when set beside their counterparts from the capital area, but they are interesting for the way in which, while owing much to the T'ang traditions, they breathe a kind of exotic atmosphere. Examples have been brought back by the Japanese Ōtani expedition and by Sir Aurel Stein, and a number are preserved in Japan.

Kōsei Andō

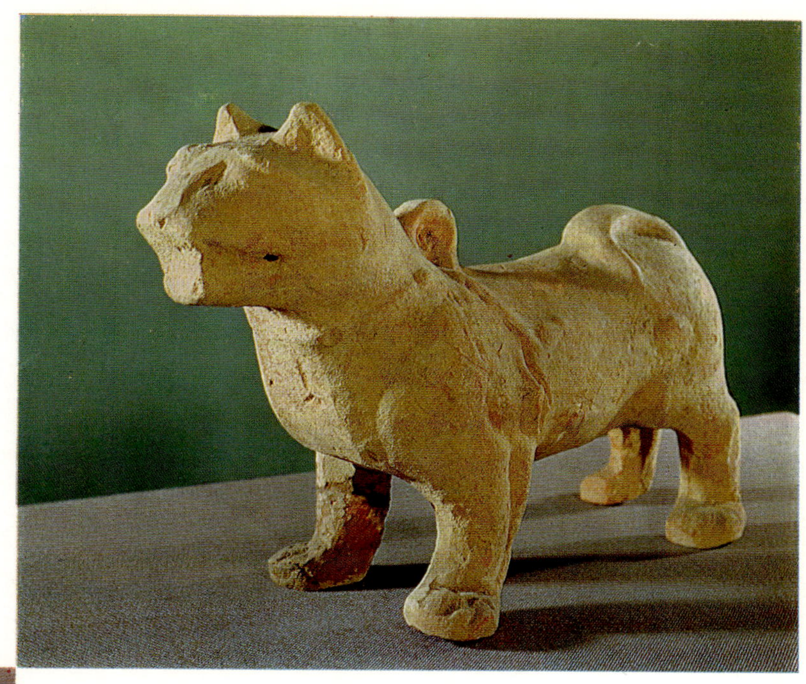

244. Dog, glazed earthenware. Later Han dynasty. Excavated at Hsiang-kuo Temple, Chiang-pei, Chungking, Szuchwan.
height: 20.0 cm. (7.9 in.); length: 27.0 cm. (10.6 in.)

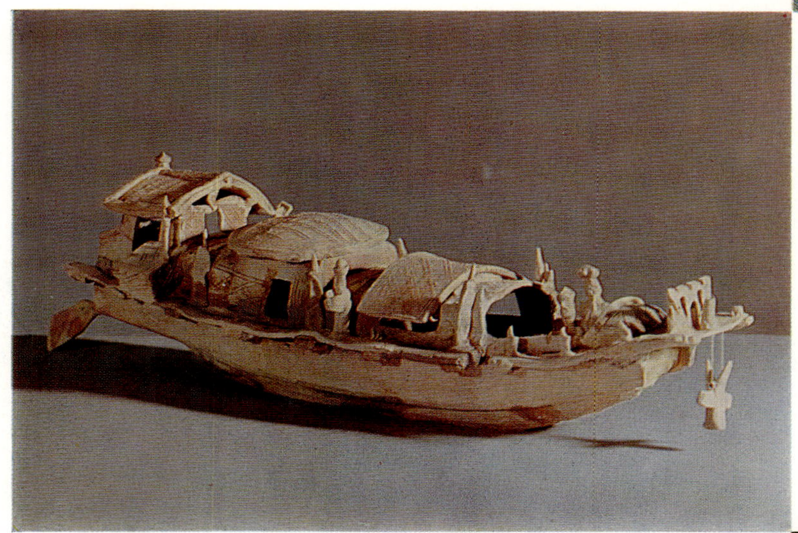

245. Boat, earthenware. Later Han dynasty. Excavated at Sha-ho-ch'ü, Kuang-chou, Canton.
length: 55.0 cm. (21.65 in.)

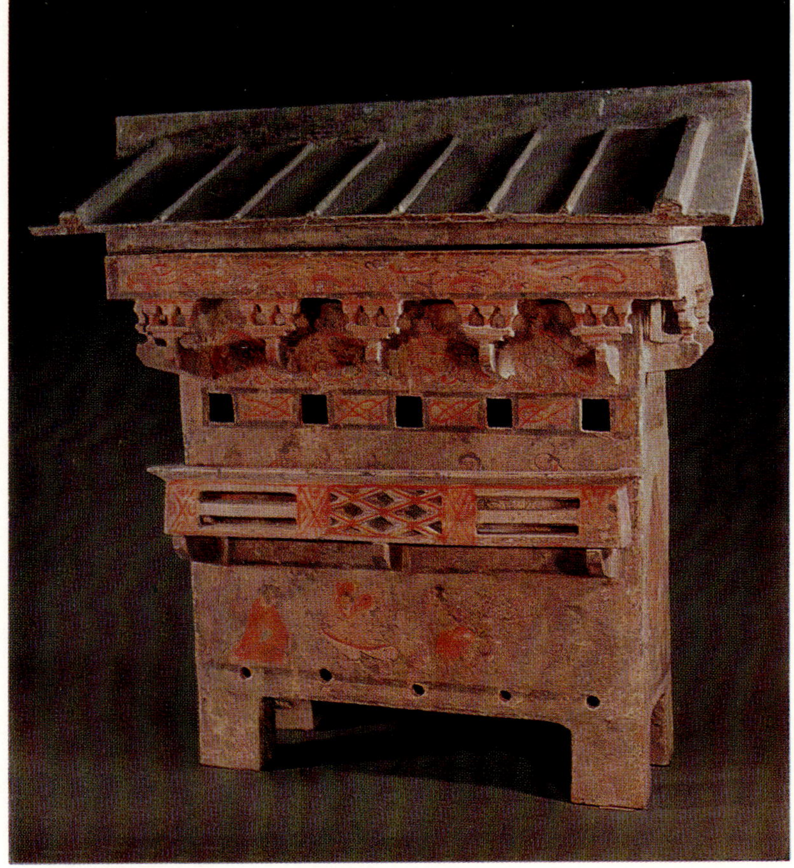

246. Building, earthenware with slip decoration. Han dynasty. Excavated at Ho-wang-ts'un, Hsing-yang District, Honan (*see* Pl. 188).
height: 77.0 cm. (30.2 in.); width: 70.0 cm. (27.6 in.); depth: 38.4 cm. (15.1 in.)

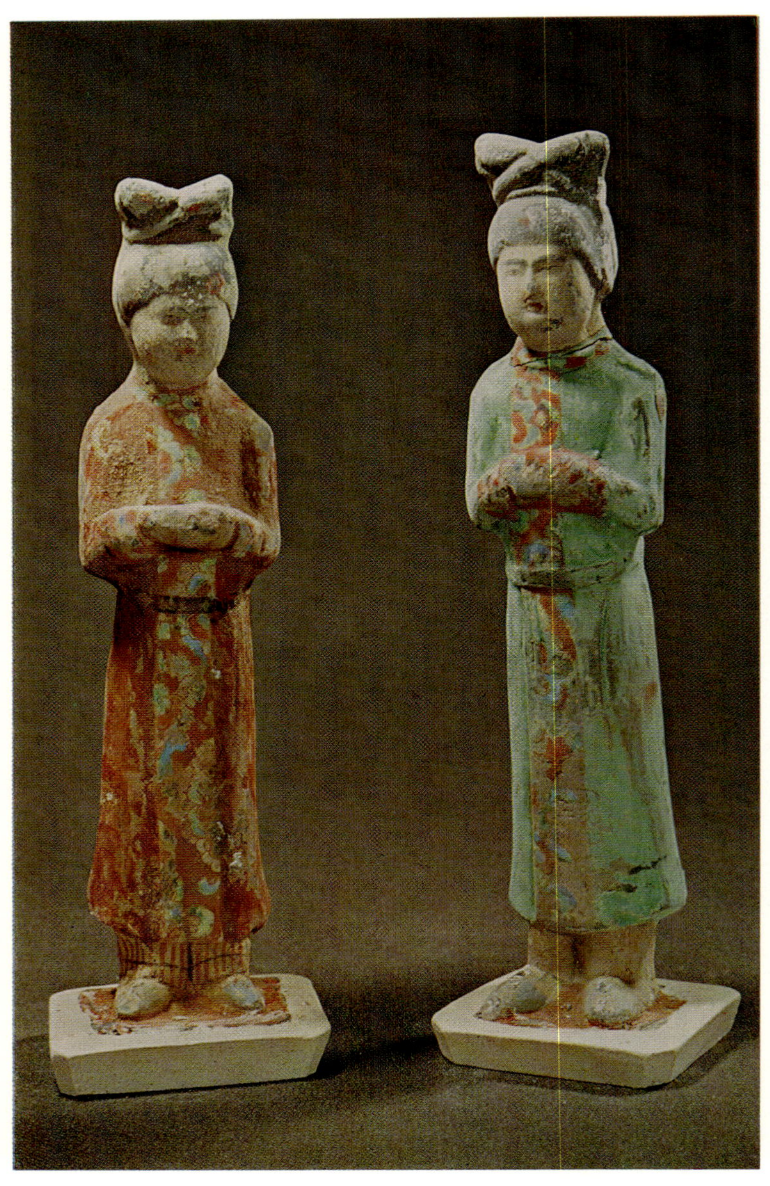

247. Ladies-in-waiting, slip-painted earthenware. T'ang dynasty. Excavated from the Princess Yung-t'ai tomb, Ch'ien District, Shensi.
height: approx. 18.5 cm. (7.3 in.)

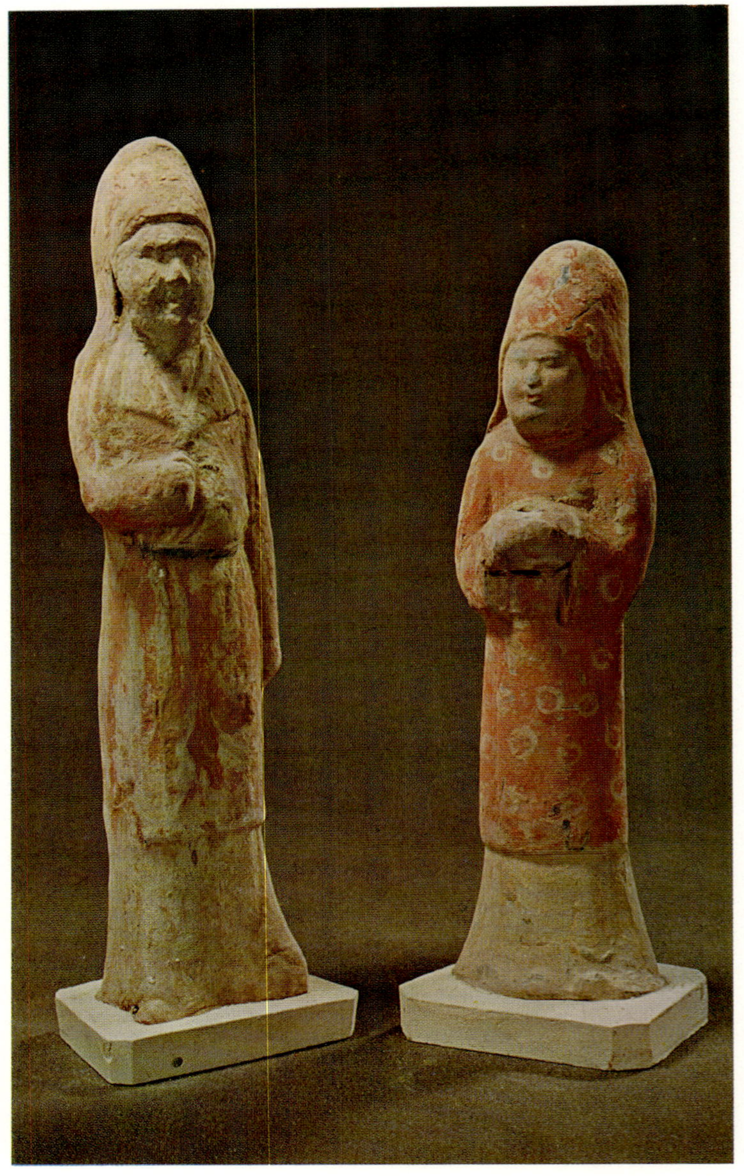

248. Men in foreign costume, slip-painted earthenware. T'ang dynasty. Excavated from the Princess Yung-t'ai tomb, Ch'ien District, Shensi.
height: 19.5 cm. (7.7 in.)

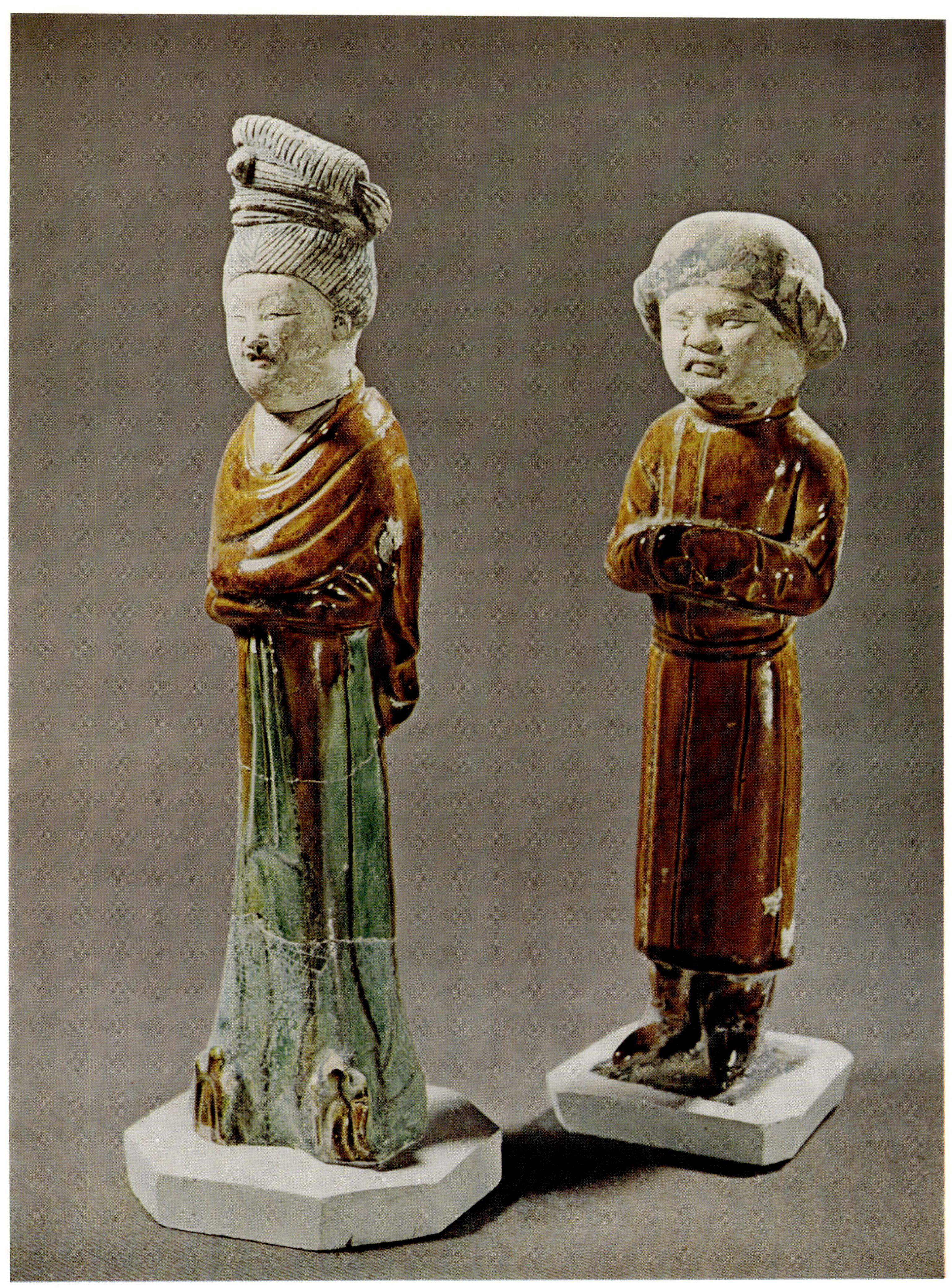

249. Lady and foreign attendant, earthenware with *san-ts'ai* glaze. T'ang dynasty. Excavated from the Princess Yung-t'ai tomb, Ch'ien District, Shensi.
Lady. height: 20.5 cm. (8.1 in.)
Attendant. height: 19.0 cm. (7.5 in.)

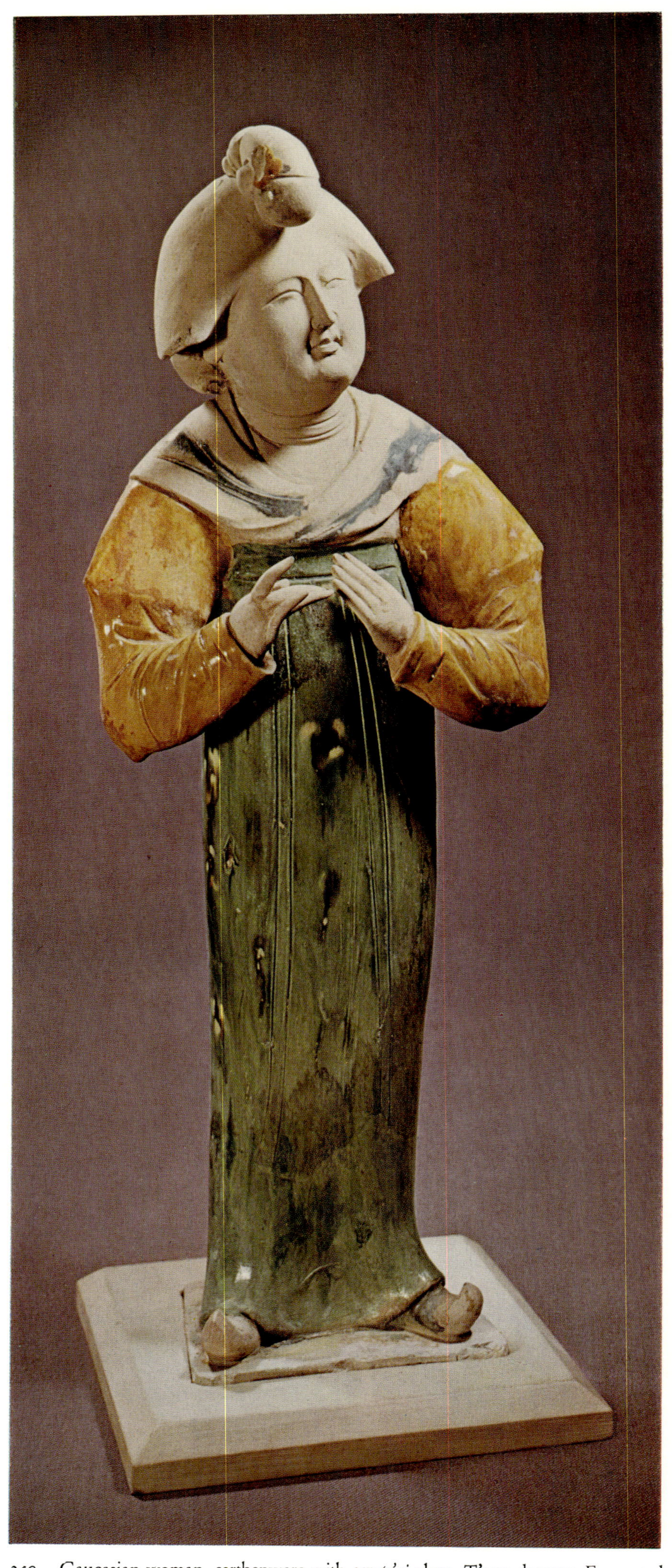

250. Caucasian woman, earthenware with *san-ts'ai* glaze. T'ang dynasty. Excavated from the Hsien-yü T'ing-hui tomb, Nan-ho-ts'un, Sian, Shensi.
length: 43.0 cm. (16.9 in.)

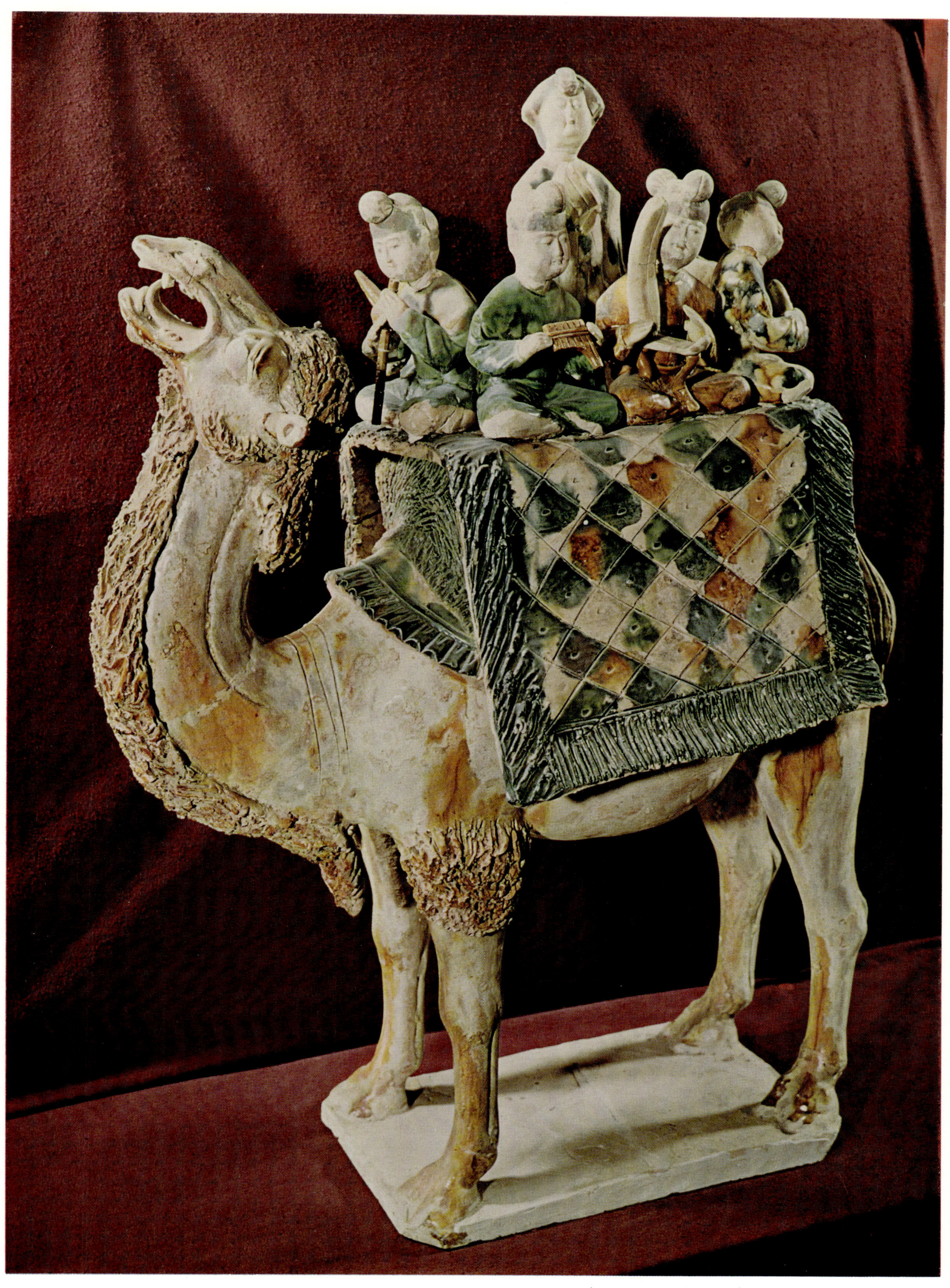

251. Camel carrying a band of musicians, earthenware with *san-ts'ai* glaze. T'ang dynasty. Excavated from the Hsien-yü T'ing-hui tomb, Nan-ho-ts'un, Sian, Shensi.
height of camel: 48.5 cm. (19.1 in.)

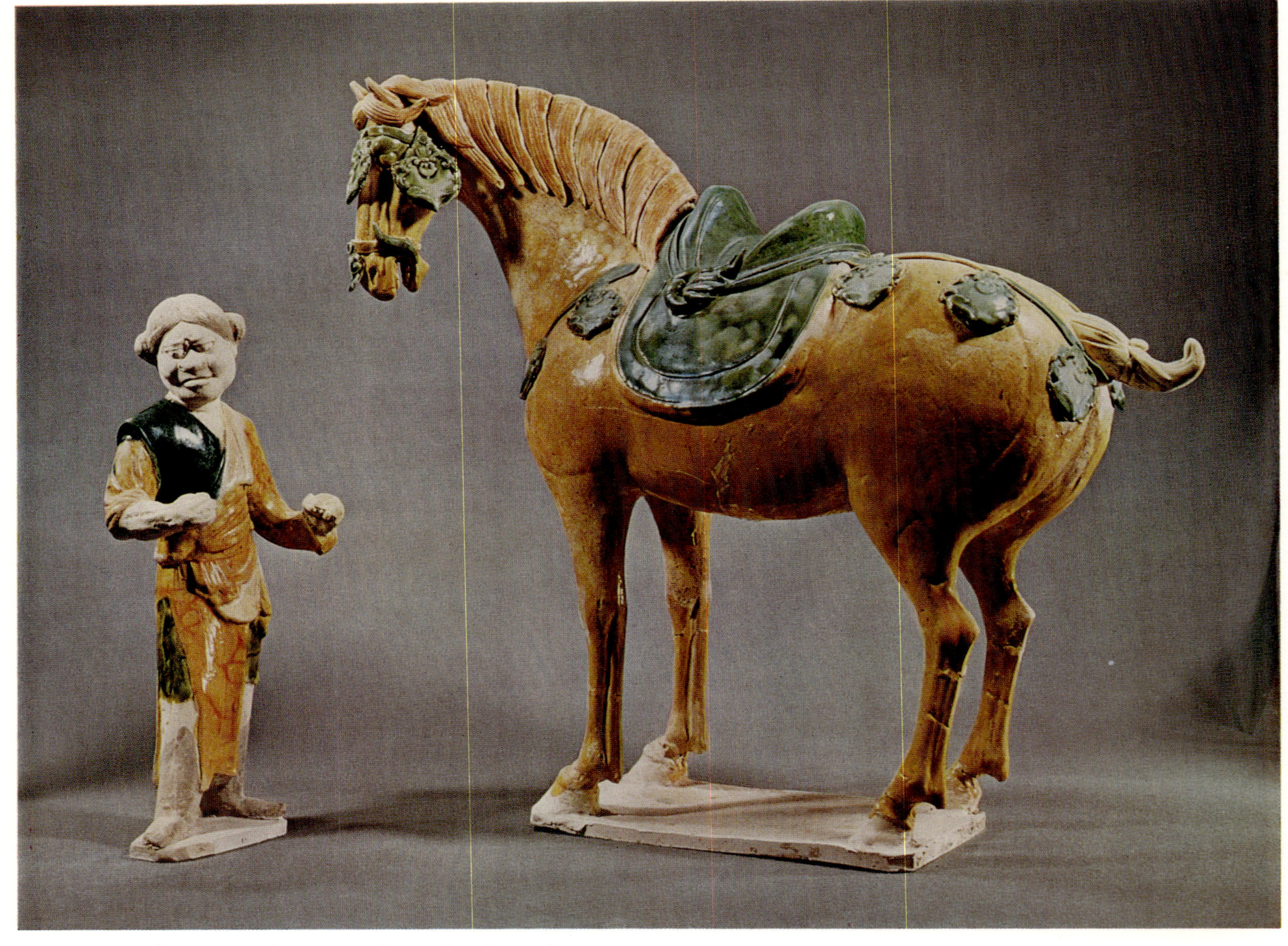

252. Horse and groom, earthenware with *san-ts'ai* glaze. T'ang dynasty. Excavated at Chung-pao-ts'un, Sian, Shensi (same as Pl. 381).
Groom. height: 28.5 cm. (11.2 in.)
Horse. height: 39.6 cm. (15.5 in.); length: 43.0 cm. (16.9 in.)

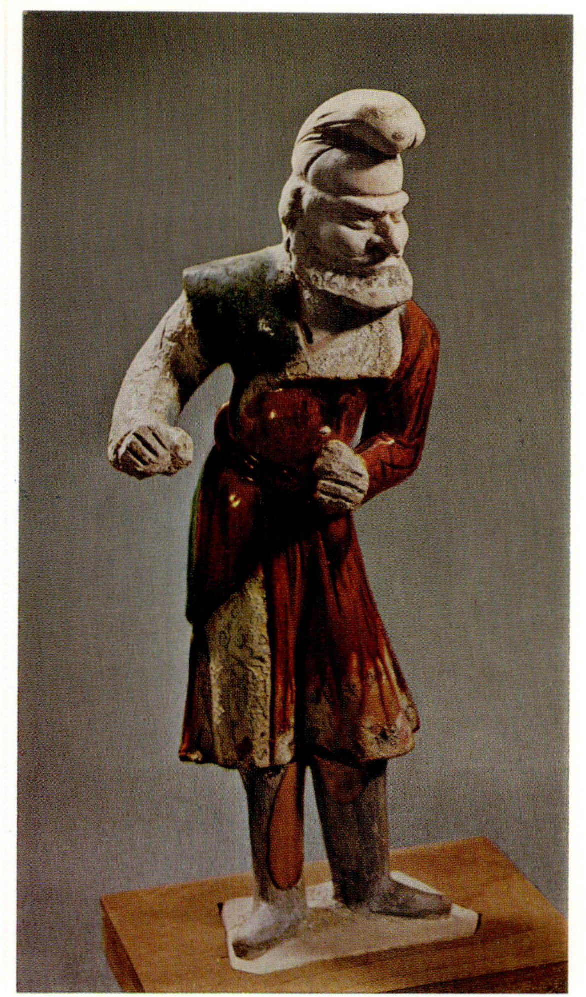

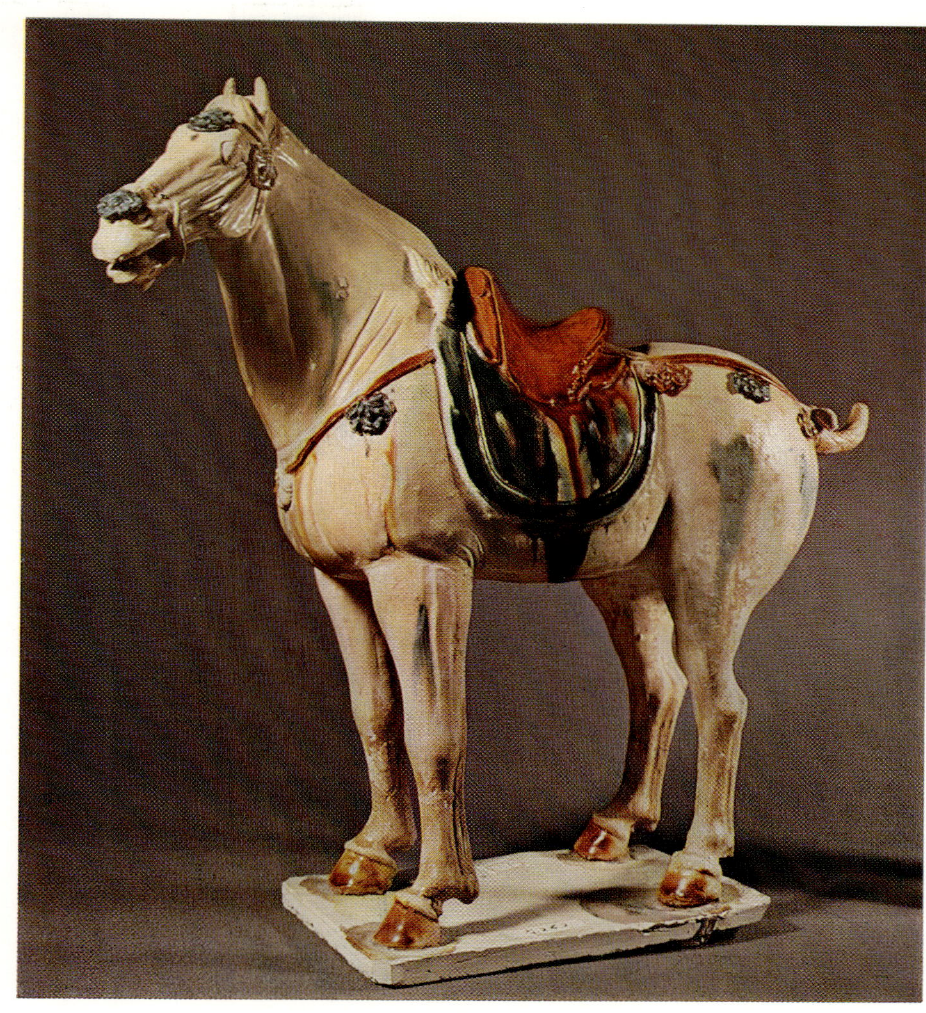

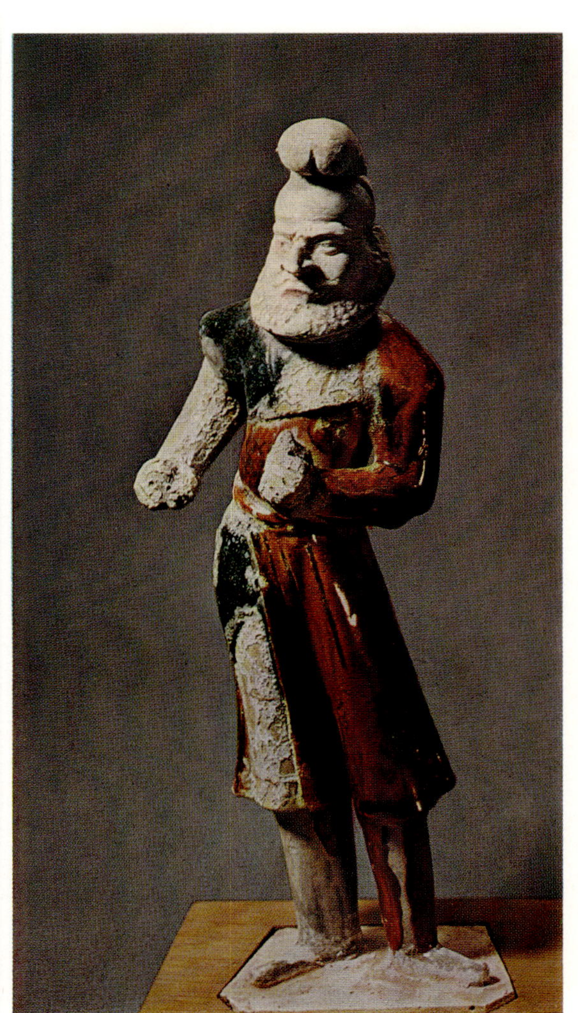

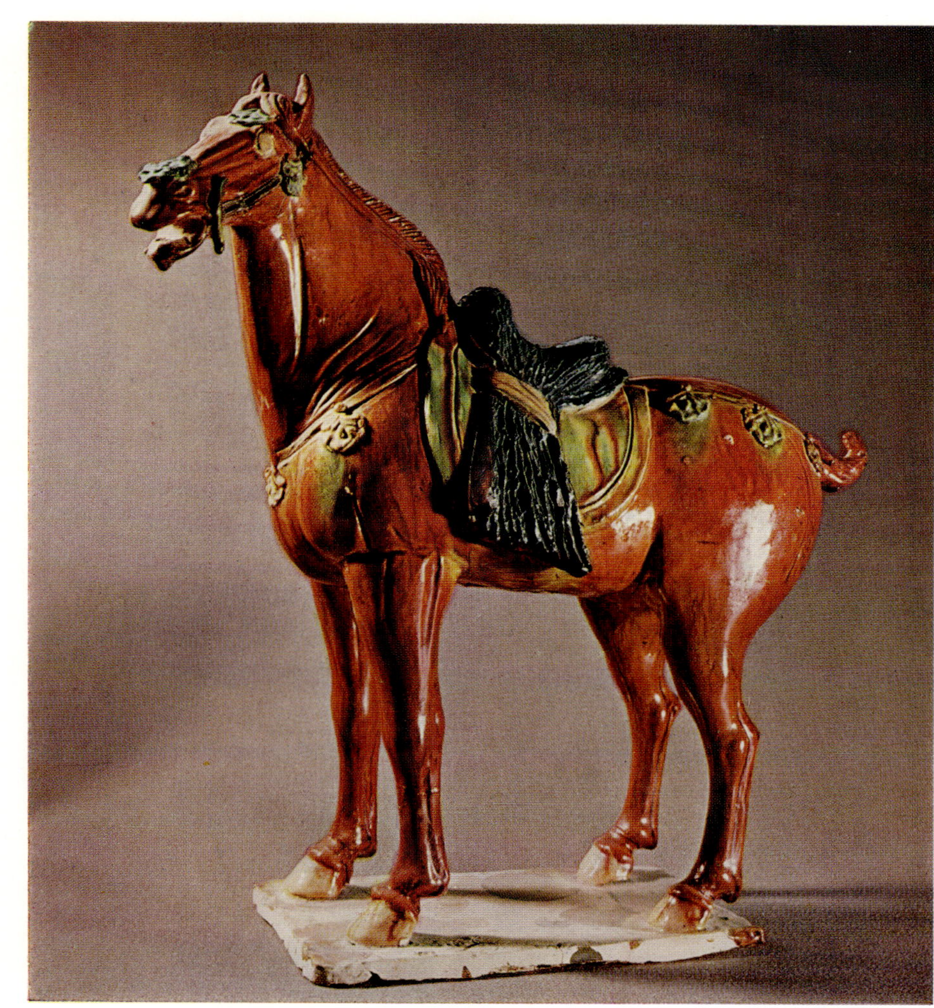

253–256. Foreign horses and grooms, earthenware with *san-ts'ai* glaze. T'ang dynasty. Excavated from tomb No. 337, Shih-li-p'u, eastern outskirts of Sian, Shensi.
Grooms. height: 29.0 cm. (11.4 in.)
Horses. height: 36.5 cm. (14.4 in.)

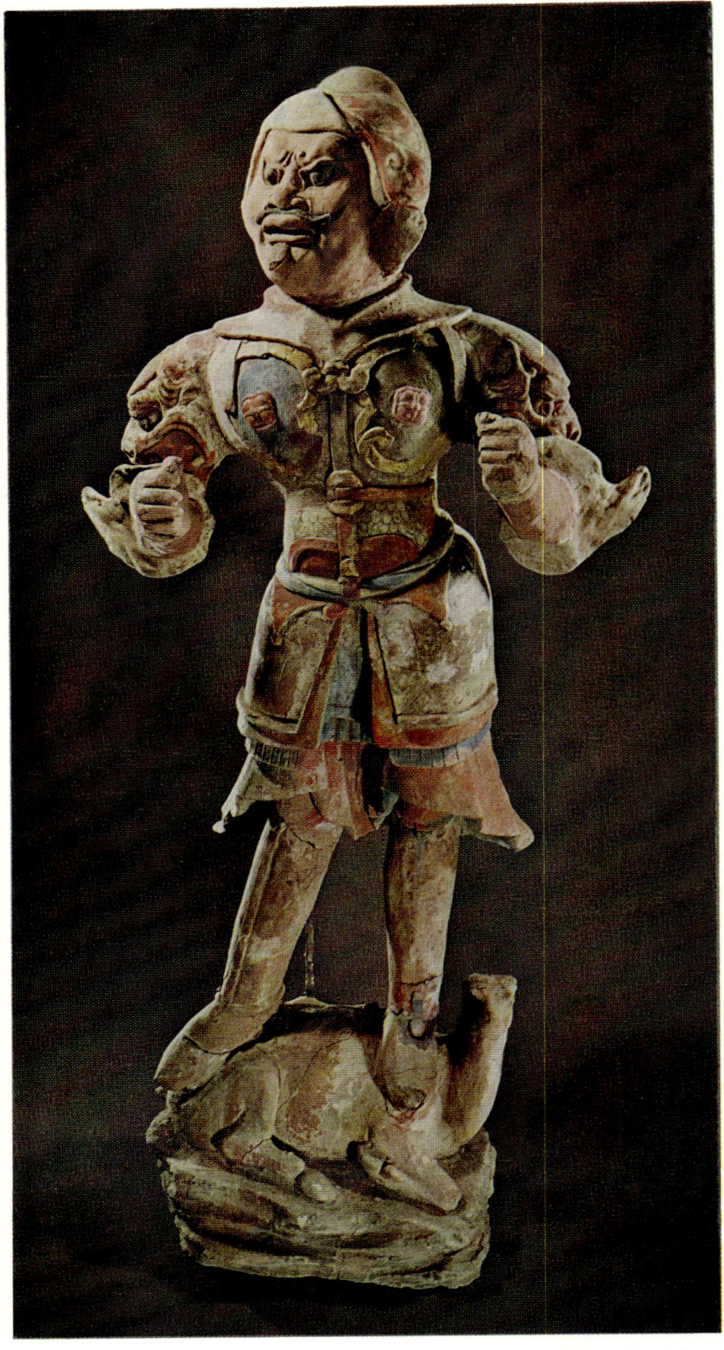

257. Heavenly Guardian, earthenware with slip decoration. T'ang dynasty. Excavated from the Li Shuang tomb, Yang-t'ou-chen, Sian, Shensi.
height: 90.0 cm. (35.4 in.)

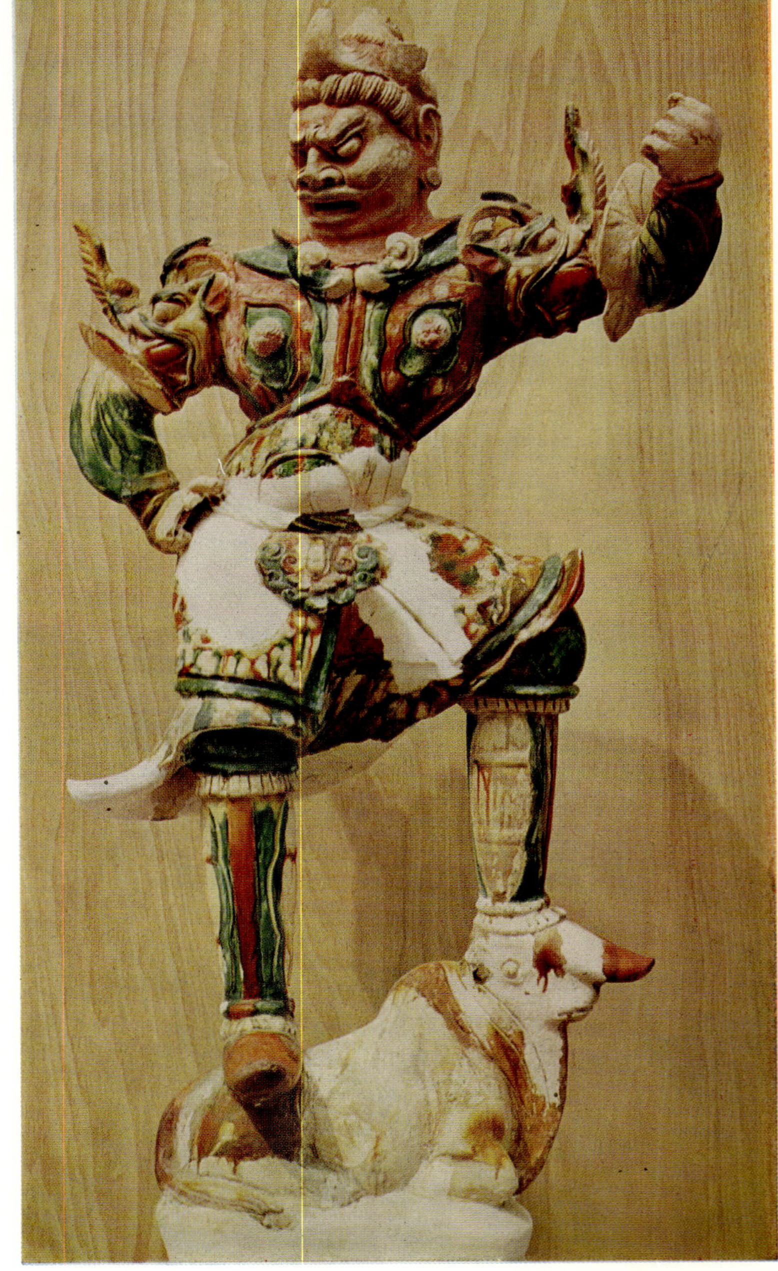

258. Heavenly Guardian, earthenware with *san-ts'ai* glaze. T'ang dynasty. Excavated at Chia-li-ts'un, Sian, Shensi.
height: 95.0 cm. (37.4 in.)

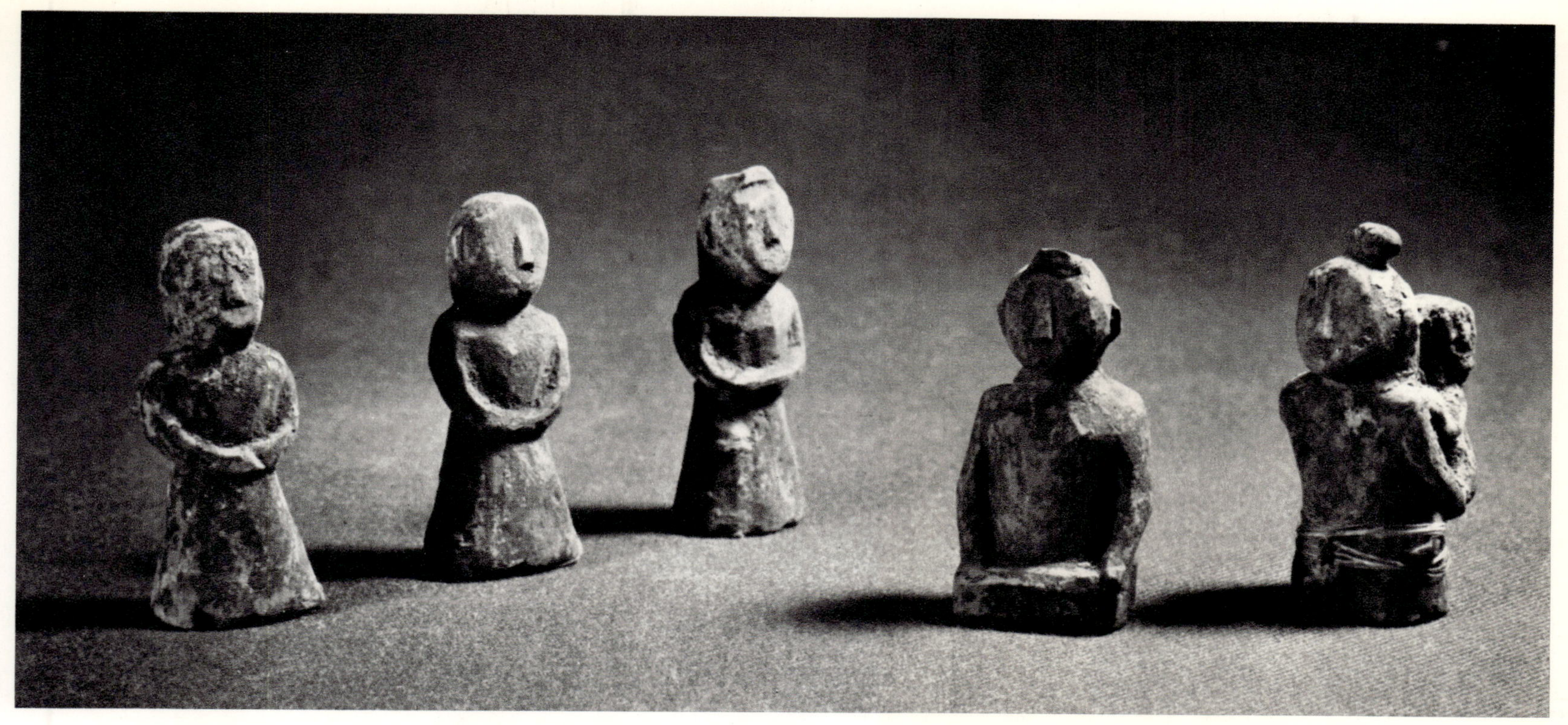

259. Figures, earthenware. Warring States period. Excavated at Fen-shui-ling, Chang-chih Municipality, Shansi.
height: 5.0 cm. (1.97 in.)

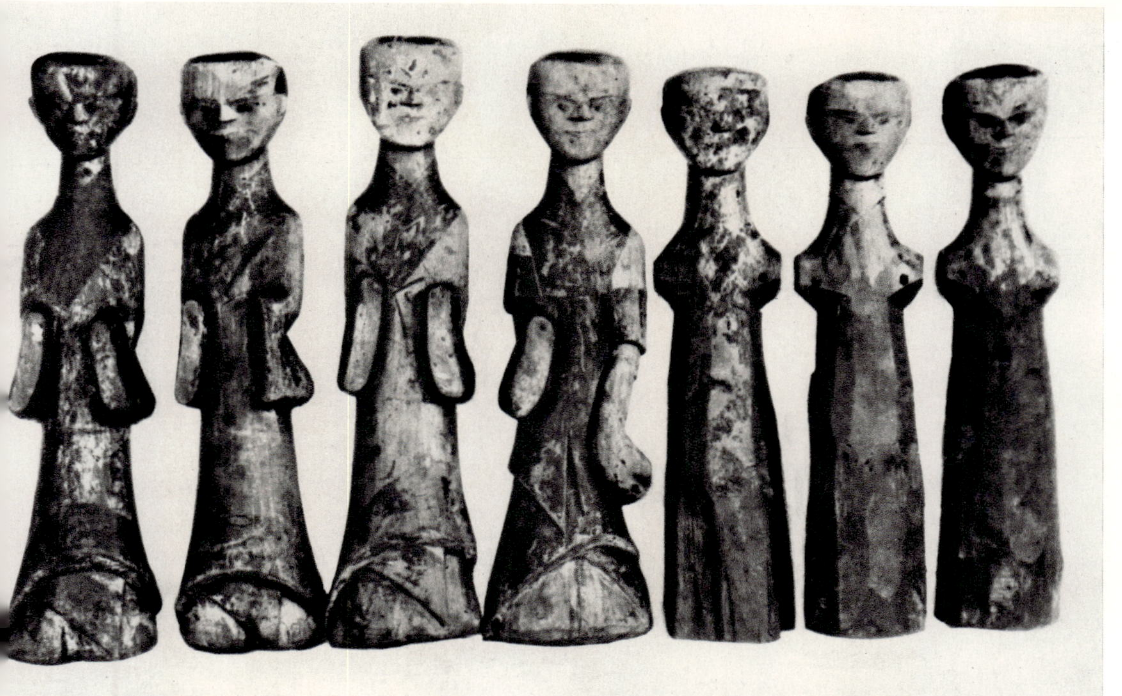

260. Figures, carved wood. Late Warring States period. Excavated at Yang-t'ien-hu, Ch'ang-sha, Hunan.
height: 50.0–53.0 cm. (19.7–20.8 in.)

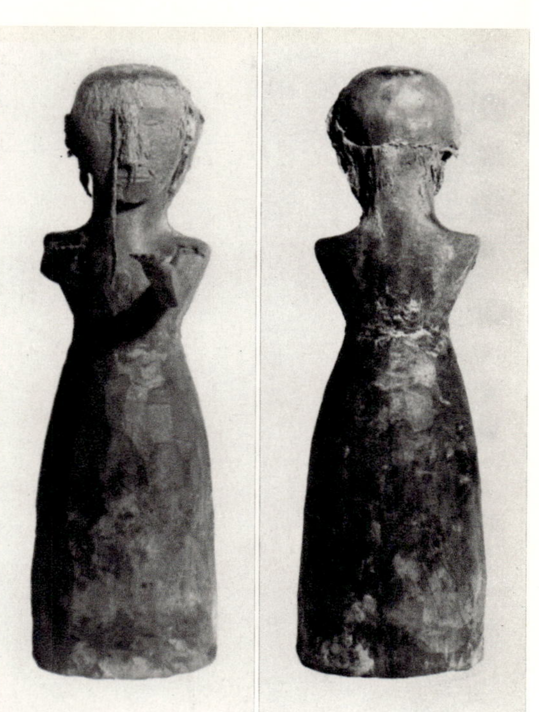

261. Figure, wood. Late Warring States period. Excavated at Huang-ni-k'eng, Ch'ang-sha, Hunan.
height: 53.0 cm. (20.8 in.)

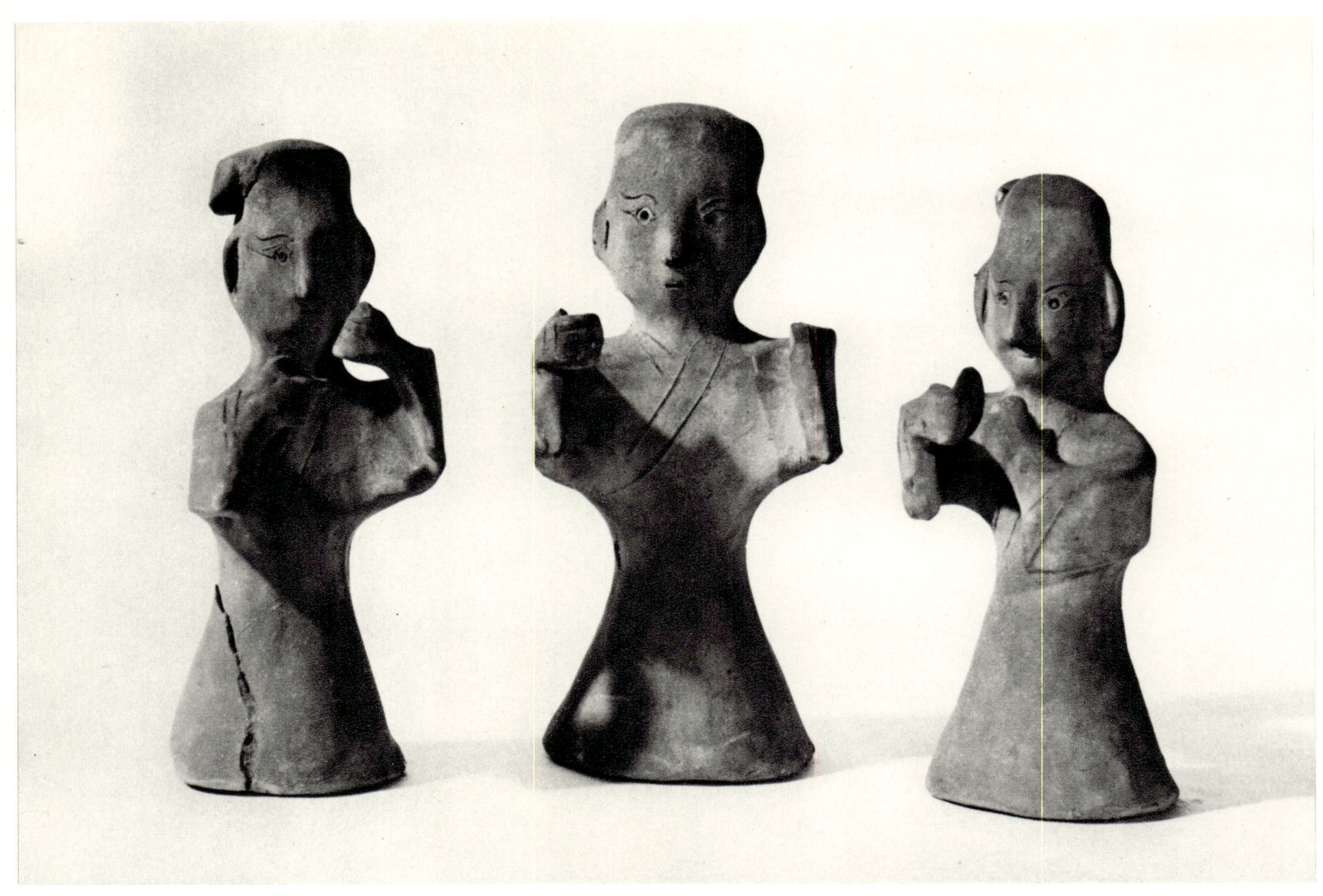

262. Figures, earthenware. Later Han dynasty. Excavated from Ma-ying-kang, Zoological Gardens, Canton.
no measurement given

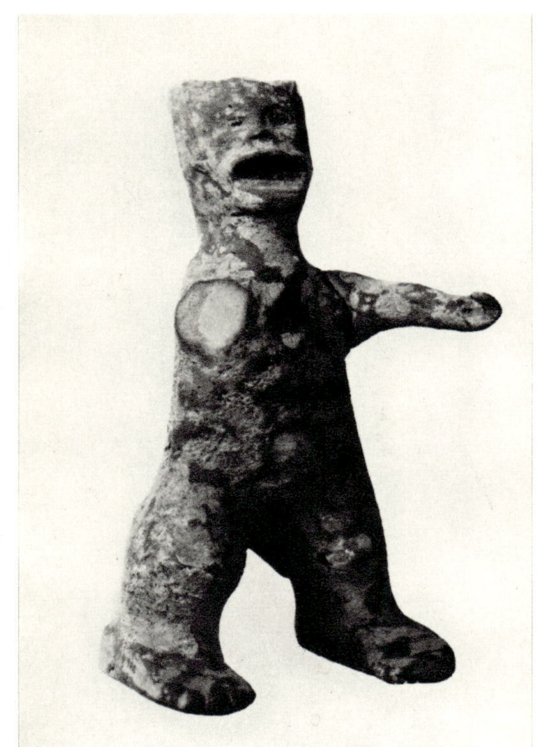

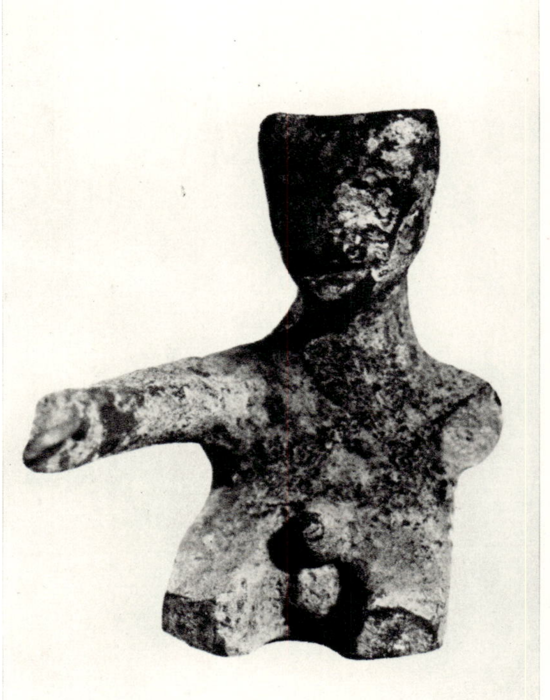

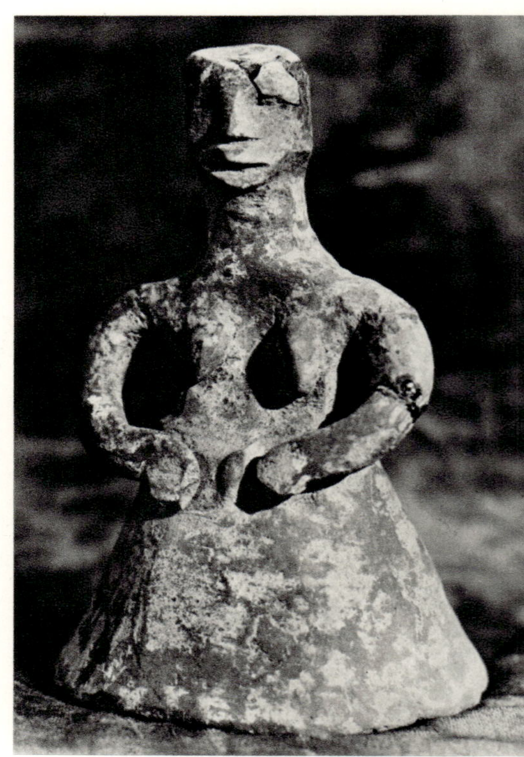

263–265. Figures, earthenware. Late Han dynasty or early Six Dynasties. Excavated from a tomb at Lü-ta Municipality, Liaoning.
heights: [263] *16.0 cm. (6.3 in.);* [264] *8.6 cm. (3.4 in.);* [265] *17.5 cm. (6.9 in.)*

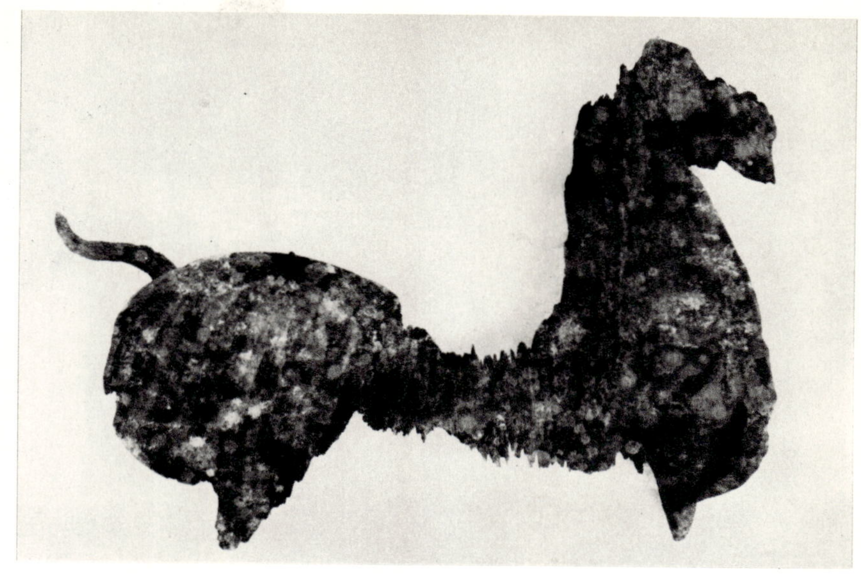

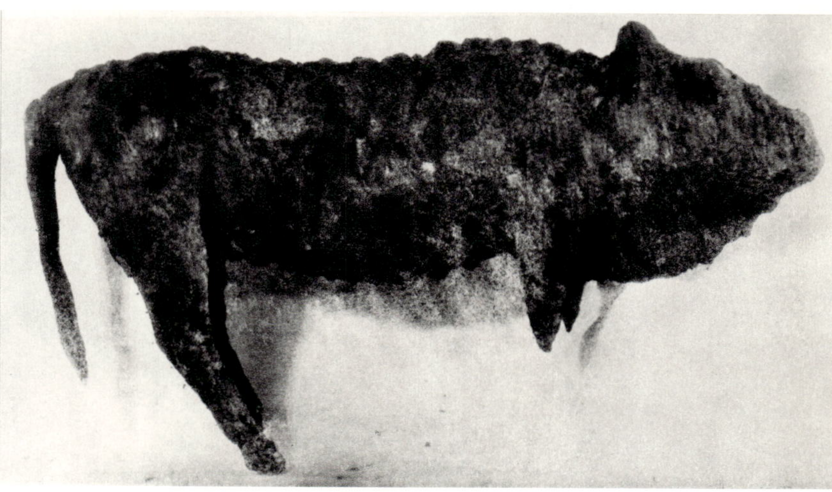

266–267. Animal figures, carved, lacquered wood. Later Han dynasty. Excavated from a wooden coffin tomb at Feng-huang-shan, Ch'eng-tu, Szuchwan.
266. Horse. present height: 32.0 cm. (12.6 in.); length: 62.0 cm. (24.4 in.)
267. Ox. height: 24.0 cm. (9.4 in.); length: 43.0 cm. (16.9 in.)

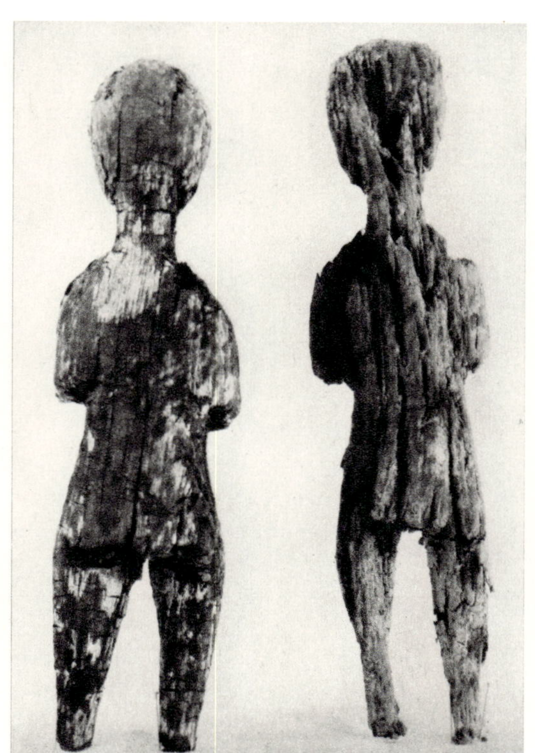

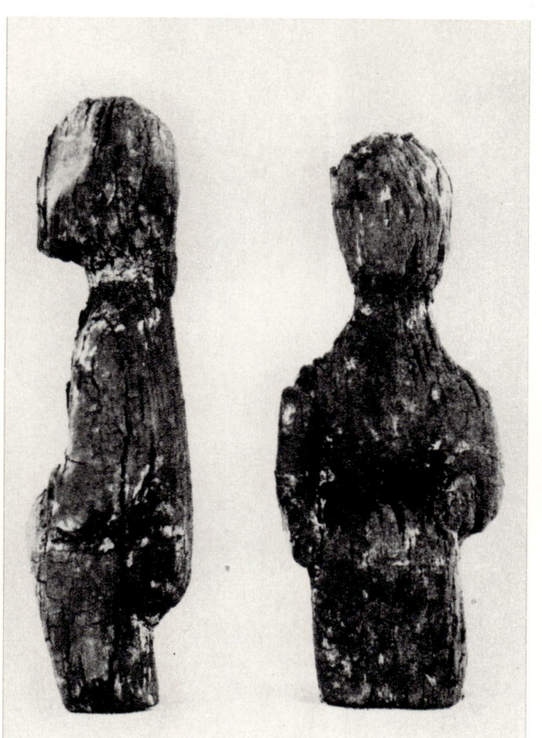

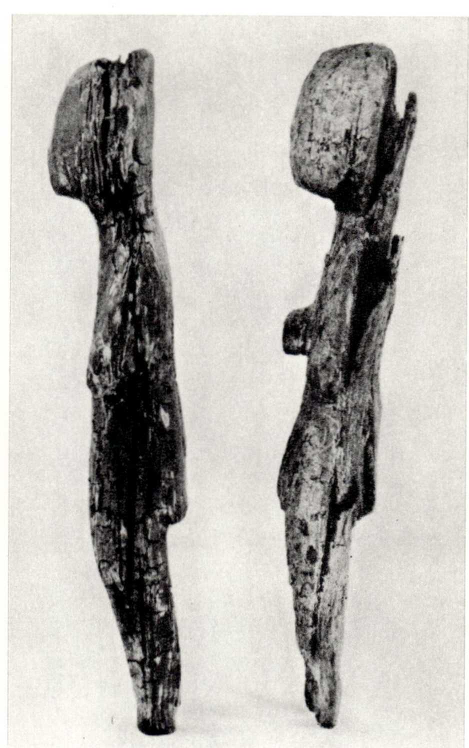

268–270. Figures, carved wood. Later Han dynasty. Excavated at Feng-huang-shan, Ch'eng-tu, Szuchwan.
height: 25.0 cm. (9.8 in.)

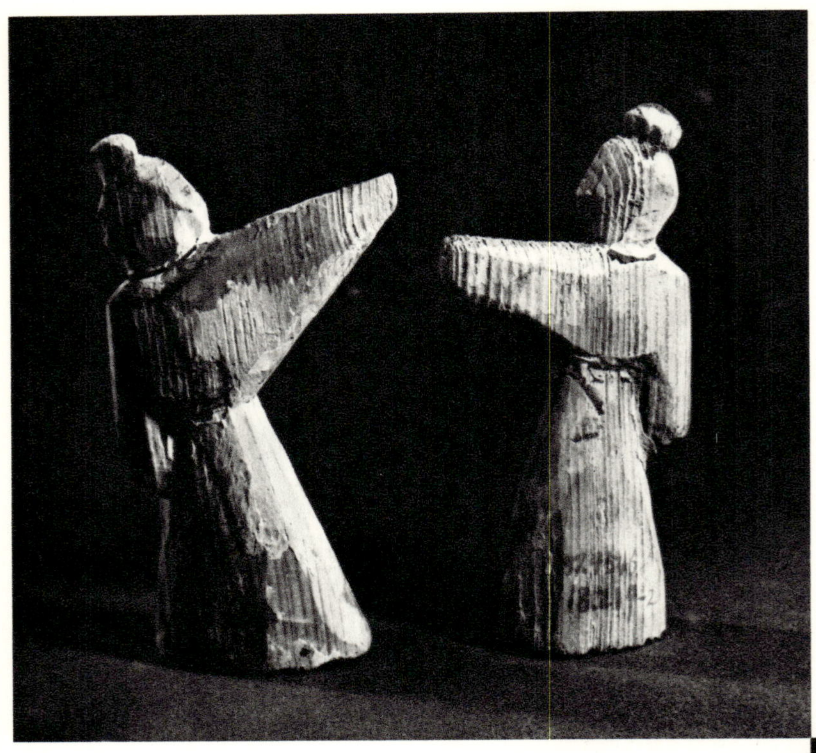

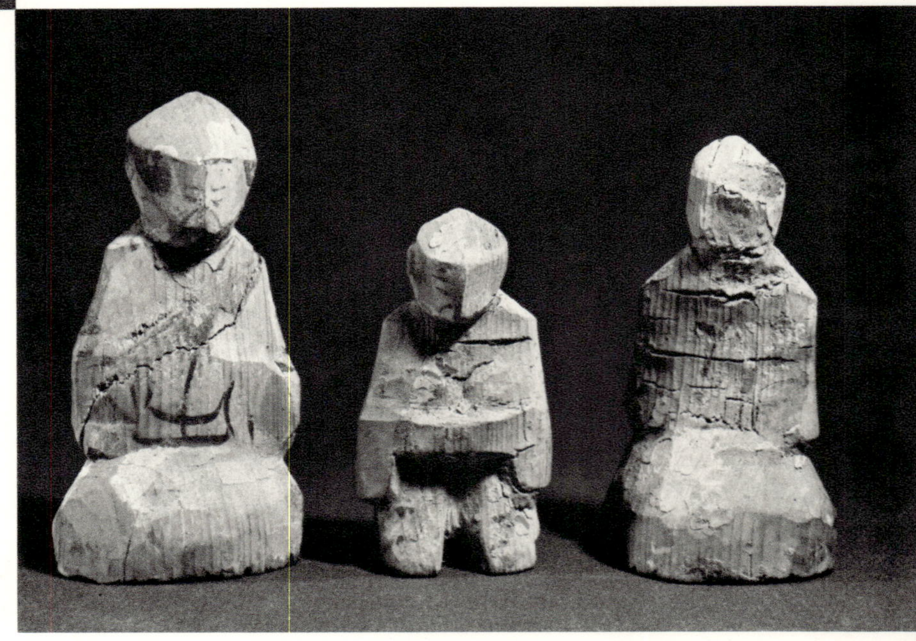

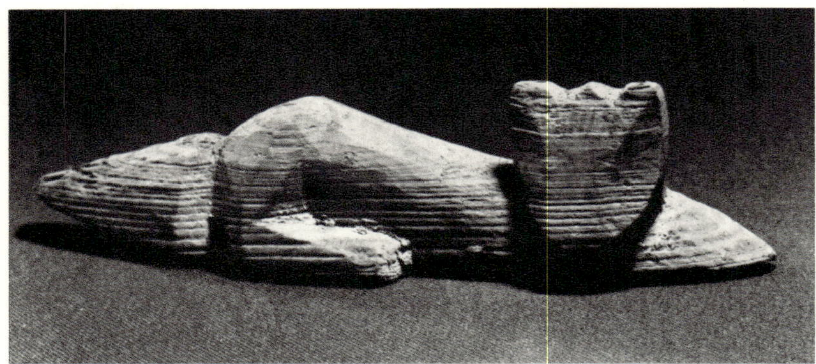

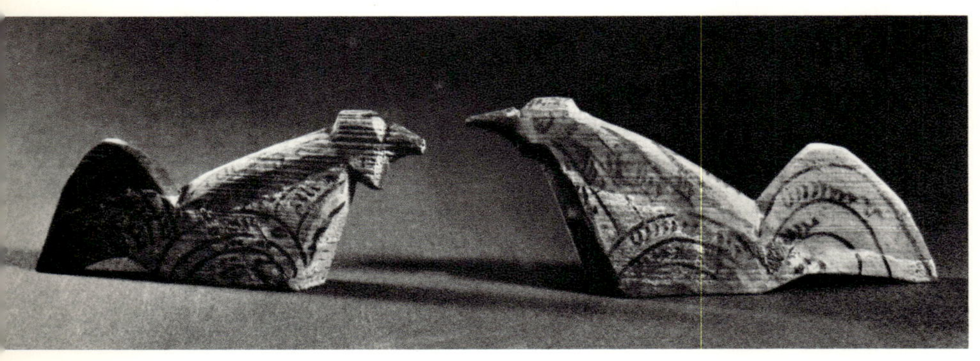

271–274. Animal and human figures, carved, plaster-coated and painted wood. Later Han dynasty. Excavated at Mo-tsui-tzu, Wu-wei, Kansu.

271. *Dancers. height: 14.5 cm. (5.7 in.)*

272. *Figures. heights (left to right): 14.0 cm. (5.5 in.); 10.0 cm. (3.9 in.); 13.0 cm. (5.1 in.)*

273. *Animal figure. height: 4.8 cm. (1.88 in.); length: 19.5 cm. (7.7 in.)*

274. *Chickens. length: 9.5 cm. (3.74 in.)*

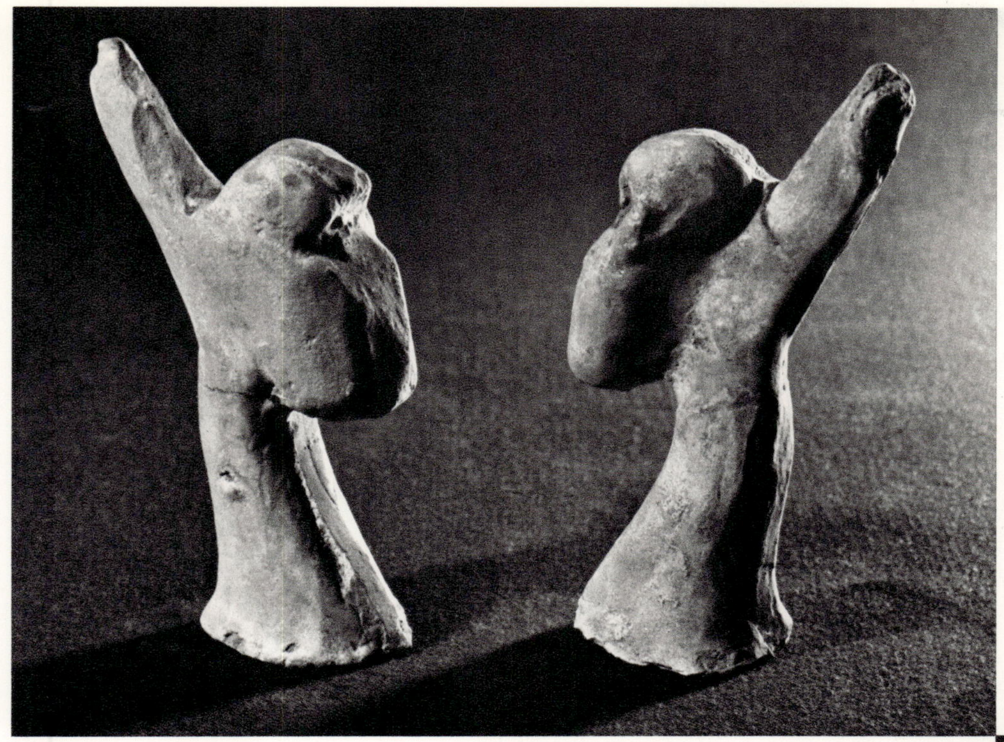

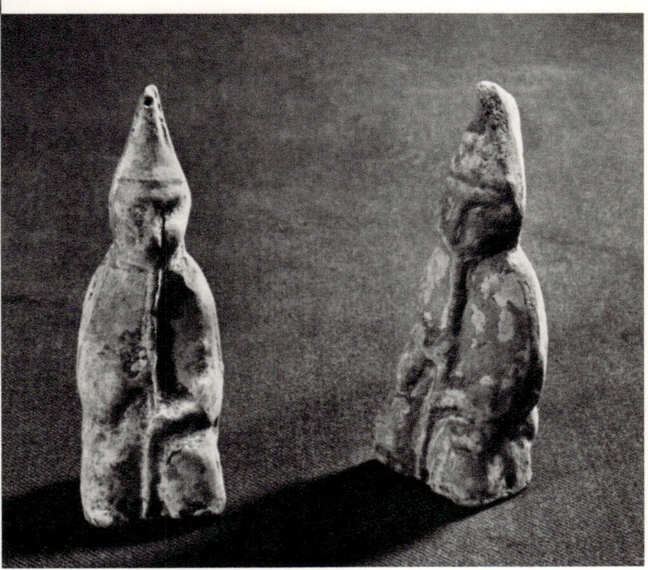

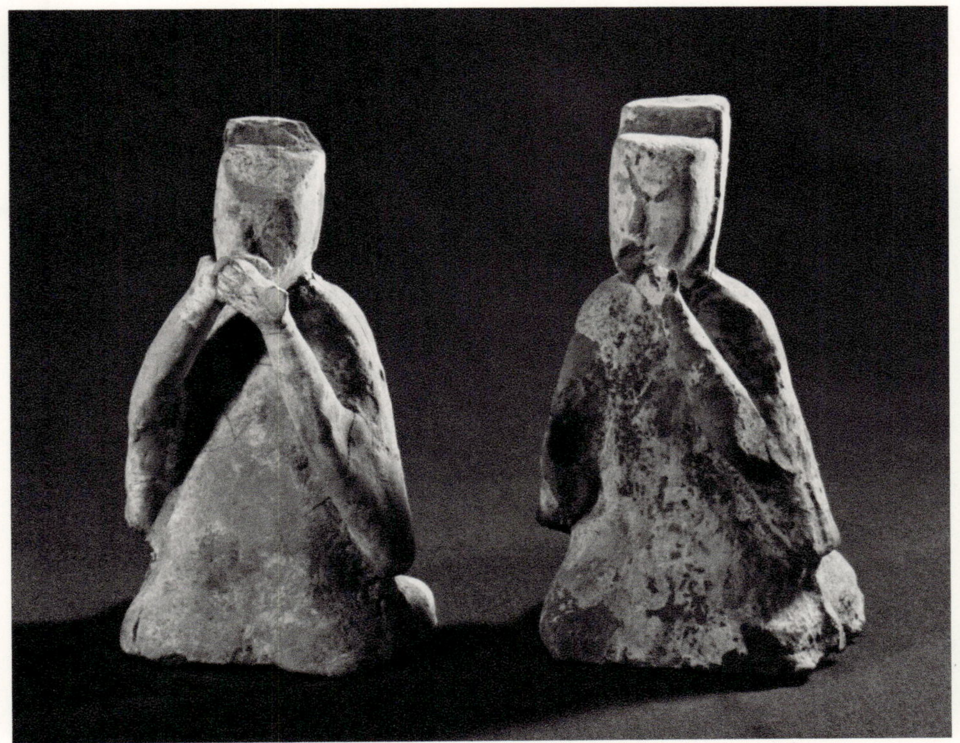

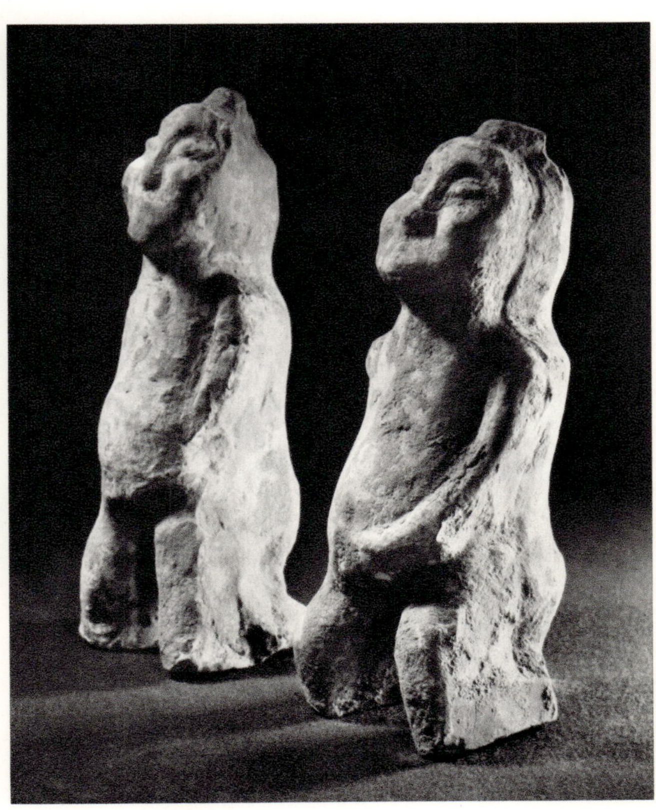

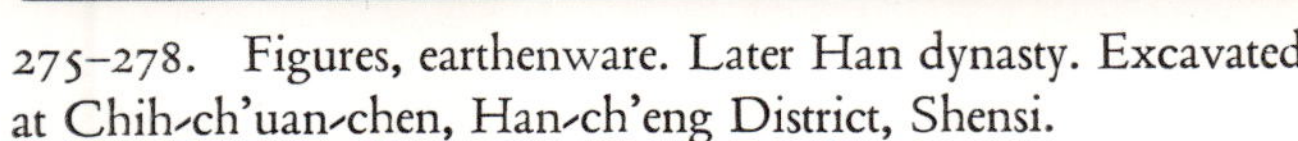

275–278. Figures, earthenware. Later Han dynasty. Excavated at Chih-ch'uan-chen, Han-ch'eng District, Shensi.

275. *Dancers. height: 12.1 cm. (4.7 in.)*

276. *Pipe players. height: 9.0 cm. (3.54 in.)*

277. *Musicians. height: 18.0 cm. (7.1 in.)*

278. *Fat-bellied figures. height: 18.0 cm. (7.1 in.)*

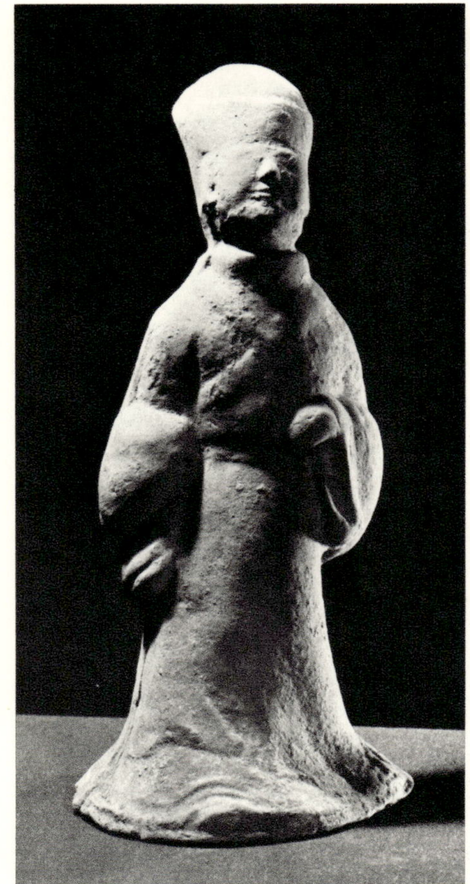

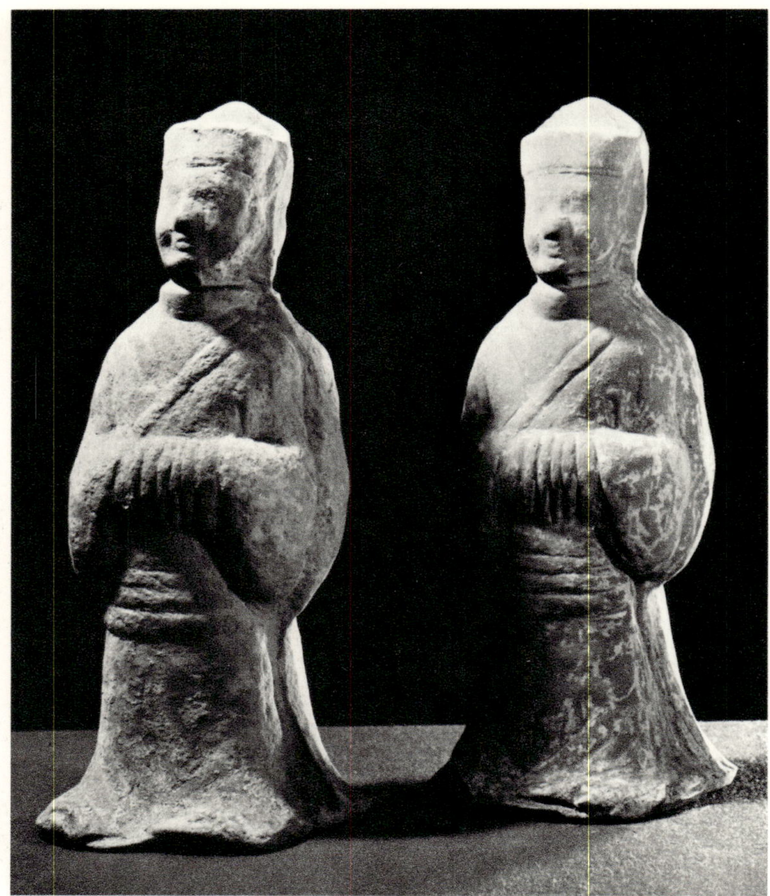

279–280. Figures, earthenware. Han dynasty. Excavated at Fo-erh-yai, Chang-ming, Szuchwan.

279. Attendant. height: 28.0 cm. (11.0 in.)

280. Scholars. height: 27.0 cm. (10.6 in.)

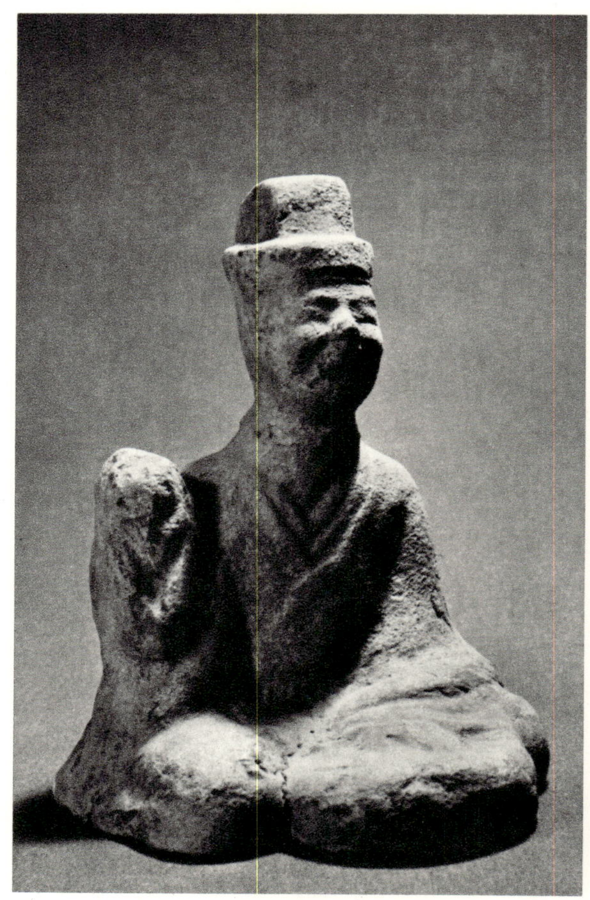

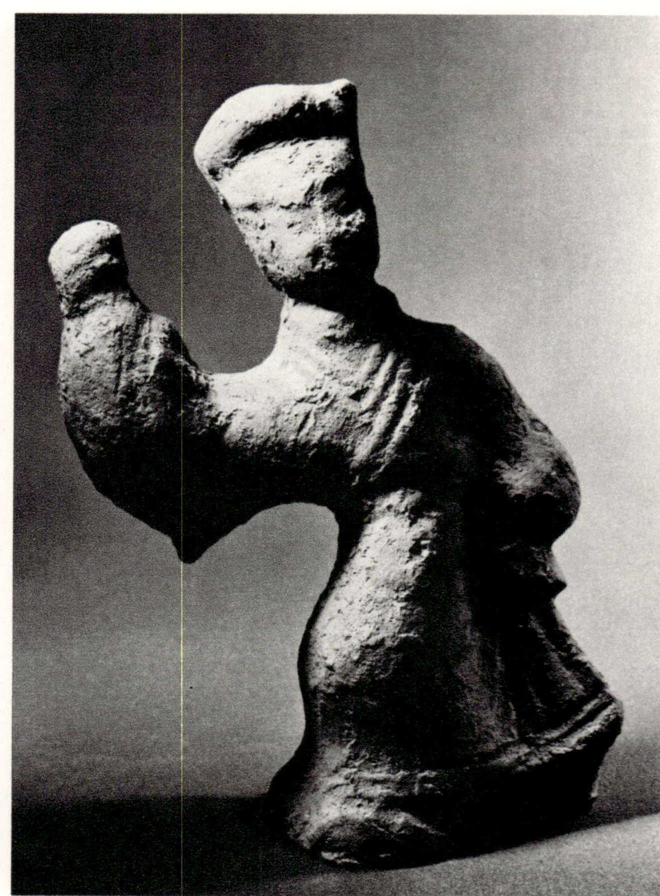

281–282. Figures, earthenware. Later Han dynasty. Excavated at Hsiang-kuo Temple, Chiang-pei, Chungking, Szuchwan.

281. Man beating a fu. height: 15.5 cm. (6.1 in.)

282. Dancer. height: 24.6 cm. (9.6 in.)

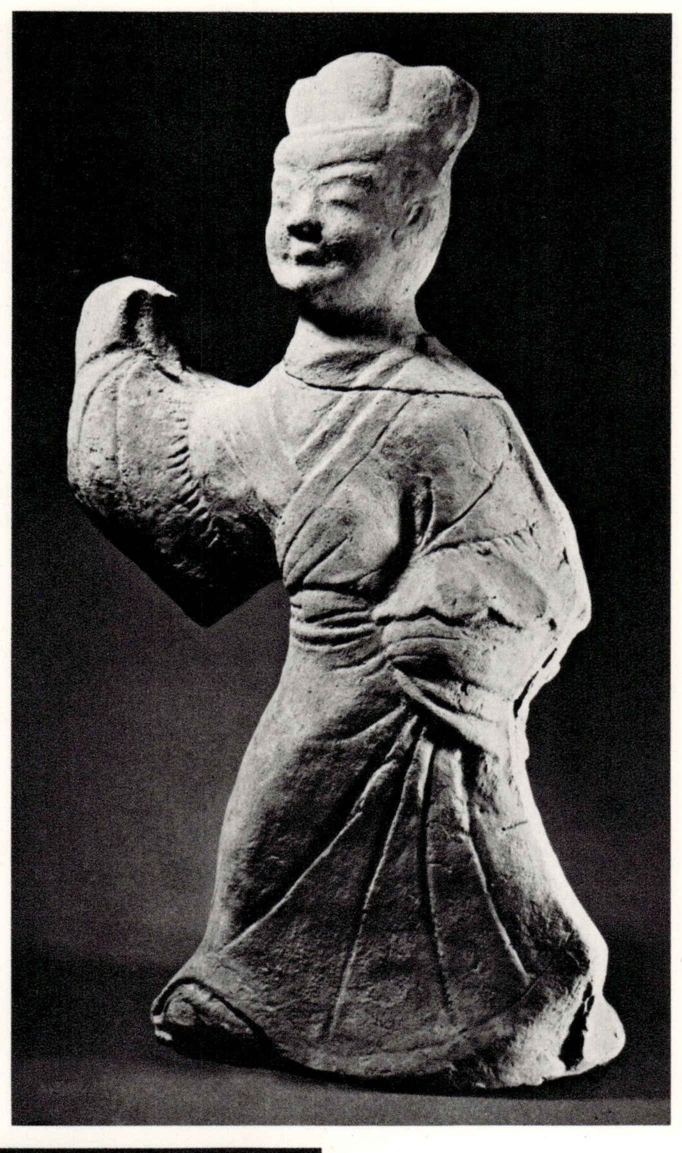

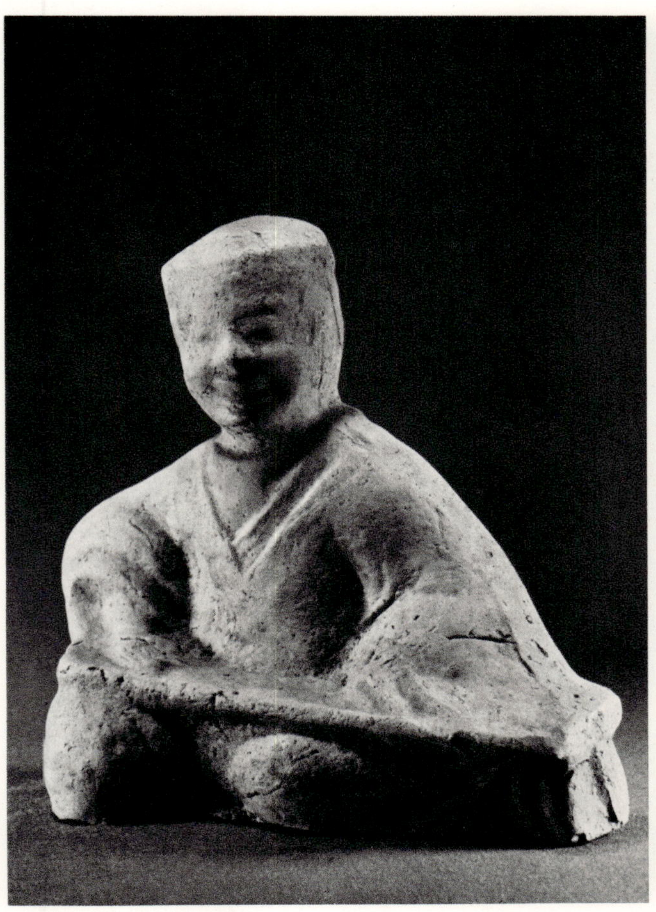

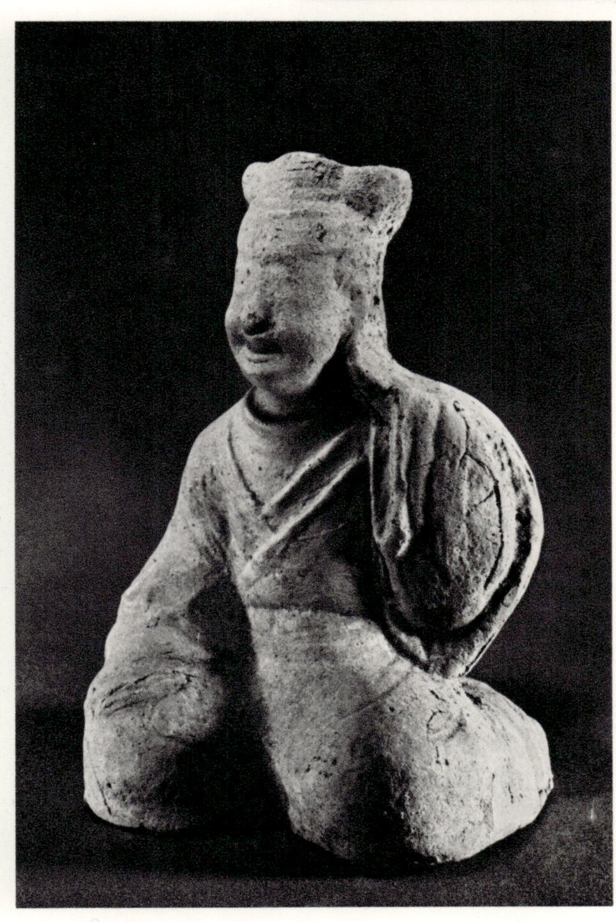

283–285. Figures, earthenware. Later Han dynasty. Excavated from the Mu-ma-shan-yai tomb, Szuchwan.
283. Dancer. height: 51.5 cm. (20.3 in.)
284. Kneeling musician. height: 23.5 cm. (9.3 in.)
285. Man listening to music. height: 25.2 cm. (9.9 in.)

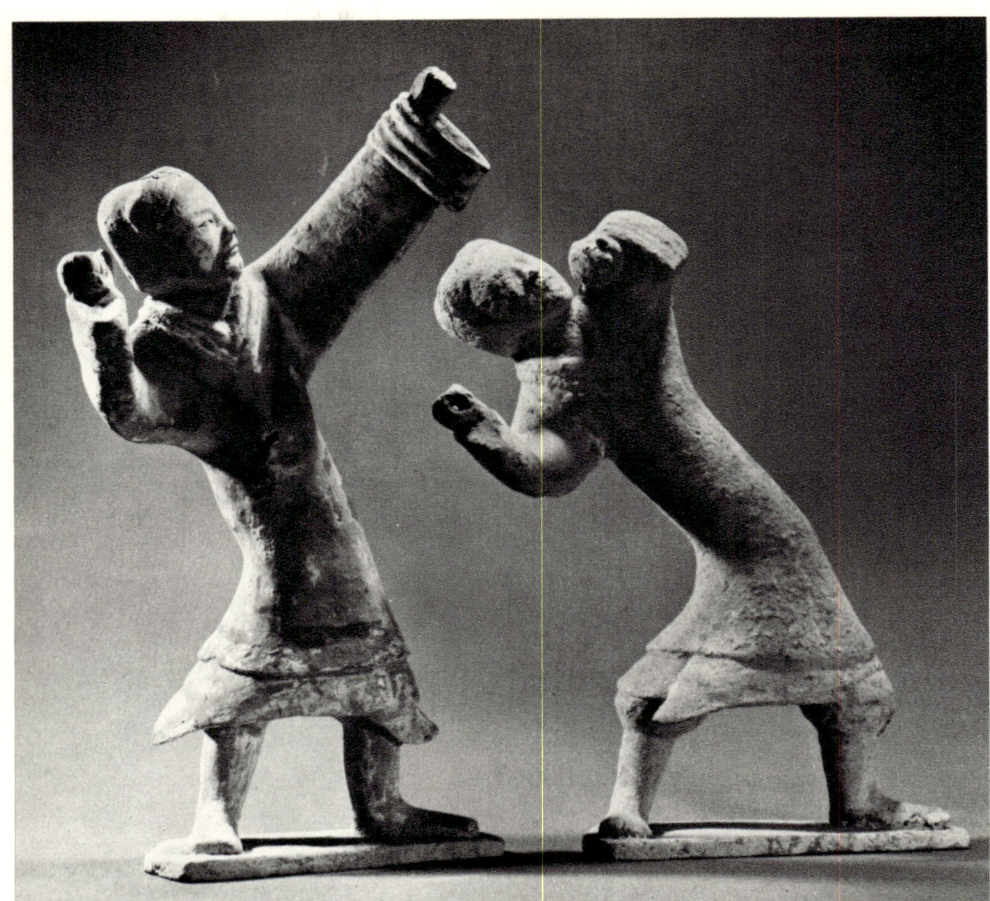

286. Figures in movement, earthenware. Han dynasty. Excavated at Lang-chia-t'ao, Shun-ling-ch'ü, Hsien-yang District, Shensi.
heights: (left) 42.5 cm. (16.7 in.); (right) 40.0 cm. (15.75 in.)

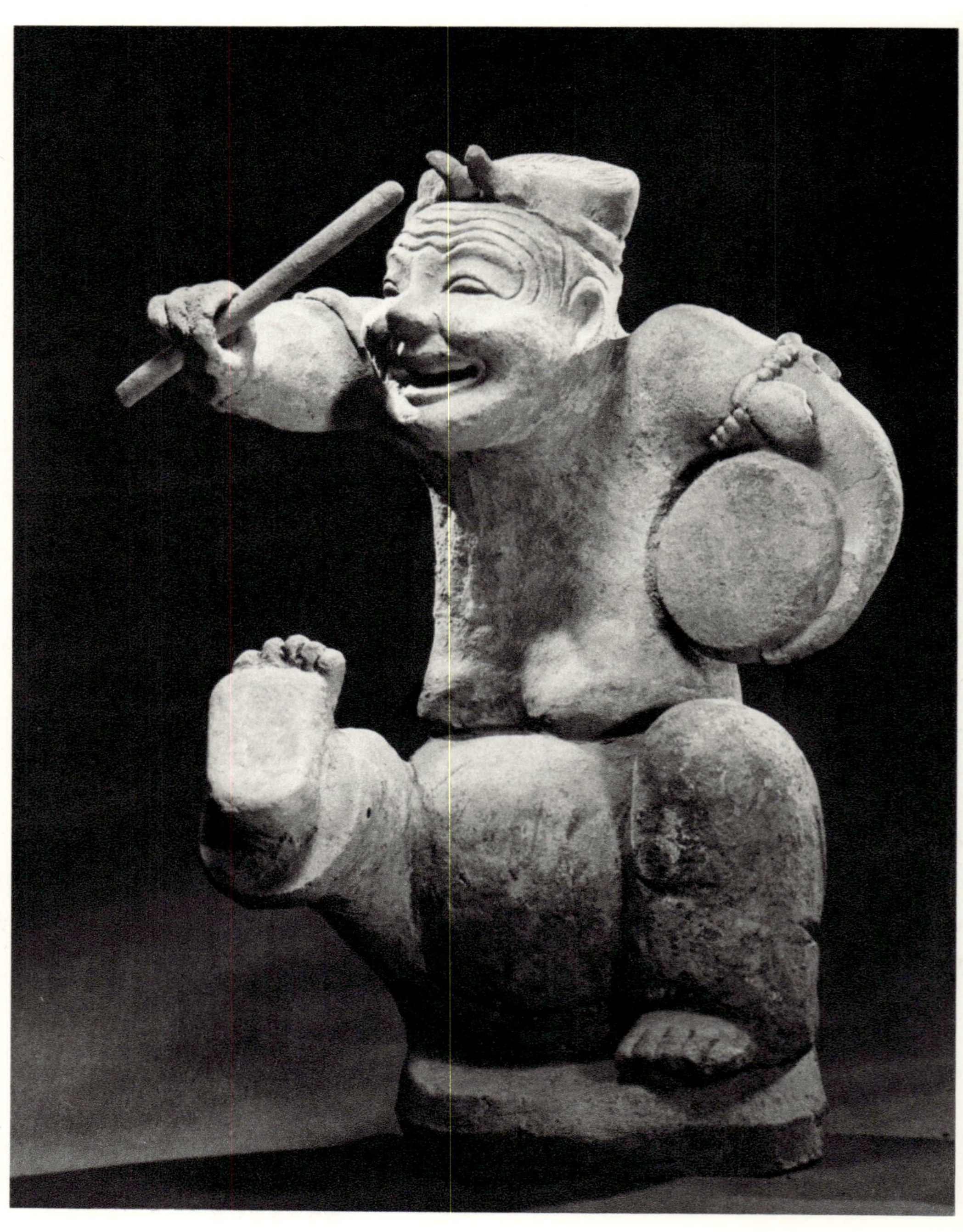

287. Storyteller, earthenware. Later Han dynasty. Excavated at T'ien-hui-shan, Ch'eng-tu, Szuchwan.
height: 56.0 cm. (22.0 in.)

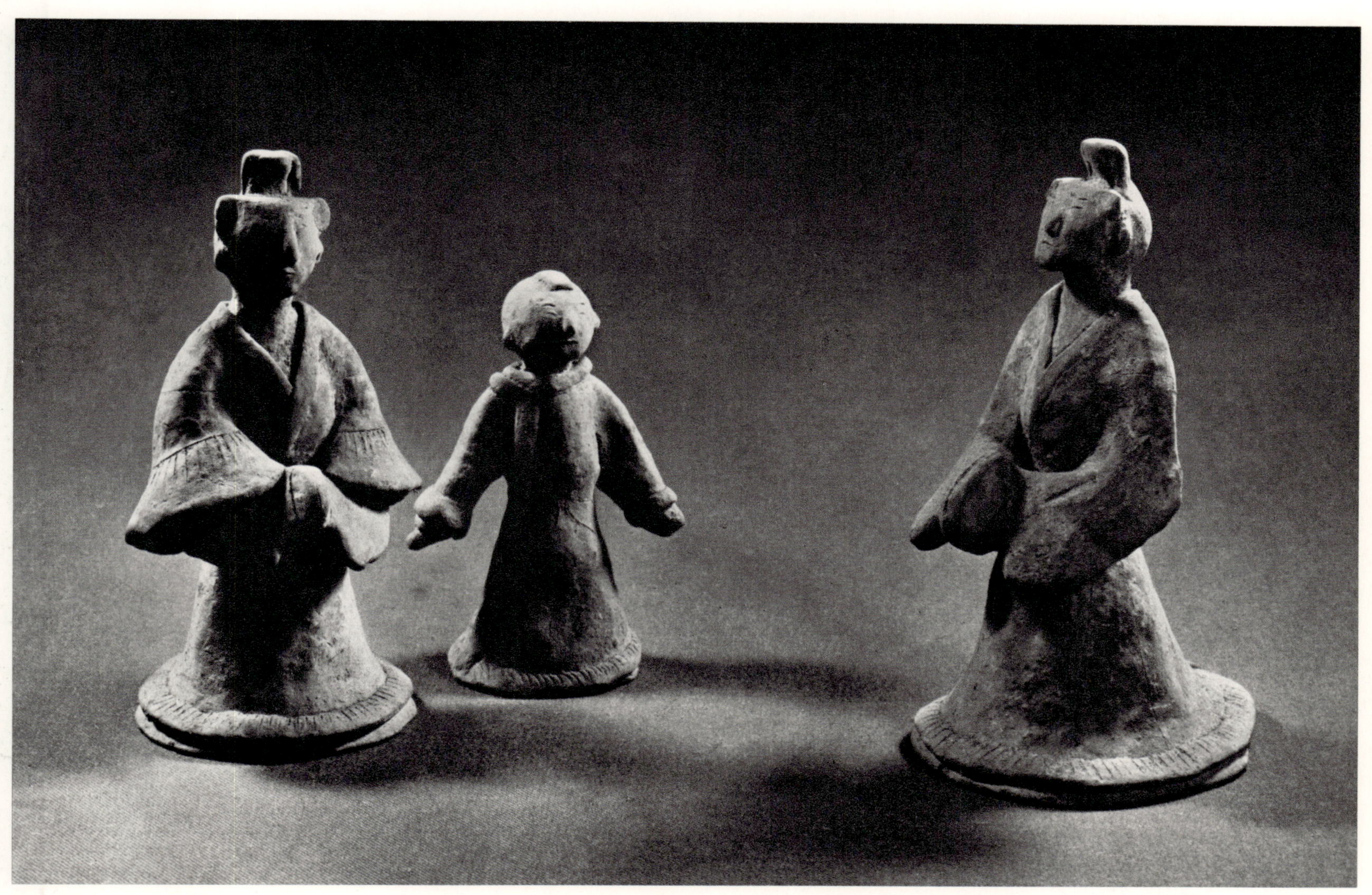

288. Figures, gray earthenware. Han dynasty. Excavated at Ch'ing-pai-hsiang, Hsin-fan, Szuchwan.
heights (left to right): 17.2 cm. (6.7 in.); 13.0 cm. (5.1 in.); 18.3 cm. (7.2 in.)

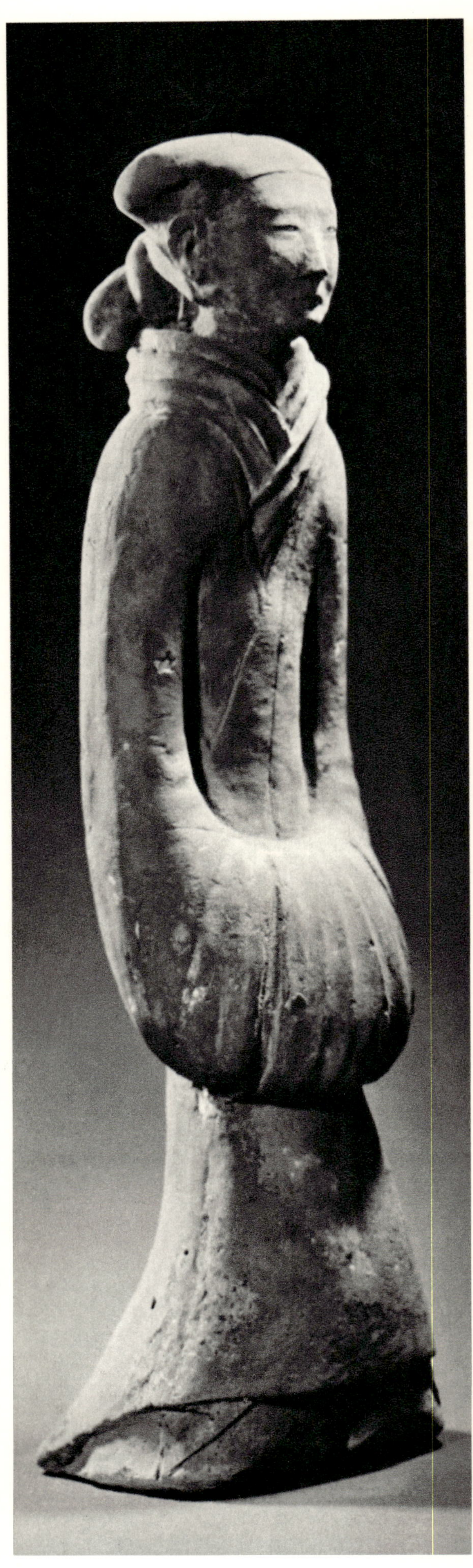

289. Female figure, gray earthenware. Later Han dynasty. Excavated from a stone chamber tomb, T'ung-shan District, Kiangsu.
height: 51.0 cm. (20.1 in.)

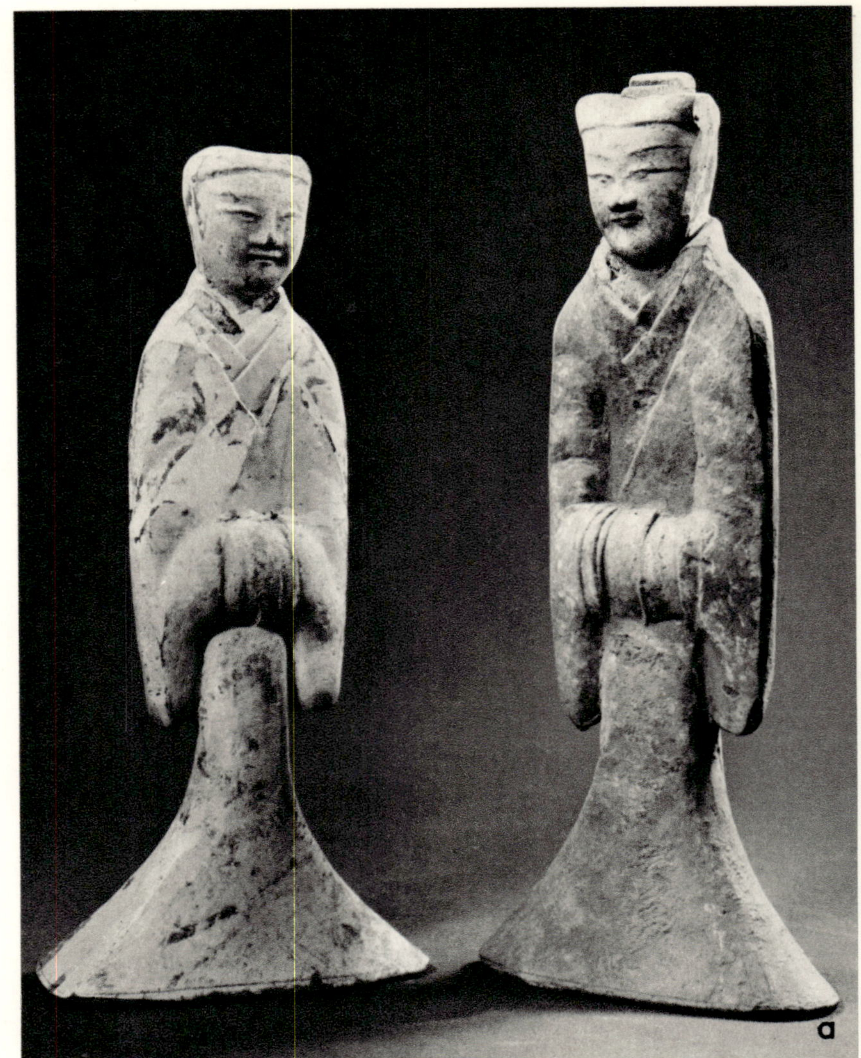

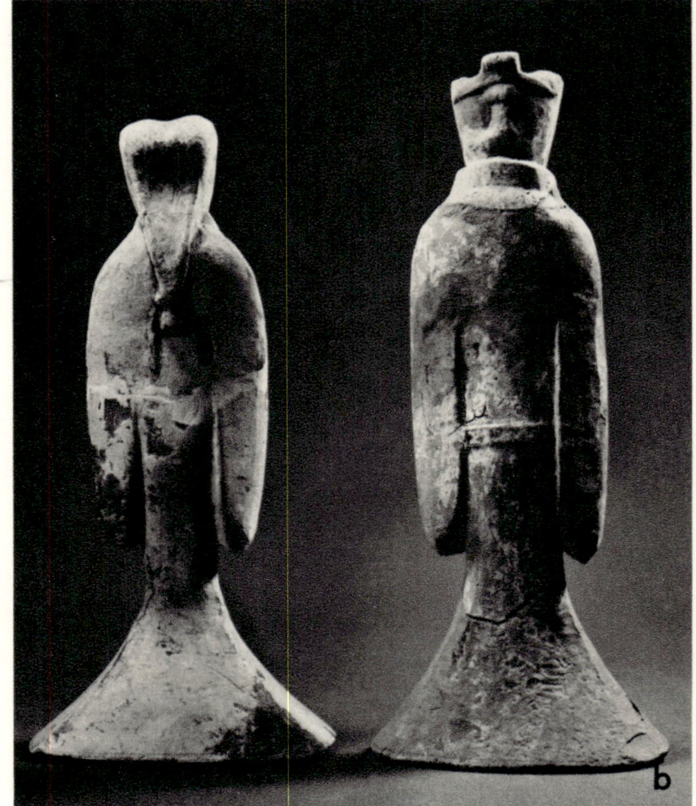

290 (a, b). Couple, slip-painted earthenware. Han dynasty. Excavated at Hung-ch'ing-ts'un, Sian, Shensi.
heights: 27.3 cm. (10.7 in.); 29.4 cm. (11.6 in.)

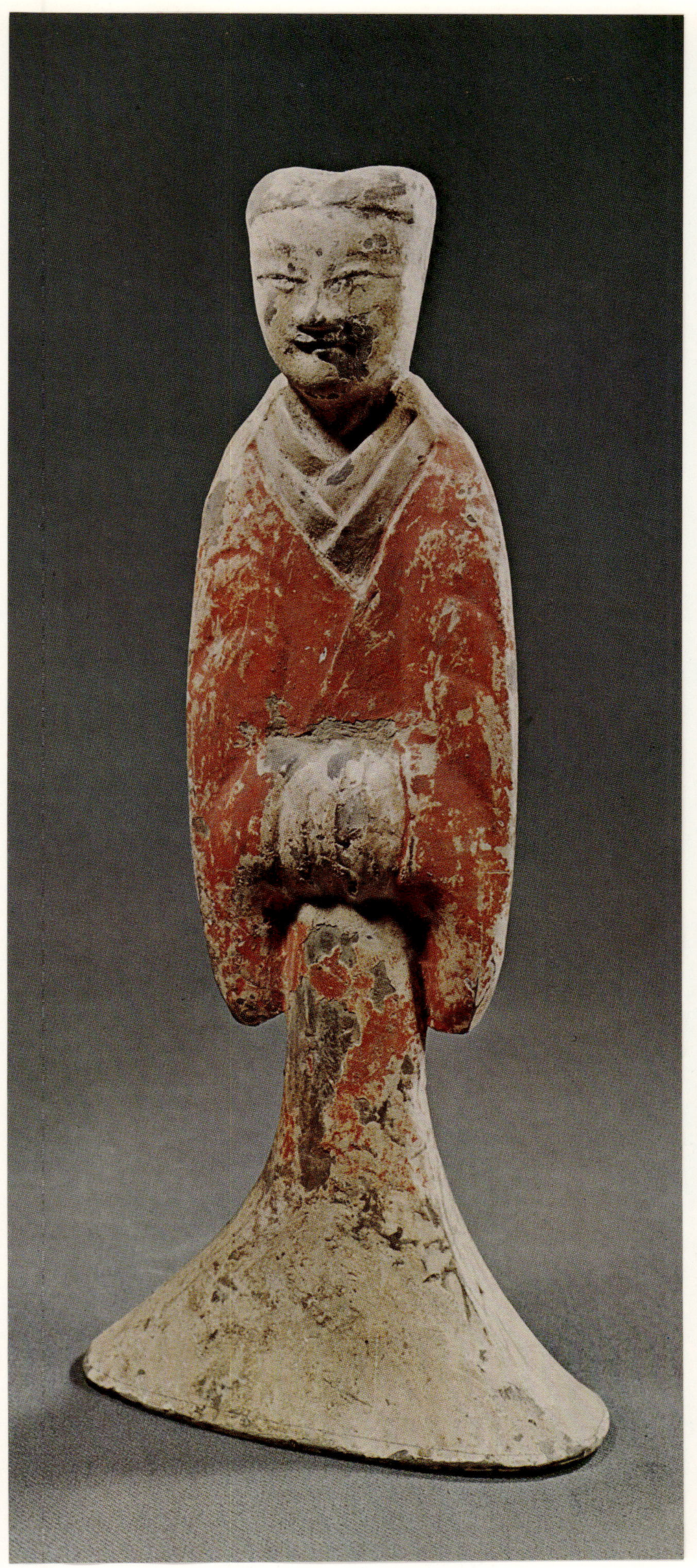

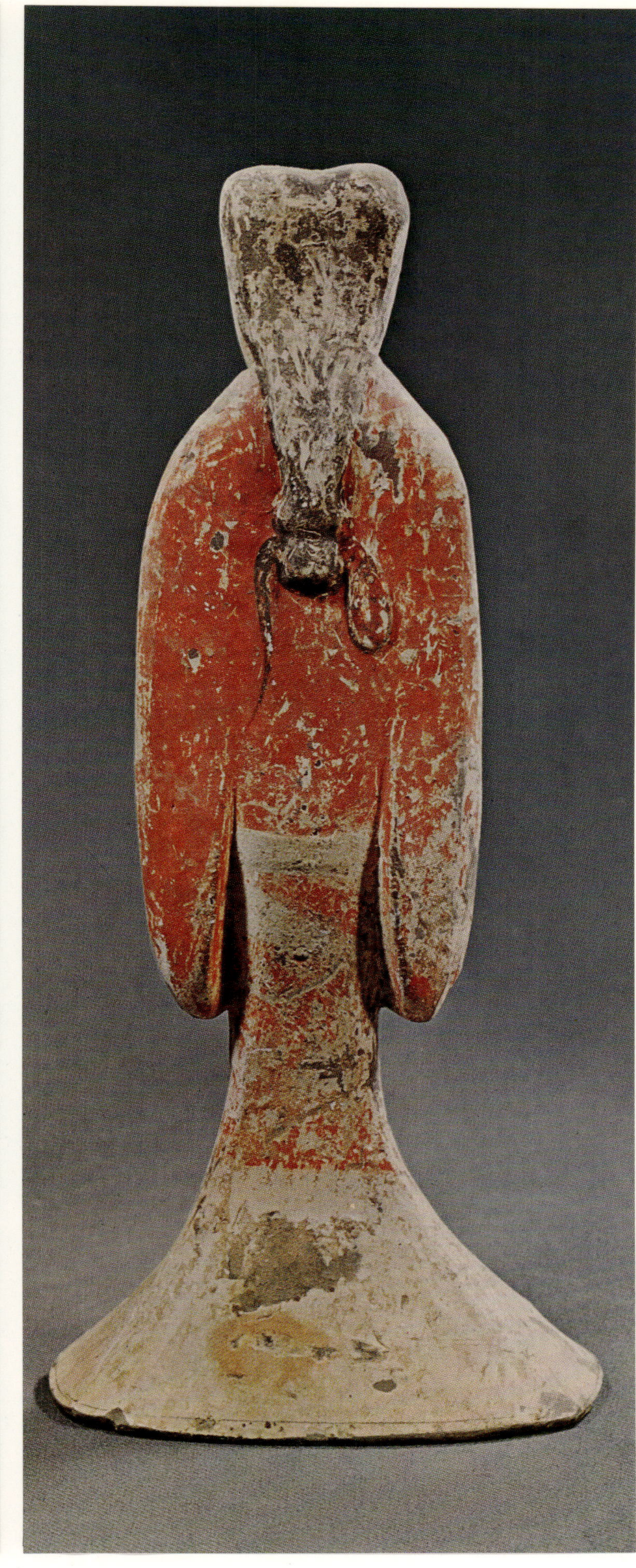

291 (a, b). Female figure, slip-painted earthenware. Han dynasty. Excavated at Hung-ch'ing-ts'un, Sian, Shensi.
height: 27.3 cm. (10.7 in.)

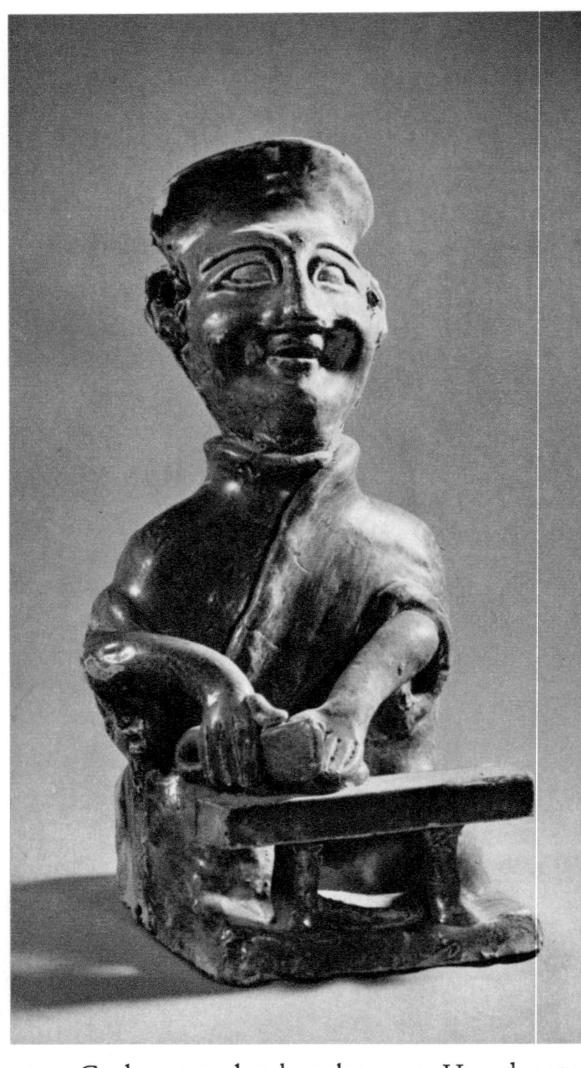

292. Cook, green-glazed earthenware. Han dynasty. Excavated at Kao-t'ang District, Shantung.
height: 29.7 cm. (11.7 in.)

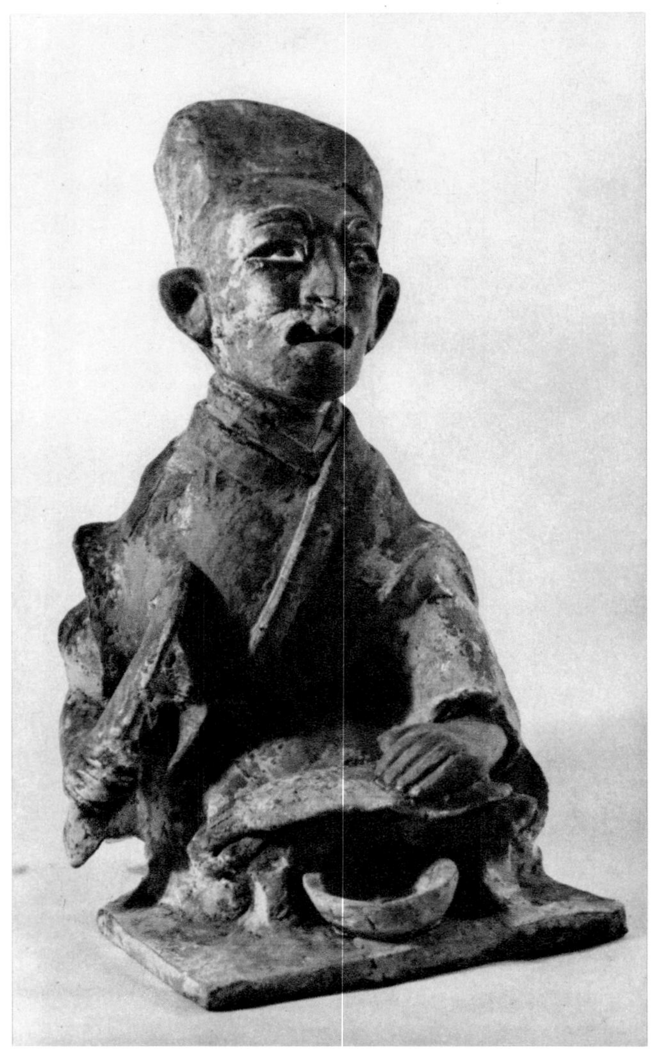

293. Cook, green-glazed earthenware. Han dynasty. Excavated at P'u-chi-chen, Chang-ch'iu District, Shantung.
height: 34.0 cm. (13.4 in.)

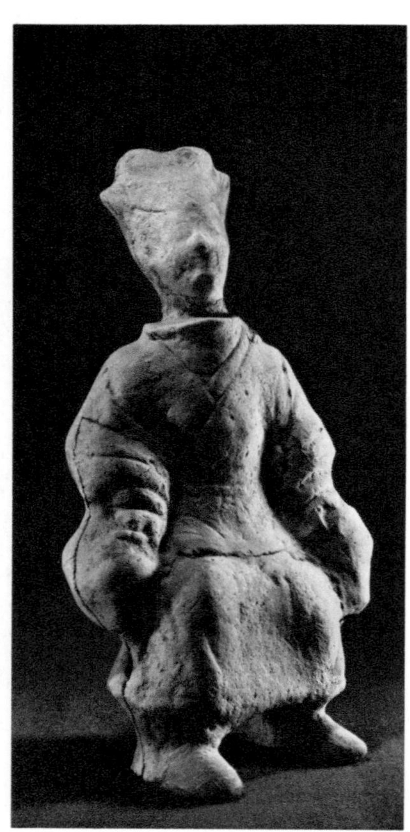

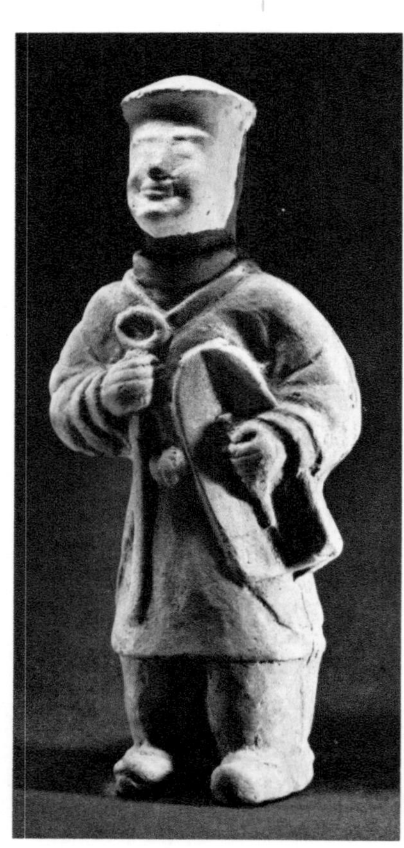

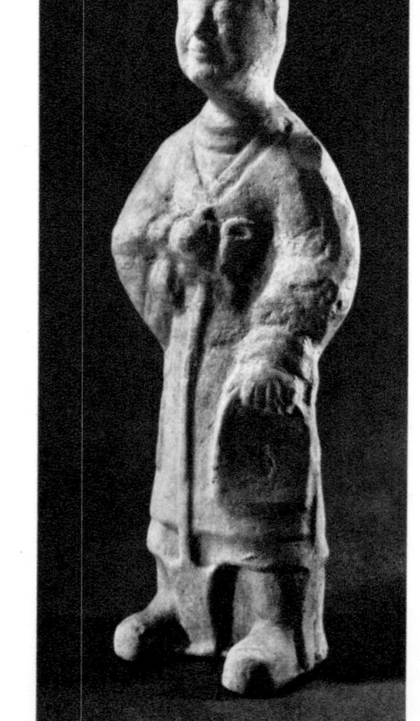

294–296. Male figures, gray earthenware. Han dynasty. Excavated at Ts'ui-p'ing-ts'un, Yi-pin Municipality, Szuchwan.
294. Man holding a hu. *height: 34.8 cm. (13.7 in.)*
295. Man holding a sword and shield. height: 38.5 cm. (15.1 in.)
296. Man holding a spade and winnow. height: 38.6 cm. (15.1 in.)

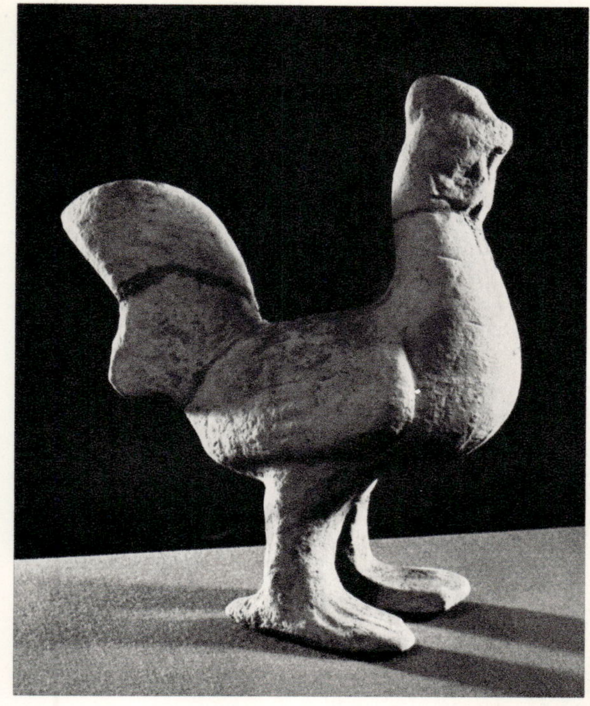

297. Cockerel, earthenware. Han dynasty. Excavated at Fo-erh-yai, Chang-ming, Szuchwan.
height: 30.3 cm. (11.9 in.)

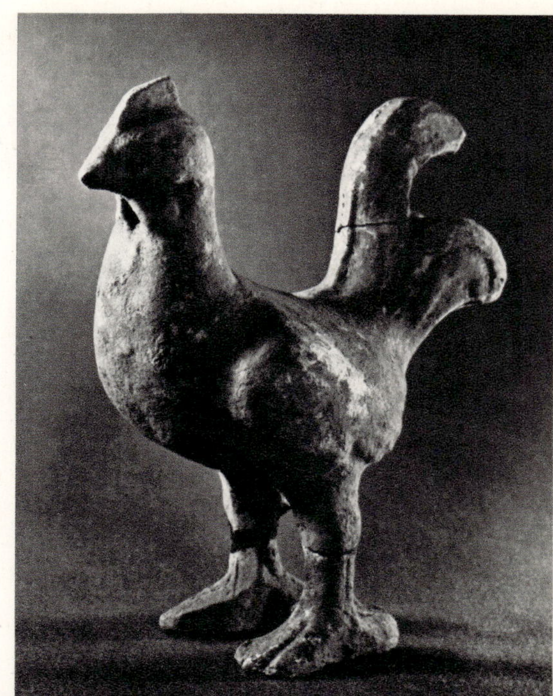

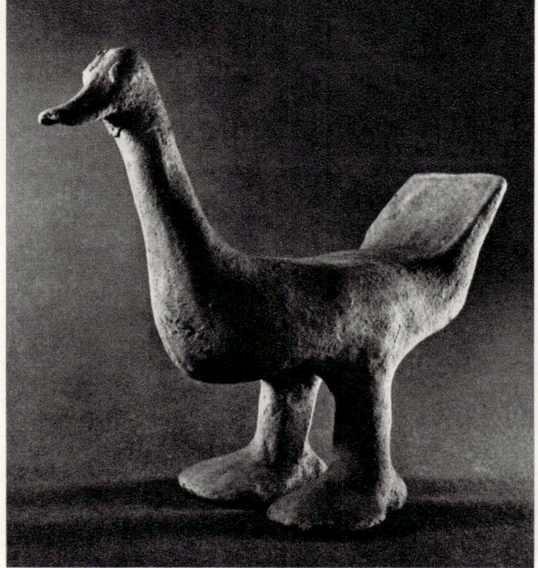

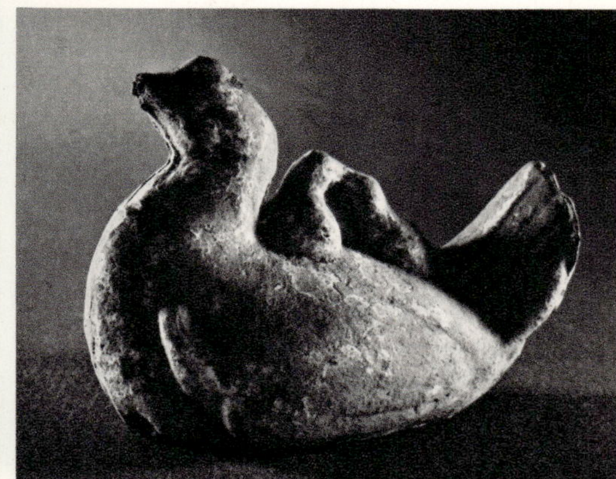

298–300. Poultry figures, earthenware. Later Han dynasty. Excavated from the Mu-ma-shan-yai tomb, Szuchwan.
298. Cockerel. height: 20.0 cm. (7.9 in.); length: 16.8 cm. (6.6 in.)
299. Drake. height: 22.0 cm. (8.7 in.); length: 23.7 cm. (9.5 in.)
300. Hen and chicks. height: 13.5 cm. (5.3 in.); length: 17.5 cm. (6.9 in.)

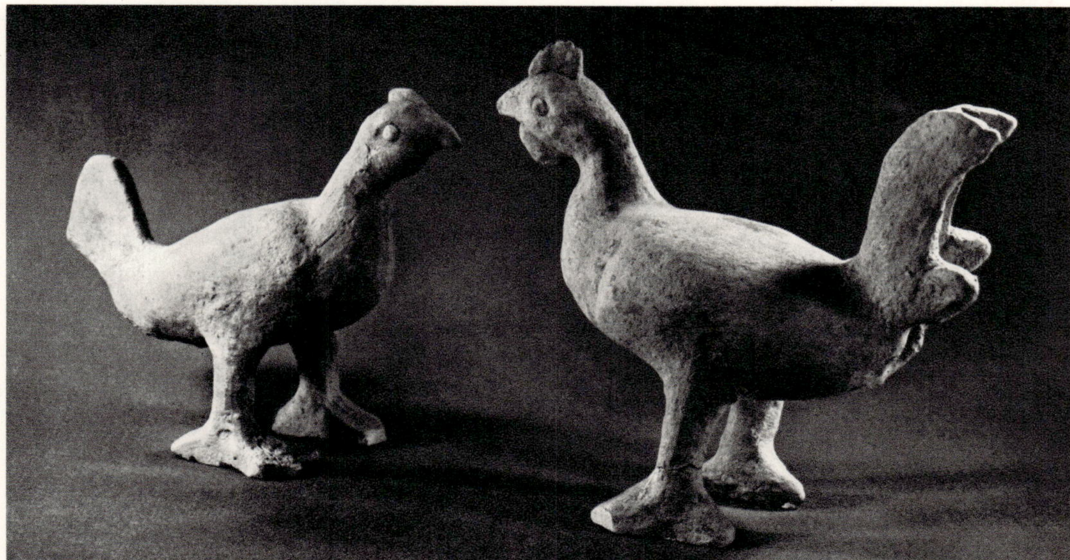

301. Cock and hen, earthenware. Han dynasty. Excavated from a tomb at Ch'ing-pai-hsiang, Hsin-fan, Szuchwan.
heights: 21.0 cm. (8.3 in.); 23.0 cm. (9.1 in.)

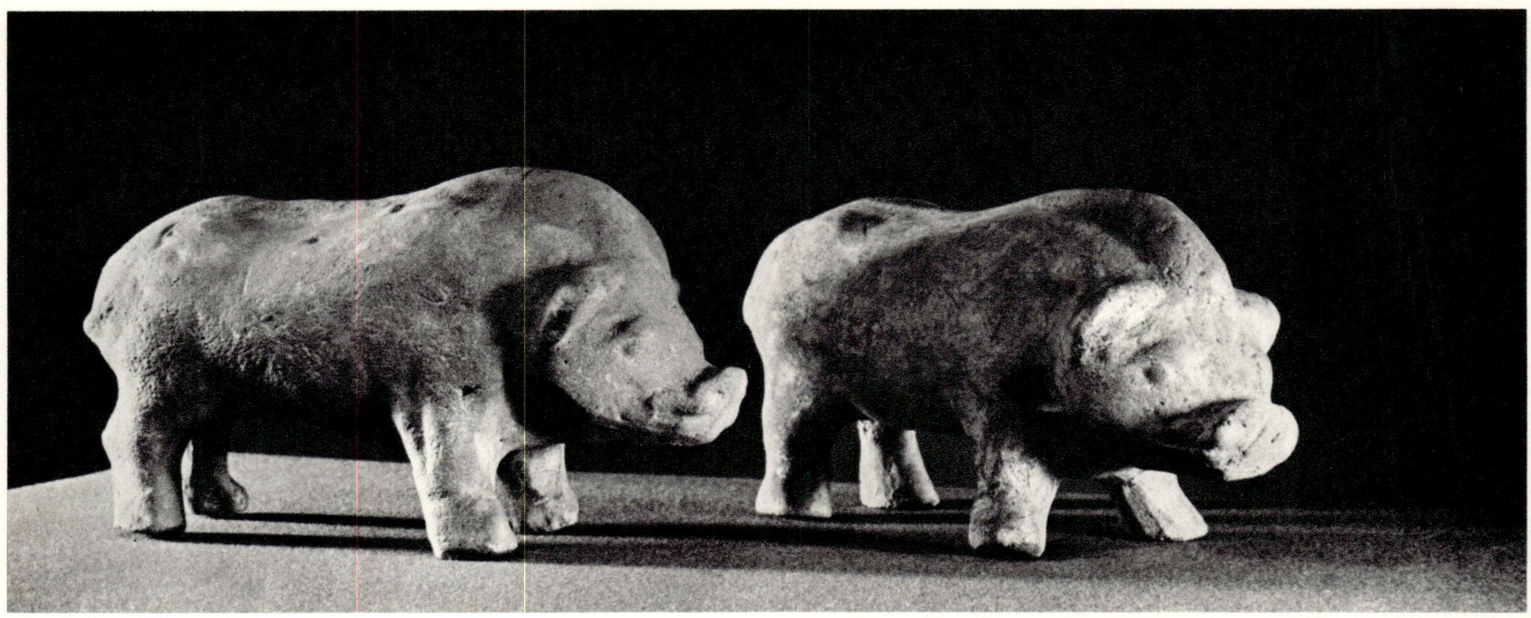

302. Pigs, earthenware. Later Han dynasty. Excavated from a tomb at the Hsiang-kuo Temple, Chiang-pei, Chungking, Szuchwan.
heights: 13.0 cm. (5.1 in.); lengths: 24.0 cm. (9.4 in.)

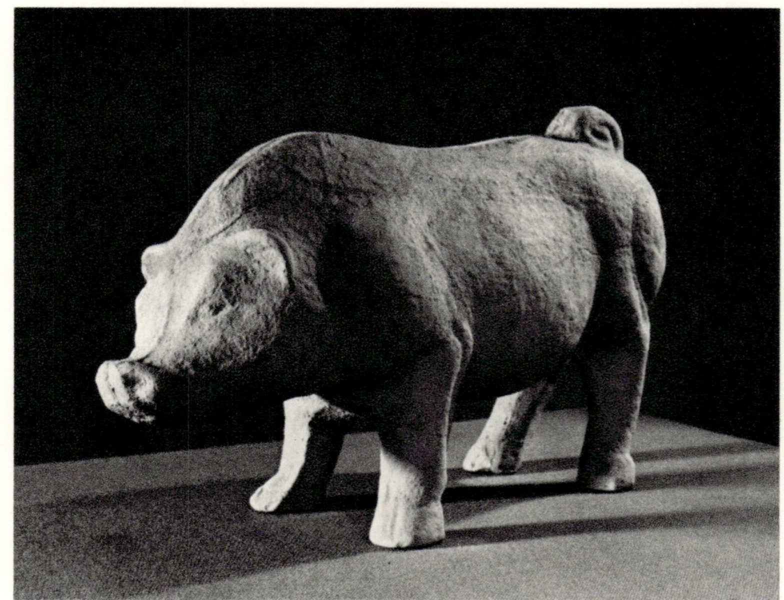

303. Pig, earthenware. Han dynasty. Excavated at Fo-erh-yai, Chang-ming, Szuchwan.
height: 19.3 cm. (7.6 in.); length: 32.0 cm. (12.6 in.)

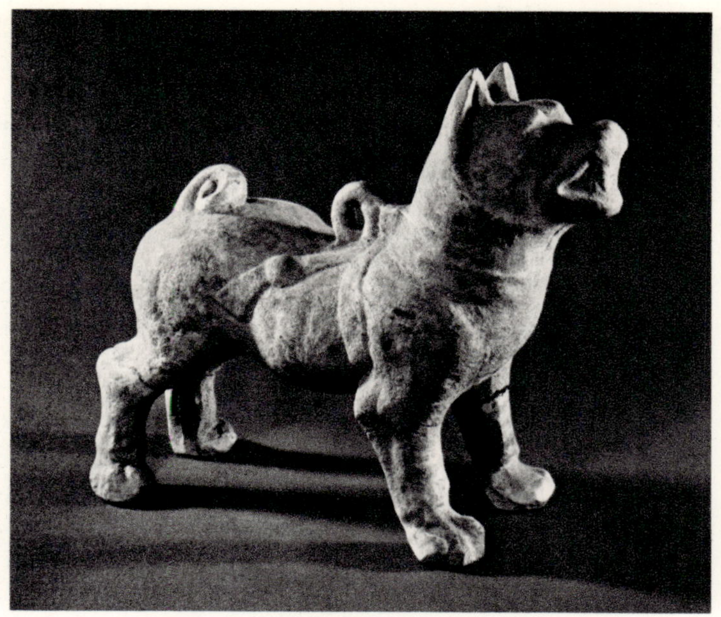

304. Dog, earthenware. Later Han dynasty. Excavated from the Mu-ma-shan-yai tomb, Szuchwan.
height: 26.0 cm. (10.2 in.); length: 30.0 cm. (11.8 in.)

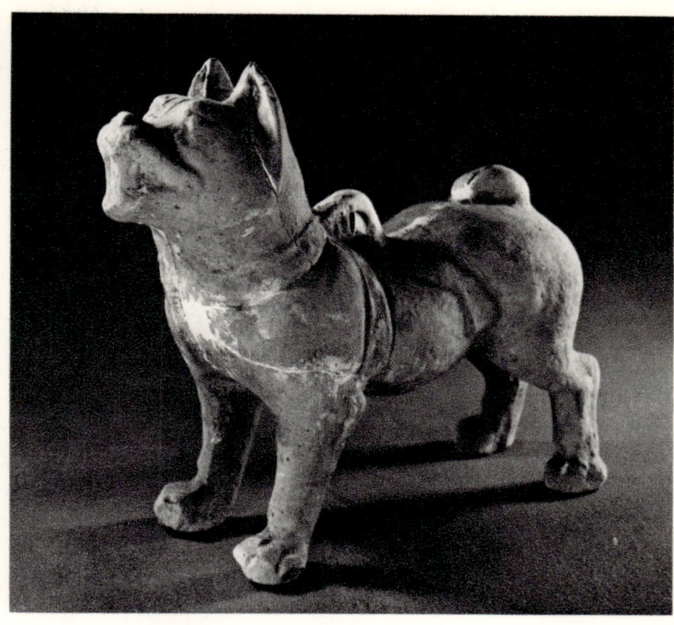

305. Dog, earthenware. Later Han dynasty. Excavated at the Hsiang-kuo Temple, Chiang-pei, Chungking, Szuchwan.
height: 20.0 cm. (7.9 in.); length: 27.0 cm. (10.6 in.)

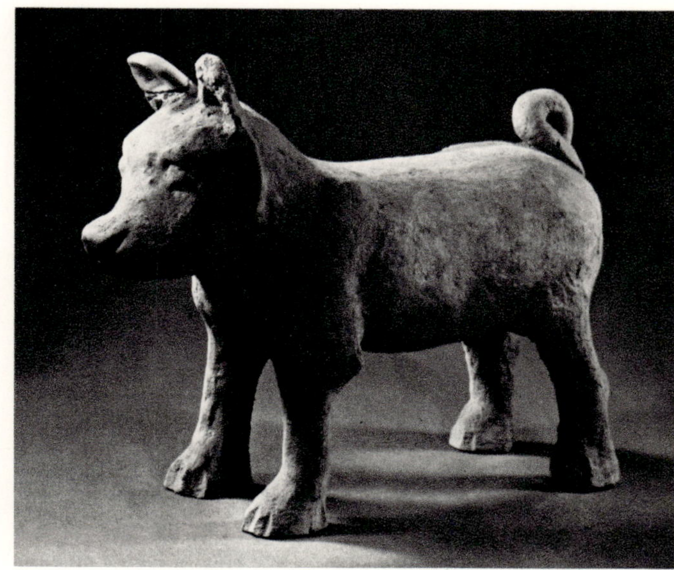

306. Dog, earthenware. Han dynasty. Excavated at Ch'ing-pai-hsiang, Hsin-fan, Szuchwan.
height: 25.0 cm. (9.8 in.); length: 33.0 cm. (13.0 in.)

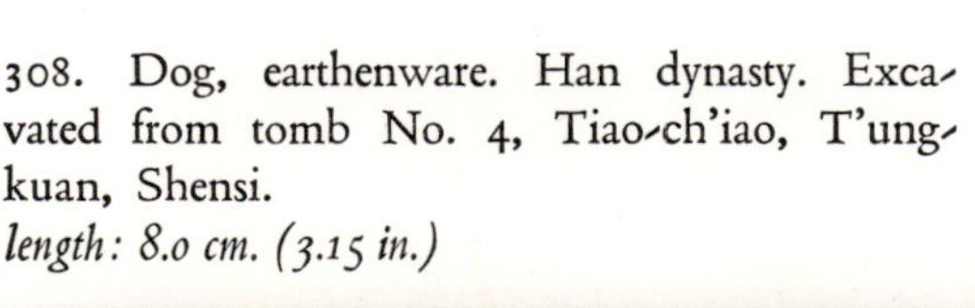

308. Dog, earthenware. Han dynasty. Excavated from tomb No. 4, Tiao-ch'iao, T'ung-kuan, Shensi.
length: 8.0 cm. (3.15 in.)

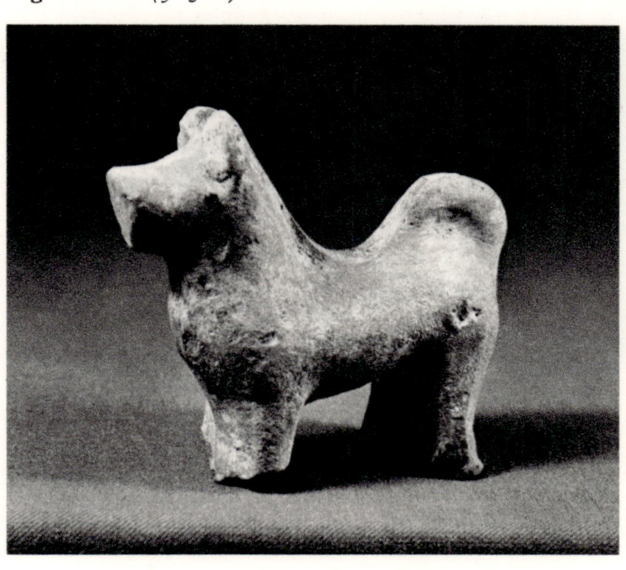

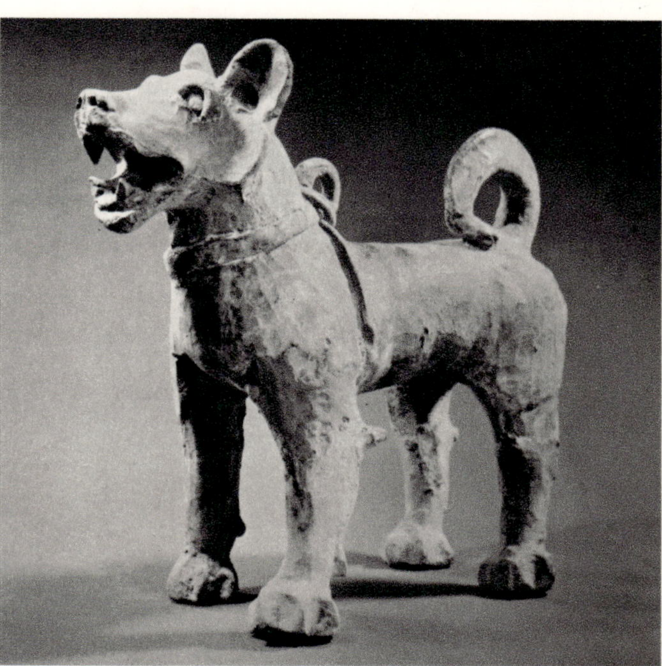

307. Dog, earthenware. Han dynasty. Excavated at P'u-chi-chen, Chang-ch'iu District, Shantung.
height: 32.5 cm. (12.8 in.); length: 33.0 cm. (13.0 in.)

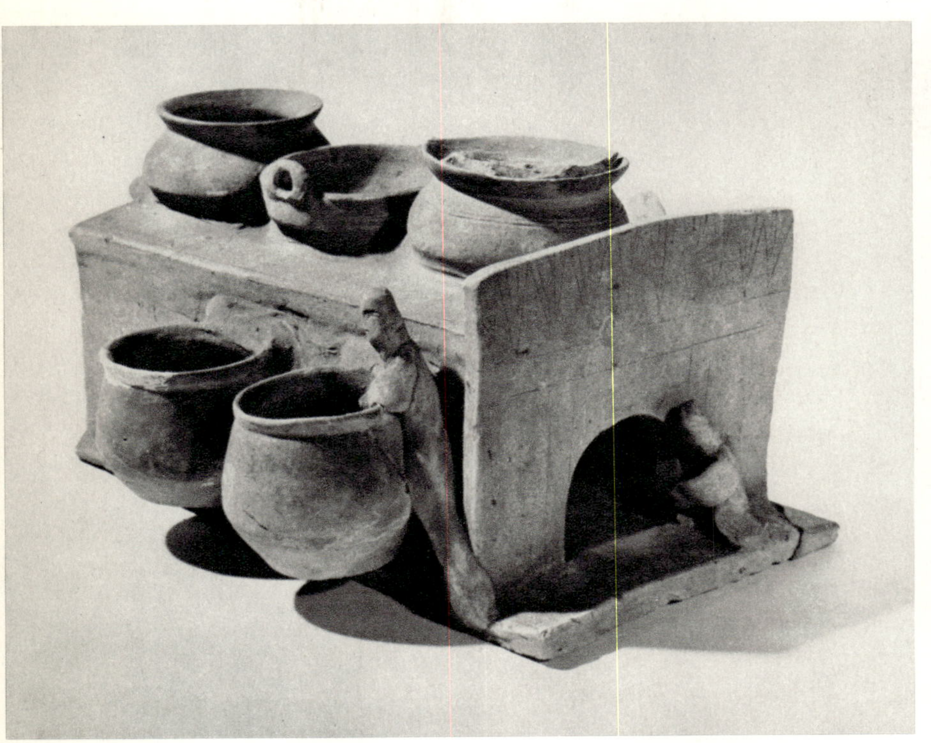

309. Cookstove with figures, earthenware. Later Han dynasty (dated 76 A.D.). From a tomb at Ma-ying-kang, Zoological Gardens, Canton.
height: 14.2 cm. (5.6 in.); length: 22.0 cm. (8.7 in.)

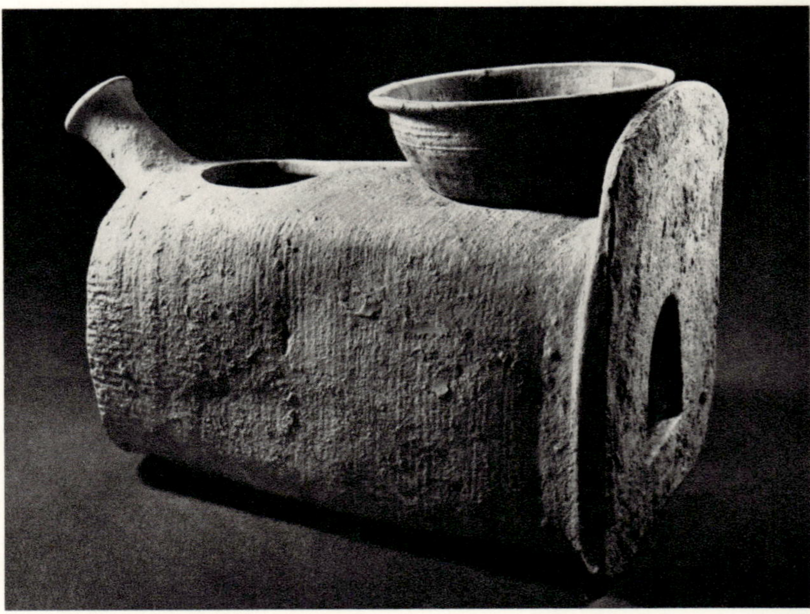

310. Cookstove, earthenware. Han dynasty. Excavated at Ch'ing-pai-hsiang, Hsin-fan, Szuchwan.
height: 18.0 cm. (7.1 in.); length: 31.0 cm. (12.2 in.)

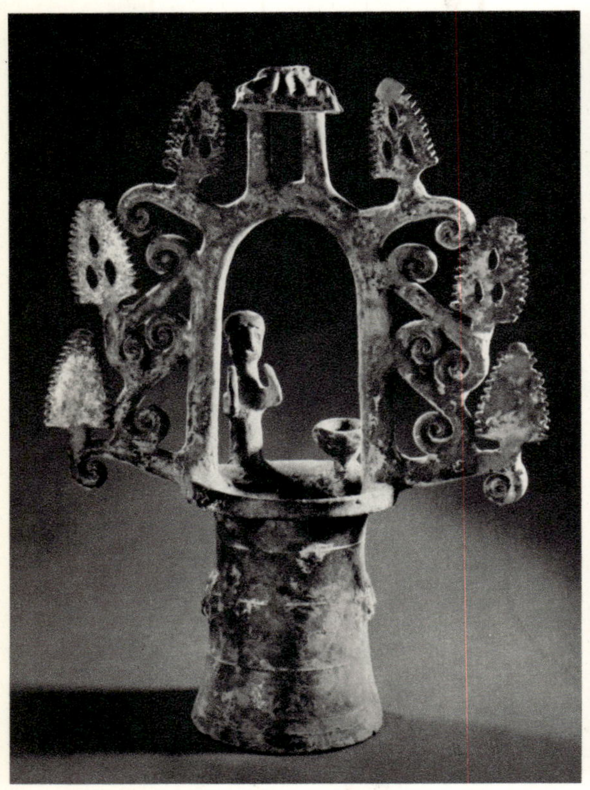

311. Well head, earthenware. Han dynasty. Excavated at P'u-chi-chen, Chang-ch'iu District, Shantung.
height: 56.0 cm. (22.0 in.); diameter at well mouth: 17.0 cm. (6.7 in.)

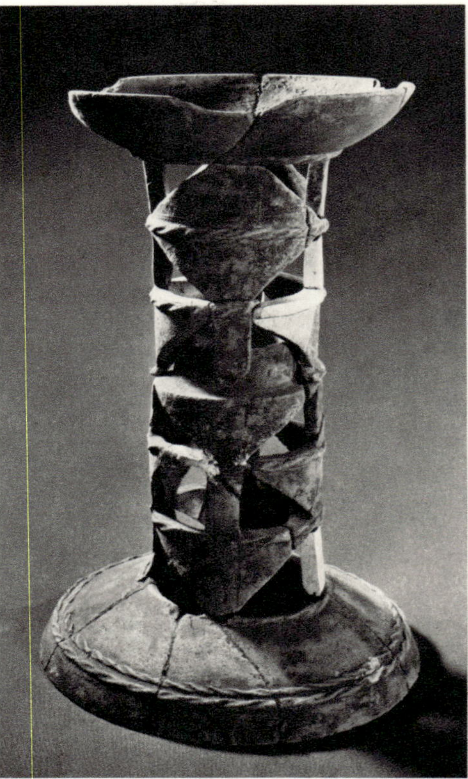

312. Columnar object, earthenware. Han dynasty. Excavated from the wooden coffin tomb at Feng-huang-shan, Ch'eng-tu, Szuchwan.
height: 23.0 cm. (9.1 in.)

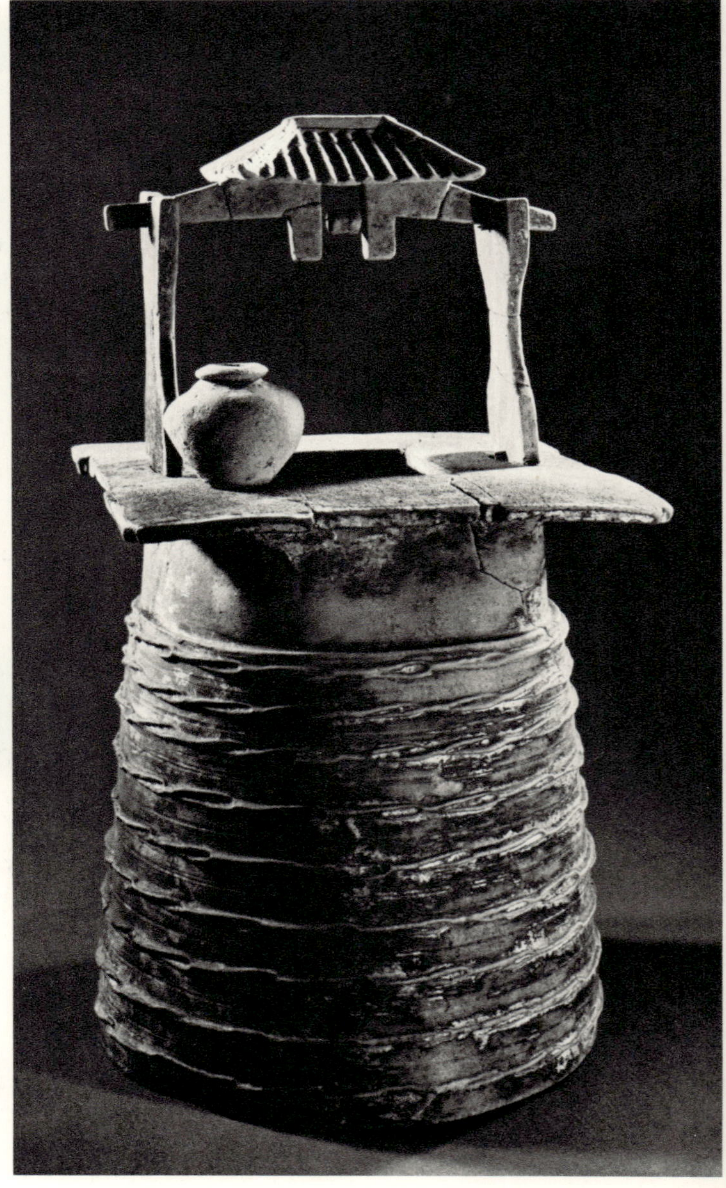

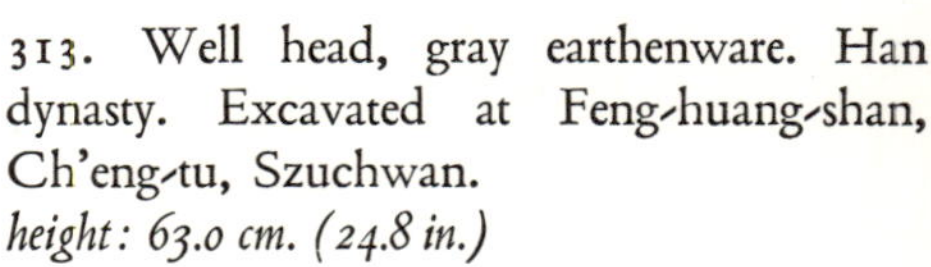

313. Well head, gray earthenware. Han dynasty. Excavated at Feng-huang-shan, Ch'eng-tu, Szuchwan.
height: 63.0 cm. (24.8 in.)

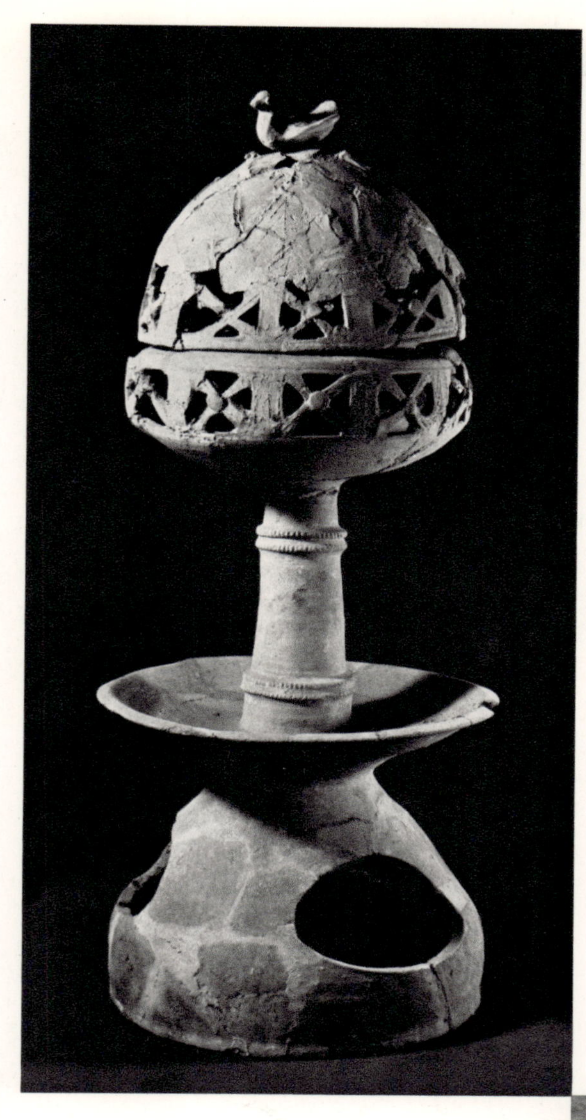

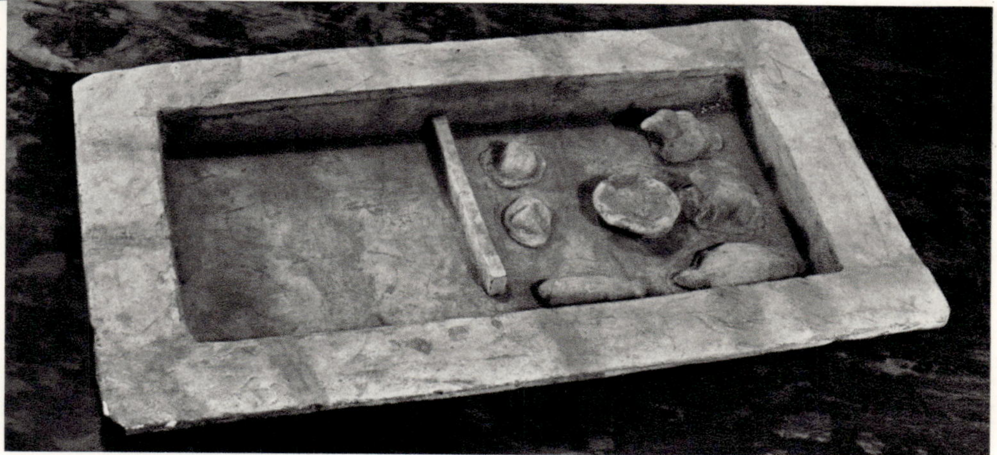

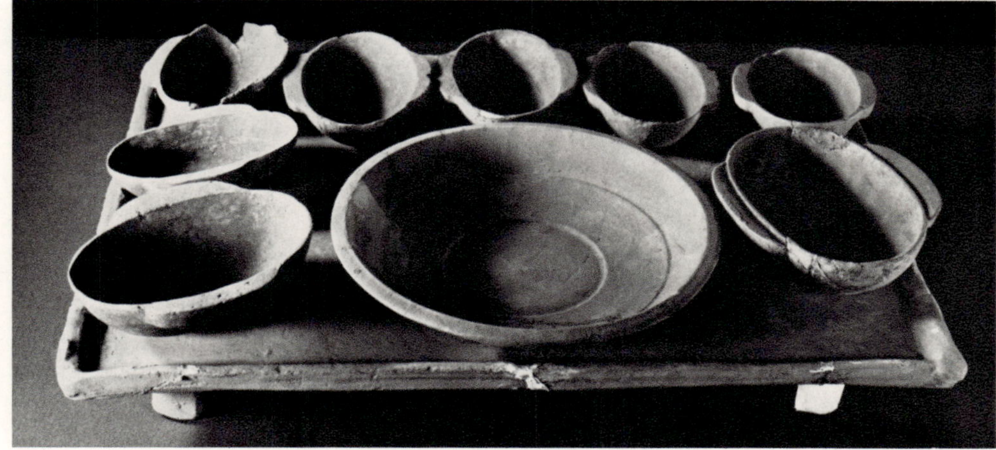

314–316. Tomb objects, earthenware. Later Han dynasty. Excavated at Hsiang-kuo Temple, Chiang-pei, Chungking, Szuchwan.

314. Incense burner. height: approx. 53.4 cm. (21.1 in.)

315. Paddy field and pond. height: 4.0 cm. (1.58 in.); length: 42.0 cm. (16.5 in.); width: 25.0 cm. (9.8 in.)

316. Oval cups and bowl on a stand. length: 48.0 cm. (18.9 in.): width: 34.0 cm. (13.4 in.)

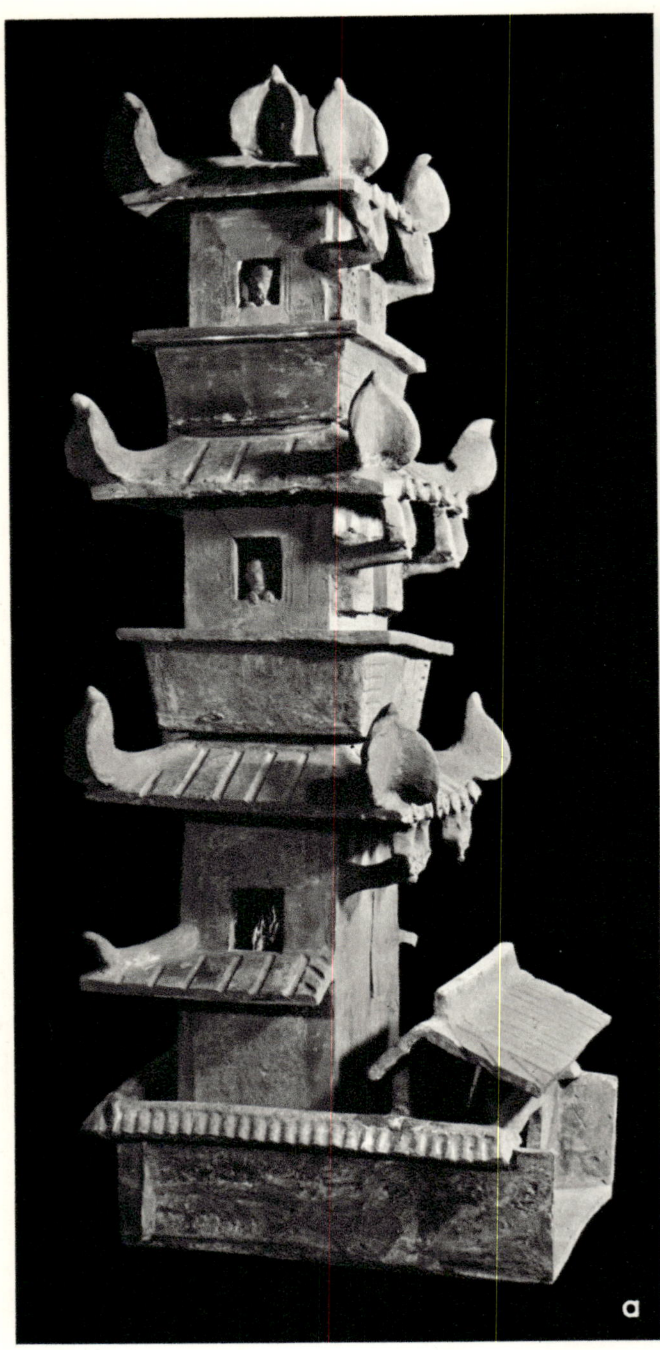

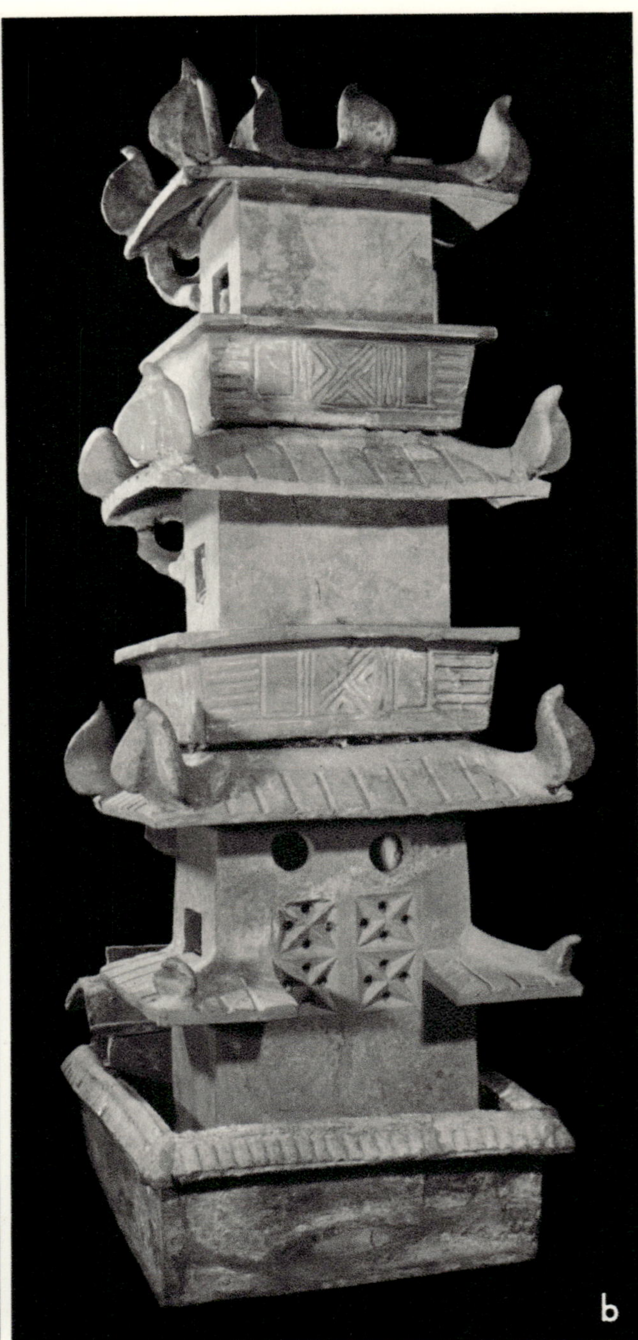

317 (a, b). Tower, earthenware. Side and back views. Han dynasty. Excavated at Tiao-ch'iao, T'ung-kuan, Shensi.
height: 117 cm. (46.1 in.)

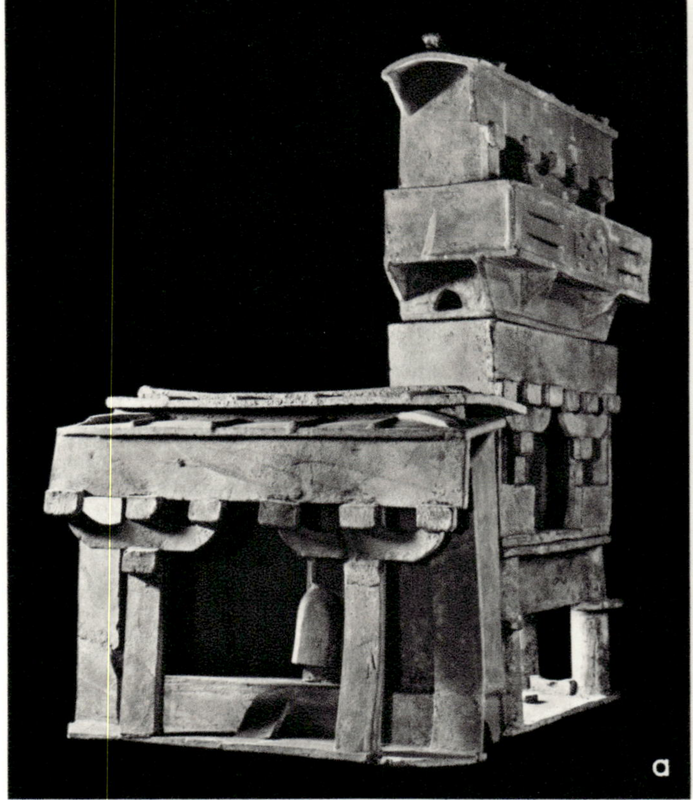

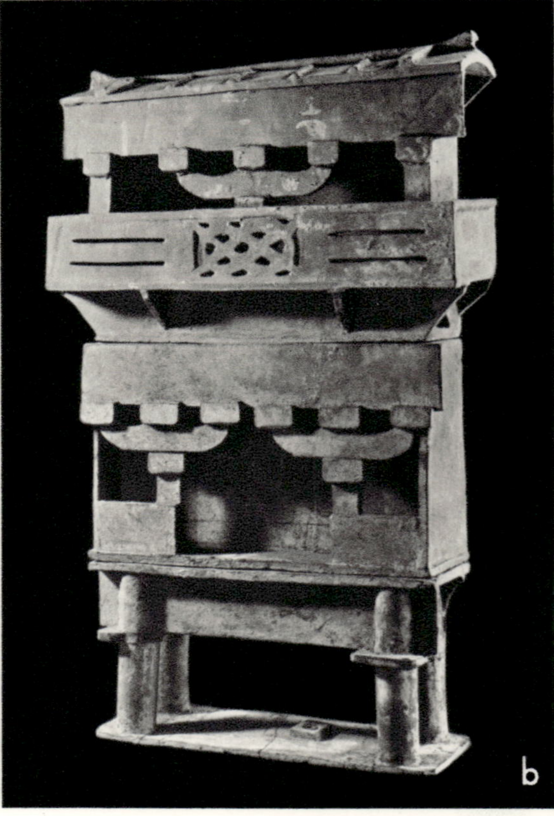

318 (a, b). One- and three-story buildings, gray earthenware. Later Han dynasty. Excavated at Hsiang-kuo Temple, Chiang-pei, Chungking, Szuchwan.
a. One-story building. height: 32.0 cm. (12.6 in.)
b. Three-story building. height: 64.5 cm. (25.4 in.)

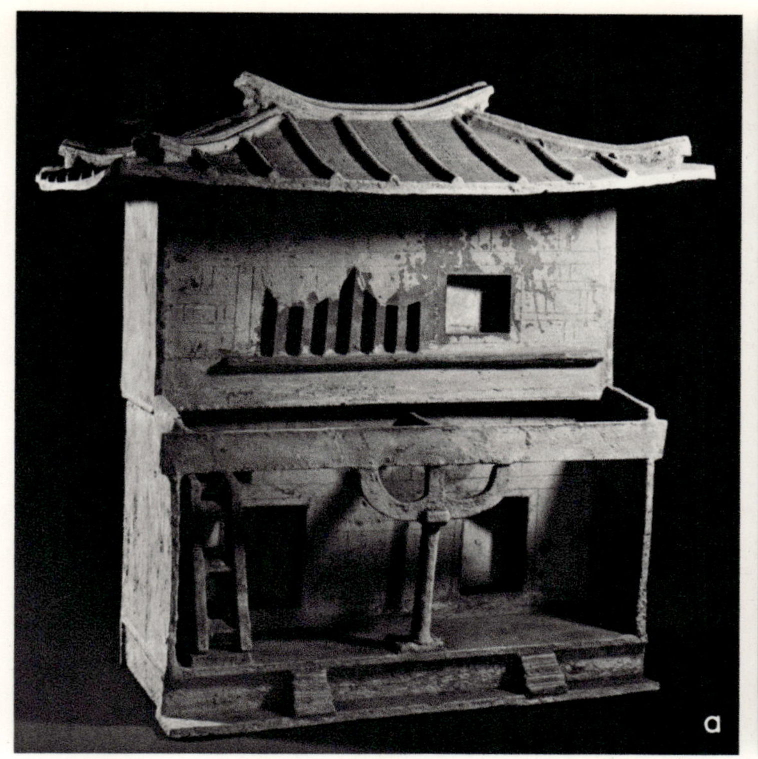

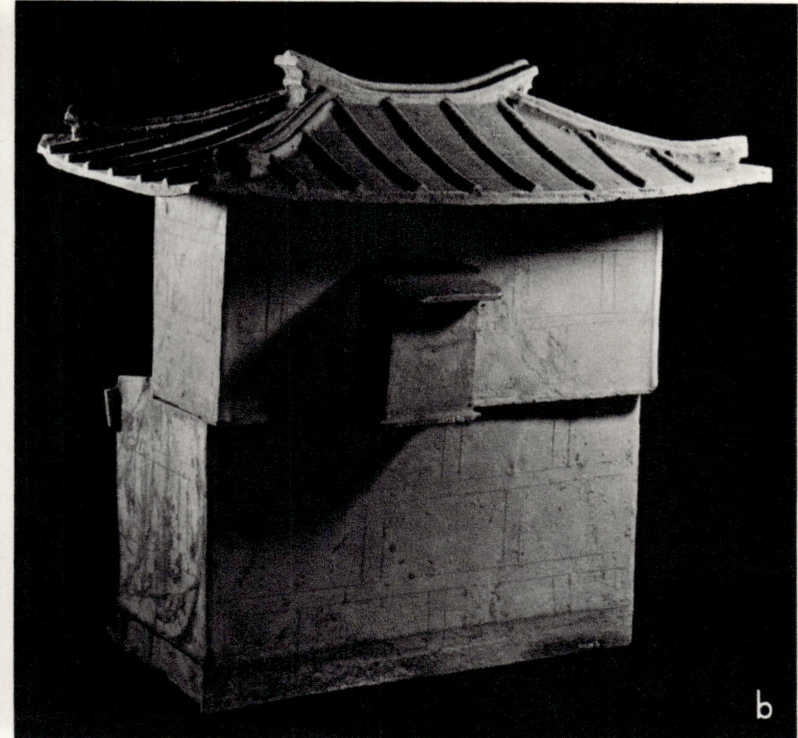

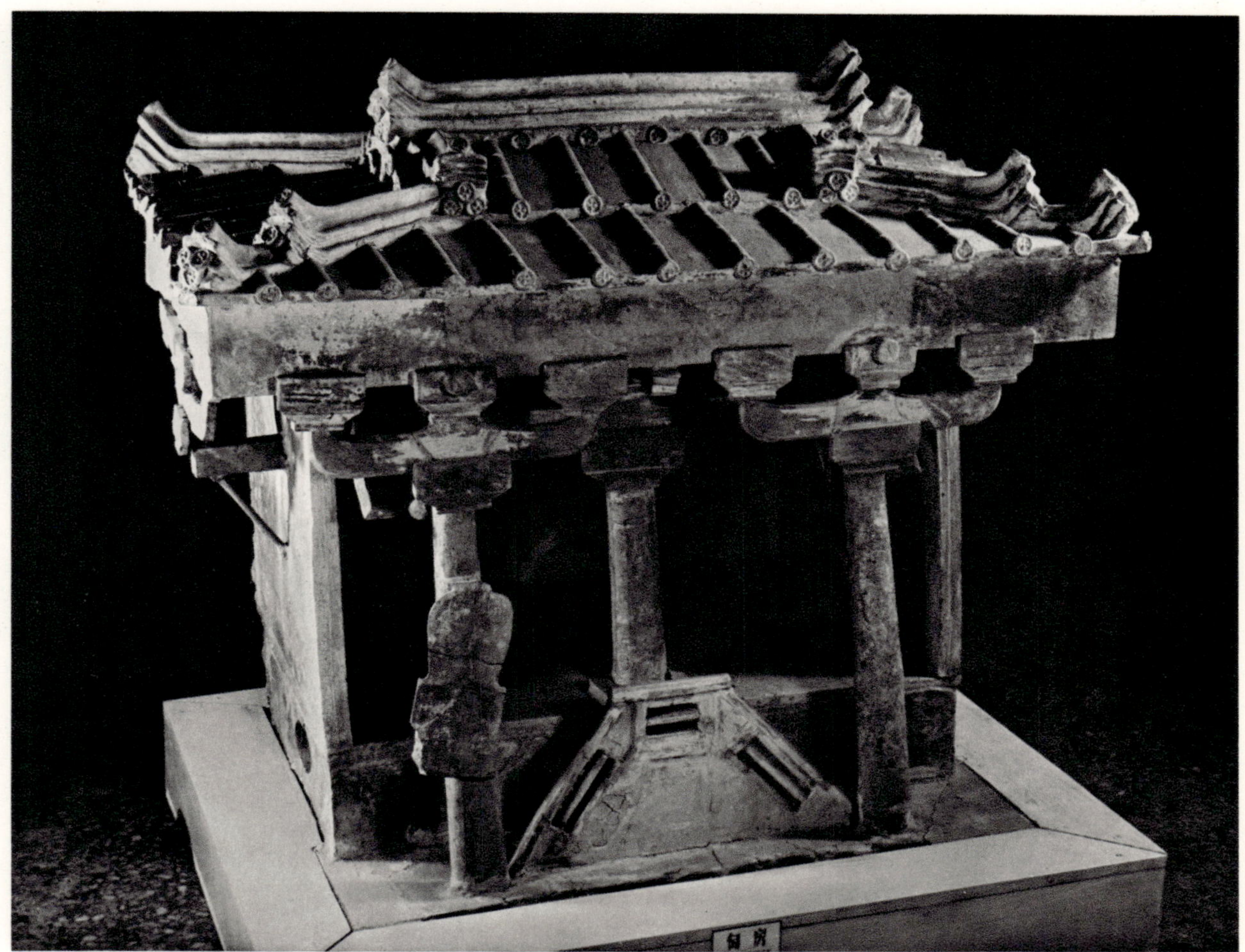

319 (a, b)–320. Building models, earthenware. Later Han dynasty. Excavated from the Mu-ma-shan-yai tomb, Szuchwan.

319 (a, b). Two-story building. height: 58.0 cm. (22.8 in.); width: 68. cm. (26.8 in.)

320. One-story building. height: 60.0 cm. (23.6 in.)

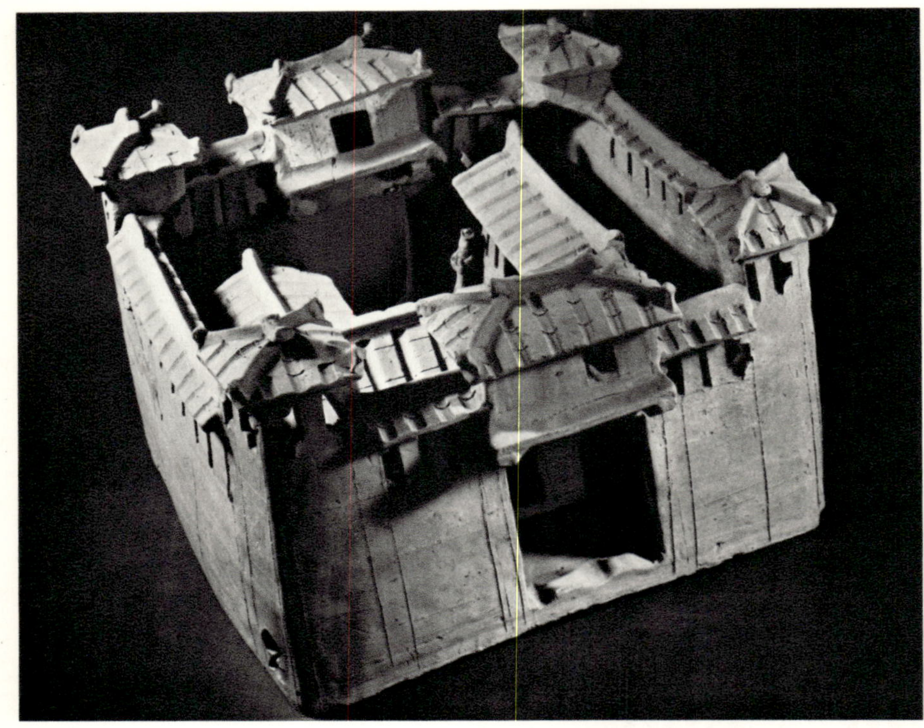

321–322. Castle with dwelling houses, earthenware. Later Han dynasty. Excavated from tomb No. 2, Ma-ying-kang, Zoological Gardens, Canton.

321. Castle. height: 29.6 cm. (11.6 in.); length: 41.2 cm. (16.2 in.); width: 40.0 cm. (15.75 in.)

322. House. height: 17.7 cm. (7.0 in.)

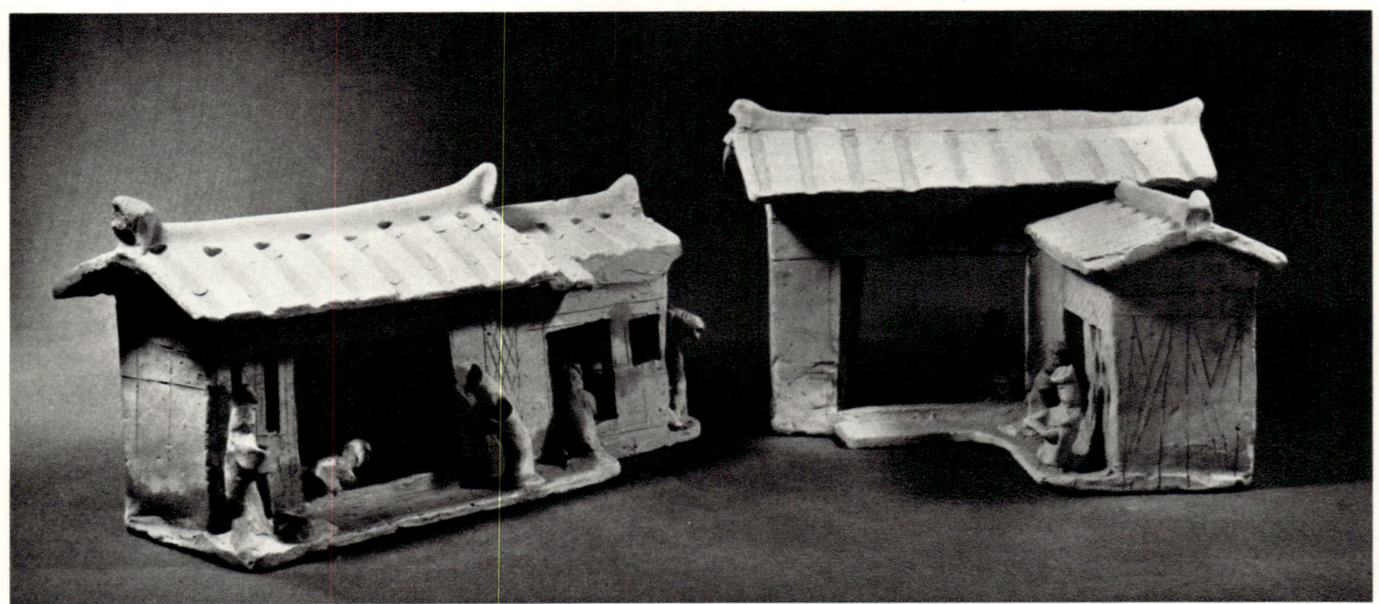

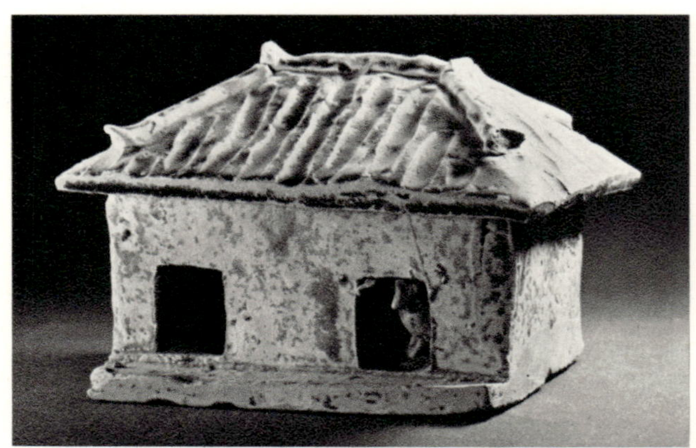

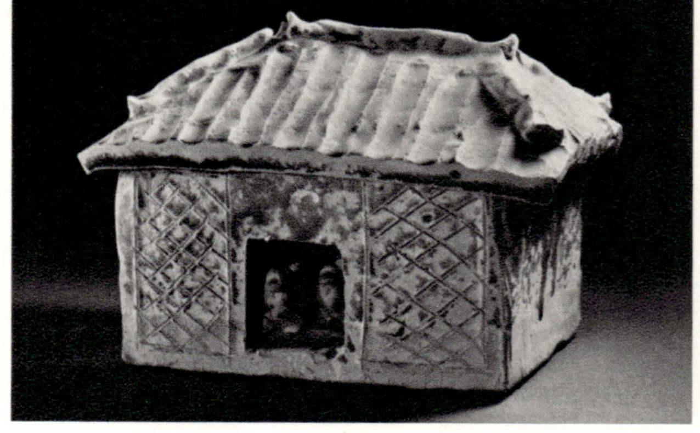

323–324. Poultry houses, earthenware. Wu dynasty. Excavated from an Eastern Wu tomb, Lien-hsi Temple, Wu-ch'ang, Hupei.

323. Chicken house. height: 13.0 cm. (5.1 in.); length: 17.2 cm. (6.8 in.); width: 13.3 cm. (5.2 in.)

324. Duck house, bluish-green-glazed earthenware. height: 28.0 cm. (11.0 in.); length: 18.0 cm. (7.1 in.); width: 12.7 cm. (5.0 in.)

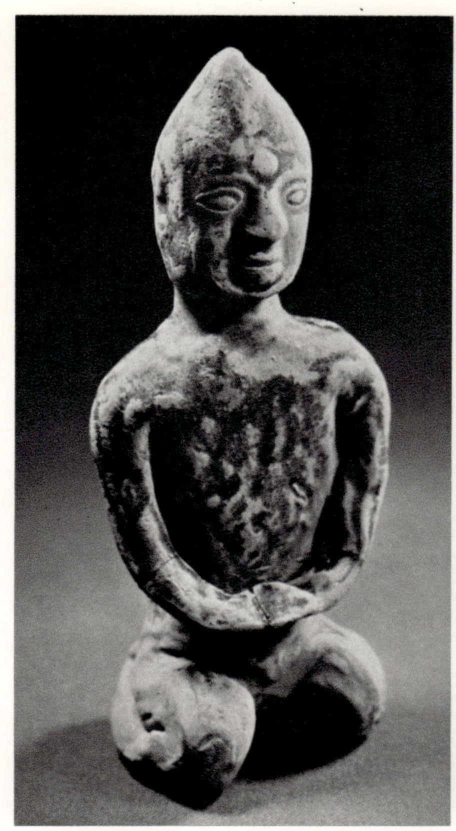

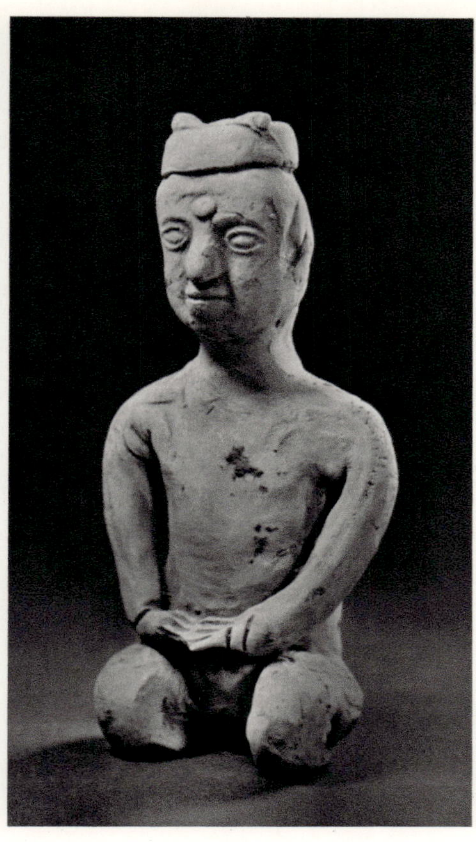

325–326. Kneeling figures, blue-glazed earthenware. Wu dynasty. Excavated at Lien-hsi Temple, Wu-ch'ang, Hupei.
325. *height: 18.0 cm. (7.1 in.)*
326. *height: 16.8 cm. (6.6 in.)*

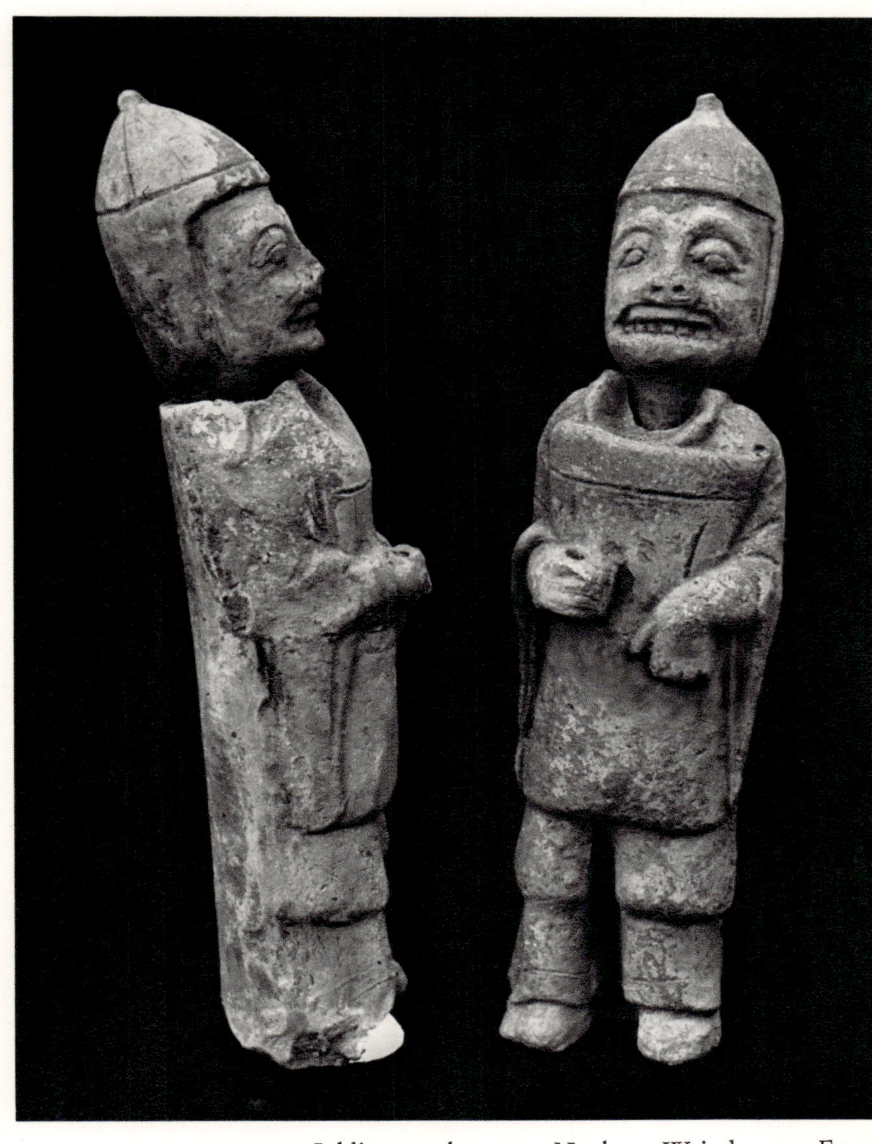

327. Soldiers, earthenware. Northern Wei dynasty. Excavated from the Shao Chen tomb, Jen-chia-k'ou, Sian, Shensi. *height: 43.0 cm. (16.9 in.)*

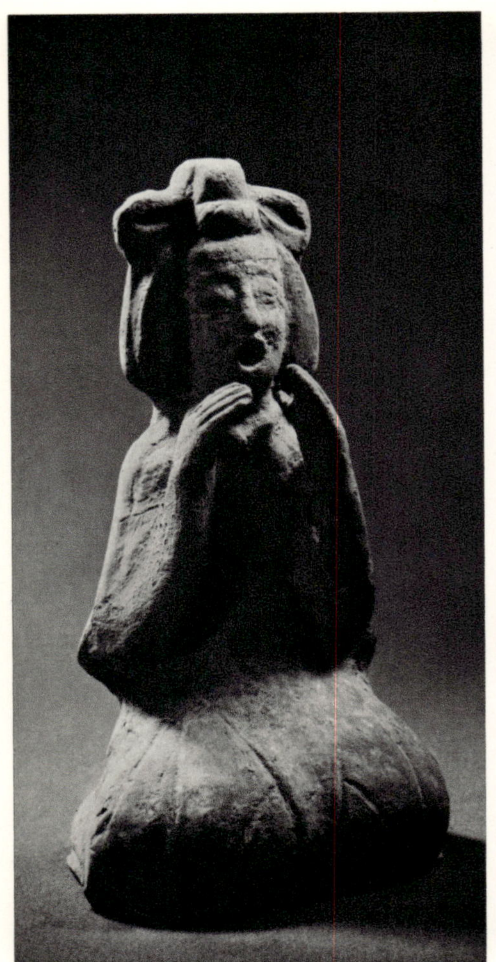

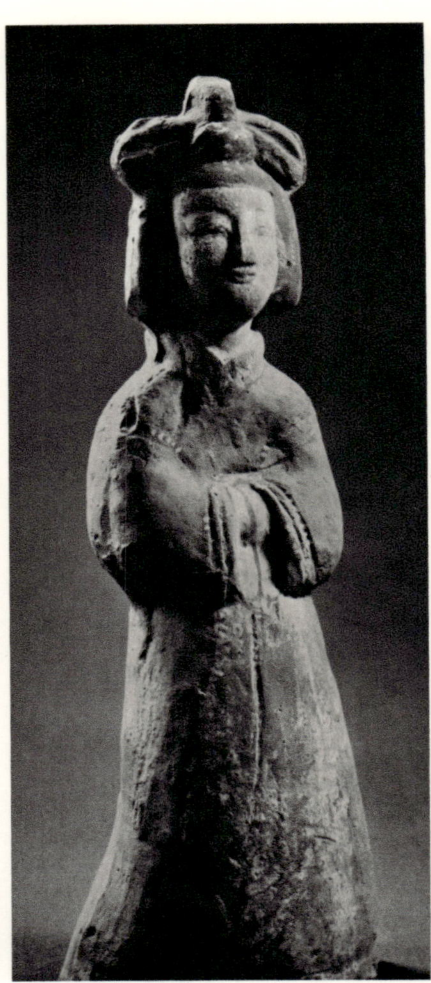

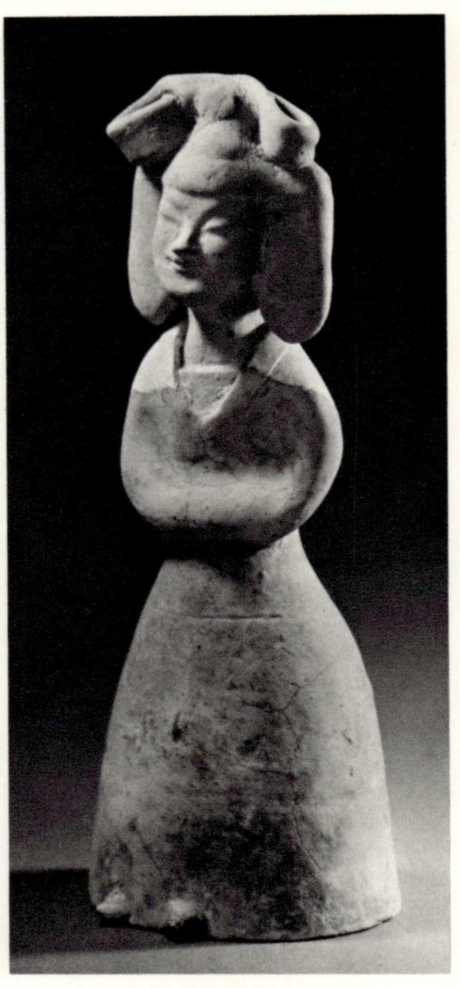

328–329. Female figures, earthenware. Northern Wei dynasty. Excavated at Ts'ao-ch'ang-p'o-ts'un, southern outskirts of Sian, Shensi.
328. Singing woman. height: 24.0 cm. (9.4 in.)
329. height: 33.5 cm. (13.2 in.)

330. Female figure, earthenware. Six Dynasties. Excavated at Mu-fu-shan, Nanking.
height: 33.0 cm. (13.0 in.)

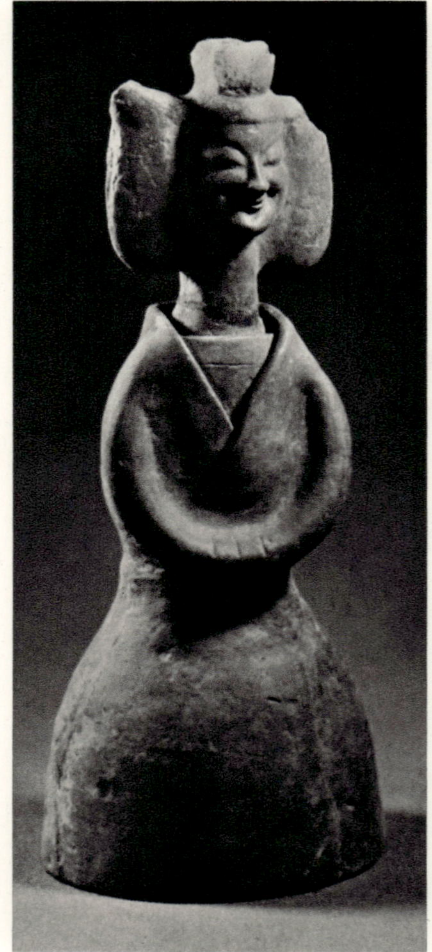

331. Female figure, earthenware. Six Dynasties. Excavated at Hsiao-hung-shan, Chung-yang-men-wai, Nanking.
height: 30.1 cm. (12.2 in.)

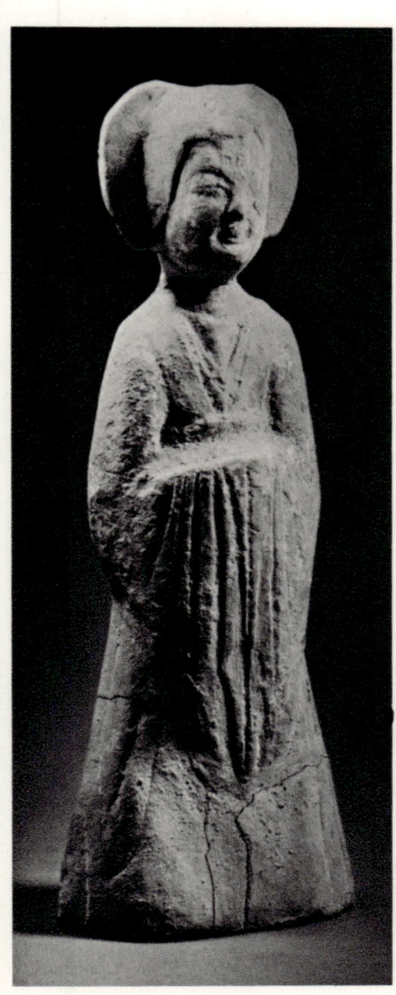

332. Female figure, earthenware. Six Dynasties. Excavated at Chang-chia-k'u, Nanking.
height: 31.2 cm. (12.3 in.)

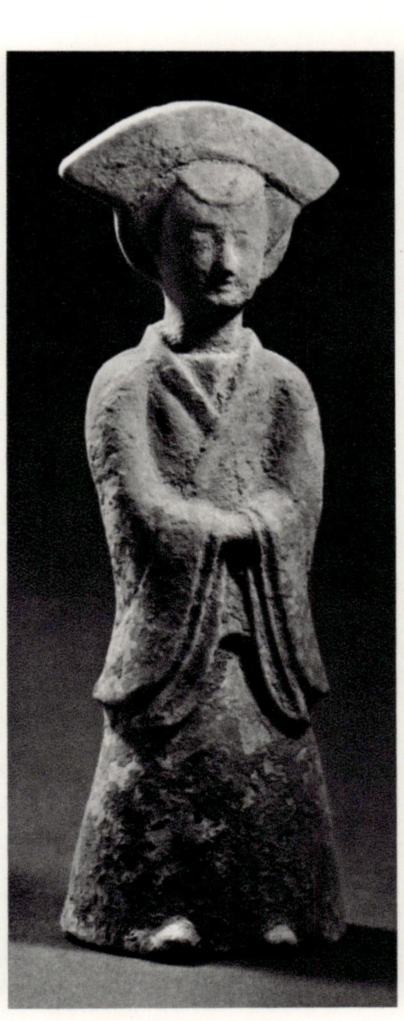

333. Female figure, earthenware. Six Dynasties. Excavated at Ssu-pan-ts'un, Nanking.
height: 31.15 cm. (12.2 in.)

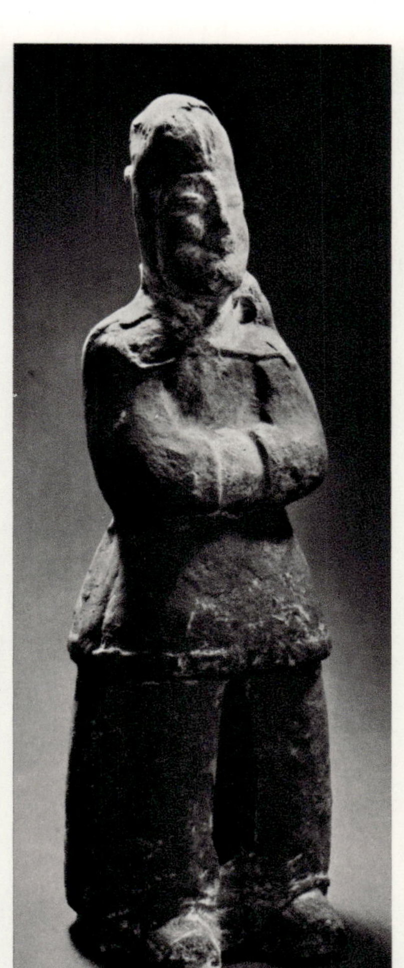

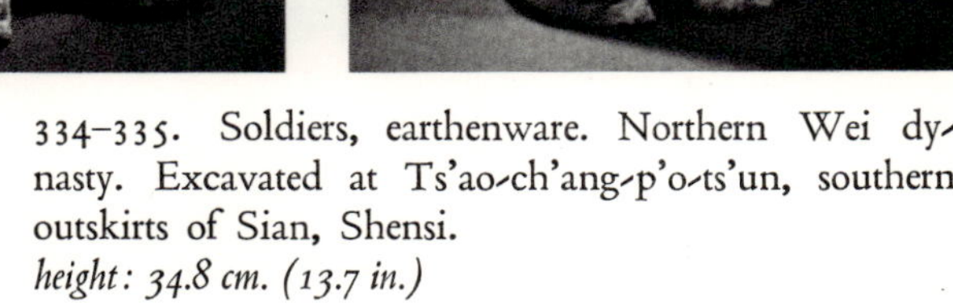

334–335. Soldiers, earthenware. Northern Wei dynasty. Excavated at Ts'ao-ch'ang-p'o-ts'un, southern outskirts of Sian, Shensi.
height: 34.8 cm. (13.7 in.)

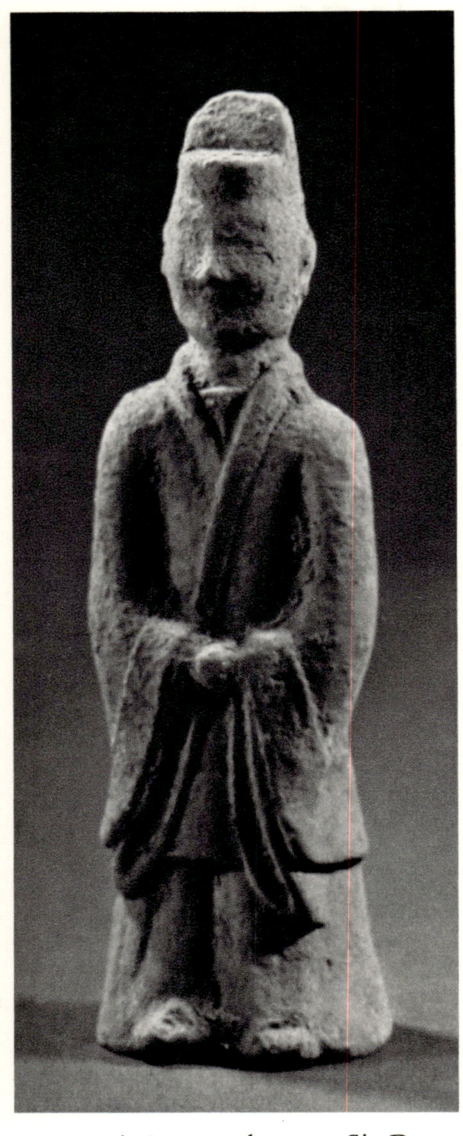

336. Male figure, earthenware. Six Dynasties. Excavated at Ssu-pan-ts'un, Nanking.
height: 27.3 cm. (10.7 in.)

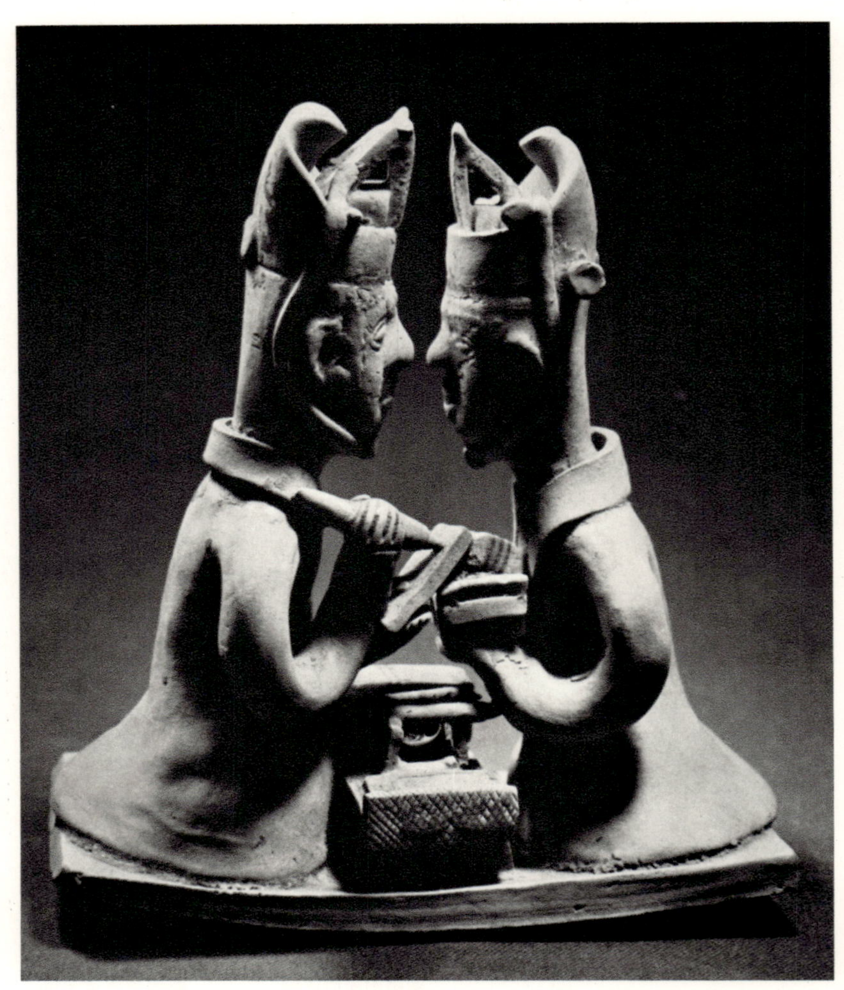

337. Scribes, earthenware. Chin dynasty. Excavated at Chin-p'en-ling, Ch'ang-sha, Hunan.
height: 19.2 cm. (7.7 in.)

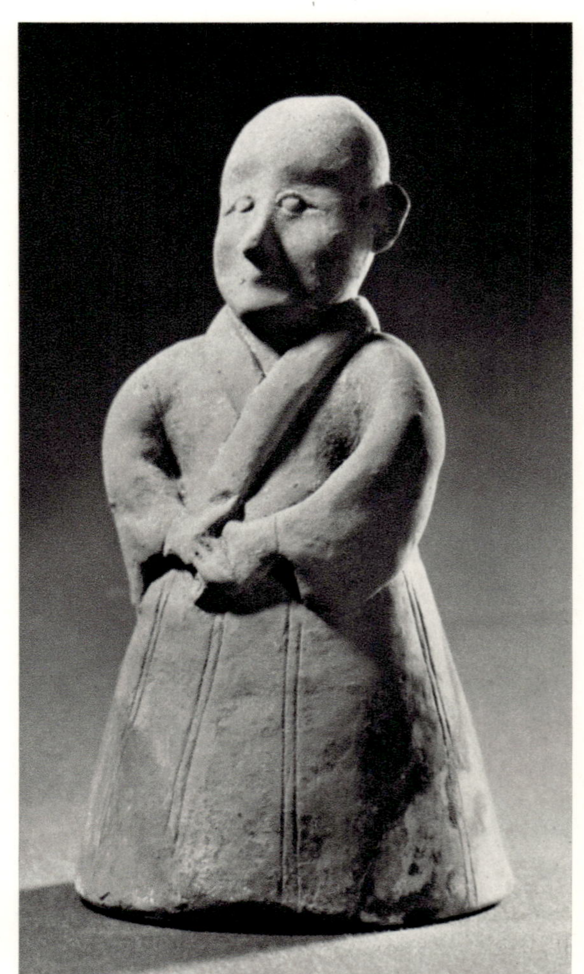

338. Scholar, earthenware. Chin dynasty. Excavated at Shih-men-k'an-hsiang, Nanking.
height: 20.0 cm. (7.9 in.)

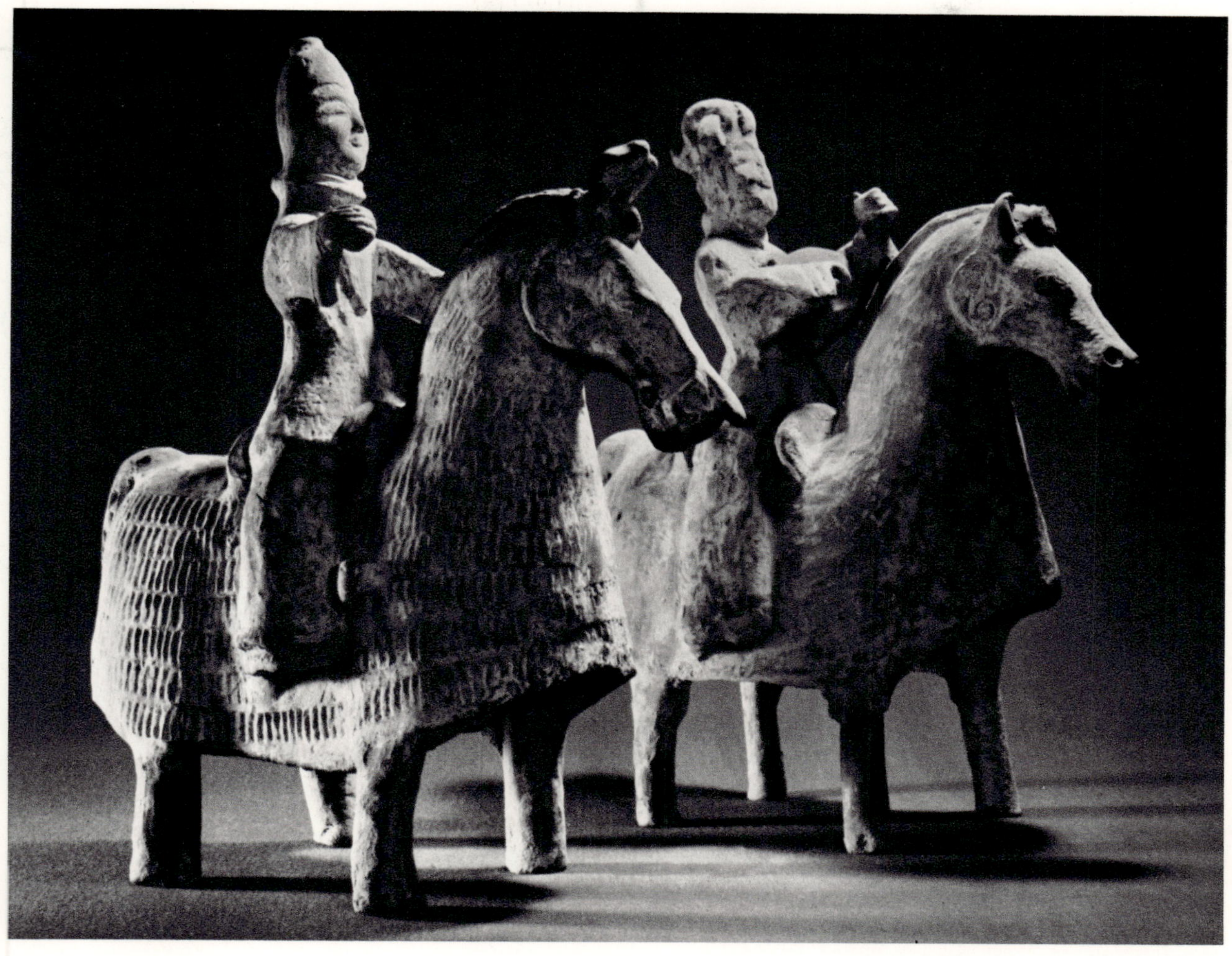

339–340. Equestrian figures, earthenware. Northern Wei dynasty. Excavated at Ts'ao-ch'ang-p'o-ts'un, Sian, Shensi.
339. height: 37.5 cm. (14.8 in.)
340. Figure blowing a horn. height: 39.0 cm. (15.3 in.)

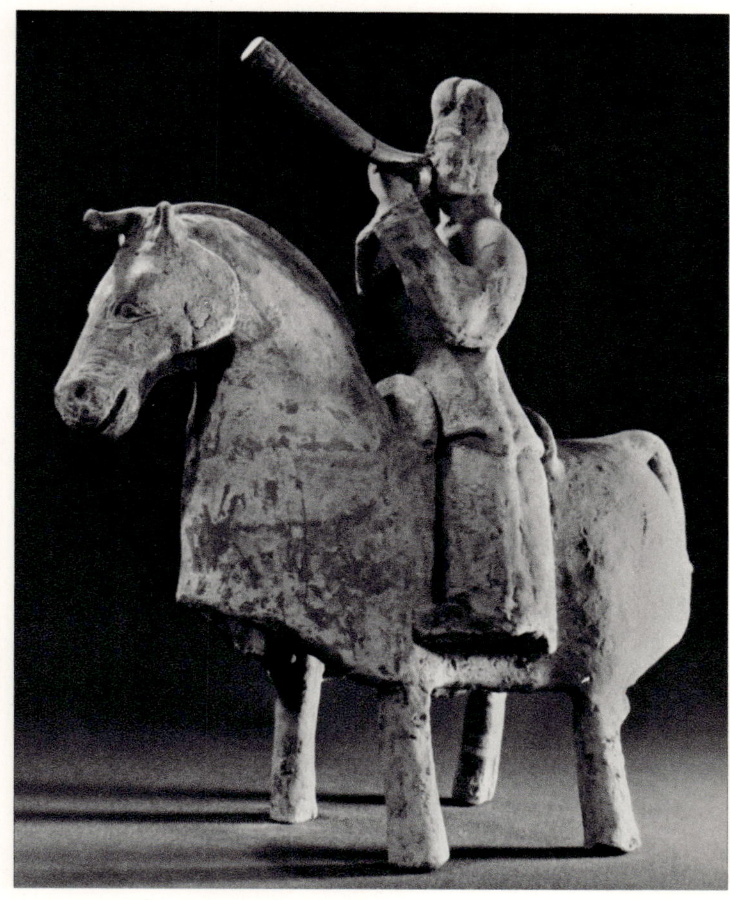

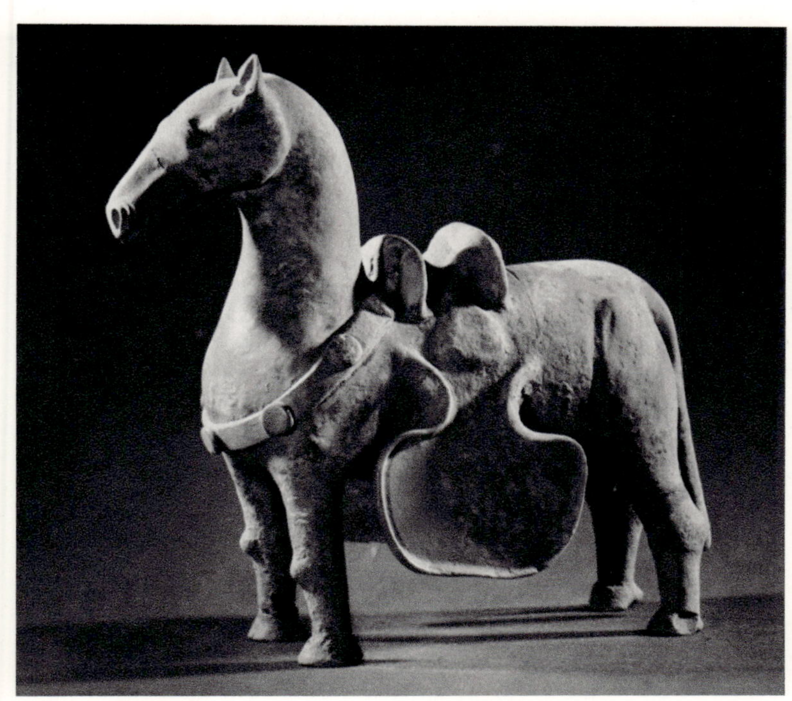

341. Horse, earthenware. Six Dynasties. Excavated at Mu-fu-shan, Chung-yang-men-wai, Nanking.
height: 28.5 cm. (11.2 in.); length: 29.5 cm. (11.6 in.)

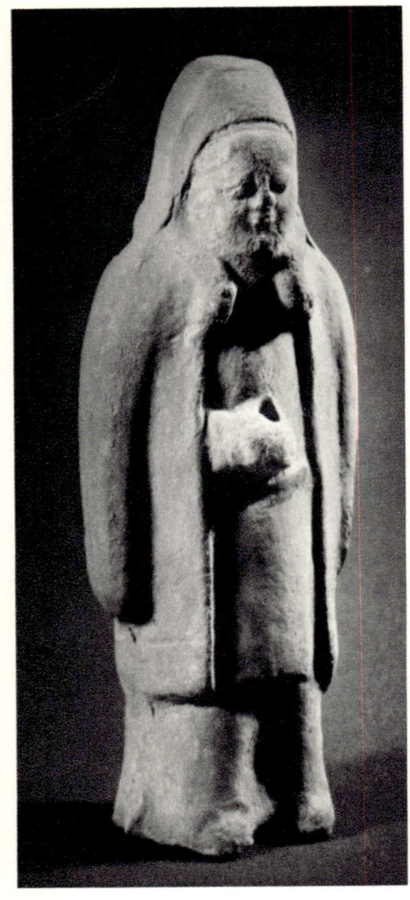
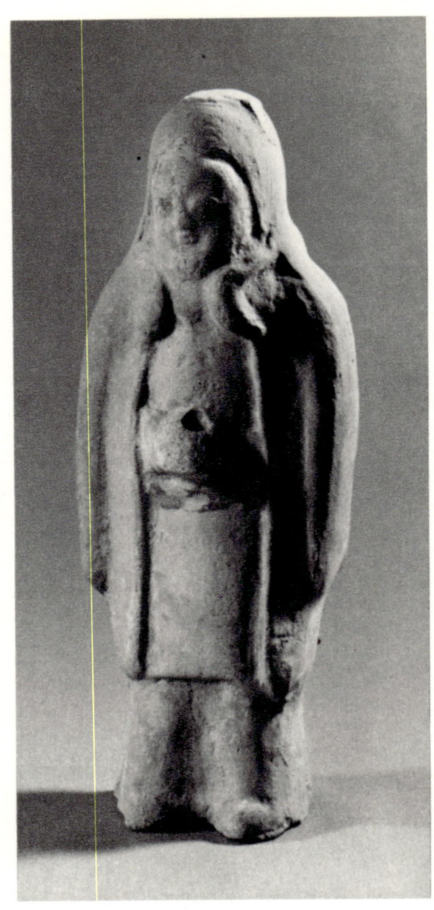

342–343. Overcoated male figures, earthenware. Sui dynasty. Excavated from the Li Ching-hsün tomb, Sian, Shensi.
heights: [*342*] *18.0 cm.* (*7.1 in.*); [*343*] *16.2 cm.* (*6.4 in.*)

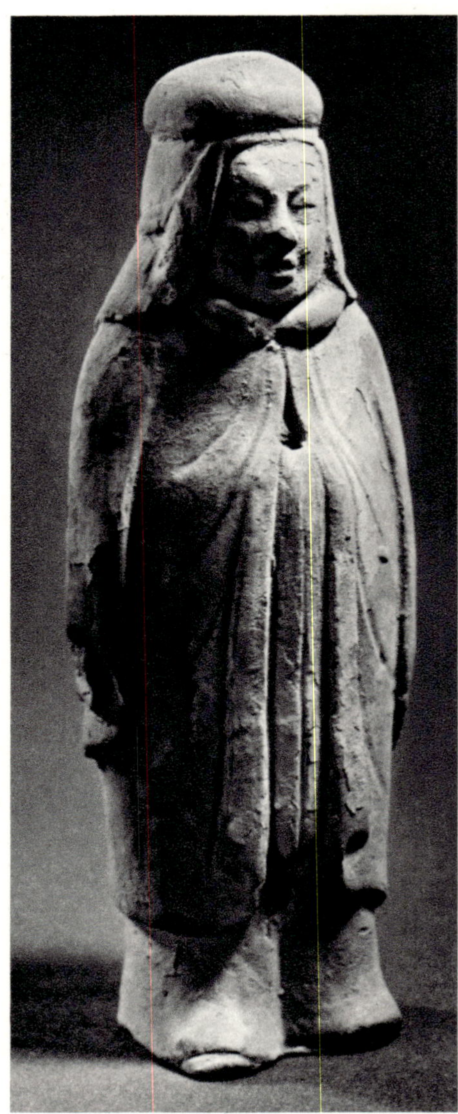
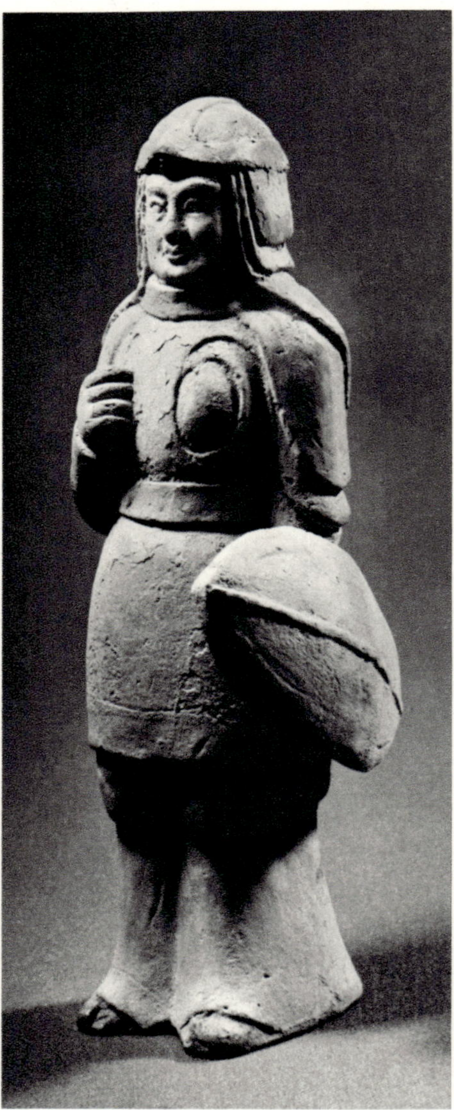
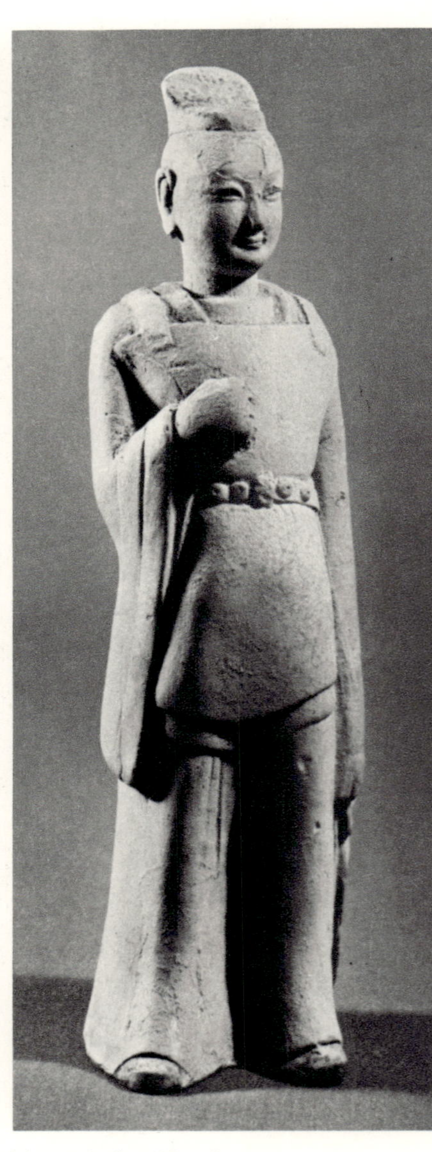

344–346. Male figures, earthenware. Sui dynasty. Excavated from the Feng family tombs, Ching District, Hopei.
344. Overcoated male figure. height: 24.2 cm. (9.5 in.)
345. Soldier holding a shield. height: 21.4 cm. (8.5 in.)
346. Military officer in armor. height: 25.8 cm. (10.1 in.)

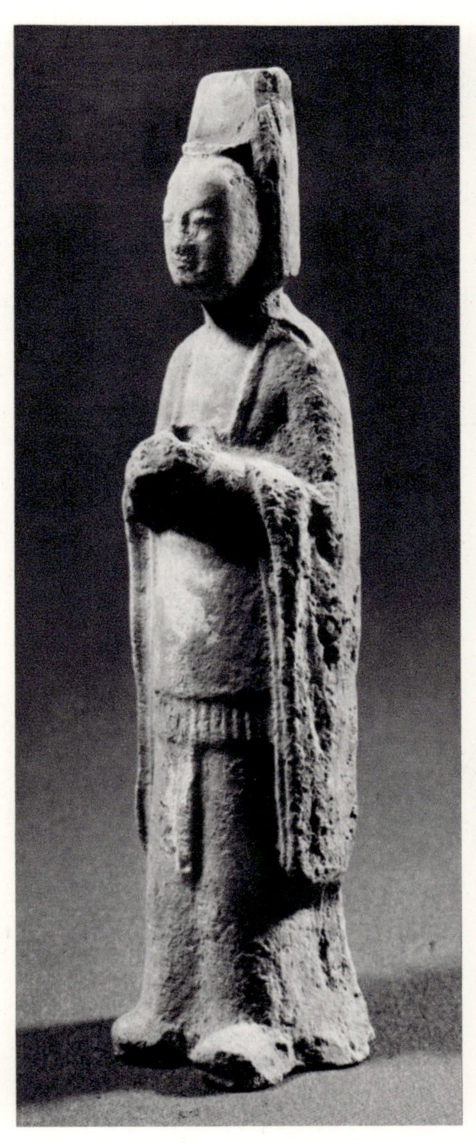
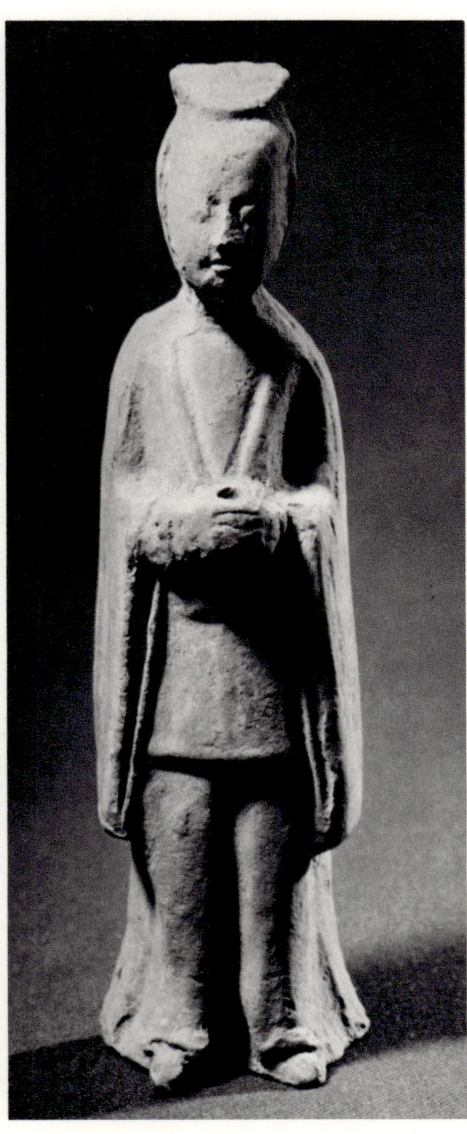
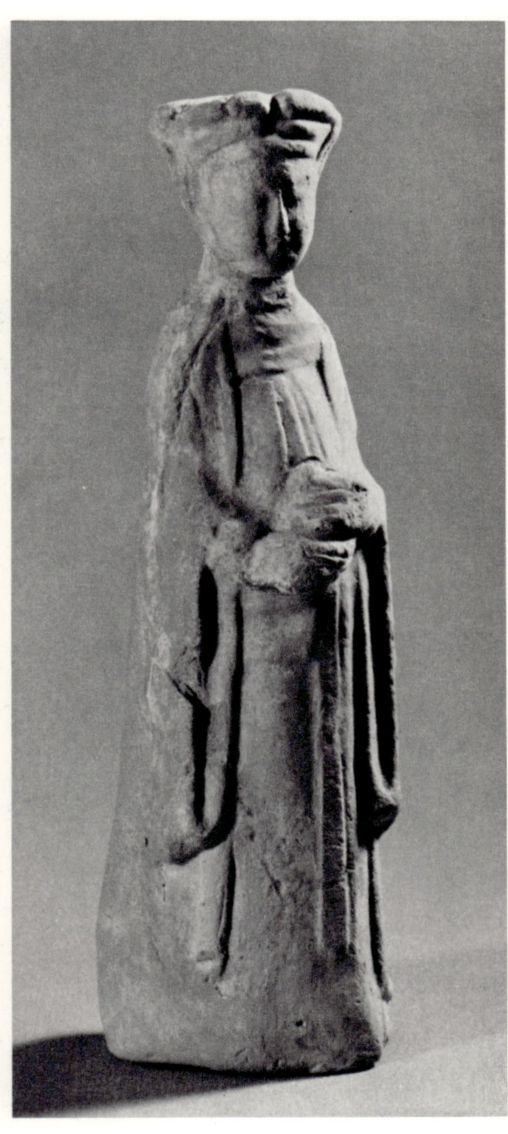

347–349. Figures, earthenware. Sui dynasty. Excavated from the Li Ching-hsün tomb, Sian, Shensi.
347. *Official wearing a woven cane cap. height: 19.4 cm. (7.7 in.)*
348. *Official wearing a small official cap. height: 18.2 cm. (7.2 in.)*
349. *Female figure. height: 18.5 cm. (7.3 in.)*

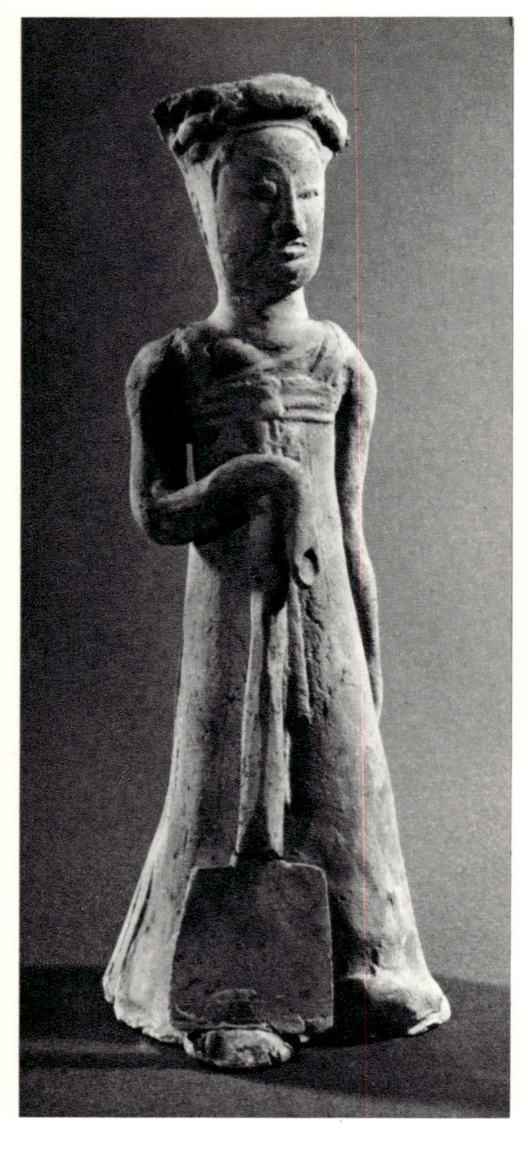

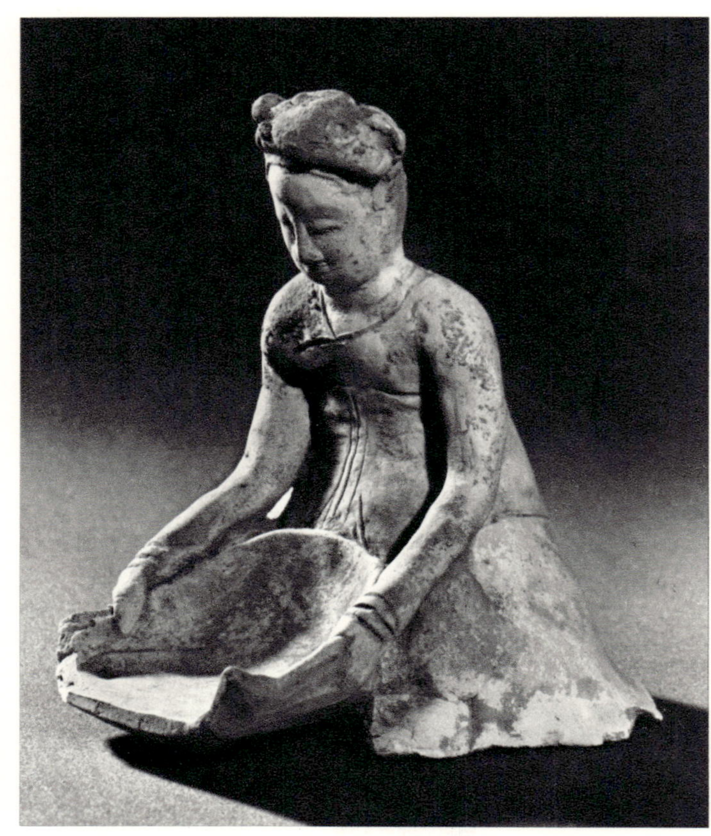

350–352. Female figures, earthenware. Sui dynasty. Excavated from the Chang Sheng tomb, An-yang, Honan.

350. Woman holding a shovel. height: 23.3 cm. (9.2 in.)

351. Woman winnowing. height: 16.5 cm. (6.5 in.)

352. Ladies-in-waiting, slip decoration. heights: 21.3–23.5 cm. (8.4–9.3 in.)

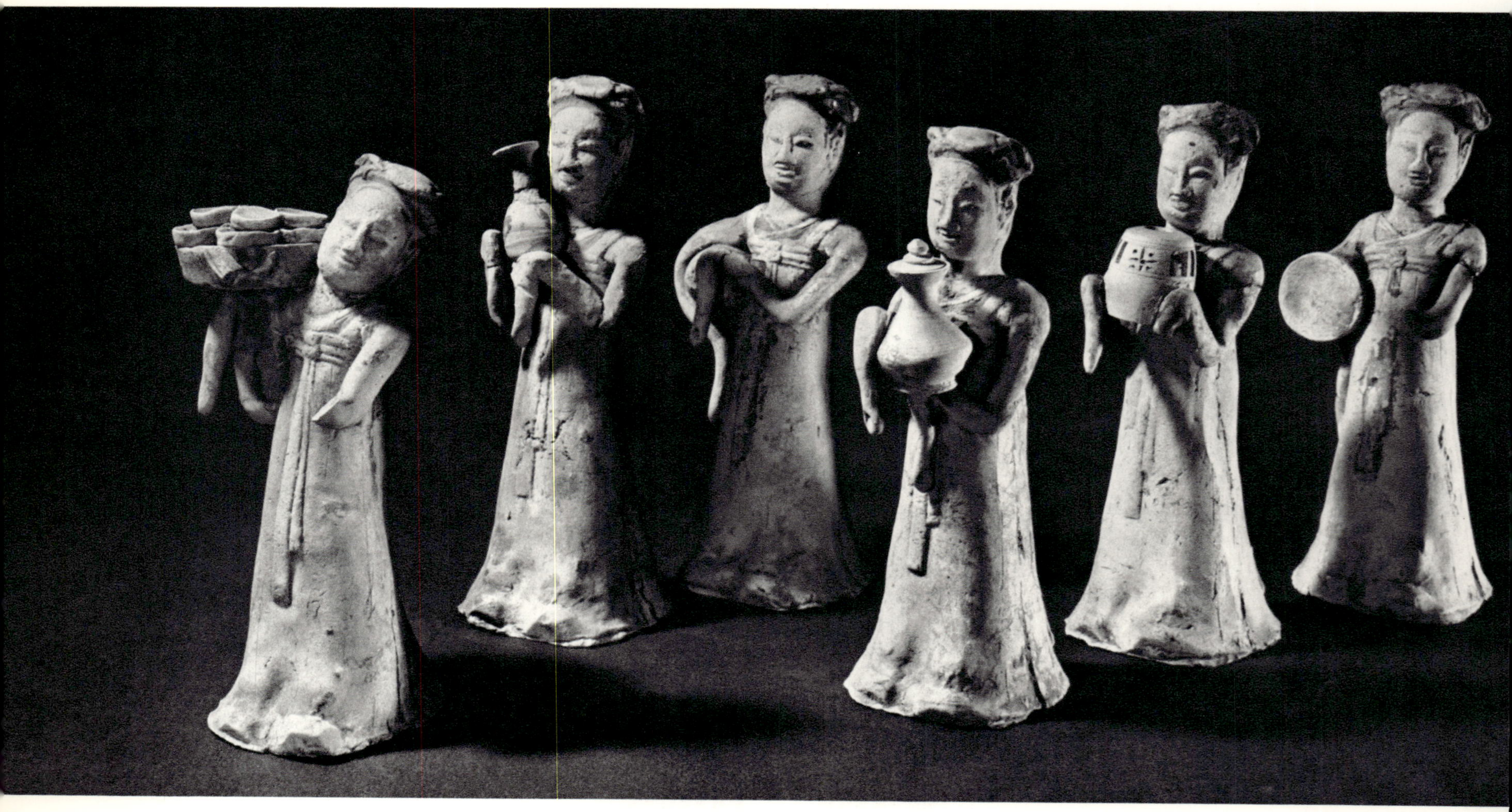

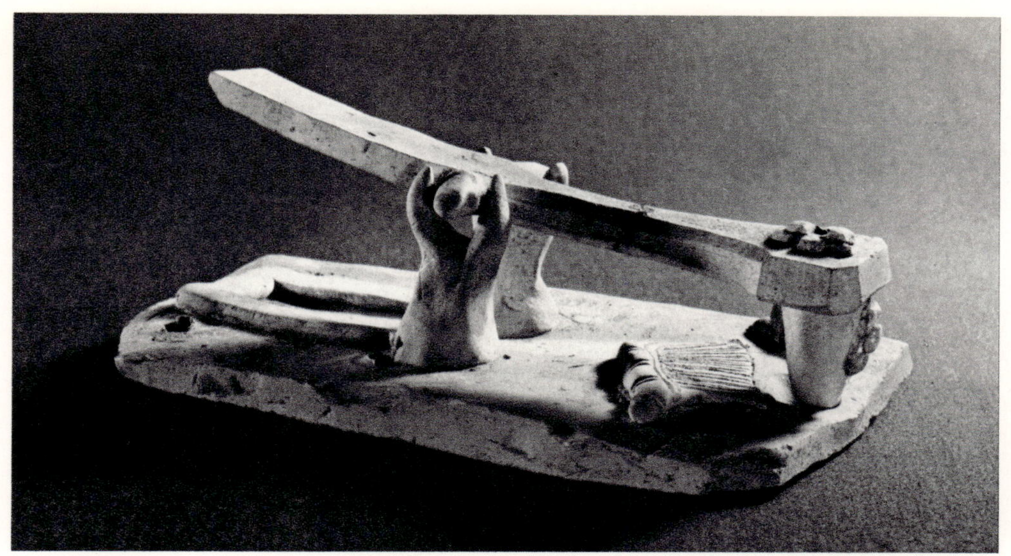

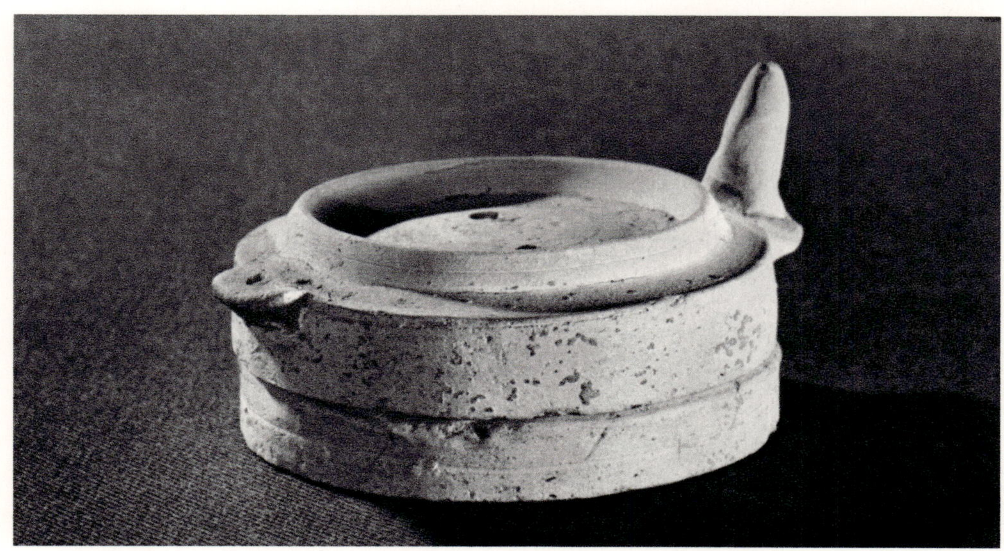

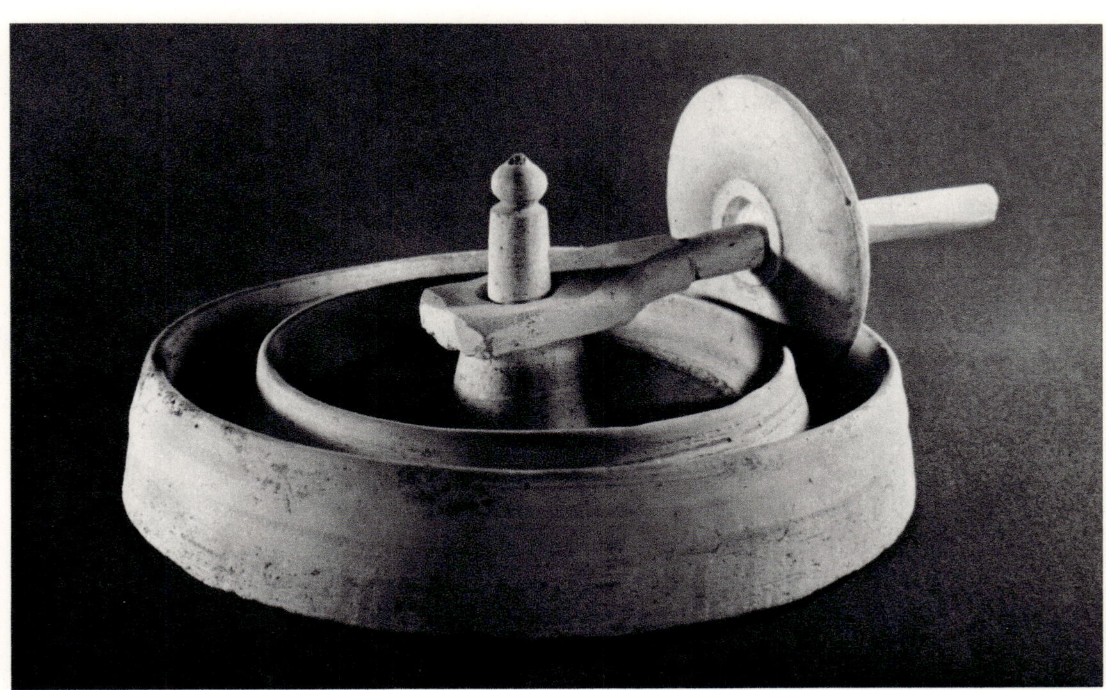

353–355. Mills, earthenware. Sui dynasty. Excavated from the Chang Sheng tomb, An-yang, Honan.

353. *Foot mill. height: 8.0 cm. (3.15 in.); length: 20.5 cm. (8.1 in.); width: 10.5 cm. (4.1 in.)*

354. *Hand mill. height: 5.5 cm. (2.17 in.); diameter: 10.8 cm. (4.2 in.)*

355. *Hand mill. height: 11.3 cm. (4.4 in.); diameter: 24.0 cm. (9.4 in.)*

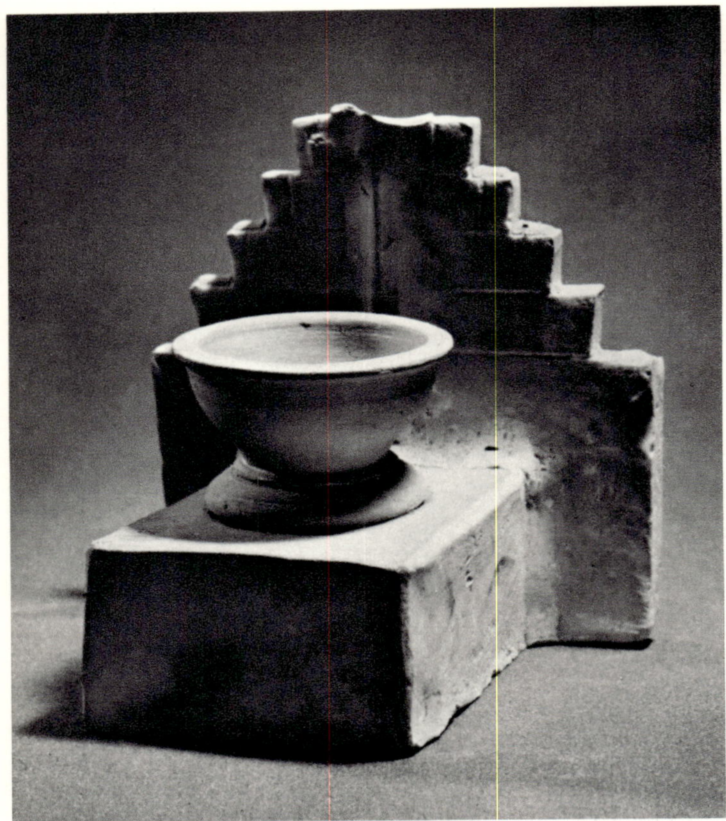

356. Cookstove, earthenware. Sui dynasty. Excavated from the Feng family tombs, Ching District, Hopei.
height: 14.5 cm. (5.7 in.)

357–358. Animals on low pedestals, earthenware with slip painting and glaze. Sui dynasty. Excavated from the Chang Sheng tomb, An-yang, Honan.
357. height: 10.5 cm. (4.1 in.)
358. height: 13.5 cm. (5.3 in.)

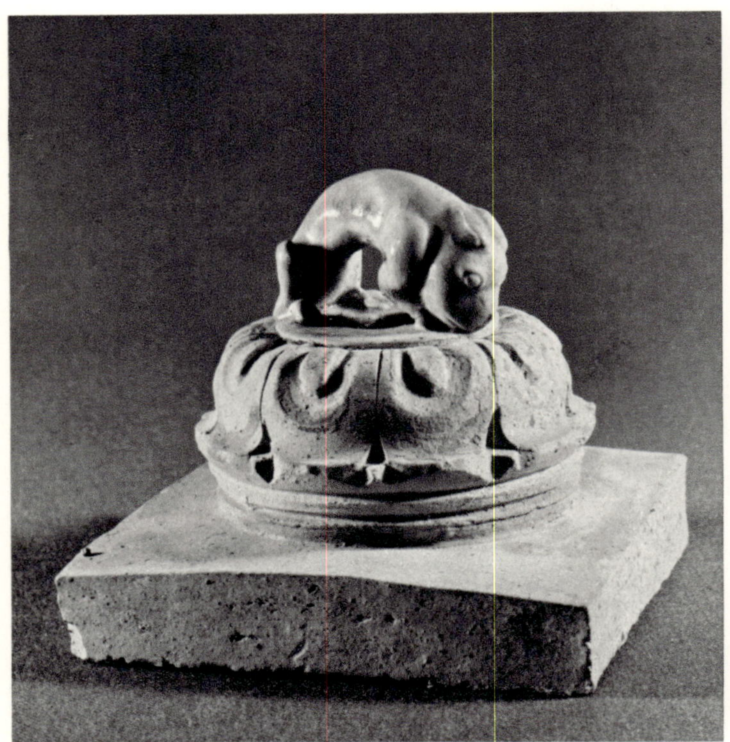

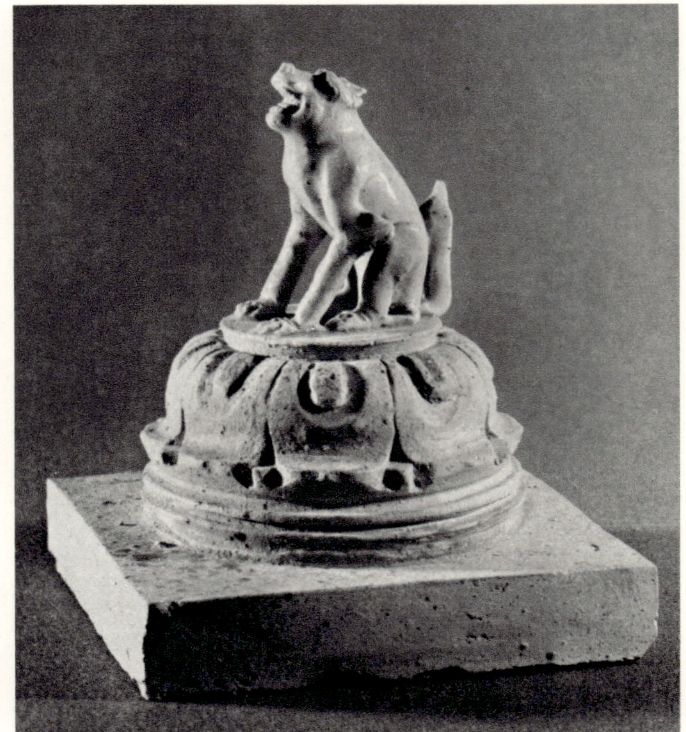

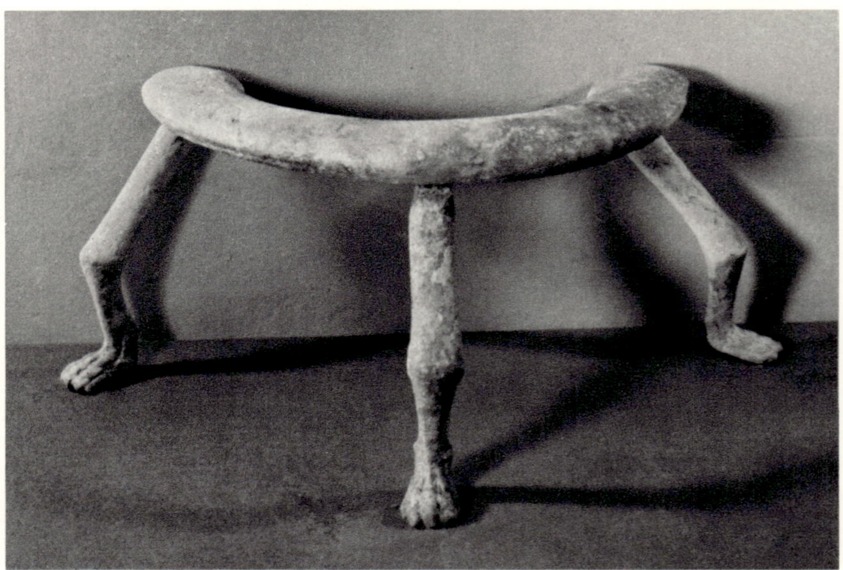

359. Armrest, gray earthenware. Six Dynasties. Excavated at Ssu-pan-ts'un, Nanking.
height: 19.0 cm. (7.3 in.); length: 33.0 cm. (13.0 in.)

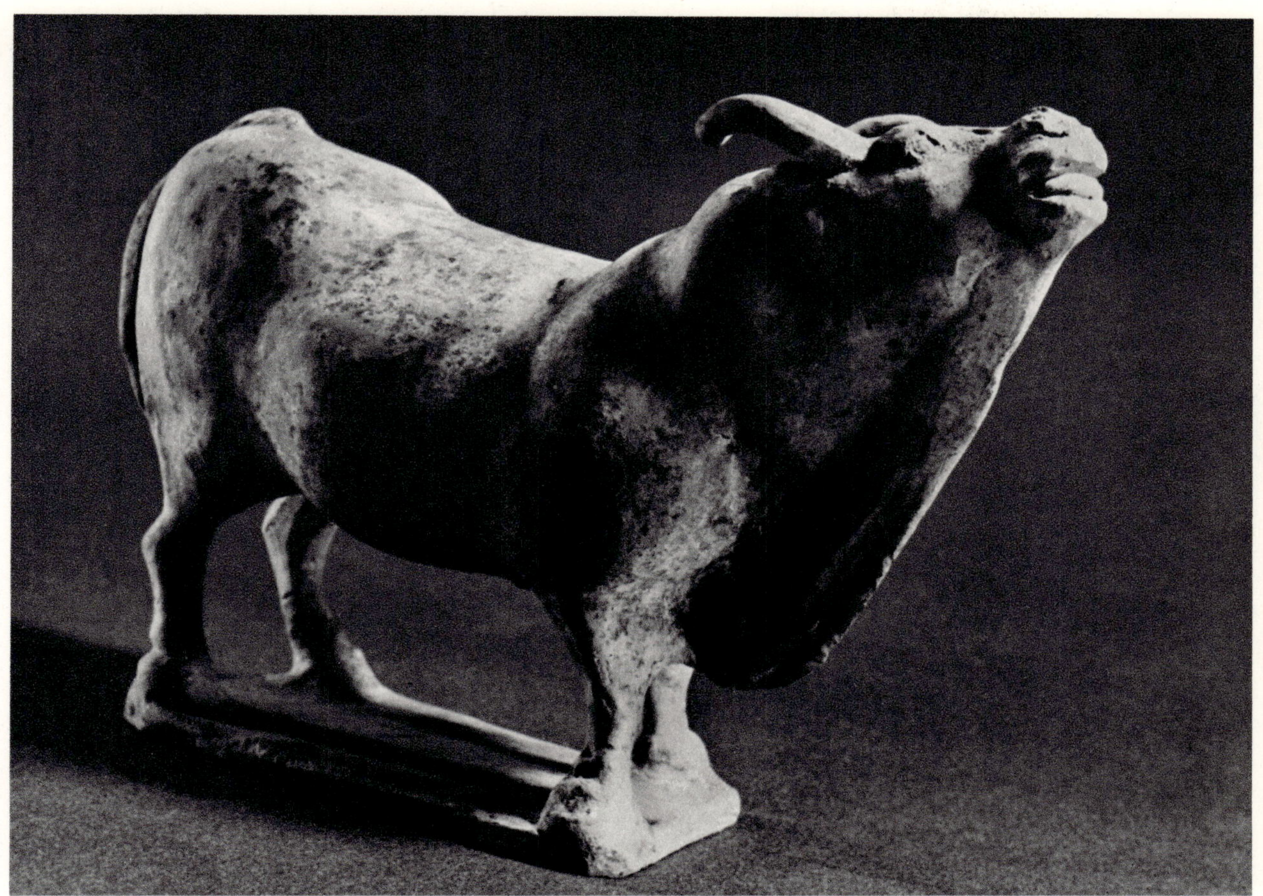

360. Ox, earthenware. Sui dynasty. Excavated from the Li Ching-hsün tomb, Sian, Shensi.
length: 27.5 cm. (10.8 in.)

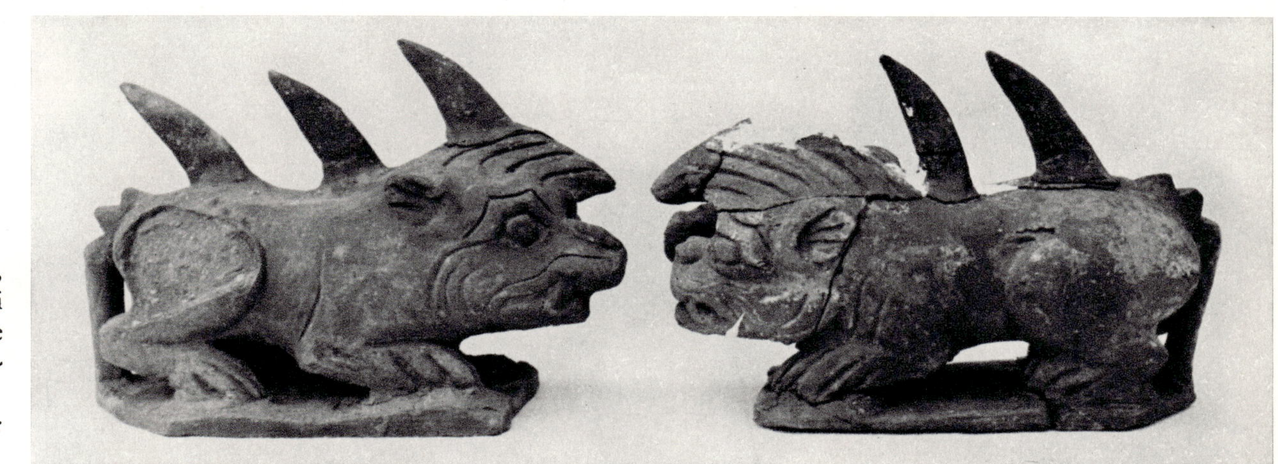

361. Tomb guardian beasts, earthenware. Northern Wei dynasty. Excavated from the Shao Chen tomb, Jen-chia-k'ou, Sian, Shensi.
height: 15.0 cm. (5.9 in.); length: 22.0 cm. (8.7 in.)

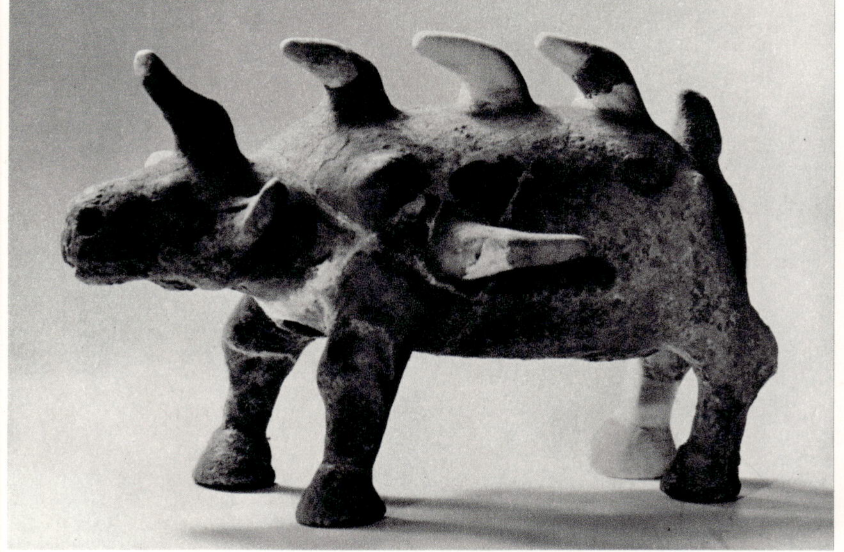

362. Mythical beast, gray earthenware. Six Dynasties. Excavated at Ssu-pan-ts'un, Nanking.
height: 15.5 cm. (6.1 in.); length: 25.0 cm. (9.8 in.)

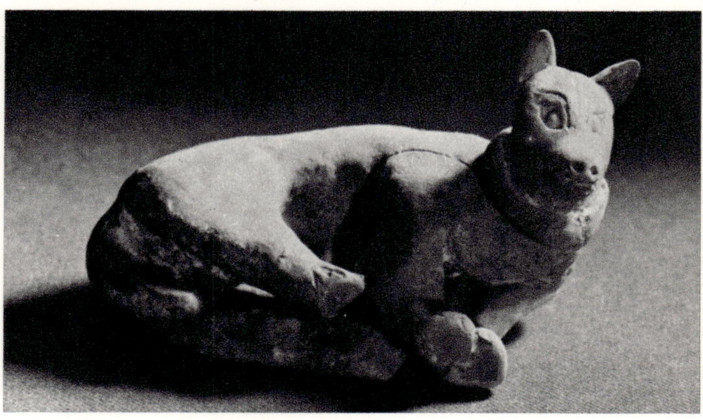

363. Dog, earthenware. Chin dynasty. Excavated from the Ts'ao Yi tomb, Ting-chia-shan, Chung-hua-men-wai, Nanking.
height: 5.5 cm. (2.17 in.); length: 11.0 cm. (4.3 in.)

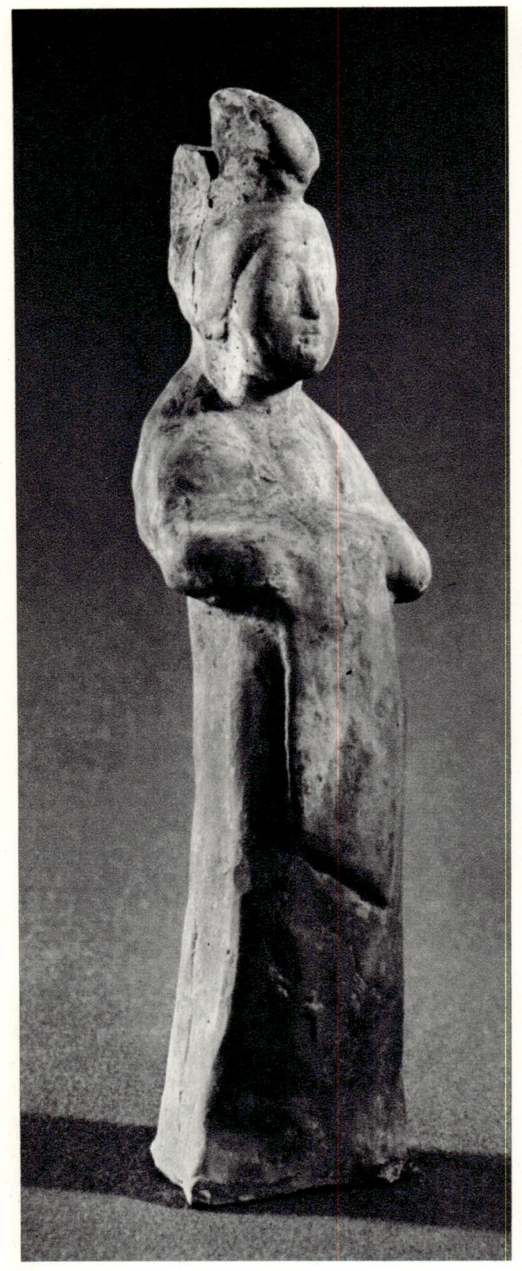

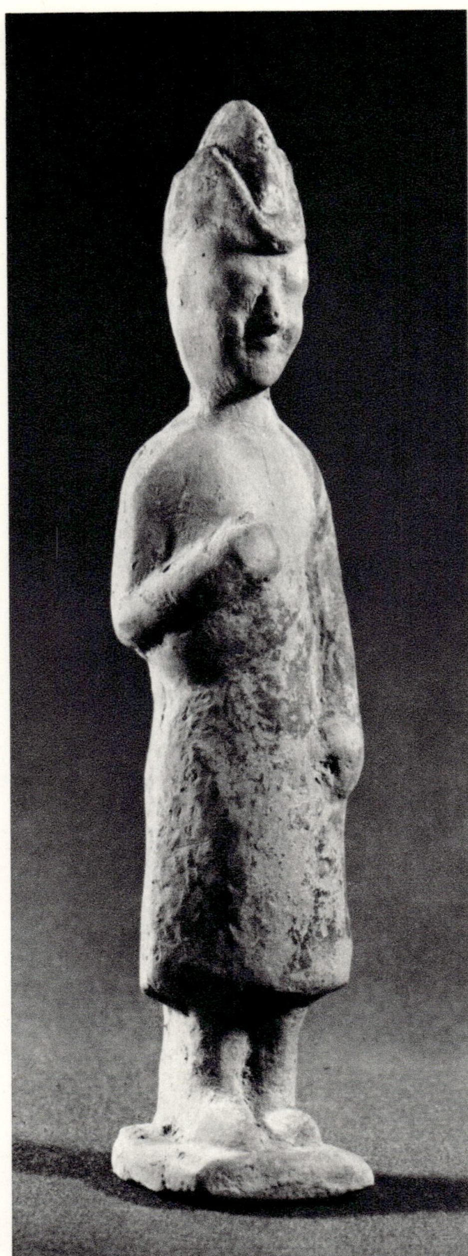

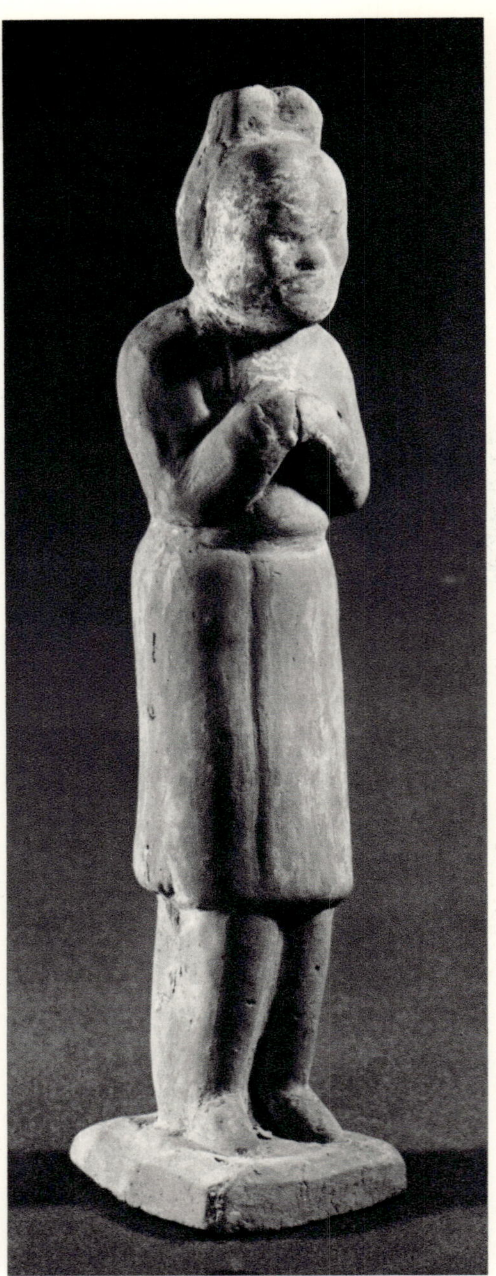

364–368. Figures, red earthenware with traces of slip painting. T'ang dynasty. Excavated from the Ts'ui Ch'en tomb, Hsin-chuang-ts'un, Yen-shih District, Honan.

364. *Female figure. no measurement given.*

365. *Male figure in foreign clothes. height: 24.0 cm. (9.4 in.)*

366. *Male figure in foreign clothes. height: 26.0 cm. (10.2 in.)*

367. *Female figures. heights: 28.0 cm. (11.0 in.); 25.0 cm. (9.8 in.)*

368. *Male figures in foreign clothes. heights: 26.0 cm. (10.2 in.); 24.0 cm. (9.4 in.)*

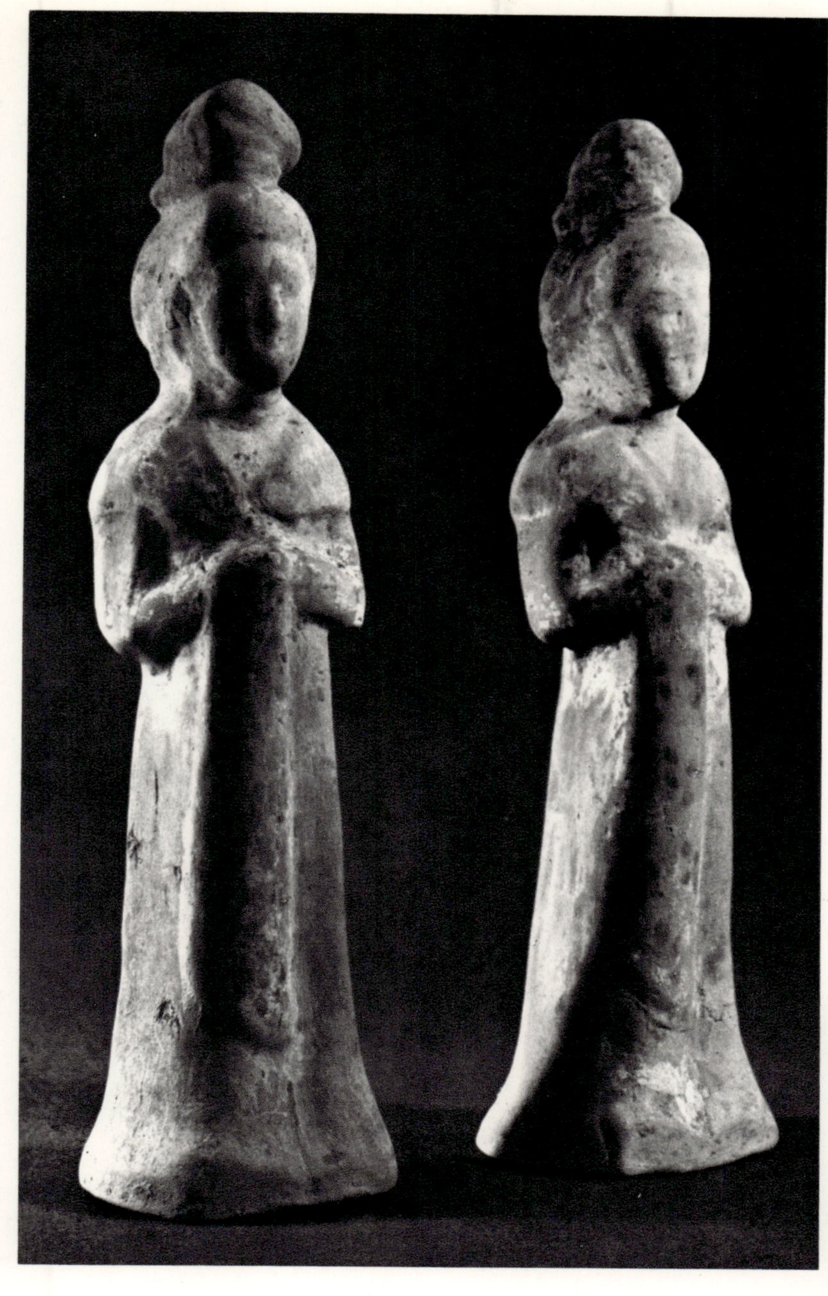

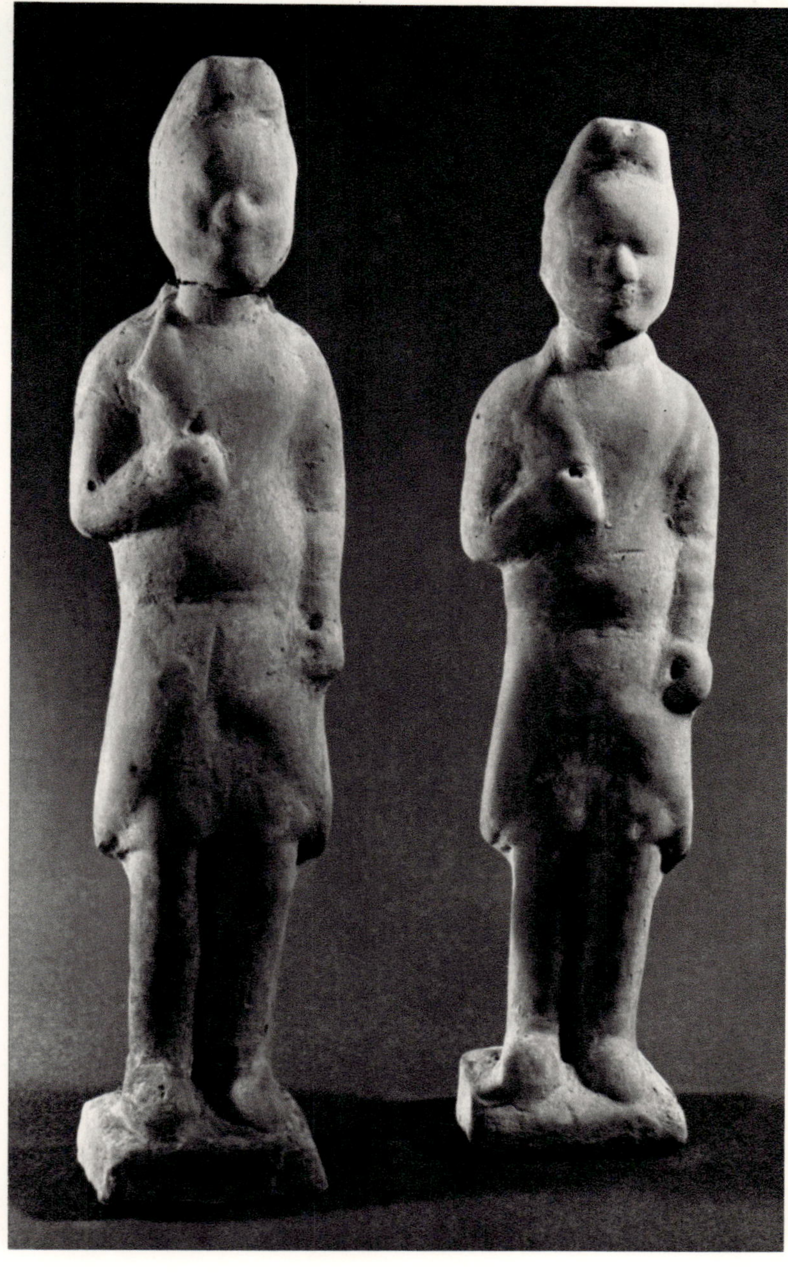

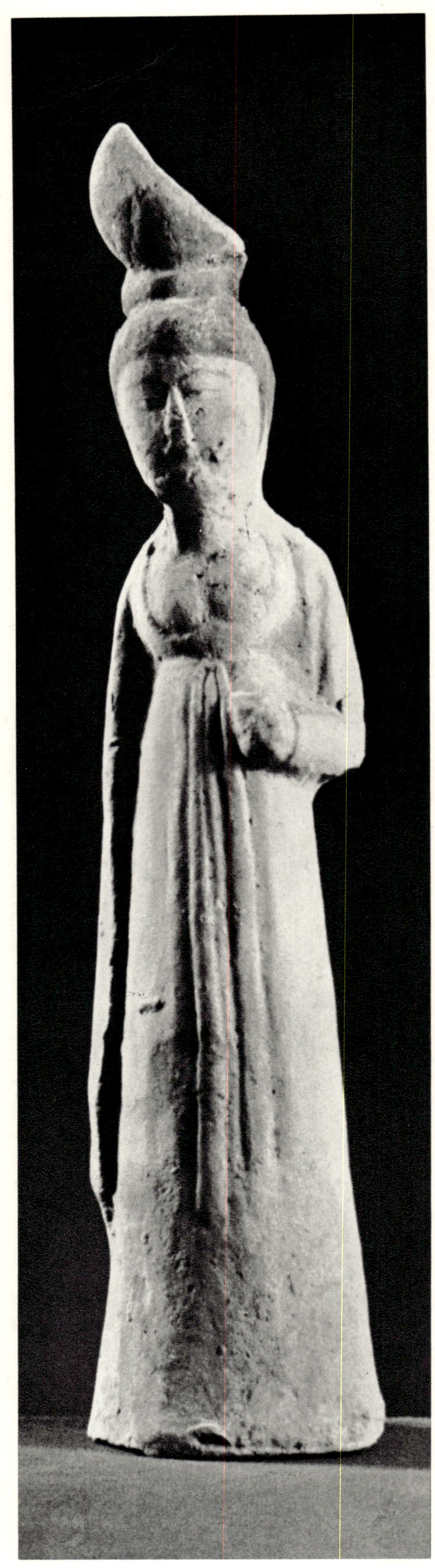

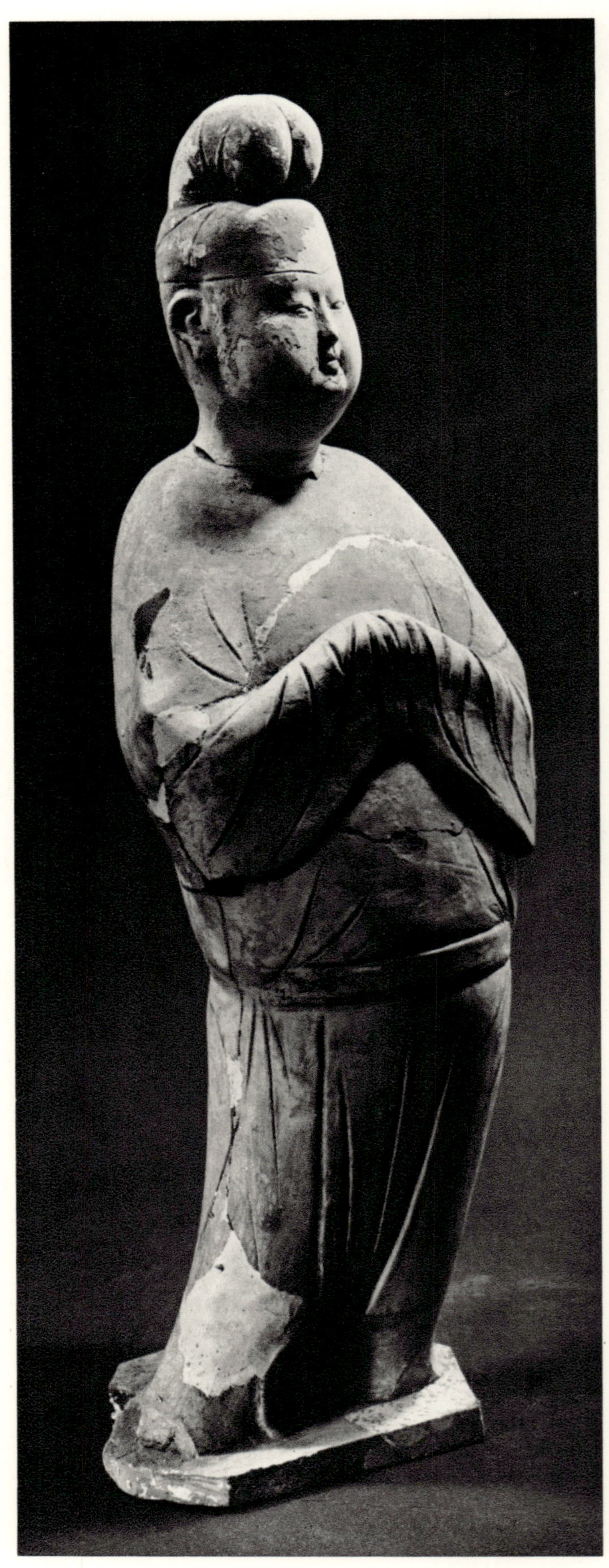

369. Female figure, earthenware. T'ang dynasty (668 A.D.). Excavated from the Li Shuang tomb, Yang-t'ou-chen, Sian, Shensi.
height: 22.0 cm. (8.7 in.)

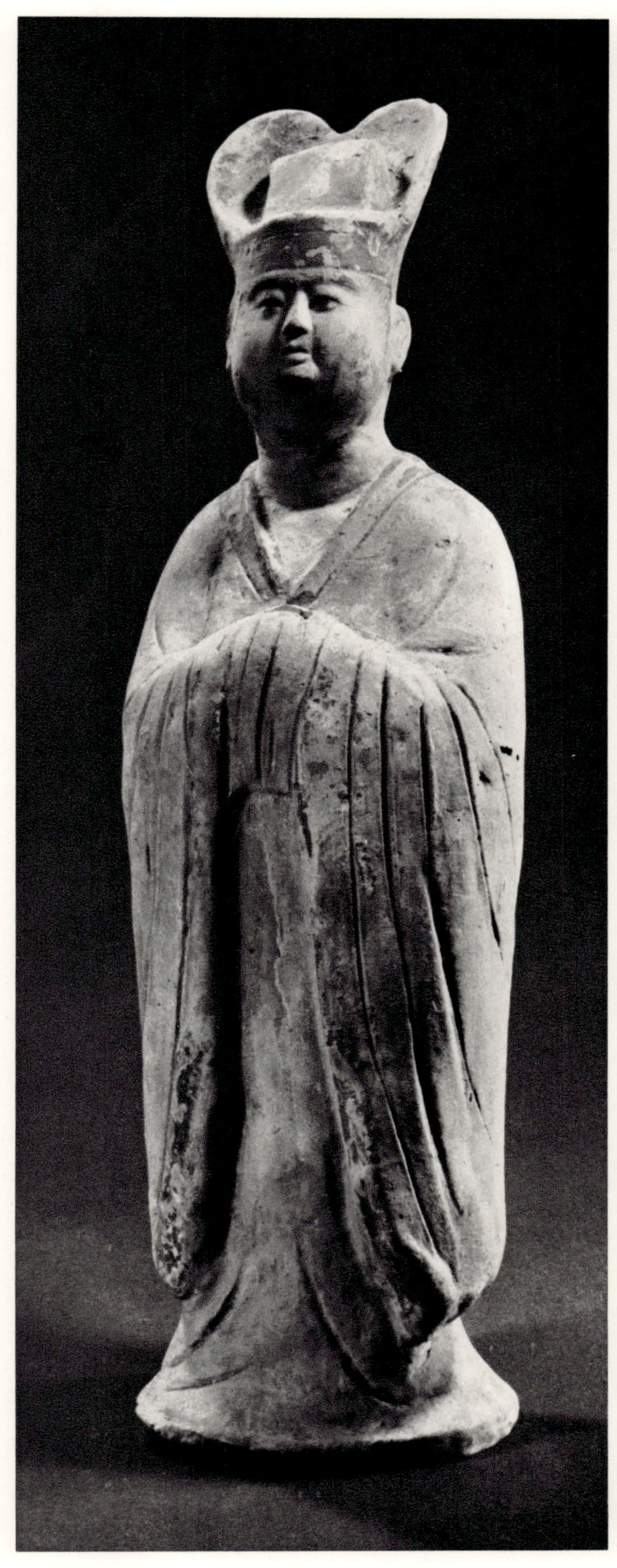

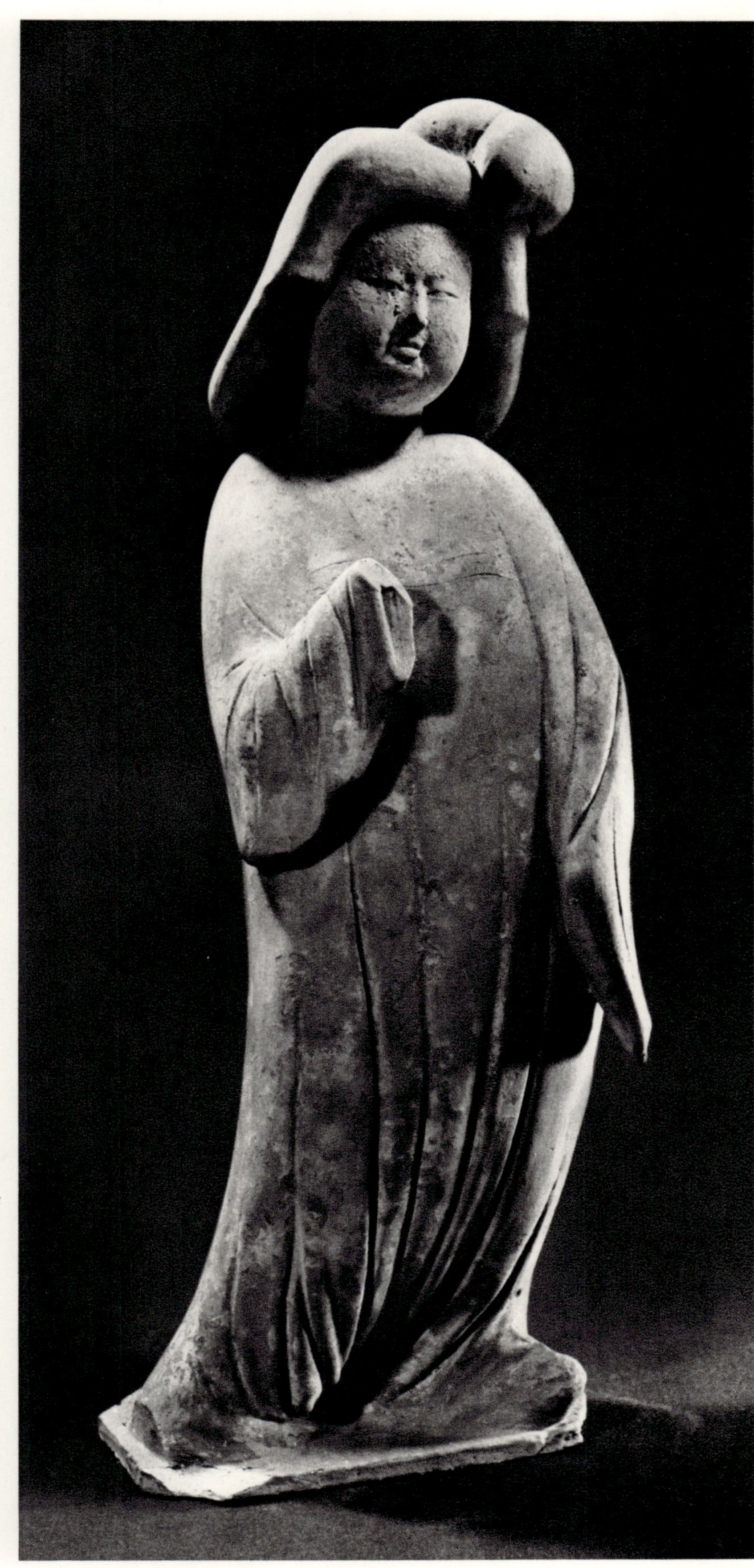

370–372. Figures, earthenware. T'ang dynasty (748 A.D.). Excavated from the Wu Shou-chung tomb, Kao-lou-ts'un, Sian, Shensi.
370 (facing page). Male figure. height: 54.5 cm. (21.45 in.)
371. Civil official. height: 51.0 cm. (20.1 in.)
372. Female figure. height: 55.5 cm. (22.85 in.)

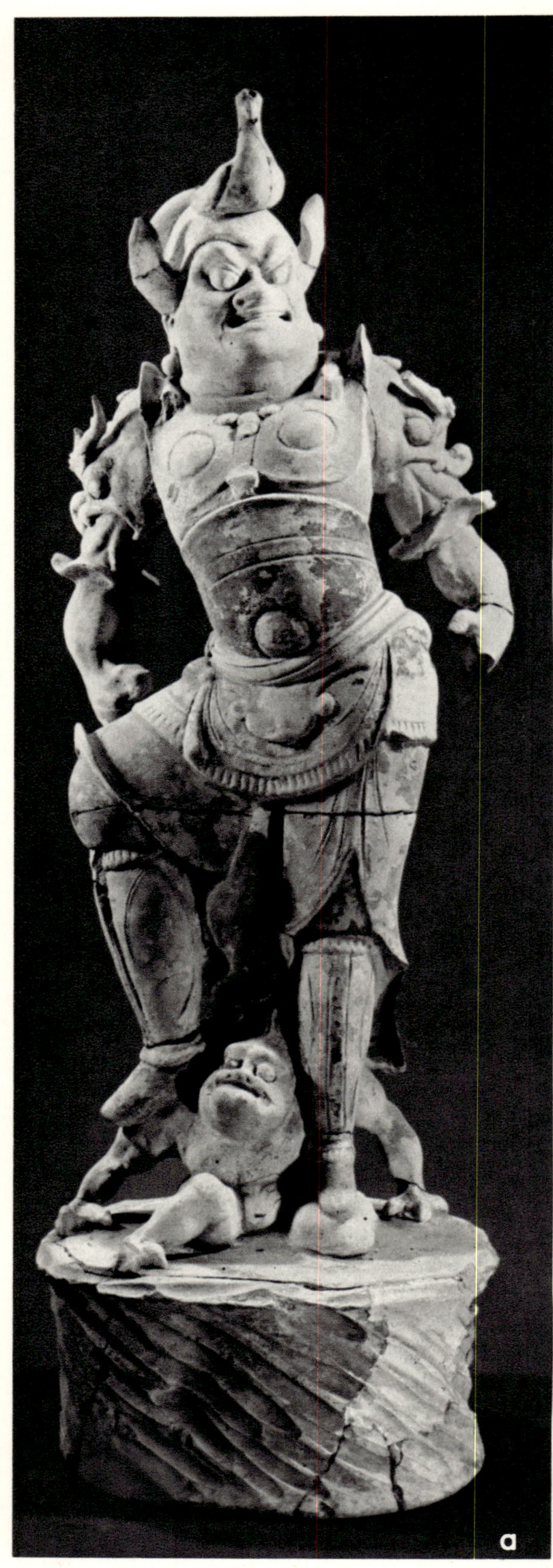

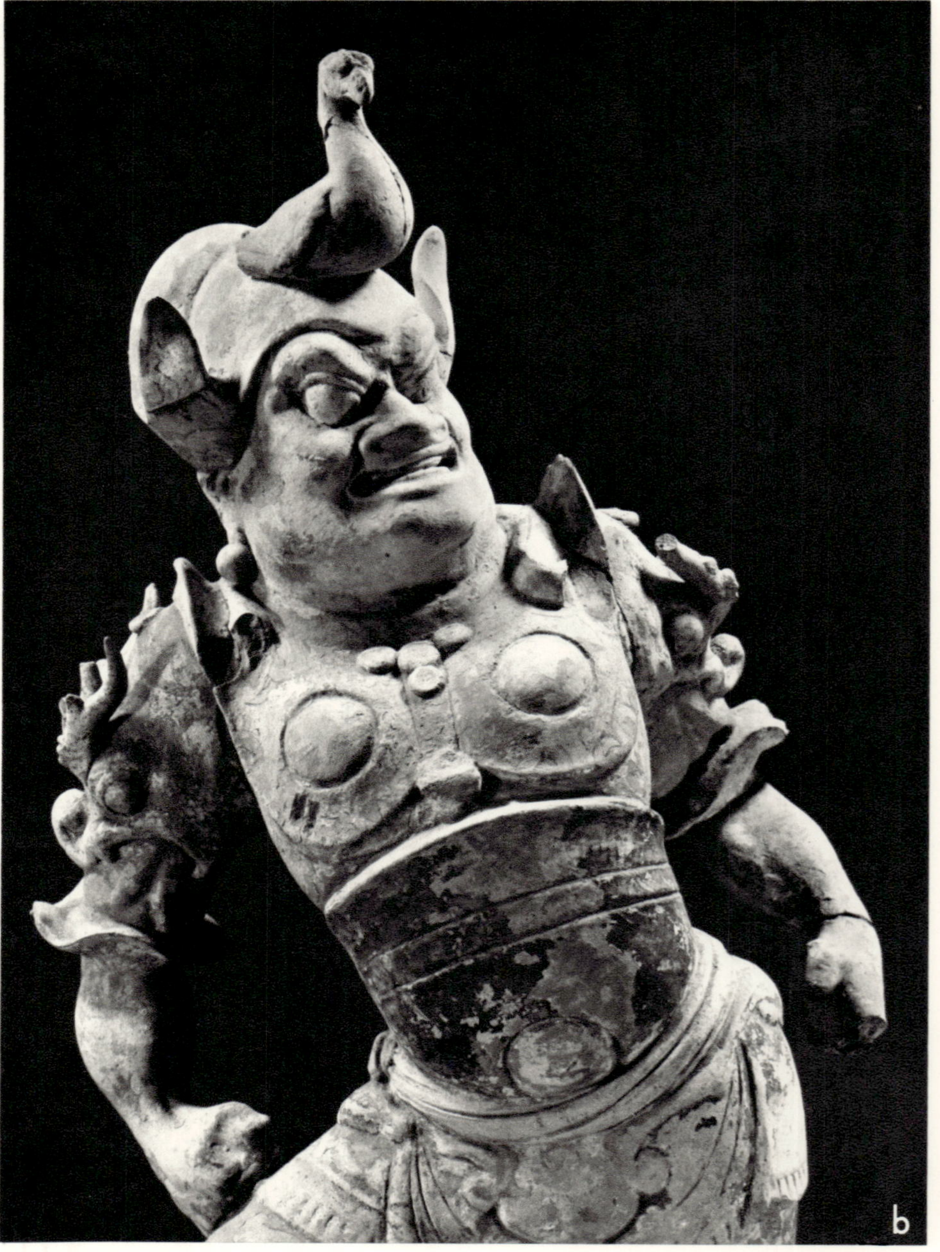

373(a, b). Heavenly Guardian, slip-painted earthenware. T'ang dynasty (748 A.D.). Excavated from the Wu Shou-chung tomb, Kao-lou-ts'un, Sian, Shensi. *height: 85.0 cm. (33.4 in.)*

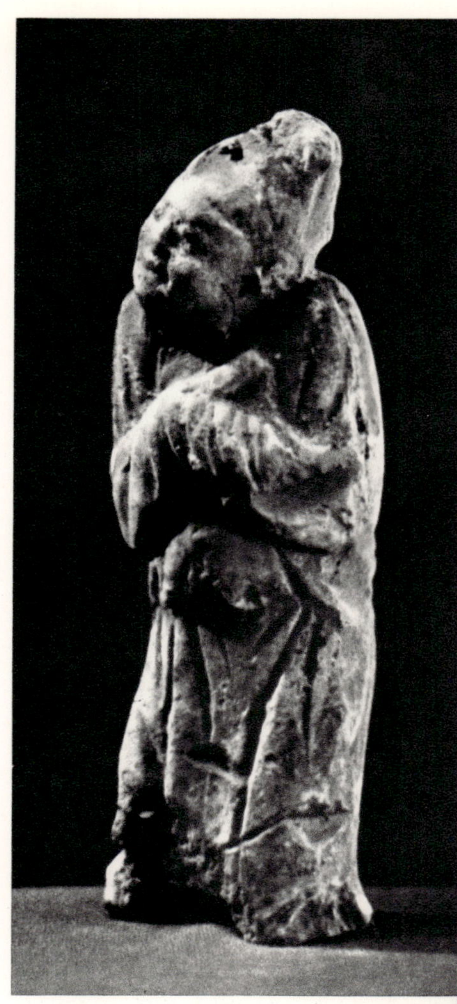

374. Comic actor, earthenware. T'ang dynasty. Excavated at Shih-li-p'u, Sian, Shensi. *height: 8.5 cm. (3.35 in.)*

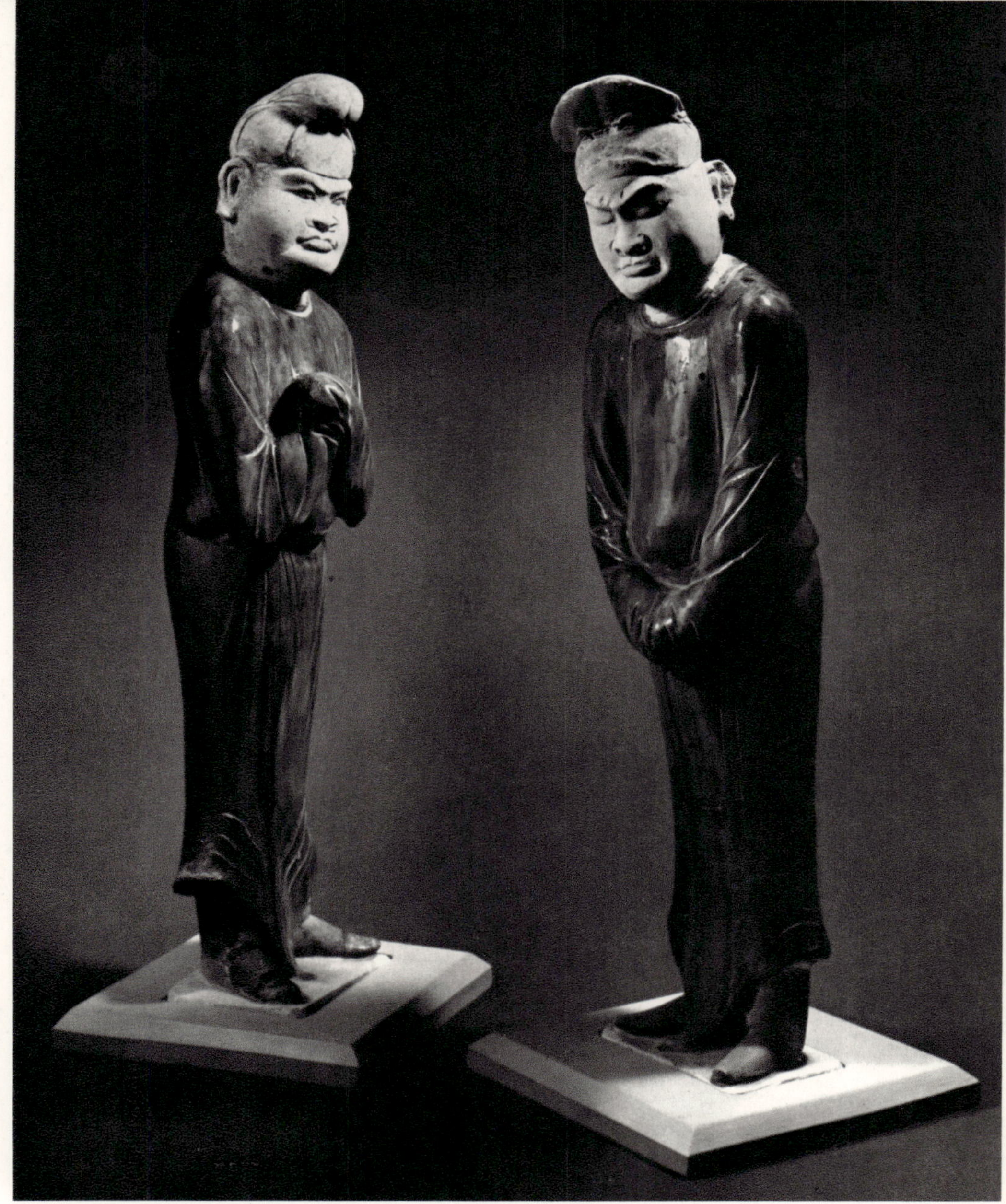

375. Two characters from a *hsi-lung* theatrical, glazed earthenware. T'ang dynasty (723 A.D.). Excavated from the Hsien-yü T'ing-hui tomb, Nan-ho-ts'un, western outskirts of Sian, Shensi. *heights: 45.0 cm. (17.7 in.); 44.6 cm. (17.5 in.)*

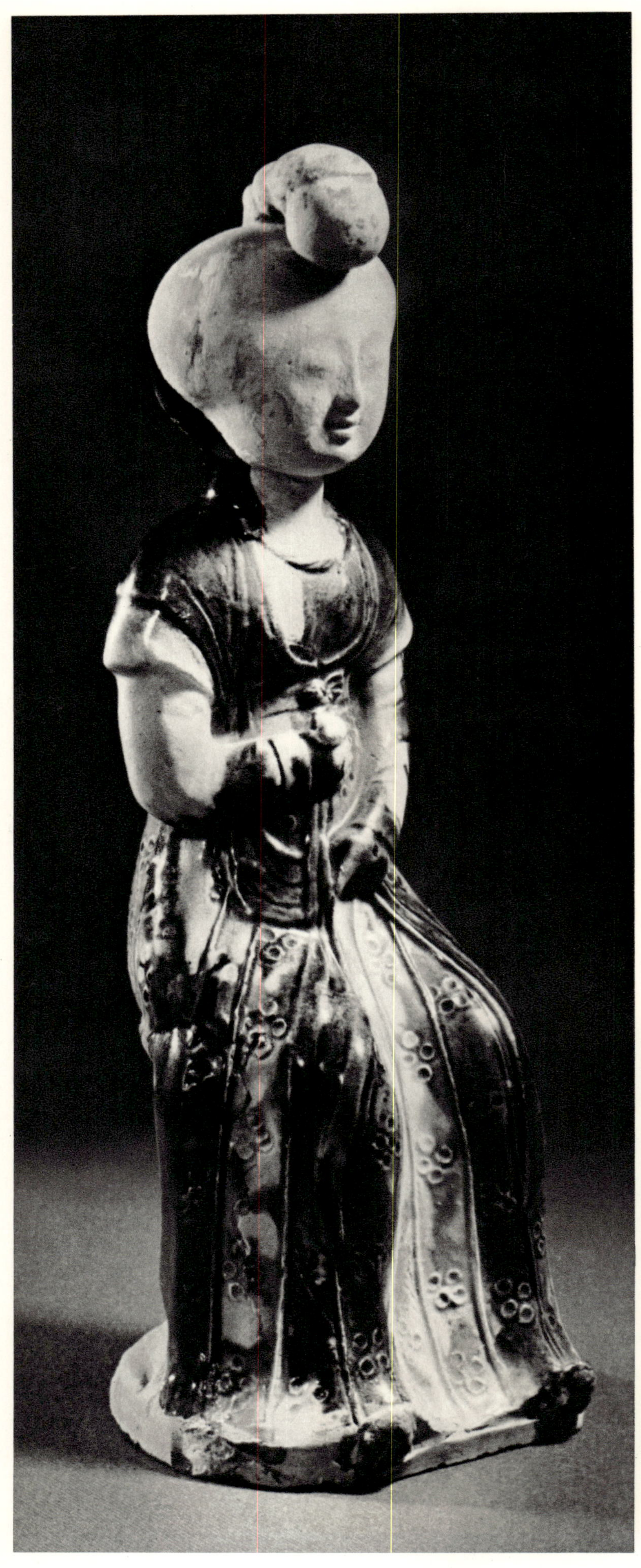

376. Seated female figure, earthenware with *san-ts'ai* glaze. T'ang dynasty. Excavated at Wang-chia-fen-ts'un, Sian outskirts, Shensi.
height: 28.5 cm. (11.2 in.)

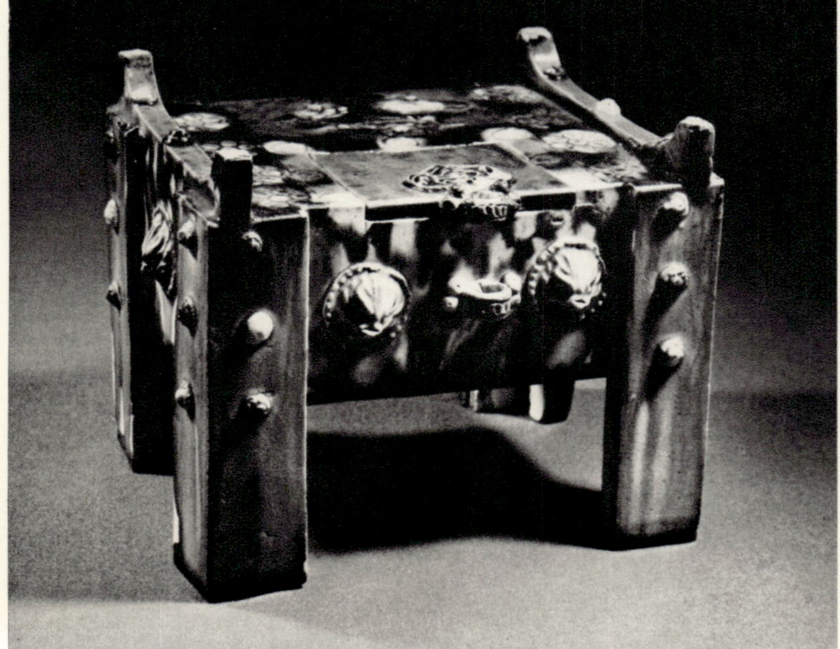

377. Money chest, earthenware with *san-ts'ai* glaze. T'ang dynasty. Excavated from tomb No. 90, Wang-chia-fen-ts'un, Sian outskirts, Shensi.
height: 13.3 cm. (5.2 in.); length: 15.5 cm. (6.1 in.); width: 12.1 cm. (4.7 in.)

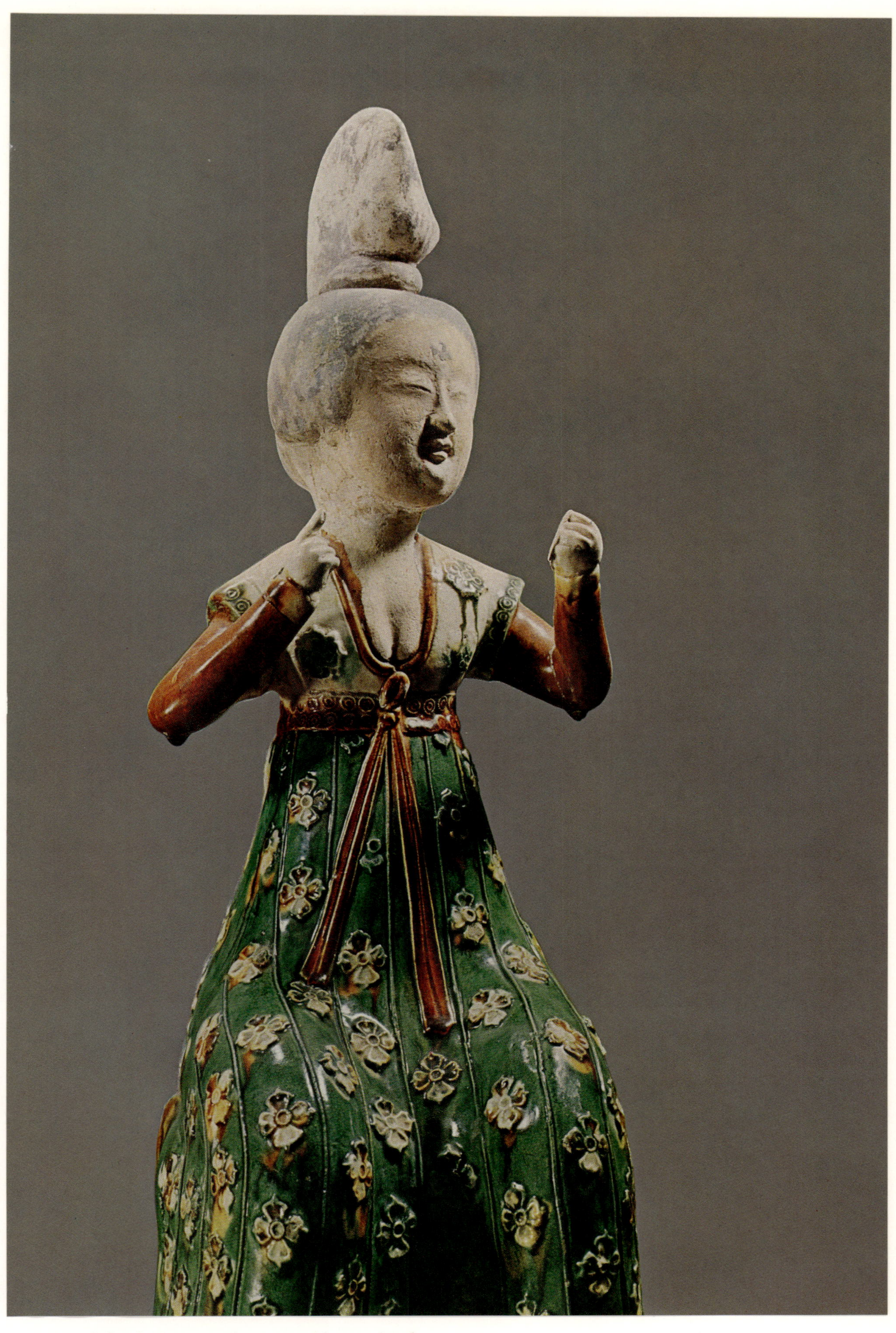

378. Seated female figure, earthenware with *san-ts'ai* glaze. T'ang dynasty. Excavated from a T'ang dynasty tomb at Wang-chia-fen-ts'un, Sian outskirts, Shensi.
height: 47.3 cm. (18.6 in.); width: 19.3 cm. (7.6 in.)

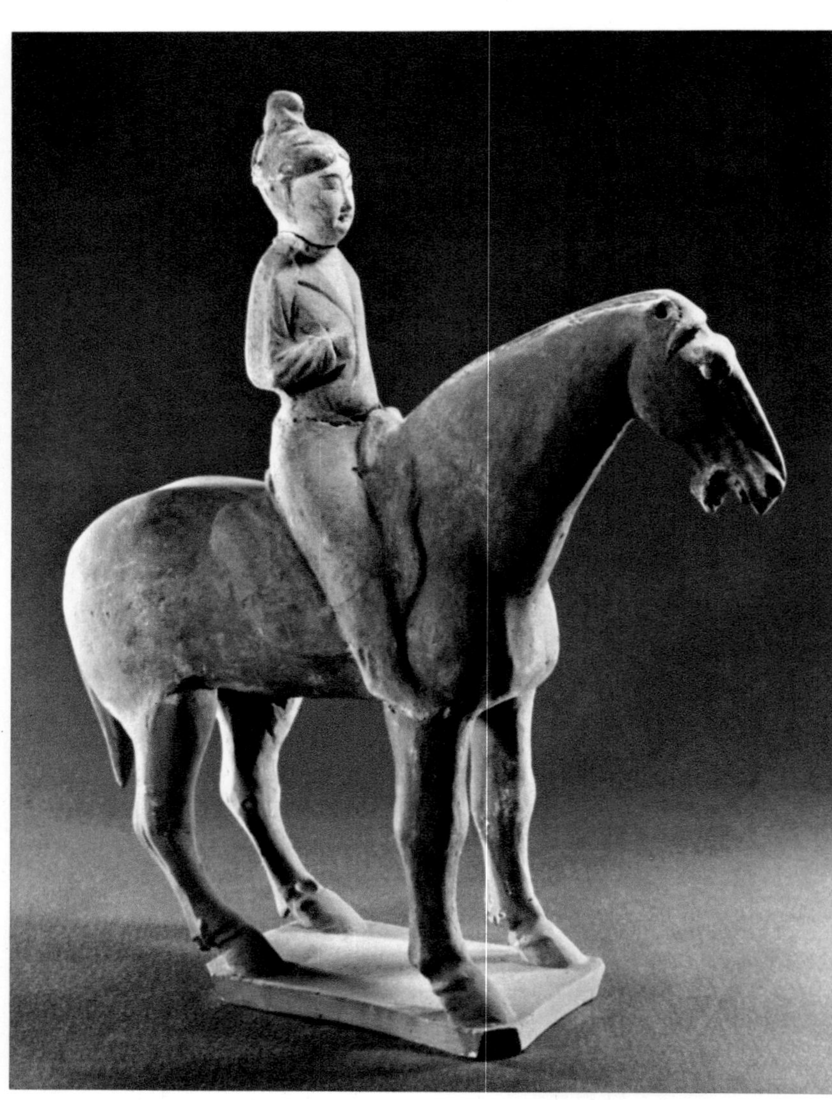

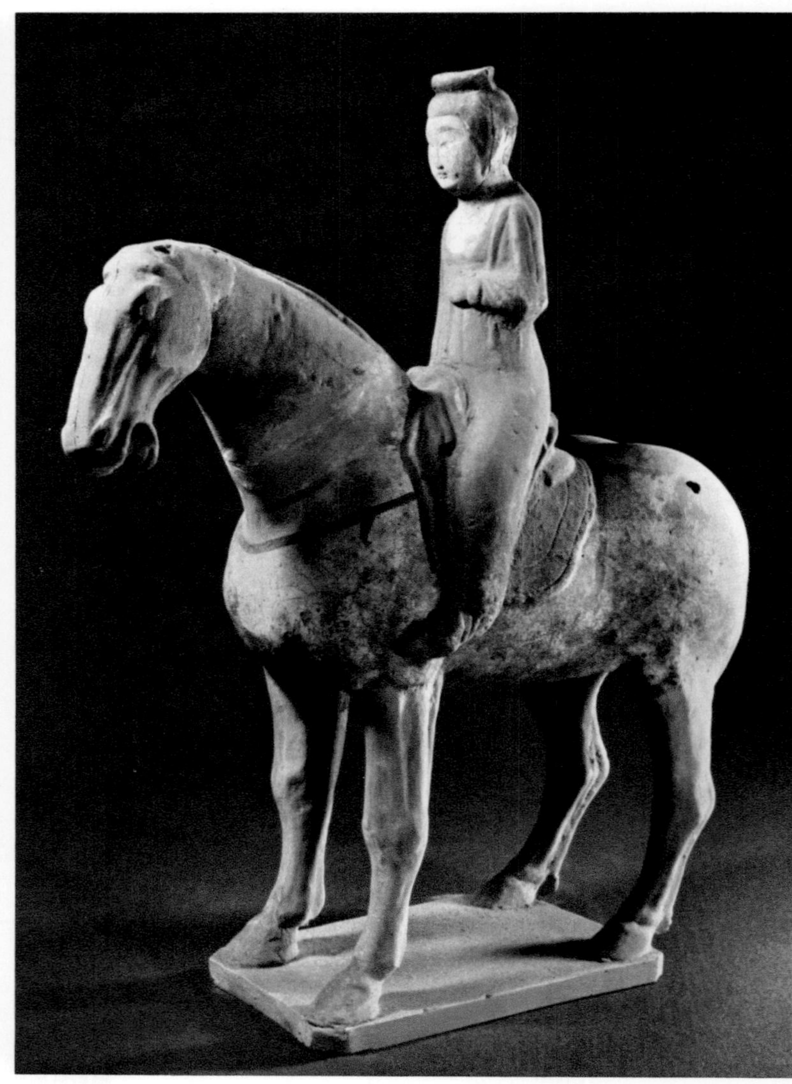

379–380. Equestrian figures, slip-painted earthenware. T'ang dynasty (668 A.D.). Excavated from the Li Shuang tomb, Yang-t'ou-chen, Sian, Shensi.
379. Male figure. height: 38.0 cm. (14.95 in.)
380. Female figure. height: 38.0 cm. (14.95 in.)

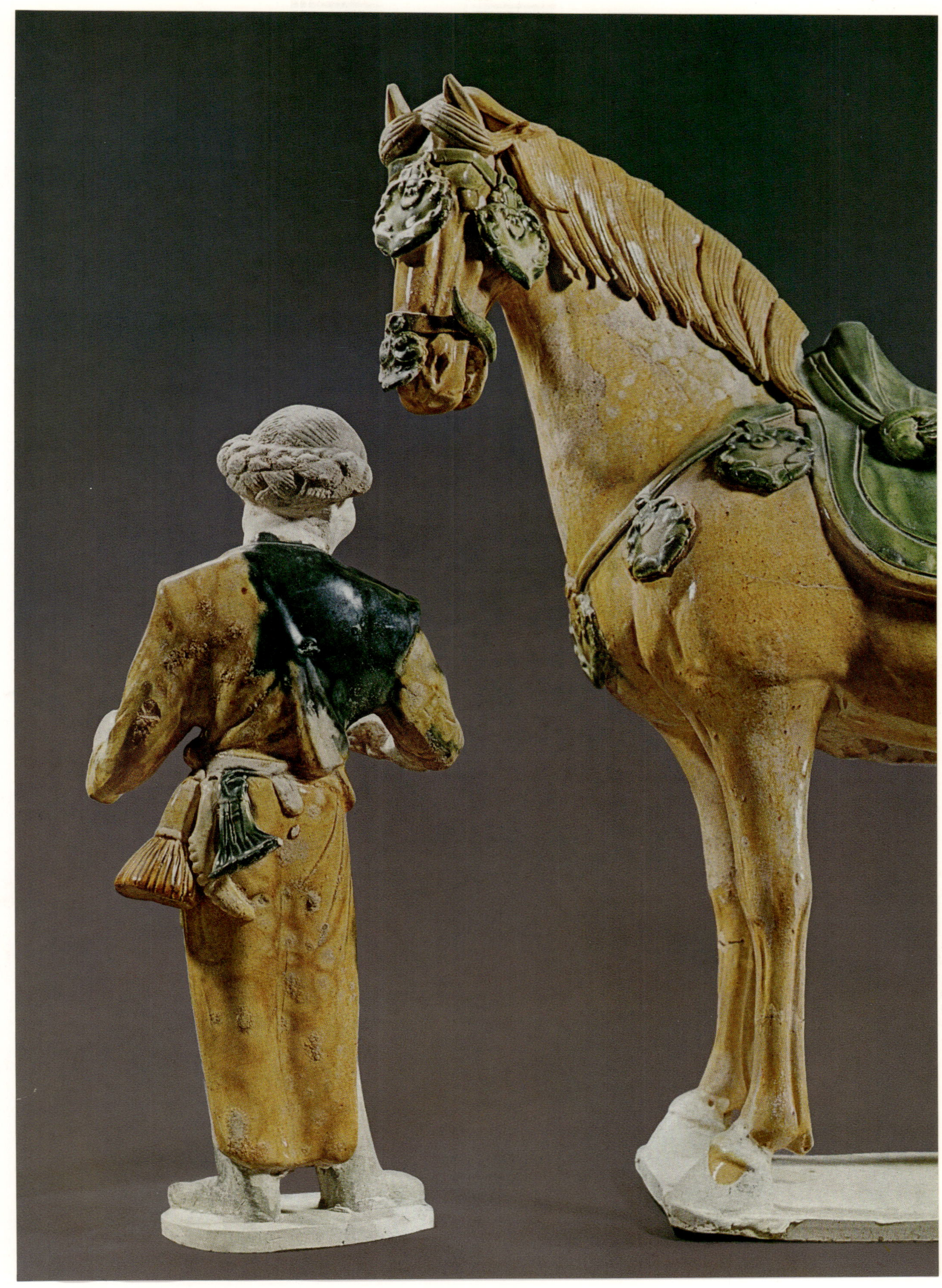

381. Horse and groom, earthenware with *san-ts'ai* glaze. T'ang dynasty. Excavated at Chung-pao-ts'un, Sian, Shensi.
Groom. height: 28.5 cm. (11.2 in.)
Horse. height: 39.6 cm. (15.5 in.); length: 43.0 cm. (16.9 in.)

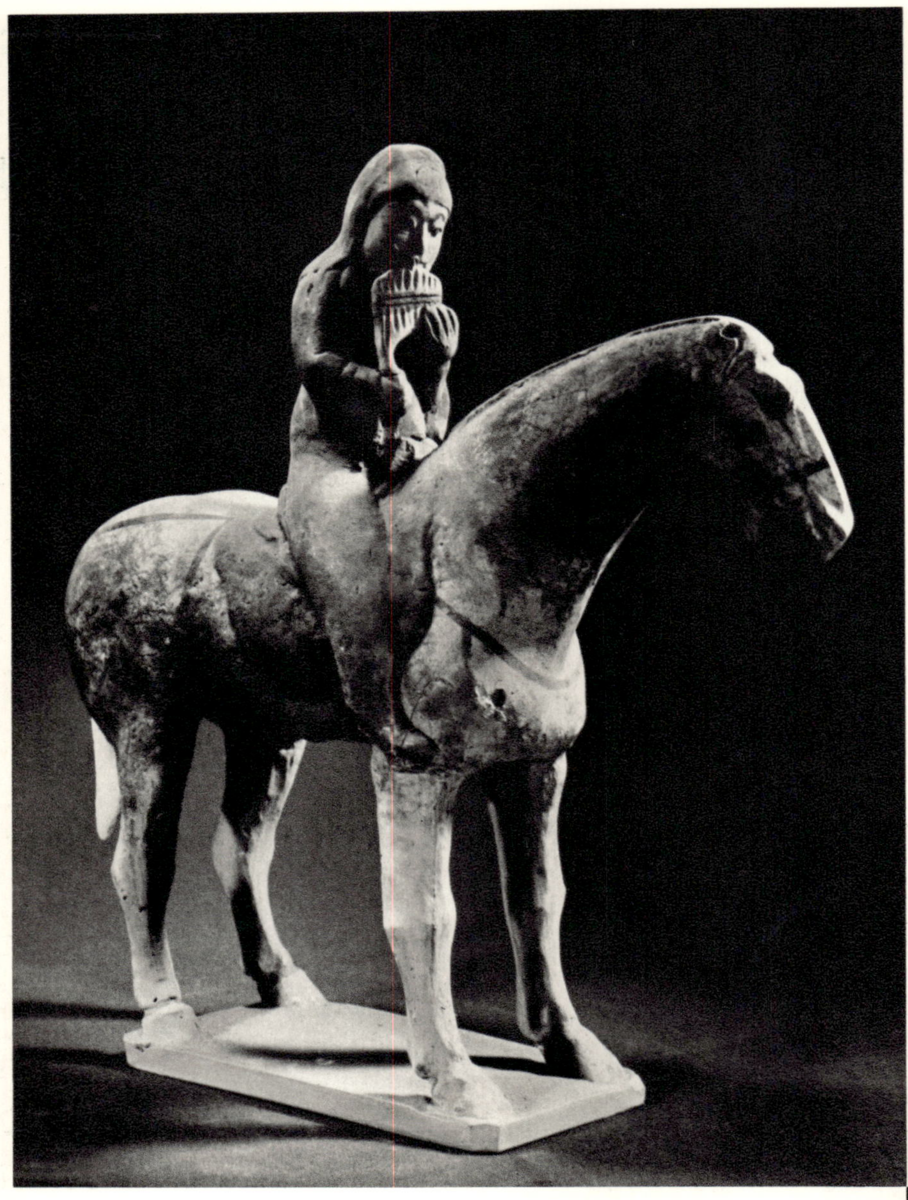

382. Equestrian musician, slip-painted earthenware. T'ang dynasty (668 A.D.). Excavated from the Li Shuang tomb, Yang-t'ou-chen, Sian, Shensi.
height: 38.0 cm. (14.95 in.)

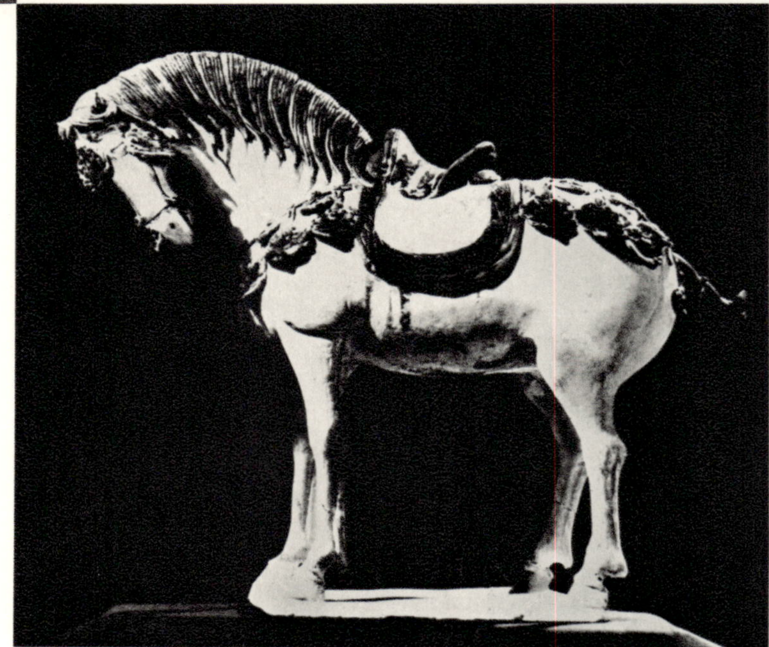

383. Horse, earthenware with *san-ts'ai* glaze. T'ang dynasty. Excavated at Chung-pao-ts'un, eastern outskirts of Sian, Shensi.
height: 40.0 cm. (15.75 in.); length: 48.0 cm. (18.9 in.)

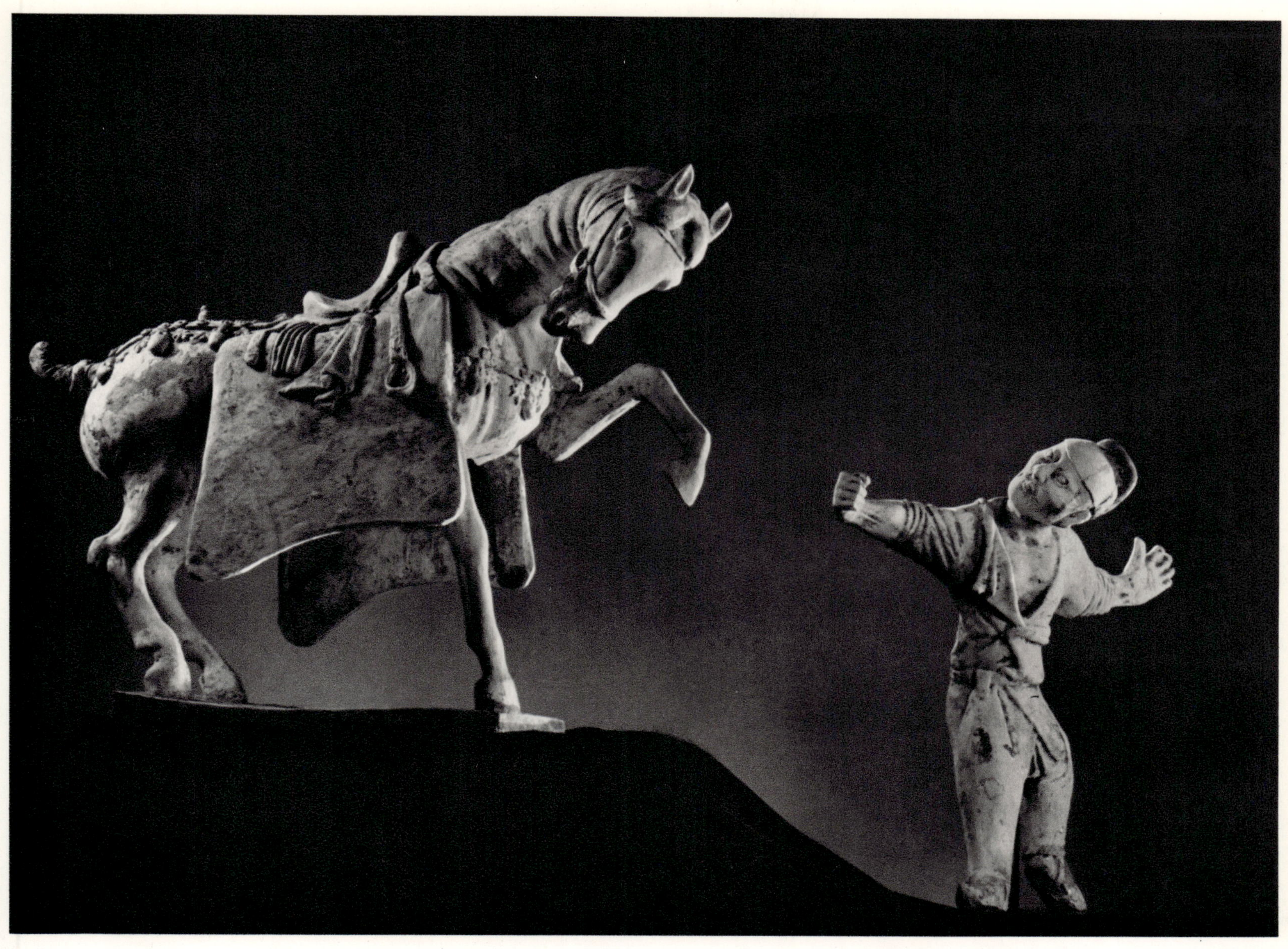

384. Horse and foreign groom, earthenware. T'ang dynasty. Excavated at Sian, Shensi.
no measurement given

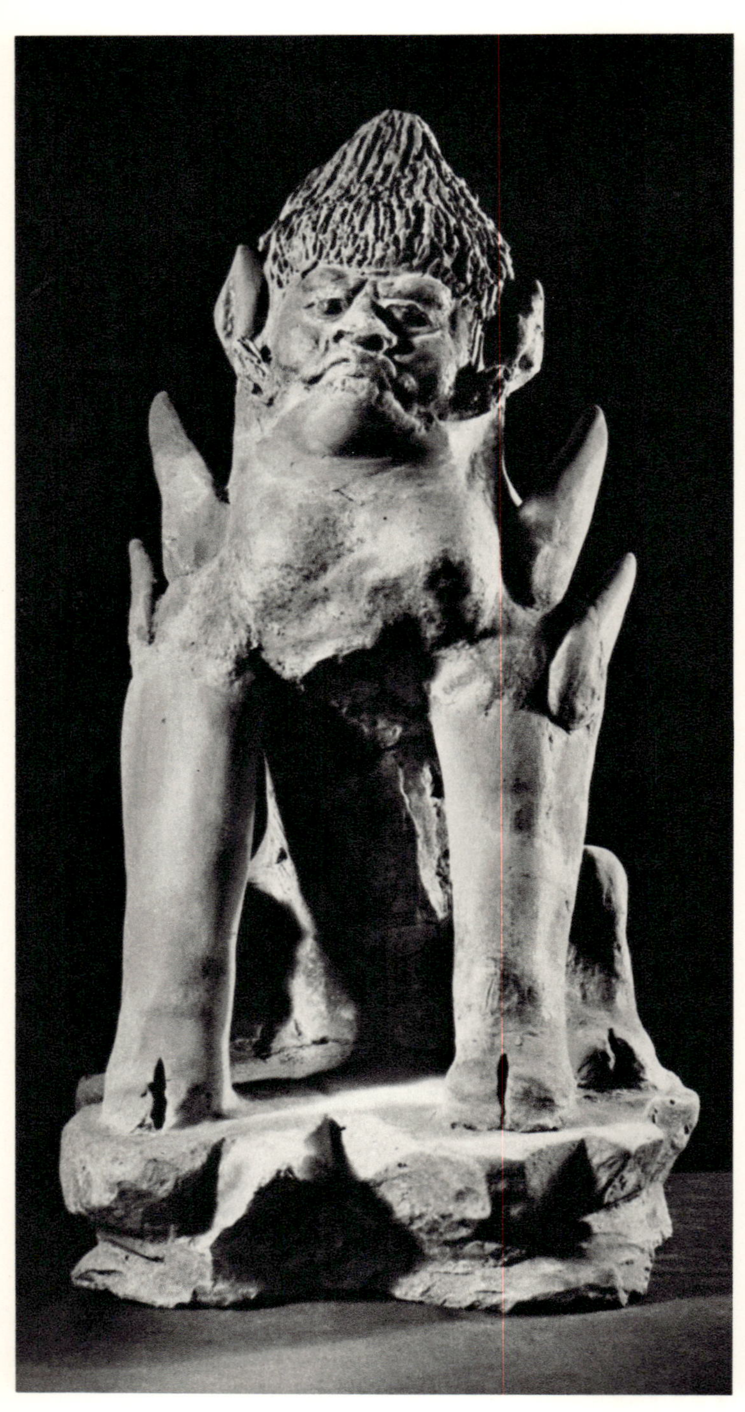

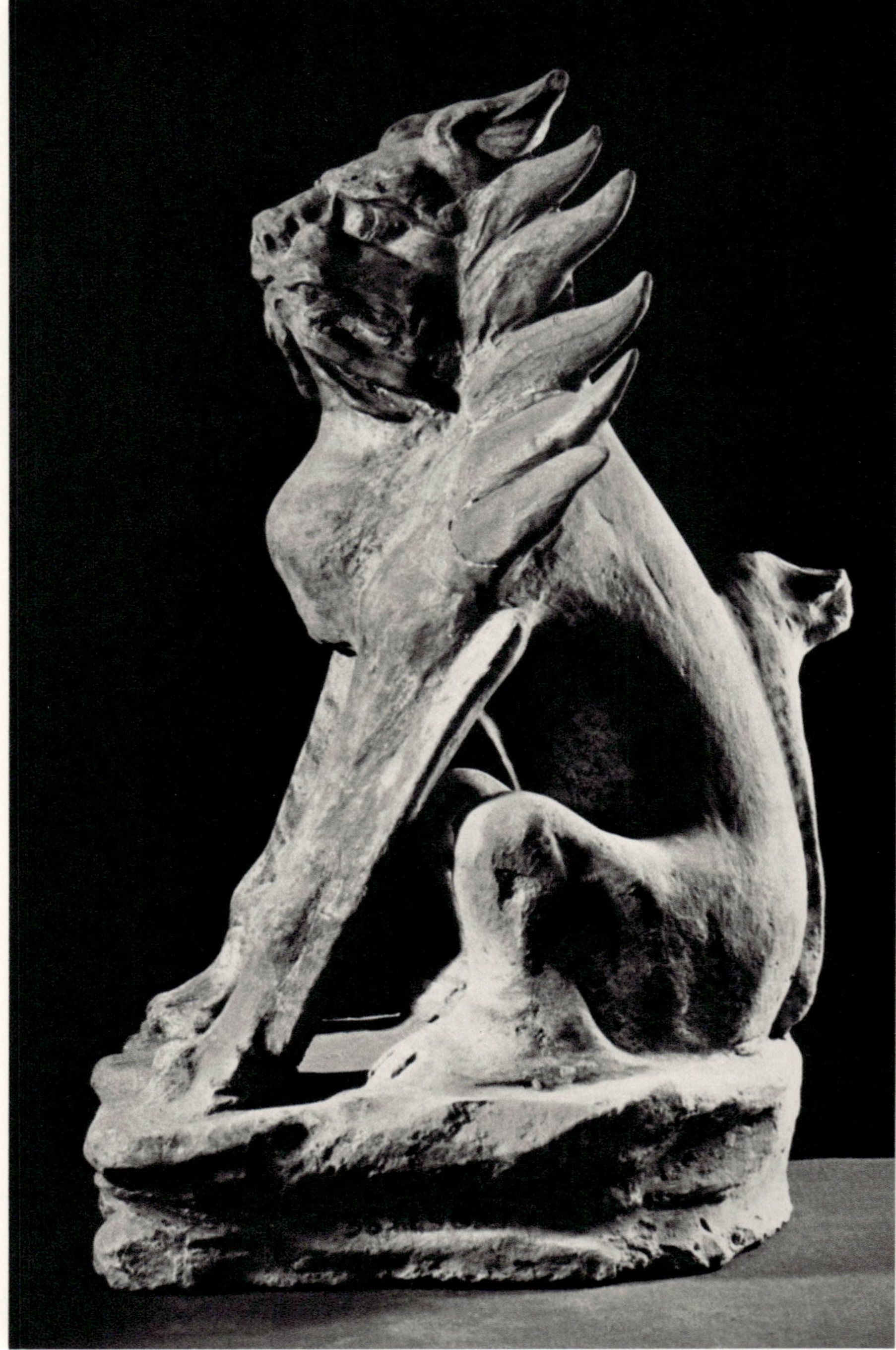

385–386. Tomb guardians, earthenware. T'ang dynasty (668 A.D.). Excavated from the Li Shuang tomb, Yang-t'ou-chen, Sian, Shensi.
385. height: 46.5 cm. (18.3 in.)
386. height: 44.0 cm. (17.3 in.)

NOTES TO THE PLATES

ABBREVIATIONS OF PERIODICALS

K	K'ao-ku 考古
KX	Kaogu Xuebao 考古学報
KT	K'ao-ku T'ung-hsün 考古通訊
W	Wen-wu 文物
WTT	Wen-wu Ts'an-k'ao Tzu-liao 文物参考資料

Notes to the Plates

I. NEOLITHIC, YIN AND CHOU—ARTS OF THE PEASANT AND ARISTOCRAT

1. *Painted Pottery bowl, red earthenware with black slip decoration. Neolithic period.*

This bowl is very similar to that shown in Plate 2, but is a little larger and the decoration motifs differ slightly. The "face" motif is not quite the same and the fish have here been replaced by a rectangular netlike motif.
Ref: *The Neolithic Village at Pan-p'o, Sian*, Pl. CXV, pp. 110-111, 163-164, 166, 175, The Institute of Archaeology of the Academia Sinica, and the Pan-p'o Museum (Sian), Peking, 1963; KT, 1956/6, pp. 81-84

2. *Painted Pottery bowl used as the cover of a jar burial, red earthenware with black slip decoration. Neolithic period.*

The well-balanced shape of this bowl is among the finest of the Yang-shao type pieces excavated from this site. The rim is finished as though on a wheel, and there are traces of the spatula used in burnishing the surface. The contrast between the black of the designs and the light-red ground is especially beautiful. The base appears to be small and flat. This bowl was used as the cover of a jar burial of a baby.

The interpretation of the motif inside the bowl is controversial. It is held by some authorities to represent a human face, but others, taking note of the fish also in the decoration and the strange motifs at the top and lower parts of the "face," regard this as some sort of aquatic insect. This design is unique among Yang-shao type Painted Pottery.
Ref: *The Neolithic Village at Pan-p'o, Sian*, Pl. I'-1, CXIV, pp. 110-111, 163-164, 166-167, 180; *ibid.*

3. *Painted Pottery cup, rede arthenware with brown slip decoration. Neolithic period.*

This very elegant cup is almost perfectly preserved; the burnished surface retains a beautiful sheen. It is typical of the geometric style of decoration of many pieces of the Yang-shao type found at this site. There is as yet no conclusive support to the widely held theory that the curvilinear style of decoration (*see* Pl. 6) preceded the rectilinear.
Ref: *The Neolithic Village at Pan-p'o, Sian*, Pl. II'-1, CXIX-4, pp. 106-107, 170, 175

4. *Painted Pottery jar, red earthenware with black slip decoration. Neolithic period.*

This exceptional Ma-chia-yao jar is quite large, well proportioned and very gracefully decorated. There are four curious projections just below the neck rim and two loop-handles on the belly below the shoulder. The surface is beautifully burnished. The elegantly painted design of circles and curved lines in slip is characteristic of the Ma-chia-yao style.
Ref: KT, 1956/6, Pl. I, p. 13; WTT, 1956/12, Cover, p. 13

5. *High-collared Painted Pottery jar, red earthenware with black and white slip decoration. Late Neolithic period or early Yin dynasty.*

This jar is the first complete piece of Painted Pottery excavated in Shantung and so is of great interest and importance. The surface is highly burnished. The decoration, in black and white slip, is of circles, spirals, triangles and dots. In general, the pottery from this site is of Lung-shan type, but it also shows characteristics of both Yang-shao and early Yin earthenwares. This decoration seems to be in the Yang-shao tradition and is thought to be of the late Neolithic period or early Yin dynasty.
Ref: W, 1959/10, p. 64; 1960/2, Cover, Pl. V

6. *Painted Pottery bowl, red earthenware with black slip decoration. Neolithic period.*

This is one of the most beautiful painted Yang-shao type pieces excavated from this site. The body is very fine, and the potting of the double curve of the sides is quite exceptional. This shape and the swirling design appear in pottery from western Honan and southern Shansi sites. They can also be seen in some of the wares of the Ma-chia-yao type from Kansu. It seems from this that there may be some connection between the wares of these two areas.
Ref: *Miao-ti-kou and San-li-ch'iao*, Pl. XXVI-1, p. 31, The Institute of Archaeology, Academia Sinica, Peking, 1959

7. *Jar, white earthenware. Yin dynasty.*

White earthenware was made as early as the Neolithic period in China, but the White Ware made in the style of bronze vessels was produced only in the Yin dynasty. It was made of a refined clay with a low iron content and was thrown on a wheel. When half dry, the surface was burnished and the design cut in the surface with a knife. This earthenware was then fired at about 1000 degrees centigrade.

This is one of the few examples of White Ware excavated in perfect condition. It is a particularly beautiful piece,

egg-shaped with vertical loop-handles on either side of the neck, and a ring-foot. The design of four *t'ao-t'ieh* is unusual; the horn of the *t'ao-t'ieh* is greatly elaborated, and each creature has hands and a triangular body. This motif may be related to the so-called "human body design" (*t'i-ch'ü-wen*) seen in the Ma-ch'ang Painted Pottery of the Kansu area.
Ref: W, 1960/1, pp. 32-33

8. Tsun, *earthenware with yellow-brown glaze over incised decoration. Western Chou dynasty.*

The shape is close to that of a bronze *tsun*. It is decorated both inside the flaring lip and over the outer surface with incised parallel lines, crisscross and wavy line patterns. There are small appliqué coiled decorations on the inner surface of the lip. The jar is glazed over the lip and down almost to the foot. The yellowish-brown and black-brown (in the incised lines) color of the glaze is due to its iron-oxide content.
Ref: KX, 1959/4, Color Plate (pp. 90-91), Pl. XIV-1, p. 67

9-10. *Ssu Mu Wu* ting, *bronze. Yin dynasty.*

This is one of the largest bronze pieces ever discovered. First found in 1939 at a farm north of Wu-kuan-ts'un, Anyang, it was thought too large to excavate in one piece. However, it was not dug up at that time for fear of losing it to the Japanese army, but it was finally excavated in one piece in 1946.

The three-character inscription reads Ssu Mu Wu (司母戊). Mu Wu seems to have been the wife of the Emperor Wu-yi and mother of the Emperor Wen-ting. But some authorities take her to be the wife of Ti-yi.

The body of the piece is six centimeters thick, is decorated with *t'ao-t'ieh*, and there are *k'uei-lung* borders on the central rectangular panels. The upper portions of the hollow legs are decorated with *t'ao-t'ieh.* The two lug-handles, which are also hollow, are decorated on the outer surface with a pair of confronted tigers, open mouthed, about to bite a man's head. At the base of each side, are added animal masks. Ch'en Meng-chia has interpreted this head as representing a slave or prisoner of war. However, it seems preferable to regard this figure as that of a harmful devil. The narrow edges of the lugs are also decorated with dragon pattern (龍文). The thickened rim and notched flanges at the angles give added weight to this massive piece, which must arouse admiration for its sheer size and the brilliance of the casting technique. It is believed that some two hundred to three hundred craftsmen may well have taken part in the various processes of the production of this huge *ting.* In the Historical Museum, Peking.
Ref: KX, VII, Pls. XL-XLIII, pp. 29-30; W, 1959/12, pp. 27-28

11. Kuei, *bronze. Western Chou dynasty.*

This *kuei* was excavated with the large bell illustrated in Plate 59, the *kuei* being found inside the bell. This bowl-shaped grain container has four vertical loop-handles at the shoulder and stands on a slightly everted foot-ring. Inside the bowl is a turtle design. Both the upper surface of the mouth rim and the foot are decorated with variants of cloud-thunder scroll (雲雷文). On each handle is a small animal mask with protruding eyes; the main surface of the body is decorated with large hook variant (鈎状文) motifs, and the spaces between filled in with cloud-thunder scroll. This is a piece of rare quality both in the dignity of the design and the exceptional quality of the casting.
Ref: W, 1960/7, pp. 48-49

12. Yü, *bronze. Late Western Chou dynasty.*

This *yü*, a deep bowl-shaped vessel for containing liquids, is typical with its two lug-handles and deep foot-ring. However, the animal-head cartouches with dependent loops are unusual. The upper and lower registers of the decoration are of *k'uei-lung*; the main zone is decorated with a combination of *hui-lung* and wave pattern (波文) or cloud-scroll (雲文). The rings and cartouches are decorated with minute scroll pattern. Many characteristics of the late Western Chou bronze work are evident in this piece.
Ref: W, 1959/11, pp. 72-73

13. *The Marquis of Ts'ai* kuei, *bronze. Ch'un Ch'iu period.*

This covered *kuei*, rather late in style, is fixed to a square stand. The cover is surmounted by a coronet of petal-like forms, and there are four animal-head cartouches around the rim. The two large ear-handles on either side of the body are also decorated with animal masks. The foot-ring is joined to the square stand. The cover is decorated with a whorl pattern (円渦文), and there are three rows of scale pattern (鱗文) on the ears. The main body of the piece is decorated with a minute intertwined-dragon pattern (蟠螭文). Inside the cover there is a six-character inscription, of which the last two characters are illegible.
Ref: *Relics Unearthed from the Tomb of the Marquis of Ts'ai at Shou District*, Pls. V-2, LXXX, pp. 7, 21, The Institute of Archaeology, Academia Sinica, Peking, 1956

14. *Gold plaque. Ch'un Ch'iu period.*

Twelve gold plaques were found in this tomb. Of these, seven round, one triangular and one rectangular piece were found around the waist of the body. The remaining three were in the western part of the tomb. The one shown here is one of the circular plaques found with the body. The whole surface is embossed with a form of intertwined-dragon pattern. The two pairs of holes on either side of this plaque perhaps indicate that it was used as a costume accessory.
Ref: *Ibid.*, Pl. XXX-1, p. 15

15. *Bronze sword with carved ivory hilt and sheath. Ch'un Ch'iu period.*

The sword is double-edged with a cylindrical shaft, but no guard. The tip has been corroded away. The hilt and sheath of ivory are decorated with minute engraved designs. The butt end of the hilt is elliptical in section, while the lower end is rhomboid and bounded by a rectangular-sectioned rib. There are four such ribs around the hilt, and between each is a panel decorated with minute intertwined-dragon pattern. The whole shaft and part of the upper blade fits into the cavity of this ivory hilt. The sheath is rhomboid in section and has a rectangular plaque pierced by three holes, presumably to take a cord to carry the sword. The surface decoration is divided into three sections. The upper

and middle sections are decorated on one side only with minute intertwined-dragon pattern and an anchor-shaped relief decoration. The lower part of the sheath is decorated on both sides with a similar intertwined-dragon pattern. This is an exceptional piece, notable particularly for the fine workmanship in the carving of the ivory.
Ref: *Chung-chou-lu, Lo-yang*, Pl. XLVI, p. 97, The Institute of Archaeology, Academia Sinica, Peking, 1959

16. *Finial in the shape of a horse's head, bronze inlaid with gold and silver. Warring States period.*

This is a finial for the harness shaft of a vehicle. Made in bronze, it is inlaid with gold and silver in spiral (渦文), scale, and parallel curved line patterns (平行曲線文), etc. The neck of the animal is hollow to take the shaft, the end of which was wrapped in fabric and then inserted into the hollow cylinder, where it was fixed by three iron nails.

This is one of the artistic masterpieces of the Warring States period, both for the lively representation and for the brilliance of the inlay technique.
Ref: *Excavations at Hui District*, Pl. L, p. 78, The Institute of Archaeology, Academia Sinica, Peking, 1956

17. *Belt hook, silver and gilt with jade and glass insets. Warring States period.*

This silver and gilt belt hook is decorated with jade and glass inlay. The broader end is in the form of an animal head, while a dragon body runs down either side, joining in one dragon head at the narrow end. Here the dragon holds in its jaws a duck-head hook of white jade. The dragon bodies seem to twine around a parrot. The three circles of jade (small *pi*) inset in the main body of this piece are engraved with the rice-grain (穀文) design, and glass-eye beads are set in the center of the two outer circles.

The complexity of the design, and the richness of the technique and the colors make this an outstanding example of the craftsmanship of the period.
Ref: *Excavations at Hui District*, Pl. LXXIV, pp. 104-105, The Institute of Archaeology, Academia Sinica, Peking, 1956

18. *Buffalo, bronze inlaid with white metal. Warring States period.*

This exquisite small piece is very naturalistically modeled. The body of the animal is decorated with a variant of the cloud spiral (雲渦文) motif peculiar to the Warring States period. The white metal of the inlay has been thought to be platinum, but to date this has not been proved. If it were platinum, this would be a very important fact in the study of metallurgical techniques of ancient China.

The four-character inscription, which is cast, reads: 大府之器. This can be translated: "the possession of the chief treasure-house" (of the king of the Ch'u state).
Ref: W, 1959/4, front inside cover, pp. 1-2

19. *Pair of tigers, carved wood with black, red and yellow lacquer decoration. Warring States period.*

This pair of tigers, back to back, is carved from a single piece of wood. The carving is lively and realistic. The whole body surface is covered with scale pattern in red and yellow lacquer. There are three rectangular holes in each animal, two in the shoulders and one in the rump.

Fragments of a drum painted with a very fine lacquer decoration were found in this same grave. Also found were four wooden curved supports shaped like animal legs, the design on which is entirely consistent with the scale pattern seen on the tigers. It has been suggested that these were originally inserted in the holes in the tigers to support the drum. This theory is supported by a painting of a similar pair of tigers supporting a drum on the stone with bas-reliefs of the Han dynasty tomb excavated at Nan-yang, Honan.
Ref: WTT, 1957/9, Color Plate, p. 21

20. *Male figure, carved and lacquered wood. Warring States period.*

This is one of a pair of standing figures discovered together. This piece shows a man wearing a long-sleeved black garment, with his hands clasped in front of him. Though the face is rather flat, the features are clearly shown. He wears his hair in a long plait. The sleeve-band of an under-garment can be seen at the edge of the outer sleeve. Below the waist in front is an indication of tied strings. The feet are not visible in front, but it is said that a pair of black shoes show at the back. Two figures of women were also found in this tomb with six other figures so far unidentified. This find presents very important material for the study of costume and ornament of the Warring States period.
Ref: KT, 1958/11, Pl. VIII, p. 80

21. *Stand surmounted by deer antlers, lacquered wood. Warring States period.*

This is a most unusual I-shaped wooden stand supporting a pair of real antlers. It is painted in black lacquer and decorated in spiral and triangle motifs in red and yellow lacquer. As in the piece shown in Plate 98, the antlers dominate this form. It is believed that antlers may have been a talisman against evil.
Ref: KT, 1958/11, Pl. VI, p. 80

22. *Covered* hu, *bronze with inlaid copper decoration. Warring States period.*

Unfortunately, much of the original copper inlay is missing. The cover is decorated with eighteen animals around the central loop-knob. There are six lappets between the two loop-handles, while the main body of the *hu* is divided into twelve rectangular sections by a twisted-rope relief. Each of these sections contains a lively hunting scene in which men armed with spears hunt animals ranging from elephants and buffalo to birds. This is an excellent example of the trend toward realism typical of the arts of the Warring States period.
Ref: KX, VI, Pl. X, pp. 83-86

23. Hu, *bronze with cast decoration, probably originally inlaid. Warring States period.* (*same as Plate 77;* see *note*)

Formerly in the Palace Museum, Peking, this round-bodied *hu* has a pair of ring-handles and stands on a foot-ring. The whole of the surface is decorated in a negative relief, presumably originally inlaid with a copper-gold alloy. All traces of the inlay are now lost. The decoration is divided in three asymmetrical registers. The upper register depicts scenes of picking mulberry leaves and hunting and shooting practice. The second register shows wildfowl hunting and a banquet scene, this last in two layers. The third register, which is also partly divided in two, shows battle scenes on land and water. The vivid representation of man and animals is a fine example of the art of this period, and the subject matter makes this piece one of exceptional value as study material for the life of the times.

A bronze vessel with a copper-gold alloy inlay battle-scene decoration similar to this piece has been excavated from a Warring States tomb in Chi District, Honan.
Ref: Yang Tsung-jung. *Painting Materials of the Warring States Period*, Pl. XX, p. 7, Peking, 1957; WTT, 1957/9, Color Plate, pp. 21, 26; 1958/1, pp. 21, 26-27

24. *Painted Pottery jar shard, earthenware with slip decoration. Neolithic period.*

This is a Yang-shao pottery shard. The design appears to have been in four roundels, one of which shows a frog or toad design. Although no information has been given on the color, one presumes that the slip painting is in black on a red body. In comparison with the frog designs of the Ma-chia-yao type pottery from Kansu, this decoration is realistic and lively. Insofar as there are very few representations of living creatures on Painted Pottery, this fragment is of some importance.
Ref: *Miao-ti-kou and San-li-ch'iao*, Pl. IX-1, p. 26, Institute of Archaeology, Academia Sinica, Peking, 1959

25. *Painted Pottery cup, earthenware with black slip decoration. Neolithic period.*

This is a beautifully made cup of a very usable size. The lattice decoration painted in black only is also typical of the Pan-shan type. If this is not merely a coincidence, this similarity may indicate some relationship between this Honan site and the Kansu, Pan-shan type.
Ref: *Ibid.*, Pl. XIV-4, p. 28

26. *Painted Pottery jar, earthenware with slip decoration. Neolithic period.*

This is a Ma-ch'ang type piece. The relationship to Pan-shan can be seen in the general form and in the wavy line at the lower edge of the decoration, but the surface, originally burnished, has lost its luster and the decoration is a rough and crude version of the earlier delicate type from which it derives.

For some time after 1949, the three great periods of Painted Pottery culture of Kansu—Pan-shan, Ma-chia-yao, and Ma-ch'ang—were known collectively as the Kansu/Yang-shao culture, but today they are generally termed the Ma-chia-yao culture. However, as there are such clear differences of style and decoration between the wares of these three periods, it is probably best that the three separate names should be retained in classification. It is evident that the Ma-ch'ang period immediately follows the Pan-shan period, for the wares of the Ma-ch'ang type are a degenerate form of the Pan-shan type. It is assumed that the period of production of the Ma-chia-yao type is contemporary with both the Pan-shan and the Ma-ch'ang periods.
Ref: KX, 1960/2, Pl. III-1 (pp. 52-53), p. 17

27. *Painted Pottery two-handled jar, earthenware with slip decoration. Stone-and-Bronze period.*

This Ch'i-chia style jar has a pair of loop-handles extending between the rim and the body, and the shoulder is decorated with straight lines in parallel and crisscross patterns. This piece shows some influence of the Ma-ch'ang style, which gives weight to a theory that the Ma-ch'ang precedes Ch'i-chia.
Ref: KT, 1956/6, Pl. III-6, p. 15

28. *Painted Pottery two-handled jar, red-slip-coated earthenware with black slip decoration. Stone-and-Bronze period.*

This T'ang-wang style jar has unusually large graceful handles. It is, however, quite roughly made. The surface is burnished and is decorated with a form of spiral over a red slip. The T'ang-wang culture, discovered after 1949, is thought to be either a little earlier than the Hsin-tien culture or to run contemporary with it, though belonging to a different branch of the Painted Pottery culture. A coffee-cup shape is also typical of the T'ang-wang type.
Ref: KX, 1957/2, Pl. I-8 (pp. 32-33), p. 26

29. *Painted Pottery jar, white-slip-coated earthenware with slip decoration. Stone-and-Bronze period.*

The long neck, sloping shoulder, small loop-handles and the double-hook design are all typical of the Hsin-tien type. The body and decoration are somewhat crude, a sign of the general deterioration in the later part of the Painted Pottery culture. Hsin-tien succeeded the Ch'i-chia culture (*see* Pl. 27 Note).
Ref: KT, 1956/6, Pl. IV-4, p. 15

30. *Painted Pottery two-handled jar, earthenware with red slip decoration. Bronze Age.*

This beautiful jar is typical of Sha-ching type wares. The small base is flat, the body is sandy and somewhat rough, and the surface is burnished and covered with a red slip over which is painted, in a darker red, a geometric pattern. The Sha-ching culture is independent of any other Kansu cultures mentioned and is regarded as one of the last survivals of the Painted Pottery culture in this region.
Ref: KX, 1960/2, Pl. VI-11 (pp. 52-53), p. 23

31. *Spouted* kuei, *earthenware. Late Neolithic period.*

This spouted *kuei* form with hollow legs should be distinguished from the spouted, kettle-shaped *ho*. Both of these earthenware shapes are typical of the Lung-shan style. The *ho* was subsequently adopted as a bronze shape. Both the *kuei* and *ho* were used for heating and pouring liquid.

The spout shows some signs of repair, but otherwise this piece is in perfect condition. Though largely hand-modeled, the rim appears to have been turntable finished. The body is very thin (approximately three millimeters) and is of a relatively unrefined milky-white clay. The two relief lines above the legs have no known significance. The twisted-rope handle has three button-like fixings, two at the upper end and one at the lower, which look like rivets. This appears to be a comparatively late example of the Lung-shan pottery style.
Ref: KX, 1958/1, Pl. IV-1 (pp. 42-43), p. 40

32. *Black Pottery* hu, *burnished black earthenware. Neolithic period.*

This piece shows strong influence of the Shantung Lung-

shan culture. It is wheel-made, and the black body is burnished to a beautiful luster. The long neck and short body are also characteristic. It stands on a ring-foot and has vertical loops at either side of the neck through which a cord was probably threaded. It is evident that this *hu* was made after a bronze shape, and judging from its shape it could even be as late as the Yin-Chou period. However, the makers of this kind of *hu* were not yet using bronze vessels.
Ref: WTT, 1956/2, p. 25

33-35. *Black Pottery stemmed cups, burnished black earthenware. Neolithic period.*

Found in three different tombs, these pieces are all wheel-made of fine clay. The body is one to two millimeters thick, and the surface is burnished to a fine luster. The beautiful form, with variations in the design of the stem, is very unusual in Black Pottery. They were probably used as drinking goblets.

Goblets of a similar shape were produced by potters of the later Lung-shan culture during the late Neolithic and early historic period.
Ref: KX, 1959/4, Pls. IV-1, IV-3, IV-4 (pp. 30-31), p. 24

36. *Cup, earthenware with incised decoration. Neolithic period.*

This small, hand-formed cup has an oval-sectioned body. The incised design has been identified by Chinese scholars as a *t'ao-t'ieh* mask, but this seems doubtful. It seems incredible that in the Neolithic period such a symbol of the ruling classes should be used on a drinking cup for the ordinary people. A few fragments of Chou dynasty jade and bronze were found at this site, but their relationship to and relative position vis-à-vis this cup is not clear. If the cup is related, and so is in fact of the Chou period, this design might well be a faint echo of a *t'ao-t'ieh* reproduced by a craftsman from memory. It is, in any case, a very unusual and strange design. There are two holes in the base of the cup. The reason for these is not clear, and it seems unlikely that they were made during the restoration of this piece.
Ref: WTT, 1955/8, p. 83; KT, 1956/3, p. 17

37. Tou, *red earthenware. Neolithic period.*

This *tou* is hand formed, and the surface is unburnished. The disproportion of foot to bowl is characteristic of the type. The foot is decorated with pierced holes of about four centimeters in diameter cut through the body, which is about five millimeters thick. The Ch'ing-lien-kang culture, in which this type of *tou* appears, is one of the three Neolithic cultures of the Yangtse River basin. The other two are the Ch'u-chia-ling and Liang-chu cultures.
Ref: WTT, 1954/4, pp. 18, 27; 1954/9, pp. 76-77

38. *Gecko in high relief on a rough, red earthenware shard. Neolithic period.*

This fragment showing a gecko in high relief is very unusual. Perhaps inspired by seeing a gecko on the shoulder of a jar, the potter has represented it in a most realistic and lively manner. The piece is interesting as it shows a realism in the work of the early artists, and it is a masterpiece among the few examples of Yang-shao sculptural art.

Ref: *Miao-ti-kou and San-li-ch'iao*, Pl. XXXVIII-2, p. 42, Institute of Archaeology, Academia Sinica, Peking, 1959

39. *Horned owl mask, earthenware. Neolithic period.*

No information is available about the back of this piece, so that it is not possible to judge the use of such a modeled mask. The two holes appear to have held feather tufts like those seen on the horned owl. The expression also quite vividly suggests this bird. Chinese authorities have identified it as a hawk, but the expression and the evidence of the tufts seem to point much more to its being an owl. This is another example of the sculptural technique and skill of the Yang-shao craftsmen.
Ref: K, 1959/11, Pl. VIII-3

40. *Human mask, coarse earthenware shard. Neolithic period.*

A surface find, the left ear of this mask is missing. The wry expression of the face is simply yet effectively achieved with the modeling of the drooping eyes and curved mouth. The purpose of the projection above the right eye is not evident. This is an unusual example of Yang-shao art, and will be valuable material in anthropological studies.
Ref: K, 1959/11, Pl. VIII-1 p. 589

41. Chüeh, *bronze. Yin dynasty.*

The *chüeh*, a three-legged vessel used for heating liquids, is characterized by the spout, the raised point at the rear, the posts on either side of the spout, and the handle, always to the right of the spout. However, this example is peculiar in its elliptical body and the thin, crude casting. Also notable are the exceptionally small posts and the spindly legs set at the edge of the flat base. The *t'ao-t'ieh*, which is on the side opposite the handle, and thus not shown in the photograph, is in thread relief and surprisingly simple. Many of the distinctive characteristics of this class of bronzes can also be seen in Plate 42. Very little is known about the dating of such pieces, and there are two conflicting theories. One theory regards this group of thinly cast, somewhat crude pieces as prototypes of the classic bronzes, and so dates them in the middle Yin dynasty. The other theory, regarding the crudeness of technique as indicating degeneration, dates them in the late Yin dynasty or even early Western Chou.
Ref: *Excavations at Hui District*, Pl. XIII-4, p. 24, Institute of Archaeology, Academia Sinica, Peking, 1956

42. Chia, *bronze. Yin dynasty.*

A *chia* was also used for heating liquids and is similar to the *chüeh* except that it has a simple flaring lip with no spout or raised point at the rear. The posts on the lip have spreading caps, and the handle, of triangular section, is comparatively thin. The legs, which are rhomboid in section, are hollow, and open into the base. The base is flat, another typical feature of this class (discussed in the note to Plate 41). The decoration is in two registers and comprises one band with *k'uei-lung* motif and one of six simple circle motifs. It is thought that this piece was used, since it shows signs of burning on the outside and there is a whitish deposit on the inside.
Ref: WTT, 1955/10, pp. 29, 34; KX, 1957/1, Pl. III-3 (pp. 74-75), p. 71

43. Tsun, *bronze. Yin dynasty.*

The most striking feature of this beautifully cast *tsun* is the design of the double-bodied tiger biting the head of a man, which may represent a devil harmful to human beings. Although this motif is not uncommon on bronzes of this period, the representation of the tiger is unusually realistic and marks this as an exceptional piece.
Ref: W, 1959/1, both sides of the cover

44. *Chime, stone. Yin dynasty.*

This chime was found on the west side of a tomb coffin chamber. Made of a bluish-white stone, it is one of the oldest known musical instruments of China. In use it would be suspended by a cord threaded through the hole, and be struck with a hammer. The open-mouthed animal is somewhat like a tiger (*see* Plate 43) with the eyes of a *t'ao-t'ieh.* The surface decoration on the body of the animal is very similar to the decorative motifs found on the contemporary bronzes.
Ref: *Chung-kuo K'ao-ku Hsüeh-pao,* V, Pl. VIII (pp. 62-63), p. 25

45. *Rectangular* ting *with human mask decoration, bronze. Late Yin dynasty.*

This *ting* was found among scrap metal in Ch'ang-sha in 1959. It was subsequently discovered that it had been recently dug up in Ning-hsiang District, some forty kilometers west of the city. The striking similarity of style between this piece and the Ssu Mu Wu *ting* (Pls. 9, 10) has led to dating this piece also in the late Yin dynasty. A rectangular *ting* with very slightly sloping sides, this piece has striking human masks in relief on each side panel. The features are modeled quite realistically, with protruding cheekbones and lips, while the ears are represented by stylized motifs to either side of the face. The reason for the modeling of this mask is unclear, but its features may be of some anthropological interest.
Ref: W, 1960/10, Cover, pp. 57-59

46. Li, *bronze. Yin dynasty.*

The *li,* a vessel with hollow, udder-like legs, was used for heating liquids, sometimes forming the lower part of a steamer for grain. This piece appears at first glance to be a *ting,* but since the legs are hollow, it must be regarded as a *li,* although an unusual one. Below the rim, the band of decoration is composed of three *t'ao-t'ieh* motif units, which have been dissolved to such an extent that the eyes alone are discernible. Two ears stand atop the rim, one directly above one leg, and the other midway between two legs. A raised, parallel-line design forms a zigzag pattern from a point beneath the two eyes to the joint of the legs.
Ref: *Excavations at Hui District,* Pl. XIV-1, pp. 23-24, Institute of Archaeology, Academia Sinica, Peking, 1956

47. Chih, *bronze. Yin dynasty.*

A *chih* is a wine vessel. It is somewhat similar to the *ku* (*see* Pl. 48), but is shorter, with a swelling body. This *chih* is elliptical in section, and the body is decorated in three registers. The main section is covered by a large *t'ao-t'ieh* design, while the bands around the neck and the foot-ring bear designs of *k'uei-lung* and *k'uei-feng* respectively. In each of these bands a cicada-like motif appears between the animals.
Ref: *Illustrated Catalogue of the Exhibition of the Cultural Relics Unearthed in the Course of Basic Constructions Throughout the Country,* Pl. LV, Peking, 1954

48. Ku, *bronze. Yin dynasty.*

A *ku* is a wine goblet with a wide flaring mouth and also a flaring, tall foot. This is a tall, slender example of the most highly developed *ku* of the late Yin dynasty. The surface decoration is in three sections. The outer surface of the trumpet mouth is decorated with four spear-like shapes filled with minute thunder-scroll. The lower two registers are divided by four vertical flanges. The middle register is decorated with *t'ao-t'ieh* motifs and the lower with a narrow band of *hui-lung* above another *t'ao-t'ieh.* There is a pictorial inscription inside the hollow foot that shows a horse and a man carrying a halberd on his shoulder.
Ref: KX, IX, Pl. IX (pp. 90-91), pp. 48-49

49. Hu, *burnished earthenware with impressed design. Yin dynasty.*

This is a very beautiful wheel-made pot, the surface of which has been highly burnished. The band of *t'ao-t'ieh* design just below the shoulder is similar to that found on bronzes of this period. It has been impressed into the clay, probably using a clay mold similar to those found at Ch'eng-chou. Next to the White Ware (*see* Pl. 7), this type of earthenware is the most elaborate, and is thought to have been intended for the use of the ruling class.
Ref: KX, 1957/1, Pl. II-7 (pp. 74-75), p. 61

50. Tsun, *earthenware with yellowish-green glaze. Yin dynasty.*

This handsomely potted *tsun* has a finely shaped rim and shoulder and a small, flat base. It is a relatively high-fired piece and is hard-bodied and heavy. The body and base of the pot are covered with an impressed pattern, presumably made by striking a piece of wood (on which the crisscross design is carved) against the side of the vessel. This was one of the most primitive ways of making impressed designs. The whole surface is coated with a yellowish-green glaze. This is unquestionably an intentionally applied glaze, and not a fortuitous ash glaze. It is the earliest piece of glazed earthenware found in China to date and as such is of the greatest interest.
Ref: *Erh-li-kang, Cheng-chou,* Pl. X-6, p. 30, The Institute of Archaeology, Academia Sinica, Peking, 1959; K, 1960/8, Pl. X-6, p. 27

51. *Three-legged* ting, *gray earthenware. Yin dynasty.*

The clay of this piece is not very fine and has a considerable amount of white sand mixed with it. It was fired at a rather high temperature, resulting in a very hard surface and a bluish-gray color. The piece is small-mouthed, round-shouldered, and deep-bellied, and is covered all over with a twisted-rope design. The legs are of a flat, triangular shape and carry four rows of twisted-rope pattern in the shape of a "V" on both sides. The outermost of these lines forms a vertical ridge on the wall of the vessel. The piece is perfectly preserved and is extremely rare in shape and design.

Ref: KX, 1960/1, Pl. VII-1 (pp. 50-51), pp. 43-44

52. *Three-legged* ting, *bronze. Early Western Chou dynasty.*

This *ting* weighs almost one hundred kilograms and is the largest bronze found in Shensi recently. The band of *k'uei-lung* motifs forms a variant of the *t'ao-t'ieh*, and another variant is also seen on the legs. The outer surface of each lug-handle is decorated with realistically represented tiger motifs. A six-character inscription on the inner surface of the rim reads: 外叔乍宝尊彝. As this piece is very similar to the famous *yü ting* of the K'ang Wang reign (excavated in Shensi before 1900) it is regarded as being of the early Western Chou period.
Ref: W, 1959/10, pp. 84-85

53. Lei, *bronze. Middle Western Chou dynasty.*

A *lei*, shaped very much like a *hu* but with two ring-loop handles, was used for storage of liquids. The decoration, in three main registers, is composed of attenuated *k'uei-lung* and *k'uei-feng* motifs with whorl pattern, and the background is filled with thunder-scroll. There is a fourteen-character inscription, arranged in three lines, within the rim. It reads: 繁作且己□尊彝、其子々□孫々永宝。戈
Ref: KX, 1957/1, Pl. II-2 (pp. 86-87), pp. 78-79, 81

54. *The Marquis of Yen* yü, *bronze. Western Chou dynasty*

With a slightly everted lip, two loop-handles and a deep foot-ring, the whole surface of this *yü* is decorated with very beautifully engraved *k'uei-feng* motifs. The five-character inscription in the base reads: 匽侯作餴盂 ("Rice bowl made by Marquis of Yen"). The character 匽 is used for 燕, and 餴 is used for 飯. Although a *yü* is usually regarded as a vessel for liquid, this example would seem to have been used for cooked grain. Sixteen pieces of bronze were found at this site, including two unfortunately destroyed during excavation.
Ref: WTT, 1955/8, pp. 21, 27

55. *Covered* hu, *unglazed earthenware. Western Chou dynasty.*

This pot is made very close to a bronze shape. It has a long neck, a potbelly and a tall, everted foot-ring. The decoration around the neck, between the small ear-handles, is an incised, wide zigzag, and the background is filled with simple, incised vertical lines. The body of the piece is decorated with bold, horizontal grooves. The bottom of the cover is made to fit in the mouth of the jar, and the top is a handle in the form of an inverted foot-ring.
Ref: *Excavations at Feng-hsi (1955-1957)*, Pl. LXXIII-2, p. 125, The Institute of Archaeology, Academia Sinica, Peking, 1963

56. *Covered* ting, *bronze. Ch'un Ch'iu period.*

Although this was excavated in a Ch'un Ch'iu tomb, it is very close to the style of the Warring States. The cover, with three small ring-handles, has a large whorl medallion in the center surrounded by three concentric rings of decoration. The inner of these is of thunder-scroll and the outer two of intertwined-dragon patterns. The decoration of the body does not match this: it is divided by a double-twisted-rope relief into two main zones, each decorated with an interlacing thunder-scroll pattern. The surfaces of the lug-handles are decorated with triangular spiral and twisted-rope-spiral (絡縄渦文) motifs. The legs, which are much damaged, are made of a copper-lead alloy quite different from that of the body. They appear to be a later repair. The carbon on the outer surface of the base indicates that this piece had been in everyday use.
Ref: *Chung-chou-lu, Lo-yang*, Pl. LVIII-1, pp. 89, 92, The Institute of Archaeology, Academia Sinica, Peking, 1959

57. *Marquis of Ts'ai* hu, *bronze. Late Ch'un Ch'iu period.*

The shape of this piece shows a complex movement from the rectangular foot to the rounded body and then to the rectangular neck and mouth. The openwork petal-shaped coronet on the cover, and the elaborate animal handles with thin, swinging ring-loops, and the four animal feet add further elaboration, making this a very distinctive piece. The body, divided by horizontal and vertical relief strips, is decorated with a minute intertwined-dragon pattern. A six-character inscription inside the neck is thought to read: 蔡侯龖之□□ (*see* Plate 13 Note). This piece and those discovered at Hsin-cheng District, Honan, are all typical in style of the late Ch'un Ch'iu period.
Ref: *Relics Unearthed from the Tomb of the Marquis of Ts'ai at Shou District*, Pl. VII, VIII, p. 8, The Institute of Archaeology, Academia Sinica, Peking, 1956

58. Ting, *bronze. Ch'un Ch'iu period.*

The sixty-five bronze *ting* excavated at this site have been classified into eight large categories. The example comes within the category IV-A. It is typified by the hemispherical body, ears standing on the rim, and slightly cabriole legs. The decoration is in two registers, the upper band in scrolls derived from *k'uei* forms. The decoration of the lower part of the body is a band of spiral variant (渦状) consisting of somewhat dissolved animal motifs (獣帯文).
Ref: *The Cemetery of the State of Kuo at Shang-ts'un-ling*, Pl. LVIII-1, p. 13, The Institute of Archaeology, Academia Sinica, Peking, 1959

59. Chung, *bronze. Western Chou dynasty.*

Two molds have been used in casting this bell, the cross section of which is a pointed oval. The cylindrical handle is hollow, the cavity continuing into the bell itself. There is a swelling in the handle, but no ring to suspend the bell. The decoration on the handle is cloud-thunder scroll and hook variant (鈎状文) patterns, while two protruding knobs suggest the eyes of an animal mask. The main body of the bell is covered with a very fine cloud-thunder scroll and by thirty-six protruding nipples. The tone of the bell could be adjusted by scraping these down. The thickened, rectangular shape at the lip of the bell is the striking area. This is a typical example of fine bronze work of the first half of the Western Chou dynasty.
Ref: W. 1960/7, pp. 48-49

60. Yi, *bronze. Ch'un Ch'iu period.*

The *yi*, which is a water pouring vessel used in the washing of hands, seems to be very similar to the *kuang* (*see* Pl. 66). The handle is animal-headed and the legs are also in animal form. The decoration consists of a band of overlapping

scale pattern around the rim and a horizontally ribbed body. This well-proportioned *yi* seems to follow closely the style of the bronzes of the Western Chou.
Ref: *The Cemetery of the State of Kuo at Shang-ts'un-ling*, Pl. XVII-3, pp. 14, 18-19, The Institute of Archaeology, Academia Sinica, Peking, 1959

61. *Covered* ling, *bronze. Ch'un Ch'iu period.*

The *ling* is a liquid container very similar to the *hu*. It typically has a narrow neck, swelling body and flattened base. This unusual piece has a cover and two animal loop-handles with dependent rings. The cover is in the form of a wide-mouthed cup placed upside down on the mouth of the vessel. The whole outer surface is decorated with horizontal grooves.
Ref: *Selected Pieces from the Relics Discovered in Shantung Province: General Survey*, p. 43, The Shantung Province Bureau for the Superintendence of Cultural Properties and the Shantung Province Museum, Peking, 1959

62. P'an, *bronze. Ch'un Ch'iu period.*

The *p'an* is usually considered to be a water container. This example has a band of fish motifs running around the inside of the rim, while the inner surface of the basin is filled with a large, coiled, dragon design. Outside, the sides of the basin are decorated with oblique cloud-scrolls. The tall foot is pierced by four rectangular holes. The *p'an* first appeared as a bronze vessel in the late Yin dynasty. At that time it was rather tall in proportion to its width and had no ear-handles. Later it became gradually wider and lower, and the ear-handles were added. This form became complete in the later Western Chou period.
Ref: *The Cemetery of the State of Kuo at Shang-ts'un-ling*, Pl. XVIII, p. 18, The Institute of Archaeology, Academia Sinica, Peking, 1959

63. *Covered jar, gray earthenware. Ch'un Ch'iu period.*

This wide, squat jar appears heavy. It is unusual in that it has a cover, which is in the form of a footed cup with a slightly inverted mouth, fitting upside down in the mouth of the jar. The shoulder of the jar has an incised double zigzag decoration very similar to that used on Yin dynasty gray wares. This piece also appears to be gray ware, but there is no information on the firing.
Ref: *Ibid.*, Pl. VI-1, pp. 8, 10

64. T'an, *glazed earthenware with impressed design. Ch'un Ch'iu period.*

A *t'an* is a wine jar. This one appears to have originally had a cover, to judge by the groove around the neck. The body is covered with a feather pattern in eight horizontal bands. This has been impressed, and mistakes and erasures have been corrected so that the overall effect is uneven. The whole piece is glazed, although there is no indication of the color. This piece comes within the category of "impressed, hard earthenware."
Ref: KT, 1957/3, Pl. 4

65. *Horse-shaped* tsun, *bronze. Western Chou dynasty.*

This horse-shaped vessel was intended to hold liquid, and has a covered opening on the back. There seem to have been a pair of these horses, but unfortunately only the cover of the other one has been found. The animal is realistically modeled, and is decorated with a medallion containing scroll motifs on either side. The cover and chest of the horse bear a long inscription. This records the granting of two horses by the king to a high-ranking official named Lu. The date is generally accepted as being during the reign of Yi Wang (934-909 B.C.). Two *tsun* were made to commemorate this honor. The realism of the representation is unusual for this early period and resembles the Warring States horse found at Chin-ts'un, Lo-yang.
Ref: KX, 1957/2, Pl. I-1 (pp. 6-7), pp. 1-4; WTT, 1957/4, p. 5

66. *Covered* ssu kuang, *bronze. Early Western Chou dynasty.*

This is one of the group of twelve bronze pieces found at the foot of Yen-tun Mountain. These objects are an important indication of the extension of the early Western Chou power as far south as the Chiang-nan region. The *ssu kuang* is so called because it was originally made of horn, reputed to be the horn of the *ssu*. This creature is described as a one-horned, bovine animal, the female of the *hsi* (犀), which is today the name used for the rhinoceros. Such drinking vessels as the *ku*, *chih* and *kuang* were all first made in horn and later produced in bronze.

This piece in the form of a buffalo has a cover on the back and a loop-handle at the rear. The upper part of the body of the vessel is decorated with a large *k'uei-feng* design. This is regarded as an example of the comparatively degenerate form of the *ssu kuang*.
Ref: WTT, 1955/5, p. 60; KX, 1956/2, Pl. IV (pp. 94-95)

67-68. *Animal-shaped* tou, *bronze. Ch'un Ch'iu period.*

This is an unusual *tou* placed on the back of an animal. It is a humorous piece, and no comparable examples have been found. The lip of the *tou* is inverted, and the curved surface of the cup is decorated with a variant of animal pattern in the form of oblique cloud-scroll in rectangular units. The whole of the body surface is decorated with thunder-scroll and scale pattern. The general appearance of this cup, with its thick base, suggests the Yin-Chou style. The animal is hollow, the base of the feet being open. It may represent a rabbit-like creature, with its long ears.
Ref: *The Cemetery of the State of Kuo at Shang-ts'un-ling*, Pl. XLIII-1, XLIII-2, pp. 16, 18, The Institute of Archaeology, Academia Sinica, Peking, 1959

69. *Male figure, jade. Western Chou dynasty.*

This small piece is quite flat-backed, but carved in the round at the front; the whole figure tapers away from the large head. The two projections on the head are probably topknots of hair. The hair itself is indicated by incised lines, and is cut straight and short at the back. Judging by the thick eyebrows and large features, this is thought to be the figure of a man. The broad-edged garment is worn wrapped around, with the left side over the right, and tied around the waist with a narrow sash. There seems to be an indication of an apron worn in front. This unusual jade carving is of great interest in the observation of the manners and costume of the time. There is no indication of the quality or color of the jade.
Ref: K, 1959/4, Pl. IV-1-3, p. 188

70. *Necklace, stone and jade. Ch'un Ch'iu period.*

Four ring-shaped ornaments were found in one tomb: three on the corpse and one on the coffin. This circlet was found at the neck and so may safely be regarded as a necklace. It consists of 101 beads of a "chicken's-blood stone" and ten hoof-shaped stone beads, one oblong jade bead and two other stone ornaments. It would seem that the "chicken's-blood stone" of the report refers to a red agate. This red makes a fine color contrast with the white stone and jade beads.
Ref: *The Cemetery of the State of Kuo at Shang-ts'un-ling*, Pl. I; pp. 37-41, The Institute of Archaeology, Academia Sinica, Peking, 1959

71. *Ornaments, stone and jade. Ch'un Ch'iu period.*

The upper row shows a serpentine dragon on the left and a double-headed animal ornament on the right.
Ref: *Ibid.*, Pls. XXIX-6-8, 11, p. 22

72. *Ornaments, stone and jade. Ch'un Ch'iu period.*

The four small split rings in the upper row are *chüeh.* These are similar to *pi*, but are distinguished by the small opening in the ring. Some 290 such *chüeh* were found in this tomb. They can be classified into three broad categories: a) simple and flat (as the center two); b) flat but with a small hole drilled in the ring (as in the first and fourth); c) cylindrical. The flat ones are not quite even in section, and the surface may be decorated as in the second from the right. As the majority have been found either by the ears of the corpse or close to the head, these rings are thought to have been earrings. They closely resemble the Japanese Jōmon period ear ornaments. Of course, the Japanese ones considerably predate these Chinese examples, and there is no known relationship between them.
Ref: *Ibid.*, Pls. XXIX-1-5, 9, 10, 12, pp. 22-23

73. *Mirror, bronze. Ch'un Ch'iu period.*

This mirror was found to the right side of the legs of an encoffined corpse. Two other mirrors found in another tomb at this site had no decoration. The three together are extremely important as the oldest mirrors yet discovered in China. A flat, circular bronze with a knob on one side was reported before 1937, found at Hou-chia-chuang, An-yang, Honan, but there is no further information to identify this as a mirror. The present example is quite flat, with a pair of arching loops. The decoration around these loops is of two tigers, a deer and a bird. The technique is archaic, and the design different both from the bronze vessels of the period and from the mirrors of the Warring States.
Ref: *Ibid.*, Pl. XL-2, p. 27

74. *Relief, "replica" mold for bronze casting, earthenware. Late Ch'un Ch'iu or early Warring States period.*

This figure with hands raised wears a long robe wrapped right over left. The robe is tied around the waist with a narrow sash, the ends being held behind the knot. The robe has a striped pattern of triangular cloud-scroll. A crescent-shaped headdress hides the hair, but judging from the gentle expression and long skirt, this is presumed to be the figure of a woman.
Ref: W, 1960/8, 9, pp. 7, 14

75. *Relief, "replica" mold for bronze casting, earthenware. Late Ch'un Ch'iu or early Warring States period.*

This figure with its arms raised also wears a short robe, folded right over left and tied at the waist with a narrow sash. The robe is decorated with a thunder-scroll design. The legs appear to be uncovered. A cap on the head is indicated by a band of vertical lines. Possibly this represents the figure of a man.
Ref: *Ibid.*

76. *Relief, "replica" mold for bronze casting, earthenware. Late Ch'un Ch'iu or early Warring States period.*

This pair, forming a semicircular shape, is carved in very fine relief. The two creatures with serpents in their mouth are cleanly carved and form a strong composition. The bodies of the animals are entirely covered with minute scale, feather, thunder-scroll and spiral patterns. These, though replica molds, are very fine works of art in themselves.
Ref: *Ibid.*, pp. 8, 14; W, 1962/4, pp. 6, 37-42

77. Hu, *bronze with cast decoration. Warring States period. (same as Plate 23;* see *note)*

b) This banqueting scene is chiefly of interest for the construction of the stand of the musical instruments.
c) This part of the neck of the vessel shows mulberry leaf picking and, in the lower part, a hunting scene. In the upper right-hand corner of the picture, just above the dividing line, there seems to be a sheaf of straw used as an archery target. The hunting scene shows archers shooting a goose-like bird, apparently using the method known as *chiao* (繳) whereby a line is attached to the arrow. There are fish in the pool.
d) The water battle here seen about to commence shows two warships with men rowing and four men armed with lance and halberd. In the water three men are swimming among turtles and fish.
Ref: Yang Tsung-jung. *Painting Materials of the Warring States Period*, Pl. XX, p. 7, Peking, 1957; WTT, 1957/9, Color Plate, pp. 21, 26; 1958/1, pp. 21, 26-27

78. *Fragments of a bronze vessel thought to be a* chien. *Warring States period.*

These fragments are displayed in the Palace Museum, Peking. They appear to be parts of a water container known as a *chien*, but it is impossible to reconstruct it. Stylistically, the decoration is very close to the Warring States piece shown in Pl. 23, and so this is regarded as being of similar date. The very delicately drawn, fine-line engraved decoration on the inner surface depicts a building, horses and carriages, humans and animals, birds and plants. It is of special interest that the carriages already have four wheels. Warring States bronze vessels with similar decoration engraved in a fine line have been found at Ch'ang-ch'ih Municipality, Shansi and at Hui District, Honan.
Ref: W, 1962/2, pp. 3-4, 52

79. *Circular stand with tiger-shaped legs, bronze. Warring States period.*

This is one of many unusual bronze objects found in Warring States tombs. Though it is clearly a stand, its exact purpose is not known. It is in the form of an openwork floral disc supported by four strongly modeled

tigers. The tigers stand on their hind legs and rest their forepaws on the disc. There are four frogs in relief in the center of the disc. This is a masterly work, particularly in the modeling of the tigers.
Ref: WTT, 1958/11, front inside cover, p. 78

80. *Openwork ornament, bronze. Early Warring States period.*

One of two similar pieces excavated from a tomb said to be of the Warring States period, this disc, with four loop-ears around the edge, has a crosswise trace of wood across the back. The use of such pieces is unknown. There is a band of cowrie decoration around the rim. The curious central openwork design shows a scaly dragon-like creature holding naked human figures in its forepaws and serpentine creatures with its hind legs. The large feathers to either side seem to belong to the dragon. Mr. Minao Hayashi has put forward the theory that the dragon is grasping devils and snakes, both of which are harmful to human beings.
Ref: *Chung-chou-lu, Lo-yang*, Pl. LXIX-1, p. 105, The Institute of Archaeology, Academia Sinica, Peking, 1956

81. Lien, *bronze. Warring States period.*

Although the term *lien* usually refers to a container for mirrors or cosmetics, this bucket-shaped openwork piece appears to be a brazier of some sort. It has a rim slightly wider than the base, which is also of openwork, and stands on three legs. The rendering and design of the sides is very beautiful. The cloud-dragon scroll design is comprised of one vertical unit repeated five times around the piece.
Ref: WTT, 1958/1, p. 12

82. *Mirror with quatrefoil decoration, bronze. Warring States period.*

The mirrors shown in Plates 82, 84-86 are typical of the Warring States mirrors from Ch'ang-sha. They are thin and flat with a curved rim, and the central loop, except in Plate 86, is small.

A quatrefoil motif within a broken diamond forms the unit of this decoration. The background surface is covered by a feather-like animal pattern (羽状獣文) in very fine relief, which makes a sharp contrast with the bold lines of the upper motifs. The surface is almost free of verdigris, making the mirror look very fresh and bright.
Ref: KX, 1959/1, Pl. VI-4 (pp. 60-61), p. 50

83. *Mirror with multiple loop-handles, bronze. Warring States period.*

Five such mirrors were found at this site; two each in tombs 1 and 2 and one from tomb No. 3. The present piece is the one from tomb No. 3. It is fairly thick and quite flat, with a line of three loop-handles off-center on the back. The geometric decoration is carried out in simple thread relief lines on the surface. These mirrors are of very much the same type as those found in Liaotung, the Siberian coastal region, Korea and western Japan; indeed these Liaoning pieces might be the prototype of the widely spread northern finds.
Ref: KX, 1960/1, Pl. VI-2 (pp. 72-73), p. 70

84. *Mirror with* shan *pattern, bronze. Warring States period.*

The design on this mirror is known in China as either the *shan* (山) or "reversed *ting*" (丁) pattern. There is no established theory of the meaning of the design. The background is covered with feather-like animal pattern, and the small knob is in a square seat that has a simple leaf embellishment at each angle.
Ref: KX, 1959/1, Pl. VI-6 (pp. 60-61), p. 50

85. *Mirror, bronze. Warring States period.*

A wide, plain square offset for the small loop has a single leaf motif in the center of each side. The remainder of the surface of the mirror is covered with feather-like animal pattern, which is very similar to that used on bronze vessels of this period. Careful analysis shows that it consists of a single repeated unit.
Ref: *Ibid.*, Pl. VI-2 (pp. 60-61), p. 50

86. *Mirror with hemispherical, openwork knob and intertwined-dragon pattern, bronze. Late Warring States period.*

This mirror has a large hemispherical knob that is decorated with an elaborate openwork design. The background of the main field of the mirror is covered with a form of cloud-thunder scroll made up of minute spirals, dots and lines. The main pattern over this is an intertwined-dragon pattern of beautiful curved lines. Mirrors of this kind with such refined decoration may sometimes have an inscription in Former Han style script. For this reason they are thought to be of the last phase of the Warring States style.
Ref: *Ibid.*, Pl. VII-5 (pp. 60-61), p. 50

87. Ho, *earthenware with slip decoration. Warring States period.*

The *ho* was a vessel in which wine and water were mixed and heated. A typical *ho* has a spout at the front, a loop-handle at the back, and stands on three or four legs. This example is unusual in that it has a large strap-handle over the top, and for this reason some authorities have called it a *chiao.* Since bronze *ho* were made at this period, it is thought that the ceramic version is a replica of the metal shape. The spout and legs are both of animal form. The cover is decorated with circles, the neck with S-shaped designs, and the whole body is covered with a scale pattern. No indication is given of the color of this piece.
Ref: W, 1959/9, pp. 67, 69

88. *Jar, unglazed earthenware with impressed design. Warring States period.*

This piece belongs to the category of "impressed hard earthenware." The short, rounded shape, termed a *p'ou* (瓿) stands on a foot-ring. Although the clay is rough and unrefined, it has been fired very hard. The body surface is decorated with an impressed "stepped" design applied with a carved wooden or earthenware beater on the coil-built piece. The effect is both to bind the clay and make a clear design. It is perhaps the simplest and most effective method of making an impressed decoration.
Ref: KX, 1958/1, Pl. III-1 (pp. 86-87), p. 80

89. *Covered* ting, *dark-gray earthenware with "graphite" decoration. Warring States period.*

The earthenware *ting* excavated at this site have been classified in nine categories, of which this piece is an example of type I. The very dark-gray body has been burnished to leave a so-called graphite decoration of triangular, spiral variant, wave variant and S-shaped motifs on the cover, ears and rim. This effect is produced by a burnishing of the surface with a spatula before the body is quite dry. After firing, the burnished surface thickens in color and turns shiny. This class of ware was probably made specifically for burial.

Ref: *Erh-li-kang, Cheng-chou*, Pl. XXI-1, p. 58, The Institute of Archaeology, Academia Sinica, Peking, 1959

90. *Details of the engraved decoration on a lacquered* lien. *Warring States period.*

These are parts of a lacquered *lien* decorated with a very fine-line, needle-engraved design. Tigers, deer-like animals, and waterfowl are depicted among cloud-spirals. The vivid drawing of the animals and the fluent, fine line of the scrolls show admirably the light and lively quality typical of the painting of the Warring States period.

Ref: *Illustrated Catalogue of the Exhibition of the Relics of the State of Ch'u*, pp. 19-20, The Peking Historical Museum, Peking, 1954; Yang Tsung-ying. *Painting Materials of the Warring States Period*, Pls. XV-1, XV-2, Peking, 1957; WTT, 1967/7, pp. 50-51

91. *Tiger-headed waterspout, earthenware. Warring States period.*

This water or drainage pipe may have been used in a palace building. In the form of a tiger-like animal, the body is thinned to make the connecting joint. The lighthearted treatment of this animal contrasts with the *t'ao-t'ieh* of the eave end-tile (*see* Pl. 95).

Ref: W, 1959/10, pp. 5, 12; K, 1962/1, Pl. VI-1, p. 15

92-94. *Semicircular eave end-tiles, earthenware. Warring States period.*

92) This is a strange design, since the "eyes" are so emphatic it is thought to represent a much simplified *t'ao-t'ieh*. This motif was first used in the decoration of tiles in the Yen state, so that this piece from the Lo-yang area must be in some way related. However, this relationship need not be very direct, since *t'ao-t'ieh* motifs are present also in the tile decorations of the Ch'i and Lu states.

Ref: *Chung-chou-lu, Lo-yang*, Pl. XVIII-14, p. 33, The Institute of Archaeology, Academia Sinica, Peking, 1965

93) The identification of these confronted writhing animals as dragons is supported by the bronze dragon found near Lao-mu-t'ai at the site of Yen-hsia-tu. This powerful and lively design is among the best examples of eave end-tiles of the Yen state.

Ref: KX, 1957/6, Pl. V-3, p. 25

94) It is difficult to understand what this represents. The design itself would probably not be assigned to the Warring States period. The report says, "It is composed of one complete cartouche and two half cartouches." A cartouche is an animal-shaped metal seat on a bronze vessel on which is attached a ring-handle. Looking at this tile with this in mind, elements corresponding to eyes, ears, and a nose can be found, suggesting an animal head. But when it is compared to other designs, it would seem better to take it as an extremely dissolved *t'ao-t'ieh*.

Ref: *Chung-chou-lu, Lo-yang*, Pl. XVII-4, p. 32, The Institute of Archaeology, Academia Sinica, Peking, 1956

95-97. *Semicircular eave end-tiles, earthenware. Warring States period.*

95) The *t'ao-t'ieh* was the most popular decoration for eave end-tiles in the Yen state. In this very handsome example, the mask is surmounted by two confronted animals. This addition, probably an adaptation to fit the semicircular space, is quite successful.

Ref: KX, 1957/6, Pl. III-1, p. 23

96) The stepped design called in Chinese *yün-shan-wen* (雲山文) is a variant of the classic *fu-wen* (黼文). This is a design based on an ax motif and associated with official insignia. The present version of this motif is an extended form of one element. It is sometimes also known by the expressive term, "motif in the shape of the character *t'u*" (凸字様文). The *fu-wen* was a favorite motif in the decoration of flat and curved tiles of the Yen state.

Ref: *Ibid.*, Pl. VII-4, p. 26

97) The decorating of flat and curved tiles apparently was peculiar to the Yen state. The *fu-fu-wen* (黼黻文) derives from a double decorative device more usually associated with very formal embroidery in black, white and blue and seen most clearly among the imperial insignia embroidered on official robes of later ages. The *fu* (黼) motif of the hatchet has been discussed in Note 96. It is shown here in the decoration of the end sections. Associated with it is the *fu* (黻) usually described as two characters, either 己 or 弓, back to back. In the present example, one of these parts is repeated three times to form the decoration of the central section, although the form is unusual in that the characters all face the same way.

Ref: K, 1962/1, Pl. VI-5, p. 15

98. *Horned animal eating a snake, carved and lacquered wood. Warring States period.*

This is a carving of a mysterious animal placed at a tomb to ward off evil spirits. The antlers are real. The creature sits like a man and grasps a snake in its hands. The huge red eyes and pointed ears seem to denote anger, and the hanging tongue is grotesque. This tongue and the antlers may have had some magic significance, as also may have had the gesture of eating a live snake.

The whole piece, the back of which is carved with spiral patterns, has been painted with black lacquer. The scale pattern covering the creature is added in three-color lacquer. It would seem that the tusk-like shapes on the thighs represent the toenails of the hind feet. This fine carving is not only a masterpiece of wood carving and lacquer painting of the period, but also is an important study piece in the consideration of the beliefs and culture of the time.

Ref: WTT, 1957/9, Color Plate, p. 22

99. Lien, *black and red lacquer. Warring States period.*

After 1949, many Warring States tombs were excavated in the Ch'ang-sha area. This *lien* is a fine example of the large quantity of lacquer found in these excavations. It has gilt-bronze legs and handle, and the body is covered with black lacquer on which the design in five registers is painted in red. The first, third and fifth of these are decorated in a cloud-scroll pattern typical of the Warring States period. The second and fourth show scenes of men hunting birds and animals. The lively drawing of the running huntsman in the upper scene and the man walking with a

monkey-like creature on a leash in the lower typify the realistic style of the Warring States and give some clue to the pictorial arts of the period.
Ref: KX, 1959/1, Color Plate (pp. 60-61), Pl. XIII-3, p. 55

100. *Wooden box, black and red lacquer. Warring States period.*

This box was wrapped in a silk cloth when excavated. The surface is covered with black lacquer, and the extremely stylized phoenix design on the cover is painted in red, creating a striking color contrast. It contained an undecorated bronze mirror when excavated, with the cord through the loop-knob in good condition.
Ref: WTT, 1954/12, pp. 6, 15; KX, 1957/1, Pl. II-5 (pp. 102-103), p. 94

101. *Twenty-five-stringed* se, *wood with lacquered end sections. Warring States period.*

Although no details are given of this *se* (瑟), the description of a similar one found in tomb No. 1 at this site explains the structure. It is made of one piece of wood, the two end sections of which are decorated with lacquer painting, while the center is left quite bare. Seventeen bridges remain, but originally there were twenty-five, one for each string. These strings were gathered on four pegs at one end and then on two fittings on the underside of the instrument. The bridges stand on two legs and have a small nick to carry the string. The pegs have octagonal heads and fit firmly into square holes. This piece is very similar to the *se* found at Ch'ang-sha, differing only in the pegs.
Ref: KT, 1958/11, Pl. X-1, p. 80

102. *Inner surface of leather shield, red, yellow and black lacquer. Warring States period.*

This is one of two shields excavated in Ch'u state tombs. It is lacquered black on both sides with complex decoration in red and yellow. This beautifully decorated piece seems too sumptuous to have been for practical use, and so is thought to have been for ceremonial use in dancing or processional rites.
Ref: *Excavations at Ch'ang-sha*, Color Plate II, pp. 57-58, The Institute of Archaeology, Academia Sinica, Peking, 1957

103-104. *Armrest, carved lacquer. Warring States period.*

This piece has been identified as a table, but I regard the curved surface as making this possibility unlikely. The height is just right for an armrest for a man sitting on a thick cushion, and the widening at the center makes it comfortable for that use. The top is decorated with a beautiful, carved cloud-scroll pattern, and the four simple strut legs at either end are typical of both tables and armrests of the period. This very beautifully made and decorated piece of furniture suggests the elegant life of the period.
Ref: WTT, 1957/9, Cover, p. 22

105. *Phoenixes, lacquered wood. Warring States period.*

The two birds are removable, the legs fitting into holes on the shoulders of the animals on which they stand. It appears that each bird has been carved in three parts: head, body and wings. A mortise joint is visible on the back of the birds. In contrast to the formalism of the animals, the birds, with heads held high and holding "pearls" in the beaks, are quite realistically carved. The piece has been entirely lacquered black and the design in red and possibly yellow painted over it. The purpose of this piece is unknown, but by comparison with other similar animal pieces, it can be presumed to be a stand (*see* Pl. 19).
Ref: KT, 1958/11, Pl. IV, p. 80; W, 1963/2, pp. 10-12; 1964/9, pp. 23-26

106. *Table, lacquered wood. Warring States period.*

This table is preserved in almost perfect condition. Only the four legs are separated. The whole piece is lacquered black, the edge is decorated with a form of spiral design, and the whorl medallions on the top are a late form of cloud-scroll. No information is given on the color, but it is assumed that the decoration is in red.
Ref: *Illustrated Catalogue of the Exhibition of the Relics of the State of Ch'u*, p. 16, The Peking Historical Museum, Peking, 1954

107. *Openwork panel, wood. Warring States period.*

This is an example of the carved wooden panels found under the coffin in many tombs in the Ch'ang-sha area. This very handsome design of interlacing strips and rings, incorporating six sheep-like heads, is one of the finest pieces of wood carving of the period.
Ref: WTT, 1954/3, pp. 53-54; KX, 1957/1, Pl. IV-3 (pp. 102-103), p. 100

108. *Set of thirteen bells, bronze. Warring States period.*

Although the bells were in almost perfect condition when they were excavated, the rack shown here has been reconstructed. The thirteen bells are graded in size and musical tone. There seems some possibility that the complete set would have included one more bell between numbers twelve and thirteen; this theory is supported by a tonal interval between these two bells that is inconsistent with the scale produced by the others. However, an inscribed bamboo slip found in this tomb reads: "one musical instrument, chime of thirteen bells" (楽人之器一架□首鐘少大十又三), thus confirming that, at least at the time of burial, the chime consisted of thirteen bells only. The form of the bell is typical of the period. The rack is lacquered black and both painted and carved in spirals and triangular thunder-scroll motifs, and the bells hang on copper animal-mask hooks. Two wooden hammers were found with this chime, and the well-preserved one is shown. This is of the greatest interest, since it shows quite unquestionably the method by which such chimes were sounded.
Ref: WTT, 1957/8, Cover; 1958/1, pp. 7, 13

109. Huang, *white jade. Warring States period.*

This is an unusually large *huang* (semicircular jade gem) consisting of seven pieces of carved white jade. The center three pieces are carved with cloud-dragon scroll, and there is a dragon-head piece on either side. These five pieces are hollow and are threaded with a copper strip to the gilded copper *t'ao-t'ieh* holding the jade pieces at either end in their mouths. The animal-shaped projections on the center piece are pierced, apparently to take the thread for suspending

the *huang*. The beautiful composition and exquisite carving make this a masterpiece of the period.
Ref: *Excavations at Hui District*, Pl. LIII-2, pp. 80-81, The Institute of Archaeology, Academia Sinica, Peking, 1959

110. *Reconstructed coffin, lacquered wood. Warring States period.*

There is a black lacquer undercoating to the red, and the design is painted in black-bordered figures in four registers around the sides. The first and fourth registers show continuous rectangular figures within which S-shaped dragons appear; the second and third registers show angular spiral patterns within continuous triangular figures. These figures are filled in alternately with yellow and purple lacquer. There are twelve gilt copper ring-handles suspended from animal-mask plaques. This reconstruction, with its brilliant colors and shining metal fittings, gives a most striking impression of the richness of the lacquers of this time in their original state.
Ref: *Ibid.*, Pl. XLV-3, p. 73

111. *Bamboo basket containing writing tools and other objects. Warring States period.*

The weaving of the split bamboo is in a chevron pattern very similar to that used today. The basket contains, among other things: a balance, ring-shaped weights, bamboo slips and a brush for writing, an iron knife with wooden handle, a cylindrical bamboo container, a wooden comb, spatula and divining sticks and an imitation gold coin in clay. It was perhaps a writing box. As this was found completely submerged in water, the state of preservation is surprisingly good.
Ref: WTT, 1954/12, pp. 7, 14; KX, 1957/1, Pl. I-6 (pp. 102-103), pp. 95

112. *Fragment of yellowed silk. Warring States period.*

This silk fragment was found beneath the head in a coffin. It is of special interest for the traces of embroidery remaining. Silk and hemp textiles found in the Ch'u state tombs of the Ch'ang-sha region indicate a high quality in both spinning and weaving techniques of this period.
Ref: *Excavations at Ch'ang-sha*, Pl. XXXIII-B, pp. 63-64, The Institute of Archaeology, Academia Sinica, Peking, 1957

T. Sekino

II. HAN TO T'ANG—TRANSITION AND INNOVATION IN ART

113-114. *Jar, earthenware with slip decoration. Former Han dynasty.*

This earthenware jar is in the shape of a bronze *chung*. It is one of a set of jars made as burial pieces to contain grain. The slip decoration on the neck and shoulder is arranged in bands of a variety of motifs carried out in a very beautiful combination of red, green, blue and black.

115. *Horsehoof-shaped box, lacquer on cloth. Former Han dynasty.*

An example of *chia-chu* or hemp-cloth-bodied lacquer ware. The design is in red lacquer painted on black and is similar to a piece excavated in a Warring States tomb in Ch'ang-sha Municipality, Hunan. The box was a container for women's combs and other toilet articles.
Ref: W, 1957, No. 7

116. *Axle caps, bronze with gold and silver inlay. Han dynasty.*

These are the bronze caps for the axle ends of a chariot or cart. The caps are fixed with an iron pin just below the rim. The decoration is carried out in gold and silver inlay. The end surface is decorated with an animal motif and the sides have four registers of decoration: the outer band is of birds; the second, of feathered men, monsters and tigers; the third, deer, sheep and long-tailed birds; the fourth is again of feathered men and long-tailed birds. These are fine examples of the industrial arts of the Han dynasty and also of the quality of horse trappings and chariot fittings of the period.
Ref: K, 1959, No. 11.

117-119. *Fragments of embroidered silk. Han dynasty.*

In each case this embroidery is carried out in chain stitch, the traditional form of embroidery in China. This elaborate embroidery seems adequate justification for the valuing of embroidery more highly than brocade at this period.

Plate 117 shows a cloud-scroll motif on reddish-brown silk, Plate 118 a human figure and Plate 119 cloud-scroll motifs and a very vividly drawn leaping rabbit, also on reddish-brown silk.

120. *Detail of brocade from a man's jacket. Later Han dynasty.*

This is a brocade in yellow, red, and blue, in which a four-character felicitious inscription is incorporated in a "flowing" cloud-scroll. The inscription reads: "May you have ten thousand generations of descendents, may all your wishes be granted" (万世如意). Because the weft threads are thin and the warp thick, this is called "warp brocade" (経錦). This piece was found in a Later Han tomb in the ruins of Nia (Ming-feng District), where Aurel Stein had worked before the war. With the two other famous brocades, one from Noin Ula and the other from Lou-lan, in which similar phrases of good wishes are incorporated in the design, this piece is of the greatest importance in the study of Han textiles. The piece from Noin Ula in Outer Mongolia bears the phrase 新神霊廣成寿萬年, and the piece from Lou-lan,Sinkiang reads: 韓仁繡文丸者子孫無極.
Ref: W, 1960, No. 6

121. *Incense burner, Greenware. Chin dynasty.*

Here a three-legged incense burner is placed in a three-legged dish. The incense burner is spherical in form with triangular holes cut through the body and a bird with spread wings on top. It is probably a copy of the Po-shan-lu type of bronze incense burner (*see* Pl. 137). The potting is of fine quality and the glaze very even and smooth. The body and glaze are the same as the Greenware found at a Greenware kiln site at Ting-shou-chen, Yi-hsing District, Kiangsu, and it is considered that this piece may be a product of this kiln.
Ref: KX, 1957, No. 4

122. *Large jar, Greenware. Northern Dynasties.*

The body of this piece is gray and the glaze green. The use of appliqué for the lotus motif is an innovation from the West and quite new to China. The Feng family was one of the rich families of the Hopei region in the Northern Dynasties and the tombs have yielded much treasure of the period. As a kiln producing Greenware of the Sui period has been found in Hopei, it is possible that this piece may have been produced in the north, also.
Ref: KT, 1957, No. 3

123. *Jewelry, gold, coral and turquoise. T'ang dynasty.*

The eight outer petals are of a beaded-gold filigree enclosing turquoise and coral. The central bird is made of gold filigree wire and stands with outspread wings and head folded on its breast. The hole just below the bird's feet was probably intended for a fastening. Perhaps this piece is a hair ornament such as those picturesquely described in Po Lo-t'ien's poem, "Song of Everlasting Sorrow" (長恨歌) The tomb from which this piece came is dated 750 A.D.
Ref: W, 1959, No. 8

124. *Necklace, gold, pearls and semi-precious stones. Sui dynasty.*

This necklace is formed of twenty-eight gold and pearl beads with blue stones set in the fastening, the center one being carved with a deer motif. Red and blue stones in a pearl and gold setting are at the center of the necklace. The design accords remarkably with modern taste. Li Ch'ing-hsün was a granddaughter of the eldest sister of Emperor Yang-ti of Sui and died at the age of nine. One wonders if perhaps this necklace was worn and treasured by the little girl.
Ref: K, 1959, No. 9

125. *White jade cup and gold, stemmed cup. Sui dynasty.*

The elegant white jade cup has a deep foot and the rim is bound with gold. The shape is similar to cups of Greenware or glass of the period, but the milky-white jade made it specially fit for an emperor's use. The stemmed, gold cup is finely proportioned, and is a fine example of the splendor that marked the reign of Yang-ti of Sui.
Ref: *Ibid.*

126. *Stemmed bowl, green-white ware. T'ang dynasty.*

The foot and base of the bowl have a lotus relief decoration, while the first and third registers bear rectangular lotus cartouches alternating with oval medallions. The alternate

register is decorated with impressed florettes. This piece, now in the Shensi museum, came from a tomb dated 667 A.D.
Ref: 新中国的考古収獲, 1962

127. *Bird-headed ewer, Greenware. T'ang dynasty.*

The body is very pale gray and the glaze has overtones of a very pale blue-green and straw color. The glaze is glassy where it runs thick. The cover is in the form of a phoenix head, and a dragon standing on its hind legs forms the handle. There are relief medallions around the body, each enclosing the figure of a wrestler. This shape, called in Chinese 胡瓶 ("foreign ewer"), was introduced to China from the West, where it is found in Persian glass- and metal-wares. This shape is also represented in lacquer ware in the Shōsōin collection.
Ref: WTT, 1958, No. 2

128. *Mirror, nickel with mother-of-pearl and traces of lacquer. T'ang dynasty.*

The decoration is composed in mother-of-pearl on nickel. The pearl motifs of birds, flowers and human figures are further delineated with a fine line engraving. In the upper part of the composition, among the flowers, there is the remains of lacquer filling. Mirrors decorated with mother-of-pearl are mentioned in Chinese records such as the *An Lu-shan Biography* (安禄山事蹟), and a few are preserved in the Shōsōin collection. However, this is the first example to be found in China, and, as such, is of very great interest.
Ref: WTT, 1956, No. 5

129. *Small bowl, marbled ware. T'ang dynasty.*

The body is a mixture of dark and light clays used to make a wood-grain effect. The straw-colored glaze is very thin. This shape is often seen in silver wares. It is interesting to see such an amalgam of techniques achieving a pleasing result.

130. *Stemmed lamp, white-glazed stoneware. T'ang dynasty.*

This has a white body and transparent glaze. It is a well-balanced and finely finished piece consisting of a tall stem and double bowl to hold wick and oil. The stem is wheel-made and the foot deeply decorated with lotus-petal relief. A vase of similar white ware has also been found at San-men-chia. A kiln for white ware has been found recently in Kung District, Honan, and has increased our knowledge of the production of this type of ware.
Ref: WTT, 1958, No. 11

131. *Parrot-shaped ewer, green- and yellow-glazed earthenware. T'ang dynasty.*

This is a handled ewer, the body of the bird being hollow. The head and breast are glazed yellow, and the body and stand, green. The parrot is realistically represented with incised details of feathers. T'u-ch'eng-tzu in Horin Ghol is the site of the Shan-yü Tu-huo-fu castle of T'ang. The tomb from which this piece comes is thought to date from before the Liao dynasty, but though the piece is a late T'ang date, it was probably a prototype of the Liao-style ceramics.
Ref: W, 1961, No. 9

132. *Lamp and spoon, bronze. Han dynasty.*

A great variety of metal lamps were made in the Han dynasty. Here a man holds the stems of the oil saucers aloft. The spoon is also bronze.
Ref: 新中国的考古収獲, 1962

133. *Covered jar, earthenware with slip decoration. Former Han dynasty.*

This jar, in the shape of a bronze *chung*, is a kind of *ming-ch'i* in which grain was placed for use in the next world. The surface is decorated with lively slip designs (*see* Pls. 113, 114, 136, 186).

134. Lien, *bronze. Han dynasty.*

A *lien*, a container for cosmetics and mirrors, may be made of a variety of materials, of which lacquer and bronze are perhaps the most common. This is an excellent example, with especially fine engraved surface decoration. The center band of animal designs, including dragon and deer, is bordered by geometric bands.
Ref: WTT, 1954, No. 6

135. Chung, *bronze. Han dynasty.*

This has a tall foot with eight ridges. Horizontal grooves decorate the body of the jar and there are animal-mask ring-handles on the shoulder. Complex motifs such as the *t'ao-t'ieh* motif of the Yin and Chou had by this time been dropped and simplicity of style and decoration were in favor. Together with the *ting* and the *Po-shan-lu*, the *chung* was the most popular shape in use in the Han dynasty. Indeed, the *chung* and *ting* were regarded as a pair for ritual purposes and referred to together as a two-character phrase.
Ref: WTT, 1956, No. 12

136. *Jar, earthenware with slip decoration. Han dynasty.*

This is probably a replica of a bronze *chung* shape. There are two animal-mask cartouches on the shoulder. The striking feature of the ceramic version is, of course, the painted polychrome decoration. Carried out in black, red, and blue slip colors, the decoration is in nine horizontal zones. These range from geometric to freely flowing forms. The most striking of these is the band around the shoulder in which a white tiger and a wolf-like creature are beautifully drawn among cloud-scrolls. The light touch of the painting is equally successful in the scrolls and the lively animals. The whole gives a strong and well-balanced effect.

137. *Hill-shaped incense burner, bronze. Han dynasty.*

The stem of the incense burner rises from the wide saucer base on which lies a serpentine dragon coiled around the stem and grasping it in its mouth. Above the dragon spreads a quatrefoil motif below the bowl of the burner itself. The hill-shaped cover is surmounted by a phoenix with spread wings. This hill shape, known in China as *Po-shan-lu*, persisted after the more classic *chung* and *ting* shapes had been discontinued.
Ref: WTT, 1956, No. 12

138. *Cowrie container, bronze. Former Han dynasty.*

Bronze drums were made by the people living around Lake

Tien, Yünnan, and authority was measured by the number of such drums. The scene depicted on top of this cowrie container probably represents one of their festivals. There are 127 human figures in the scene. Among these, one particularly large female figure sits on a platform of one of the houses. On the veranda of this house there are sixteen drums, and two larger ones in the yard. Many cowrie shells, which were used as money, were found inside this drum.
Ref: 新中国的考古収獲, 1962

139. *Men dancing with saucers, bronze. Former Han dynasty.*

This high-spirited representation of two men dancing is cast in bronze. They each wear a long sword and there is a large snake beneath their feet. Many animals and human ornaments in bronze have been found in the Han dynasty graves of the minority ethnic groups of the Lake Tien area of Yünnan. These give us some clue to their life and crafts.
Ref: *Ibid.*

140. *Belt buckle, gold relief with agate, turquoise, and silver-foil inlay. Former Han dynasty.*

The winged tiger is vividly modeled in gold relief. The legs and feathers are minutely engraved, and the eyes are orange agate. The whole surface is enriched with silver-foil inlay and tiny turquoise insets. This is as important as the magnificent buckle found in mound No. 9 at Lo-lang in Korea.
Ref: 石寨山報告, p. 107

141. *Iron sword with bronze handle and gold-decorated sheath. Former Han dynasty.*

This sword has an iron blade, bronze handle and gold decoration on the sheath. This decoration is simple and very typical of the work of the tribes of this region at this period. It is possible that the blade was brought from the central area of China, but the hilt and sheath are clearly in the local style.
Ref: 新中国的考古収獲, 1962

142. *High-relief mirror, bronze. Later Han dynasty (dated 205 A.D.).*

The inner field of decoration is in high relief, consisting of figures of immortals and mythical animals. The arrangement of these in lines across the mirror is contrasted with the more usual concentric arrangement around the central knob. The immortals to the top and bottom of the composition are winged, while the other figures seem to be attendants. There are two sets of three-character inscriptions reading 君宜官, which is a title. These appear directly above and below the loop knob. The long inscription around the rim contains the date 建安十年 (*Chien-an shih-nien*), corresponding to 205 A.D. *Chien-an* refers to a period in the reign of Hsien-ti, (189-220 A.D.) the last emperor of the Later Han dynasty. The complete forty-character inscription reads: 建安十年 造作大吉 吾作明竟 幽湅官商 周羅万象 五帝天王 白牙単琴 黄帝除兇 朱鳥玄武 白虎青龍
Ref: WTT, 1956, No. 11

143. *High-relief mirror, bronze. Later Han dynasty.*

Centering around the animal-mask knob is a deep relief decoration of four immortals and four animals. The immortals wear feathered robes, and each animal holds a ring-handled knife in its jaws, with eight teats visible beneath. The rectangular cartouches around this field bear an inscription similar to that in Plate 142 beginning: 吾作明鏡, 幽東三商 .... The outer rim is decorated with two concentric bands of intricate motifs. The casting of the piece is good, and the style was first made in the southern area (Chiang-nan) at the end of the Later Han period, being continued into the Southern Dynasties as is borne out by a similar mirror bearing the date 498 A.D. from the Southern Ch'i dynasty.
Ref: KT, 1955, No. 6

144. *Mirror, bronze. Wang Mang interregnum, Han dynasty.*

The outer rim is decorated with a "flowing" cloud-scroll motif, and the inner field contains "angles and circles" in association with the four animals of the directions (Green Dragon, White Tiger, Red Phoenix, Black Tortoise) and birds and beasts in thread relief. This style is typical of the mirrors made around the time of the Wang Mang interregnum (8-23 A.D.). The inscription, in seven-character phrases, reads: 杜氏作竟四夷服 多賀新家人民息 胡虜殄滅天下復 風雨時節五穀熟 長保二親受大福 伝告後世子孫力 官位高. The term 新家 implies that this is a Wang Mang period production. It is usual for the inscription to start with the name of the government office supervising mirror production, but this piece begins with an individual's name (杜氏).
Ref: 陝西省出土銅鏡, 1949

145-147. *Sword fittings, carved jade. Han dynasty.*

Swords of this period decorated with jade were, according to contemporary records, very highly valued and were termed "jade accoutered swords" (玉具剣). Plate 147 shows a sword guard, which would be placed between the blade and hilt; Plate 146 shows a pommel decoration to be fitted to the head of the hilt; and the piece shown in Plate 145 fits on the tip of the sheath. All these are carved in high relief with openwork carving in some cases. They seem to be a set and show the richness of such fittings at this period.
Ref: KT, 1958, No. 5

148. P'ei, *carved jade. Wang Mang interregnum, Han dynasty.*

This *p'ei* is carved with great precision from white jade. Many similar examples have been found in Han tombs as far apart as Lo-lang in Korea and Canton in Kwangtung, and it seems probable that jade *p'ei* were worn very widely at this time.
Ref: W, 1960, No. 3

149. Yüan, *jade. Han dynasty.*

The three categories of jade rings are classified by the relative size of the overall diameter to the central hole. This present piece is classified as a *yüan* and is decorated with a fine intertwining-viper motif. Compare this with the similar example shown in Plate 158, which is greenish in color and has a rice-grain motif. Such rings are thought to have been worn as a costume decoration.
Ref: KT, 1960, No. 3

150. *Green silk embroidered with animal and flower motifs in polychrome chain stitch. Han dynasty.*

The animal bodies are curved in whorls with conventionalized, flame-like limbs. This fragment was attached to the lower end of a pair of man's trousers. Another piece of embroidered silk of the Han dynasty, found at Noin Ula in Outer Mongolia, is embroidered with a honeysuckle motif.
Ref: W, 1960, No. 6

151. *Inkstone, gray-blue stone. Han dynasty.*

This very fine example of Han dynasty writing equipment consists of two parts. The inkstones of the Han period are of two types, the flat rectangular and the flat circular; there is no indentation for the ink pool in either. It is believed that since inksticks were not yet in common use, a vegetable black was made by grinding pine soot. This piece has a double animal-handle and the outer surface is decorated with cloud-scroll and engraved line decoration of horses, dogs and fish. The three legs are decorated with bear's-head masks.
Ref: WTT, 1958, No. 12

152. *Urinal, Greenware. Wu dynasty (dated 251 A.D.).*

This urinal has a cocoon-shaped body, animal-shaped handle and four short legs. This type of urinal, with the mouth at one end, is called a *hu-tzu* (虎子). The inscription on the side reads: 赤烏十四年会稽上虞陳長冝作. This gives the date as 251 A.D. and the place of production as Shao-hsing.
Ref: KX, 1957, No. 1; WTT, 1960, No. 7

153. *Lamp, Greenware. Wu dynasty (dated 256 A.D.).*

The oil cup is supported by an animal standing in the basin. This animal may be a bear and is somewhat humorously represented. An inscription on the base reading 甘露元年 refers to the reign of King K'uai-chi and gives the date as 256 A.D.
Ref: W, 1959, No. 10; K, 1960, No. 7

154. *Ram-shaped water pots, Greenware. Wu dynasty.*

These are water vessels. The glaze is a clear green and they are finely modeled.
Ref: 新中国的考古収獲, 1962

155. *Urn, Greenware. Chin dynasty (from a tomb dated 300 A.D.).*

Models of human figures and buildings stand on the two projecting flanges around the neck. The cover, in the form of a hipped roof, is fixed to the mouth. Cartouches of dragon, phoenix and human reliefs around the body complete the decoration. As the cover is fixed, this is taken to be a ritual burial piece. The tomb from which it was excavated was built in the first year of Yung-k'ang (300 A.D.).
Ref: WTT, 1956, No. 2

156. *Ram-spouted jar, Greenware. Six Dynasties.*

The ram's-head spout is quite unusual and is very naturalistically modeled.
Ref: WTT, 1956, No. 6

157. *Chicken-spouted ewer, Greenware. Liu-Sung dynasty.*

The whole piece, including the base, is covered with a thick, bluish-green glaze that is slightly crazed and flawed. It is a finely made chicken-spouted ewer, typical of the period in such details as the square loop-handles and the small spout. It was excavated with other Greenwares from a tomb dated 447 A.D. in the Liu-Sung dynasty (one of the Southern Dynasties).
Ref: KX, 1958, No. 1

158. *Ring with "rice-grain" pattern, jade. Northern and Southern Dynasties* (see *Pl. 149).*
Ref: KT, 1960, No. 3

159. *Incense burner, Greenware. Chin dynasty.* (see *Pl. 121)*
Ref: KX, 1957, No. 4

160. *Belt fittings, metal. Western Chin dynasty.*

These are buckle fittings for leather belts. They are beautifully wrought with an openwork dragon motif. It is reported that the metal contains a high proportion of aluminum. Similar belt fittings, of gilded copper, have been found in a Western Chin tomb in the vicinity of Lo-yang, in an Eastern Chin tomb in Ta-tao-shan, Kwangtung and in the Samita burial mound at Nara in Japan. It is thought that these fittings were produced at the time of the change from the traditional Chinese belt hooks (*see* Plate 18) to the belt buckle of the northwest Asiatic tribes, though the dragon motif marks these as being of Chinese workmanship.

161. *Cooking vessel model, Greenware. Western Chin dynasty.*

This is a model of a type of cooking vessel, the outer pan standing in the fire and the three-legged bowl being used for serving soup. This piece was found with many other tomb models of objects and buildings of Greenware in the same tomb.
Ref: KX, 1957, No. 4

162. *Glass bowl. Northern Dynasties.*

Mostly a greenish-blue, this glass has touches of purple and yellow. There is a very shallow foot. The string-like decoration is similar to pieces found at the Golden Crown Tomb in Kyongju, Korea. This cup was excavated from the tomb of Feng Mo-nu, who died in 493 A.D., the tomb being constructed in 531 A.D. in the Northern Wei dynasty. The manufacture of glass in the Northern Wei state is recorded, and this bowl and its provenance are therefore of especial interest.
Ref: KT, 1957, No. 3

163. *Glass bowl. Northern Dynasties.*

The bowl is mostly blue-green with touches of yellow, purple, and red. It is valuable in the study of glassware of the Northern Dynasties.
Ref: *Ibid.*

164. *Double-bodied ewer, white clay body with transparent glaze. Sui dynasty.*

This strangely shaped ewer has a single neck and two

bodies, and there is a dragon-headed handle at either side of the neck. It is a well-made piece in spite of its eccentricity of shape.
Ref: K, 1959, No. 9

165. *Bottle, green transparent glass. Sui dynasty.*

This round-bodied bottle has a foot-rim. A transparent blue glass cup was excavated from the same tomb and, with this bottle, appears to be part of a set. The design has a contemporary feeling even today.
Ref: *Ibid.*

166. *Rectangular mirror, bronze. Sui dynasty.*

With an animal mask at each corner, the main field is decorated with four different running-animal reliefs. The inscription is literary in style by comparison with those of the Han mirrors. The inscription reads: 楊府可則 盤龍斯鋳 徐稚経磨 孫承晋賦 散池菱影 開雲桂樹 玉面方窺 仙刀永故.
Ref: 陝西省出土銅鏡, 1959, Pl. 80

167. *Chicken-spouted ewer with dragon handle, Greenware. T'ang dynasty.*

This dragon-handled, chicken-spouted ewer has two sets of loop-handles on the shoulder. The Li Shuang tomb was built in 668 A.D.
Ref: WTT, 1959, No. 3

168. *Spouted jar, pale-gray clay body with greenish-yellow glaze and dark-brown splashes. T'ang dynasty.*

The four relief cartouches depict butterflies, birds, a lion and flowers. The character 長 (*chang*), which is incorporated in the center of the cartouche motif, is probably the name of the craftsman or kiln owner. The products of the Wa-cha-p'ing area are much in the style of the Yo-chou kilns and are characteristic of the Greenwares of South China in the T'ang dynasty.
Ref: W, 1960, No. 3

169. *Four-handled jar, Greenware. T'ang dynasty.*

The exposed body is a purplish gray, and the glaze, gray green. There is unevenly distributed crazing on the body. Probably this is an everyday pot such as might have been used in Ch'ang-an in the T'ang dynasty.
Ref: W, 1959, No. 3

170. *Plate fragment, silver and gilt. T'ang dynasty.*

Only half of the plate now remains. It was excavated at the site of the Hsing Ch'ing Palace, built by Hsüan-tsung, in which many a gorgeous banquet was held. This plate may perhaps have been used on such an occasion. The central motif is a phoenix, and the border is of lotus leaves. The legs and feathers of the bird have been most minutely worked. This is an exquisitely finished, exceptionally fine work.

171. *Mirror with animal decoration, bronze. T'ang dynasty.*

The gods of the four directions (Green Dragon, White Tiger, Red Phoenix, and Black Tortoise) appear around the central square, while the twelve animals of the Chinese zodiac are around the outer rim. The decoration is considerably more realistic in style than that of the Han. This particular decoration is thought to be a revival of the "squares and circle" (or TLV) type of the earlier period (*see* Pl. 144 Note). The date is believed to be either Sui or early T'ang in view of the inscription reading: 仙山竝照 智水斉名 花朝艶采 月夜流明 龍盤五瑞 鸞舞双情 伝聞二寿 始験銷兵. The Jen-shou (仁寿) era mentioned refers to the last part of the reign of Wen-ti of Sui (601-605 A.D.). This would give the earliest limit to the date of production.
Ref: 湖南, 60; WTT, 1956, No. 2

172. *Mirror with animal, bird, and flower decoration, bronze. T'ang dynasty.*

Flying crane, horse, phoenix and lion circle the central field, while the border is decorated with birds and flowers. These are carried out in very fine relief and composed in an exceptionally beautiful design. A similar but larger mirror (diameter: 70 cm.) was found at Haraf in Jerusalem and is now in an Istanbul art museum.
Ref: 陝西省出土銅鏡, Pl. 127

173. Ch'ien-ch'iu *mirror, bronze. T'ang dynasty.*

This is a very finely cast mirror with eight lobes. A writhing dragon and cloud-scrolls fill the main field, with sharp detail in the claws and scales. The quality alone makes clear the reason for the title "emperor's mirror" given to this type of writhing-dragon mirror. There are two rectangular motifs and two flowers in the lobes of the rim. One flower bears the character 千 (*ch'ien*), and the other, 秋 (*ch'iu*). The phrase *ch'ien-ch'iu* ("one thousand autumns") stands the Ch'ien-ch'iu Festival established in 729 A.D. to mark for the birthday of the Emperor Hsüan-tsung. In 743 A.D. the name of this festival was changed to T'ien-ch'ang-chieh (天長節). The use of the earlier title appears to mark this as an earlier piece that may have been made for presentation to the Emperor at the festival.
Ref: *Ibid.*, Pl. 146

174. *Mirror with bird and flower decoration, bronze. T'ang dynasty.*

Fabulous birds, dancing with flowers in beak and claws, confront each other. Sprays of auspicious flowers appear above and below the knob. This is a favorite style of the second quarter of the T'ang dynasty. The present mirror is one of the finest of those excavated in the Ch'ang-an area.
Ref: *Ibid.*, Pl. 128

175. *Mirror with hunting scene, bronze. T'ang dynasty.*

Two of the mounted huntsmen carry bows and arrows, one a spear and the fourth a throwing rope. Deer and other animals are shown between them. This is a fine representation of a courtly hunting scene in the T'ang dynasty.
Ref: *Ibid.*, Pl. 116

176. *Eight-lobed mirror, bronze. T'ang dynasty.*

The spreading acacia tree, placed right over the knob, makes the central feature of this composition. The hare with pestle and mortar, the toad, and the flying figure are all inhabitants of the moon in Chinese mythology.
Ref: *Ibid.*, Pl. 120

177. *Eight-lobed mirror, silver plate on white bronze body. T'ang dynasty.*

This magnificent mirror is decorated with a rich design of animals, birds and grapevine-scroll. The central knob is in the shape of a lion. The decorated surface is a silver plate attached to the white bronze body of the mirror.
Ref: *Ibid.*, Pl. 124

178-179. *Six-lobed cup stand, silver and gilt. T'ang dynasty.*

Signs of wear inside the cup seem to point to use before burial. Seven such stands were excavated together at this site. This stand bears the inscription: 大中十四年八月造成 ... ("completed in the eighth month of the fourteenth year of Ta-chung"), which fixes the date of production at 860 A.D. An inscription on another stand (左策使宅茶庫一 ...) indicates that they had belonged to an official. This is a representative piece of the silverwork of the mid-T'ang period.

180. *Six-lobed dish on three legs, silver and gilt. T'ang dynasty.*

The decoration consists of a central figure of a howling lion and a border decoration of flower motifs. The dish stands on three bronze legs, one of which is lost. Four silver spoons were found with this fine dish. These bear dated inscriptions equivalent to 743 A.D. and 751 A.D. Since Pa-fu-chuang is in the southwestern area of the Eastern Inner Park of the Ta-ming Palace of the T'ang dynasty, it is thought that these pieces may have been buried for security at the time of the An Lu-shan uprising (765 A.D.). A similar gilt-covered silver dish with a deer decoration is in the collection of the Shōsōin in Japan.
Ref: WTT, 1957, No. 4

181-183. *Covered box, silver and gilt. T'ang dynasty.*

Decorated on the top with dancing figures among arabesques, this box has fine line engraving on the bottom. The latter shows a man and woman, with the touching inscription 二人同心 ("two people in perfect accord").
Ref: W, 1959, No. 8

184. *Brocade fragment, woven in blue, green, and red on a yellowish-orange base. T'ang dynasty.*

The pairs of "heavenly horses" confront each other, some with head up and some eating grass. The pattern is in the Sassanian style, and is thought to have been made after the manner of Persian brocade in the early T'ang or even in the Sui dynasty. This fragment was found in a tomb, where it had been used as a veil and breast decoration.
Ref: WTT, 1960, No. 6

T. Okazaki

III. PAINTING—THE EMBELLISHMENT OF TOMBS

185 (a-d). *Fragments of a lacquered* se. *Warring States period.*

The fragments of this *se* comprise about one-third of the instrument, which is a larger version of the *ch'in* (*see* Plate 101 Note). The motifs shown in these paintings vary greatly: there are men, one shouting with his arms raised (a); a hunter carrying his game on a pole (c); a man shooting an arrow (b); and a monster with an animal head and human body (d). The animals include deer, dog, snake, anteater, dragon and birds. Theories of the meaning of this decoration are conjectural and range from the depiction of legends and myths to the representation of some magic ritual of the time. The gestures and garments of the human figures and the slender, graceful animals are of the greatest interest both artistically and anthropologically.
Ref: 我国考古史上的空前発現信陽長台発掘一座戦国大墓, WTT, 1958, No. 6

186. *Jar, earthenware with slip decoration. Former Han dynasty.*

Many beautiful and colorful pots, used as grain containers for the dead, have been excavated from Han tombs in the vicinity of Lo-yang. In some cases, the designs, in red and white slip, have been painted directly on the gray body of the jar. In others, the surface has been coated with white slip on which the design is first drawn in black ink. In this example, the guardians of the four directions appear around the body with bands of formal decoration above and below. The drawing of the animals is lively and the touches of pure red add pleasant accents to the composition.

187. Lien, *lacquer on wood. Han dynasty.*

Among the numerous lacquer wares excavated from Warring States and Han tombs in the Ch'ang-sha area there is much material for the study of painting of the period. This small *lien* shows the light and vivid Han period style found in this area. The horse and carriage are clearly moving through a landscape, which is indicated by the white and green hill. Painted on a red lacquer ground, the whole picture is picked out with freely drawn black lines. The representation is skillful and lively in its simplicity, and although the composition is characteristically diagrammatic in conception, the whole picture fits with pleasant balance within the space, showing a subtle awareness of problems of pictorial composition.
Ref: 漢代絵画選集, Peking, 1955; 戦国漆器花紋与戦国絵画, WTT, 1957, No. 7; 長沙出土古代漆器図案選集, Peking, 1954

188. *Ceramic building, detail. Han dynasty.*

Two similar ceramic buildings were found in 1958 in the excavation of a Han dynasty tomb near the Ho-wang-ts'un dam. For the photograph, the "balcony" between the first and second floors has been removed (*see* Pl. 246), as also have the *tou-kung* from the top.

The decoration, which is painted in colored slip over a white slip coating, shows two registers. In the upper register, the second man from the left appears to be a superior before whom three men are kneeling. In the lower register, a woman in a long-sleeved garment and a man naked to the waist dance, while musicians are depicted at either end. The movement of the figures is directly expressed by the simplest of means.
Ref: WTT, 1958, No. 10

189-190. *Mold-impressed bricks from the coffin chamber and passageway of a tomb. Southern Dynasties (fifth century).*

This Southern Dynasties tomb (fifth century), excavated in March, 1958, at Teng District, attracted great interest among scholars for the molded decoration on the bricks of the coffin chamber and passageway of the tomb. All the bricks are now in the National Historical Museum in Peking. They are in beautiful colors and show a wide variety of subjects. Several pieces bear inscriptions that give meaning to the picture, as in the felicitations 千秋 and 萬歲, ("one thousand autumns" and "ten thousand years"), at either side of the curious creatures in Plate 190. In Plate 215 the inscription given as 南山四皓 should probably read 商山四皓, the piece showing four old hermits in the Shang Mountains. All kinds of subjects, real and imaginary, are depicted. Examples shown here include the soldiers in Plate 214, musicians (Pl. 189), and a sprite riding a spirited mythical beast (Pl. 216). All these mold-impressed pictures are of great interest, but perhaps the most valuable are those where figures are shown in landscape settings; the treatment of trees and mountains provides valuable material for the historical study of landscape painting in China.
Ref: 鄧県彩色画象磚墓 Peking, 1958

191. *Tomb wall painting. T'ang dynasty (706 A.D.).*

This wall painting in the tomb of Princess Yung-t'ai (excavated 1960) is of the finest quality and most exquisite composition of any T'ang dynasty wall painting excavated to the present. Princess Yung-t'ai, whose personal name was Li Hsien-hsün, was the seventh daughter of the Emperor Chung-tsung. She was murdered at the age of seventeen with her husband and brothers because she had offended against the usurping Empress Tse-t'ien. However, when the Empress died and the Emperor Chung-tsung regained the throne in 705 A.D., he built this grand tomb for his daughter at the foot of Liang Mountain, Ch'ien District, Shensi, in the following year. At the time the grandeur of the tomb was much admired because it was built on the scale of that of an emperor or empress. This confirms the modern estimation of the high quality of the paintings in comparison with other contemporary tombs.

The tomb is unusually complex in plan, having both a "tomb path" at the entrance and an "inner passage" linking the two chambers. The width of the tomb is seventeen meters, while the length from the entrance to the tomb path to the back wall of the inner chamber is eighty-seven meters. The walls of the inner passage are decorated with paintings of warriors and male servants, while the walls of both the chambers are covered with paintings of beautiful servant girls. Unfortunately, these paintings have been severely damaged by tomb robbers and the section reproduced from the east wall of the front chamber shows the best preserved of the remaining paintings. This east wall is divided by a red pillar into a group of seven girls to the north and a group of nine to the south. Both groups of girls face the pillar as though they were moving toward the center of the room. The first lady in each group is drawn larger and more meticulously than her companions, who are all elegantly dressed and carry offerings. It is interesting

Decorated Bricks Tomb (Figure accompanying Note 189–190)
Teng District, Honan

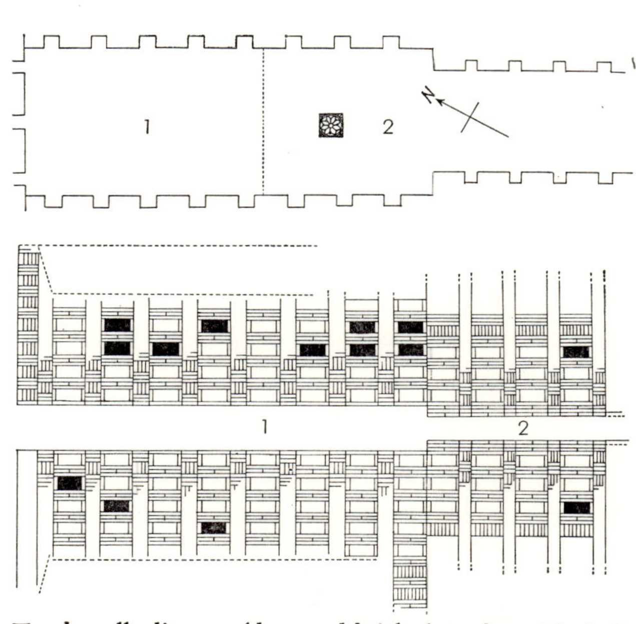

Tomb walls diagram (decorated bricks have been blacked out)

1. Coffin chamber 2. Inner passageway

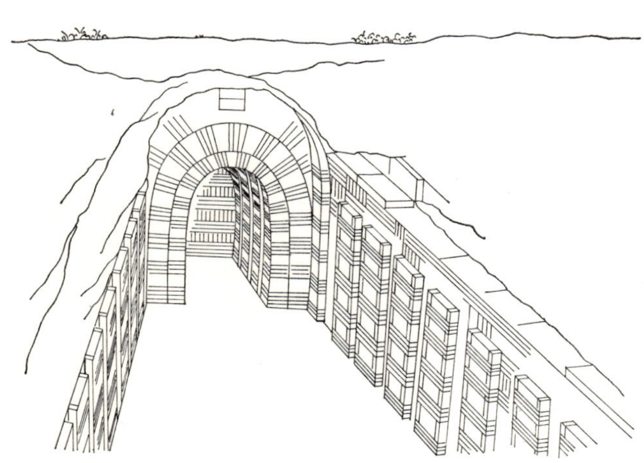

Diagram showing brick tomb construction; looking from coffin chamber out into inner passageway

Princess Yung-t'ai Tomb (Figure accompanying Note 191)
Ch'ien District, Shensi

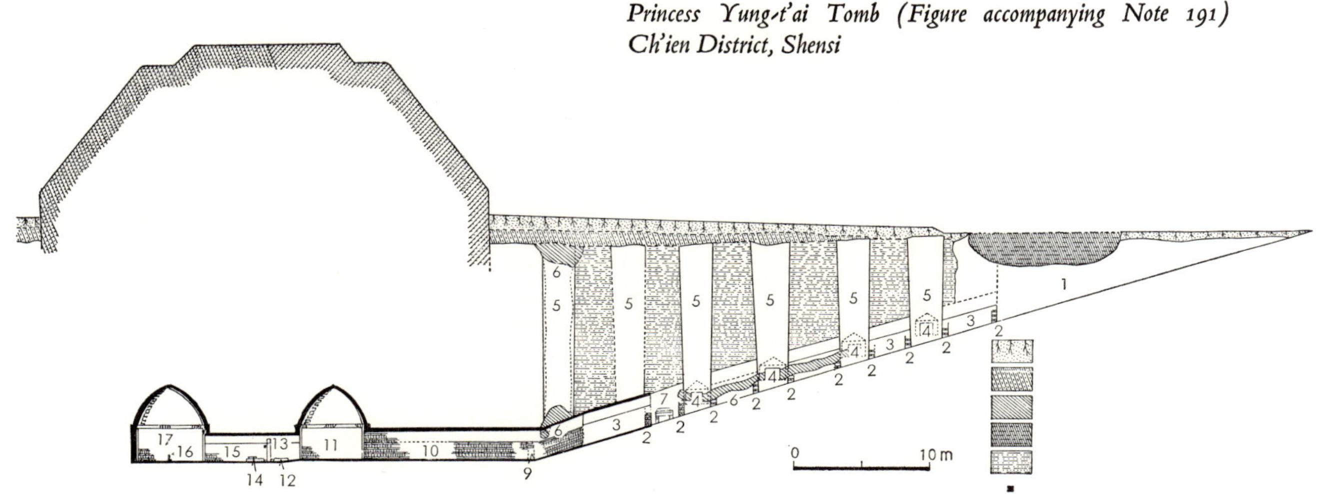

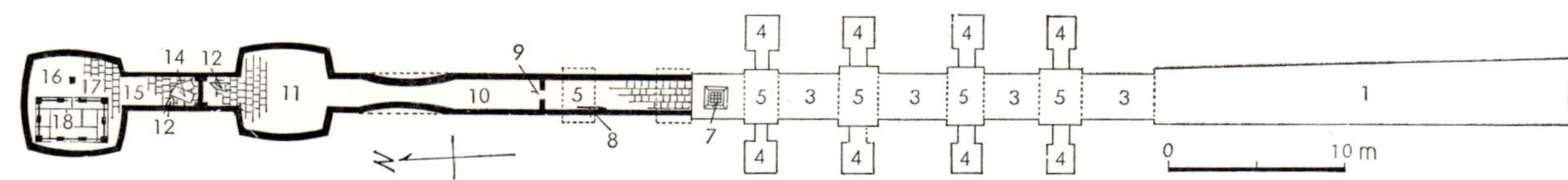

1. Grave path	7. Stone tablet	13. Stone doorframe
2. Sealing walls (brick)	8. Iron pole	14. Stone door
3. Outer passageway	9. Remains of wooden door	15. Empress' passageway
4. Niches	10. Inner passageway	16. Stone screen support
5. Ceiling shafts	11. Antechamber	17. Empress' chamber
6. Secret passageway	12. Remains of stone lintel	18. Stone coffin

that the last girl in each group is dressed as a man. The beautifully balanced poses of the first three girls of the group give an effective rhythm to the whole composition.

The technique used, as shown in the frontispiece, is that of a first drawing in brown and a final statement in a black ink line. This masterly use of a sensitive line to express all the individuality and variety of character, physical form, dress and hairstyle of the figures shows that the T'ang dynasty line drawing technique had almost reached perfection as early as the beginning of the eighth century.

Ref: 唐永泰公主墓壁画集, Peking, 1963; 唐永泰公主墓発掘簡报, W, 1964, No. 1; 唐永泰公主墓誌銘, W, 1963, No. 1; Kitagawa, Momoo, "*Eitai Kōshu no Haka—Seian Kikō,*" *Kobijutsu*, 1965, No. 10

192-193. *Tomb wall paintings. T'ang dynasty (668 A.D.).*

According to the epitaph, Li Shuang, whose last title was Yin-ch'ing Kuang-lu Tai-fu, died at the age of 76 in 668 A.D. The tomb was excavated in 1956.

The coffin chamber is 3.9 meters by 6.5 meters and 6.5 meters high in the center of the domed ceiling. Four men and women attendants are painted on the north, east and west walls respectively, a total of twelve attendants standing among red pillars and beams painted on the walls. These attendants carry offerings or play musical instruments. The girl shown in Plate 226 is one of these figures from the north wall, while the girl wearing a red dress and holding a tray of dishes (Pl. 192) comes from the west wall. An old man (Pl. 193) and a lady-in-waiting are found at either side of the inner tomb passageway. The man holds a tablet and bows in worship, while the lady stands with hands folded, facing him. The painting of the attendants is in a soft, rich ink line, while the old men are character paintings of more individuality.

Ref: 西安羊頭鎮唐李爽墓的発掘, W, 1959, No. 3

194-196. *Tomb wall paintings. T'ang dynasty (745 A.D.).*

According to the epitaph on this tomb, excavated in 1952, it was built for Su Ssu-hsü, who was buried there in 745 A.D. In this tomb there are paintings found on the walls of the inner passageways and coffin chamber. Among them is this one of musicians and dancers (Pl. 194) from the east wall of the coffin chamber. The center of the three sections shows an Iranian-type dancer with deep-set eyes and a high-bridged nose, wearing a long-sleeved garment and dancing energetically. To either side of the dancer, musicians sit on yellow carpets. The group of musicians on the right are playing the *shu-ti* (flute), *ch'in* (koto), *k'ung-hou* (harp), and *p'ai-hsiao* (panpipes); on the left the musicians play the *p'i-p'a* (lute), *sheng*, *nao-pa* (cymbals), *heng-ti* (transeverse flute) and *p'ai-pan*. Each group contains a singer who appears to be keeping the rhythm with his outstretched arm. The west wall of this chamber is divided into six sections, in each of which a man is depicted below a tree (Pl 229). This series is thought to represent the life of hermits in the mountains. Although the relative complexity of the composition in the groups of figures would typify the more developed art of this later period, the poor quality of the drawing and slight treatment of the figures seem to point to the work of a second-rate artist.

Ref: *Excavation of the Tomb of Su Ssu-hsü (T'ang Dynasty) in the Eastern Suburb of Sian*, K, 1960, No. 1

197. *Tomb wall painting. T'ang dynasty (710 A.D.).*

Lady Hsüeh, daughter of Hsüeh Chao and Princess T'ai-p'ing, died at the age of twenty-four in 710 A.D. Her tomb, which is richly decorated with wall paintings, was excavated in 1953. The figures of attendants are painted along both sides of the inner passage. This present example, which is now in the Historical Museum, Peking, is particularly beautiful. The figure is elegantly posed, with her hands folded in her stole. She has a lovely pink-and-white complexion, and her costume and hairdress are both elegant and lively. The skirt and upper garment are green, and it would seem that the stole was originally bright blue or purple. Both this detail and the man's head in Plate 228 show the greater painting skill of the eighth century, during which period a lively sketch technique developed as compared to the works of the previous hundred years.

Ref: 唐墓壁画, W, 1959, No. 8; 從出土文物展覧看卓越的瑛唐墓室壁画, WTT, 1954, No. 10

198. *Detail of the "Tribute Office Scroll," color on silk. Copy (1077 A.D.) of the original by Hsiao Yi (539 A.D.).*

Hsiao Yi was the seventh child of the Emperor Wu-ti of Liang, one of the Southern Dynasties. He was renowned as a painter, calligrapher and writer, and was given the epithet *san-chüeh* in his day. Before he ascended the throne as Yüan-ti, he was stationed as an official at Ching-men (present-day Chiang-ling, Hupei). During this time he drew studies of the messengers and tribute bearers from the many states paying tribute to the prosperous Liang state. When foreigners came to Ching-men he would paint them himself, but if they went to the capital, Chien-k'ang (Nanking), Hsiao sent his men to observe them and would then paint his picture from their reports. Adding a preface to these paintings, he produced the first Chin-kung-t'u ("Tribute Office Scroll") in Chinese painting. It is thought that this scroll was completed about 539 A.D. Unfortunately, only the preface of this original work is preserved in Volume 55 of the *Yi-wen-lei-chü* (藝文類聚). However, a copy was made of the painting in 1077 A.D. This is recorded as being in the collection of Liang Chiao-ling at the beginning of the Ch'ing dynasty, from whom it was acquired for the Imperial Ch'ing Collection. It was subsequently lost for some time, but recently came into the possession of the Nanking Museum and was shown in the Historical Museum in Peking. The details shown here are photographs of the Sung dynasty copy. It is understood that the original "Tribute Office Scroll" of Hsiao Yi contained at least thirty-five separate figures with explanatory notes. In the early Ch'ing dynasty it is recorded that the Sung copy consisted of twenty-five such figures, but today only thirteen entries have survived, representing the following countries: Hua Kuo, Persia, Pai-chi Kuo, Kucha, Japan, Tang-ch'ang Kuo, Kang-ya-hsiu Kuo, Teng-chih Kuo (state of Teng; i.e. Hupei), Chou-ku-ko Kuo, Ko-pa-t'an Kuo, Hu-mi-tan Kuo, Pai-t'i Kuo, and Mo Kuo. Even in this incomplete and damaged condition, it is a very interesting document both of the peoples of the sixth century and of the painting style of the Liang dynasty. The scroll was used as the basis for the chapter on foreigners of the *Liang Shu* (*Book of Liang*). The remains of the Northern Sung copy contains much that was not included in this record and so makes invaluable study material.

Plate 198 is the oldest painting extant in China of a

Li Shuang Tomb (Figure accompanying Note 192–193)
Sian, Shensi

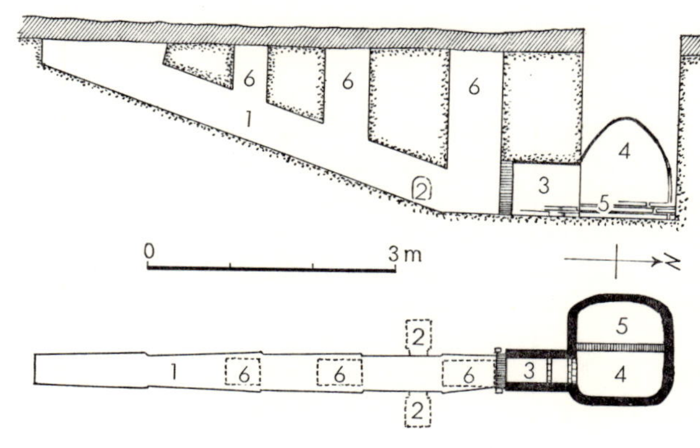

1. Outer passageway
2. Niches
3. Inner passageway
4. Coffin chamber
5. Coffin platform
6. Ceiling shafts

West wall

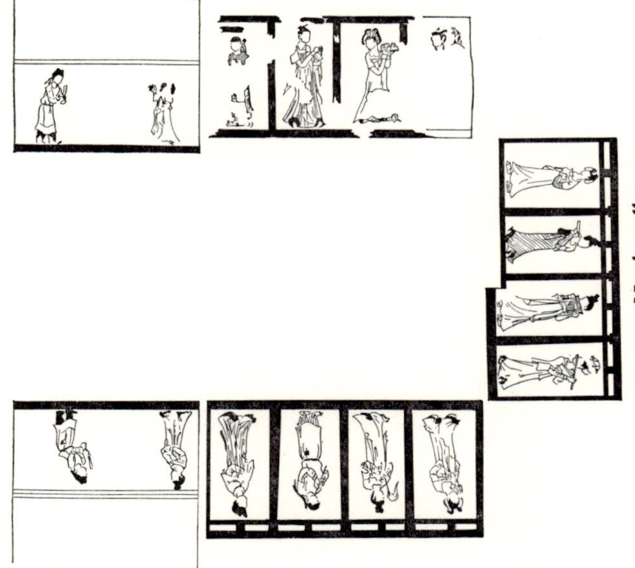

East wall

Su Ssu-hsü Tomb (Figure accompanying Note 194–196)
Sian, Shensi

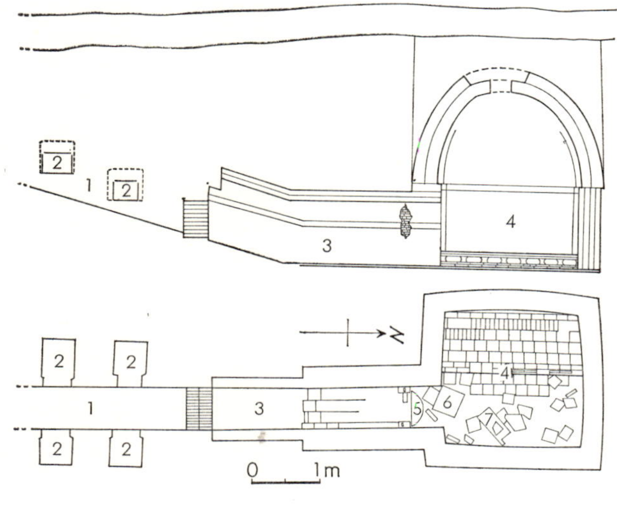

1. Outer passageway
2. Niches
3. Inner passageway
4. Coffin chamber
5. Half-moon-shaped lintel
6. Inscribed memorial tablet
7. Stone gate

Japanese. The barefooted figure, dressed in a headcloth and two tied and draped cloths seems to accord with an early description of Japanese costume in the *Wei-chih Wo-jen Chuan* (魏志倭人伝) and other writings. Here the Japanese are said to "wear cotton head coverings and costumes of wide pieces of material with almost no sewing, being joined by tying at the front . . . they all go barefoot." We know from our own archaeological studies that this is not an accurate description of the Japanese costume of the sixth century. Since there was no official contact between China and Japan at this time, it is probable that Hsiao Yi painted his study from some such fanciful description.

Ref: 職貢図的時代与作者, W, 1960, No. 7

199. *Detail of "Ladies-in-Waiting" scroll by Chou Fang, ink and color on silk. T'ang dynasty.*

Unfortunately I missed a chance of seeing this scroll at Shen-yang (formerly Feng-t'ien) on a recent visit to China.

The ladies-in-waiting in this detail stand in elegant poses, wearing filmy costumes and floral hair decorations. The composition is very much in the style of the Hui-tsung copy of Chang Hsüan's "Ladies Preparing Silk" in the Museum of Fine Arts, Boston, and the Chou Wen-chü "Palace" scroll in the Fogg Museum, Cambridge, Massachusetts. The costumes are of T'ang style, and very similar to the Yakushiji Srimakadevi paintings. The hair styles are similar to those in the Hui-tsung scroll mentioned and to the Yin-lu P'u-sa scroll found at Tun-huang and now in the British Museum. The only difference is in the flower decoration, but this seems of little significance, for, according to the Ch'ing dynasty scholar Chao Yi, flower decorations were worn in the hair by both men and women of the T'ang and Sung dynasties. This painting was first recorded in the *Ta-kuan Lu* (大観録) by Wu Sheng of the Ch'ing dynasty.

Ref: 唐周昉簪花仕女図的商榷, WTT, 1958, No. 6

200. *Copy of a painting on silk. Warring States period.*

This is painted on a very thin, evenly woven silk. The drawing is indistinct because of the worn condition of the silk, but one can see a phoenix with outspread wings in the upper part of the picture and a dragon rising from the lower left corner. A woman with her hand outstretched and looking upward stands to the right. The figure, with neatly dressed hair, wears a smooth sash around her long, flowing gown. This gown appears to be two-colored and to have a decoration around the collar and cuffs. The meaning of this picture is a mystery, but it has great value as one of the earliest Chinese paintings on silk in existence.

Ref: 戦国絵画資料, Peking, 1957

201-202. *Reconstructed details of lacquer painting on a* lien. *Han dynasty.*

These plates show the design from the side of a *lien.* Sitting figures in houses alternate with standing figures. The red ground is bordered at top and bottom by cloud-scroll patterns (not shown here) in red and green on a black ground. Plate 201 is the decoration in its present condition, while Plate 202 is a restoration.

Ref: 漢代絵画選集, Peking, 1955; 戦国漆器花紋与戦国絵画, WTT, 1957, No. 7; 長沙出土古代漆器図案選集, Peking, 1954

203. *Carriage procession, copy of a tomb wall painting. Later Han dynasty.*

This Later Han stone tomb, excavated in 1953, consists of an outer and inner chamber on a north-south axis. The wall paintings are in the outer chamber on the east, west and south walls. This copy is of the painting on the west wall. Supernatural beings and a phoenix appear above a procession of carriages. The center carriage seems to be that of the occupant of the tomb, as indicated by the inscription above it: 淳于謁卿車馬 ("horses and carriage of of the Lord Ch'un-yü). The surface of the wall is prepared with a plaster finish, and although there is a certain rhythmic beauty in the drawing of the carriages, the color and treatment of the whole is perfunctory and almost crude.

Ref: WTT, 1955, No. 5; 山東文物選集, Pl. 203

204. *Reconstruction of the painting on a tomb gateway. Southern Dynasties (fifth century).*

In addition to the painted, molded bricks of the interior of the tomb (*see* Pls. 189, 190), there is a very interesting painting on the entrance gate to this tomb. This has been preserved in much of its original freshness by a brick wall built to block the entrance. The technique of the wall painting is of interest: the brick surface was prepared with a gesso ground; the design, first pricked out, was drawn in red; the colors, seven in all, were laid on, and the black strengthening lines added as the final touch.

The grotesque animal mask holds a ribbon-draped weapon in its jaws; *apsaras* to either side float over the heads of the soldiers who guard the gate. This is drawn with strength and sharpness and even in the copy is useful in the study of Southern Dynasties period painting. This reconstruction, made by Ch'en Ta-chang, is shown as a restoration in the Historical Museum, Peking.

Ref: 鄧県彩色画象磚墓, Peking, 1958

205. *Detail of a tomb wall painting. Han dynasty.*

This stone coffin tomb was excavated in 1944. The coffin was placed in a small stone enclosure in the center of the main, rectangular stone chamber (5.15 meters by 4.85 meters). This is very similar to the stone coffin tomb found at Pang-t'ai-tzu, also in Liao-yang (*see* Pls. 206, 207). In both, the main chamber is flanked by side rooms to the north, south and east with the tomb entrance in the west wall. The walls of all the chambers are decorated with painting. The detail illustrated comes from the west wall of the main chamber. The lively representation of a carriage procession can be usefully compared with a similar subject in the Liang-shan District tomb (Pl. 203), but this Liao-yang painting seems the more sophisticated in the interpretation of depth in the drawing of the carriages and in the subtlety of color used.

Ref: 漢代絵画選集, Peking, 1955

206-207. *Details of a tomb chamber wall painting. Han dynasty.*

This tomb was discovered by chance in 1944, but scientific investigation was not undertaken until after the 1949 revolution. There are three stone coffins in the tomb chamber, which measures 6.6 meters by 8.0 meters. A small room is found on the right and on the left of this chamber. All the walls are decorated with paintings. The

details shown are taken from the wall to the right of the tomb entrance. A similar composition is on the opposite side of the doorway. The right-hand wall shows twenty-three human figures in three rows. The upper row (Pl. 207) consists of four musicians and five singers seated before trays of food. The lower two rows are entertainers, acrobats, jugglers and dancers (Pl. 206). These paintings are admirable study material for the customs of the time.
Ref: WTT, 1955, No. 5

208. *Rubbings of the engraved decoration on a cowrie container, bronze. Former Han dynasty.*

A large-scale excavation of tombs at Shih-chai-shan, Yünnan, carried out between 1955 and 1958, has brought to light much of the interesting culture developed in this area through the contacts between the metropolitan Han culture and the indigenous Tien (滇) culture. The money-cowrie containers for burial are worthy of study for the content of the decoration alone (*see* Pl. 138). The design here is carried out in negative, engraved relief in two registers on a container similar in shape to the one pictured in Plate 138. In one register there is a procession in which figures carry bundles on their heads and lead animals, with birds flying overhead. Two men are carried in litters. In the other register there is a double row of figures, placed one above the other. There are storehouses, and figures carrying objects move to and from them. The costume and hair style of the people is typical of the Tien culture and are repeated in the other bronze images found at this site. The storehouses are similar to the proto-historic period houses of Japan.

209-210. *Painted bricks. Han dynasty.*

Altogether twenty-four Han graves were excavated from this site near Chiu-ch'üan in 1950. The painted bricks of tomb No. 1 are of particular interest. This tomb consists of two chambers set on an east-west axis and measuring 10.12 meters in length. The whole is built of soft, red, rectangular brick. The floors are also of the same brick, but square and arranged in a floral design. There are sixty-four painted wall bricks in the tomb. The subjects of the pictures vary greatly, ranging from farmers and hunters to animals. The two examples—the man with the lantern standing beside a tree and the humorous elephant—illustrate well the Han dynasty free style of drawing. Interestingly, this style was popular as far west as Kansu.
Ref: 酒泉下河清第1号墓和第18号墓発掘簡報, W, 1959, No. 10

211. *Detail of a tomb wall painting. Later Han dynasty.*

Two similar Han tombs of complex construction were found at Wang-tu District. No. 1, excavated in 1952, has three main chambers laid out on an east-west axis with side rooms to the north and south of the first two and a small niche in the north wall of the third. The total length of the tomb is 20.35 meters. The paintings on the walls of the first chamber and of the passage connecting it to the center chamber are particularly fine. Those on the east and west walls (wall height: 140 cm.) of the first chamber are divided in two; in the upper register figures of officials stand looking toward the inner chamber; in the lower register there are auspicious birds and animals.

The walls have been prepared with a thick, white plaster ground on which the design is sketched, and the colors—red, blue and yellow—filled in. The black ink line is the final addition. Each wall bears a title inscription written in the square (*li*) style script. The example illustrated from the northern part of the east wall is entitled 辟車伍佰八人 ("five hundred and eight charioteers").

212. *Relief brick. Later Han dynasty.*

The freedom of expression and the variety of subject matter of the relief bricks found in Szuchwan have radically changed the conception of Han dynasty art. The salt manufacture shown in this example is being carried out by the "well" method, which has been used in this area to this day. Brine is dredged up from the well and conducted by bamboo pipes to pans, where the water is evaporated and the salt collected. The whole of this process, including the collection of fuel, is shown clearly. A deer hunt is taking place in the middle of the composition. Among the trees of the receding planes of mountains animals of many kinds are depicted with great vivacity.
Ref: 漢代絵画選集, Peking, 1955

213. *Relief brick. Later Han dynasty.*

This relief brick is an excellent illustration of everyday activities of the Han period. In the lower part, farmers work in the paddy, reaping with scythes, while the man on the left seems to be bringing food for the workers. In the upper section, hunters beside a well-stocked lake shoot at flying wildfowl. All animals and human figures are expressed with great life and freedom.
Ref: *Ibid.*

214-216. *Mold-impressed bricks from the coffin chamber and passageways of a tomb. Southern Dynasties (fifth century) (*see *Pls. 189-190 Note).*

217. *Rubbing of impressed-brick wall decoration. Late Eastern Chin or Liu-Sung dynasty (early fifth century).*

This brick tomb, excavated in 1960, has a long, narrow chamber set on an east-west axis (6.85 meters by 3.1 meters). There is a large, raised, wall-to-wall platform filling two-thirds of the chamber, on which there were two coffins. Of special importance is the impressed brick decoration, located fifty centimeters from the floor, on the two long walls. This shows eight wise men living in seclusion among trees. The hermits are named: on the south wall, left to right, Chi K'ang (playing the *ch'in*), Juan Chi, Shan T'ao (seen with the accouterments of one who likes strong spirits), Wang Jung (with the backscratcher); on the north wall, from right to left, Hsiang Hsiu, Liu Ling, Juan Hsien (who plays the round musical instrument known by his name and attributed to his invention), and Jung Ch'i-kuei. The first seven are the group known as the "Seven Worthies of the Bamboo Grove," while the last is a famous hermit of the Warring States period. The figures are individually expressed as though they were portraits, and the trees that surround them (gingko, pine, willow) are equally sensitively drawn. All show the special features of Southern Dynasties art. The technique of making this large composition shows considerable sophistication: the whole was drawn on a wooden block, which was

then carved, and the design then impressed on numbered bricks that were fired and built up to form a wall.
Ref: 南京西善橋南朝墓及其磚刻壁画, W, 1960, Nos. 8-9

218. *Details of the "Tribute Office Scroll," color on silk. Copy (1077 A.D.) of the original by Hsiao Yi (539 A.D.)* (see *Pl. 198 Note)*

219-225. *Engraved slabs from a stone coffin case (details) and wall paintings from a coffin chamber (details). T'ang dynasty (dated 708 A.D.).*

Wei Chiung was the younger brother of Lady Wei, the Empress of the Emperor Chung-tsung. He died in 692 A.D. at the age of sixteen, but in 708 was honored posthumously by the Emperor with the title of Huai-yang-wang and reburied. This tomb was excavated in 1959, and was found to be decorated with exceptionally fine wall paintings and to contain a magnificent gabled stone coffin case. The walls of this are of ten slate-blue slabs, which are decorated with very fine engraved designs. These, besides depicting the gate and windows on the outside of this house-like structure, show graceful ladies-in-waiting inside. One of these ladies dresses as a man (*see* Pl. 191 Note), while another wears a wide-collared foreign dress. All carry offerings.

The paintings originally covered the walls of the antechamber, passage, and coffin chamber of this tomb, which is on an east-west axis. However, most have been damaged and only the decorated ceiling and north and west walls of the coffin chamber now remain in good condition. Red pillars and beams painted on the walls framed single figures of men and women places alternately. On the north wall of the coffin chamber, a man plays the *p'i-p'a* (Pl. 222) on the left, a woman (Pl. 223) is in the center, with another man on the right. On the west wall, there are two women and a man. The woman in Plate 225 is on the left of this set. These paintings have been roughly sketched in on the plaster-coated wall and then drawn in with bold black lines; the freely painted color is red and green. The results are very animated paintings of highly individual human beings.
Ref: 長安県南里王村唐韋洞発堀記, W, 1959, No. 8

226. *Tomb wall painting. T'ang dynasty (668 A.D.)* (see *Pls. 192-193 Note).*

227. *Tomb wall painting. T'ang dynasty (658 A.D.).*

This is the earliest T'ang dynasty tomb painting known. It was painted in 658 A.D. and excavated in 1957, and is now preserved in the Historical Museum, Peking. The figure is drawn in black lines with the simple addition of a reddish-brown color. The very simplicity of technique seems to enhance the liveliness and freedom of movement expressed. It is of interest that Chih Shih Feng Chieh, buried in the tomb, was a Turkic servant of the T'ang dynasty.
Ref: 唐墓壁画, W, 1959, No 8; Akiyama, Terukazu, "*Chōan no Tōbō Hekiga,*" *Sansai,* 1961, No 135

228. *Tomb wall painting. T'ang dynasty (710 A.D.)* (see *Pl. 197 Note).*

229. *Tomb wall painting. T'ang dynasty (745 A.D.)* (see *Pls. 194-196 Note).*

230. *Tomb wall painting. T'ang dynasty (706 A.D.)* (see *Pl. 191 Note).*

231-232. *Details of a tomb wall painting. Early T'ang dynasty.*

Probably because it was the place of origin of the T'ang dynasty, T'ai-yüan was regarded as the northern capital during that dynasty, and a number of T'ang tombs have been found in the area. As in the tombs at Sian, there are many wall paintings, but the T'ai-yüan examples are noticeably of a cruder quality. This tomb is brick, and all the walls of the square tomb chamber (2.13 meters by 2.2 meters) are painted with human figures among a framework of painted red pillars and beams. The south wall has male attendants with drawn swords at either side of the entrance. The southern parts of the east and west walls show female attendants, each accompanied by a young girl (Pl. 231). In each of the eight panels between the nine pillars lining the northern part of the chamber, an old man is depicted standing under a tree (Pl. 232). Perhaps these men represent noblemen of the period in their mountain retreats. The brushwork is crude and the conception somewhat naive, particularly in comparison with comtemporary tombs of the metropolitan area.

As the inscription of this tomb is lost, there is no way of identifying it. The sole method of dating is by comparison with another tomb found at Tung-ju-chung-hsin-ts'un, which is dated at 696 A.D. Here the wall paintings are very similar. Tomb No. 4 is thus thought to be also of an early T'ang date.
Ref: "Two T'ang Dynasty Tombs at Chin-sheng-ts'un, T'ai-yüan, Shansi," K, 1959, No. 9

233-234. *Rubbings of stone line engravings of Buddhist figures, warriors and guardians. T'ang dynasty (663 A.D.).*

These engravings of human figures, from the pedestal of the memorial stela erected in 663 A.D. to the monk Tao-Yi, are very important examples of the characteristics of T'ang dynasty painting. They differ from the tomb paintings or engravings in that here Buddhist themes are used, and the style is entirely different. Perhaps they belong more properly to a later discussion, but the brilliant portrayal of the strange features of the figures shows something of the high standard of painting at this time.
Ref: 閻立本与尉遲乙僧, W, 1940, No. 4

235-236. *Rubbings of stone line engravings. T'ang dynasty.*

Wei Hsü was a nobleman who died in 718 A.D. The tomb was robbed in the late Ch'ing dynasty, and at one time some of the stone slabs were used as steps in the nearby Ta-hsiang-tzu (Taoist) Temple. These were rediscovered in 1942, and today twelve slabs and the tomb inscription are in the Shensi museum. As in the Wei Chiung tomb, the ladies-in-waiting are shown in a setting of birds and flowers (*see* Pls. 219-221), and the details of dress decoration are minutely engraved.
Ref: 唐代的石刻綫画, WTT, 1956, No. 4

T. AKIYAMA

Notes to Plates 185, 200 by T. Sekino; Plate 198 by Sadao Nishijima; Plate 199 by Y. Yonezawa

Tomb at Hsi-shan-ch'iao, Nanking (Figure accompanying Note 217)

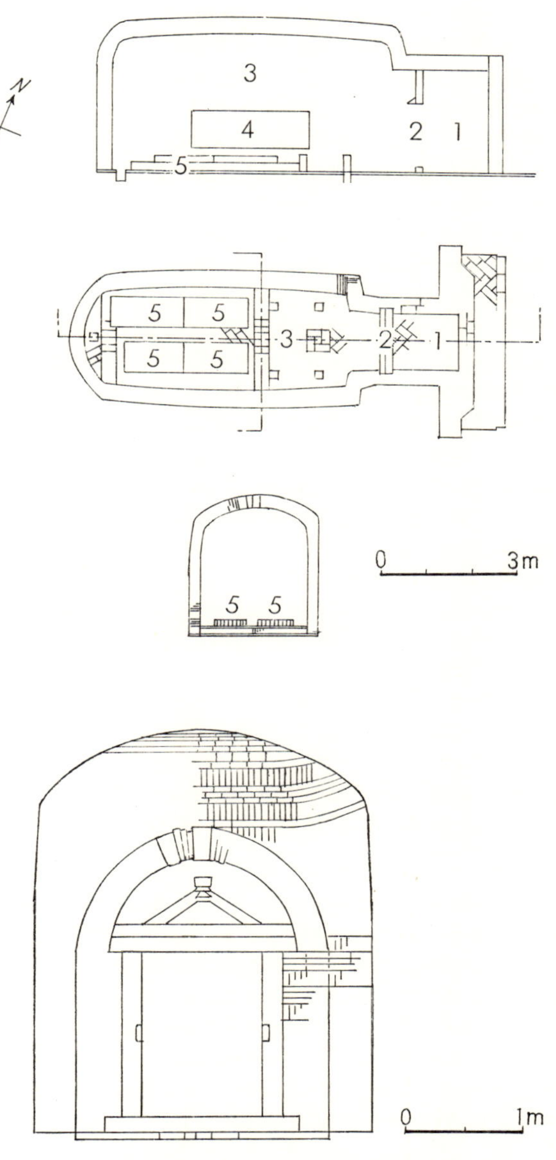

Diagram of gate as seen from the coffin chamber

1. Inner passageway
2. Gate
3. Coffin chamber
4. Impressed brick decoration
5. Coffin platforms

Wei Chiung Tomb (Figure accompanying Note 219–225)
Ch'ang-an District, Shensi

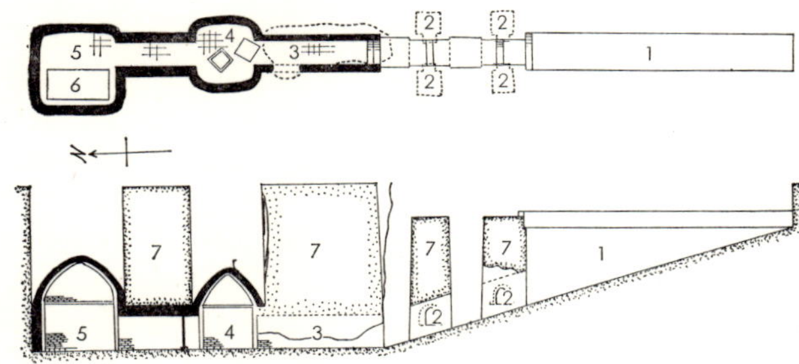

1. Outer passageway
2. Niches
3. Inner passageway
4. Antechamber
5. Coffin chamber
6. Coffin platform
7. Ceiling shafts (filled)

IV. MONUMENTAL ANIMAL SCULPTURE

237. *Horse standing over a captive, stone. Former Han dynasty (*ca. *117 B.C.).*

Huo Ch'ü-ping was a brave general of the Han Emperor Wu-ti (140-86 B.C.). This stone sculpture, one of many animals placed in front of the tomb, is thought to have been carved about 117 B.C. when Huo Ch'ü-ping died. It is the earliest known piece of true sculpture in China. Here the horse stands over a man, thought to be a foreigner. The carving is straightforward, if somewhat two-dimensional.

Ref: 陝西興平県霍去病墓前的西漢石雕藝術, W, 1964, No. 1

238. *Mythical animal, stone. Southern Ch'i dynasty (*ca. *498 A.D.).*

Although this horned animal has been much damaged and the legs lost, it is a very fine piece of great vitality. The formalized hair and the crisp tautness of line are typical of the sculpture of this period. This piece comes from the tomb of the Southern Ch'i dynasty Emperor Ming-ti, who died in 498 A.D., and it is presumed to have been carved at about this time.

239. *Mythical animal, stone. Liang dynasty (*ca. *526 A.D.).*

This is one of a pair excavated in 1956. The other one is extensively damaged. Although usually called a lion, this creature has wings, and so should perhaps be classed as a *pi-hsieh*. It is one of the finest of all the stone tomb animals of this period and a very powerful piece of sculpture.

Hsiao Hung was a younger brother of Wu-ti of Liang and died in 526 A.D. It is therefore probable that the tomb dates from near this time.

Ref: 修復南京六朝陵墓古蹟中重要発現, WTT, 1957, No. 3

240. *Tiger, stone. T'ang dynasty (*ca. *635 A.D.).*

The pair of stone tigers at this tomb of Kao-tsu of T'ang are typical of the stone animal sculpture of the early T'ang. Realistically represented, they show a sensitive observation of live animals, but still retain the strength and plasticity of the earlier carvings.

241. *The "White-Hoofed Horse" of T'ai-tsung, stone relief carving. T'ang dynasty (seventh century).*

This is one of the famous six horses of T'ai-tsung of the T'ang dynasty. The Chao *ling*, in which both T'ai-tsung and his Empress Wen-te were buried, was built about the middle of the seventh century. These reliefs were originally inside the north gateway of the tumulus. The inscriptions on each piece are now illegible, but old records show that this horse was called the "White-Hoofed Horse" and was the one that T'ai-tsung rode in his defeat of the armies of Hsüeh Jen-kuo.

242. *Winged horse, stone. T'ang dynasty (*ca. *684 A.D.)*

The tomb of the Emperor Kao-tsung, called the Ch'ien *ling*, is thought to have been constructed during his lifetime or immediately at his death (683 A.D.). There were a number of stone sculptures—human figures, lions and ostriches—at this tomb. This fine seventh century winged horse shows signs of a florid formalization in the carving of the wings.

243. *Mythical animal, stone. T'ang dynasty.*

This winged and horned creature should properly be termed a *t'ien-lu* or mythical animal. The style is very typical of this period, with its static, heavy formalism. The Shun *ling* is the tomb of Lady Yang, mother of the usurping Empress Wu Tse-t'ien who reigned from 684 to 705 A.D. The tomb was built in the later part of this reign.

Ref: 唐順陵勘査記, W, 1964, No. 1

S. Matsubara

V. BURIAL OBJECTS—MODELS OF WORLDLY COMFORT

244. *Dog, glazed earthenware. Later Han dynasty.*

This is a typical Han dog, probably an indigenous breed, with broad jaw and sturdy body and legs.
Ref: WTT, 1955, No. 3

245. *Boat, earthenware. Later Han dynasty.*

This mat-covered, fully manned boat is a model typical of the Kwangtung waterways. China's coastline is short in relation to the land mass, and so boats and reminders of life on and by water are rare in *ming-ch'i.* This is thought to be a product of the Later Han period, although the clay is quite different from that of pieces of similar date further north. This piece is of special interest in that it shows that the customs of the Han, i.e. that of burying *ming-ch'i,* had reached this southern part of the country by the Later Han. Another boat *ming-ch'i* excavated in the Canton area is a wooden one found in the wooden coffin tomb of the Emperor Kang of the Former Han period.
Ref: WTT, 1955, No. 4

246. *Building, earthenware with slip decoration. Han dynasty (*see *Pl. 188 Note).*

Two such house-shaped models were excavated from this tomb. As the roof is removable, this piece may have been intended as a vessel rather than a replica. The front beam is supported by five composite brackets, and the beam at the side, by two. In the front, a balustrade runs the full length of the building about halfway up the wall, and a row of ventilation holes is pierced through the wall almost at ground level. At first glance, this appears to be a single-story building, but, in view of the proportions, it might be a multi-story one. I cannot agree with the report's classification of this as a *lou* or "tower," since the windows are too high in relation to the balustrade and no entrance is visible. It is very similar to a house-shaped *ming-ch'i* with bear's feet, in the Fujii Yūrinkan, Kyoto, Japan.
Ref: WTT, 1958, No. 10

247. *Ladies-in-waiting, slip-painted earthenware. T'ang dynasty.*

The women, probably ladies-in-waiting, wear high-necked garments and have their hair dressed in two horns, a style very popular at this period. This same hairstyle is seen in the "Beauty in Foreign Costume" brought from Turfan in Sinkiang Province by the Ōtani expedition. As the Princess Yung-t'ai tomb can be dated at 706 A.D., it is inferred that this hairstyle was popular in both Shensi and Sinkiang in the early eighth century.
Ref: W, 1963, No. 1

248. *Men in foreign costume, slip-painted earthenware. T'ang dynasty.*

The taller of these figures wears a coat with lapels and a tall hat. The deep-set eyes mark this as the representation of a foreigner. The bases have been added since excavation. Similar pieces had been excavated previously from the Sui dynasty tomb of Li Ching-hsün at Sian.
Ref: *Ibid.*

249. *Lady and foreign attendant, earthenware with* san-ts'ai *glaze. T'ang dynasty.*

To judge by her ease and air of nonchalance, the lady appears to be of high rank.
Ref: *Ibid.*

250. *Caucasian woman, earthenware with* san-ts'ai *glaze. T'ang dynasty.*

This standing figure wears a yellow-sleeved blouse and a long, green skirt; the white dots on this are probably achieved by wax resist. She stands gracefully, gently smiling. Her hair is loosely swept back at the sides, with a heavy coil brought forward along the crown of the head. From her high-bridged nose and the general cast of her features, she seems to be a Caucasian. There were white women, popularly known as *hu-chi* ("foreign concubines"), in Ch'ang-an and Lo-yang at this time. Although many foreign men appear, there are strangely few figures of such women among the *ming-ch'i.* This is therefore a valuable example.
Ref: KT, 1958, No. 1; 新中国的考古収獲, 1962

251. *Camel carrying a band of musicians, earthenware with* san-ts'ai *glaze. T'ang dynasty.*

Although many fine *san-ts'ai ming-ch'i* of camels have been found, this is certainly one of the finest and most elaborate. There are six musicians on its back, which is covered by a large carpet. The band is made up of men and women playing a variety of instruments of the period. They appear to be a very cheerful group. Possibly this represents a band in a procession. A mate to this piece was found in the same tomb, but the musicians are all male. These pieces seem to represent a gaiety quite unlike the somber grief of the Han tomb models. This change in character of the *ming-ch'i* is very striking, and marks a significant difference between the two periods.
Ref: *Ibid.*

252. *Horse and groom, earthenware with* san-ts'ai *glaze. T'ang dynasty.*

According to the report, the grave from which these figures came is similar to two other tombs at Shih-li-p'u, also in Sian: tomb No. 337, and the Hsien-yü T'ing-hui tomb. It seems likely that these tombs are all of the second quarter of the T'ang dynasty.

Three horses and two grooms were found among the *ming-ch'i* of this tomb. The horse and groom shown here were chosen at random; the same groom with a different horse is shown in Plate 130 of the report. This man wears foreign dress and carries brushes for his horse. The green shoulder pad makes a fine accent for this beautiful figure. Ten female figures of the "Beauty Under the Tree" type were found in this same tomb.
Ref: K, 1960, No. 3

253-256. *Foreign horses and grooms, earthenware with* san-ts'ai *glaze. T'ang dynasty.*

Two grooms and horses were all excavated from the same site. This tomb, dated in the third quarter of the T'ang dynasty, was investigated in March and April, 1955, and proved extraordinarily rich in *ming-ch'i* of all kinds, among

them a great variety of outstanding *san-ts'ai* figures of animals and humans. The men here shown, both foreign grooms, wear open-necked coats without a right sleeve. Perhaps convenient when riding, this coat without a right sleeve is thought to have been customary wear for grooms at this period. However, they do wear a shoulder pad on the right shoulder. The horses, though similar, are subtly different in that the white one stands quiet while the red one is neighing. There is no indication in the report as to which horse belongs to which groom.
Ref: WTT, 1956, No. 8; 五省出土重要文物展覧圖録, 1958

257. *Heavenly Guardian, earthenware with slip decoration. T'ang dynasty.*

The helmet appears to be made of leather. This is a particularly beautiful figure of a Heavenly Guardian, reminiscent of the Japanese *Jūni Jinshō* ("Twelve Heavenly Guardians"). The typical T'ang representation of these figures is mannered and pretentious, but this example is a masterpiece of dignity and composure. This tomb, excavated in April, 1956, contained a great many models and wall paintings (*see* Pls. 192, 193, 226, 369, 379, 380, 382, 385, 386). It can be dated at 668 A.D. by the burial tablet.
Ref: W, 1959, No. 3; 陝西省出土唐俑選集, 1958

258. *Heavenly Guardian, earthenware with* san-ts'ai *glaze. T'ang dynasty.*

Such armored figures produced in the T'ang dynasty represent either human soldiers or Heavenly Guardians, and it is not always easy to be sure of the difference. In this case, he is a Heavenly Guardian, since he stands on an animal. Such a piece was presumably placed near the entrance of a tomb to ward off evil spirits.

259. *Figures, earthenware. Warring States period.*

A total of eighteen such images were excavated from the same tomb. There are signs of a spatula having been used in the modeling, and the surface is coated with iron oxide, giving a red color. Although the representation is extremely simple, with a nose as the only facial feature, there are a great variety of poses. The hairstyles and sashes are valuable anthropological data. The base of the figures is flat and pierced by a small hole. Possibly they were originally grouped and fixed on pegs on a wooden board. There has long been controversy about the provenance of such pieces, but this excavation at least confirms one site.
Ref: KX, 1957, No. 1

260. *Figures, carved wood. Late Warring States period.*

These figures are like Japanese *kokeshi* dolls with a little carving added. The faces, clothes, etc. are painted in color on a white base. Figures thought to be a little earlier than these are in the Waseda University and the Tenri Sankōkan collections in Japan. These wooden figures must have been developed from those to which Confucius objected, saying that to bury them seems too much like the immolation of living people.
Ref: KX, 1957, No. 2

261. *Figure, wood. Late Warring States period.*

This figure stretches both arms forward, perhaps holding an offering. Among the wooden figures found in Ch'angsha, there are others in which, as here, the arms have been made separately and attached to the body.
Ref: KX, 1956, No. 6

262. *Figures, earthenware. Later Han dynasty.*

The long garments flare to the feet, and the faces are large, with well-defined eyes and eyebrows. The tombs from which these figures were excavated were built in 76 A.D.
Ref: W. 1959, No. 11

263-265. *Figures, earthenware. Late Han dynasty or early Six Dynasties.*

The Lü-ta area in the northeast of Liaotung was under strong Han influence. However, while the structure of the tombs and the house-shaped tomb models are in the same tradition, the human figures show little similarity and lack the life and sophistication of the more central area. These figures somehow recall the *haniwa* of Japan. In general, the figures in this northeastern area are larger and cruder than those further south. The woman in Plate 265 is half nude, with a long skirt flaring to the ground. The date of this tomb is given as late Han or Six Dynasties.
Ref: KT, 1956, No. 3

266-267. *Animal figures, carved, lacquered wood. Later Han dynasty.*

A number of wooden figures were excavated from the wooden coffin tomb at Feng-huang-shan, Szuchwan. They are painted with black lacquer. This example bears faint traces of lacquer. In spite of the damaged condition, the animals show an intense liveliness in contrast to the earthenware horse models of the period.
Ref: K, 1959, No. 8

268-270. *Figures, carved wood. Later Han dynasty.*

In the Warring States period, wooden figures of human beings were seldom shown with legs, but were usually dressed in a long skirt that covered the figure to the feet. With these figures, the legs are clearly shown, though the bodies still retain the flatness characteristic of the earlier carvings. It is perhaps because Szuchwan is so far away from the metropolitan area of China that this style was carried forward into the Han period.
Ref: *Ibid.*

271. *Dancers, carved, plaster-coated and painted wood. Later Han dynasty.*

These very simple but animated figures are in a sense a development from the black earthenware figures of the previous period, with the same vitality but replacing curves with straight lines.
Ref: WTT, 1958, No. 11

272. *Figures, carved, plaster-coated and painted wood. Later Han dynasty.*

Wooden figures are rare among the human-figure *ming-ch'i* of the Later Han period. Many wooden *ming-ch'i* were found in this tomb, and all are equally simple in their

technique. These carvings remind one of certain folk-art carvings in Japan. The surface is coated with a fine, white lime plaster on which lines are painted in red and black. Such features are of importance in any discussion of the development of Ch'ang-sha wooden figures.
Ref: *Ibid.*

273. *Animal figure, carved, plaster-coated and painted wood. Later Han dynasty.*

The surface of this piece is painted with a white lime plaster and the lines are black.
Ref: *Ibid.*

274. *Chickens, carved, plaster-coated and painted wood. Later Han dynasty.*

These creatures are carved out of flat boards. The feathers and tail are drawn in red and black on a white ground.
Ref: *Ibid.*

275. *Dancers, earthenware. Later Han dynasty.*

Vividly portrayed in the action of the dance, these figures in their vitality are in no way inferior to the black earthenware figures of the Warring States, and have an even greater fluidity.
Ref: K, 1961, No. 8

276. *Pipe players, earthenware. Later Han dynasty.*
Ref: *Ibid.*

277. *Musicians, earthenware. Later Han dynasty.*

Many models of musicians playing in groups were made during the Han dynasty and continued to be made until the eighth or ninth century.
Ref: *Ibid.*

278. *Fat-bellied figures, earthenware. Later Han dynasty.*
Ref: *Ibid.*

279. *Attendant, earthenware. Han dynasty.*

The ceramic models of Szuchwan shown in this and the later plates are already modeled in the round, without the old flatness, and have a sense of flowing movement. In this, they are quite different from the contemporary pieces from the central area of China. The discovery of tomb models in Szuchwan has done much to correct the mistaken view that the carving and modeling of the Chinese in the Han dynasty was all naive or crude.
Ref: KT, 1955, No. 6

280. *Scholars, earthenware. Han dynasty.*
Ref: *Ibid.*

281. *Man beating a* fu, *earthenware. Later Han dynasty.*

A number of musician figures have been excavated from this brick tomb. All are cheerful, smiling figures. This man beats a *fu* (拊), an instrument similar to a *ku* (鼓) drum.
Ref: WTT, 1955, No. 3

282. *Dancer, earthenware. Later Han dynasty.*

This figure seems to be dancing in a slow tempo. The bagginess of the sleeve gives a weight and volume to the figure entirely characteristic of this type.
Ref: *Ibid.*

283. *Dancer, earthenware. Later Han dynasty.*

This dancer lifts his skirt in a manner similar to the figurine in Plate 282. The tooled representation of the folds is very effective.
Ref: K, 1959, No. 8

284. *Kneeling musician, earthenware. Later Han dynasty.*

This smiling musician playing a *ch'in* across his knees is a typical Han *ming-ch'i* of the Szuchwan area.
Ref: *Ibid.*

285. *Man listening to music, earthenware. Later Han dynasty.*

Kneeling with his right hand on his knee and left hand raised to his ear, this figure with head slightly on one side has been said to be singing. Other authorities have said that he is listening to the *ch'in.* Since a singing figure was also found in this tomb, I consider that this man is indeed listening with a smile of satisfaction on his face.
Ref: *Ibid.*

286. *Figures in movement, earthenware. Han dynasty.*

These figures appear to be dancing together. They are among the masterpieces of Han human figures.
Ref: WTT, 1955, No. 4

287. *Storyteller, earthenware. Later Han dynasty.*

A masterpiece among the modeled tomb figures of Szuchwan, the old man is shown in full action as he tells his story. The immense vitality of this figure shows the marked advance in expressiveness and technical skill of the makers of *ming-ch'i* in Szuchwan through the Han dynasty. This is undoubtedly the most individual piece discovered in the area.
Ref: W, 1959, No. 10; 新中国的考古収獲, 1962

288. *Figures, gray earthenware. Han dynasty.*
Ref: WTT, 1955, No. 12

289. *Female figure, gray earthenware. Later Han dynasty.*

This was excavated in 1954. It is a far more lifelike representation that the two Han figures in Plate 290, and is one of the masterpieces of this type of standing figure.
Ref: KT, 1956, No. 3

290. *Couple, slip-painted earthenware. Han dynasty.*

The woman stands on the left. The pair represents a considerable development in the Ch'ang-sha type of standing figure. A certain flatness is still retained, but the exaggerated flaring of the skirt around the feet is characteristic of the Han period.
Ref: WTT, 1955, No. 7

291. *Female figure, slip-painted earthenware. Han dynasty.*

This is a typical gray earthenware tomb figure of a standing woman. The gray body is covered with a white slip. The slender figure, wearing two undergarments beneath her red gown, stands quietly with her skirt fanning wide at her feet. Her eyes are slanting and her lips curve in a gentle smile.

292. *Cook, green-glazed earthenware. Han dynasty.*

The cook is chopping on a block. The head is disproportionately large and the features exaggerated.

293. *Cook, green-glazed earthenware. Han dynasty.*

Though very similar to the figures from Kao-t'ang District, Shantung, this is a better quality piece.
Ref: KT, 1955, No. 6

294. *Man holding a* hu, *gray earthenware. Han dynasty.*
Ref: KT, 1957, No. 3

295. *Man holding a sword and shield, gray earthenware. Han dynasty.*
Ref: *Ibid.*

296. *Man holding a spade and winnow, gray earthenware. Han dynasty.*

Probably this figure shows a typical farmer of the region. All the Han figures of Szuchwan have the same mildness of style with nothing emphatic in the modeling, but compared with the figures in, for example, Plates 281 and 283, this figure lacks a sense of rhythm.
Ref: *Ibid.*

297. *Cockerel, earthenware. Han dynasty.*

Ming-chi'i chickens are always represented with thick and clumsy legs, but in the Szuchwan area, even a figure such as this cockerel has a rounded, contented air that does not preclude liveliness.
Ref: KT, 1955, No. 6

298. *Cockerel, earthenware. Later Han dynasty.*

Both a cock and hen model were found in this tomb. The cock here shown is plump and stands firmly, with high, plumed tail.
Ref: K, 1959, No. 8

299. *Drake, earthenware. Later Han dynasty.*

Figures of both a duck and drake were found in the tomb, the duck in charge of a duckling. The balance and rhythm of the modeling of the neck and breast of the drake shown here are particularly fine.
Ref: *Ibid.*

300. *Hen and chicks, earthenware. Later Han dynasty.*

This is a very lively representation of a hen crouching over one chick with another beneath her wing, and illustrates the keen observation of the Szuchwan craftsmen.
Ref: *Ibid.*

301. *Cock and hen, earthenware. Han dynasty.*

The cock stands on the right. A very similar model of a cock was found in a tomb at Mu-ma-shan. They appear clumsy, but actually capture the movements of real chickens very accurately.
Ref: WTT, 1955, No. 12

302. *Pigs, earthenware. Later Han dynasty.*

These are domesticated pigs. Both figures were placed at the entrance to the tomb, on a bed of speckled pebbles.
Ref: WTT, 1955, No. 3

303. *Pig, earthenware. Han dynasty.*

A more realistic representation than that of Plate 302.
Ref: KT, 1955, No. 6

304. *Dog, earthenware. Later Han dynasty.*

A little bigger than the figure shown in Plate 305, this is a fine contrast to the thin dog excavated at tomb No. 1, Pai-chüan, Hui District, Szuchwan.
Ref: K, 1959, No. 8

305. *Dog, earthenware. Later Han dynasty.*

This species of dog seems to have been popular in Han times, and similar models have been found throughout China. But, as might be expected, the pieces from Szuchwan show a particular keenness of observation.
Ref: WTT, 1955, No. 3

306. *Dog, earthenware. Han dynasty.*
Ref: WTT, 1955, No. 12

307. *Dog, earthenware. Han dynasty.*

A particularly fine example of a favorite theme of Han *ming-ch'i*, this barking dog is vividly represented.
Ref: KT, 1955, No. 6

308. *Dog, earthenware. Han dynasty.*

This is a very roughly made model. The front legs are joined, as are the back legs. There is no representation of the features of the face.
Ref: W, 1961, No. 7

309. *Cookstove with figures, earthenware. Later Han dynasty (dated 76 A.D.).*

This cookstove is equipped with three pans on the top and two large water jars standing beside it. One figure is stoking the fire while the other appears to be washing something in one of the jars. Such cookstoves complete with human figures are rare.
Ref: W, 1959, No. 11

310. *Cookstove, earthenware. Han dynasty.*

There is a chimney at the end of the stove and a wide pan on top. This is very simple in comparison with other models from Szuchwan.
Ref: WTT, 1955, No. 12

311. *Well head, earthenware. Han dynasty.*

This well must originally have had a wooden wheel and rope, both of which have decayed away. Although many

such wells appear in *ming-ch'i*, this is the most elaborate example seen so far.
Ref: KT, 1955, No. 6

312. *Columnar object, earthenware. Han dynasty.*

In two sections, it is not clear just what this model represents. Possibly an incense burner or a lamp stand.
Ref: K, 1959, No. 8

313. *Well head, gray earthenware. Han dynasty.*

A variety of well-head shapes were in use in China at this time, but this is the one most typical of the period. It has a roof, and wheel and ropes to hold the bucket. The outer surface of the well is decorated with spiral rope motif in relief.
Ref: *Ibid.*

314. *Incense burner, earthenware. Later Han dynasty.*

Here the incense burner is in the shape of a *tou* on a tall, pierced stand. The hemispherical cover is surmounted by a bird with spread wings. Many *ming-ch'i* of incense burners are unpierced, since they were intended solely as models. However, this example, elaborately pierced in the bowl, has indeed been used; the report mentions ashes of incense inside it.
Ref: WTT, 1955, No. 3

315. *Paddy field and pond, earthenware. Later Han dynasty.*

Models of scenes of everyday life were not unusual among Szuchwan *ming-ch'i.* The paddy field is divided into two sections, one being a pool in which there is a fish, snail, frog, turtle, water chestnut and lotus leaf. The dividing barrier is left incomplete so that the water can reach the paddy.
Ref: *Ibid.*

316. *Oval cups and bowl on a stand, earthenware. Later Han dynasty.*

It is customary for such a stand to have cups and a bowl with it. The oval-eared cups and bowl are here arranged on the stand just as they were placed in the tomb. The interior of the cups and the legs of the stand are coated with a red color.
Ref: *Ibid.*

317. *Tower, earthenware. Han dynasty.*

This is a *ming-ch'i* model of an ancient four-story building with a covered gateway at the front. The main purpose of such tall buildings was to gain a panoramic view, and indeed, a man is standing at each window of this model looking out. Although it may not be a model of an actual tower, the apricot-leaf decorations at the roof angles are extremely interesting.
Ref: W, 1961, No. 1

318. *One- and three-story buildings, gray earthenware. Later Han dynasty.*

Excavated in 1954, these two buildings were found arranged as shown in the left-hand plate. The top floor of the tall building has a veranda around three sides. In each building the beams are supported by brackets. There is a funnel-shaped drainage hole in the ground floor of the three-story building. The one-story building has a floor raised four centimeters above ground level and a half-open door to the room on the right. These buildings probably represent the main building of a residence of the type often represented in Szuchwan art.
Ref: WTT, 1955, No. 3

319. *Two-story building, earthenware. Later Han dynasty.*

A great variety of house models appear among the Szuchwan *ming-ch'i.* This two-story house is built on a raised platform. The beam of the first floor is supported by a large bracket in the center. There are probably two rooms on the ground floor, and a ladder leads up to the second floor. The roof has a gentle slope and the roof beam is artfully curved upward at the ends. Perhaps this is a fairly faithful representation of an ordinary house of the area.
Ref: K, 1959, No. 8

320. *One-story building, earthenware. Later Han dynasty.*

The roof is tiled and the ridges covered with triple tiles. The frontal beam is supported by two sets of brackets on round pillars. The side beams are also supported by brackets. A double staircase with a balustrade between the two pillars leads to the raised platform of the building. On this platform, a third round pillar also supports a set of brackets. The rectangular hole in the side wall is a ventilator. Generally speaking, *ming-ch'i* of buildings cannot be regarded as faithful models, but in this case the brackets at least seem to be true copies of those used in the wooden buildings of the time. To judge by its massive construction, this would appear to be a part of a palace or temple building.
Ref: *Ibid.*

321-322. *Castle with dwelling houses, earthenware. Later Han dynasty.*

Castle models are very unusual. This elaborate piece shows high walls with a gate front and back and six lookout towers, one at each corner and over each of the two gates. Inside the walls, ladders lead up to the towers. Plate 322 shows the two houses that were found within the walls. A total of eleven people and a horse are in these models.
Ref: W, 1959, No. 11; 新中国的考古収獲, 1962

323. *Chicken house, earthenware. Wu dynasty.*

The construction is quite simple, but there are two entrances and a platform that projects at the front. The body material and glaze are similar to those of the duck house found in the same tomb (Pl. 234).
Ref: K, 1959, No. 4

324. *Duck house, bluish-green-glazed earthenware. Wu dynasty.*

This is made of purplish-gray earthenware and is glazed with a bluish-green glaze. A lattice design is incised on the walls. There are three ducks at the entrance. This piece was excavated with a lead tag bearing the date 永安五年 ("fifth year of Yung-an"), which corresponds to the year 262 A.D.
Ref: *Ibid.*

325-326. *Kneeling figures, blue-glazed earthenware. Wu dynasty.*

Four human figures of this type have been excavated from Wu tombs. Two wear pointed caps, as in Plate 325, and the others flat ones. They all sit on their heels with hands folded in the lap. The meaning of the round protruberance on the forehead, like a Buddhist *ŭrnă*, is unknown. The modeling is naive and somewhat mild.
Ref: *Ibid.*

327. *Soldiers, earthenware. Northern Wei dynasty.*

These figures were excavated in 1955. Shao Chen was a governor of Ho-yang, and his tomb is dated as contructed in 520 A.D. Since the *ming-ch'i* seem to have been undisturbed since burial, this excavation is of special interest. These soldiers were door guards for the main chamber and stood at either side of the entrance. The right hand of each figure appears to have been holding something, and the left is tucked into the apron. The heads are made separately and fixed into a socket at the neck.
Ref: WTT, 1955, No. 12

328-329. *Female figures, earthenware. Northern Wei dynasty.*

This hairstyle of braids arranged in a cross on the top of the head seems to have been the fashion of this period. In contrast with the vehemence typical of other northern figures, the group of figures found at Ts'ao-ch'ang-p'o-ts'un, Sian, show a marked mildness of style, and are similar in feeling to those of Mu-fu-shan, Nanking (Plate 330).
Ref: K, 1959, No. 6

330. *Female figure, earthenware. Six Dynasties.*

Numerous other Wu and Chin figures have been excavated from tombs in the Mu-fu-shan, Chao-shih-kang and Ting-chia-shan areas of Nanking. They all have a gentle mildness of expression that sets them apart from the *ming-ch'i* of the north. This figure is useful material in the study of sculpture of the Southern Dynasties.
Ref: WTT, 1955, No. 8; 南京六朝墓出土文物選集, 1957

331. *Female figure, earthenware. Six Dynasties.*

In style and technique, this figure is very similar to the Mu-fu-shan piece (Plate 330).
Ref: 南京六朝陶俑, 1958

332. *Female figure, earthenware. Six Dynasties.*
Ref: K, 1961, No. 8

333. *Female figure, earthenware. Six Dynasties.*
Ref: K, 1959, No. 3

334-335. *Soldiers, earthenware. Northern Wei dynasty.*

Many similar figures have been excavated from this tomb since 1953. The chamber is of a considerably older style than that at Jen-chia-k'ou (523 A.D.), and resembles a late Han tomb, so that even assuming it belongs to the Northern Wei dynasty, it must be very early. The rounded, mild style of modeling is typical of figures from this tomb. As already discussed (*see* Plate 329 Note), the female figures show similarities with those of the Nanking area. The summary modeling of the horses' legs (*see* Plates 339, 340) is a feature that distinguishes these models from Han *ming-ch'i*, and the large horn that the rider is blowing in Plate 340 marks him as a member of a northern army.
Ref: K, 1959, No. 6

336. *Male figure, earthenware. Six Dynasties*
Ref: K, 1959, No. 3

337. *Scribes, earthenware. Chin dynasty.*

These are quite unusual pieces. In spite of the poor modeling technique, there is a mysterious power of expression in the two figures.
Ref: KX, 1959, No. 3; 新中国的考古収獲, 1962

338. *Scholar, earthenware. Chin dynasty.*

Although very simply executed, the impression of a wise, intelligent man is skillfully realized.
Ref: KT, 1958, No. 9

339. *Equestrian figure, earthenware. Northern Wei dynasty.*
Ref: *Ibid.*

340. *Equestrian figure blowing a horn, earthenware. Northern Wei dynasty.*

The artist seems to have been more interested in the man blowing the horn than in the horse. However, in spite of the casual modeling, the whole effect is lively.
Ref: K, 1959, No. 6

341. *Horse, earthenware. Six Dynasties.*

Although the legs are disproportionately short, the observation and representation of the horse is very lively. The saddle with its cloth and the alert head of the horse are skillfully suggested. This is a very gentle, likeable piece of work.
Ref: WTT, 1955, No. 8; 南京六朝陶俑, 1958

342. *Overcoated male figure, earthenware. Sui dynasty.*

This figure of a man in trousers, long robe and overcoat seems to have originally held something in the right hand. It was excavated from the tomb of Li Ching-hsün, in August, 1957. Li Ching-hsün was a daughter of a nobleman, and died at the age of nine in 608 A.D. Many other figures, including tomb guardians, soldiers and men and women were found in this tomb. They are all mold-made of red earthenware, and some are slip decorated.
Ref: K, 1959, No. 9

343. *Overcoated male figure, earthenware. Sui dynasty.*

A great many such figures of men wearing coats in a Caucasian manner have been found in tombs of the Sui and early T'ang periods. This piece is valuable because the date of production can be determined.
Ref: *Ibid.*

344. *Overcoated male figure, earthenware. Sui dynasty.*

As in the figures shown in Plates 342 and 343, this man wears an overcoat and hood. He does not put his arms into the sleeves of the coat, but folds them on his chest.

Apparently this piece was excavated from the tomb of Feng Tzu-hui, (*see* Pl. 346 Note).
Ref: WTT, 1957, No. 3

345. *Soldier holding a shield, earthenware. Sui dynasty.*
Ref: KT, 1957, No. 3

346. *Military officer in armor, earthenware. Sui dynasty.*

This man wears a suit of armor over his trousers and jacket. He also wears an official cap.

In the Ching District of Hopei there is a group of tombs of the Feng family. Over the centuries, farmers in the area respected these graves and even held rites for the dead. However, in 1948, discarding their superstitions, they dug up four of the tombs, removing the contents to their own homes. The four tombs are as follows: Feng Mo-nu (封魔奴), reburied on the thirtieth day of the tenth month of 521 A.D.: Feng Yen-chih (封延之), buried on the twenty-third day of the tenth month, 541 A.D., and his wife, buried on the twenty-sixth day of the second month, 589 A.D.; Feng Tzu-hui (封子絵), buried on the seventh day of the second month, 565 A.D., and his wife, buried on the fifteenth day of the second month, 583 A.D.; and Tsu Shih (祖氏) (only the cover of the burial tablet was found). It will be noted that the dates extend over the Northern Wei, Ch'i, Western Wei and Sui dynasties.

The contents of the tombs have now been collected by archaeologists and placed in the Ching District government office. However, though the burial markers survive, the dating of the finds is now uncertain, since the excavation was uncontrolled. A Sui dynasty date has been given to this piece, although many stylistic features indicate a Northern Wei date.
Ref: *Ibid.*

347. *Official wearing a woven cane cap, earthenware. Sui dynasty.*

This type of woven cane official cap was much worn in the Northern Wei dynasty, but as this comes from a tomb dated 608 A.D., it was clearly still in use in early Sui times.
Ref: K, 1959, No. 9

348. *Official wearing a small official cap, earthenware. Sui dynasty.*

It is interesting that this tomb was built in the same year (608 A.D.), which almost certainly makes this figure contemporary with the construction of the Hōryūji Temple, Japan.
Ref: *Ibid.*; 新中国的考古収獲, 1962

349. *Female figure, earthenware. Sui dynasty.*

The hairstyle is flat, and the gown very high-waisted. This figure, produced in 608 A.D., has an almost severe expression, with none of the voluptuous beauty often associated with female figures of the T'ang dynasty.
Ref: *Ibid.*

350. *Woman holding a shovel, earthenware. Sui dynasty.*

This woman holds a *ch'an* (鏟), a kind of shovel, and seems to be working outdoors. The hairstyle and costume are the same as with the ladies-in-waiting in Plate 352.
Ref: K, 1959, No. 10

351. *Woman winnowing, earthenware. Sui dynasty.*

Many figures of women sitting winnowing were produced during and after the Six Dynasties period. This piece is particularly beautiful for its volume and grace.
Ref: *Ibid.*

352. *Ladies-in-waiting, earthenware with slip decoration. Sui dynasty.*

Excavated in May, 1959, this tomb of Chang Sheng and his wife was built in 595 A.D. near Sha-ch'ang, Yü-pei, An-yang District. According to the report of the excavation, stoneware figures of soldiers and guardian animals, and earthenware figures of men and women, ladies-in-waiting, dancers, musicians, foreigners, priests, and domestic animals and birds were found. Also, there were various articles, or models of articles, used in everyday life. It is noteworthy that forty-nine of the actual everyday objects are of Greenware.

The group of figures are presumably ladies-in-waiting at work. The costume includes a long, loose skirt tied high at the breast with long sashes hanging down the front. The long sleeves hang down over the hands. The color shcemes include a green blouse with red skirt, and brown and yellow blouse with green skirt. The hairstyles are flat, apparently with ornamental pins at the back.
Ref: *Ibid.*

353-355. *Mills, earthenware. Sui dynasty.*

The object pictured in Plate 353 is a foot mill, while the objects in Plates 354 and 355 are models of hand mills. The foot mill was made in 608 A.D.
Ref: *Ibid.*

356. *Cookstove, earthenware. Sui dynasty.*
Ref: KT, 1957, No. 3

357-358. *Animals on low pedestals, earthenware with slip painting and glaze. Sui dynasty.*

The animals are set on "lotus stands" very similar to those used for Buddhist figures. The stands are slip-painted in red, yellow, green, black and white, while the animals are glazed. The dog in Plate 358 appears to be barking. The report classifies these as objects for everyday use, but the purpose is unknown.
Ref: K, 1959, No. 10

359. *Armrest, gray earthenware. Six Dynasties.*

Unlike the usual armrest, this has three legs and seems a more substantial rest on which one can lean the full weight of the body.
Ref: K, 1959, No. 3

360. *Ox, earthenware. Sui dynasty.*
Ref: K, 1959, No. 9; 新中国的考古収獲, 1962

361. *Tomb guardian beasts, earthenware. Northern Wei dynasty.*

These were placed to either side of the main chamber of the tomb and accompanied the guard soldiers pictured in Plate 327.
Ref: WTT, 1955, No. 12

362. *Mythical beast, gray earthenware. Six Dynasties.*

The hornlike projections on the back and flanks probably represent hair on this imaginary animal, which was probably suggested by the rhinoceros.
Ref: K, 1959, No. 3

363. *Dog, earthenware. Chin dynasty.*

This dog appears to have just awakened and shows some displeasure. The tomb was built in 285 A.D.
Ref: WTT, 1955, No. 8

364. *Female figure, red earthenware with traces of slip painting. T'ang dynasty.*

This woman wears a blouse and skirt and a long stole, under which she hides her hands. The hairstyle is similar to that of the figures in Plate 367, and is often shown in wall paintings of this date. This is probably a lady-in-waiting. The tomb is dated 706 A.D.
Ref: WTT, 1958, No. 8

365. *Male figure in foreign clothes, red earthenware with traces of slip painting. T'ang dynasty.*

Similar in pose to Plate 366, but wearing a tall hat.
Ref: *Ibid.*

366. *Male figure in foreign clothes, red earthenware with traces of slip painting. T'ang dynasty.*

This tomb, excavated in 1957, contained a great variety of models, including men on horseback, women, soldiers, dogs, cows, bullock carts, sheep, chickens, ducks and tomb guardians. All are mold-made of reddish earthenware, and were originally slip painted. The decoration has largely worn off.
Ref: *Ibid.*

367. *Female figures, red earthenware with traces of slip painting. T'ang dynasty (*see *Plate 364 Note).*
Ref: *Ibid.*

368. *Male figures in foreign clothes, red earthenware with traces of slip painting. T'ang dynasty.*

These two figures stand very straight and may have held a banner or flag in their hands.
Ref: *Ibid.*

369. *Female figure, earthenware. T'ang dynasty (668 A.D.).*

With a décolleté blouse and long skirt tied at the waist with a long sash, this lady wears her hair dressed high on top of her head and has a stole draped around her shoulders. There are women with exactly similar clothing and hairstyle in the wall paintings in this same tomb, which is dated 668 A.D. Perhaps this is a typical lady-in-waiting of the period.
Ref: W, 1959, No. 3

370. *Male figure, earthenware. T'ang dynasty (748 A.D.).*

A typical male figure of the second quarter of the T'ang dynasty, this figure was made in 748 A.D. The man wears an official cap and a long, collarless garment tied at the waist with a sash.
Ref: WTT, 1955, No. 7; 陝西省出土唐俑選集, 1958

371. *Civil official, earthenware. T'ang dynasty (748 A.D.).*

This tomb was excavated in March, 1955. A great variety of *ming-ch'i* was found in it, many of which were damaged. The report stresses the vivid colors of those still in good condition, which include human and animal figures, human figures with heads of the zodiacal creatures, Heavenly Guardians, guardian beasts, and mounted figures.
Ref: *Ibid.*

372. *Female figure, earthenware. T'ang dynasty (748 A.D.).*

This plump figure is standing in a graceful swaying pose, slightly bending back, with her head tilted to the left. This is a female figure of the type known in Japan as "Beauty Under the Tree," after the painting in the Shōsōin repository.
Ref: *Ibid.*

373. *Heavenly Guardian, slip-painted earthenware. T'ang dynasty (748 A.D.).*

The report classifies this model as a soldier, but the glaring eyes and foot resting on a demon mark him clearly as a Heavenly Guardian. The skin is painted reddish brown, and the features are drawn in black ink. There is a bird ornament on the front of the helmet. As this is a dated tomb (748 A.D.), this piece is of importance in the consideration of styles of Buddhist statues of Heavenly Guardians and *t'ien-wang* ("Heavenly Kings") of this period.
Ref: *Ibid.*

374. *Comic actor, earthenware. T'ang dynasty.*

With shrugged shoulders and hands folded, this clowning actor grins sheepishly.
Ref: W, 1959, No. 8; 陝西省出土唐俑選集, 1958

375. *Two characters from a* hsi-lung *theatrical, glazed earthenware. T'ang dynasty* (723 A.D.).

The *hsi-lung* (戲弄) was a very popular entertainment in the T'ang dynasty with a very simple plot, and included singing, dancing and dialogue. Among titles of *hsi-lung* known are "San-chün-hsi" (参軍戯), "Hsi-liang-chi" (西涼伎) and "Lan Ling Wang" (蘭陵王). The Chinese scholar T'ien Chin identifies these two figures as characters from the "San-chün-hsi." He bases this premise on the costume and expressions and the fact that the figures appear as a pair. They are exceptionally fine glazed figures. This tomb is dated 723 A.D.
Ref: *Ibid.*; KT, 1958, No. 1; 新中国的考古収獲, 1962

376. *Seated female figure, earthenware with* san-ts'ai *glaze. T'ang dynasty.*

Although this is very similar to the figure shown in Plate 378, and although they were both excavated at Wang-chia-fen-ts'un, Sian, they come from different tombs. The stole is glazed blue, and the skirt, brown, with impressed floral decoration.
Ref: WTT, 1954, No. 10; 陝西省出土唐俑選集, 1958

377. *Money chest, earthenware with* san-ts'ai *glaze. T'ang dynasty.*

This chest was found placed in front of the seated woman illustrated in Plate 376. There is a hinged lid, which has a loop corresponding to one on the body of the chest. These two loops appear to have taken a lock, as in a similar chest in the St. Louis Art Museum. The top of the chest bears a floral design, and the sides, animal masks. The legs are heavily studded. There is a narrow slit in the top of the chest, which probably accounts for the classification in the report as a money box. It may, however, represent a cosmetic chest for toilet articles or other personal belongings.
Ref: WTT, 1956, No. 8; 五省出土重要文物展覽圖錄, 1958

378. *Seated female figure, earthenware with* san-ts'ai *glaze. T'ang dynasty.*

This figure was excavated in March, 1955. She seems to have been holding a mirror, now lost, in her left hand and raising her right to adjust her makeup. The prunus decoration on the forehead was a fashion of the day. The lady has a very high dressed coiffure and beautiful flower-patterned blouse and skirt. The figure was found placed before a *san-ts'ai ming-ch'i* of a chest. The report regards this figure as representing the occupant of the tomb because it is thought to be too grand to be a servant and because no other human figures were found in the tomb.

379-380. *Equestrian figures, slip-painted earthenware. T'ang dynasty (668 A.D.).*

Forty-seven models of men and women on horseback were found in the side chambers on either side of the approach to this tomb. The horses are slip-painted in red or white with the harness drawn in black ink. The horses' legs had been strengthened with a metal wire armature, but, in spite of this, they were damaged when found. These examples have been restored. The women's faces are painted white and their costume is red or green. The tomb is dated 668 A.D.
Ref: W, 1959, No. 3

381. *Horse and groom, earthenware with* san-ts'ai *glaze. T'ang dynasty (*see *Plate 252 Note).*
Ref: K, 1960, No. 3

382. *Equestrian musician, slip-painted earthenware. T'ang dynasty* (668 A.D.).

Many of the equestrian figures from this tomb are musicians (*see* Plates 379-380 Note). Most of the male figures are dressed in an open-necked, foreign-style garment, which is painted red or blue. The faces of the men are usually red. The horse is very similar to that in Plate 379.
Ref: W, 1959, No. 3

383. *Horse, earthenware with* san-ts'ai *glaze. T'ang dynasty.*

This model shows a horse with a long mane, as also seen in Plates 252 and 381. The more usual trim during the T'ang dynasty was for the mane to be clipped, and the forelock parted in two. The left-hand lock was grasped by the rider when mounting.
Ref: K, 1960, No. 3; 新中国的考古収獲, 1962

384. *Horse and foreign groom, earthenware. T'ang dynasty.*

This is an unusually lively example of a subject that is not uncommon among tomb models.

385-386. *Tomb guardians, earthenware. T'ang dynasty (668 A.D.).*

These two figures were placed one on either side of the entrance to the burial chamber to ward off evil spirits. The figure in Plate 385 has an animal body and a ferocious lion face with exaggerated mane. The mate to it in Plate 386 has an animal body with cloven hoofs and a human face. The most typical tomb guardians of T'ang usually show two horns on a lion face and one horn on a human face, but these seem to have none.
Ref: W, 1959, No. 3

K. Ando

Archaeological Site Map

1. Liaoning
2. Shen-yang, Liaoning
3. Liao River
4. Liao-yang, Liaoning
5. Lü-ta
6. Hopei
7. Luan River
8. T'ang-shan, Hopei
9. Peking, Hopei
10. Yung-ting River
11. Yi District (Yen-hsia-tu), Hopei
12. T'ien-chin, Hopei
13. Tzu-ya River
14. Wang-tu District, Hopei
15. Ch'ü-yang, Hopei
16. Ching District, Hopei
17. Hsing-t'ai, Hopei
18. Han-tan (Chao-wang-ch'eng), Hopei
19. Tz'u District, Hopei
20. Inner Mongolia Autonomous Region
21. Hou-ho-hao-t'e, Inner Mongolia Autonomous Region
22. Shansi
23. Yün-kang, Shansi
24. Hun-yüan, Shansi
25. Yellow River
26. T'ai-yüan, Shansi
27. Fen River
28. Ch'ang-chih, Shansi
29. Hou-ma, Shansi
30. Shensi
31. Han-ch'eng District, Shensi
32. T'ung-kuan, Shensi
33. Hua District, Shensi
34. Pan-p'o-ts'un, Shensi
35. Hsien-yang District, Shensi
36. Ch'ien District, Shensi
37. Ch'i-shan District, Shensi
38. Pao-chi, Shensi
39. Sian (Ch'ang-an), Shensi
40. Hsing-p'ing District, Shensi
41. Fu-feng District, Shensi
42. Mei District, Shensi
43. Wei River
44. Ning-hsia Mohammedan Autonomous Region
45. Yin-ch'uan, Ning-hsia Mohammedan Autonomous Region
46. Kansu
47. Chiu-ch'üan, Kansu
48. Wu-wei, Kansu
49. Lan-chou, Kansu

(continued on page 242)

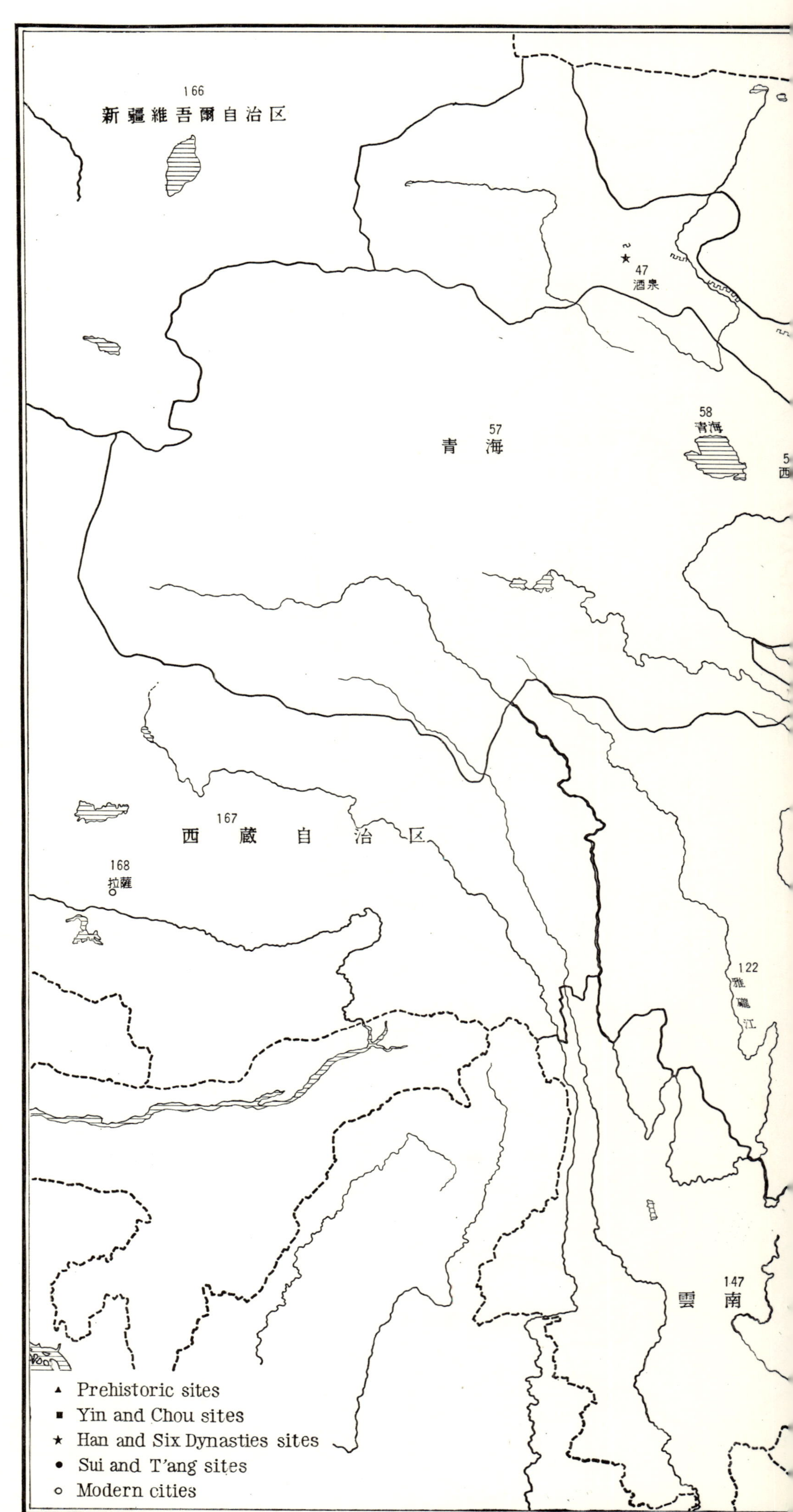

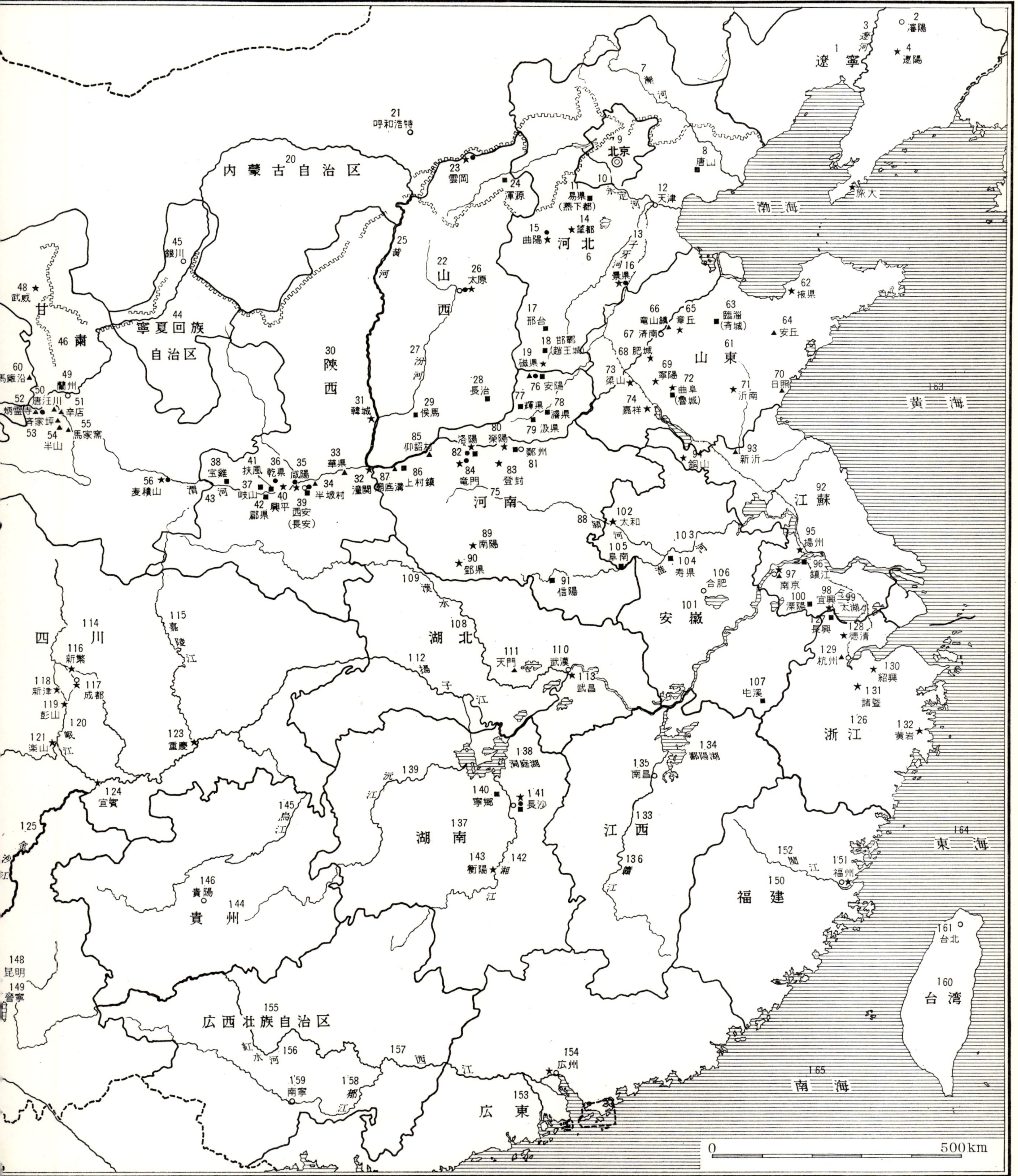
1 遼寧
2 瀋陽
3 遼河
4 遼陽
7 灤河
8 唐山
9 北京
10 永定河
11 易県（燕下都）
12 天津
13 子牙河
14 望都
15 曲陽
6 河北
16 景県
17 邢台
18 邯鄲（趙王城）
19 磁県
20 内蒙古自治区
21 呼和浩特
22 山西
23 雲岡
24 渾源
25 黄河
26 太原
27 汾河
28 長治
29 侯馬
30 陝西
31 韓城
32 潼関
33 華県
34 半坡村
35 咸陽
36 乾県
37 岐山
38 宝雞
39 西安（長安）
40 興平
41 扶風
42 鄠県
43 渭河
44 寧夏回族自治区
45 銀川
46 甘粛
48 武威
49 蘭州
50 唐汪川
51 辛店
52 炳霊寺
53 斉家坪
54 半山
55 馬家窯
56 麦積山
60 馬廠沿
61 山東
62 掖県
63 臨淄（斉城）
64 安丘
65 章丘
66 竜山鎮
67 済南
68 肥城
69 寧陽
70 日照
71 沂南
72 曲阜（魯城）
73 梁山
74 嘉祥
75 河南
76 安陽
77 輝県
78 濬県
79 汲県
80 滎陽
81 鄭州
82 洛陽
83 登封
84 竜門
85 仰韶村
86 上村鎮
87 廟底溝
88 潁河
89 南陽
90 鄧県
91 信陽
92 江蘇
93 新沂
94 銅山
95 揚州
96 鎮江
97 南京
98 宜興
99 太湖
100 溧陽
101 安徽
102 太和
103 淮河
104 寿県
105 阜南
106 合肥
107 屯溪
108 漢水
109 漢水
110 武漢
111 天門
112 揚子江
113 武昌
114 四川
115 嘉陵江
116 新繁
117 成都
118 新津
119 彭山
120 岷江
121 楽山
123 重慶
124 宜賓
125 金沙江
126 浙江
127 呉興
128 徳清
129 杭州
130 紹興
131 諸曁
132 黄岩
133 江西
134 鄱陽湖
135 南昌
136 贛江
137 湖南
138 洞庭湖
139 沅江
140 寧郷
141 長沙
142 湘江
143 衡陽
144 貴州
145 烏江
146 貴陽
148 昆明
149 晉寧
150 福建
151 福州
152 閩江
153 広東
154 広州
155 広西壮族自治区
156 紅水河
157 西江
158 郁江
159 南寧
160 台湾
161 台北
163 黄海
164 東海
165 南海
渤海
旅大
0
500km

50. T'ang-wang-ch'uan, Kansu
51. Hsin-tien, Kansu
52. Ping-ling-ssu, Kansu
53. Ch'i-chia-p'ing, Kansu
54. Pan-shan, Kansu
55. Ma-chia-yao, Kansu
56. Mai-chi-shan
57. Ch'ing-hai
58. Ch'ing-hai Lake
59. Hsi-ning, Ch'ing-hai
60. Ma-ch'ang-yan, Ch'ing-hai
61. Shantung
62. Yeh District, Shantung
63. Ling-tzu (Ch'i-ch'eng), Shantung
64. An-ch'iu District, Shantung
65. Chang-ch'iu District, Shantung
66. Lung-shan-chen, Shantung
67. Chi-nan, Shantung
68. Fei-ch'eng, Shantung
69. Ning-yang District, Shantung
70. Jih-chao District, Shantung
71. Yi-nan, Shantung
72. Ch-ü-fu (Lu-ch'eng), Shantung
73. Liang-shan District, Shantung
74. Chia-hsiang, Shantung
75. Honan
76. An-yang, Honan
77. Hui District, Honan
78. Chün District, Honan
79. Chi District, Honan
80. Hsing-yang District, Honan
81. Ch'eng-cho, Honan
82. Lo-yang, Honan
83. Teng-feng, Honan
84. Lung-men, Honan
85. Yang-shao-ts'un, Honan
86. Shang-ts'un-ling, Honan
87. Miao-ti-kou, Honan
88. Ying River
89. Nan-yang, Honan
90. Teng District, Honan
91. Hsin-yang, Honan
92. Kiangsu
93. Hsin-yi District, Kiangsu
94. T'ung-shan District, Kiangsu
95. Yang-chou, Kiangsu
96. Chen-chiang, Kiangsu
97. Nanking, Kiangsu
98. Yi-hsing District, Kiangsu
99. T'ai Lake (T'ai-hu)
100. Li-yang District, Kiangsu
101. Anhui
102. T'ai-ho District, Anhui
103. Huai River
104. Shou District, Anhui
105. Fu-nan District, Anhui
106. Ho-fei, Anhui
107. T'un-hsi, Anhui
108. Hupei
109. Han River (Han-chiang)
110. Han-k'ou (Wu-han), Hupei
111. T'ien-men, Hupei
112. Yangtze River
113. Wu-ch'ang, Hupei
114. Szuchwan
115. Chia-ling River
116. Hsin-fan, Szuchwan
117. Ch'eng-tu, Szuchwan
118. Hsin-chin, Szuchwan
119. P'eng-shan, Szuchwan
120. Min River
121. Lo-shan, Szuchwan
122. Ya-lung River
123. Chungking, Szuchwan
124. Yi-pin, Szuchwan
125. Chin-sha River
126. Chekiang
127. Ch'ang-hsing District, Chekiang
128. Te-ch'ing, Chekiang
129. Hangchow, Chekiang
130. Shao-hsing, Chekiang
131. Chu-chi District, Chekiang
132. Huang-yen District, Chekiang
133. Kiangsi
134. Po-yang Lake
135. Nan-ch'ang, Kiangsi
136. Kan River
137. Hunan
138. Tung-t'ing Lake
139. Yüan River
140. Ning-hsiang District, Hunan
141. Ch'ang-sha, Hunan
142. Hsiang River
143. Heng-yang, Hunan
144. Kueichou
145. Ch'ien River
146. Kuei-yang, Kueichou
147. Yünnan
148. K'un-ning, Yünnan
149. Chin-ning District, Yünnan
150. Fuchien
151. Fu-chou, Fuchien
152. Min River
153. Canton
154. Kuang-chou, Canton
155. Kuanghsi T'ungtsu Autonomous Region
156. Hung-shui River
157. Hsi River
158. Yü River
159. Nan-ning, Kuanghsi T'ung-tsu Aut. Region
160. Taiwan
161. T'aipei, Taiwan
162. Po-hai
163. Yellow Sea
164. East China Sea
165. South China Sea
166. Uighur Autonomous Region, Sinkiang.
167. Tibet Autonomous Region
168. Lhasa, Tibet Autonomous Region

Chronology of Archaeological Sites

The numbers in parentheses ( ) refer to entries on the Archaeological Site Map

YANG-SHAO SITES
(33) Hua District, Shensi
(41) Fu-feng District, Shensi
(34) Pan-p'o-ts'un, Sian, Shensi
Pai-tao-kou-p'ing, (49) Lan-chou, Kansu
San-p'ing, Lin-hsia District, Kansu
(55) Ma-chia-yao, Lin-yao District, Kansu
(87) Miao-ti-kou, Shan District, Honan
(85) Yang-shao-ts'un, Min-chih District, Honan
Pao-t'ou, (69) Ning-yang District, Shantung

LUNG-SHAN SITES
Ching-chih-chen, (64) An-ch'iu District, Shantung
Ch'eng-tzu-yai, (66) Lung-shan-chen, Li-ch'eng District, Shantung
Liang-ch'eng-chen, (70) Jih-chao District, Shantung
Liang-chu-chen, (129) Hangchow, Chekiang

OTHER NEOLITHIC SITES
Tung-chia-t'ai, T'ien-chu District, Kansu
Tu-chia-ts'un, Kuo-chia-p'ing, } Lin-t'ao District, Kansu
(50) T'ang-wang-ch'uan, Tung-hsiang Autonomous Region, Kansu
Shih-chia-ho, T'ien-men District, Hopei
Hua-t'ing-ts'un, (93) Hsin-yi District, Kiangsu

YIN SITES (1700–1050 B.C.)
Erh-li-kang, Pai-chia-chuang, } (81) Cheng-chou Municipality, Honan
Ch'i-li-p'u, Shan District, Honan
Hou-chia-chuang, Hsiao-t'un, Ta-shih-k'ung-ts'un, Wu-kuan-ts'un, } (76) An-yang District, Honan
Liu-li-ko, (77) Hui District, Honan
(140) Ning-hsiang District, Hunan
(105) Fu-nan District, Anhui
Ch'ing-hua-chen, (37) Ch'i-shan District, Shensi
Ts'ao-yen-chuang, (17) Hsing-t'ai, Hopei
Chu-chia-ch'iao, Ping-yin District, Shantung

WESTERN CHOU SITES (1050–770 B.C.)
Ch'i-chia-ts'un, (41) Fu-feng District, Shensi
(37) Ch'i-shan District, Shensi
P'u-tu-ts'un, Chang-chia-p'o, } (39) Ch'ang-an District (Sian), Shensi
Li-ts'un, (42) Mei District, Shensi
Hsin-ts'un, (78) Chün District, Honan
Tung-chiao, (82) Lo-yang, Honan
Yen-tun-shan, (96) Chen-chiang Municipality, Kiangsu
Ma-ch'ang-kou, Ling-yüan District, Liaoning
Shang-ts'ao-lou-ts'un, (127) Ch'ang-hsing District, Chekiang
(107) T'un-hsi Municipality, Anhui

CH'UN CH'IU SITES (770–403 B.C.)
Chung-chou-lu, (82) Lo-yang, Honan
Kuo state cemetery, (86) Shang-ts'un-ling, Shan District, Honan
Marquis of Ts'ai tomb, (104) Shou District, Anhui
Yi-shui District, Shantung
Chen-tse District, Kiangsu
Tung-chou ruins, (29) Hou-ma Municipality, Shansi

WARRING STATES SITES (403–249 B.C.)
Ch'en-chia-ta-shan, Huang-ni-k'eng, Yang-t'ien-hu, Wu-li-p'ai, Tso-chia-kung-shan, Yen-chia-tsui, Tzu-tan-k'u, Yüeh-liang-shan, Liao-chia-wan, } (141) Ch'ang-sha, Hunan
Ku-wei-ts'un, (77) Hui District, Honan
Erh-li-kang, (81) Cheng-chou Municipality, Honan
site of Eastern Chou capital, Chung-chou-lu, Chin-ts'un, } (82) Lo-yang, Honan
Hou-ch'uan, Shan District, Honan
Shan-piao-chen, (79) Chi District, Honan
Chang-t'ai-kuan, (80) Hsin-yang District, Honan
Yen-hsia-tu, (11) Yi District, Hopei
Chao-wang-ch'eng, (18) Han-tan, Hopei
Tung-tung-ts'un, Hsing-t'ai Municipality, Hopei
Chia-ko-chuang, (8) T'ang-shan Municipality, Hopei
Fen-shui-ling, (28) Ch'ang-chih Municipality, Shansi
She-chu, (100) Li-yang District, Kiangsu
Shih-erh-t'ai-ying-tzu, Chao-yang District, Liaoning
Ch'iu-chia Hua-yüan, (104) Shou District, Anhui
Pan-p'o-ts'un, (39) Sian, Shensi
(63) Lin-tzu (Ch'i-ch'eng), Shantung

FORMER HAN SITES (205—8 B.C.)
Shao-kou, (82) Lo-yang, Honan
General Huo Ch'ü-ping tomb, (40) Hsin-p'ing District, Shensi
(141) Ch'ang-sha, Hunan
Feng-huang-ho, (95) Yang-chou Municipality, Kiangsu
Feng-huang-shan, (117) Ch'eng-tu, Szuchwan
Shih-chai-shan, (149) Chin-ning District, Yünnan
(154) Kuang-chou, Canton
(39) Sian (Ch'ang-an), Shensi
(127) Ch'ang-hsing District, Chekiang

WANG MANG INTERREGNUM SITES (8 B.C.–23 A.D.)
Ho-chia-ts'un, (39) Sian, Shensi
Wu-li-p'ai, (141) Ch'ang-sha, Hunan

Later Han sites (23–220 a.d.)

Yang-tzu-shan,
T'ien-hui-shan, } (117) Ch'eng-tu, Szuchwan
Feng-huang-shan,
Mu-ma-shan-yai tomb, Szuchwan
Hsiang-kuo Temple, Ching-pei, (123) Chungking, Szuchwan
Mo-tsui-tzu, (48) Wu-wei, Kansu
(5) Lü-ta Municipality, Liaoning
(94) T'ung-shan District, Kiangsu
Sha-ho-ch'ü, (154) Kuang-chou, Canton
Ma-ying-kang, Zoological Gardens, Canton
Min-feng District, (166) Uighur Autonomous Region, Sinkiang
Li-chu, (130) Shao-hsing Municipality, Chekiang
Che Shan, Wu-hu Municipality, Anhui
So-yao-ts'un, (14) Wang-tu District, Hopei
Hou-yin-shan, (73) Liang-shan District, Shantung
Chih-ch'uan-chen, (31) Han-ch'eng District, Shensi
(4) Liao-yang, Liaoning
(71) Yi-nan, Shantung

Han sites (no specified period)

Kao-t'ang District, Shantung
Ning District, Shantung
Pu-k'ou-ts'un, Chu-ch'eng District, Shantung
Shuang-shan-ch'u, Yi District, Shantung
P'u-chi-chen, (65) Chang-ch'iu District, Shantung
Ch'ing-pai-hsiang, (116) Hsin-fan, Szuchwan
Fo-erh-yai, Chang-ming, Szuchwan
Ts'ui-p'ing-ts'un, (124) Yi-pin Municipality, Szuchwan
Lang-chia-t'ao, Shun-ling-ch'ü, (35) Hsien-yang District, Shensi
Hung-ch'ing-ts'un, (39) Sian, Shensi
Tiao-ch'iao, (32) T'ung-kuan, Shensi
Pei-yüan,
Pang-t'ai-tzu, } (4) Liao-yang, Liaoning
Jung-yüan, (141) Ch'ang-sha, Hunan
Chiang-chia-shan, (143) Heng-yang Municipality, Hunan
Ho-wang-ts'un, (80) Hsing-yang District, Honan
Huai-an District, Shansi
Li-ko-tuo, (102) T'ai-ho District, Anhui
(47) Chiu-chüan, Kansu

Wu sites (220–280 a.d.)

Chao-shih-kang, Kwang-men-wai,
Ch'ing-liang-shan, } (97) Nanking
Lien-hsi Temple, (113) Wu-ch'ang, Hupei

Chin sites (3rd and 4th centuries a.d.)

Shih-men-k'an-hsiang,
Hsi-shan-ch'iao,
Ts'ao Yi tomb, Ting-chiu shan, } (97) Nanking
Chung-hua-men-wai,
(98) Yi-hsing District, Kiangsu
(131) Chu-chi District, Chekiang
Chin-p'en-ling, (141) Ch'ang-sha, Hunan

Northern Dynasties sites (386–581 a.d.)

(Northern Wei) Ts'ao-ch'ang-p'o-ts'un,
(Northern Wei) Shao Chen tomb, Jen-chia-k'ou, } (39) Sian, Shensi
Hsüeh-chuang-ts'un, (90) Teng District, Honan
Feng family tombs, (16) Ching District, Hopei

Southern Dynasties sites (420–589 a.d.)

Hsiao-hung tomb, Ch'i-lin-men,
Hsiao-hung-shan, Chung-yang-men-wai, } (97) Nanking
Hsi-shan-ch'iao,
(Southern Ch'i) Hsing-an *ling*, Tan-yang, Kiangsu
(Liu-Sung) Hsiu-shui-ling, (132) Huang-yen District, Chekiang

Six Dynasties sites (no specified period) (220–589 a.d.)

Chang-chia-k'u,
Ssu-pan-ts'un, } (97) Nanking
Mu-fu-shan, Chung-yang-men-wai,

Sui sites (581–618 a.d.)

Li Ching-hsün tomb,
Kuo-chia-t'an, } (39) Sian, Shensi
Chang Sheng tomb, (76) An-yang, Honan

T'ang sites (618–907 a.d.)

Chia-li-ts'un,
Chung-pao-ts'un,
Hsien-yü tomb, Nan-ho-ts'un, } (39) Sian, Shensi
Ho-p'ing-men-wai,
Han-sen-chai,
Kao-lou-ts'un,
Kuo-chia-t'an,
Li Shuang tomb, Yang-t'ou-chen,
Pa-fu-chuang,
The Priest Tao-yin tablet,
Pei-lin,
Shih-li-p'u, } (39) Sian, Shensi
Su Ssu-hsü tomb, Ching-wu-lu,
Wei Hsü tomb,
Wei Chiung tomb, Nan-wang-ts'un,
Wang-chia-kung,
Wang-chia-fen-ts'un,
Wu Shou-chung tomb, Kao-lu-ts'un,
Yang-t'ou-chen,
Ch'ien *ling*, (36) Ch'ien District, Shensi
Princess Yung-t'ai tomb, (36) Ch'ien District, Shensi
Shun *ling*, (35) Hsien-yang District, Shensi
Lady Hsüeh tomb, Ti-chang-wan, (35) Hsien-yang District, Shensi
Chao *ling*, Li-ch'üan District, Shensi
Emperor Kao-tsu tomb, Hsien *ling*, San-yüan District, Shensi
(79) Chi District, Honan
(82) Lo-yang, Honan
San-men-chia, Shan District, Honan
Ts'ui Ch'en tomb, Hsin-chuang-ts'un, Yen-shih District, Honan
Wa-cha-p'ing kiln site,
Ssu-mao-ch'ung } (141) Ch'ang-sha, Hunan
T'u-ch'eng-tzu, Horin Gohl, (20) Inner Mongolia Autonomous Region
Astana, Turfan, (166) Uighur Autonomous Region, Sinkiang
Chin-sheng-ts'un, (26) T'ai-yüan, Shansi

Bibliography

General:

中国科学院考古研究所「新中国的考古収獲」(考古学専刊、甲種第 6 号) 文物出版社 1962, Peking

五省出土重要文物展覧籌備委員会「五省出土重要文物展覧図録」文物出版社 1958, Peking

中国科学院考古研究所編著「洛陽中州路—西工段—」(考古学専刊、丁種第 4 号) 科学出版社 1959, Peking

中国科学院考古研究所編著「長沙発掘報告」(考古学専刊丁種第 2 号) 科学出版社 1957, Peking

湖南省博物館編「湖南出土銅鏡図録」文物出版社 1960, Peking

四川省博物館・重慶市博物館合編「四川省出土銅鏡」文物出版社 1960, 北京朱傑勤著「秦漢美術史」商務印書館 1957, Shanghai

中国科学院考古研究所編「考古学基礎」科学出版社 1958, Peking

「全国基本建設工程中出土文物展覧図録」中国古典藝術出版社 1955, Peking

山東省文物管理処・山東省博物館「山東文物選集—普査部分—」文物出版社 1959, Peking

詹蕙娟他編「中国古文物」国際書店 1962, Peking

鄭振鐸編「偉大的藝術伝統図録」1951

洛陽区考古発掘隊「洛陽焼溝漢墓」(考古学専刊、丁種第 6 号) 科学出版社 1959, Peking

雲南省博物館編「雲南晋寧石寨山古墓群発掘報告」文物出版社 1959, Peking

四川省博物館編「四川船棺葬発掘報告」文物出版社 1960, Peking

山西省博物館「太原壙坡北斉張粛墓文物図録」中国古典藝術出版社 1958, Peking

Prehistoric period:

中国科学院考古研究所編「廟底溝與三里橋」〔黄河水庫考古報告之二〕(考古学専刊、丁種第 9 号) 科学出版社 1959, Peking

馬承源著「仰韶文化的彩陶」上海人民出版社 1957, Shanghai

浙江省文物管理委員会、浙江省博物館編「浙江新石器時代文物図録」浙江人民出版社 1958, Hangchow

Yin and Chou dynasties:

中国科学院考古研究所編「著上村嶺虢国墓地」〔黄河水庫考古報告之三〕(考古学専刊、丁種第 10 号) 科学出版社 1959, Peking

安徽省文物管理委員会・安徽省博物館編著「寿県蔡侯墓出土遺物」科学出版社 1956, Peking

中国科学院考古研究所編著「輝県発掘報告」(考古学専刊、丁種第 1 号) 科学出版社 1956, Peking

中国科学院考古研究所編著「灃西発掘報告—1955～1957 年陝西長安県灃西郷考古発掘資料—」(考古学専刊、丁種第12号) 文物出版社 1962, Peking

河南省文化局文物工作隊編「河南信陽楚墓出土文物図録」河南人民出版社 1959, Chengchow

河南省文化局文物工作隊編著「鄭州二里岡」(考古学専刊、丁種第 7 号) 科学出版社 1959, Peking

郭宝鈞著「山彪鎮與琉璃閣」科学出版社 1959, Peking

蔣玄佁著「長沙—楚民族及其芸術—」(美術考古專刊之一) 第 1 巻 漆器 今古出版社 1949, Shanghai

蔣玄佁著「長沙—楚民族及其芸術—」(美術考古專刊之二) 第 2 巻 図騰、遺蹟、絹画、彫刻。美術考古学社 1950, Shanghai

商承祚編「長沙出土楚漆器図録」上海出版公司 1955, Shanghai

北京歴史博物館編「長沙出土古代漆器図案選集」人民美術出版社 1954, Peking

楊宗栄編「戦国絵画資料」中国古典藝術出版社 1957, Peking

容庚・張維持著「殷周青銅器通論」科学出版社 1958, Peking

陝西省博物館・陝西省文物管理委員会編「扶風斉家村青銅器羣」文物出版社 1963, Peking

Han to T'ang dynasties, Industrial Arts:

陝西省文物管理委員会編「陝西省出土銅鏡」文物出版社 1959, Peking

洛陽市文物管理委員会編「洛陽出土古鏡—両漢部分—」文物出版社 1959, Peking

王士倫編「浙江出土銅鏡選集」中国古典藝術出版社 1957, Peking

沈従文編「唐宋銅鏡」中国古典藝術出版社 1958, Peking

江蘇省文物管理委員会編「南京出土六朝青瓷」文物出版社 1957, Peking

聞宥「古銅鼓図録」上海出版公司 1954, Shanghai

Han to T'ang dynasties, Painting:

常任俠編「漢代絵画選集」朝花美術出版社 1956, Peking

曾昭燏・蔣宝庚・黎忠義合著「沂南古画像石墓発掘報告」中央人民政府文化部文化管理局 1956, Shanghai

常任俠編著「漢画藝術研究」上海出版公司 1955, Shanghai

北京歴史博物館・河北省文物管理委員会編輯「望都漢墓壁画」中国古典藝術出版社 1955, Peking

河北省文化局文化工作隊編「望都 2 号漢墓」文物出版社 1956, Peking

陝西省博物館・陝西省文物管理委員会合編「陝北東漢画象石刻集」文物出版社 1959, Peking

黄文弼著「吐魯番考古記」(考古学特刊、第 3 号) 中国科学院出版 1954, Shanghai

江蘇省文物管理委員会編著「江蘇徐州漢画象石」科学出版社 1959, Peking

重慶市博物館編「重慶市博物館蔵四川漢画像磚選集」文物出版社 1957, Peking

聞宥「四川漢代画象選集」羣聯出版社 1955

劉忘遠編「四川漢代画象磚藝術」中国古典藝術出版社 1958, Peking

河南省文化局文物工作隊第 1、2 隊編「河南出土空心磚拓片集」人民美術出版社 1963, Peking

河南省文化局文物工作隊「鄧県彩色画象磚墓」文物出版社 1958, Peking

劉凌源編著「唐代人物画」中国古典藝術出版社 1958, Peking

馬采著「顧愷之研究」上海人民美術出版社 1957, Shanghai

兪剣華・羅叔子・温肇桐編著「顧愷之研究資料」人民美術出版社 1962, Peking

Han to T'ang dynasties, Burial Objects:

秦廷棫「中国古代陶塑藝術」著者出版 1955, Shanghai

王志敏・朱江・李蔚然編「南京六朝唐俑」中国古典藝術出版社 1958, Peking

陝西省文物管理委員会「陝西省出土唐俑選集」文物出版社 1958, Peking

陳万里編「陶俑」中国古典藝術出版社 1957, Peking

沈仲常・馮国定・周楽欽編「四川漢代唐俑」朝花美術出版社 1963, Peking

広州市文物管理委員会編「広州出土漢代陶屋—附：陶倉、陶井、陶灶—」文物出版社 1958, Peking

Han to T'ang dynasties, Sculpture:

王子雲編「中国古代石刻画像選集」中国古典藝術出版社 1957, Peking

陝西省博物館編「陝西省博物館蔵石刻選集」文物出版社 1957, Peking

Related Publications

考古学報 科学出版社, Peking

考古通訊→考古「考古」雑誌社, Peking

文物参攷資料→文物 文物出版社, Peking

美術 人民美術出版社, Peking

美術研究 上海人民出版社, Shanghai

Chinese Chronology

Year	Dynastic Chronology		Historical Events: China	Historical Events: India, Korea, Japan
3000–2000	NEOLITHIC PERIOD Yang-shao culture Lung-shan culture			
1700	YIN Ch'eng-chou culture An-yang culture		Yin capital established at An-yang (*ca.* 1300)	
1050			Yin conquered by Wu Wang of Chou (*ca.* 1050)	
1000–800	WESTERN CHOU			
770	EASTERN CHOU	CH'UN CH'IU	Removal of Chou capital east (770)	
700–500			Compilation of *Ch'un Ch'iu Annals* by Confucius (481)	Birth of Gautama Buddha (557)
403		WARRING STATES		
300	256			Enthronement of King Aśoka (273)
221	CH'IN		Unification of China by Shih Huang-ti of Ch'in (221)	
205	FORMER HAN (Western Han)		Destruction of Ch'in; Liu Pang enthroned as Kao-tsu of Han (206 B.C.) Chang Ch'ien departs on expedition to Central Asia (138 B.C.)	Founding of kingdom of Sylla by King Hyŏkkŏse (57 B.C.) Founding of Kingdom of Koguryŏ by King Tongmyŏngsŏng (37 B.C.) Founding of Kingdom of Paekche by King Onjo (18 B.C.) Founding of Japanese sphere in Karak (southern Korea) (ca. 42 A.D.)
B.C. 0 A.D. — 8	HSIN (Wang Mang)		Wang Mang usurps Han throne (9 A.D.)	Establishment of Kushan dynasty in India (45 A.D.)
25–200	LATER HAN (Eastern Han)		Transmission of Buddhism to China (variously dated 2 B.C. or 68 A.D.) Unification of China under Emperor Kuang-wu (Liu Hsiu), Later Han established (25 A.D.) Suppression of western regions by Pan Ch'ao (74)	King of Wakoku (Japan) sends envoy to court of Later Han (57 A.D.) King of Wakoku again sends envoy to Later Han (107) Enthronement of King Kanishka in India (*ca.* 123) Flourishing of Gandhara art in India (2nd century)

Year	Dynastic Chronology	Historical Events: China	Historical Events: India, Korea, Japan
200	LATER HAN —220—	Ts'ao Ts'ao becomes king of Wei state (216) Ts'ao Ts'ao defeated by Liu Pei; establishment of capital at Ch'eng-tu (219) Collapse of Later Han, beginning of period of the Three Kingdoms (Shu-Han, Wei, Wu) (220)	Envoy of Yamato Empress Miyako arrives at Wei (234)
	SHU-HAN —263— | WEI —265— | WU —280—		
	WESTERN CHIN		
300	—304— | —316—		Ajanta cave monasteries dug in India (4th century) Rise of Paekche (346) Rise of Sylla (356) Introduction of Buddhism into Koguryŏ (372)
	FIVE BARBARIANS AND SIXTEEN KINGDOMS | 386 | EASTERN CHIN	Flourishing of Buddhism in China (4th century) Wang Hsi-chih (321–377); T'ao Yüan-ming (365–427); Wang Hsien-chih (344–383); Ku K'ai-chih (392–467); Hsieh Ling-yün (385–433)	
400	—420—	Beginning of Fa-hsien's journey to India (399)	
	—439—		
	NORTHERN DYNASTIES | SOUTHERN DYNASTIES		
500	Six Dynasties period		King Sŏngmyŏng of Paekche presents Japan with Buddhist images, banners, and scriptures (552)
	—581— | —589—	China united under Sui (589–618)	
600	SUI		Ono Imoko dispatched to Sui (607)
	—618—	China united under T'ang (618–907)	
		Journey of Hsüan-chuang to India (629–645)	Japan begins sending envoys to T'ang (630)
			Unification of Korea under Sylla (668)
700	T'ANG	K'ai-yüan and T'ien-pao reigns of Emperor Hsüan-tsung of T'ang (713–755)	Kingdom of Po-hai founded (Manchuria) (713–926)
		Culture of western regions absorbed into T'ang (8th century) Wang Wei (699–759); Li Po (701–762); Yen Chen-ch'ing (708–784); Tu Fu (712–770); Liu Tsung-yüan (773–819); Han Yü (768–824); Po Chü-yi (772–846)	
800			Saichō and Kūkai enter T'ang (804)
			Sending of Japanese envoys to T'ang stopped (894)
900	—907—		Rise of Koryŏ (918) Collapse of Sylla (935)

Selected Glossary

An Lu-shan 安禄山: (d. 757 A.D.) A peasant of Turkic descent, he became a favorite at the court of the T'ang Emperor Hsüan-tsung, against whom he led a rebellion and declared himself emperor for a short period. He was assassinated by his own son.

An-yang, Honan 安陽 河南

Ch'a-chia-ling, Ch'ang-an, Shensi 查家陸 長安 陝西

Ch'a Ching 茶經: The *Classic of Tea* by Lu Yu 陸羽 (d. 804 A.D.). A treatise on all aspects of tea drinking.

cha-chu 夾紵: Lacquer ware with a woven hemp body.

ch'an 鏟: A type of shovel.

Chang-chia-k'u, Nanking, Kiangsu 張家庫 南京 江蘇

Chang-chia-p'o, Ch'ang-an, Shensi 張家坡 長安 陝西

Ch'ang-chih Municipality, Shansi 長治市 山西

Chang Ch'ü-she tomb, Ti-chang-wan, Hsien-yang, Shensi 張去奢墓 底張湾 咸陽 陝西

Chang Sheng tomb, An-yang, Honan 張盛墓 安陽 河南

Ch'ang-t'ai-kuan, Hsin-yang District, Honan 長台関 信陽県 河南

Chang-te 彰徳

Chan Kuo Ts'e 戰国策: *Annals of the Warring States*

Chao-shih-kang, Kwang-hua-men-wai, Nanking, Kiangsu 趙史岡 光華門外 南京 江蘇

Chao-yang, Liaoning 朝陽 遼寧

Chen-ch'ih District, Kiangsu 震沢県 江蘇

Ch'eng-chou, Honan 鄭州 河南

Ch'eng-tu, Szuchwan 成都 四川

Ch'eng-tzu-yai, Lung-shan-chen, Li-ch'eng District, Shantung 城子崖 龍山鎮 歷城県 山東

Che-shan, Wu-hu Municipality, Anhui 赭山 蕪湖市 安徽

Che-shui District, Shantung 浙水県 山東

chi 戟: A three-pointed lance, developed from the *ko* dagger-ax.

chia 斝: Bronze vessel shape similar to a *chüeh* but with four legs. Popular in the late Yin and early Chou periods.

Chia-ko-chuang, T'ang-shan Municipality, Hopei 賈各荘 唐山市 河北

Chia-li-ts'un, Sian, Shensi 嘉里村 西安 陝西

Chiang-chia-shan, Heng-yang Municipality, Hunan 蔣家山 衡陽市 湖南

Chiang-nan 江南

Chiang-tso-chien 将作監: Official craft inspectorate of the T'ang dynasty.

chiao 鐎: A spouted, tripod bronze vessel similar to a *ho*.

Ch'i-chia-ts'un, Fu-feng District, Shensi 斉家村 扶風県 陝西

Chi-chou, Chi-an, Kiangsi 吉州 吉安 江西

chien 鑑: Bronze vessel shape; a deep basin with ring-handles.

ch'ien 錢: Unit of money.

Ch'ien *ling*, Ch'ien District, Shensi 乾陵 乾県 陝西

ch'ien-ch'iu 千秋: "One thousand autumns"; the title of a festival instituted in the T'ang dynasty.

Chien-ho, Lo-yang, Honan 澗河 洛陽 河南

chih 觶: Bronze vessel shape; a simple goblet with flaring lip.

Chih-ch'üan-chen, Han-ch'eng District, Shensi 芝川鎮 韓城県 陝西

Chih-shih 織室: "Textile office"

Chih-shih Feng-chieh tomb, Kuo-tu-chen, Sian, Shensi 執失節墓 郭杜鎮 西安 陝西

Ch'i District, Honan 汲県 河南

ch'i-lin 麒麟: A mythical beast with a horse's head, scaly body and plumed tail.

Ch'i-li-p'u, Shan District, Honan 七里舗 陝県 河南

chin 錦: "brocade"

ch'in 琴: Five- or seven-stringed musical instrument.

Ching-chih-chen, An-ch'iu District, Shantung 景芝鎮 安邱県 山東

Ching District, Hopei 景県 河北

Ch'ing-ching-shan, Nanking, Kiangsu 清凉山 南京 江蘇

Ch'ing-hua-chen, Ch'i-shan District, Shensi 青化鎮 岐山県 陝西

Ch'ing-pai-hsiang, Hsing-fan District, Szuchwan 清白郷 新繁県 四川

Ching-te-chen, Kiangsi 景徳鎮 江西

Ch'i-shan, Shensi 岐山 陝西

Chin-ts'un, Lo-yang, Honan 金村 洛陽 河南

Ch'iu-chia-hua-yuan, Shou District, Anhui 邱家花園 寿県 安徽

Chou Li 周礼: *Rites of Chou;* suppressed in 213 B.C.; republished in the Han dynasty.

chou-tzu-wen 舟字紋: Dot in a circle decorative motif.

Chu-chia-ch'iao, P'ing-yang District, Shantung 朱家橋 平陽県 山東

Chu-chi District, Chekiang 諸暨県 浙江

chüeh 玦: Jade ring from which a segment has been cut.

chün 郡: "commandery"

Ch'un Ch'iu 春秋: "Spring and Autumn" period (722–484 B.C.). The name of the Annals of the state of Lu attributed to Confucius.
chung 鍾: Shouldered jar very similar in shape to a *hu*.
Chung-chou-lu, Lo-yang, Honan 中州路 洛陽 河南
Chung-pao-ts'un, Sian, Shensi 中堡村 西安 陝西
Chung Yo tomb, Sung-shan, Teng-feng District, Honan 中岳墓 嵩山 登封県 河南
Chu-t'i, Szuchwan 朱提 四川
Chü-yung District, Kiangsu 句容県 江蘇
Erh-li-kang, Ch'eng-chou, Honan 二里岡 鄭州 河南
Feng Fan-chou tomb, Erh-chi-fu, Hsi-kao, Shensi 馮潘州墓 二機福 西高 陝西
Feng-huang-ho, Yang-chou Municipality, Kiangsu 鳳凰河 揚州市 江蘇
Feng-huang-shan, Ch'eng-tu, Szuchwan 鳳凰山 成都 四川
Feng family tombs, Ching District, Hopei 封氏墓 景県 河北
Fen-shui-ling, Ch'ang-ch'ih, Shansi 分水嶺 長治 山西
Fo-erh-yai, Chang-ming, Szuchwan 仏児崖 彰明 四川
Fu-feng District, Shensi 扶風県 陝西
Fu-nan District, Anhui 阜南県 安徽
Han-shen-chai, eastern outskirts of Sian, Shensi 韓森寨 西安東郊 陝西
ho 盉: Bronze vessel shape; a kettle on three or four legs.
Ho-chia-ts'un, western outskirts of Sian, Shensi 賀家村 西安西郊 陝西
ho-ch'i-chu 火斉珠: A form of glass.
Ho-p'ing-men-wai, Sian, Shensi 和平門外 西安 陝西
Hou-chia-chuang, An-yang, Honan 侯家荘 安陽 河南
Ho-ch'uan, Shan District, Honan 后川 陝県 河南
Hou-ma Municipality, Shansi 侯馬市 山西
Ho-wang-ts'un, Yung-yang District, Honan 河王村 滎陽県 河南
hsi 洗: Basin-shaped bronze vessel similar to a *chien*.
Hsiang-kuo Temple, Chiang-pei, Chungking, Szuchwan 相国寺 江北 重慶 四川
Hsiao Hsiu tomb, Yao-hua-men, Nanking, Kiangsu 蕭秀墓 堯化門 南京 江蘇
Hsiao-hung-shan, Chung-ying-men-wai, Nanking, Kiangsu 小洪山 中央門外 南京 江蘇
Hsiao-t'ang-shan, Shantung 孝堂山 山東
Hsieh Lung tomb, Ch'i-lin-men, Nanking, Kiangsu 蕭宏墓 麒麟門 南京 江蘇
Hsien-ling, Shan-yuan District, Shensi 獻陵 三原県 陝西
Hsien-yü T'ing-hui tomb, Nan-ho-ts'un, Sian, Shensi 鮮于庭誨墓 南河村 西安 陝西
Hsing-an-ling, Tan-yang, Kiangsu 興安陵 丹陽 江蘇
Hsing-ch'ing Palace 興慶宮
Hsin-kuo District, Honan 新鄭県 河南
hsiung-ch'i 凶器: Tomb models.
Hsiu-shui-ling, Huang-yen District, Chekiang 秀水嶺 黄岩県 浙江
Hsüan-tsung 玄宗: Sixth emperor of the T'ang dynasty (685–762 A.D.). Also known as Ming-Huang 明皇.
Lady Hsüeh tomb, Ti-chang-wan, Hsien-yang, Shensi 薛氏墓 底張湾 咸陽 陝西
hu 壷: High-shouldered, vase-shaped bronze.
Hua District, Shensi 華県 陝西
Huai-an, Shansi 懐安 山西
Huai District, Honan 懐県 河南
huan 環: Jade or glass ring (see *pi*). The central hole is proportionately larger than that of the *pi*.
huang 璜: Jade musical stone.
Huang-ni-k'eng, Ch'ang-sha, Hunan 黄坭坑 長沙 湖南
Hua-t'ing-ts'un, Hsin-che District, Kiangsu 花廳村 新浙県 江蘇
hua-wen-chin 華文錦: Multicolored brocade.
Hui District, Honan 輝県 河南
hui-lung 虺竜: Serpentine dragon.
Hung-ch'ing-ts'un, Sian, Shensi 紅(洪)慶村 西安 陝西
Hung-chou, Nan-yang Municipality, Kiangsi 洪州 南陽市 江西
hu-yi 胡姨: Foreign concubine.
Ju-chou, Chin-hua District, Chekiang 務州 金華県 浙江
Kao K'o-ts'ung tomb, Hsi-kao, Shensi 高克従墓 工地 西高 陝西
K'ao-kung-shih 考工室: Office concerned with the manufacture of articles for the imperial family.
Kao-lou-ts'un, eastern outskirts of Sian, Shensi 高楼村 西安東郊 陝西
Kao-t'ang District, Shantung 高唐県 山東
Kao Tsung-kan *ling*, Ch'ien District, Shensi 高宗乾陵 乾県 陝西
Kao Yi tomb, Ya-an District, Szuchwan 高頤墓 雅安県 四川
Kao Yüan-kuei tomb, Yi-chi-fu, Hsi-kao, Shensi 高元珪墓 一機福 西高 陝西
ko 戈: Dagger-ax; bronze weapon typical of the late Yin and early Chou periods.
ku 觚: Bronze vessel shape; tall, flaring beaker typical of the late Yin and early Chou periods.
kuang 觥: Bronze vessel resembling a *yi* but covered, often with an animal-shaped cover. Typical of the late Yin dynasty.
kuei 簋: Bronze vessel shape; deep, circular bowl, usually with two handles and often on a foot-ring or stand that may be rectangular. Typical of the late Yin and Chou periods.
kuei-ch'i 鬼器: "Supernatural objects," i.e. tomb models.
k'uei-feng 夔鳳: *K'uei* phoenix; bird motif used on Yin and Chou bronzes.
k'uei-lung 夔龍: *K'uei* dragon; motif used on Yin and Chou bronzes.
Kung District, Honan 鞏県 河南
kung-ling 宮綾: "Palace damask"
Kuo-chia-p'ing, Lin-t'ao District, Kansu 郭家坪 臨洮県 甘粛
Kuo-chia-t'an, eastern outskirts of Sian, Shensi 郭家灘 西安東郊 陝西
Kuo state cemetary, Shan-ts'un-ling, Shan District, Honan 虢国墓 上村嶺 陝県 河南
Kuo-tu-chen, Sian, Shensi 郭杜鎮 西安 陝西
Ku-pi-ts'un, Tzu District, Hopei 賈壁村 磁県 河北
ku-wen 穀紋: "Rice-grain motif"; used on jade.

Ku-yüan-ts'un, Hui District, Honan 固囲村 輝県 河南

lan-t'ai 籃胎: Lacquer ware with plaited bamboo basket body.

Lang-chia-t'ao, Shun-ling-ch'u, Ho-yang District, Shensi 狼家淘 順陵区 咸陽県 陝西

lei 罍: Bronze vessel shape; jar similar to a *hu* but wider bodied with a narrow foot. Typical of the Yin dynasty.

lei-wen 雷文: "Thunder-whorl" motif; rectangular spiral used in the background of bronze decoration.

li 鬲: Bronze vessel shape; tripod bowl with hollow legs.

Liang-ch'eng-chen, Jih-tsao District, Shantung 兩城鎮 日照県 山東

Liang-chu-chen, Hangchow, Chekiang 良渚鎮 杭州 浙江

Liao-chia-wan, Ch'ang-sha, Hunan 廖家湾 長沙 湖南

Li-ch'eng District, Shantung 梁山県 山東

Li Ching-hsün tomb, Sian, Shensi 李静訓墓 西安 陝西

Li-chu, Shao-hsing, Chekiang 漓渚 紹興 浙江

lien 奩: Bronze vessel shape; cylindrical with three legs and a cover. Container for cosmetics or mirrors.

Lien-ch'i-shih, Wu-chang, Hupei 蓮溪寺 武昌 湖北

Li-ko-tu, T'ai-ho District, Anhui 李閣多 大和県 安徽

ling 鐳(鑐): Squat, round bronze vessel with contracted mouth.

ling 綾: Silk damask.

lin-wen 鱗紋: Scale motif used on bronzes of the Yin dynasty.

Li Shuang tomb, Yang-t'ou-chen, Sian, Shensi 李爽墓 羊頭鎮 西安 陝西

liu-li 琉璃: Glass

Liu-li-ko, Hui District, Honan 琉璃閣 輝県 河南

Ma-ch'ang-kou, Ling-yuan District, Liaoning 馬廠溝 淩源県 遼寧

Ma-ying-kang, Zoological Gardens, Canton 麻鷹崗 動物園 広州

Miao-ti-kou, Shan District, Honan 廟底溝 陝県 河南省

ming-ch'i 明器: "Spirit objects"; tomb models.

Min-feng District, Sinkiang 民豊県 新疆

Mo-fu-shan, Nanking, Kiangsu 幕府山 南京 江蘇

Mo-tsui-tzu, Wu-wei, Kansu 磨嘴子 武威 甘粛

Mu-ma-shan-yai tomb, Szuchwan 牧馬山崖墓 四川

ni-hsiang 泥像: Clay figurines for burial.

Ning District, Shantung 寧県 山東

Pa-fu-chuang, northeastern outskirts of Sian, Shensi 八府荘 西安東北郊 陝西

Pai-chia-chuang, Ch'eng-chou, Honan 自家荘 鄭州 河南

Po-chüan, Hui District, Honan 百泉 輝県 河南

Pai-tao-kou-p'ing, Lan-chou, Kansu 白道溝坪 蘭州 甘粛

Pa-li-t'ai, Lo-yang 八里台 洛陽

Pan-shan, Kansu 半山 甘粛

Pao-t'o, Ning-yang District, Shantung 堡頭 寧陽県 山東

p'ei-yü 佩玉: Jade pendants, including three categories of flat rings: *pi*, *yüan* and *huan*.

pi 璧: Glass or jade disc ring; the central hole is approximately one-third of the ring diameter.

pi-liu-li 璧琉璃: Colored glass; usually abbreviated to *liu-li*.

p'i-p'a 琵琶: Stringed musical instrument resembling a lute.

po 鉢: Round-bodied jar.

po-li 玻璃: Glass

Po-shan-lu 博山炉: Incense burner with a hill-shaped, conical cover.

P'u-chi-chen, Chang-ch'iu, Shantung 普集鎮 章邱 山東

Pu-k'o-ts'un, Chu-ch'eng District, Shantung 埠口村 諸城県 山東

P'u-tu-ts'un, Ch'ang-an, Shensi 普渡村 長安 陝西

San-men-chia, Shan District, Honan 三門峡 陝県 河南

San-pan, Lin-hsia District, Kansu 三坪 臨夏県 甘粛

san-ts'ai 三彩: "Three colors"; referring to the polychrome low-fired glazes used from the T'ang dynasty onward. The colors vary in grouping, but are typically green, yellow, and purple.

se 瑟: Twenty-five-stringed musical instrument, similar in shape to a *ch'in*.

Sha-ching, Kansu 沙井 甘粛

Sha-fu-chien 少府監: Craft inspectorate of the T'ang dynasty.

Sha-ho-ch'u, Canton 沙河區 広州

Shang-fang 尚方: Agency making objects for the imperial family.

Shang-ts'ao-lu-ts'un, Chang-hsing District, Chekiang 上草楼村 長興県 浙江

Shang-ts'un-ling, Shan District, Honan 上村嶺 陝県 河南

Shao-kou, Lo-yang, Honan 燒溝 洛陽 河南

Shih-chai-shan, Chin-ning District, Yünnan 石寨山 晉寧県 雲南

Shih-chia-ho, T'ien-men District, Hopei 石家河 天門県 河北

Shih-li-p'u, Sian, Shensi 十里舗 西安 陝西

Shih-men-k'an-hsiang, Nanking, Kiangsu 石門坎郷 南京 江蘇

Shih-p'an-ts'un, Nanking, Kiangsu 四板村 南京 江蘇

Shih-tzu-ch'ung, Tzu-chin-shan, Ch'i-lin-men, Nanking, Kiangsu 獅子沖 紫金山 麒麟門 南京 江蘇

Shou-chou, Huai-nan District, Anhui 寿州 准南県 安徽

Shuang-shan-ch'u, Yi District, Shantung 双山区 掖県 山東

Shun-ling, Yang District, Shensi 順陵 陽県 陝西

Ssu-mao-ch'ung, Ch'ang-sha, Hunan 絲茅冲 長沙 湖南

Sung-tzu tomb, Nan-yang Municipality, Honan 宋資墓 南陽市 河南

Su Ssu-hsü tomb, Ching-wu-lu, Sian, Shensi 蘇思勗墓 東郊経五路 西安 陝西

Ta-hsing-ch'en 大興城: Another name for Ch'ang-an 長安

T'ai-sung, Li-ch'uan District, Shensi 太宗 醴泉県 陝西

t'an 罈: General term for a round-bodied jar shape.

T'ang-lang, Szuchwan 堂狼 四川

T'ang-wang-ch'uan, Tung-hsiang-tzu-ch'ih District, Kansu 唐汪川 東鄉自治県 甘粛

t'ao-t'ieh 饕餮: Animal-mask motif associated with early bronze decoration.

Ta-shih-k'ung-ts'un, An-yang, Honan 大司空村 安陽 河南

Teng District, Honan 鄧県 河南

Tiao-ch'iao, Tung-kuan, Shensi 吊橋 潼関 陝西

T'ien-hui-shan, Ch'eng-tu, Szuchwan 天廻山 成都 四川

T'ien Lake, Yünnan 滇池 雲南

t'ien-lu 天禄: Fabulous creature, sometimes with one horn.

ting 鼎: Bronze vessel shape; three- or four-legged cauldron.

to-chin 綴錦: Brocade patchwork.

tou 科: Long-stemmed cup or bowl with a cover.

Ts'ai Hou (Marquis of Ts'ai) tomb, Shou District, Anhui. 蔡侯墓 寿県 安徽

tsang-yü 葬玉: Burial jades to be placed on the bodily orifices.

Ts'ao-ch'ang-po-ts'un, southern outskirts of Sian, Shensi 草廠坡村 西安南郊 陝西

Ts'ao-yen-chuang, Hsing-t'ai, Hopei 曹演荘 邢台 河北

Ts'ao-yi tomb, Ting-chia-shan, Chung-hua-men-wai, Nanking, Kiangsu 曹翌墓 丁申山 中華門外 南京 江蘇

Tsi-an District, T'ung-kou, Korea 輯安県 通溝

Tso-chia-kung-shan, Ch'ang-sha, Hunan 左家公山 長沙 湖南

Tsui-p'ing-ts'un, Yi-pin Municipality, Szuchwan 翠屏村 宜賓市 四川

Ts'ui Ch'en tomb, Hsin-chuang-ts'un, Yen-shih District, Honan 崔沈墓 新荘村 偃師県 河南

tsun 尊 (*tsun-yi* 尊彝): General term for bronze vessels, or specifically a beaker-shaped vessel.

Tuan Po-yang tomb, Sian, Shensi 段伯陽墓 西安 陝西

T'u-ch'eng-tzu, Horin Gohl, Inner Mongolia 土城子 和林 格爾 内蒙古

Tu-chia-ts'un, Lin-t'ao District, Kansu 杜家村 臨洮県 甘粛

Tun-ch'i Municipality, Anhui 屯渓市 安徽

Tung-chia-t'ai, T'ien-chu District, Kansu 董家台 天祝県 甘粛

Tung-chou-yi-chih, Hou-ma Municipality, Shansi 東周遺址 侯馬市 山西

Tung-ou, Chekiang 東甌 浙江

Tung-tung-ts'un, Hsing-t'ai Municipality, Hopei 東董村 邢台市 河北

Tung-yüan-chiang 東園匠: Han imperial factory for *ming-ch'i*.

Tun-k'o-tun, Inner Mongolia 扽克扽 内蒙古

Tzu-t'an-ku, Ch'ang-sha, Hunan 子弾庫 長沙 湖南

Wang-ch'eng Park, Lo-yang 王城公園 洛陽 河南

Wang-chia-fen-ts'un, Sian outskirts, Shensi 王家墳村 西安郊外 陝西

Wang-tu, Hopei 望都 河北

Wei Chiung tomb, Nan-li-wang-ts'un, Sian, Shensi 韋洞墓 南里王村 西安 陝西

Wu-an, Honan 武安 河南

Wu-kuan-ts'un, An-yang, Honan 武官村 安陽 河南

Wu-li-p'ai, Ch'ang-sha, Hunan 五里牌 長沙 湖南

Wu Shou-chung tomb, Kao-lou-ts'un, Sian, Shensi 呉守忠墓 高楼村 西安 陝西

Wu-tu Commandery, Szuchwan 武都郡 四川

Yang-chia-wan, Ch'ang-sha, Hunan 楊家湾 長沙 湖南

Yang-chou Municipality, Kiangsu 揚州市 江蘇

Yang Kuei-fei 楊貴妃: Famous concubine of the T'ang Emperor Hsüang-tsung.

Yang-shao-ts'un, Min-ch'ih District, Honan 仰韶村 澠池県 河南

Yang-t'ien-hu, Ch'ang-sha, Hunan 仰天湖 長沙 湖南

Yao-chou, T'ung-shan District, Shensi 耀州 銅山県 陝西

Yen-hsia-tu, Yang District, Hopei 燕下都 易県 河北

yi 匜: Bronze vessel shape; uncovered sauce-boat-shaped, low ewer on three or four legs.

Yi-hsing, Kiangsu 宜興 江蘇

Yi-nan, Shantung 沂南 山東

Ying-ch'eng-tzu, Liaoning 営城子 遼寧

yi-wen-p'ao 異文袍: Figured robes.

Yo-chou, Hunan 岳州 湖南

yü 盂: Bronze vessel shape; deep bowl used for water and other liquids.

yüan 環: Jade or glass flat ring (see *p'ei yü*).

Yüeh-liang-shan, Ch'ang-sha, Hunan 月亮山 長沙 湖南

yung 俑: Wooden models of human figures made for burial.

Princess Yung-ts'ai tomb, Ch'ien District, Shensi 永泰公主墓 乾県 陝西

Yung-yang District, Honan 滎陽県 河南

Yung-yüan, Ch'ang-sha, Hunan 容園 長沙 湖南

MARY TREGEAR

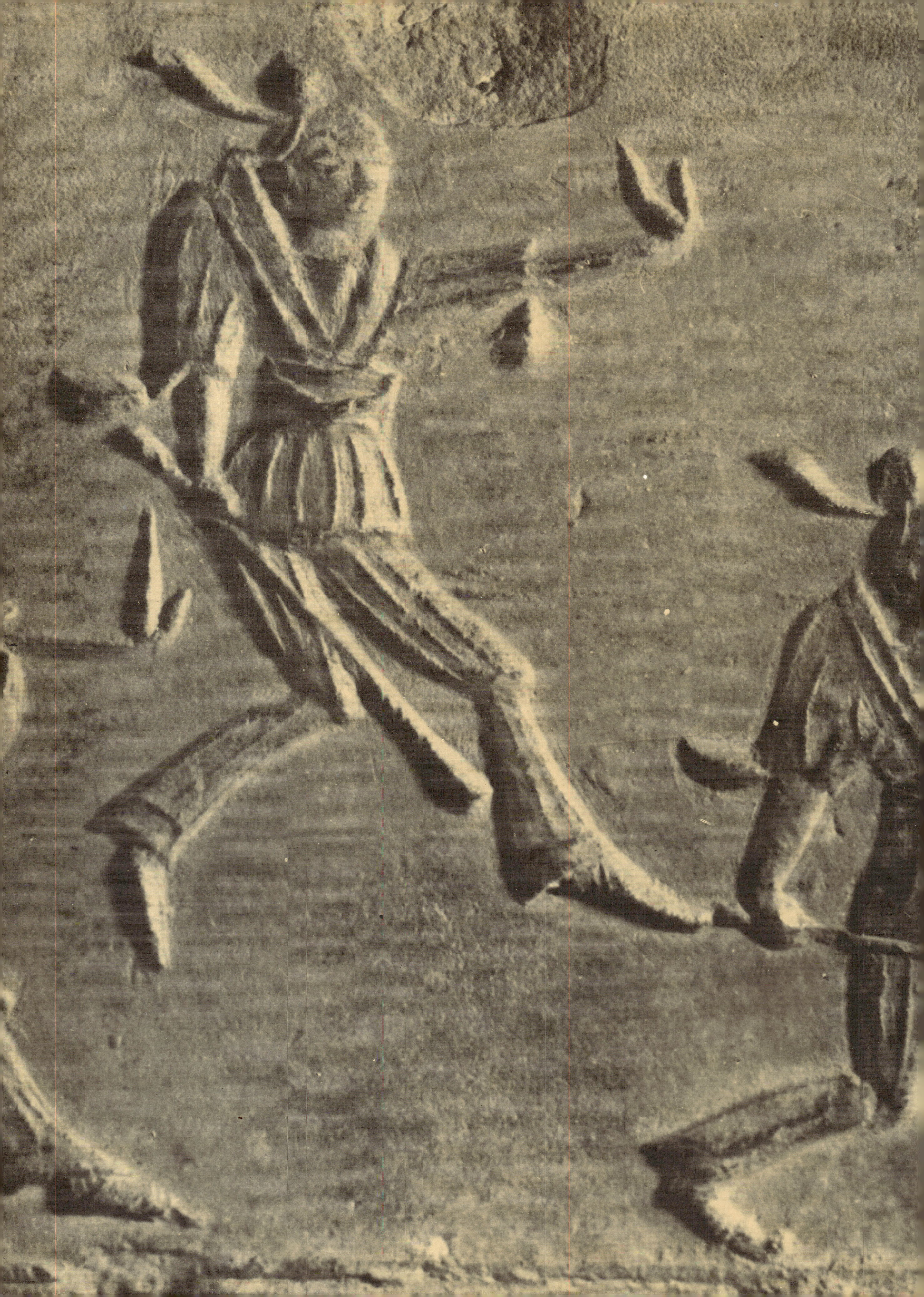